The Handbook of Bird Photography

rockynook

Markus Varesvuo
Jari Peltomäki
Bence Máté

The Handbook of Bird Photography

Publisher: Gerhard Rossbach
Editor: Jocelyn Howell
Copyeditor: Jeanne Hansen
Translation from Finnish to English: Minna Lindroth
Layout: Petra Strauch
Cover Design: Helmut Kraus, www.exclam.de
Printer: Everbest Printing Co. Ltd through Four Colour Print Group, Louisville, Kentucky
Printed in China

ISBN 978-1-937538-10-1

Title of the Finnish original: Lintukuvauksen Käsikirja
ISBN 978-951-0-37640-9

1st Edition (2nd Printing, Jan 2014)

Rocky Nook, Inc.
802 E. Cota Street, 3rd Floor
Santa Barbara, CA 93103

www.rockynook.com

Library of Congress Cataloging-in-Publication Data

Varesvuo, Markus.
The handbook of bird photography / by Markus Varesvuo, Jari Peltomäki, Bence Máté. -- 1st edition
pages cm
ISBN 978-1-937538-10-1 (soft cover : alk. paper)
1. Photography of birds--Handbooks, manuals, etc. I. Peltomäki, Jari. II. Máté, Bence. III. Title.
TR729.B5V37 2013
779'.328--dc23
2012034897

Distributed by O'Reilly Media
1005 Gravenstein Highway North
Sebastopol, CA 95472

TABLE OF CONTENTS

INTRODUCTION

Just as nature and wildlife have the capacity to inspire and intrigue, so does photography. Bird photography is a fantastic way to combine being in the great outdoors with observing and photographing the natural world, be it for documentation or for artistic purposes.

The three of us authors have different backgrounds, careers, perspectives, and working styles. Each of us has his own particular strengths, visions, and expertise. Out of this divergence grew the idea to combine it all into one book, especially because we share the same passion for bird photography—we all know what a fantastic hobby it is and how challenging it is as a profession.

We have been out photographing together several times and have learned that even when the subject and the circumstances are the same for each photographer, different approaches can yield surprisingly different outcomes. One of the main aims of this book is to encourage photographers to find their own individual approach to bird photography.

Although this book outlines equipment and techniques, the main emphasis is on fieldwork. It also made sense to leave digital image processing and computer work out of the book altogether. Each of these topics merits enough space to be an entire book itself, and many excellent guides have already been written.

We want to share our experience, views, and skills in the most down-to-earth and practical manner possible, with a wealth of photos to support our words. We don't just talk it; we have walked every step of it.

We split up the topics to correspond to our strengths, and we each hand picked our images. We are not always in loving harmony with one another when it comes to bird photography, but we share the same passion for birds and bird photography, the same joy in great nature photography, and the same burning ambition to take better pictures.

This handbook is a hefty tome with tons of bird photography know-how, but the photos offer a respite from words,

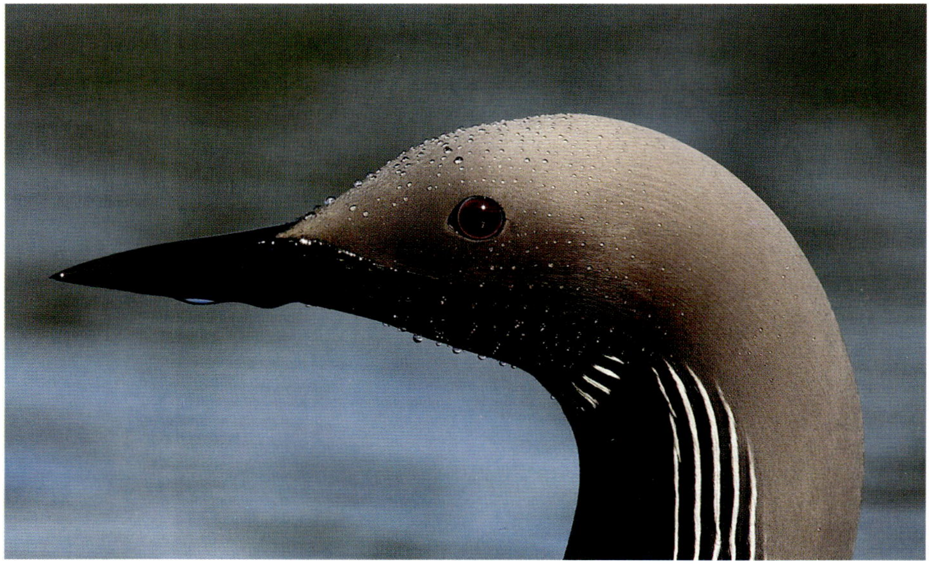

Markus Varesvuo

Black-throated Diver/ Arctic Loon *(Gavia arctica)*
Canon EOS-1Ds Mark III 500mm f/4.0 plus 1.4x extender, 1/500 second, ISO 500, Gitzo tripod, Manfrotto 501 video head, blind. Vaala, Finland, June 2008.

leading into the exciting visual world of birds. We could have reduced the book to a more field-friendly size by minimizing the number of images, but we wanted to create a balanced mix of informative reading and enjoyable viewing. With the photos we hope to help raise awareness about the world of birds and share their beauty.

Getting it right is still such a rush, even after decades of photographing birds. It is still fun and exhilarating even though it is a full-time job. Gaining new insights, like a new angle or a fresh composition idea, when shooting a common and familiar species is just as uplifting as adventures in new locations or working with a species for the first time. Even if we are well versed in the art and craft of bird photography, it is a never-ending road to the perfect photo.

Wishing you sweet moments of success, photography trips full of fun, and unforgettable, unique photographs,

Markus Varesvuo
As a specialist in wintertime and bird action photography, Markus has faith in the natural light.

Jari Peltomäki
Although he specializes in owl photography, Jari easily turns his camera toward other wildlife subjects too.

Bence Máté
As a master of composition, Bence specializes in shooting from within a photography blind and working with flash.

LEARN ABOUT YOUR SUBJECT

Knowledge in bird behavior and biology helps improve your photography.

Nowadays quite a few people start bird photography with no previous knowledge of birds. It's clear that anyone who is just starting bird photography is in a different position than those who have spent decades observing birds, even if they are new to photography. Studying bird behavior, phenology (the rhythm of biological phenomena and the effect of various factors on this rhythm), and bird songs and calls, by spending time in the field observing and learning why and when birds do what they do, yields a wealth of information that cannot be found in books. Besides being fun, fieldwork gives you experience, and it gets easier to recognize one-off situations that are rarely seen, let alone photographed. These situations deserve more time and effort than most other events that you come across.

One way for a fledgling bird photographer to cut many corners is to hook up with a more experienced bird photographer. Many veterans have at least tried, probably many times, to photograph any species that you are starting with. Some of them are happy to share their knowledge. Another way to learn the ropes is by taking part in photography courses and workshops run by other photographers who give much-needed advice and support to beginners and advanced photographers alike. Workshops are also a great way to meet other people with similar interests. Some photographers prefer to roam the wilderness alone, but in my opinion cooperation and the exchange of information about locations yield better results.

Bird watchers observe birds with binoculars and telescopes. Binoculars are an essential tool for a bird photographer too, whether for following a bird in its nest-building activities or looking for places where birds are feeding. Sometimes your eyes are not enough for locating birds and you need a good pair of binoculars to spot, for example, a flock of partridges feeding in the middle of a field, or a Snowy Owl perching on the edge of a ditch. Binoculars will also help you determine if anything, like a twig, is obscuring your shot and help you see if there is a better view from a different angle.

As a rule of thumb, photographers should let birds approach them, not the other way around. You will soon learn that birds will move away from you or fly away completely if you try to get close to them. At least, this is the case in countries where birds are hunted. By nature birds are shy and wary, so you must outsmart them if you wish to get close. A photography blind is perfect, but sometimes it is enough to blend in with your surroundings by wearing camouflage clothes or by throwing a camouflage net over yourself and your camera equipment. Birds will lose their wariness and return to their normal activities as soon as you disappear from sight. Shooting from a blind can yield photos of bird behavior that would otherwise be impossible to witness or capture.

The chapter "How to Build and Use a Blind" elaborates, but in short, photography blinds work best in places where birds gather naturally, such as display grounds, breeding sites, and feeding and resting places. It is best to leave your

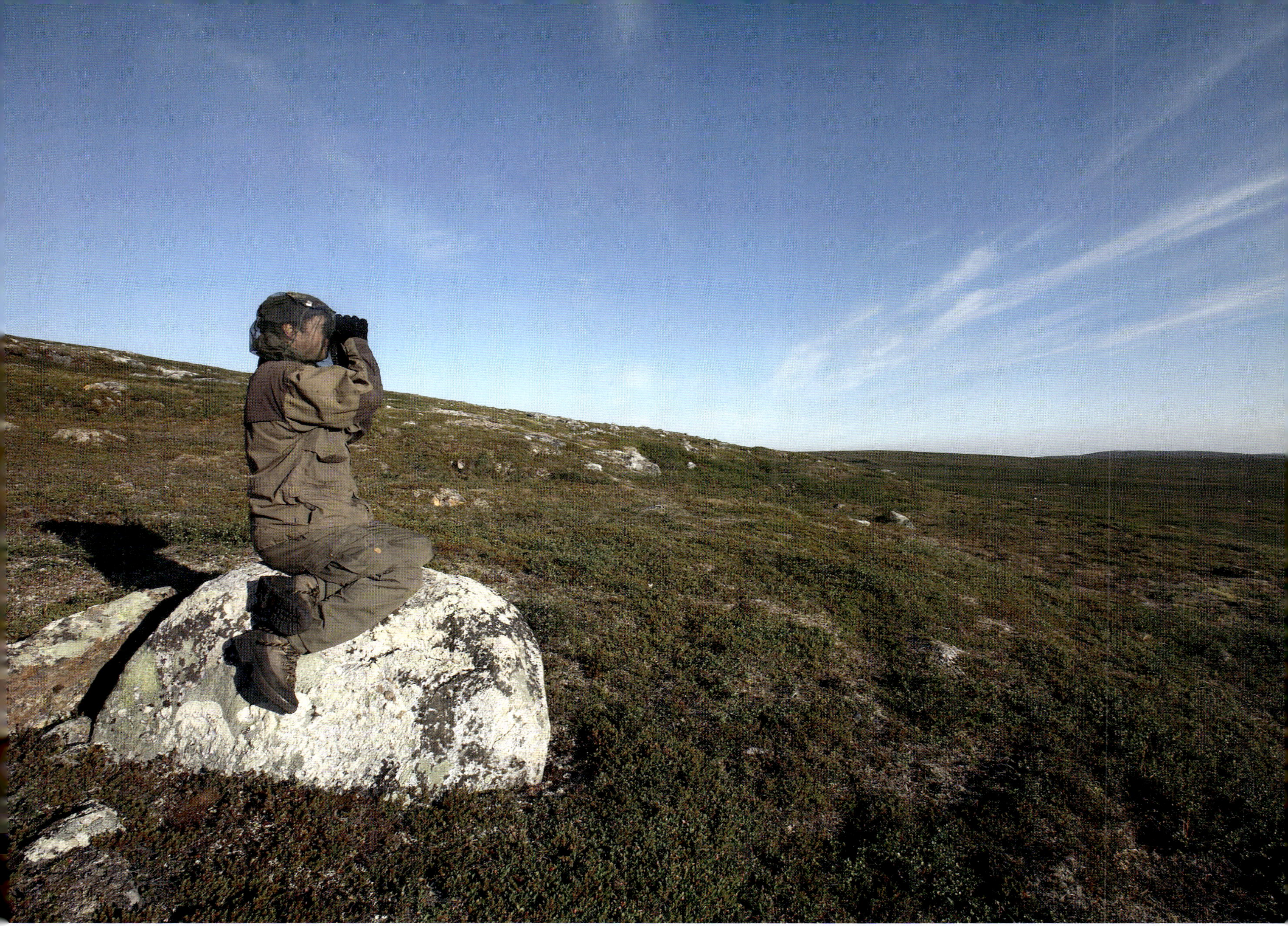

Scanning the arctic terrain in the Finnish Lapland,
looking for Snowy Owls

Jari Peltomäki

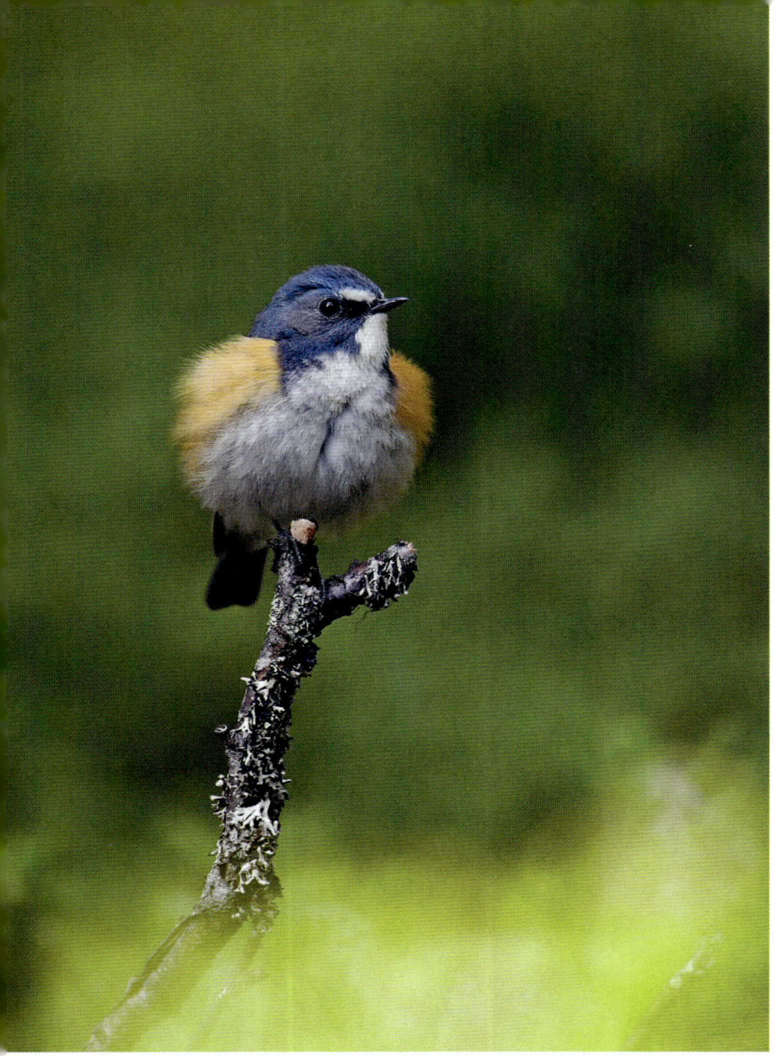

Jari Peltomäki

A Red-flanked Bluetail in the taiga *(Tarsiger cyanurus)*
Canon EOS-1D Mark II, 500mm f/4.0, 1/160 second, f/5.0, ISO 200, one-shot focus with one focusing point, Gitzo tripod, Manfrotto 501 video head. Kuusamo, Finland, June 2005.

blind in the same place for a period of time because birds will soon get used to it. You need to have an escort to see some species and to go into some areas, such as nesting sites. But no escort is needed on a stretch of shore full of feeding waders. Read more about the different ways to get a bird to come close to your blind in the chapter "Attracting Birds."

It is worth knowing that even migrating birds can be territorial. Small birds have their own feeding territories and keep coming back to the same spot to look for food, even to the same branch. By observing such sites and behavior and calmly waiting nearby, you can get some great shots of small birds, which are usually elusive and super fast. Time and patience usually work in your favor!

What, Where, and When?

You should study bird phenology to learn about the timing of events in birds' life cycles that recur on a yearly basis. It is especially important for a bird photographer to know when to photograph a certain species or behavior. Take, for example, most songbirds, like the Red-flanked Bluetail, which inhabits the taiga. They are easiest to photograph right when they return in the spring, because that is when they sing the most enthusiastically. The same applies to many other passerine species. After their singing season is over, they become more secretive and hard to spot.

You should lay out a time frame on a calendar by marking down the best times for photographing the species you are after. Your knowledge and understanding of what type of places draw the most birds in different seasons will grow with experience. The Capercaillie, for instance, has a relatively long displaying season, but the best week for photography is when the females arrive to the lek for mating. In southern Finland this is usually at the end of April, but the farther north you go, the later it takes place until finally in Arctic Inari they mate in mid-May. Your time frame can never be exact, though, because birds take their cues from the seasonal changes in weather, mainly from the pace of the snow melt and the changes in temperature. Whatever kind of schedule you can give yourself for photography, try making it as flexible as possible.

Most bird species try to nest out of sight, and many make their nests deep in the vegetation or hidden inside a hole in a tree. It requires extensive knowledge and lots of field time to find the nests of small birds, and it takes true expertise to find a nest with a Common

A Great Reed-Warbler feeding a young Common Cuckoo *(Acrocephalus arundinaceus, Cuculus canorus)*
Nikon D200, 300mm f/2.8, 1/1000 second, f/4.0, ISO 400, one-shot focus, Gitzo tripod and video head. Hungary, June 2006.

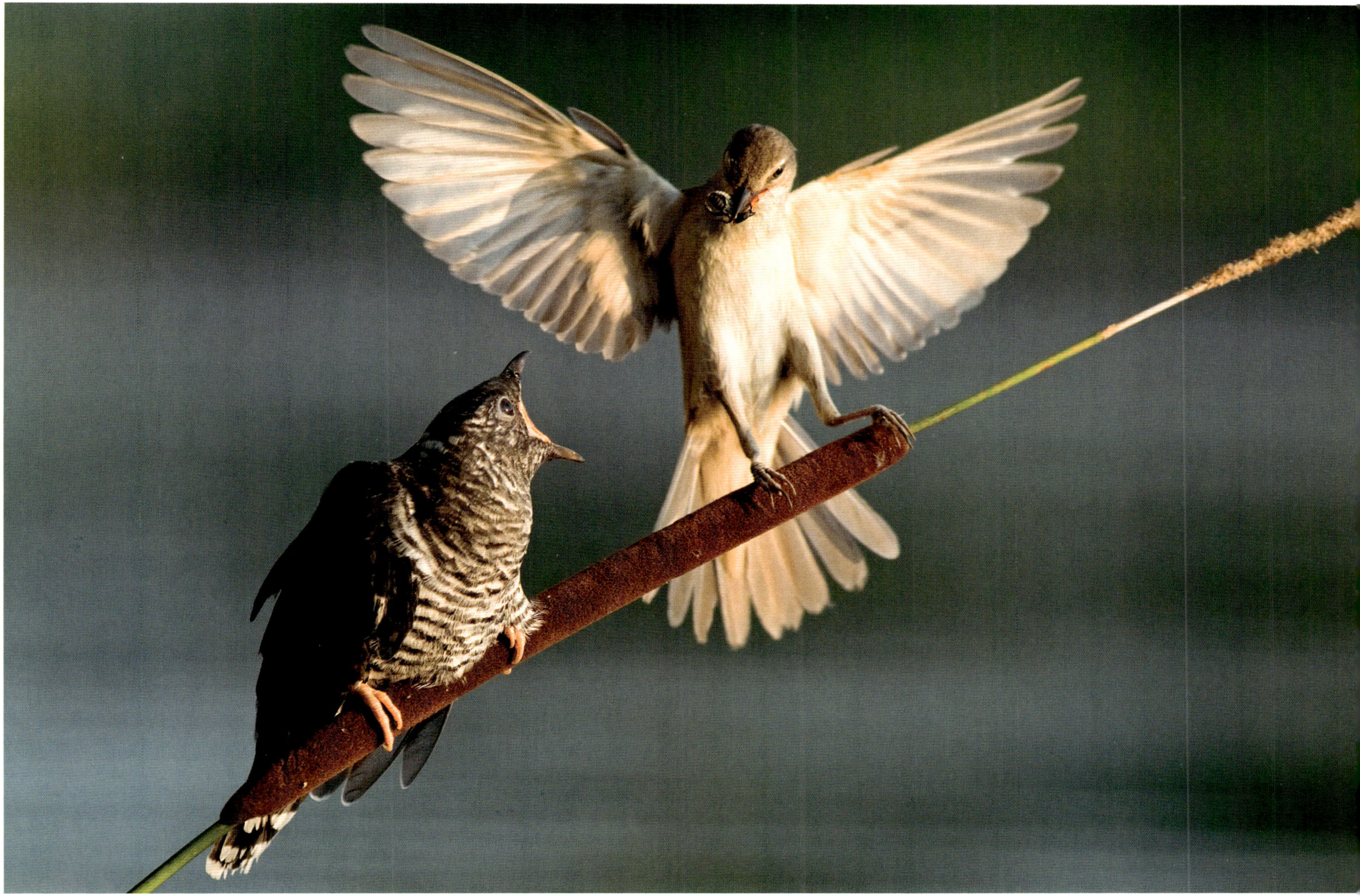

Bence Máté

Cuckoo's egg. In Finland, the Common Cuckoo's host species is usually a Redstart, whereas in the Pusztaszer area in Hungary, a Common Cuckoo will lay its egg in the nest of a Great Reed-Warbler. To find a Common Cuckoo nest, you need to know the host. You can read more about nest photography in the chapter "Photographing at Nests."

The start of the nesting season varies from one year to another, depending on whether spring starts early or late and also on the food situation. In a good vole year owls start breeding weeks earlier than when the vole population is low. If the vole numbers are at an all-time low, owls may skip breeding altogether.

Different species migrate at different times. Each species has a so-called peak migration, which is when the largest numbers migrate. In spring, adult waders are in a hurry to reach their breeding grounds in the Siberian tundra, and they stop for only the shortest possible breaks along their migration routes. On their autumn migration, which takes place in July, they are less hurried and are relatively easy to photograph in breeding plumage while feeding on popular wader shores. Highly visible formations like headlands, waterways, and mountain ranges are the leading lines that channel birds in their migration flight, and staging sites along these routes draw migrating birds every year for much-needed rest and food. These are good locations for photographing migrating birds.

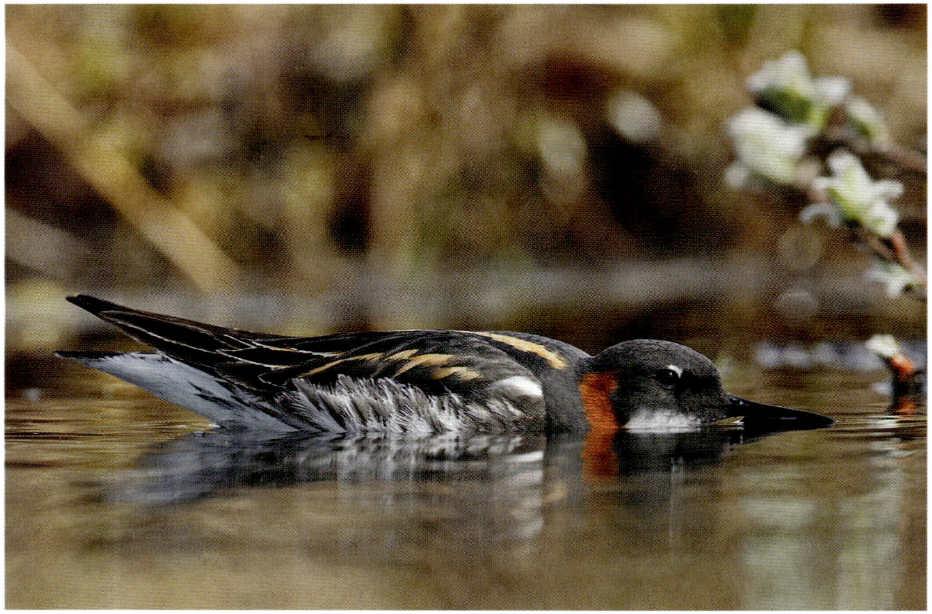

A Red-necked Phalarope flattens itself against the surface of the water as a Gyrfalcon circles above *(Phalaropus lobatus)*
Canon EOS-1D Mark II N, 500mm f/4.0, 1/500 second, f/11.0, ISO 400, one-shot focus with one focusing point, ground pod. Varanger Peninsula, Norway, June 2006.

Jari Peltomäki

Bird Behavior

Birds have excellent eyesight; they can spot a predator circling up above far quicker than we can. Birds keep an eye on the sky by tilting their heads sideways. In the picture, a Red-necked Phalarope was feeding on a pond in the arctic tundra when suddenly it flattened itself down against the water's surface. It tilted its head sideways and looked up into the sky. This helped the photographer spot a Gyrfalcon circling above! Other waders behave in the same way when they're on open shores. Similarly, small birds stop dead in their tracks when they hear a warning call or see a predator.

Another useful piece of information is that birds take off into a headwind. This is handy to know when you prepare to take flight shots or when you approach birds, which is best done with the wind behind you or at your side. You should never chase birds into flight. Instead, you should check the wind direction and stay in a good spot to wait for the birds to take off. This way they may fly past you at close range. Most birds indicate clearly when they are about to take off. Geese, for example, shake their heads a couple of times, and cranes make coughing noises and perform a specific sequence of steps just prior to lifting off.

Bird Songs and Calls

Knowing bird songs and calls is a huge advantage, especially in the woods. A Common Crossbill's alarm call can lead a photographer to a napping owl. The very secretive Red-flanked Bluetail's gentle alarm, *tschak*, can reveal its nest to a bird photographer who has keen ears. If you hear a Curlew male give its unmistakable, plaintive, and lonely *cour-leee*, you can expect Curlew mating to take place soon.

It is easy to learn birds' songs from recordings, but many of their calls and alarms can be heard only out in the field. The importance of these little sounds cannot be overstated because the many little clicking sounds, agitated chatterings, squeaks, and shrill whistles can help a bird photographer navigate toward interesting subjects and exciting action.

Sitting in a blind and waiting for something to happen can be tiresome, and you may find your eyes just won't stay open. Try to keep your snooze to a light catnap, though, because ravens will tell you when an eagle is flying. It pays to stay tuned to the sounds that carry into the blind because they will help you be ready when something starts to happen. The action is fast and often doesn't last long, like an eagle chasing ravens as it arrives at a carcass.

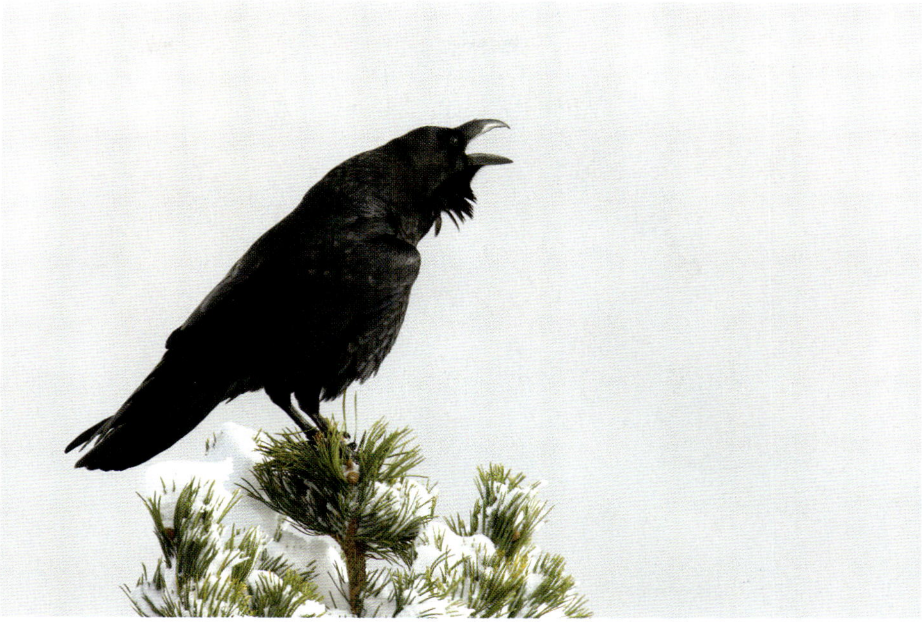

Markus Varesvuo

Ravens have different calls for different predators *(Corvus corax)*
Canon EOS-1Ds Mark III, 800mm f/5.6 plus 1.4x extender, 1/320 second, f/16, ISO 800, one-shot focus with a central focusing point, Gitzo tripod, Manfrotto 501 video head, blind. Spain, November 2010.

Ravens have a rich and complex repertoire of sounds, and there is a certain call for different dangers, like an eagle flying, or Goshawks and Gyrfalcons. You will learn to discern the ravens' many alarm calls, and after a while you will know without looking out from the blind which predator is causing the commotion.

Listening to what is going on outside is also useful in a goose blind. Geese pair up while migrating north, so when they land on any of the stopover or staging sites along their routes they feed and

A Golden Eagle chases Common Ravens from a carcass *(Aquila chrysaetos, Corvus corax)*
Canon EOS-1D Mark III, 300mm f/2.8, 1/1250 second, f/3.2, ISO 1600, continuous focus with 45 focusing points, Manfrotto 501 video head, blind. Utajärvi, Finland, January 2008.

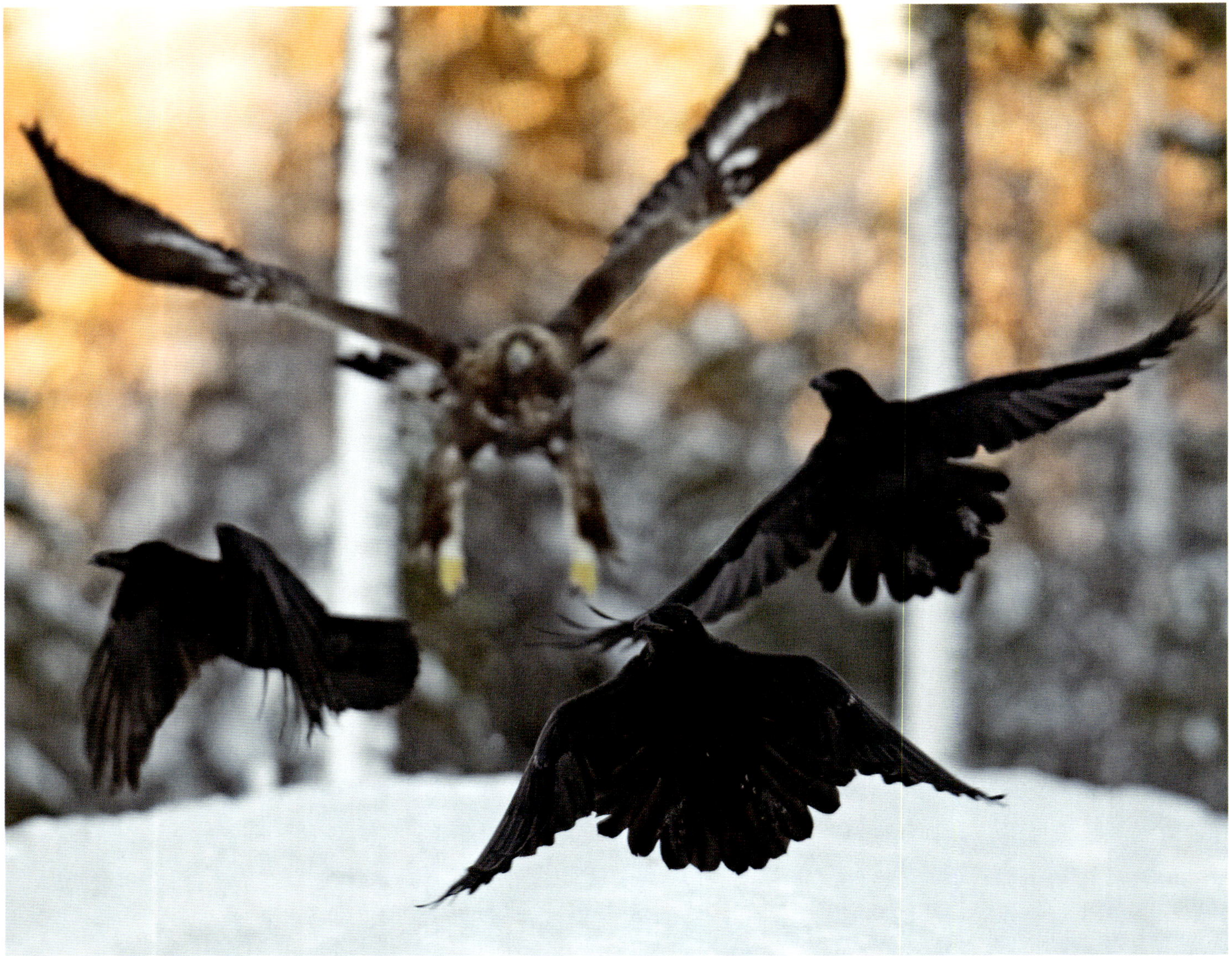

Markus Varesvuo

By keeping an eye on the Common Ravens and listening to their calls, you won't be caught by surprise when something happens ***(Aquila chrysaetos, Corvus corax)***

Nikon D3S, 400mm f/2.8, 1/500 second, f/4.0, ISO 1600, continuous focus with 51 focusing points, Manfrotto 501 video head attached to a blind. Utajärvi, Finland, January 2011.

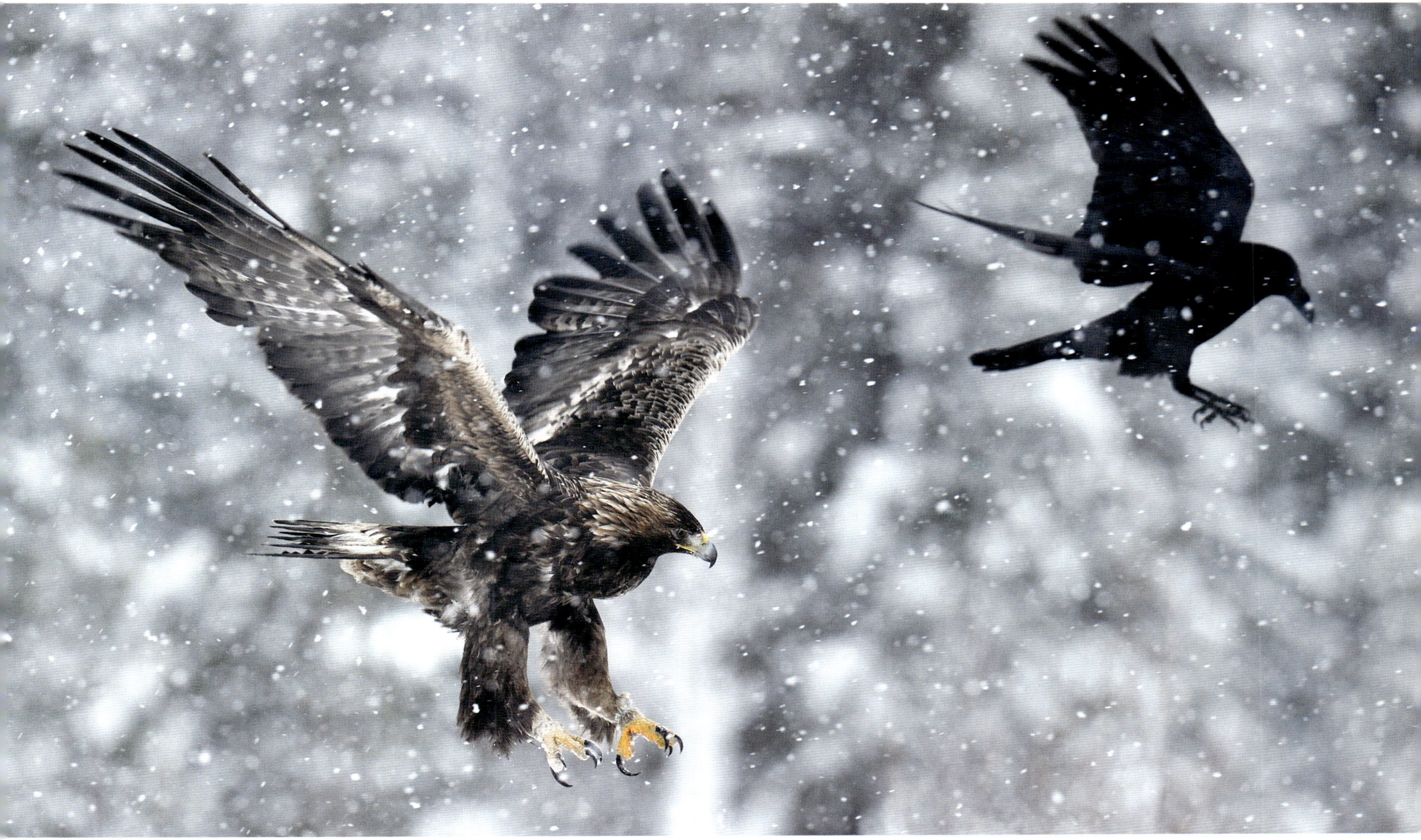

Jari Peltomäki

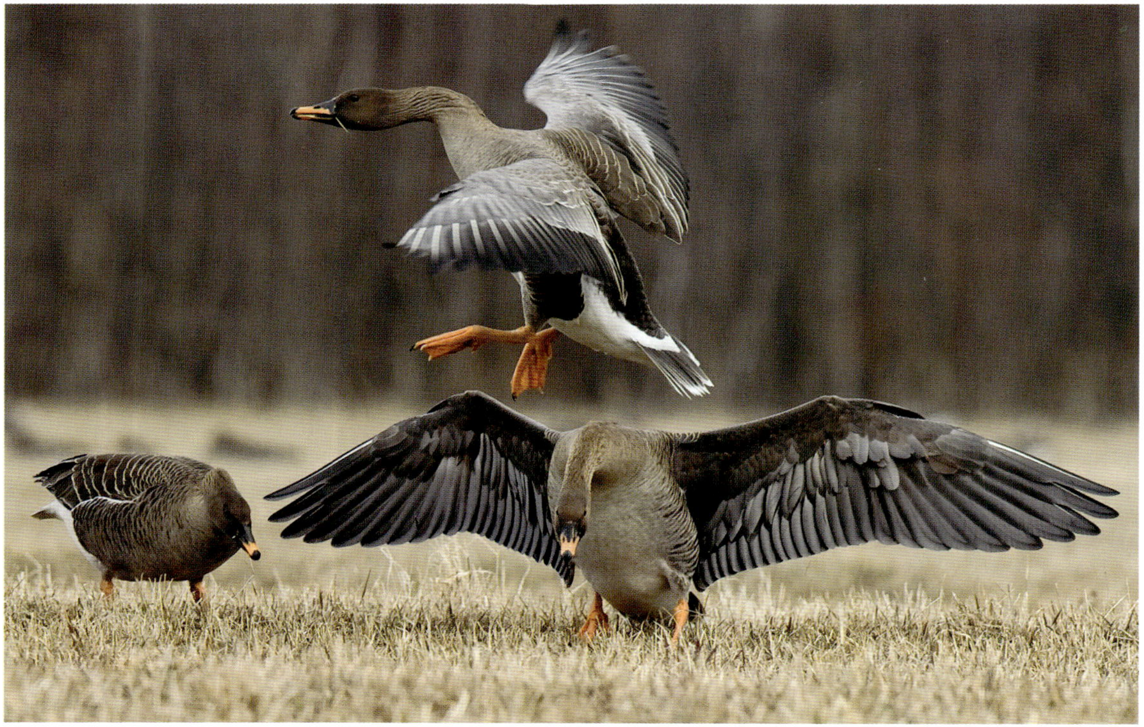

Jari Peltomäki

Bean Geese squabbling and feeding on a field in spring *(Anser fabalis)*
Canon EOS-1D Mark II, 300mm f/2.8, 1/1000 second, f/5.6, ISO 200, continuous focus with 45 focusing points, ground pod. Liminka Bay, Finland, April 2004.

chat with one another in a calm fashion. If their communication becomes excited, you know that something is about to happen; they might be getting ready to take off, or maybe a neighboring male has come too close to a paired female and there will be a chase or a fight. These are opportunities you should not miss!

Every piece of information you glean about your subject raises your chances of getting better photos. You should start by knowing where to find your subject and how to photograph it—this comes only through years of fieldwork. And then you should be prepared to have patience and give your projects the time they need. This is a good recipe for taking successful shots, and when you add a pinch of luck, you can take a winning shot!

JARI PELTOMÄKI

YEARS VARY AND CIRCUMSTANCES CHANGE

Tap into the opportunities each year offers.

Each bird year is different, and many factors affect them. Weather causes essential changes from one year to another, but the food situation has the biggest effect on where and when birds move and where they settle. As an example, in some years rowan trees have very good berry crops. These years are ideal for photographing berry-eating birds. In some years the vole populations decline, so owls become very easy targets for photography. Seasoned bird photographers know how to use these different phenomena to their advantage.

With bird photography, you should strike when the iron is hot. Whenever a normally hard-to-photograph species is for some reason emerging in greater numbers, you should invest time and effort into photographing it. More time should be taken with less photographed species and special situations or actions related to them. Take as varied a selection of shots as possible with different focal lengths and angles, even of the same bird. You never know what type of images will be most useful. The future use of your image may rely on a small difference, such as if the bird is perching in just the right position or on just the right branch. You might also get the chance to photograph something that has rarely—if ever—been photographed before. The more time you spend with a subject, the better your photographs get.

Spring Floods and the First Open Waters

In latitudes where it snows, some winters are more spectacular than others. You should not miss the opportunity to concentrate on snow when you can, be it in your own country or somewhere else. A snow-related phenomenon to pay attention to is spring flooding, especially when spring is advancing fast after a snow-rich winter and floods hit flat fields and low estuaries and shores. These areas are favored by geese and swans. These floods are over in a couple of days, so you should carefully follow the situation; ideally, take your blind to the shooting site well in advance. During cold springs the waters open up slowly, giving photographers good opportunities to shoot a variety of species at close ranges. You can help waterbirds find the spot in front of your blind by placing grain on the ground for them to feed on.

The fields around Liminganlahti Bay in Oulu, Finland, offer good opportunities for photographing geese—like

A lightweight and low tarp blind on a flooded field in spring

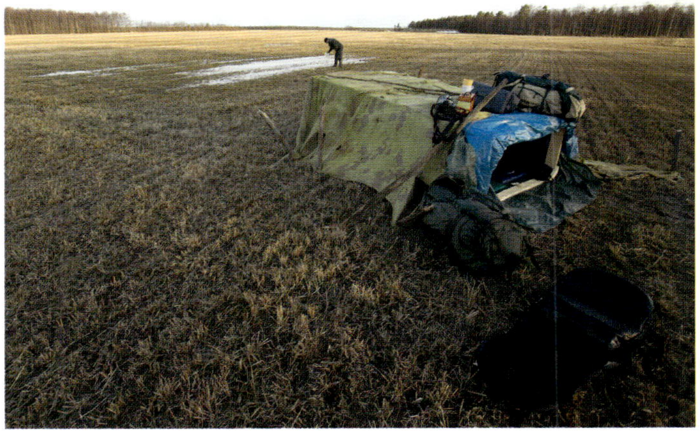

Jari Peltomäki

Graylag Geese and Bean Geese have arrived in spring, finding the first open patches of water *(Anser anser, Anser fabalis)*
Canon EOS-1D Mark III, 500mm f/4.0, 1/1000 second, f/9.0, ISO 400, Manfrotto 501 video head, ground pod, blind.
Lumijoki, Finland, April 2008.

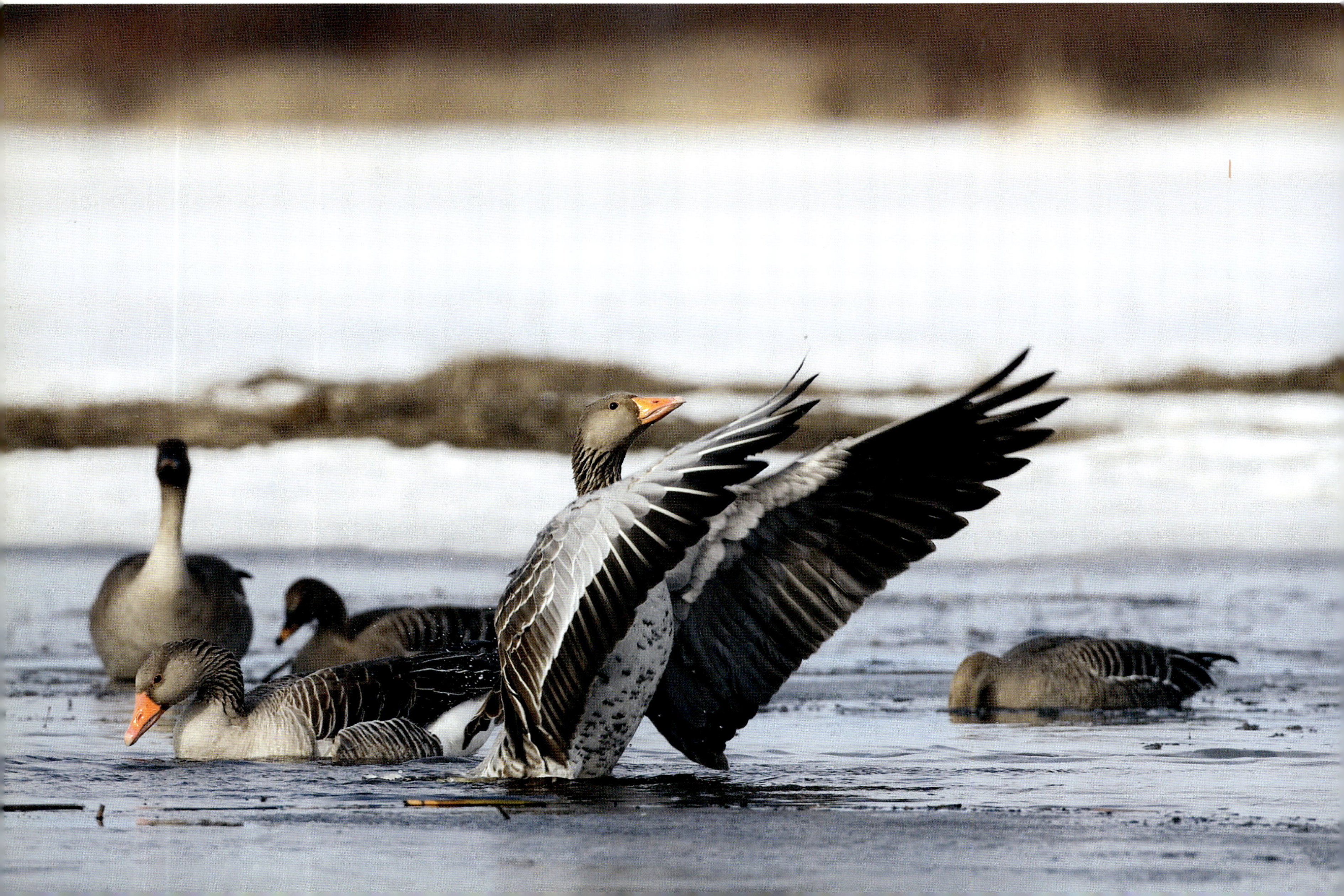

Jari Peltomäki

Graylag, Bean, Greater White-fronted, and Pink-footed—at close range. Lightweight tent blinds or other portable constructions with tarpaulin covers are the photographer's choice in these fields because it is important to be able to move them easily. Barley scattered on the ground in front of the blind helps attract the birds closer, and in about a day or two the normally shy geese get used to the blind.

Vagrant Birds

In some autumns there can be a lot of vagrant birds. An especially successful breeding season causes the surplus birds to erupt out of their normal range in search of food, sometimes in great numbers. The best places to photograph them are capes, spits, islands, and ridges between the inland waterways. The tip of the Hanko Peninsula is one of Finland's best-known spots for wandering birds. Typical vagrant species are the

Markus Varesvuo

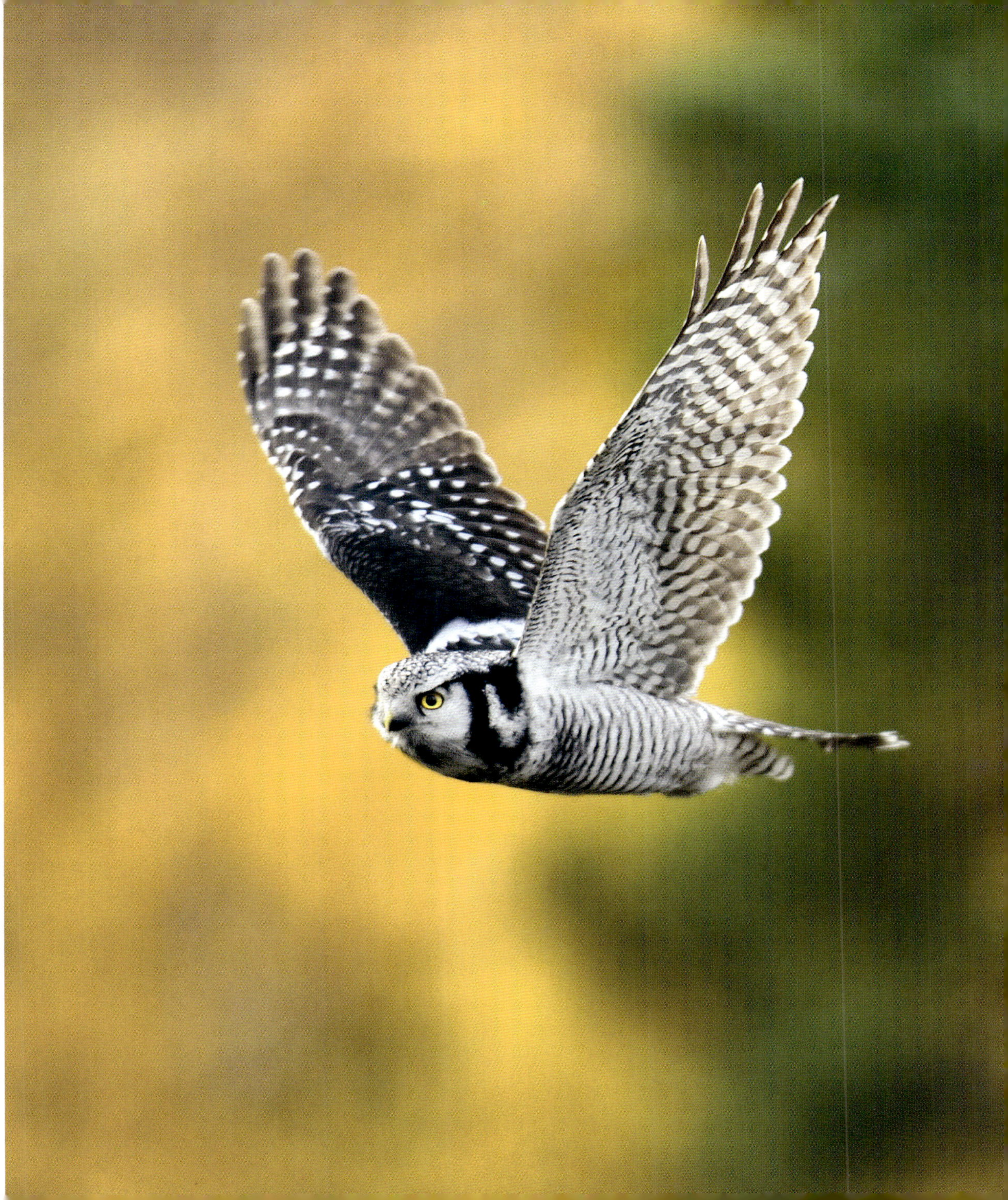

A Northern Hawk Owl on autumn migration *(Surnia ulula)*
Canon EOS-1D Mark II, 300mm f/2.8, 1/1600 second, f/2.8, ISO 800, continuous focus with 45 focusing points, handheld camera. Helsinki, Finland, October 2005.

Erkki Toppinen

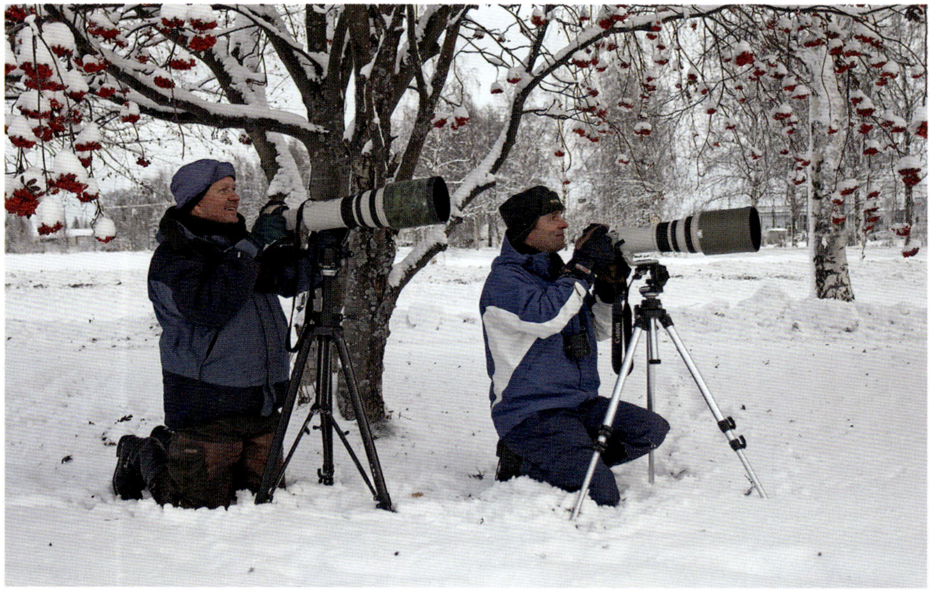

Bird photographers with an excellent opportunity to photograph berry-eating birds

Long-tailed Tit and other tits, woodpeckers, jays, nutcrackers, and nuthatches.

Owls can also take to nomadic behavior as they search for new hunting grounds, and they can be out and about during daylight. A Northern Hawk Owl stayed for months in a park in Helsinki, offering great opportunities for photographing it (overleaf). The autumn foliage helps indicate that the owl is an autumn vagrant. And as always, autumn colors give your shots an elegant touch!

Berry-Eating Birds

The success of rowanberry crops makes a big difference in terms of how easy it is to photograph birds like waxwings, Pine Grosbeaks, and thrushes. Every few years the rowans yield very good crops, bringing an influx of berry-eating birds to the area, and this is when you should concentrate your photographic efforts on them. The birds start from the tops of the trees and gradually work their way down. You should be ready because by that time the birds, focused on eating, are quite fearless and are easily photographed. This is a good example of an opportunity not to be missed!

Much more rarely, maybe only once or twice in a decade, you get to photograph birds feeding on snow-covered berries. The action-packed foraging and eating, combined with the elements of berries and snow, offer you many chances at being creative in your photography. Don't forget that light reflects off snow and hits the birds from a low angle; this is a nice element in your images, especially in flight shots.

When the rowans are doubling over with berries, you can harvest some and

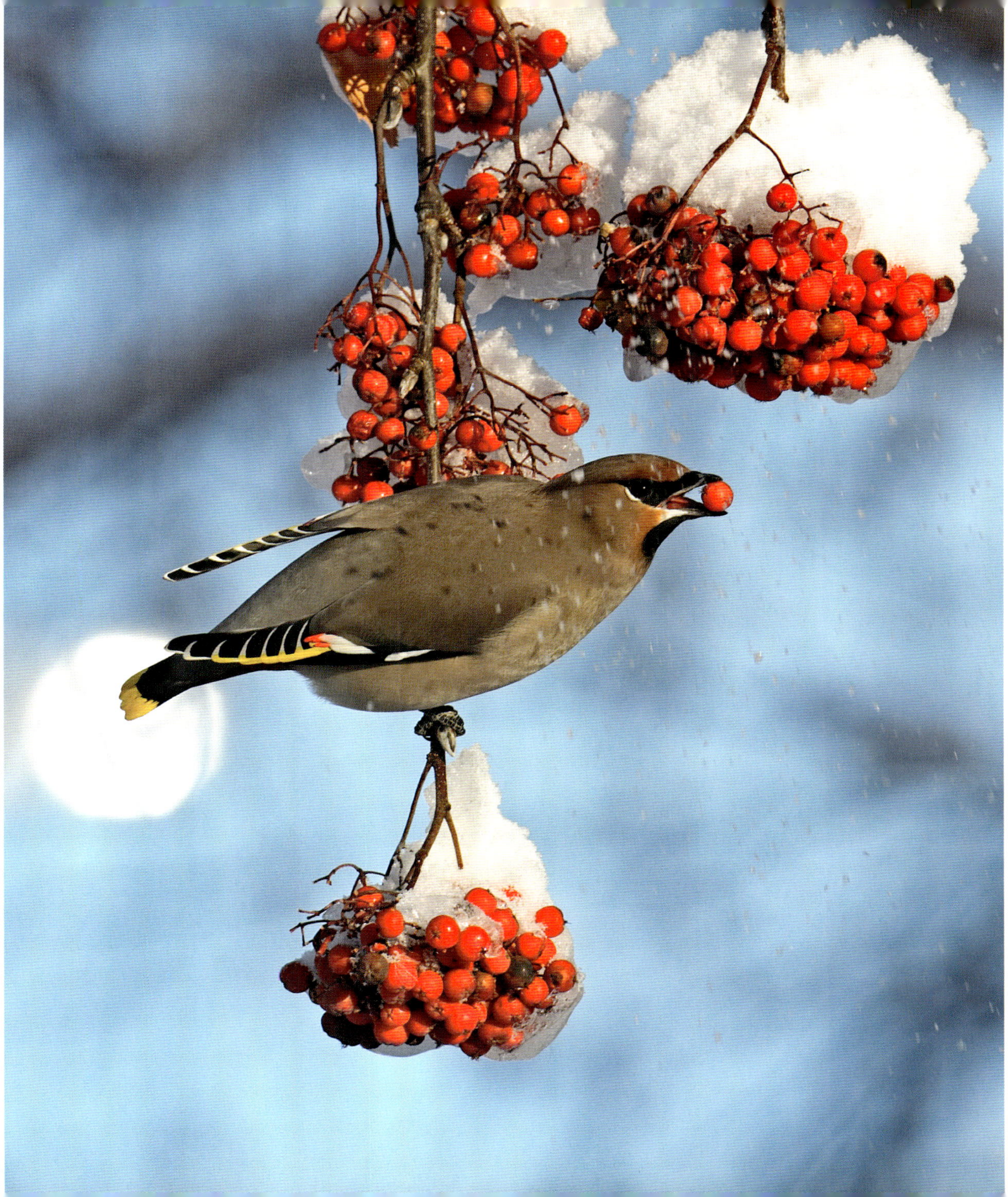

Jari Peltomäki

Bohemian Waxwing with snowy rowanberries *(Bombycilla garrulus)*
Canon EOS-1D Mark II N, 500mm f/4.0, 1/1000 second, f/8.0, ISO 400, one-shot focus with one focusing point, Manfrotto tripod, Manfrotto 501 video head. Liminka, Finland, November 2006.

stock them in your freezer. You can use the frozen berries to attract berry-eating birds to your feeding stations. Many great images of berry-eating birds have been taken in simulated situations.

Owl Years

Just as berry crops affect berry-eating birds, fluctuations in vole populations affect owl behavior and how easily they can be photographed. Vole populations fluctuate in roughly four-year cycles, and most owls breed during population rises or peaks. Years when the vole populations are on the rise are especially good because it helps the young owls fledge and find food throughout their first year. Peak years, on the other hand, can be difficult because the vole populations often decline during the breeding season or in the autumn, making survival through their first winter unlikely for the young owls.

So how do the vole populations affect the life of a bird photographer? Well, the cycles differ from one area to another, and keeping track of the vole population development in your locale helps you plan owl projects. A local raptor center will probably have information about the voles. You can also find information from forest research centers, which can often give estimates for a wider area.

When the owls are having a good breeding year, you have the opportunity to witness and document the entire breeding phase, with the males bringing food to the nestlings and, later, the dispersed owlets. Sometimes, with the necessary precautions and preparations, you can photograph breeding owls, but remember to make sure that your photographic actions do not cause the birds any harm! If you are at all unsure how to go about it, find out before trying on your own. You can turn to bird guides or other bird experts.

Nowadays extremely rare in Scandinavia and Finland, the Snowy Owl sometimes breeds in the region, depending on the lemming populations. For unknown reasons, lemmings have fluctuated in very uneven cycles, and peak years are few and far between, making the Snowy Owl a rare breeder in this part of the arctic range. Photographing breeding Snowy Owls requires a license from the authorities. In 2007 roughly 10 Snowy Owl pairs attempted breeding in the Finnish Lapland, and another 10 or so in Finnmark, northern Norway. Most of the nests perished due to a dramatic decline in the lemming populations at a crucial time in the breeding season. Some parents were able to adapt to the situation and

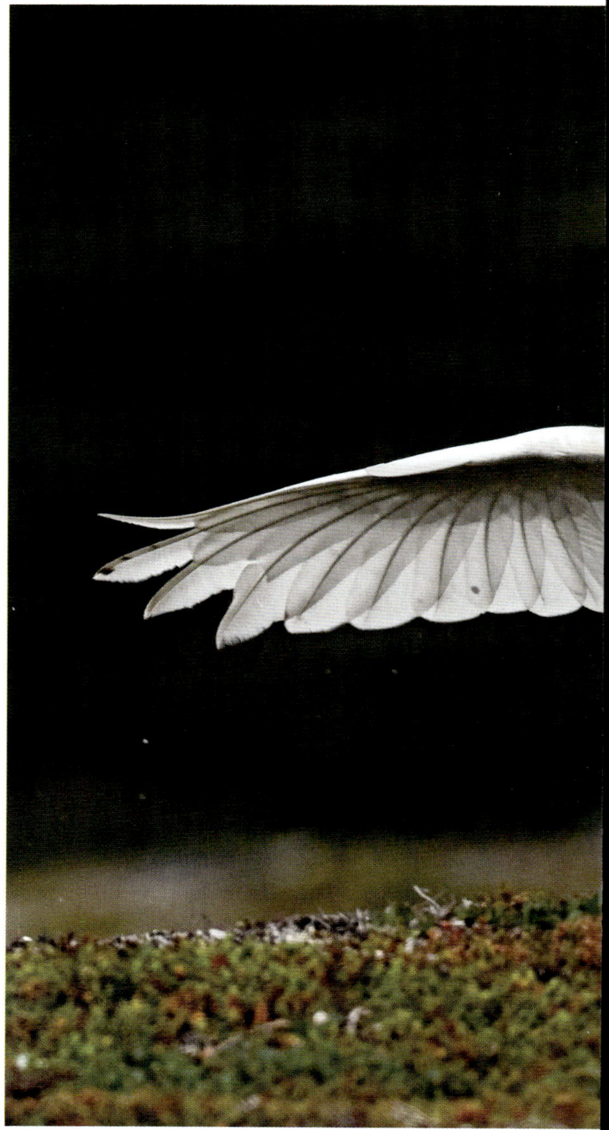

Jari Peltomäki

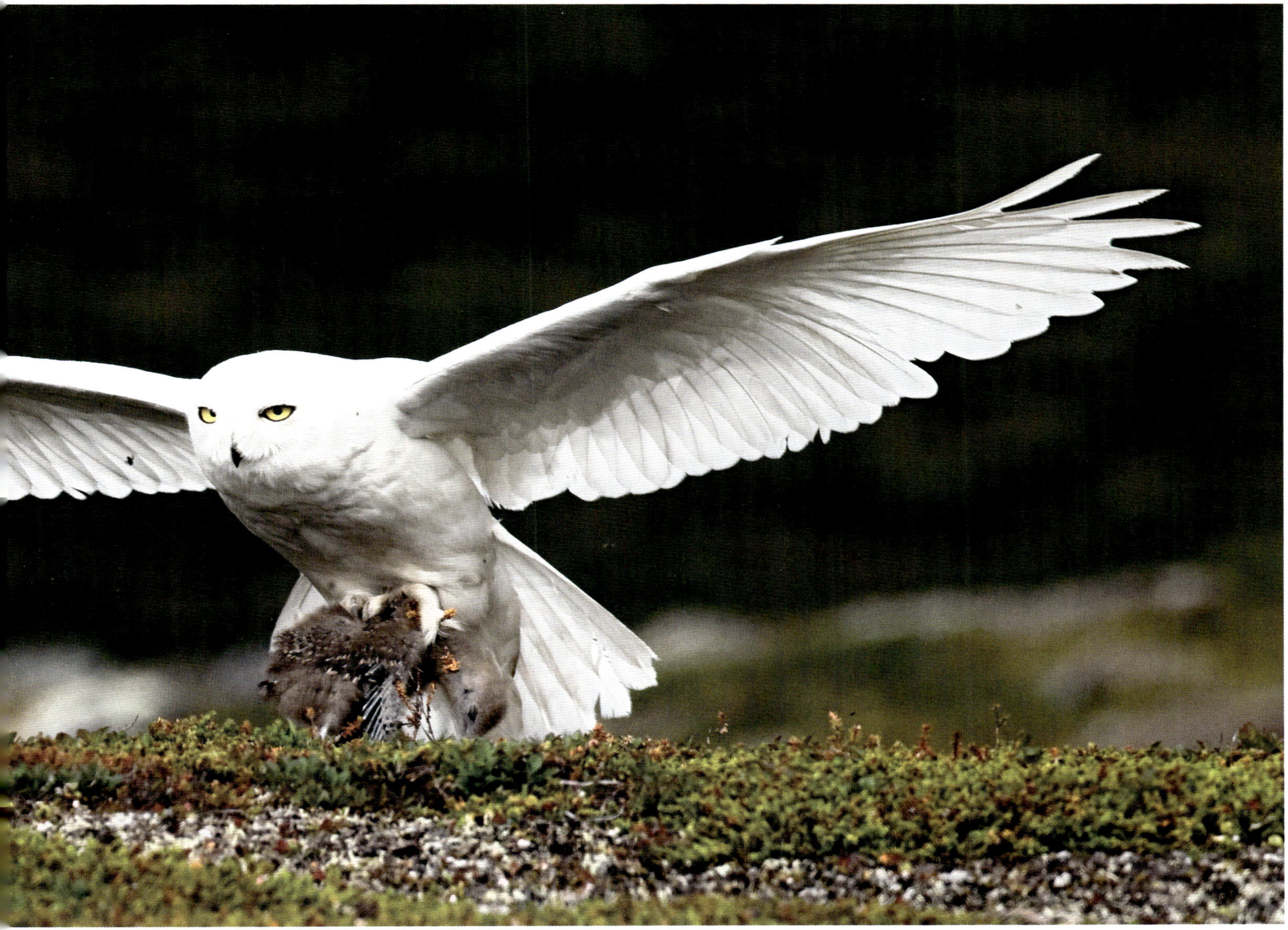

A Long-tailed Jaeger chick caught by a male Snowy Owl
(Bubo scandiacus, Stercorarius longicaudus)
Canon EOS-1D Mark III, 500mm f/4.0, 1/1250 second, f/13.0, ISO 800, continuous focus with an extended central focusing point, Gitzo tripod, Manfrotto 501 video head, dome tent blind. Finnish Lapland, July 2007.

Minna Rautio

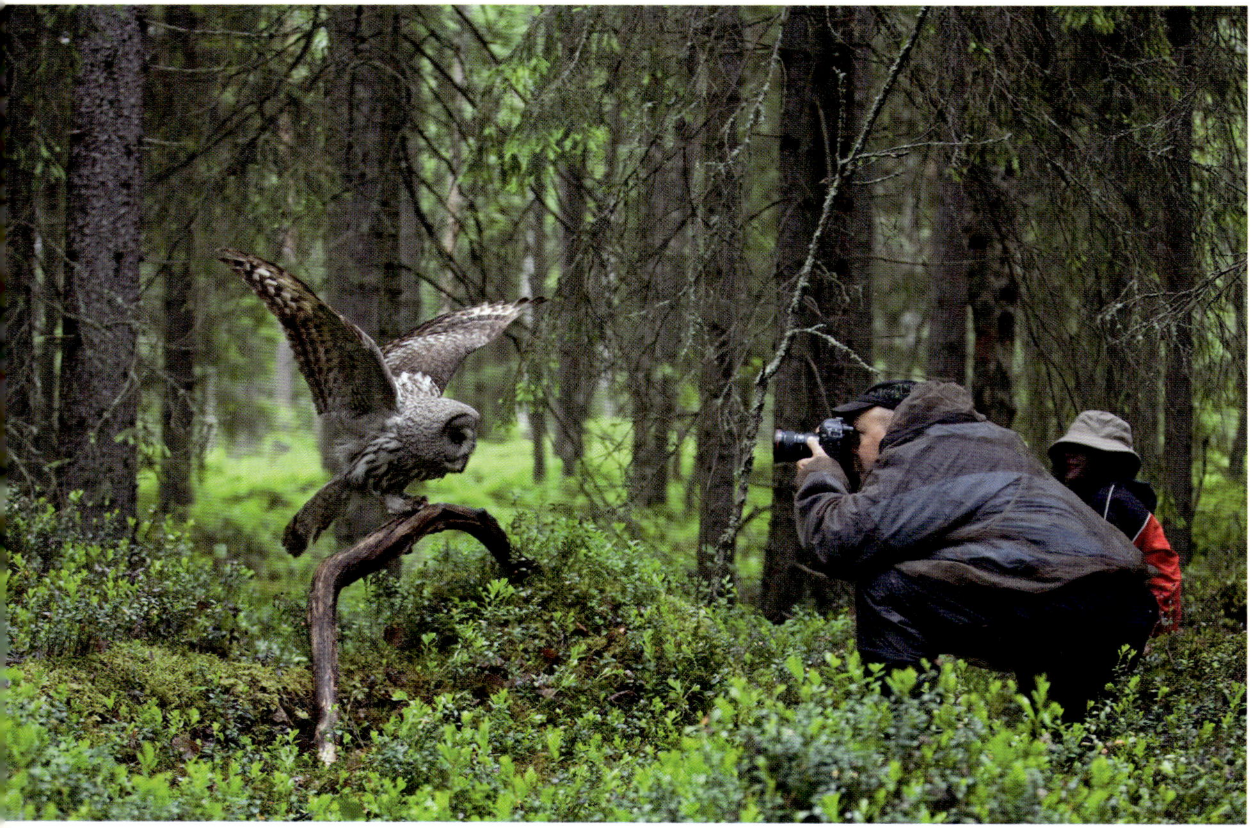

A female Great Gray Owl, wild and free *(Strix nebulosa)*

started feeding their young with other birds. At least chicks of Common/Black Scoters, Wood Sandpipers, and Meadow Pipits plus their chicks, and adult Long-tailed Jaegers/Skuas ended up on the Snowy Owls' menu!

Owls can be more readily photographed when the vole populations are low because you can feed breeding owls with dead rodents and even with pieces of meat or minced meat. Sometimes, in situations like these, female owls seem to become temporarily tame, which makes photographing them very easy, whereas the males and the chicks retain their innate shyness. The females return to their wild selves by the time the special circumstances are over.

Sometimes owls are forced to wander in the winter due to scarcity of food, and they can become active in the daytime. As they gravitate to open areas to hunt, they become easier to photograph. By spending a lot of time along the edge of a field you can get spectacular shots of owls hunting in authentic, unsimulated situations. Changes in the temperature and the weather conditions can at times cause the snowpack to become really hard, making it difficult or impossible for the owls to strike through to get their prey, or an owl can be close to starvation and have no energy left for hunting. Bird photographers can start feeding these owls with dead voles or mice. Many an owl has been helped through the winter, or even saved from starvation, and in exchange the photographer gets beautiful shots of owls flying low over snowy fields.

A starved female Great Gray Owl was fed in Tornio, northwest Finland, in the winter of 2008–2009 for several months, with dead rodents and pieces of pork heart. Dozens of photographers from all over the world had the chance to photograph it.

A Great Gray Owl hunting ***(Strix nebulosa)***
Canon EOS-1D Mark III, 70–200mm f/2.8, 1/2000 second, 75mm, f/8.0, ISO 800, continuous focus with one focusing point, handheld camera. Tornio, Finland, March 2009.

Jari Peltomäki

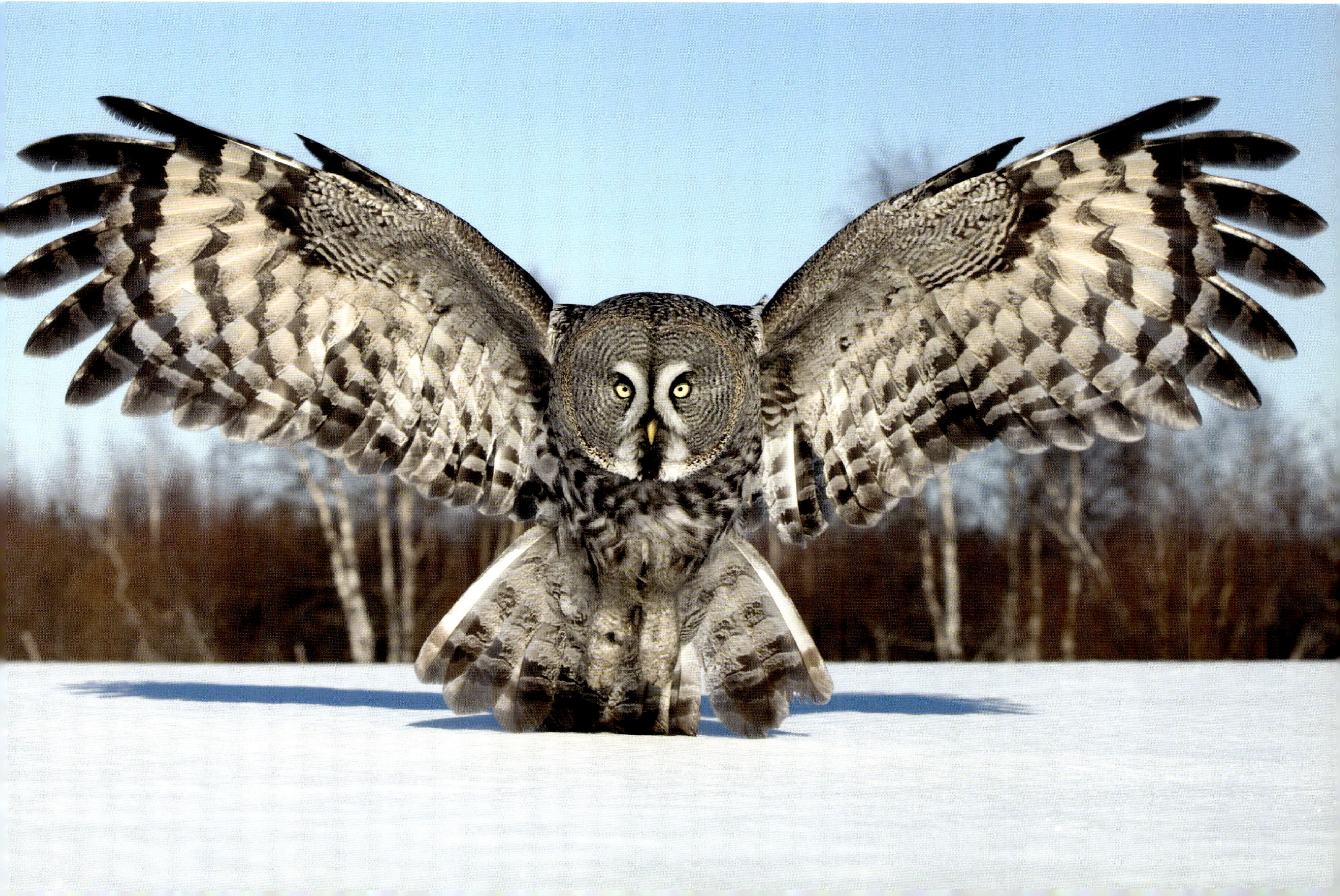

MARKUS VARESVUO

LOOK FOR NEW ANGLES

Birds are being photographed more than ever before.

The advance of digital cameras has fundamentally changed photography; for example, bird photographers easily take 10 times as many pictures as they did with film cameras. The expense of buying and developing film used to be a limiting factor, whereas now, after the initial and undeniably hefty investment, photography costs practically nothing. Taking hundreds of frames in a good situation is not a problem anymore, nor does it matter if the chances of success are slim.

It is easier to get good shots with a digital camera than with a film camera. The results can be checked instantly on the preview screen, and any changes needed to improve the shot can be made on the spot and the picture can be taken again. Small errors in exposure can be fixed afterwards in image editing software, in stark contrast to the finality of pressing the shutter release of a film camera, where nothing could be done to alter the result afterwards—at least not without a time-consuming and possibly expensive scanning process that inevitably resulted in worse picture quality. The best digital cameras allow ISO values that were never possible before without loss of image quality. All of this has made it easier for people to take pictures of birds, and the number of new photographers has risen exponentially in the past 10 years.

Thousands of enthusiastic photographers roam far and wide with cutting-edge equipment. Sparing no time, effort, or wear and tear on their shutter release, they strive for good images. As a result we are inundated with an unprecedented number of high-quality bird photos that are published on websites that anyone can set up.

Take time to explore the current inventory and quality of bird photography on the Internet. The best material is just a mouse click away. You can browse any picture library that is dedicated to wildlife photography and the hundreds of websites created by active hobbyists and professional photographers. In just a few hours it becomes crystal clear that practically every species is covered with technically good, basic portraits that are usually taken with a long telephoto lens in typical midday light. Every once in a while you will come across delightfully unique and spectacular bird photos.

Set Your Sights High

People who are new to bird photography take great pleasure in sharp images of a familiar species spotted in familiar settings. A little further down the road their appetites grow, and they begin to want more range and variety, either for their own pleasure or to reach a wider audience. Adding a little extra to a photo, like the light of a beautiful evening, dramatic backlight, or an interesting background, can elevate a picture from mediocre to intriguing. A presentation based on a series of good but basic portraits will soon begin to bore both the photographer and the audience. A presentation improves rapidly when it is spiced with elements like backlight, landscape, action, super closeups, rain, creative framing, and so on.

A Siberian Jay in a winter wonderland *(Perisoreus infaustus)*
Canon EOS-1D Mark III, 24mm f/1.4, 1/250 second, f/11.0, ISO 800, prefocus, Gitzo tripod, Manfrotto 501 video head, remote control. Kuusamo, Finland, February 2010.

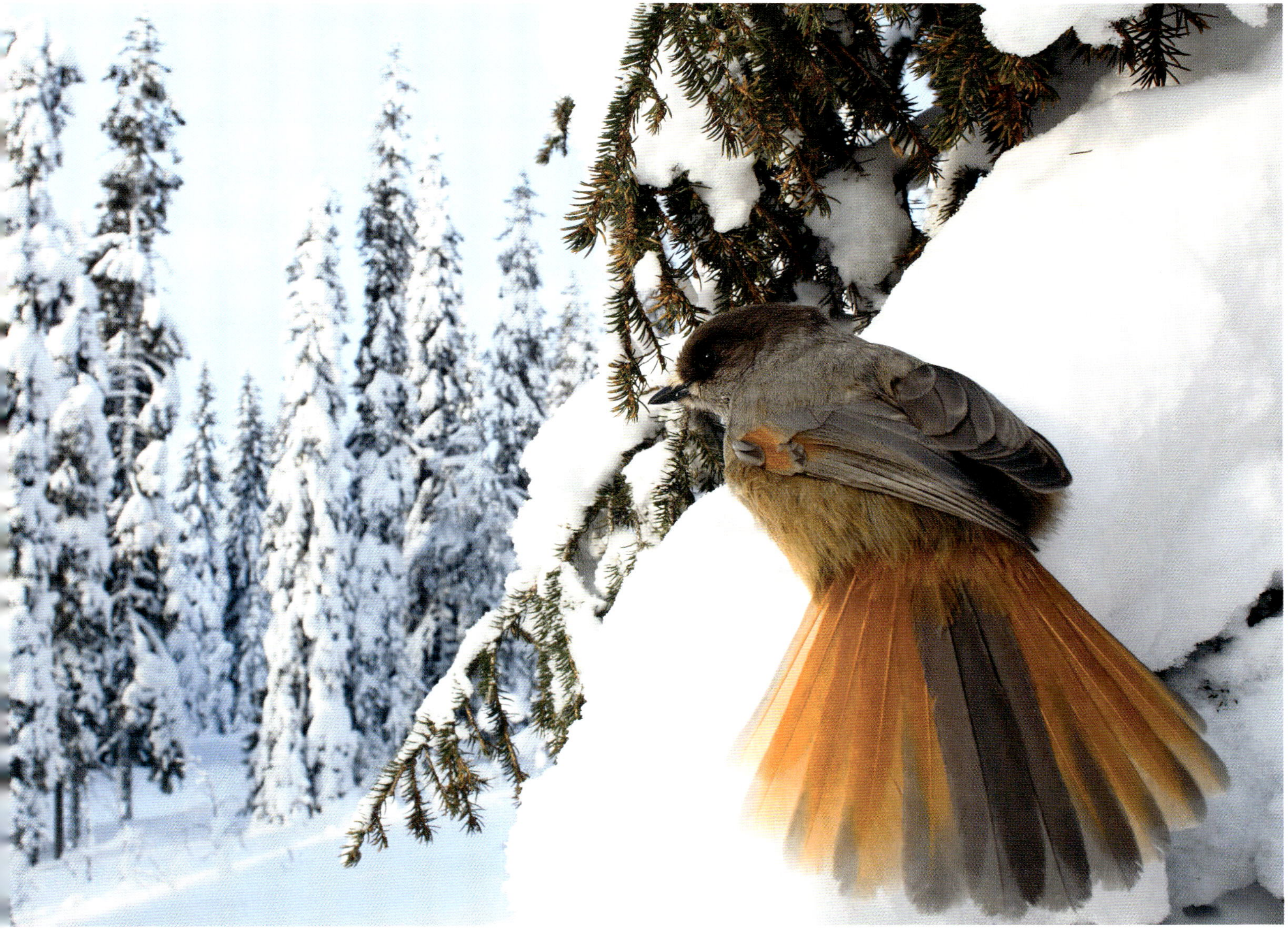

Markus Varesvuo

If you want to get your photos in magazines or books on a regular basis, your material should be extensive and original. Technically flawless quality is a starting point—your creative skill and talent will set you apart from others.

Getting your work accepted by the best nature photo agencies is not easy. An agency might ask you to submit a portfolio of 100 photos so they can evaluate whether your material would add any essential or new value to their collection. On top of having a varied and individual set of photos, success in international photo competitions or some other form of acclaim can help an agency make a decision in your favor.

The following examples outline various angles to approach bird photography.

Taking a good photo of a bird in a landscape is harder than one would think. The basic idea is to shoot with a short focal length to get a full landscape, the bird's habitat, or perhaps its feeding ground. A visually pleasing background is easily achieved in a closeup, but it gets remarkably more difficult in wide landscapes. The challenge is further amplified with efforts to include a cautious bird in the frame; they are not easily approached at the best of times, let alone with a short lens.

I used a 24mm lens and remote control to capture a Siberian Jay in its wintery woodland home. Having placed the camera at an ideal distance from a branch where I had sprinkled some raisins, I framed the image and prefocused my camera. Then, stepping back with the remote control ready, I waited for the birds to arrive and discover the feast.

A 24mm lens has a good depth of field, even with the widest aperture, but if you want to have both the bird big in the picture and your background sharp, you need to stop down to gain the necessary depth of field.

I spent a full day with this project (January days in the north are short) and got a few shots with all the elements I had hoped for.

Some birds are not bothered by people and thus are easy to work with because they mostly ignore humans and provide good opportunities to try shots of birds in a landscape. Big seabird colonies have tens of thousands of birds, and short focal lengths are best for highlighting the size of the huge flocks.

The photo of the flock of flying Common Murres was taken in optimal conditions with a 24mm lens. The birds were flying toward me, into a headwind, directly above my head, with the closest bird nearly touching my hood as they passed the nesting cliff, and the sunlight was coming from behind me. The snow was reflecting light back into the air, which softened the already hard mid-morning light.

I find a 70–200mm zoom lens handy and versatile for taking photos of birds in a landscape. You can be farther from the subjects than with a wide-angle lens, and the zoom offers more opportunities for framing the picture.

The Smew photo is an excellent example of a 70–200mm zoom at work. The pair is perching on spring ice by a small opening in the water, waiting for the ice to melt on their nesting lake. The birds are within a few yards of each other, yet by zooming the lens to a focal length of 85mm the photographer captured the birds, the opposite shoreline, and the mist rising from the icy lake into the spring-heated air.

In portraits, the background also plays an important role. Portraits are normally taken with a telephoto lens to get the subject sharply in focus, while the background is blurred into a uniform canvas. More often than not, the best background is darker than the subject because it allows the subject to stand out in the picture.

Water is a playful element and provides many opportunities for taking pictures with a more personal touch. I once got the chance to shoot Red Phalaropes

Common Murres over their nesting cliffs *(Uria aalge)*
Canon EOS-1Ds Mark III, 24mm f/1.4, 1/2000 second, f/4.5, ISO 250, continuous focus with 45 focusing points, handheld camera. Vardø, Norway, April 2009.

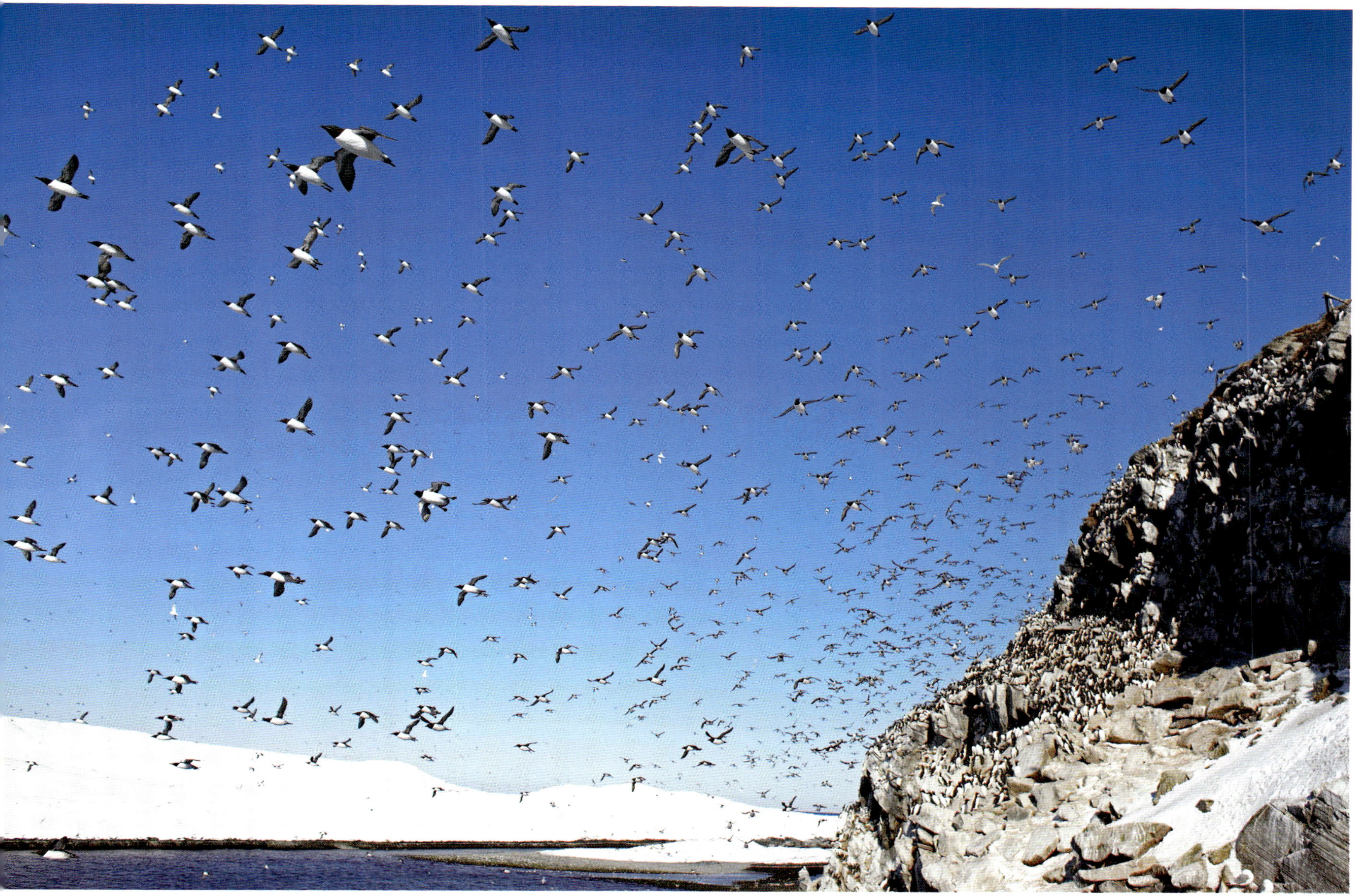

Markus Varesvuo

Jari Peltomäki

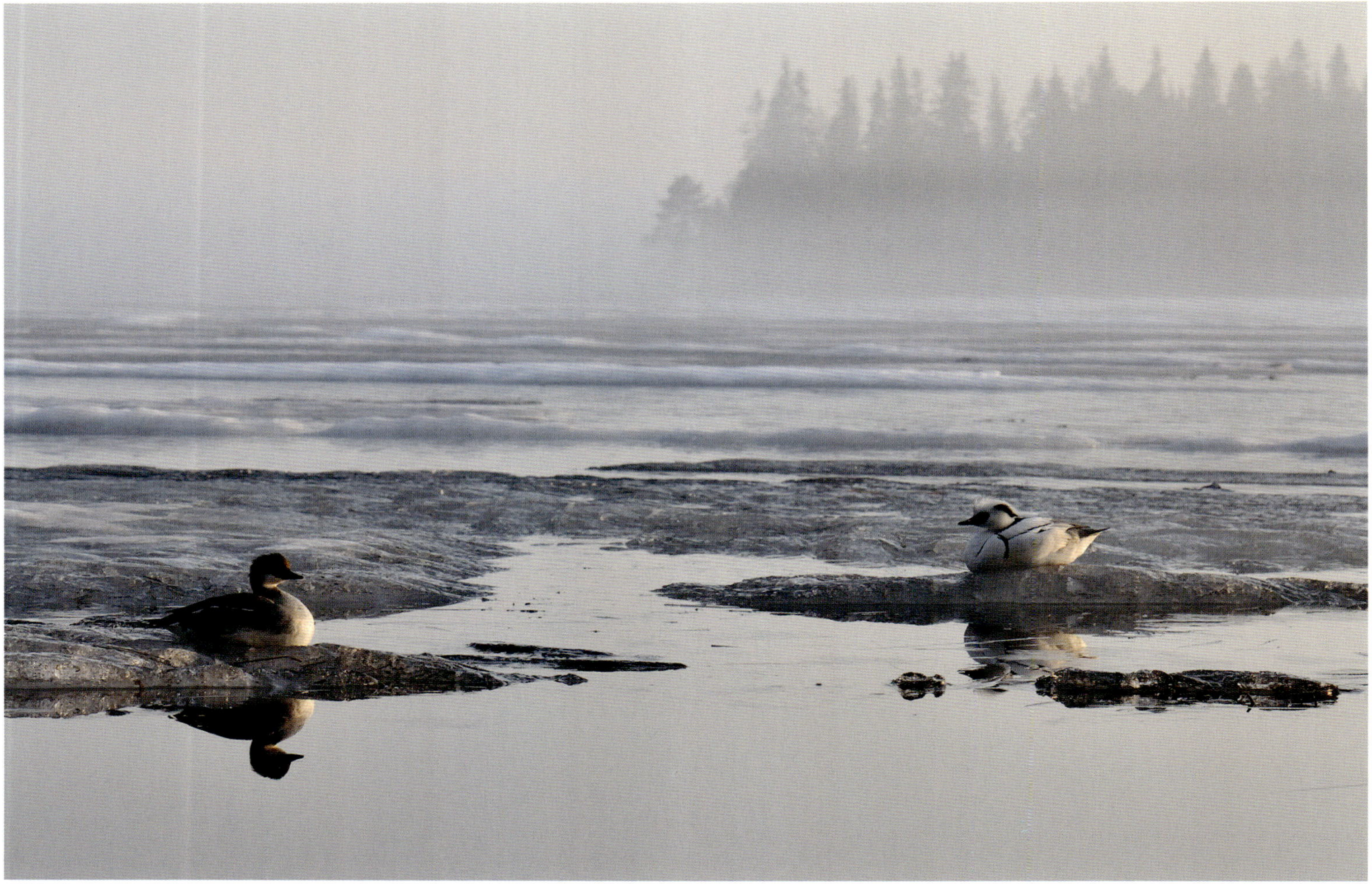

Smews on spring ice *(Mergellus albellus)*
Nikon D300S, 70–200mm f/2.8, 1/500 second, 86mm, f/9.0, ISO 800, one-shot focus with a central focusing point, ground pod, Manfrotto 501 video head, blind. Kuusamo, Finland, May 2010.

Markus Varesvuo

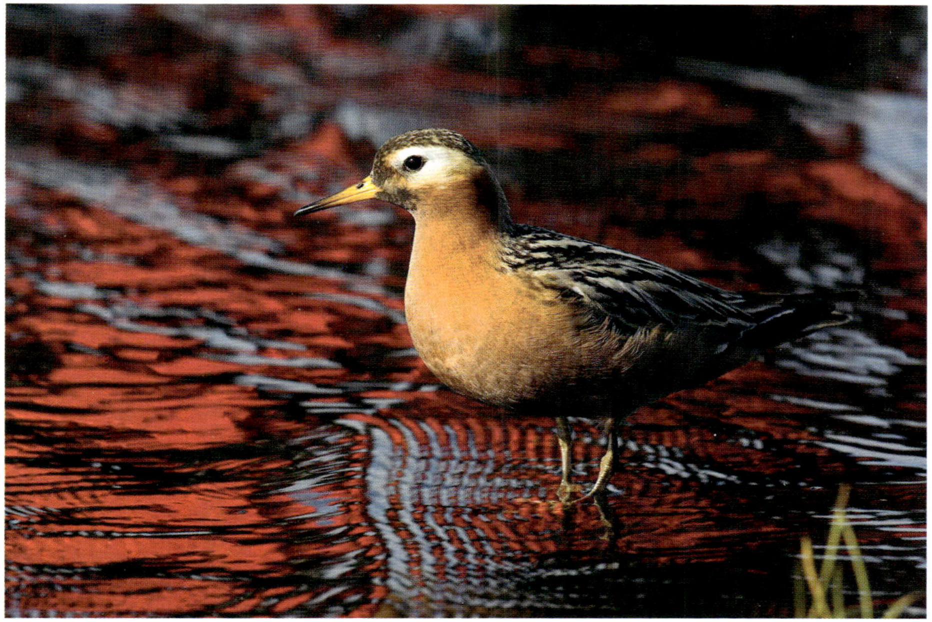

Red Phalarope with a red reflection *(Phalaropus fulicarius)*
Canon EOS-1D Mark II, 500mm f/4.0, 1/200 second, f/14, ISO 250, one-shot focus, Gitzo tripod, Manfrotto 501 video head. Iceland, June 2006.

in good settings for several hours. At first I took traditional closeups with the blue sky or some darker land formation reflecting in the surface of the shallow water. Then I noticed that the reflection from my travel partner's bright red coat was creating interesting patterns in the small irregular ripples across the water. I positioned myself to better get the red into the picture so it entirely framed the bird.

A tight crop that partially shows the subject and unusual light can transform a basic portrait. The Cinereous Vulture is backlit by the soft rays of the evening sun and is framed with a beautiful golden rim of light. The dark uniform background further emphasizes the effect.

If your subject is engaged in some activity, it will immediately raise the impact of your photo. It may not end up being used in a field guide, but it will more likely find its way into other publications, like magazines and books, than a bird that is just sitting there.

As usual, at the end of the summer I was photographing migrating birds. The southern and southwestern areas of the Finnish archipelago are along the migration routes, and birds stop on the islands to rest and feed before continuing their journeys. This time I was working on Utö Island when a young Spotted Redshank landed on the shore right in front of my blind. It foraged for a while, and then it started to preen. After cleaning its feathers thoroughly, it stretched its wings. Because I had witnessed this behavior before and knew what to expect, I turned my camera upright in anticipation of just this type

Markus Varesvuo

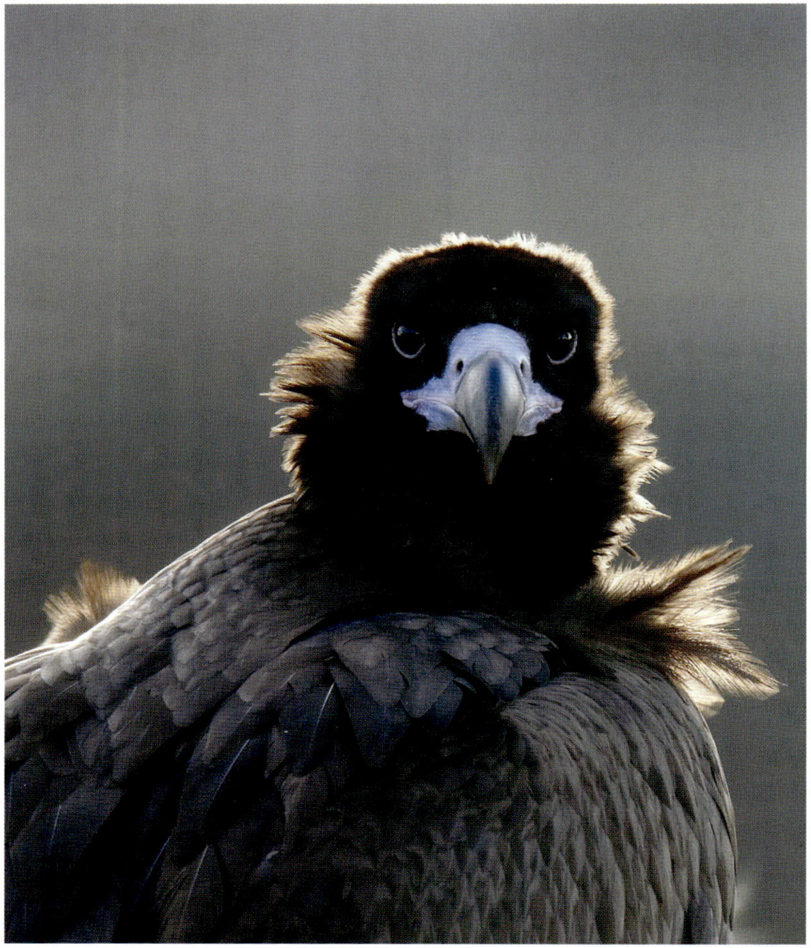

Cinereous Vulture edged in gold *(Aegypius monachus)*
Canon EOS-1Ds Mark III, 800mm f/5.6 plus 1.4x extender, 1/160 second, f/8, ISO 800, one-shot focus, Gitzo tripod, Manfrotto 501 video head, blind. Spain, December 2009.

of action. Being ready is important because the moment is brief.

Maybe closest to my own heart is taking action shots of birds. Flying, feeding, displaying, mating, fighting, and other forms of action are an essential part of a bird's life. Successfully taking action shots of birds is still a challenge, even with the most current professional camera bodies. Automatic focusing has advanced by leaps and bounds since the early days, but flying birds, especially against a background other than a uniform blue sky, are clearly still a problem.

I categorize action shots into three types:

1. Photos where movement is totally frozen
2. Photos with the head and body sharp, and the wings show movement
3. Photos that aim for a more artistic impression by showing the whole bird in a flurry of movement

I prefer photos of birds that are at least partially in sharp focus. Over the years I have seen really great shots belonging to the third category. Although I can appreciate them, it is not a trend that I follow in my own work.

The lighting conditions were excellent when I was taking the Bohemian Waxwing photo, allowing me to use a very short exposure time and completely freeze the bird's movement all the way to the wing tips. Light was reflecting off the snow and projecting back up toward the bird's underside, which helped even out the powerful spring light. Complete with the rowan tree in the background,

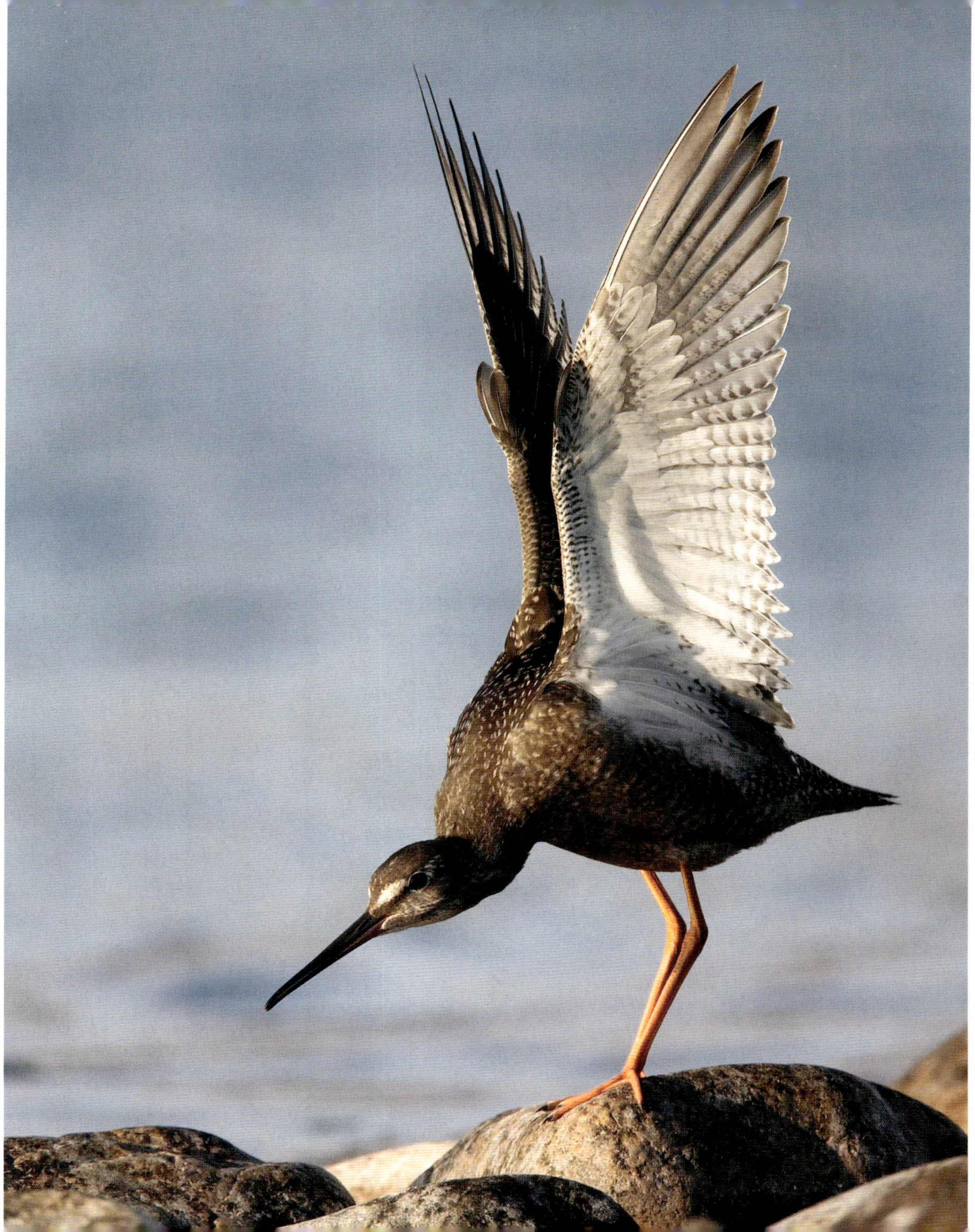

Markus Varesvuo

Spotted Redshank stretching *(Tringa erythropus)*
Canon EOS-1Ds Mark III, 800mm f/5.6 plus 1.4x extender, 1/1000 second, f/8, ISO 800, one-shot focus, Gitzo tripod, Manfrotto 501 video head, blind. Parainen, Finland, August 2009.

Bohemian Waxwing in flight *(Bombycilla garrulus)*
Canon EOS-1D, 300mm f/2.8, 1/5000 second, f/3.5, ISO 200, continuous focus with 45 focusing points, handheld camera. Helsinki, Finland, March 2003.

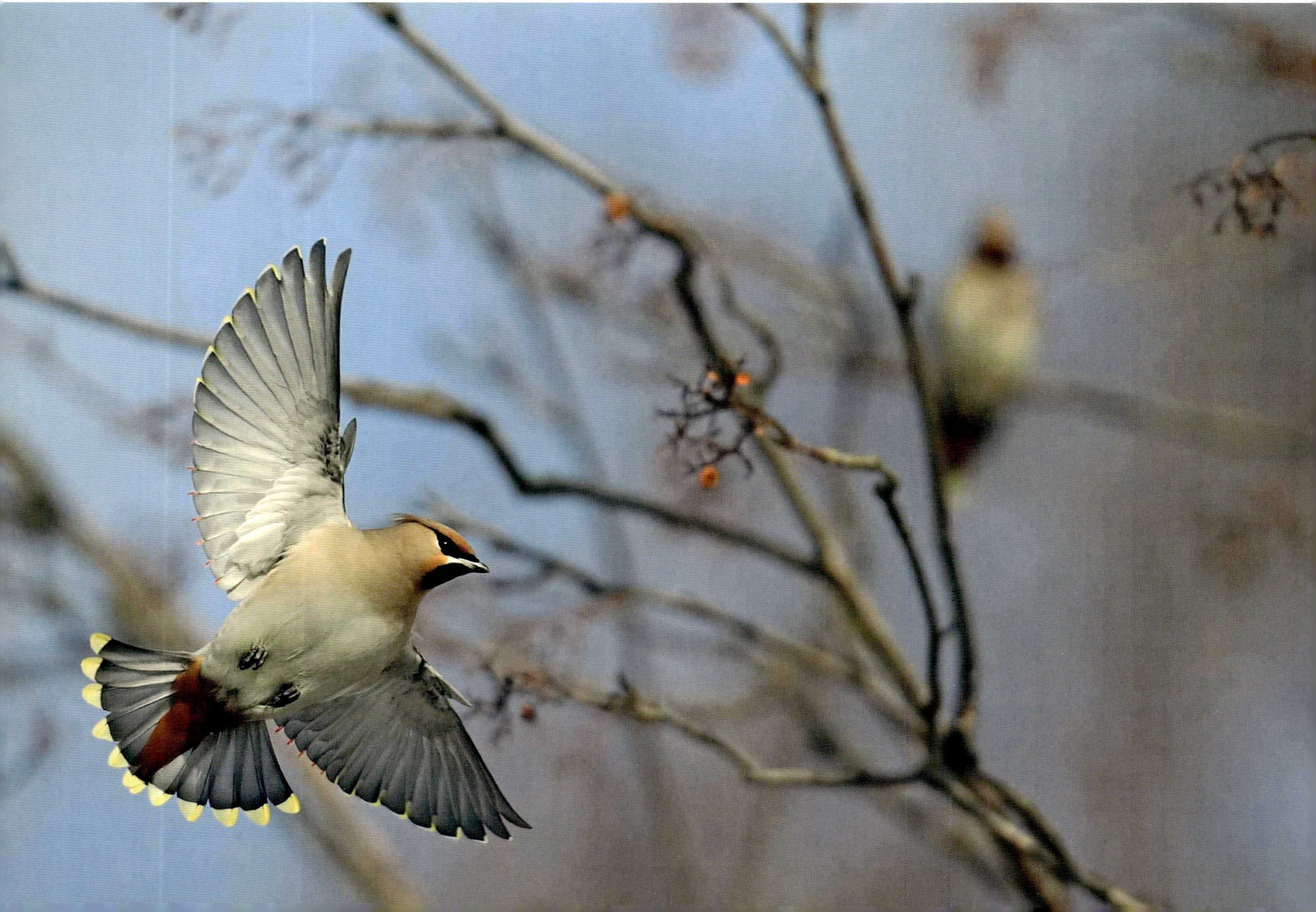

empty of berries, I knew I had taken a powerful photo. Despite many attempts over the years, I have never taken a better shot of a Bohemian Waxwing in flight.

The exposure time in the Black Grouse photo was fast enough to freeze the bird's head and body, yet slow enough to leave some movement in the wings. The light hitting the tip of the right wing emphasizes the effect.

Barnacle Geese are a fairly new sight in the southern Finnish landscape. Their population has quickly grown in the past 10 years, and in its immediate surroundings Helsinki now has thousands of Barnacle Geese in the autumn, feeding on the fields and fattening themselves for the upcoming migration.

The geese continue eating for about half an hour after sunset before they lift off and head toward their roosting sites on the Gulf of Finland. I wanted to capture the atmosphere of that moment—the fading daylight and the rising moon with hundreds of geese flying low on fast wings—without attempting to freeze a single bird.

Birds can be photographed in many different ways. It is possible to take unique shots of even the most common and most frequently photographed species as long as you don't settle for a basic portrait. Don't be afraid to take risks and do things differently; give your creativity a chance.

Markus Varesvuo

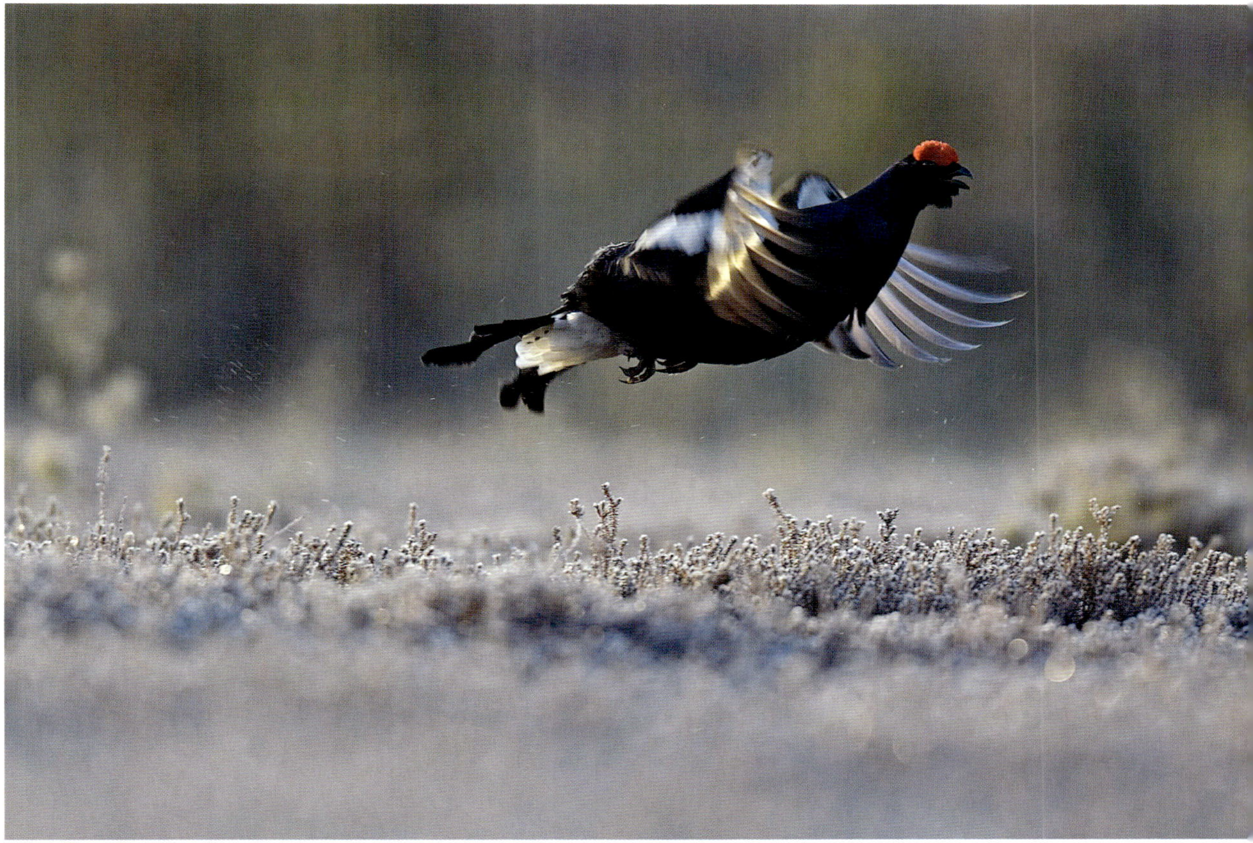

Markus Varesvuo

Black Grouse taking off *(Tetrao tetrix)*
Canon EOS-1D, 300mm f/2.8, 1/500 second, f/2.8, ISO 200, continuous focus with 45 focusing points, blind, beanbag.
Liminka, Finland, April 2003.

Barnacle Geese on an evening flight *(Branta leucopsis)*
Canon EOS-1D Mark III, 35 mm f/2.0, 1/50 second, f/2.0, ISO 3200, prefocus, handheld camera. Helsinki, Finland, October 2008.

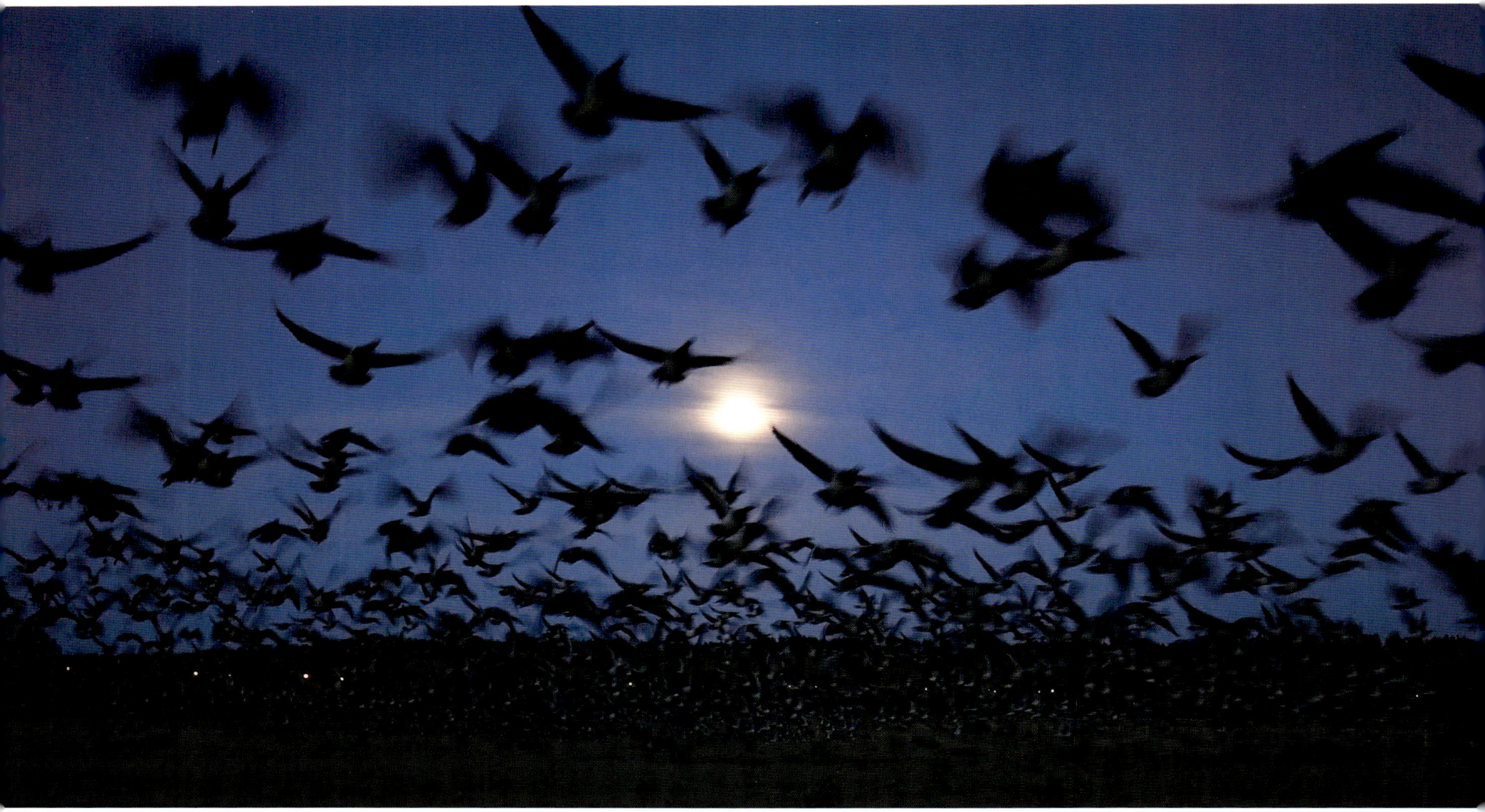

Markus Varesvuo

MARKUS VARESVUO

PERSEVERANCE PAYS OFF

Don't give up before you have the photo you want.

There are many ways to get good photos. One of the easiest is to frequent good birding sites and shoot whenever something interesting happens. This way, if you have good equipment and good photography skills, you can amass a nice collection of decent photos over the years, and with a bit of luck you can also get some excellent shots.

I have found that the best photos are the result of spending long stretches of time with one species. This way I learn more about their behavior and where and how they move. Usually, after I have studied a species well and gotten to know its ways, a vision of the type of photo I want to capture starts to take shape in my mind. The vision can originate from the bird's habitat, certain light conditions, the background, or the bird's behavior. Having first envisioned the photo in my mind, all that is needed for bringing the vision to life is tenacity and skill.

Often, in order for an envisioned photo to become a reality, you will need many repeated opportunities to take it. Many parts must fall into place: weather with the right lighting conditions, perfect exposure and focusing, and the subject has to rise to the occasion, too.

The following are three accounts of how I made a photograph out of a vision in my mind.

European Bee-eater

In May 2008 I was in Hungary on a mission from the Wild Wonders of Europe initiative, photographing the charismatic and colorful birds of the Hungarian puszta, with the European Bee-eater as one of my main target species. I photographed it mostly from a blind near a breeding colony. Within a couple of days I had many photos of courtship rituals, mating, nest hole digging, feeding, and flying.

While photographing I noticed how Bee-eaters liked to perch on a favorite branch and dart off in hot pursuit when an insect flew past them, and they often returned to the same branch with an insect in their bills. Next they would beat the insect against the branch until it was lifeless. If the insect was big, the Bee-eater had to get it inside its bill a certain way to swallow it; this was often done by tossing the insect in the air a couple of times until it was in an ideal position.

I started envisioning a rather tight closeup of a Bee-eater tossing a dragonfly, a beetle, or a bee.

Such an image, a closeup of a rather small bird, would require moving the blind to within about 5 m (16 ft) of a Bee-eater's perch, and a 500mm telephoto lens would bring the bird to the viewfinder at just the right size.

It took the birds next to no time to get used to my relocated blind, and they resumed their hunting activities from the perch. During the ensuing two days I used the best light, which is early morning and late evening, to take the image I envisioned. To freeze the action I needed a shutter speed of 1/2000 second. Even though I set the ISO to 1600, the depth of field was quite shallow at f/6.4.

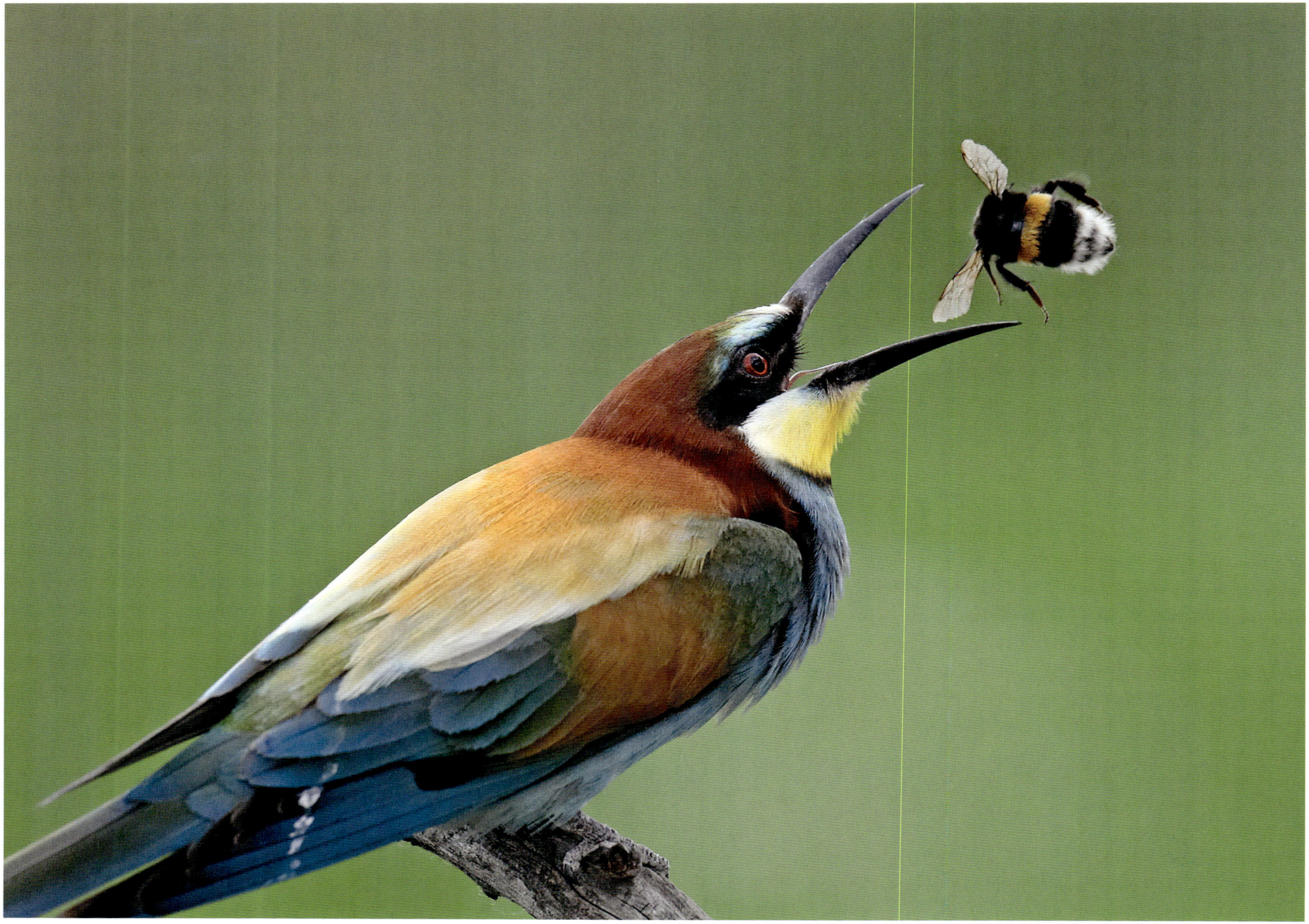

Markus Varesvuo/Wild Wonders of Europe

A European Bee-eater and a bee
(Merops apiaster)
Canon EOS-1D Mark III, 500mm f/4.0, 1/2000 second, f/6.4, ISO 1600, continuous focus with an extended central focusing point, Gitzo tripod, Manfrotto 501 video head, blind. Hungary, May 2008.

First I tried prefocusing on the Bee-eater's bill, but I soon realized that while they were handling their prey, the birds moved their heads constantly, which caused blurred images. Using continuous focus with an extended central focusing point yielded much better results, and by the second day everything fell into place.

A Bee-eater returned with a big bee in its bill and settled on the perch in a good angle toward me. After smashing the bee, the Bee-eater tossed it in the air a couple of times before swallowing it. I got two good frames of the situation, and one of them was pretty much what I had envisioned.

Bearded Reedling

The Bearded Reedling is a bit of an oddity in the Finnish avifauna. It is the only species that lives in Finland throughout the year in a reed bed. In summer it eats insects, and in winter it eats reed seeds almost exclusively. The best time to photograph Bearded Reedlings in Finland is in the winter, when you can walk on the ice and approach the flocks that winter in the dense reed beds.

During some exceptionally good winters with lots of snow, I have invested several weeks in photographing the species as extensively as possible. I have closeups, actions shots of feeding and drinking, and landscape and sunset shots—even a few images with a late evening moon.

Bearded Reedlings have short wings that are tailor made for shorts spurts inside the dense reed beds. I had some reasonably good flight shots of the species but was missing the really good ones.

In 2009 I decided to put all my efforts into taking flight shots. This is not an easy task because the birds fly mainly inside the reed beds and the spurts are only a few yards long.

I followed a flock for a couple of days, moving as inconspicuously as possible, and had my camera settings tweaked to capture flight at all times. Freezing the action of a flying Bearded Reedling requires a very fast shutter speed; 1/3200 second is needed to freeze the movement all the way to the tips of the wings, but it is possible to get good results even with 1/2500 second. I used continuous focus with 45 focusing points, because one or even an extended central focusing point would not be enough to keep the fluttering bird inside the focusing area among the reeds.

It did not take long to learn to read the birds' behavior and to anticipate their next move. They would usually stop eating and start measuring up the next reed's seed head. After several days of relentless trying, I got one great flight shot and a couple of good ones. The rest were mostly blurred because the camera liked to focus on the reeds.

Seabirds against the Moon

For about 30 years I have followed and photographed the arctic waterbirds and geese on their migration over the Gulf of Finland to the Russian tundra. This takes place primarily in May, and the birds are busiest in the mornings and evenings.

During migration peaks it is possible to see up to half a million birds in one day. On such days the traffic is heaviest

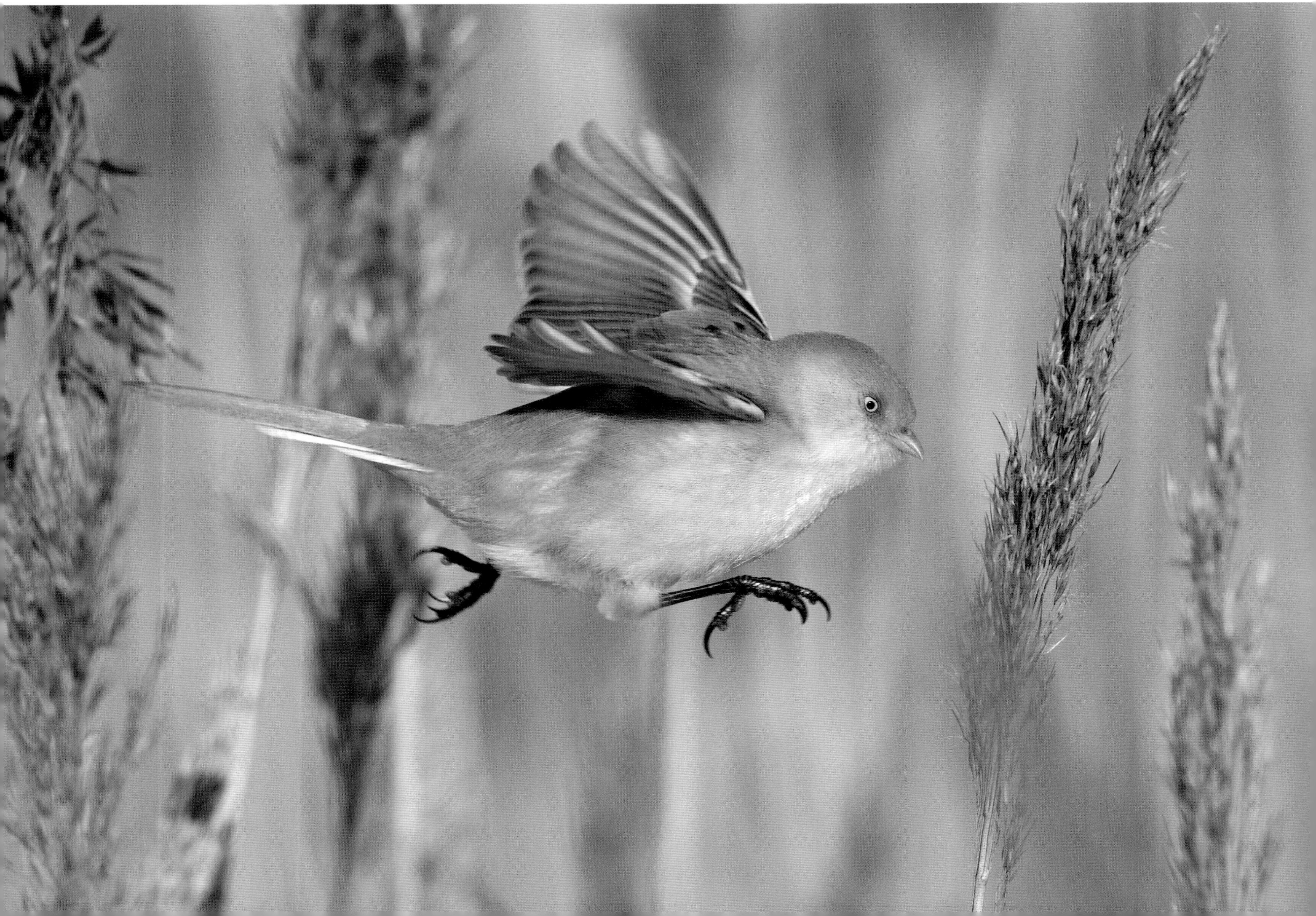

A Bearded Reedling in flight
(Panurus biarmicus)
Canon EOS-1D Mark III, 800mm f/4.0, 1/2500 second, f/9.0, ISO 800, continuous focus with 45 focusing points, Gitzo tripod, Manfrotto 501 video head. Espoo, Finland, February 2009.

in the evening and lasts all night. Over the years I have witnessed the night-time migration of Long-tailed Ducks and Common Scoters with the moon shining in the sky a couple of times. At the latitude of Helsinki, Finland, the May nights are light. In the darkest hours the flocks are visible in the sky only if they fly against the moon. With a film camera, photographing this sight was only a distant dream, because neither my equipment nor the available film speeds could have produced the images I wanted.

The vision lived on in my mind, and by 2006, when I was on my boat photographing the migration along the Gulf of Finland, I decided to try to create the images with digital technology and a powerful telephoto lens.

As before, the migration went on well into the night, and with the moon graciously shining in the right place, I had optimal conditions for my project.

I had my camera on a tripod aimed toward the moon. My friend was doing a migration count, and because he was constantly gazing at the sky he could tell me when a flock was likely to pass in front of the moon.

During the three hours that I photographed them, more than 10 flocks of all sizes passed the moon, but the main part of most flocks flew either just above or just below the moon. Luckily, in a couple of frames I captured a flock flying right across the moon. A dream come true!

Markus Varesvuo

Common Scoters migrating *(Melanitta nigra)*
Canon EOS-1D Mark II, 300mm f/2.8, 1/320 second, f/2.8, ISO 1250, Gitzo tripod, Manfrotto 501 video head, manual focus. Porvoo, Finland, May 2006. →

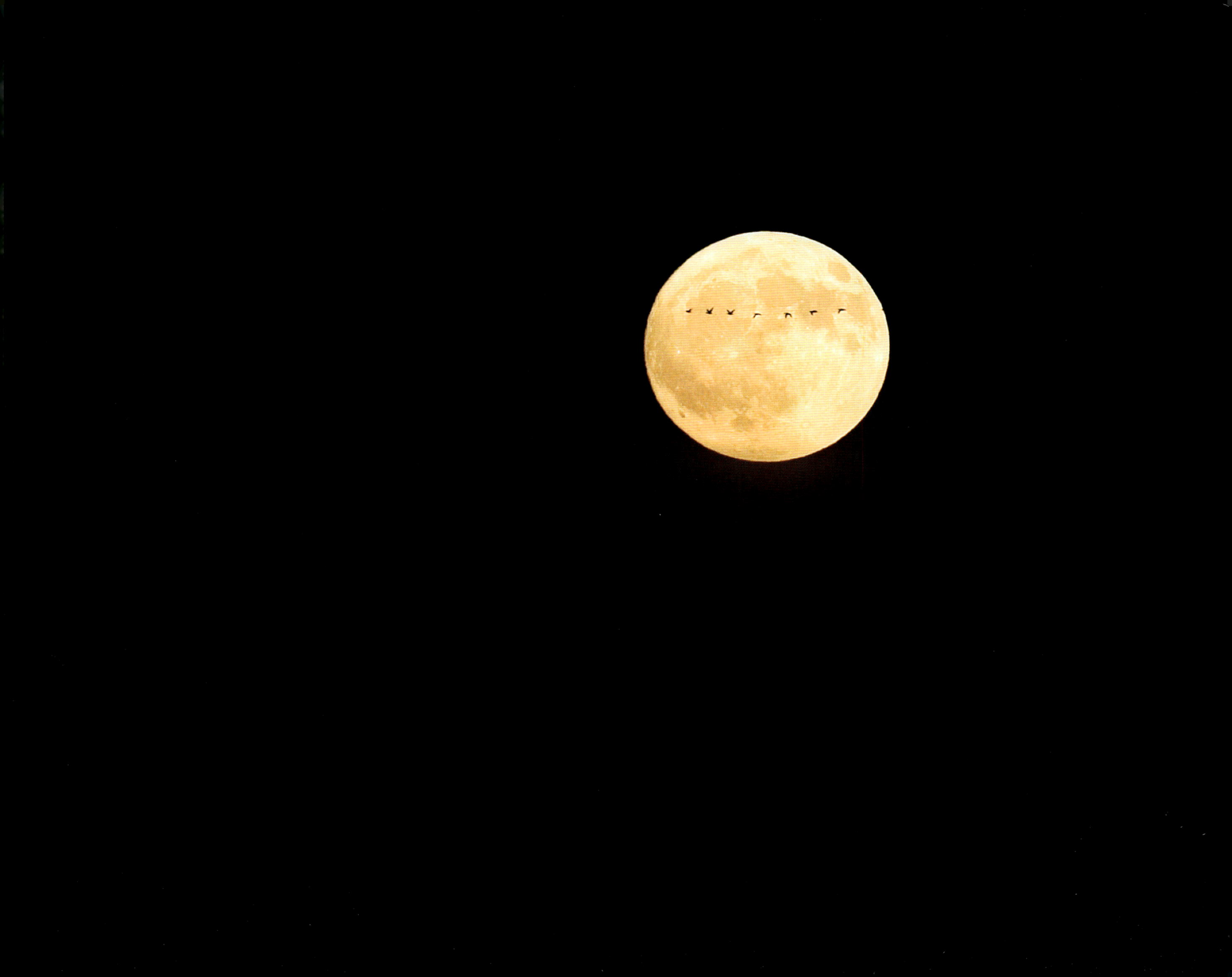

JARI PELTOMÄKI

BIRD PHOTOGRAPHER'S CAMERA

General information about digital cameras.

Most digital cameras are compact (point-and-shoot) or digital single-lens reflexes (DSLRs), depending on their ability to accommodate interchangeable lenses. Compact cameras are easy to use, and they're small and fit in your pocket, but you can't change the lens. Many birders use a compact camera coupled to a spotting scope (digiscoping), but the quality of the images is quite modest. They are good for documentation but not professional use. I use a compact camera for taking snapshots while traveling and documenting arrangements for a photo project.

DSLR cameras are bigger in size and use interchangeable lenses. The camera, the lenses, and the accessories constitute a system that gives photographers a range of options to choose from. The possibilities are many and varied, but it takes dedication to learn all of the camera's features and use them well. A DSLR is a single-lens reflex, meaning that light travels through the lens into the camera and hits a mirror that reflects the light to the viewfinder, which in turn shows you the image that you are about to photograph. In some cameras, the image in the viewfinder is a tad smaller than what will actually be captured, but this is not a problem because it's easy to crop the image in post-production.

Nowadays many camera manufacturers also offer compact superzoom cameras that have long lenses and electronic finders. They are about the size of a DSLR camera and have most of the features that you can get in a DSLR. Theoretically they are okay for bird photography, but high-end DSLRs are the most popular among bird photographers.

DSLR cameras can generally be split into three categories: (1) entry level, amateur, hobbyist, and consumer; (2) prosumer and semiprofessional; and (3) professional. The prices rise steeply with each category. As of this writing, good amateur and consumer cameras can be bought for \$600 to \$1,300, and semiprofessional cameras cost \$1,300 to \$4,000. Professional cameras cost about \$6,000 to \$8,000, so for the price of one professional camera you can get several semiprofessional cameras. There are even more expensive professional cameras, and models that fit between these very rough categories, so there are viable options for bird photographers at many price levels.

Professional camera models have metal bodies and have been designed to be sturdier and tighter than the more economical models, so professional cameras can withstand both weather conditions and harsh shooting environments better. This can be an important factor if you plan to photograph in extreme conditions.

Appetites usually grow as we make progress, and it's normal to start fantasizing about cameras made for professionals. Bear in mind, though, that a DSLR camera is not a particularly good investment because it loses value rapidly in just a few years. If you have to choose, it's better to get a high-quality, expensive lens than the latest DSLR camera with all the newest features. Good lenses keep their value far better

Markus Varesvuo

Jari Peltomäki

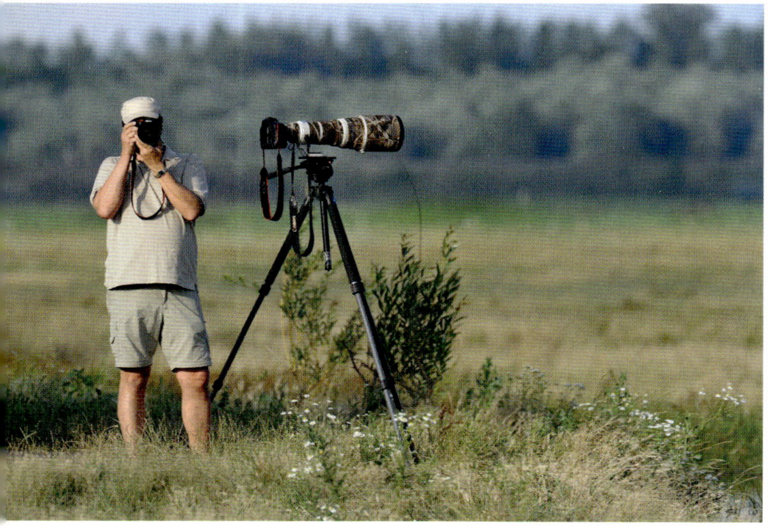

Bird photographer Olli Lamminsalo using the three-camera tactic in Hungary

than DSLRs. You can read more about this in the chapter "Bird Photographer's Lenses."

The DSLR market is much like the computer market, because they are evolving all the time. For the same price, in a couple of years you can get more and better features in the newest DSLR than what you can get today. On the other hand, if you want to start bird photography, you will eventually have to get that first good camera!

Three-Camera Tactic

Dedicated bird photographers pack two DSLR cameras and a compact camera in their bag. You can mount a wide-angle lens on one camera for flocks of birds and keep a telephoto lens on the other camera for closeups. The camera with the shorter lens can hang on your shoulder, ready for use, with straps that let you quickly grab it to point and shoot without having to first take the strap off your shoulder. Black Rapid, for example, has good straps for this purpose (http://www.blackrapid.com).

Having more than one camera is also convenient when you are photographing from a blind, plus they can help you minimize lens changes. If you can have two cameras, it's a good idea to have one with a full-frame sensor and the other with a sensor that crops the scene because you can increase the effective focal length with the latter!

Having a second camera is also a good backup measure because damage to a sole camera could completely ruin your photo trip. A second camera can save the day.

A compact camera is best for taking shots of situations that would probably not be documented otherwise. You can use these images to show where you have been or how your images were taken; these can be interesting extras in a slideshow, and sometimes they can even be handy for illustrating articles in magazines or books.

Key Camera Features

Next you need to choose a brand. Canon and Nikon have been ruling the roost for a long time among bird photographers. Both have their merits, but the absolute best bird photography camera would be created by combining the best features from these two makes. Other brands chosen by bird photographers include Olympus, Sony, Panasonic, and Pentax. In this chapter I will discuss Canon and Nikon cameras.

Selecting your system is an important decision because changing from one brand to another will be costly, so take your time to study the different makes and figure out what camera and lens features are most valuable to you. A secondhand camera is a viable option, but check how many frames have been taken because the shutter release is subject to wear and tear and will need to be replaced at some point, at a considerable cost. Also, the latest camera models have sensor cleaning functions that older models may lack.

Full-Frame Sensor versus Cropped Field of View

DSLR cameras have either a full-frame sensor (24mm x 36mm) or a sensor that crops the field of view (I'll call it a crop-frame sensor), with crop factors of 1.3 to 2.0. Also, the range of pixels varies from one camera to another; at the moment sensors come with 12–36 million pixels (megapixels).

A factor that affects the image quality in a digital camera is the physical size of the sensor. When you have two sensors that have the same resolution (the same number of megapixels), but one is physically larger than the other, then the pixels of the larger sensor are also larger and result in less noise and better image quality.

With a full-frame sensor the effective focal length of your lens and the magnification don't change. A 300mm lens will magnify your subject about six times, and a 500mm lens will magnify it about 10 times. A full-frame sensor often produces better image quality than a crop-frame sensor of the same generation, but with the rapid advancements in technology, the newest crop-frame sensors probably produce better images than older full-frame sensors. A drawback of full-frame sensors is that they utilize the lower-quality edges of lenses, which can reduce image quality in the corners.

A crop-frame sensor can benefit a bird photographer because its narrower field of view acts like an extender to the lens, but with an important difference. While an extender reduces the lens speed, a smaller sensor crops the view that the lens projects without reducing the amount of light that reaches the sensor.

The following table illustrates the effect a crop-frame sensor has on the field of view in lenses favored by bird photographers (thus extending their reach).

The size of the sensor affects the depth of field. Suppose you want the subject to be the same size in the frame of both types of camera. In a camera with a crop-frame sensor you would use a shorter focal length. If you were using the same aperture, the combination of a crop-frame sensor and a shorter focal length would give you more depth of field.

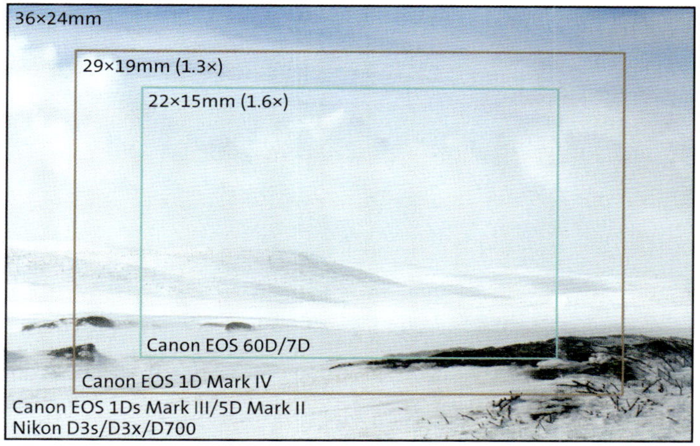

Nikon has both full-frame (FX format) sensors and crop-frame (DX format) sensors. The DX sensors have a crop factor of 1.2–1.5, which gives lenses more reach. With the DX format, the number of frames per second (fps) grows from 9 to 11, and the number of RAW files that the buffer can hold rises from 17 to 24, which means that the DX format produces smaller file sizes.

In their consumer models, Canon uses a 1.6 crop factor, and Nikon uses a 1.5 crop factor (e.g., Nikon D300S).

Crop factor and focal length

Field of view crop factor	1.3×	1.5×	1.6×	2×
Lens				
300mm	390mm	450mm	480mm	600mm
400mm	520mm	600mm	640mm	800mm
500mm	650mm	750mm	800mm	1000mm

Jari Peltomäki

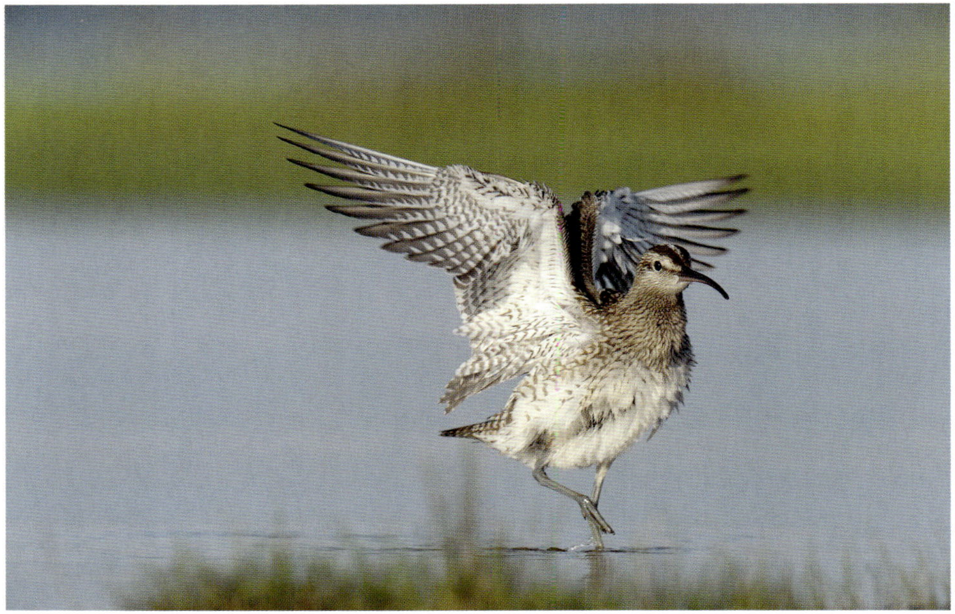

A Whimbrel's jump is fast—this is every second frame of the series *(Numenius phaeopus)*
Nikon D3S, 500mm f/4.0 plus 1.4x extender, 1/1600 second, f/8.0, ISO 800, continuous focusing with 51 focusing points, ground pod, Manfrotto 501 video head. Oulu, Finland, August 2010.

You should always use RAW format files because they give you far more freedom in post-production. Even with easy shots, the result is always better than if you had captured the image in JPEG format.

Continuous High-Speed Shooting Mode

A bird photographer who wants to take action photos appreciates how fast the camera can shoot frames and how many RAW files the buffer can hold. As of this writing, the best professional DSLR cameras reach 9–14 fps, and the buffer can hold from 45 RAW files in a Canon EOS-1D X (in the proprietary CR2 format) to 100 12-bit RAW files in a Nikon D4 (in the proprietary NDF format). The transfer rate of the memory card also affects the buffer; the faster the card, the quicker the camera is able to transmit data from the buffer to the card, thus freeing up space for new frames. The combination of a Canon EOS-1D X with a Lexar Professional 1000x 150 MB/second memory card, or a Nikon D4 with a Sony XQD 125 MB/second memory card, means that the buffer is practically limitless, even when shooting RAW files.

Both camera models are aimed primarily at sports and wildlife photographers. Speed matters. With a maximum of 14 fps on the Super High Speed setting, the Canon EOS-1D X leads in shooting speed. The Nikon D4 reaches up to 11 fps. The extra 3 fps can be vital in fast situations. At the fastest shooting rates, the exposure and focus are locked with the first frames in both cameras.

In rapid burst mode you can capture many different wing positions when you photograph a fast-moving bird—the series of three Whimbrel images is an example. The bird's jump in the air lasted less than two seconds, but with continuous high-speed shooting mode I was able to capture many varied frames, which gave me plenty of shots so I could select the best images.

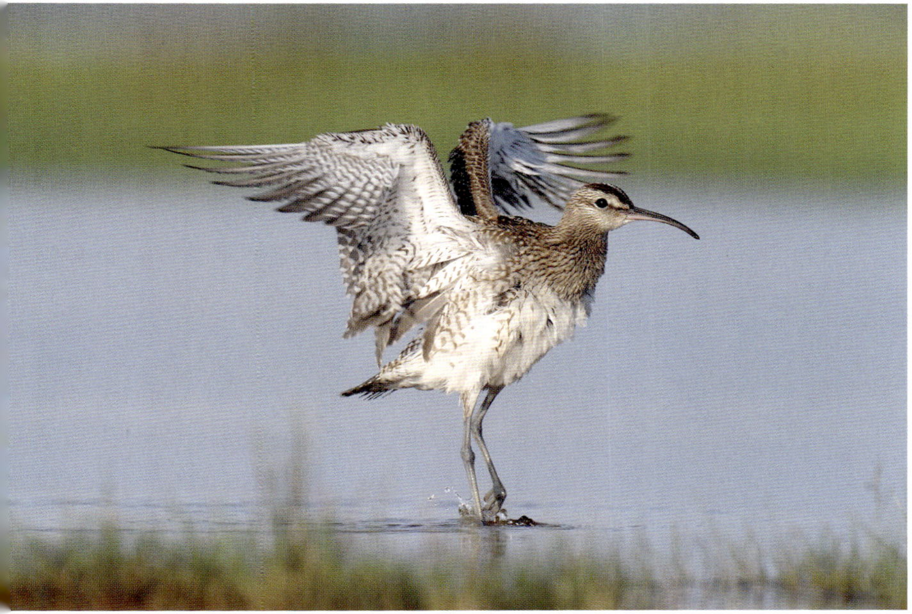

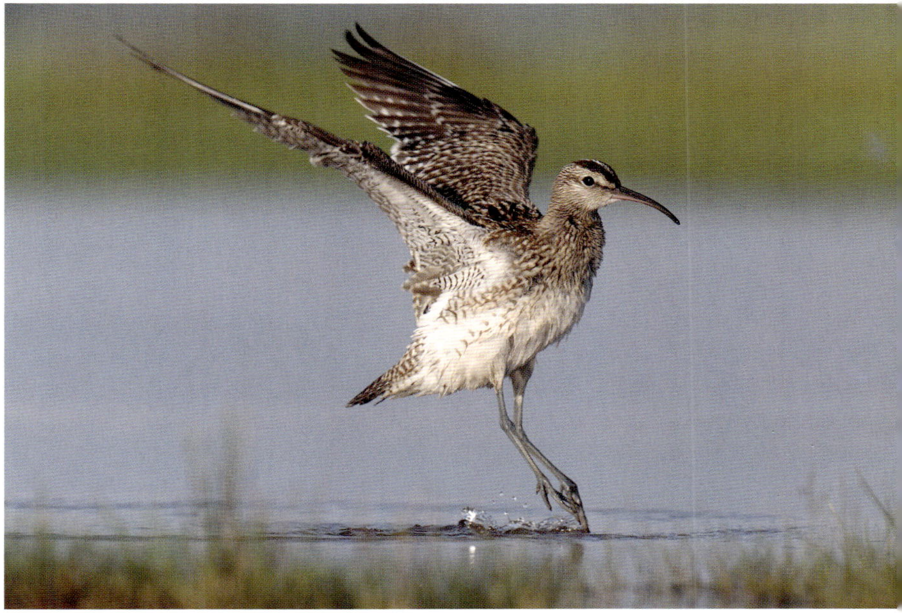

Focusing

The definitive measure of your camera's ability to take successful flight and action shots is its focusing speed. A bird flying against an even background, such as the sky, is easy for most DSLR cameras, but the more contrast there is in the background, the harder it gets for most cameras to maintain focus on your subject. The camera settings, focus tracking sensitivity, and selected focusing points, in particular, impact the success of focusing.

With my Nikon D4 I mainly use a nine-point Dynamic-area AF (autofocus), which works great with flying birds. After the camera has focused on the subject, it rarely has problems keeping it in focus, even with birds flying against challenging backgrounds. I use the 51-point Dynamic-area AF when photographing birds flying against even backgrounds. According to Nikon, the focusing capability of the D4 has been greatly improved over the D3—but I have a feeling that it is just slightly improved. However, considering all the improvements in the Nikon D4, it is by far the best Nikon camera ever manufactured.

For its new model, the EOS-1D X, Canon has successfully fixed the autofocus problems that caused trouble with some EOS-1D Mark III cameras and that weren't fully overcome in the Mark IV bodies. Markus Varesvuo says the Canon EOS-1D X is the best Canon camera so far, and he mainly uses 61 focusing points when shooting fast action, even when the birds are against busy backgrounds.

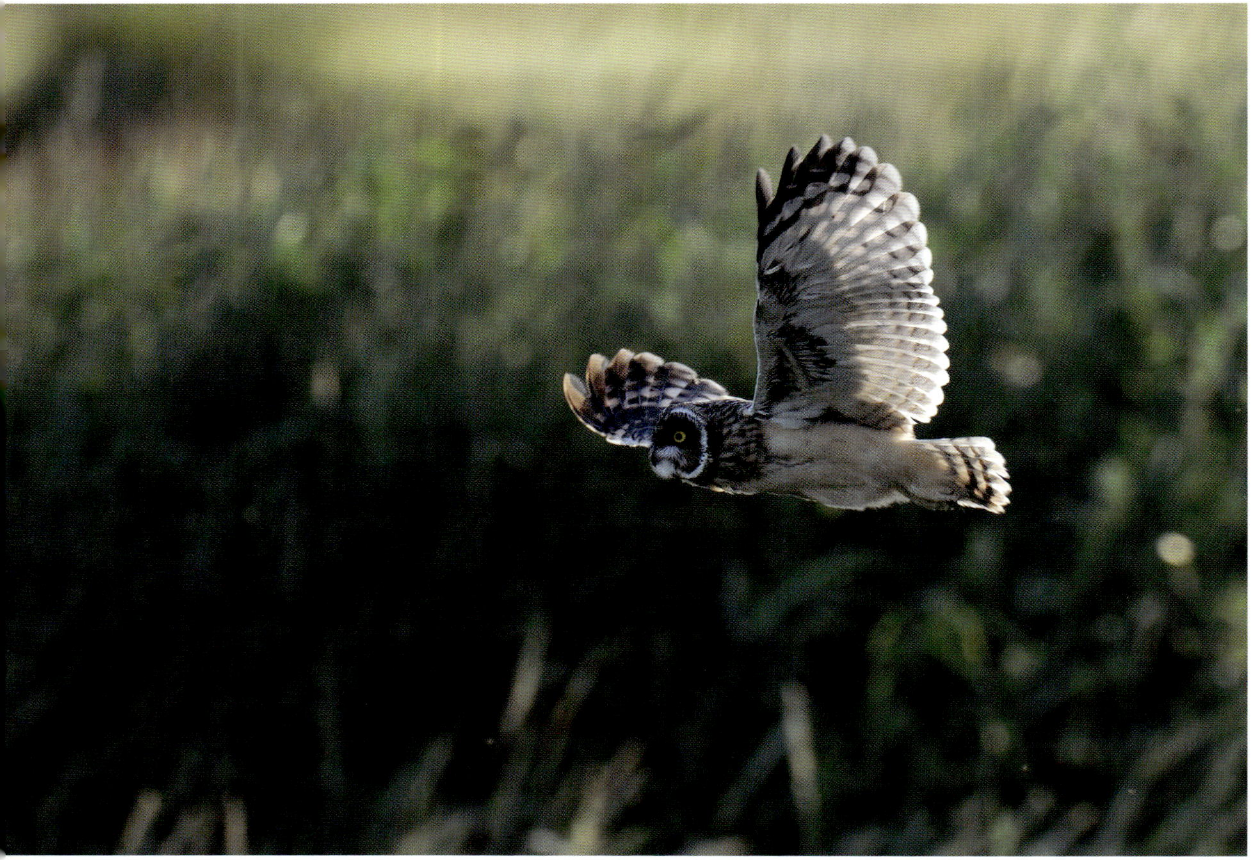

Jari Peltomäki

A young Short-eared Owl flying against a busy background is a challenge to the autofocus *(Asio flammeus)*
Nikon D3S, 500mm f/4.0 plus 1.4x extender, 1/1600 second, f/8.0, ISO 1600, continuous focusing with 51 focusing points, handheld camera. Oulu, Finland, July 2010.

Quantity and Quality of Focusing Points

The number of focusing points varies greatly among entry-level, prosumer, and professional cameras. The focusing points in Canon cameras range from 7 in entry-level cameras to 61 in professional cameras; Nikon cameras range from 3 to 51 focusing points. There is also variation in how the points are clustered. These configurations affect how you take an image and how easy it is to compose. However, for all camera makes, the central focusing point is probably the most reliable, and it is your safest choice for locking onto a subject.

The 15 cross-type focus points in the central viewfinder of the Nikon D4 are aligned to detect contrast in both vertical and horizontal lines, and each cross-type sensor is responsive in lenses with a maximum aperture of f/5.6. The Canon EOS-1D X has a 61-point AF system, with 41 cross-type sensors in f/4 and faster lenses. Both makes have AF points that are compatible with apertures down to f/8.0, allowing the use of extenders without loss of autofocus. However, where the Canon EOS-1D X allows for one cross-type central point with four supporting points at f/8.0, the Nikon D4 has a larger focusing area and more functioning focus points with cross-type sensors.

Many factors play a role in a camera's ability to track a moving target and produce sharp images, and focusing points with cross-type sensors is just one of those factors. The photographer's proficiency is also a factor.

Low-Light Modes

When it comes to a camera's low-light performance, here's a good rule of thumb: as the pixel density grows, the image quality drops. In practice this means that noise will increase as ISO values get higher. Newer cameras are better at this than their predecessors because new technology keeps improving camera sensors.

The Nikon D4 has a full-frame sensor with 16.2 megapixels. Even if I occasionally set the ISO to 12800, I can still get useable images. The Canon EOS-1D X has a full-frame sensor with 18.1 megapixels, and it produces equivalent results. There is very little difference in image quality, especially when you consider that post-production is more significant for images shot with a higher ISO. More often than not, it is difficult to make very low-light images look really good. Besides, the usability of an image is always relative; it depends both on the photographer and on how the image might be used.

Video Features

The latest DSLR cameras shoot video, even in full high-definition (HD) resolution. Videography will probably grow in popularity; it's already common for taking complementary material for slide shows. You should make sure that the camera you have your eyes set on for bird photography has a video function. Canon's latest DSLR cameras (EOS 5D Mark III and EOS-1D X) and Nikon's D4 and D800 have full HD video (1920 × 1080).

Never mind what make and model you settle on—the most important thing is to learn how to use your camera's settings and memorize all the buttons and dials so well that when you're knee deep in hot action, you don't have to think, let alone search for the right button!

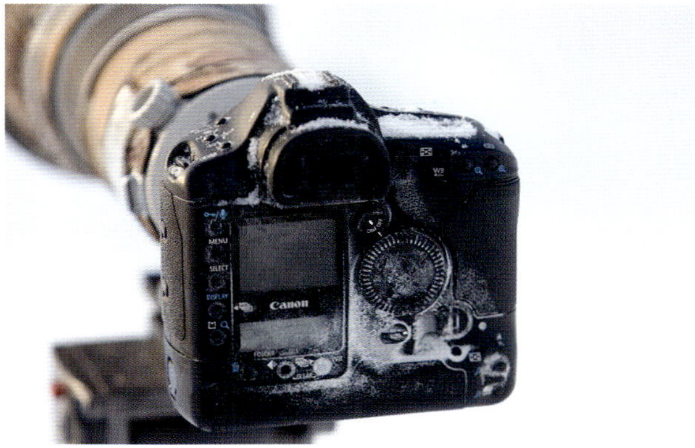

Jari Peltomäki

A frosty Canon
Even though several hours in −30°C (22°F) is extreme conditions for a camera, the cold got to the photographer first.

Golden Eagles *(Aquila chrysaetos)*
Nikon D3S, 400mm f/2.8, 1/1250 second, f/3.5, ISO 12800, continuous focus with 51 focusing points, ground pod, Manfrotto 501 video head, blind. Utajärvi, Finland, January 2011.

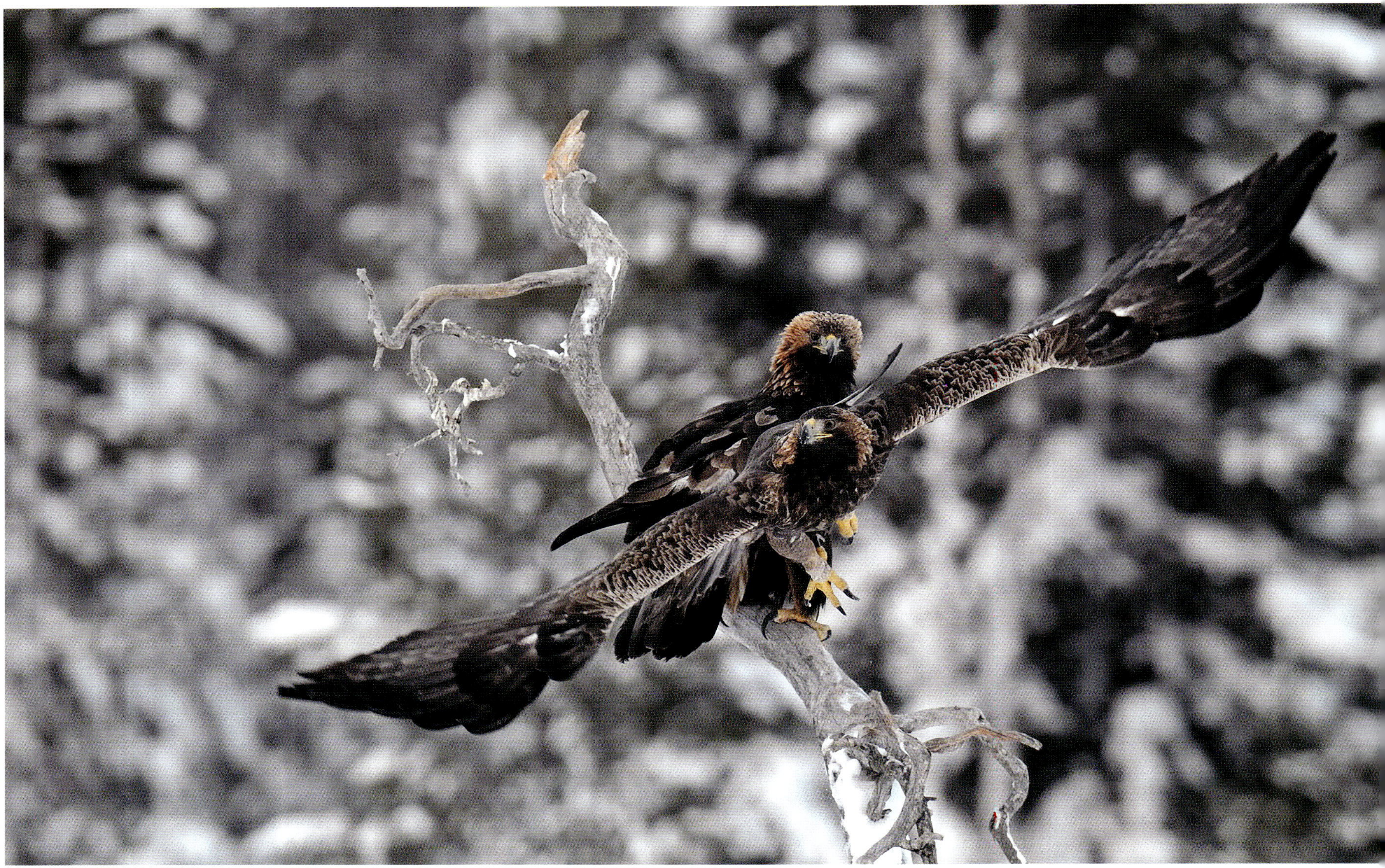

Jari Peltomäki

MARKUS VARESVUO

BIRD PHOTOGRAPHER'S LENSES

Different lenses give you different types of images.

At least in Europe it's safe to say that most birds are very wary of people, which spells trouble for a bird photographer because it's usually difficult to get close enough to the birds for photographing them. Bird photographers therefore prefer telephoto lenses with focal lengths ranging from 300mm to 600mm, even up to 800mm. This isn't to say that shorter lenses would be useless, on the contrary. An image of a bird in a landscape stands out from the mainstream, as do closeups taken with wide lenses.

During the past decade, the 500mm f/4.0 became the lens of choice among bird photographers, both dedicated amateurs and professionals. The lens is light enough to use without support for short sessions, and its focal length offers a really nice magnification, especially when coupled with a 1.4x extender. Add to that a camera with a crop factor of about 1.3, and you have a tool for getting close enough to many species, even for closeup framing, provided that you approach cautiously or settle somewhere to wait and watch.

Telephoto Lenses

You face fewer financial risks when you buy a telephoto lens than when you invest in a DSLR because lenses have been so good that there have not been any revolutionary developments for more than 10 years. I had my Canon 500mm f/4.0 lens for more than 12 years, and when I updated it to the new generation 400mm f/2.8 II lens in autumn 2011, it was still a high-quality lens. Late 2011 saw the arrival of the new generation Canon 300mm f/2.8 II and 400mm f/2.8 II lenses, and in mid-2012 the 500mm f/4.0 II and 600mm f/4.0 II were released. High-quality lenses keep their value far better than DSLRs, where major technological advances are frequent. The biggest differences with the newer lens models are that they are much lighter and have faster autofocus and better image stabilization. The image quality is only marginally better.

The main factors to consider when selecting a telephoto lens are related to focal length, lens speed, image quality, focus speed, weight, stabilization, and price. These factors are interrelated. Broadly speaking, the faster the lens (or the smaller the f-value), the faster it focuses and the better its low-light performance. Fast lenses require big lens elements, which add to the weight and raise the price. It's also good to remember that your camera plays a role in how fast your lens focuses, and especially in how good it is at keeping a moving subject in focus. The focusing capabilities of professional cameras are in a different league compared to cheaper cameras.

A stabilizer is an important asset in a telephoto lens because it significantly increases the number of sharp frames. I keep the stabilizer on all the time in my Canon lenses, set at 1, whether I am using a tripod or shooting handheld. Especially with long focal lengths and long exposures, the stabilizer gains relevance. But check your lens manufacturer's recommendations concerning the use

Harri Taavetti

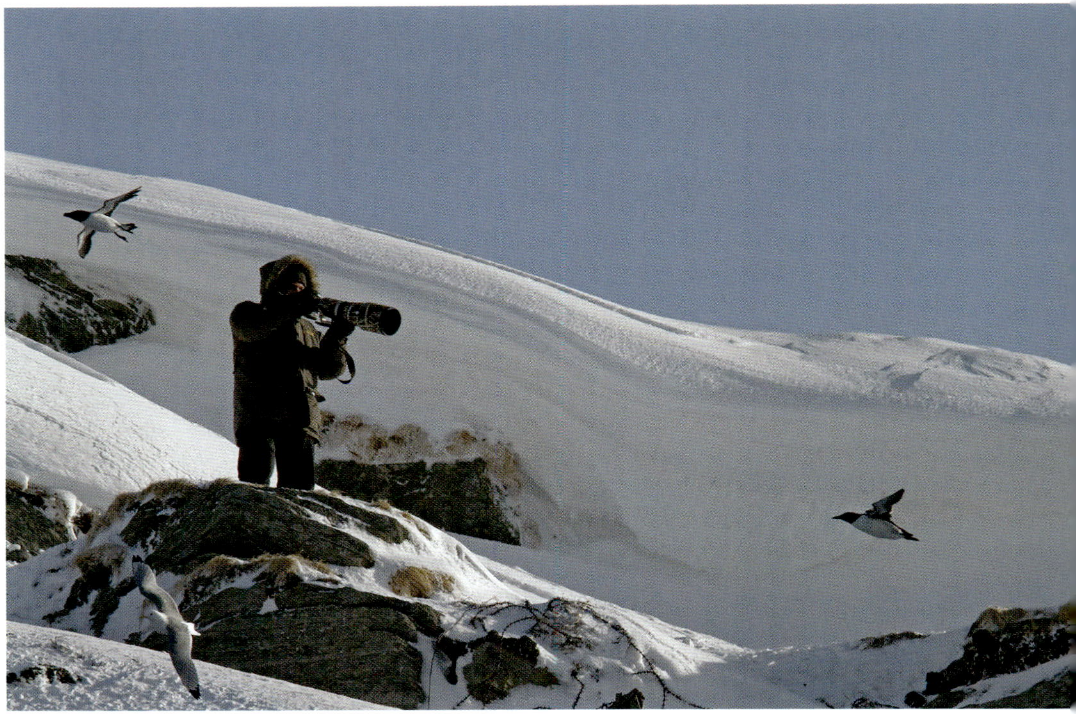

A 500mm lens doesn't stop you from photographing handheld, but it requires practice. Norway, 2010.

of image stabilization on a tripod. Some models, especially older ones, might create minimal lens shake and therefore a slight blur.

For a fledgling bird photographer with limited financial resources, I recommend starting with a 300mm f/4.0 or 400mm f/5.6 lens and getting it secondhand. And for the camera to go with that lens, get one with a crop-frame sensor, 1.5 for a Nikon or 1.6 for a Canon. The effective focal length of a 300mm lens, when coupled with Canon's 1.6 crop-frame sensor, becomes 480mm, which is getting close to magnifications needed in bird photography. The light weight of these lenses is an added bonus.

For years, the best lens for bird photography was the Canon 500mm f/4.0. The focal length of the 300mm f/2.8 is a little too short, and the 400mm f/2.8 I and 600mm f/4.0 I are way too heavy for handheld shooting. Admittedly, most bird photography is done with a tripod, but there's no way around the fact that when you have fast flight action, handheld shots often yield better results. For a long time, the lack of stabilizers was a disadvantage in Nikon's long lenses. However, the updated 500mm f/4.0 that Nikon released a couple of years ago features a stabilizer, and for a while it had the upper hand compared to Canon. This changed again in 2012 because Canon launched its new and improved 500mm, which weighs 680 g (24 oz) less than the Nikon and is at least on par with the Nikon in every way.

Both Canon and Nikon manufacture a 500mm telephoto lens, and both suit bird photography beautifully. They are fast enough, they have good stabilizers, they produce excellent image quality, they focus quickly, and with the Nikon at about 3.8 kg (8.4 lb) and the Canon at 3.2 kg (7.1 lb), they can both be handheld. If you plan to get just one lens and money is not an issue, I recommend getting a Canon 500mm f/4.0 II. At the workable weight of 3.8 kg (8.4 lb), Canon's updated 400mm f/2.8 II and 600mm f/4.0 II nips at the heels of the 500mm f/4.0 II, but in my opinion the latter is still the best lens for bird photography.

If the 500mm f/4.0 lens is too heavy, Canon's 400mm f/4.0 DO telephoto lens, which is based on new lens technology and weighs less than 2 kg (4.5 lb), is a good option. The image quality is slightly poorer than the 500mm f/4.0, but if you value light weight, this is a good choice.

In addition to my 500mm f/4.0 I and 400mm f/2.8 II, I've been using Canon's 800mm f/5.6 lens since it was launched in autumn 2008. Its range, especially with a 1.4x extender, is huge. With the 1.3 crop factor of the Canon EOS-1D Mark IV the effective focal length is 1456mm. And despite this long focal length, the image quality is excellent (as long as there is no heat haze), and the focusing works surprisingly well even in flight situations, provided that the subject is larger rather than smaller.

I used the 400mm f/2.8 II for about a year but switched back to a 500mm lens as the updated f/4.0 II was launched because the focusing distance range of 7 m (23 ft) to infinity in the 400mm isn't well suited for taking action images of birds. The lens takes too long to find the target when you hunt for it in this range, and the action can be over before the lens has settled on the target (see page 76). Even with the new Canon EOS-1D X, there was no big improvement. The new 500mm f/4.0 II has a much better focusing distance range of 10 m (32.8 ft) to infinity. Also, since it is about 600 g (21 oz) lighter, it makes handheld photography easier.

I use my 500mm and 800mm lenses about fifty-fifty. Nikon has announced it's going to release an 800mm lens in 2013.

Even though the 800mm f/5.6 is only about half a kilo (1.1 lb) heavier than the 500mm f/4.0, in my experience it doesn't suit handheld cameras well, or birds flying close. It's hard to keep a close-flying bird in the viewfinder, plus the lens has poor focusing ranges: 6 m (19.7 ft) to infinity, 6 m to 20 m (19.7 ft to 65.6 ft), and 20 m (65.6 ft) to infinity. In practice, with this lens you can photograph flying birds only with 20 m (65.6 ft) to infinity, but with small birds you ought to be able to take pictures within less than 20 m (65.6 ft), so for a bird photographer it would be nice if the lens offered a focusing range option at 15 m (49.2 ft) to infinity.

The airlines impose very strict size and weight limitations for carry-on baggage these days, meaning that sometimes you can carry on only one long telephoto lens. For shorter trips I take only the 400mm or the 500mm lens, but for longer trips I want take my 800mm lens too. One goes in my carry-on bag, and the other goes into the cargo hold, packed in a locked protective case inside a big, padded bag or a sturdy suitcase.

There are also some high-quality telephoto zoom lenses. Sigma has a 300–800mm f/5.6 zoom with a great price–quality ratio, but its image quality lags behind lenses with a fixed focal length, particularly when used at longer than 600mm. Also, the autofocus is slower, and these lenses lack stabilization, so they should always be used on a tripod.

Nikon's updated 200–400mm f/4.0 II zoom lens has a stabilizer, and its image quality and focusing speed approaches fixed focal length lenses, which makes it a good lens for photographing in a blind. Canon is coming out with a 200–400mm f/4.0 lens of its own in 2013.

Sometimes I'm glad I brought along some wider lenses too. I was photographing Rock Ptarmigans and Willow Ptarmigans on the arctic hills in the Utsjoki region in north Finland when we came across a very confident Willow Ptarmigan that was not bothered by our presence in the least. After it had finished eating, it settled into a snow burrow, where it was snug and cozy against the piercing wind and raging snowstorm. In the smaller image, a 500mm

A Willow Ptarmigan in the arctic hills *(Lagopus lagopus)*
Canon EOS-1Ds Mark II, 35mm f/2.0, 1/640 second, f/16.0, ISO 200, one-shot focus with a central focusing point, handheld camera on the ground. Utsjoki, Finland, April 2007.

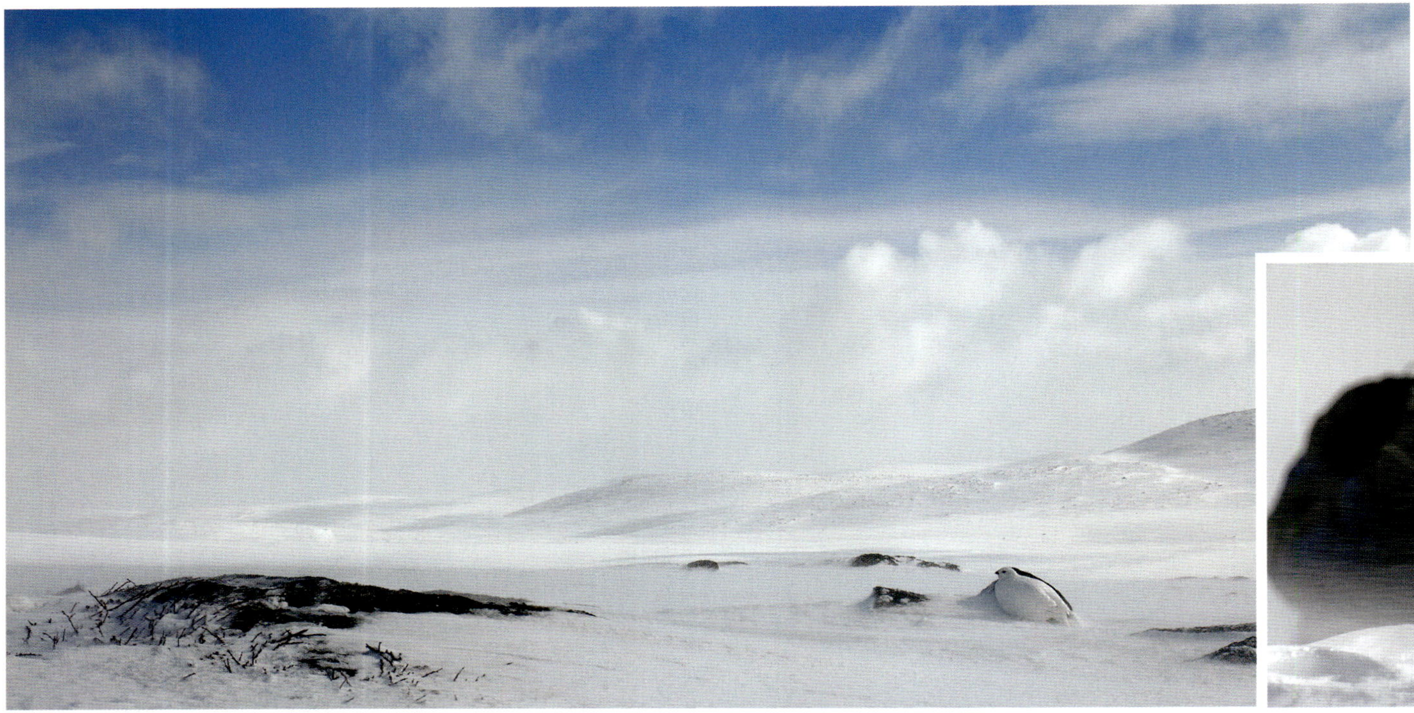

Markus Varesvuo

Markus Varesvuo

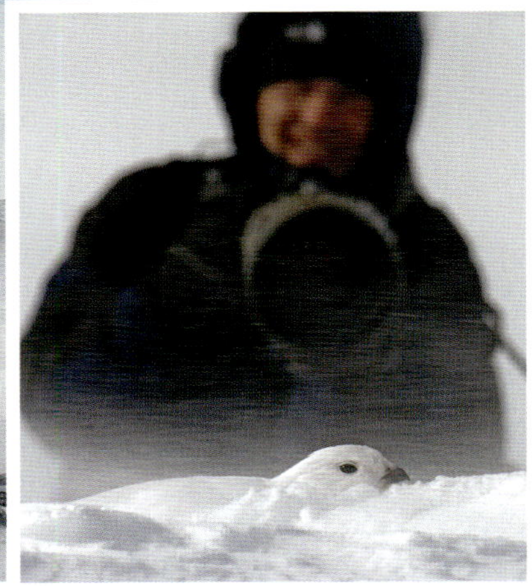

Bird photographer Tomi Muukkonen is taking a closeup of a Willow Ptarmigan using a 500mm lens *(Lagopus lagopus)*
Canon EOS-1Ds Mark II, 500mm f/4.0, 1/160 second, f/32.0, ISO 400, one-shot focus with a central focusing point, Gitzo tripod, Manfrotto 501 video head. Utsjoki, Finland, April 2007.

lens is used for taking the closeups that captured the spirit of the brave bird and the power of the storm.

Just 30 minutes later the cloud cover parted and the bird took off again. It eventually stopped in the shelter of a small rock. I mounted a 35mm lens to the full-frame camera, which allowed me to include a lot of landscape in the image. I crawled toward the bird and got to within 2 m (6.6 ft), where it allowed me to take my time composing the image and trying different exposures.

Markus Varesvuo

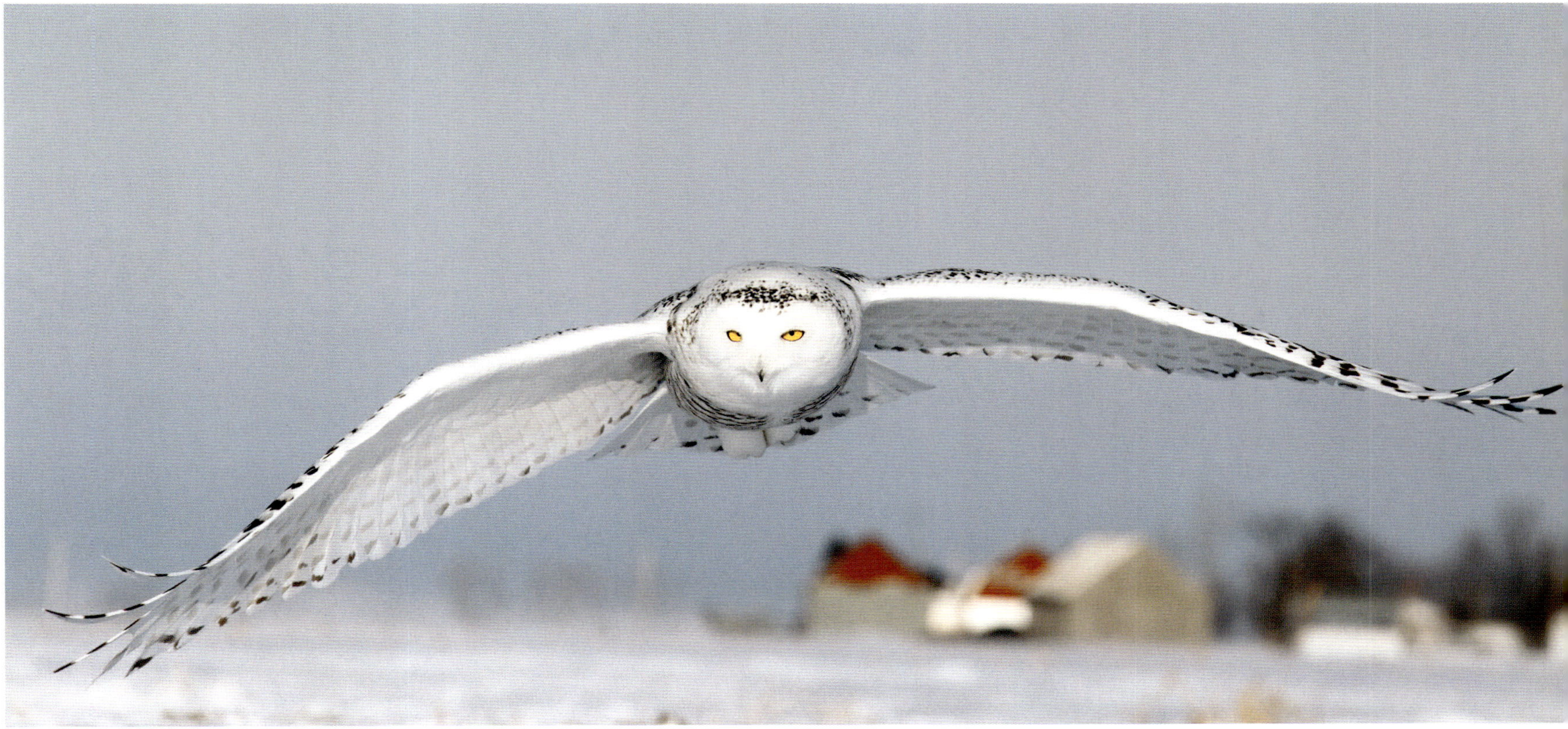

A Snowy Owl in flight at its wintering grounds *(Bubo scandiaca)*
Canon EOS-1D Mark IV, 70–200mm f/2.8, 1/2000 second, 195mm, f/9.0, ISO 1000, continuous focus with an extended central focusing point, handheld camera. Canada, February 2010.

Wide Lenses

Both Nikon and Canon have very good 70–200mm f/2.8 zoom lenses rigged with stabilizers, making them a nice complement to a bird photographer's kit in addition to the main lens. Canon has a lighter and less expensive f/4.0 version of the 70–200mm zoom, but in the trade-off for lighter weight, there's some loss in the lens speed and focus speed. There is no loss in image quality, though.

These zoom lenses are very versatile in bird photography and are useful not only for images of birds in landscapes,

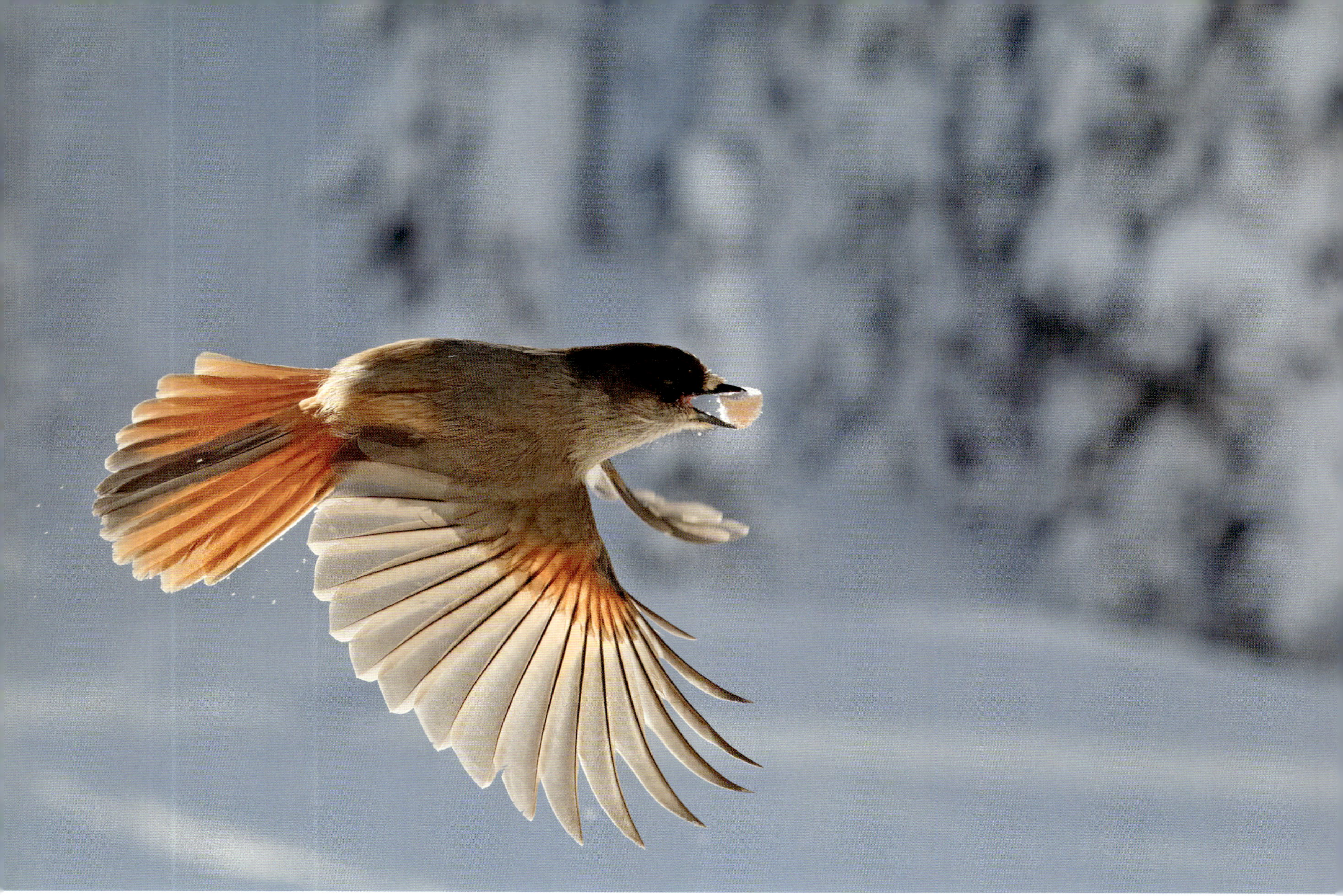

Markus Varesvuo

A Siberian Jay is heading off into the woods to stash the photo fee ***(Perisoreus infaustus)***
Canon EOS-1D Mark IV, 70–200mm f/2.8, 1/3200 second, 140mm, f/8.0, ISO 1600, continuous focus with an extended central focusing point, handheld camera. Kuusamo, Finland, March 2010.

but also for photos taken from a blind and with birds that aren't shy around people.

I also carry at least one wide-angle lens in my camera bag. If I have to tote the bag for long stretches, I choose the ultralight 35mm f/2.0 lens.

For special circumstances I pack my ultrawide 14mm f/2.8 or 24mm f/1.4 lens. These lenses require a bold bird that can be lured super close to the camera—with food, for example—or if the bird is not so bold, a remote shutter release can be used.

The Snowy Owl flight shot was taken in Canada at a typical Snowy Owl wintering ground, with colorful farms and barns dotting the wide-open fields. I used my 70–200mm zoom lens to get a tightly framed flight shot that would still include some of the elements in the owl's winter world.

Erkki Toppinen

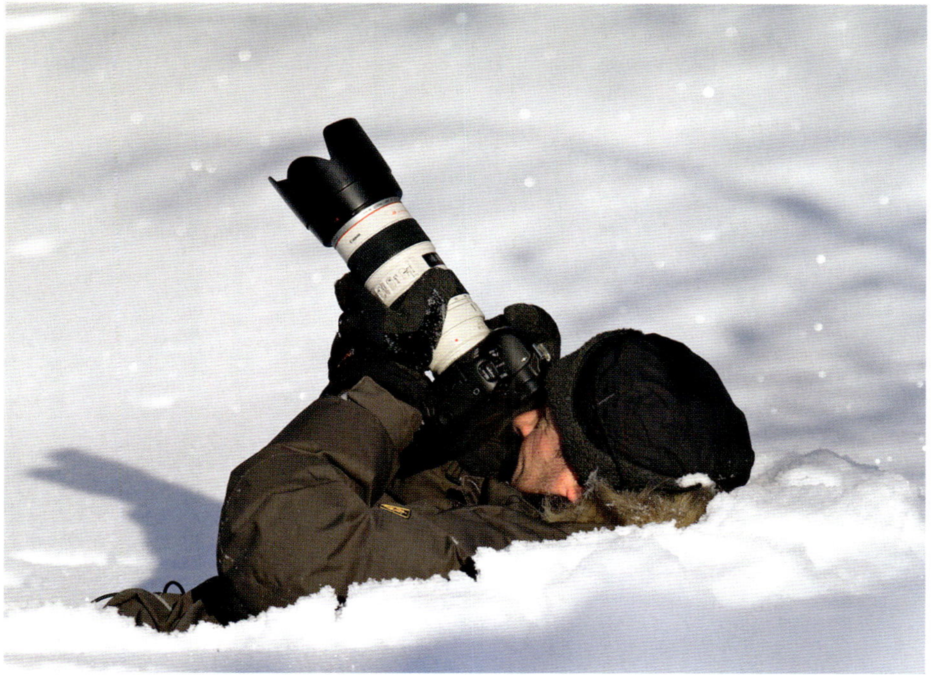

A 70–200mm zoom lens is handy for taking flight shots of confident birds

Telephoto Extenders

The most commonly used telephoto extenders increase the focal length of the lens by 1.4x or 2.0x (Nikon also has a 1.7x extender).

I use Canon's 1.4 III extender frequently; it extends my 500mm lens to 700mm with practically no loss in image quality or focus speed. The lens speed drops one stop to f/5.6.

I use the 2x extender now and then with the 500mm f/4.0 II lens. It drops the lens speed by two stops and slightly slows down the focus speed, but the image quality is still surprisingly good. The autofocus is lost when the combined speed of the lens and the extender is slower than f/8. For example, a 2x extender turns an 800mm f/5.6 lens to 1600mm with an f/11.6 lens speed, and you must use manual focus.

For the extreme closeup of the Snowy Owl, I used an 800mm lens with a 1.4x extender to get a tight, partial frame of the bird as it was about to take off.

Effect of telephoto extenders on focal length and lens speed			
Canon optic	Weight*	1.4x extender	2x extender
70–200mm f/2.8 II	1490 g (3.3 lb)	98–280mm f/4.0	140–400mm f/5.6
300mm f/2.8 II	2350 g (5.2 lb)	420mm f/4.0	600mm f/5.6
300mm f/4.0	1190 g (2.6 lb)	420mm f/5.6	600mm f/8.0
400mm f/2.8 II	3840 g (8.5 lb)	560mm f/4.0	800mm f/5.6
400mm f/5.6	1250 g (2.8 lb)	560mm f/8.0	800mm f/11.2
500mm f/4.0 II	3190 g (7.0 lb)	700mm f/5.6	1000mm f/8.0
600mm f/4.0 II	3920 g (8.6 lb)	840mm f/5.6	1200mm f/8.0
800mm f/5.6	4500 g (9.9 lb)	1120mm f/8.0	1600mm f/11.2

Note: Autofocus is lost at apertures smaller than f/8.

*These Canon weights are also good indicators for lenses by other manufacturers with equivalent lens speeds.

A Snowy Owl taking off *(Bubo scandiacus)*
Canon EOS-1D Mark IV, 800mm f/5.6 plus 1.4x extender, 1/200 second, f/11.0, ISO 800, one-shot focus with a central focusing point, Gitzo tripod, Manfrotto 501 video head. Canada, February 2010.

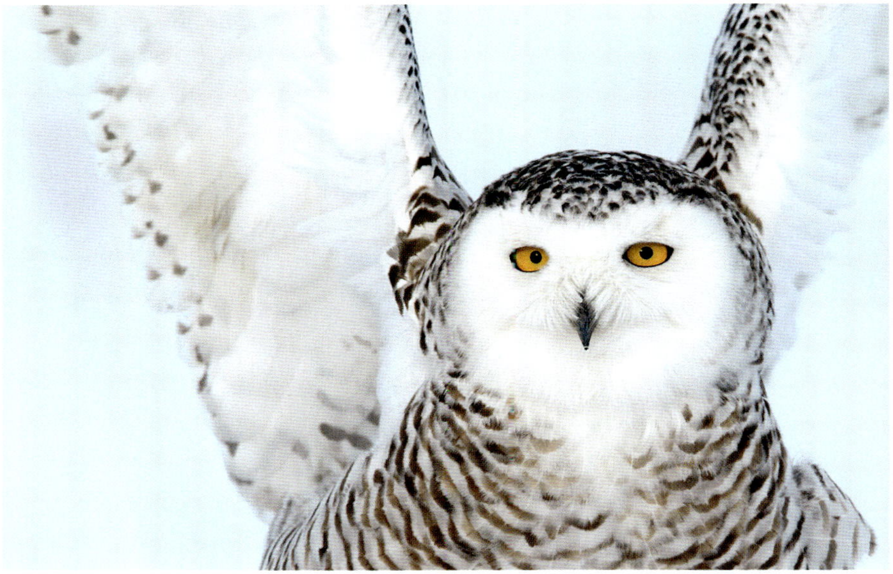

Markus Varesvuo

BENCE MÁTÉ

SOURCES OF LIGHT

Learn how artificial light can widen the range of possibilities in nature.

For some nature photographers, especially if they wish to show nature as it is, the use of artificial light can be a big no-no, but the truth is that many situations are difficult or even impossible to capture without artificial light.

Mirrors

Mirrors help to accentuate silhouettes, change the angle of light, and even fortify the intensity of ambient light, which helps reduce unwanted shadows. In a studio a fill flash would do the trick, but it is less useful in field conditions because it tends to scare off animals. Using mirrors can be challenging even in familiar settings because of the earth's rotation, which causes the direction of light to constantly change.

I first used a mirror while photographing fungi, and from there I got the idea to cast light on birds at a bird bath. I hung a mirror to a tree opposite my photography blind, tied cords to the mirror's lower corners, and trailed them into the blind. Then I was able to adjust the mirror, quietly from inside the blind, without scaring off the birds. You might notice light coming from two directions in these photos, yet the backlit details add value to the images and, in my opinion, offset any loss of realism.

I also employed mirror reflections successfully when photographing a European Bee-eater as it was digging a nest hole. The birds begin rather late in the morning, when sunlight hits the ground at an angle that is already so big that the quality of light is harsh and

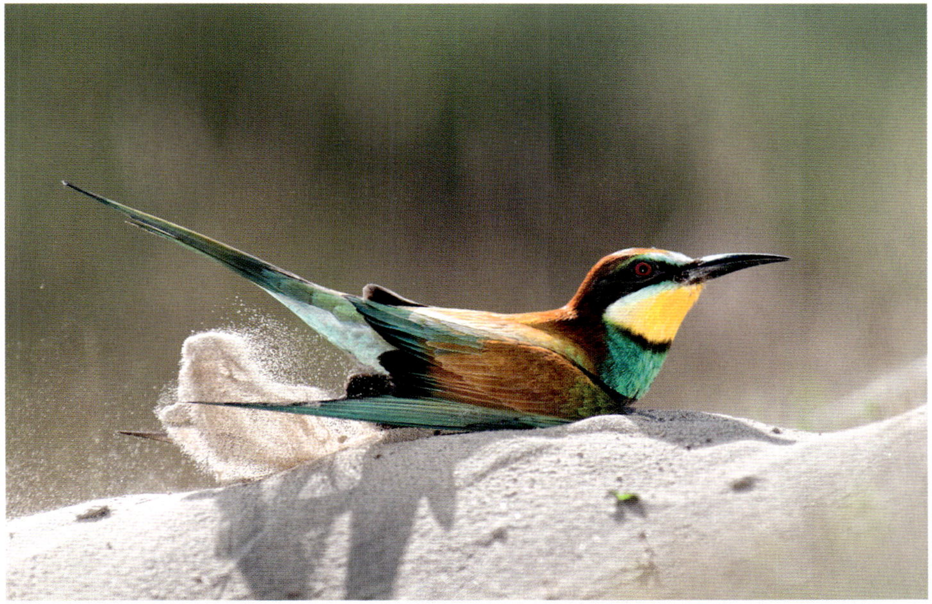

Bence Máté

European Bee-eater digging a nest hole *(Merops apiaster)*
Nikon D300, 300mm f/2.8, 1/2500 second, f/4.0, ISO 320, manual focus, Gitzo tripod and video head. Hungary, May 2008.

European Starlings bathing at a drinking station *(Sturnus vulgaris)*
Nikon D200, 300mm f/2.8, 1/60 second, f/2.8, ISO 400, manual focus, Gitzo tripod and video head.
Hungary, May 2006.

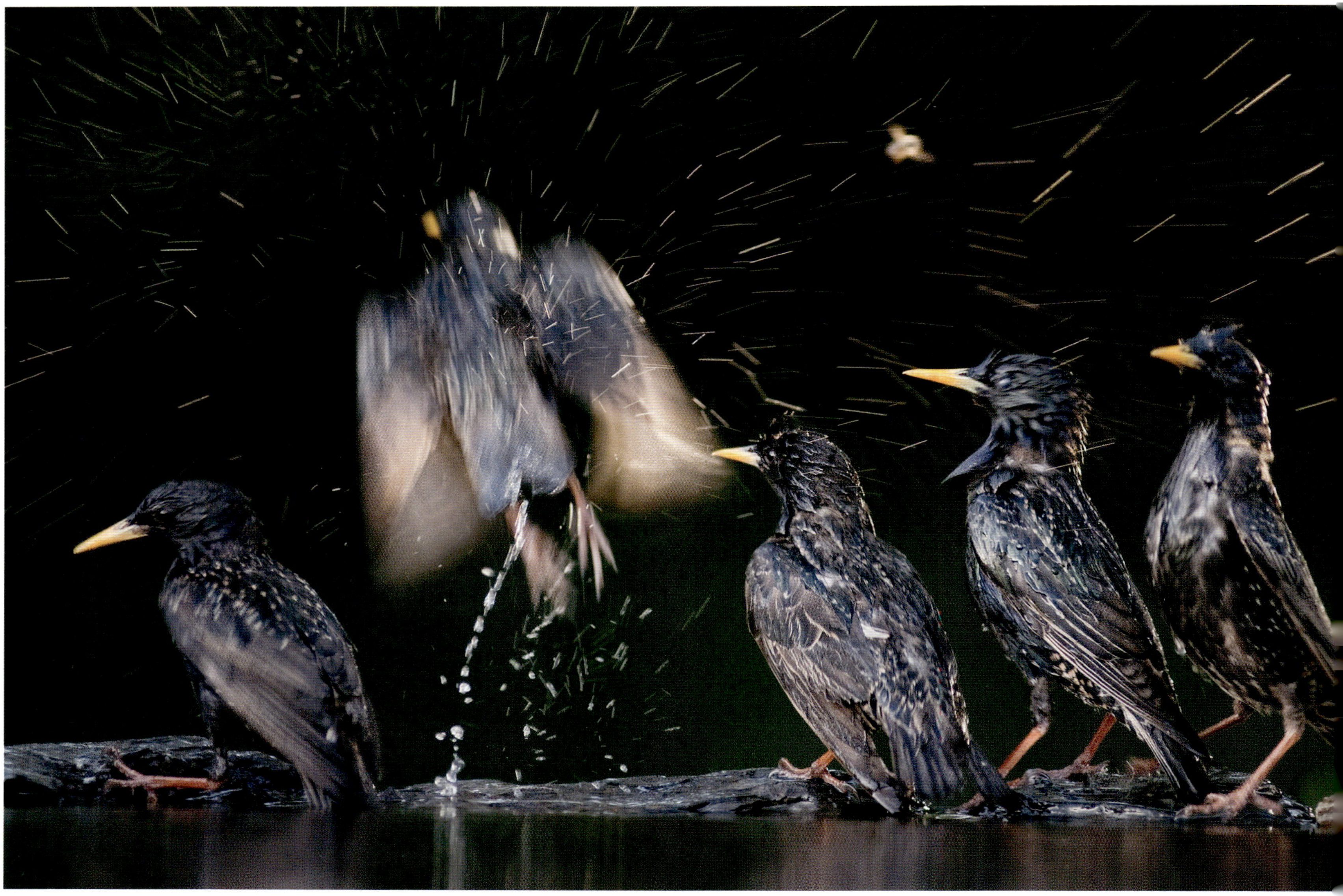

Bence Máté

causes too much contrast. I pitched my tent blind facing the rising sun so that the European Bee-eater was in a direct line between me and the sun. With the mirror propped against the blind, it reflected light on the bird from a very low angle. This softened the backlight and brought out the bird's beautiful colors.

To help prevent birds from flying into the mirror, throw a thin net over it.

Lamps

Lamps are extremely difficult to use in bird photography because lighting can be problematic to set up in the wild where electricity is usually not available. But in places where you can attract birds to a bird bath and where you have access to electricity, such as a garden, it's worth experimenting with a couple of 1000-watt lamps to create conditions identical to sunlight. I have used this technique in Norway in the winter when daylight lasted only an hour or so. Squirrels and jays visiting a bird feeder were oblivious to the 1000-watt light just a yard away from them. The lamplight mixed into the scarce ambient daylight gave the image an evening effect.

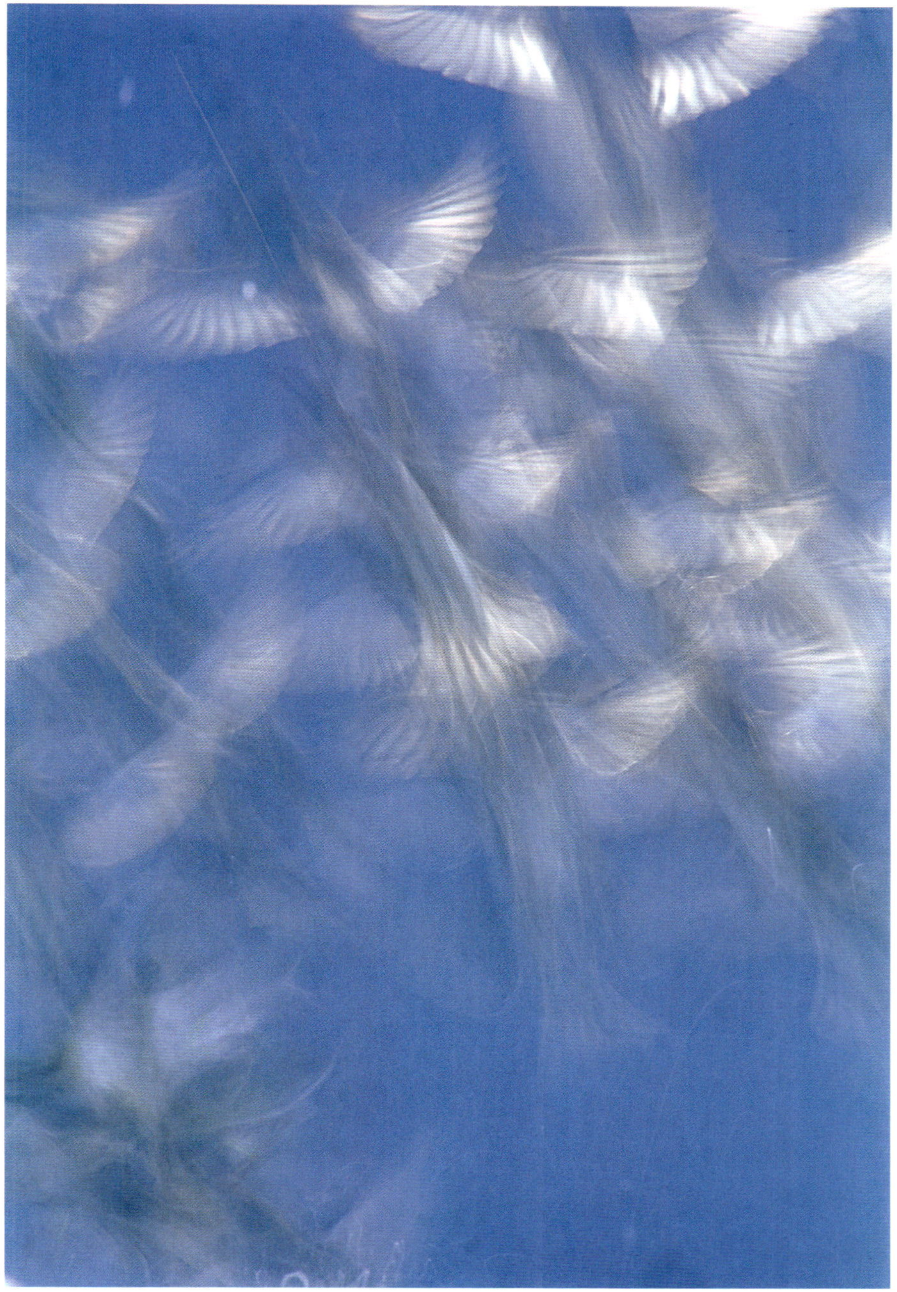

Bence Máté

A lamp behind the birds illuminates them in flight during a long exposure. European Greenfinches and House Sparrows *(Chloris chloris and Passer domesticus).*
Nikon F8008S, 300mm f/2.8, 1/2 second, f/4.0, Fuji Velvia ISO 50, manual focus, Gitzo tripod and video head. Hungary, February 2003.

A Eurasian Jay lit by a lamp *(Garrulus glandarius)*
Nikon D200, 300mm f/2.8, 1/1600 second, f/2.8, ISO 1000, manual focus, Gitzo tripod and video head, 1000-watt lamp. Norway, November 2006.

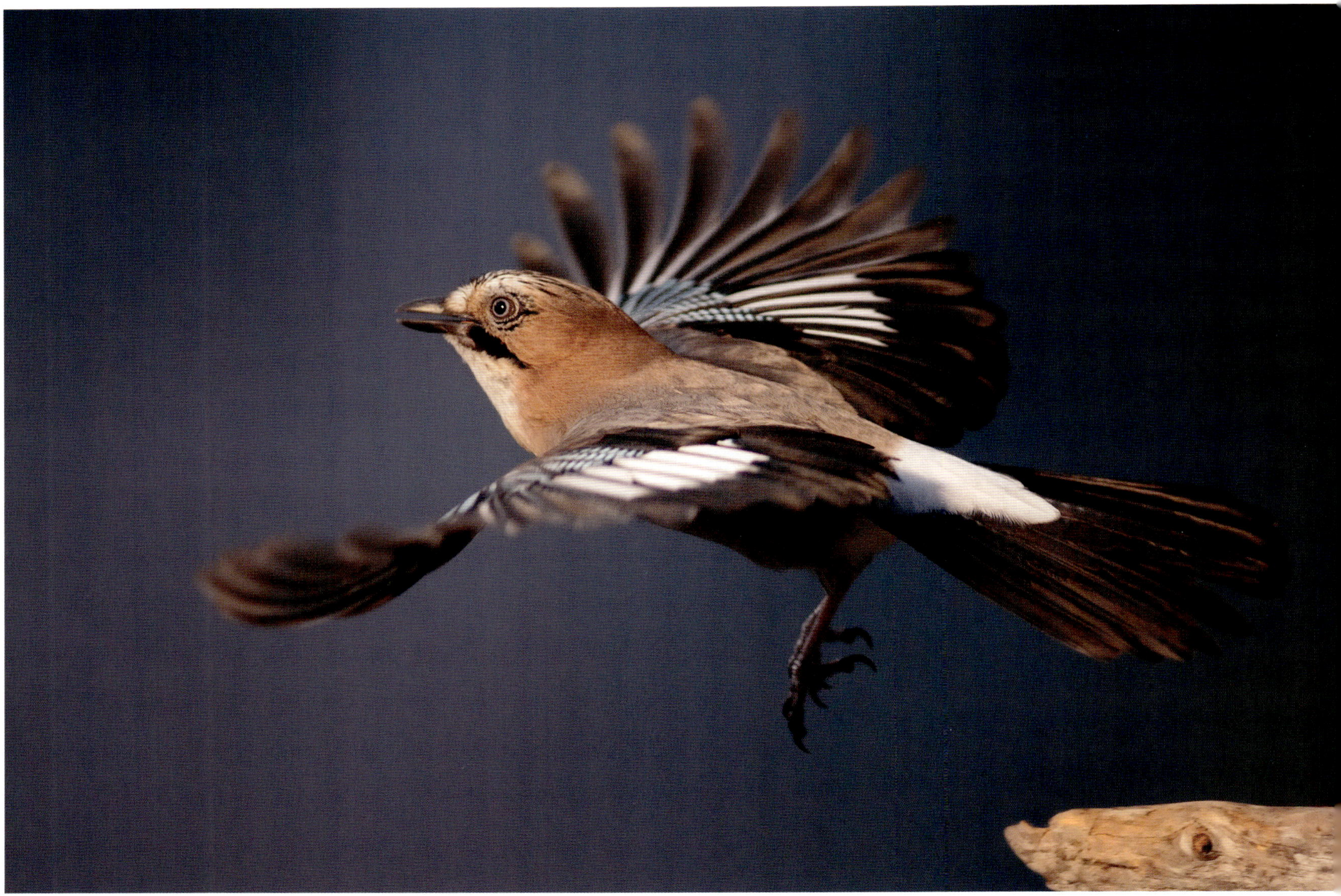

Bence Máté

Flash Photography

Flash is the most widely used source of artificial light in bird photography—but who knows, maybe in a few years action photography will resemble still photographs taken from motion pictures, which would cause stage lighting to be more common than flash.

Many photographers shy away from using flash because natural light is difficult to achieve with an artificial light source, and also because the intensity of flash light is not suited to shooting a series of frames of a quickly moving animal that is often more than 4 m (13 ft) away. Nevertheless, in the past couple of years roughly half of my pictures have been taken with flash.

Before you switch your flash on, it is worthwhile to learn some basic rules about flash photography.

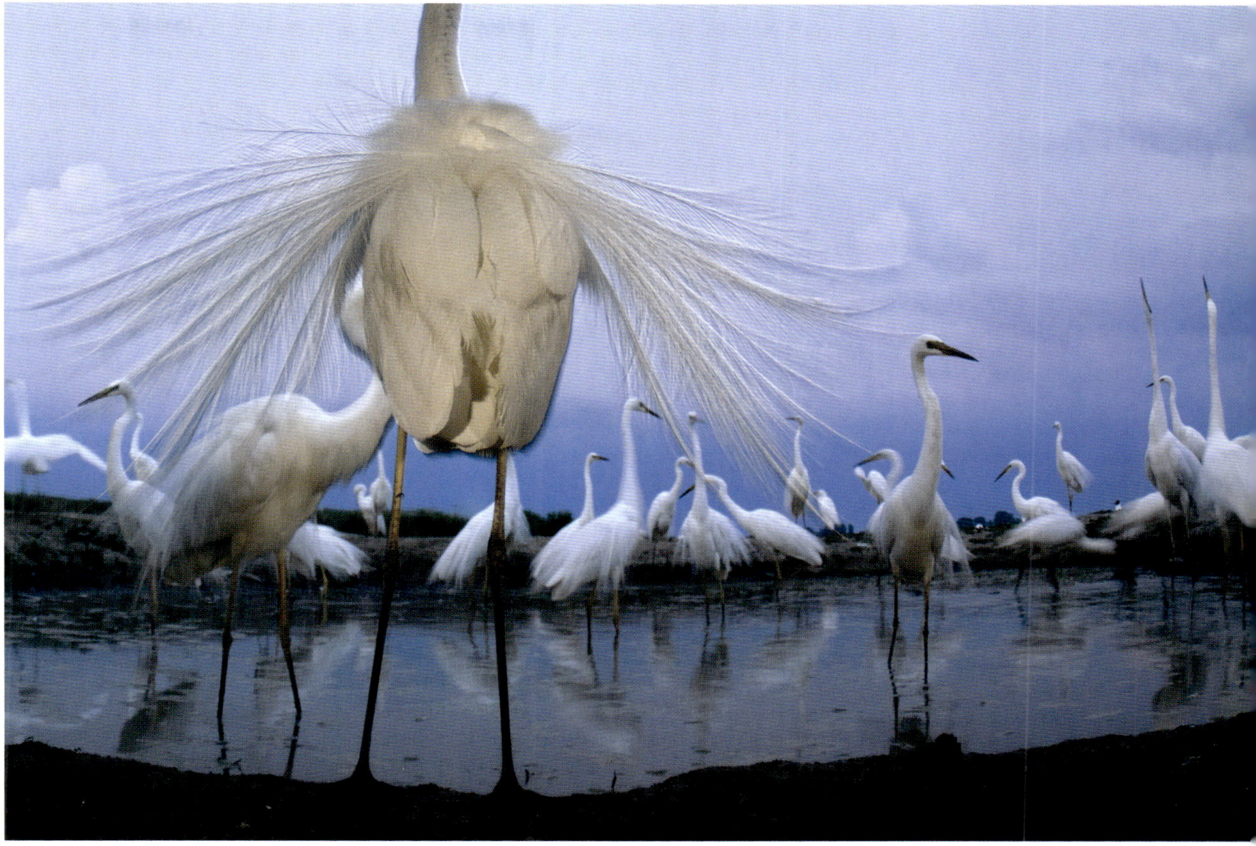

Bence Máté

Combinations of ambient light and flash yield more natural-looking results. Great Egret *(Ardea alba)*.

Nikon D300, Tokina 10–17mm fish-eye lens (10–17mm f/3.5–4.5), 1/4 second, f/4.5, ISO 100, manual focus, 8x neutral density filter, two Nikon Speedlight SB-800 flashes, handheld camera. Hungary, May 2010.

Flash Sync

The maximum flash sync speed is the fastest shutter speed at which the entire image sensor can be illuminated by the flash pulse. Most modern DSLRs have a maximum flash sync speed of 1/250 second, which is the fastest speed at which a camera has the first shutter curtain fully open before the second shutter curtains starts to close. When shutter speed is faster than sync speed, the frame is only partially open, because the sensor is covered by one curtain, or parts of both curtains, and a flash burst illuminates only part of the image.

Slow shutter speeds increase the exposure from ambient light and give a more natural feel to the image, but the risk of unwanted motion blur increases.

Then again, balancing ambient light with flash light creates interesting effects, as the Eurasian Hoopoe picture illustrates. The ghostly image of a bird flying, captured with a relatively long exposure, shows a flurry of motion, while the flash helped keep some of the details in sharp focus. I underexposed the ambient light on the main subject by 1–2 exposure values (EVs) and set the flash to 0.5 EV lower than the EV suggested by the light meter.

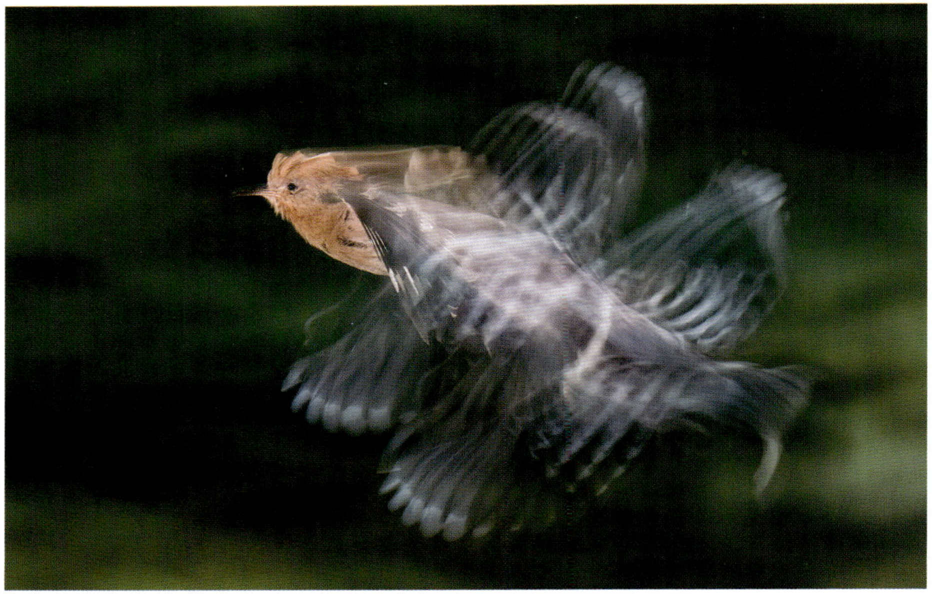

Bence Máté

With long exposures, a flash can bring out sharp details. Eurasian Hoopoe *(Upupa epops)*.
Nikon D700, 300mm f/2.8, 1/4 second, f/9.0, ISO 100, manual focus, 8x neutral density filter, two Nikon Speedlight SB-800 flashes, Gitzo tripod and video head. Hungary, May 2010.

The light hitting the birds comes from a flash, and the background is in ambient light. Green Honeycreeper and Clay-colored Thrush *(Chlorophanes spiza, Turdus grayi)*.
Nikon D700, 300mm f/2.8, 1/2500 second, f/4.0, ISO 1000, manual focus, Nikon Speedlight SB-800 flash, Gitzo tripod and video head. Costa Rica, December 2010.

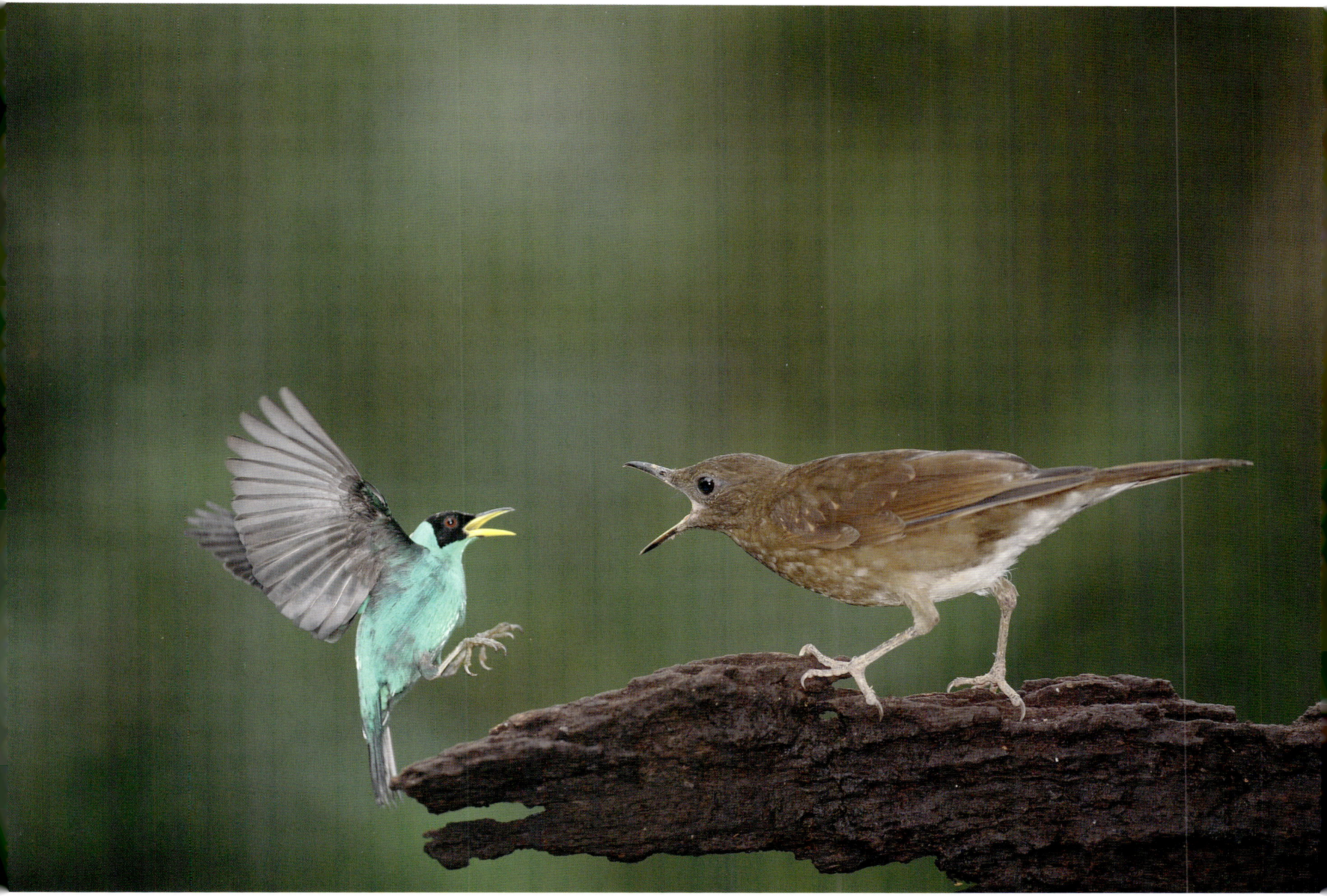

Bence Máté

Speed of Flash Bursts

When flash power is manually reduced, the duration of a flash burst diminishes along with the light intensity. This can be very useful when you set your exposure to be longer than the sync speed and freeze your subject within the short duration of the flash burst. The duration ranges of the flash burst in a Nikon SB-800 flash (and most shoe-mount flashes) are shown in the following table.

Flash burst	Power
1/1050 second	At M 1/1 (full) output
1/1100 second	At M 1/2 output
1/2700 second	At M 1/4 output
1/5900 second	At M 1/8 output
1/10,900 second	At M 1/16 output
1/17,800 second	At M 1/32 output
1/32,300 second	At M 1/64 output
1/41,600 second	At M 1/128 output

You can set your flash to a fractional power of 1/4 or 1/8 if you want to get some sharp details of moving birds. As an added bonus, with low power you can fire a series of exposures:

- 1/1 (full) power gives a series of one image
- 1/2 power gives a series of one image
- 1/4 power gives a series of three images
- 1/8 power gives a series of 6–10 images

Beyond this, with the flash at 1/16 power or less, the number of images is also determined by the power supply in your flash. If it is used with a powerful external power supply, a flash can produce more flashes than the number of images your camera can temporarily store in its buffer. So it could be said that the camera's buffer limits continuous shooting more than the flash. Remember, though, that increased power heightens the risk of overheating, so keep an eye on your flash unit.

High-Speed Flash Sync

Most of the latest DSLR cameras and flashes allow flash to be used with all shutter speeds. In a traditional flash discharge, the light intensity increases rapidly to a peak and then trails off gradually. The duration of this light impulse at full power is around 1/1000 second. In high-speed flash (flat peak), the peak of the flash burst is weaker, but the flash gives out smaller bursts continuously from the time the front curtain opens to the time the rear curtain closes, and it lights the image evenly. Unfortunately, this means that the distance between the flash and the subject has to be reduced to maintain the same light intensity as in a situation in which the flash is used at full power to light a subject that is farther away. In bird photography, where it is seldom possible to get as close to the subject as high-speed flash requires, the flash has to be dismounted and placed close to the subject. In action photography the challenges are multiplied by the fact that to fire a series of exposures, you need to reduce the flash power as previously described. This results in a further decline in light intensity, requiring even closer proximity to the subject.

You should note that high-speed flash does not freeze movement in the same way as normal flash sync; instead, the camera's shutter speed freezes the action. As long as there is no motion blur from ambient light, flash sync can produce a sharper image at 1/250 second shutter speed, because a flash impulse can be 1/10,000 second.

Front or Rear Curtain Sync

Curtain sync with a slow shutter speed and ambient light freezes movement but leaves motion blur in the image. Front curtain sync fires the flash at the beginning of the shutter duration and leaves trails ahead of the moving subject, whereas rear curtain sync fires the flash at the end of the shutter duration and leaves motion blur trailing behind the moving object. Trying to create motion blur with normal flash sync results in a rather messy general murkiness, which can also be a desired effect.

A good trick to prevent red eye is to dismount the flash, attach it to a separate arm, and raise it about 50 cm (20 in) above the camera. You will need a synch cord or an infrared or remote control.

Augmenting Flash Intensity

Increased flash speed means reduced light intensity, which makes it necessary to dismount the flash and place it closer to the subject. To operate the flash, you need a transmitter attached to the camera hot shoe and a receiver attached to the bottom of the flash, or you can use another flash (slave flash). This can be done only in prearranged settings, for example if the flash or flashes are placed near a branch where you expect a bird to land. This method is out of the question when photographing subjects whose actions cannot be predicted. Also, when the flash is dismounted, flash systems communicating via infrared light will not function if they don't detect each other. A radio wave system is a better option.

Since flashes are optimized to lenses up to 200mm, and bird photography mainly requires lenses between 300mm and 500mm, most of the flash light is wasted, and at the same time you are handicapped by insufficient light. Fortunately, there is a sensational invention to produce parallel light rays, first designed in 1818 by Augustin-Jean Fresnel, who realized that instead of using a gigantic and cumbersome convex lens, adhering bits of the bulging part of the lens on a substrate could achieve the same effect. Commercial Fresnel lenses mounted on flashes can double the light intensity when used for short distances, but there is an even better solution: large Fresnel lenses that were used in old overhead projectors. By cutting out a 12x14 cm (4.7×5.5 in) piece from the middle and placing it in front of the flash at a suitable distance, you can increase the efficiency of your flash by three stops, up to a distance of 8 m (26.2 ft)!

The numbers speak for themselves. The light intensity of a mounted flash at 1/8 power at ISO 1000 is amplified by 4 stops, making a 1/2500 second shutter speed possible at a distance of 8m (26.2 ft) in any ambient light conditions. This way the light from a shoe-mounted flash hits a surface smaller than the angle of a 400mm lens.

The best way forward in flash photography is through trial and error.

Fast action in low light—without flash, very little in this Great Reed-Warbler image would have been sharp *(Acrocephalus arundinaceus)*
Nikon D700, 300mm f/2.8, 1/160 second, f/9.0, ISO 250, manual focus, Nikon Speedlight SB-800 flash, Gitzo tripod and video head, floating blind. Hungary, May 2010. →

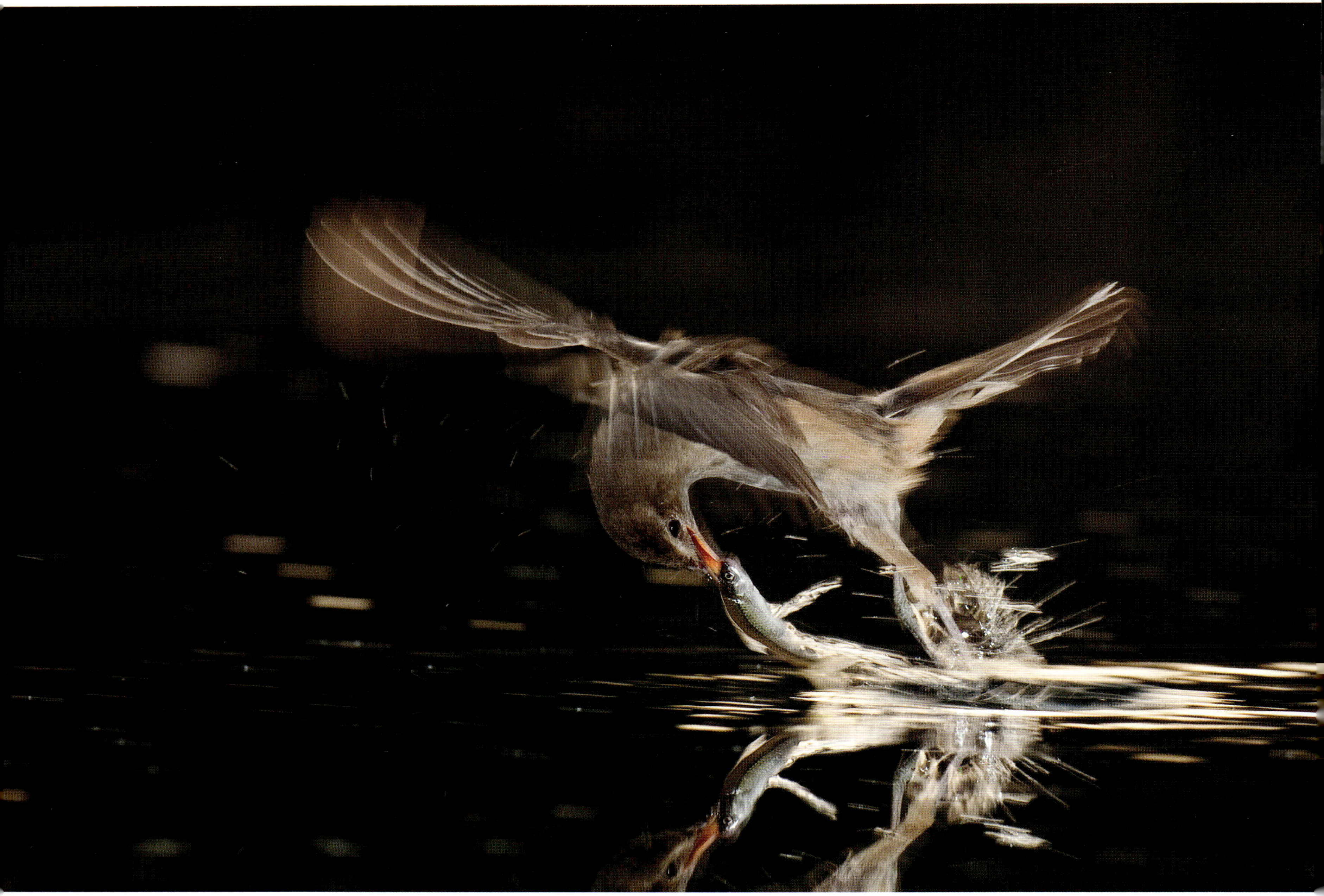

Bence Máté

BENCE MÁTÉ

REMOTE CONTROL

Remote control systems and preparations can be hard work and time consuming, but they can help you photograph subjects and events that are rarely seen.

At its simplest, remote control photography means that you mount your camera on a tripod, attach a remote control receiver to it, and put it in a place where you can attract your subject. As an example, see the Siberian Jay in the chapter "Look for New Angles."

Remote control systems are excellent for times when you either cannot get close enough to your subject or when setting up a photography blind would require excessive work. Lately, more nature and wildlife photographers have caught on to the potential of remote control techniques, mainly because experimenting is not expensive with digital cameras, not in the same way it was with film when the risks were seldom worth the trouble and success was rare.

On average, a person's reaction time is somewhere near 0.2 seconds. This means, in theory at least, that from the moment something happens, it takes about 200 milliseconds to release the shutter. This adds to the lag already present due to the electronics of the camera shutter and the remote control. The lag is an important factor to consider when choosing the most suitable remote control device—the shorter the lag, the better.

> Sometimes your subject drops a hint of forthcoming action, and you can start photographing before the action starts.

A cable release has practically no lag, but with wireless infrared and radio releases the lag is close to several tenths of a second. You can shorten the lag remarkably by pressing the shutter release halfway down. Also, it's good to select a remote control system that allows you to take a series of images as long as you apply pressure to the shutter release, and single shots by pressing the release briefly. A cable release has an extra advantage: it does not need a separate source of power because it takes power from the camera. On the other hand, a cable is always a restriction. Radio-controlled devices are handy, but they need their own power sources. Infrared devices need to have visual contact with each other, otherwise they cannot communicate and will not work. Remote controls are also good when you want to observe your surroundings more freely than you could through the camera's viewfinder. To get the Collared Aracari image I prefocused on a branch where I knew birds would land. Every once in a while more than one bird was aiming for the branch and there was a skirmish. By using the remote control I was free to keep an eye on the area and anticipate action.

When using a remote control system, you'll need to focus and set the camera in advance, so it's good to select a lens with a deep depth of field. The best partner for remote control is a wide lens, but with a wide lens you have to get close to the bird, which is usually a challenge. Sometimes you can hide the camera and the remote control in a

Collared Aracari and Montezuma Oropendola *(Pteroglossus torquatus, Psarocolius montezuma)*
Nikon D700, 300mm f/2.8, 1/2000 second, f/4.0, ISO 800, manual focus, Gitzo tripod and video head, remote control. Costa Rica, January 2010.

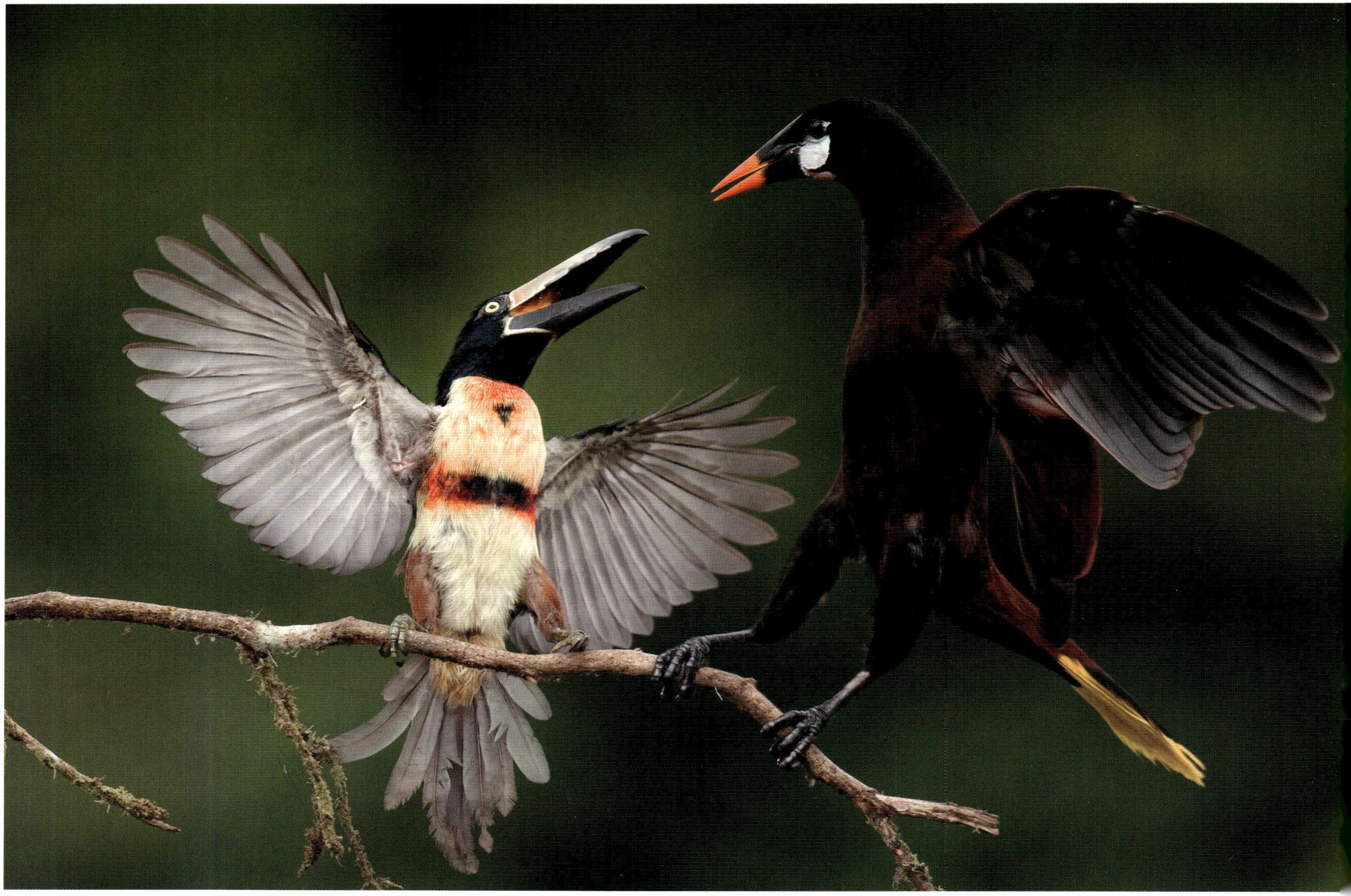

Bence Máté

A creative perspective is achieved with a remote control and a fish-eye lens, which is only 5 cm (2 in) from the bird's leg. Taken from under the wing of a Great Egret *(Ardea alba)*.
Nikon D300, 10–17mm f/3.5–4.5, 1/2000 second, f/16.0, ISO 200, self-made cable control with tripod and head. Hungary, July 2009.

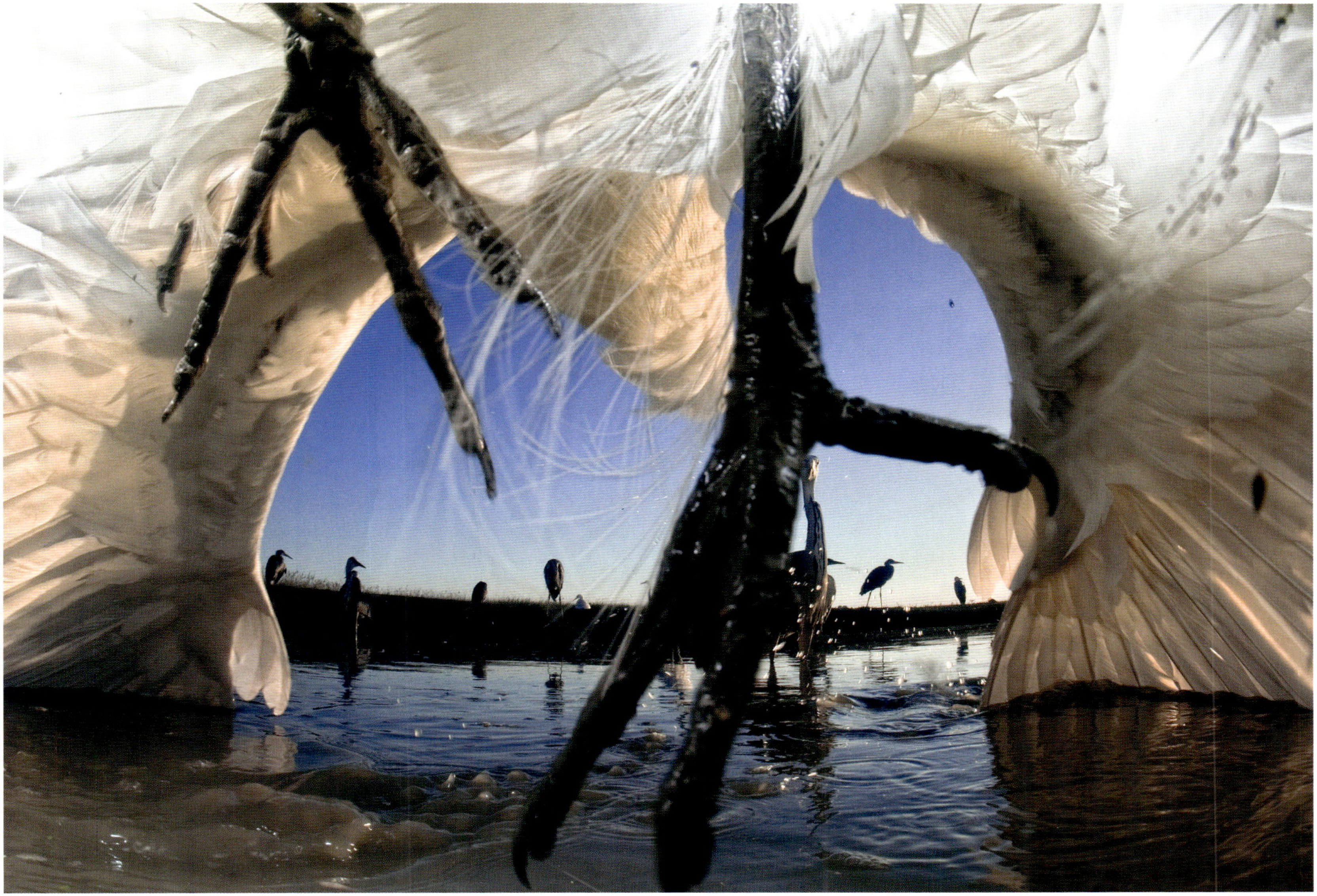

Bence Máté

protective casing, but as the angle of the light changes, the casing's shadow may hit the subject. Making the casing as small as possible can help minimize the problem.

If the remote control bug bites you and you want to invest in it properly, get yourself a motorized head for the tripod, powerful batteries, reliable wireless receivers, a weatherproof casing, and a video camera with its lens attached on the main camera's viewfinder. And prepare yourself for a lot of problems, especially if you are operating a more complex system:

- Batteries always run out in the middle of things.
- Systems with many separate interdependent items are quite vulnerable, and they are prone to malfunction.
- Everything is working fine when you are testing the system, but not during the action. Often you can repeat the session, but sometimes you have to live with the fact that you missed a unique situation.
- The sound of the shutter release or light from the flash can startle or frighten birds, especially when photographing at close range.
- If your gear is close to the birds, it tends to get dirty.

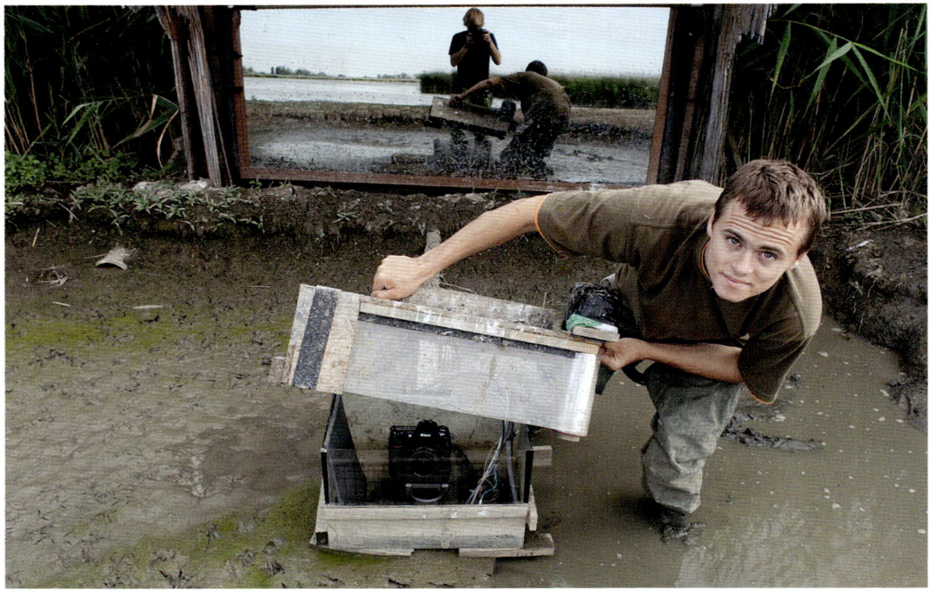

Soma Máté

An essential accessory when photographing in water with a fish-eye lens—a homemade film-feeding device that rolls out new film in front of the camera lens to prevent mud and water from ruining the images

- Make your system waterproof. It may take the birds a while to get used to the setup, and rain is common in most parts of the world. It would be very annoying to have to disassemble your system, just as the hours-long wait is about to be rewarded, because it starts to rain.

After trying many devices, often and thoroughly, I realized that to get the best results I needed to build my own system, and that I would operate it with cables. I used my own system when I photographed herons on a lake. Their movements are very quick, and I was not able to follow all the action from the viewfinder. I mounted my camera on a motorized ball head, which was hidden in a waterproof box about 4 m (13 ft) in front of my blind. The front panel of the box is made of high-quality window glass that is 2mm (0.08 in) thick. With the help of a remote joystick I operated the ball head from the blind and was able to aim my camera quickly.

I also put a small video camera inside the box and connected it to my laptop with a cable. The lens of the video camera was fixed on the viewfinder of my main camera, and it was feeding me information that helped me aim the camera. I didn't want to use the video function in my DSLR for two reasons: it produces images with a lag, and I would only be able to take single shots.

I chose to use a cable release because shutter lag would have been more of an issue had I used my computer. I rigged two flashes on either side of the box, which let me photograph when the light was poor, even at night. The biggest problem was trying to keep the box clean; between the birds and rain, the glass panel quickly accumulated muck and dirt, rendering the box useless for photography. The problem was solved by using transparent film on the glass at the front of the box. I attached a small electric engine to the top of the box, which let me roll out new, clean film in front of my camera every time it got dirty.

Vulnerability is a major drawback in this setup. With many moving parts and cables, you can be certain that something will fail right when birds are where you want them to be, the sun is shining from a low angle on the horizon, and everything is just right.

I recommend remote control photography to anyone who is interested; just make sure that you have time and plenty of patience. It helps to make it clear to yourself from the beginning that some of your projects will fail and that some days are just a royal waste of time.

Bence Máté

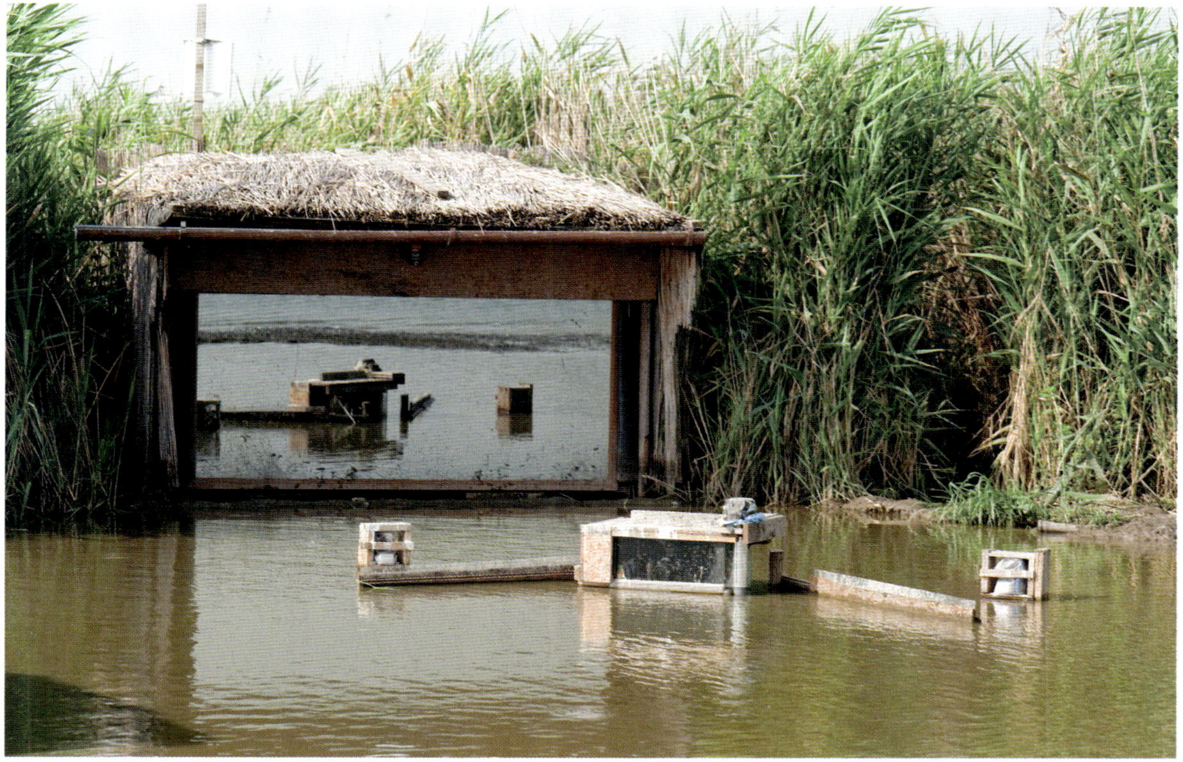

The camera is operated from the blind, which is farther away.

JARI PELTOMÄKI

BIRD PHOTOGRAPHER'S TRIPODS

Tripod or monopod? Video head, ball head, or gimbal?

All of the above are useful—but what's your best option? There is no right answer here. It's a question of different situations requiring different solutions. Sometimes one is better than the others, and another time you might benefit from another combination. Here are a few examples of how I work.

Often the easiest way to photograph flying birds is with a handheld camera. Lighter telephoto lenses (400mm f/5.6, for example) are good for following a fast-flying bird and for photographing for long periods of time without straining yourself very much. And the lighter the equipment you're lugging around in the field, the better.

However, bird photographers tend to steer toward heavier and faster lenses, those over 300mm and f/2.8–4.0. They are okay for brief shooting sessions with a handheld camera, but normally, and especially if used in a longer session, they require a tripod or a monopod. The latter is popular among sports photographers, and can sometimes be a better option than a tripod for other photographers as well.

For example, a monopod was perfect for photographing eagles from a boat outside Hokkaidō Island in Japan. Using a tripod in a boat full of photographers would have been impossible, so I chose a Gitzo carbon fiber monopod and a Wimberley Sidekick with an Arca-Swiss ball head, and voilà, following the eagles was quick and easy. Compared to handheld, photographing with a monopod is faster because the camera is at the right height all the time. The Hokkaidō photo trips were three to four hours long, and because there was no shortage of subjects to photograph, a handheld camera with a 500mm telephoto lens would have been a huge strain on my arms and back.

Tripods

The heavier the equipment, the sturdier the support needs to be. With the various alloy tripods on the market, weight tends to mean strength. Lucky for us, tripods nowadays come in carbon fiber, which makes them much lighter than metal tripods of the same caliber. The higher price is a drawback, however. Several companies manufacture carbon fiber tripods, but Gitzo is probably the most popular brand, even though they are more expensive than their competitors.

Heavy and solid metal tripods will have fans into the future, but bird photographers, the traveling kind in particular, will find that a carbon fiber tripod is the optimal choice. They are more prone to getting damaged than their metallic counterparts, so they need to be packed more carefully for traveling. Carbon fiber is nice in cold temperatures because it doesn't feel as cold to the touch as metal. The best material in cold weather is wood, and wooden tripods are indeed very steady. Some photographers prefer wooden tripods, and you often see birders use them with their telescopes. They are, however, longer than carbon fiber tripods, even when retracted, which makes them quite ill-suited for traveling.

Jari Peltomäki

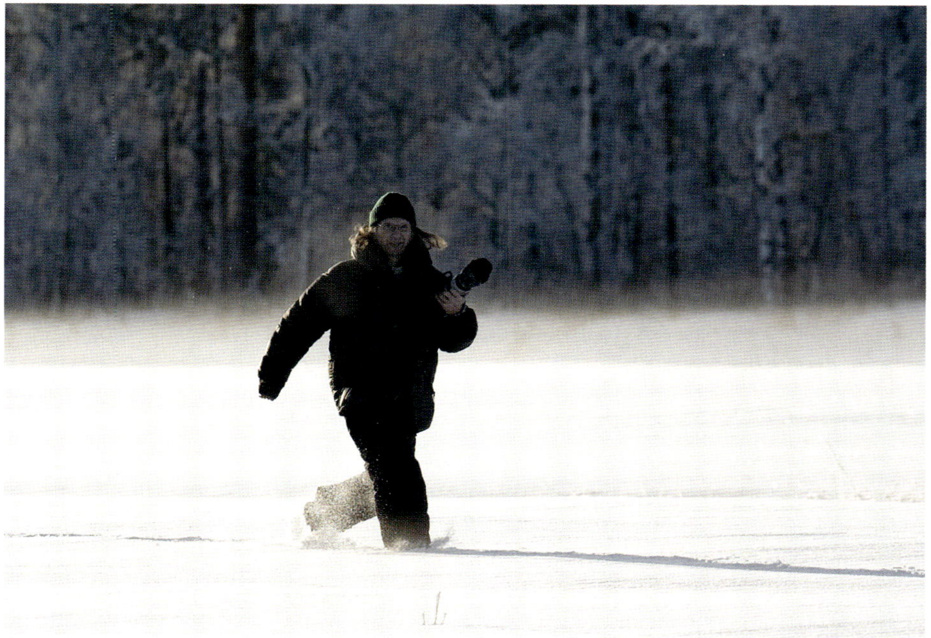

Bird photographer Jorma Luhta with a light set of photographic gear

Jari Peltomäki

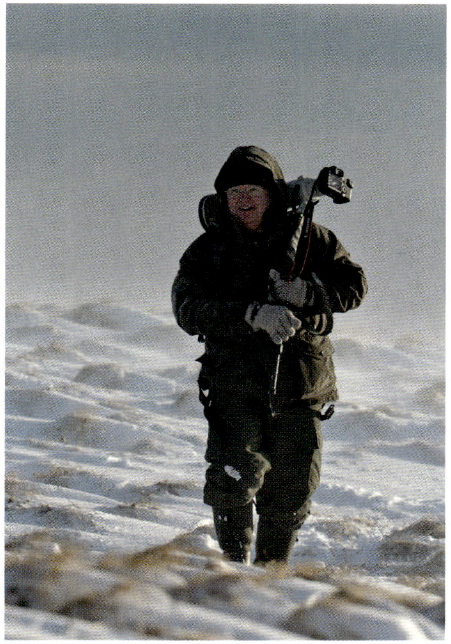

Bird photographer Tarmo Syväpuro photographing on Hornøya Island in northern Norway, equipped with a monopod

Your tripod should help your camera reach eye level without having to raise the center column because this keeps the tripod more stable. Some photographers want the tripod to spread apart to 180 degrees, allowing photography at ground level.

Video Head, Ball Head, or Gimbal?

Nature photographers use a wide variety of ball heads, but although a good ball head and side mount combination works well in bird photography, ball heads are not necessarily optimal for bird photographers.

Whatever the system between the tripod and the camera, it had better have a good quick release mechanism that lets you dismount your camera in a split second.

Side mounts—made by Wimberley and Manfrotto—are very popular with bird photographers because they help balance the camera and a heavy lens

Jari Wilenius

A metallic ground pod supports the side mount

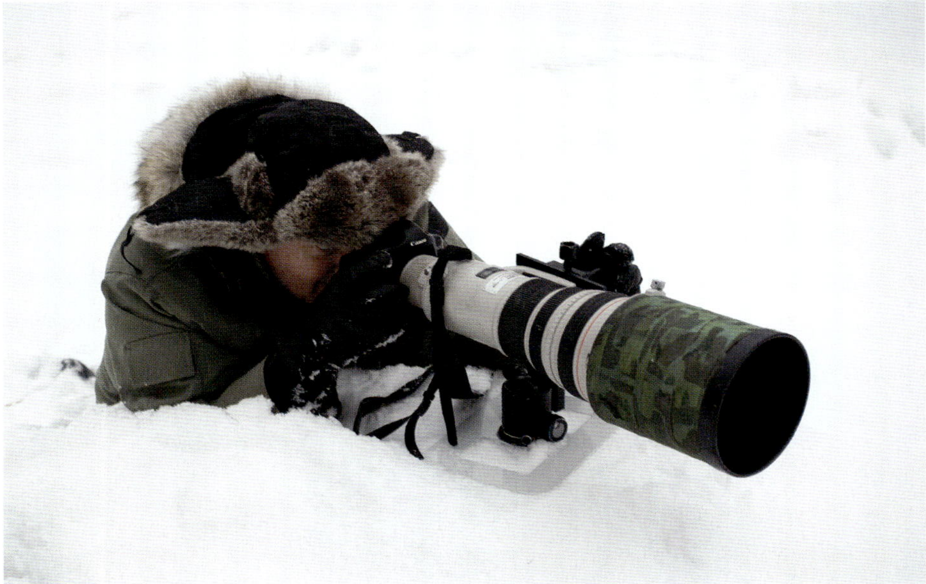

Jari Peltomäki

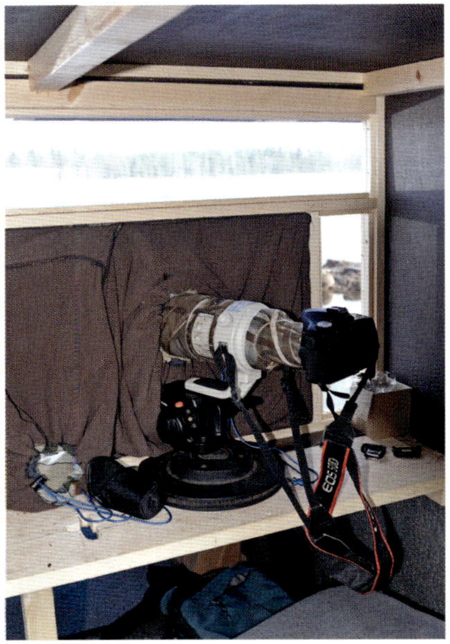

Ground pods can be used in fixed blinds

Minna Rautio

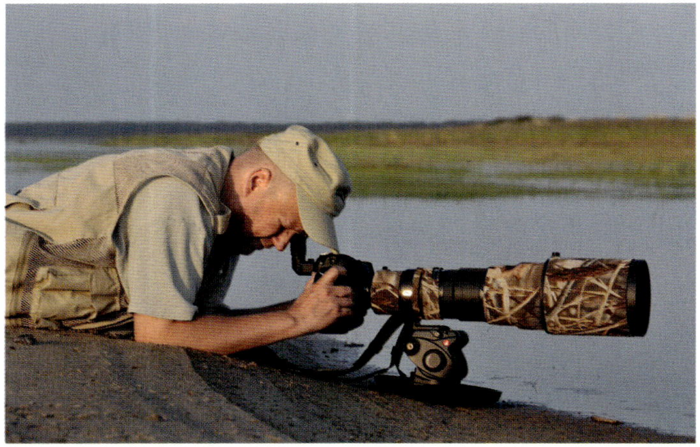

A ground pod is handy when photographing at a low angle. Shown here is a Skimmer ground pod.

on a tripod so they are light and easy to maneuver. I often use a side mount in extreme cold, when the temperatures can make my otherwise favorite video heads sluggish. The reason I choose a video head over a side mount is that side mounts do not offer enough resistance for sideways maneuvers, and I find that following a flying bird is easier with a smoothly turning video head. During most of the year I use video heads by Manfrotto and Gitzo.

A shoulder support can be a welcome addition to your kit. It gives an extra point of support for the camera, which can be particularly useful for photographing flying birds. There are a couple of commercially made shoulder supports, but the best ones I have seen were made by photographers themselves.

Ground Pod

A ground pod is very useful for photographing at ground level. It has a bolt for mounting a head of your choice, or for those who want an extremely low angle, a mount for a quick release plate is available, at least for Manfrotto, Gitzo, and Wimberley. A ground pod provides protection between the camera and the ground. Maneuvering the camera is more limited, but if you are photographing on level ground, where you need to move the camera up or down only minimally, it will be fine. Using an angle finder on your camera helps reduce the strain that the ground pod position inevitably causes on your neck.

You can also use a tripod for ground-level photography, if your tripod legs go to a full split, but a ground pod is easier to fit in crowded spaces, such as a tent blind. I also use a ground pod in a permanent blind; with the metal petal firmly attached to a shelf or table, it is easy to maneuver the camera. Again, the heavier the plate, the better the support for your camera.

There are many kinds of ground pods, made of many different materials, on the market. One of the most popular brands is Skimmer. If you are so inclined, you can make your own.

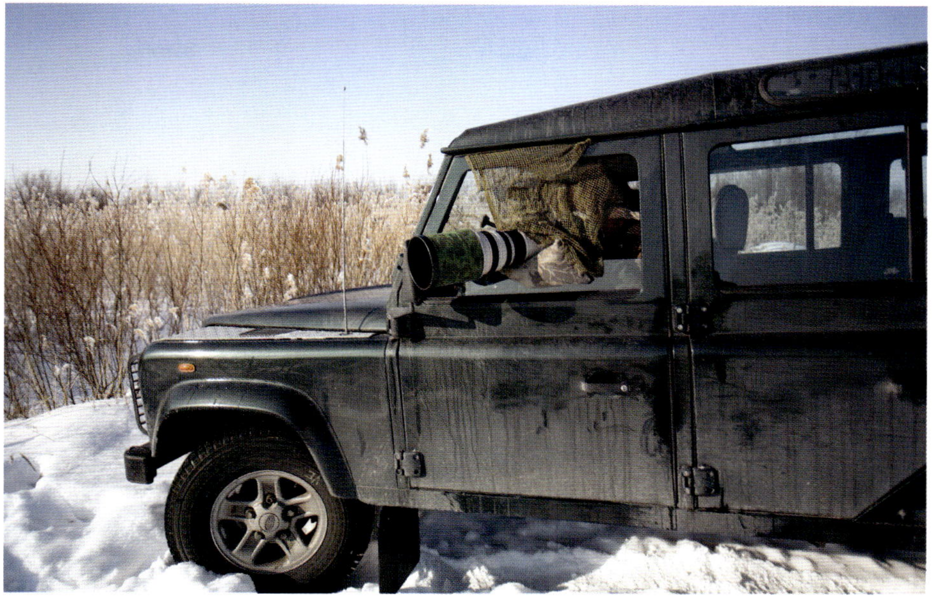

Erkki Toppinen

A beanbag is great for photographing from a car

Beanbag

Beanbags are fabulous little helpers for bird photographers, especially when photographing from a car, but they can also be used in a blind or on the ground to support a camera. You can buy beanbags or make one yourself. Dried peas make the heaviest filling; other good alternatives are sunflower seeds, grain, rice, or macaroni.

Even if handheld photography is easier than before, thanks to digital technology, some type of support is one of the most important pieces of additional equipment a bird photographer needs. You should consider all your options and weigh them against your needs. Good support is particularly important when shooting video because any shaking or other unwanted movement can be very unpleasant in video footage.

MARKUS VARESVUO & JARI PELTOMÄKI

BASIC ACCESSORIES

Basic accessories include memory cards, camera bags, and photographer's vests.

A DSLR stores images in its own buffer of RAM memory before transferring it to the memory card inserted into the camera. You can take pictures without a memory card, but they are not stored or saved anywhere. Based on my own experiences, I recommend that you adjust your camera to not function without a memory card!

When I started with digital cameras in late 2002, the highest capacity CompactFlash (CF) memory cards were 1 GB, and they cost about $500. The change has been huge; a 64 GB card at 90 MB/second now costs remarkably less.

The time it takes to transfer image data from the buffer to a memory card depends on both the camera processor and the memory card. In 2002, the rate of data transfer in cameras and memory cards was noticeably slower than today, and the image file that cameras produced was only about a quarter of the size of today's RAW files. In 10 years, buffer capacities have grown many times over, but because RAW file sizes have grown at the same time, the real increase from the early days is about three to four times. A truly remarkable change has taken place in the speed of the transfer rate. New memory cards can reach up to 150 MB/second in receiving data from the buffer, meaning that the camera is cleared faster for taking new frames. With the Lexar 1000x UDMA 7 memory card, launched in August 2012, and a Canon EOS-1D X, you can shoot about 45 RAW files before the buffer fills up, and then at about 4 fps as the files are being transferred to the card at that rate. This can make a huge difference in action photography, where the buffer tends to fill up too soon.

CF cards have no moving parts, and in my experience they are reliable and durable. I gave up the separate, portable Digital Camera Data Bank devices years ago because they were unreliable, especially in colder temperatures. And I have not needed to use the more sophisticated Multimedia Storage Viewer devices. Instead I rely on a strategy based on many high-capacity memory cards. I pack enough capacity to cover several days of intensive shooting.

It's better to have too much capacity than too little. You can be sure that whenever you need to change your card because it's full, it will be in the wrong place at the wrong time, and you will lose some great action. The bigger the card, the fewer the changes.

I have seen a CF card malfunction only once when the data was completely lost. Maybe the card did not like being dipped in bog water. It makes sense to pack the cards in watertight cases.

Card readers also have different speeds. Try to find a fast one. You will appreciate the speed after a long day's work when you are transferring your data to your computer.

Backpacks and Vests

A good camera backpack is all-important to a bird photographer. Over the

Erkki Toppinen

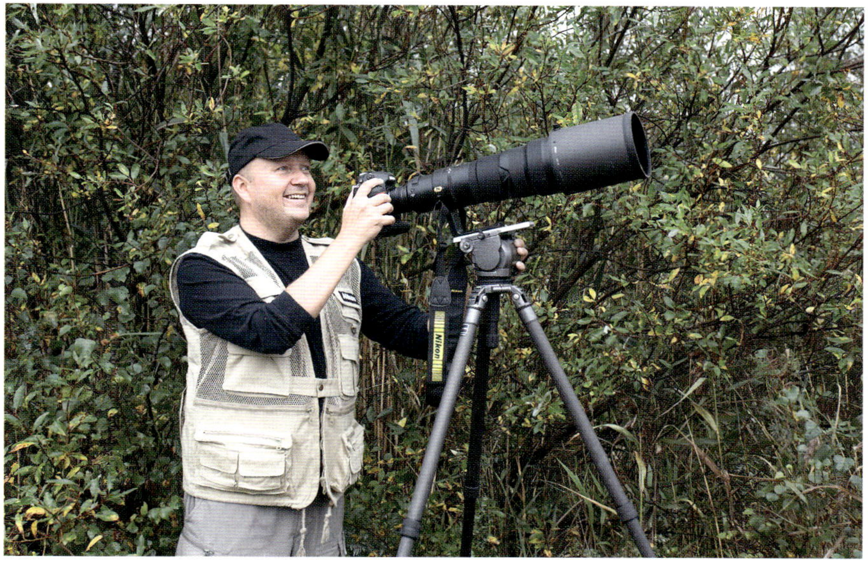

A bird photographer's vest

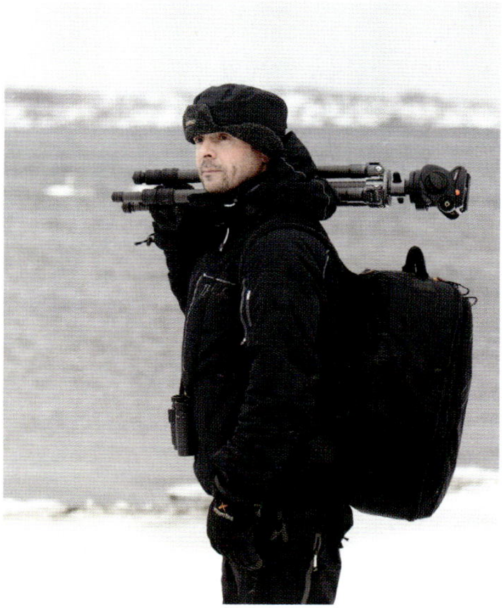

Minna Lindroth

Binoculars, a tripod, and a camera backpack are a bird photographer's basic accessories

years I have tried several models and used many of them until they almost fell apart.

The best I've found so far is Kiboko by Gura Gear, which I've been using for two years. As a bird photographer, it fills every criteria I have for a backpack. It is ultralight, made of durable materials, and has a separate rain and dust cover. In addition to one long telephoto lens (500mm or 800mm), it holds two cameras, 1.4x and 2x extenders plus extension tubes, two wide lenses, two memory card cases, a lens rain cover, an MP3 player and small speaker, and binoculars. Each of these goes into its own compartment or pocket, which helps keep my equipment orderly and safe. There is also room for drinks and snacks. What's truly important for traveling is that the backpack can be carried on to many, if not most, airplanes. The excellent design combined with very malleable and adjustable straps make carrying this backpack as comfortable as possible. You can also strap your tripod onto it. The price is quite steep, but in my opinion it's worth it.

Other good backpacks are available from, for example, Think Tank Photo, Lowepro, and Tamrac.

A vest is good for a bird photographer, although not essential. A good photographer's vest has many good-sized pockets that can hold extenders, memory cards, and a short lens. It allows you to carry your basic gear with you at all times when you're out photographing. A vest is particularly good in hot climates, where you can't wear a jacket, and a vest allows faster access to your gear than a backpack.

MARKUS VARESVUO

FOCUSING METHODS AND HOW TO USE THEM

Autofocus revolutionized flight shots less than two decades ago.

Before autofocus, focusing was done manually, and you relied on your eyesight. Trying to take sharp images of flying birds was very hard, especially when they flew close. Now you see one great action shot after another, and most of them were taken with continuous AF.

Bird images are primarily taken with autofocus. You typically use continuous focusing when photographing moving subjects and one-shot focus for subjects that are still. You occasionally need to use manual focus, which we'll talk about more at the end of this chapter.

When you use continuous focusing, you try to keep a chosen AF point, or points, locked on your subject, such as a flying bird, so that the camera processor can calculate and estimate the subject's flight path. In an ideal situation, you can admire a long series of sharp images after photographing a flying bird and decide to keep only the images in which the wing positions and the background please you most. Unfortunately, the reality is often very different, and in the most challenging situations you can count yourself lucky if you get one sharp frame.

The success ratio is best when photographing relatively large birds against an even background, such as a blue sky, and the bird is quite big in the frame. You can use one AF point because it's fairly easy to keep it locked on the bird, for example on its head. Most camera makes and models with autofocus can produce sharp images in such situations with a good success ratio, as long as the shutter speed and other adjustments are correct (read more about this in the chapter "Freezing Movement").

An essential basic adjustment to make on your lens is to select the working distance. For photographing flying birds, you should select the option with a focusing range from the largest available number of feet to infinity. This makes the focusing faster, especially the refocusing that has to happen after your subject has disappeared from your viewfinder.

When photographing a fast bird against a busy background, the success ratio drops noticeably, even with the best professional cameras. With Canon's professional models, your best option for this kind of situation is the slowest or second slowest tracking sensitivity, which helps to keep the focus steady and prevents it from switching to the background. Also, birds that fly fast in erratic paths can prove difficult, even impossible, to track with just one AF point, and you could be better off using an extended central AF point (four or eight extra points); if the central AF point loses the subject, the surrounding AF points become active and can lock onto the subject.

A Common Crane flying against a blue sky *(Grus grus)*
Canon EOS-1D Mark II N, 500mm f/4.0, 1/1250 second, f/8.0, ISO 400, continuous focus with a central focusing point, handheld camera, blind. Sweden, April 2007.

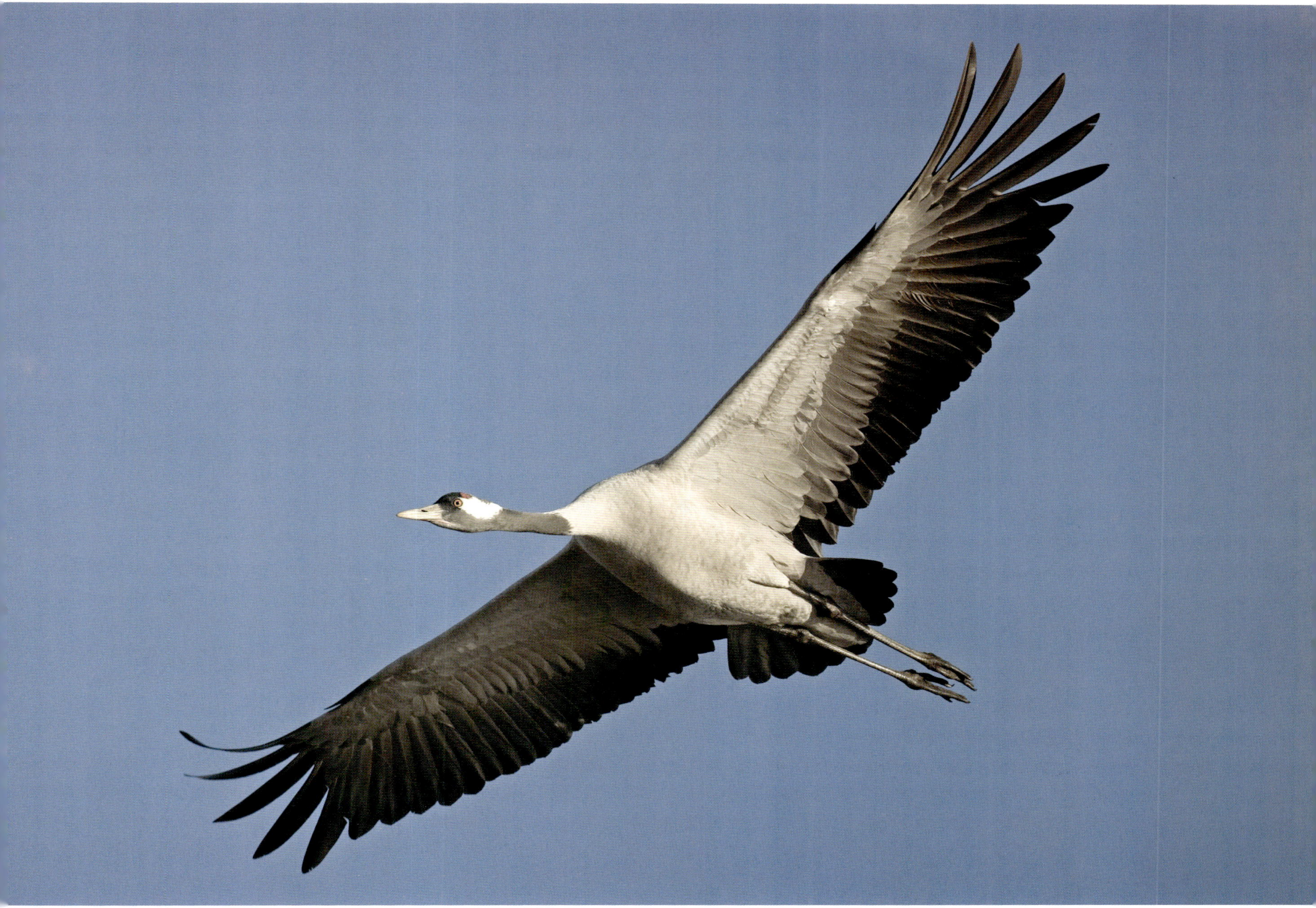

Jari Peltomäki

Markus Varesvuo

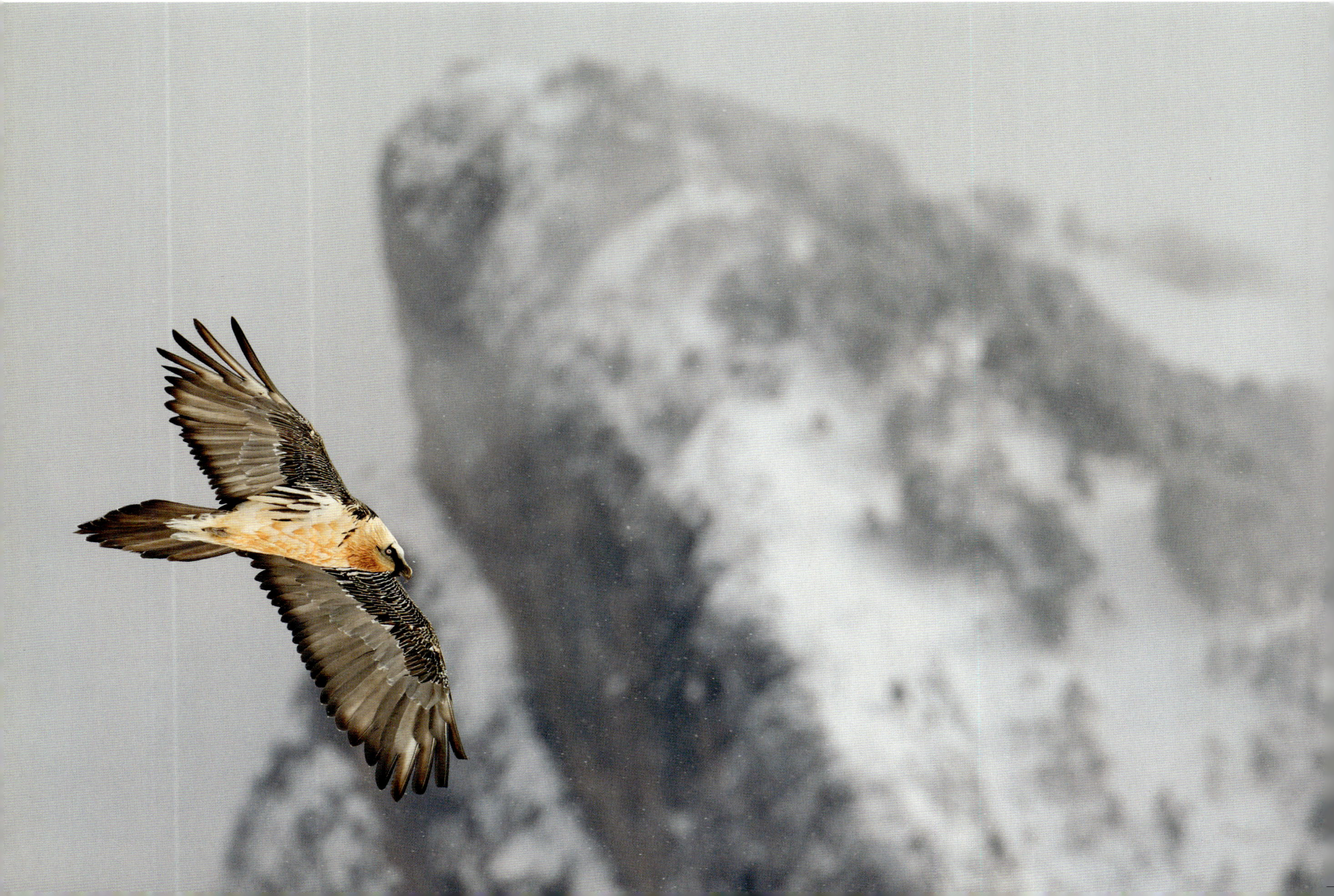

Sometimes, when the circumstances are really challenging, even the extended central AF point is not good enough to keep a flying bird in focus for any length of time, and it's better to use the largest number of AF points, such as 45 points, or 61 points with the Canon EOS-1D X. This way it's likely that at least some part of the bird is in focus, provided that it's in the viewfinder to begin with.

I used to select 45 AF points often, and in easier circumstances, with good results. This worked delightfully well in the Canon EOS-1D Mark II camera, and satisfactorily with the EOS-1D Mark IV, whereas I hardly ever used it with the EOS-1D Mark III, where the 45 AF points was hopeless. I now have some experience with the new EOS-1D X and can safely say that the 61 AF points is the best focusing system that Canon has ever engineered. It poses a serious threat to the hegemony Nikon has had over focusing in the past few years. For flying birds in demanding circumstances, the 61 points work so well that I've all but scrapped the use of one AF point or even the extended AF points. One exception, where the extended central AF point has proved better than the 61 points, is photographing fast-flying seabirds against sharp waves from a heaving boat.

Continuous focus is needed not only when the bird is flying, but also whenever it's doing something. A typical example is a waterbird swimming or a wader foraging on a shore.

One-shot focus is mainly used for birds that are still. Using one-shot focus means that you aim your AF point to the desired spot and press the shutter release halfway down. The camera focuses on the spot and locks it; you can either take several frames with the same focus by pressing the shutter release all the way down or move your camera to reframe for better composition before pressing the release fully down. To refocus, let go of the shutter release and then press it again.

Some photographers use continuous focusing even on stationary birds, but I recommend using one-shot focus because its focus is more accurate and it makes composition easier. Keep in mind that when you're taking closeups and using the largest possible aperture, the focus area is very shallow. To ensure that you will get shots where the subject, or the desired part of it, is in the focusing area, focus on the target several times and take many frames.

One-shot focus is also good when you prefocus on an area in anticipation of an action image, where continuous focus would have no chance of tracking the subject. For example, first you prefocus on a nest hole entrance, then you set your lens focus to manual. As soon as you see the bird getting close to the nest, take a series of images and hope that at least one frame has caught the bird in the right position and it's sharp in the frame. This will probably yield better results than continuous focus.

I took the Common Redstart image using one-shot focus. I followed a Common Redstart parent for a couple of days, photographing from a blind. The bird always used the same route to return to the nest with food for the young, and it always stopped on the same perch for a second or two before making a short movement, practically vertically, into the nest. First I tried using the continuous focus, but it was mostly locking on everything except the

A Lammergeier flying against an alpine background *(Gypaetus barbatus)*
Canon EOS-1D Mark IV, 500mm f/4.0, 1/2000 second, f/8.0, ISO 800, continuous focus with an extended central focusing point (the left edge of the image has been cropped), Gitzo tripod, Manfrotto 501 video head, blind. Spain, November 2010.

Markus Varesvuo

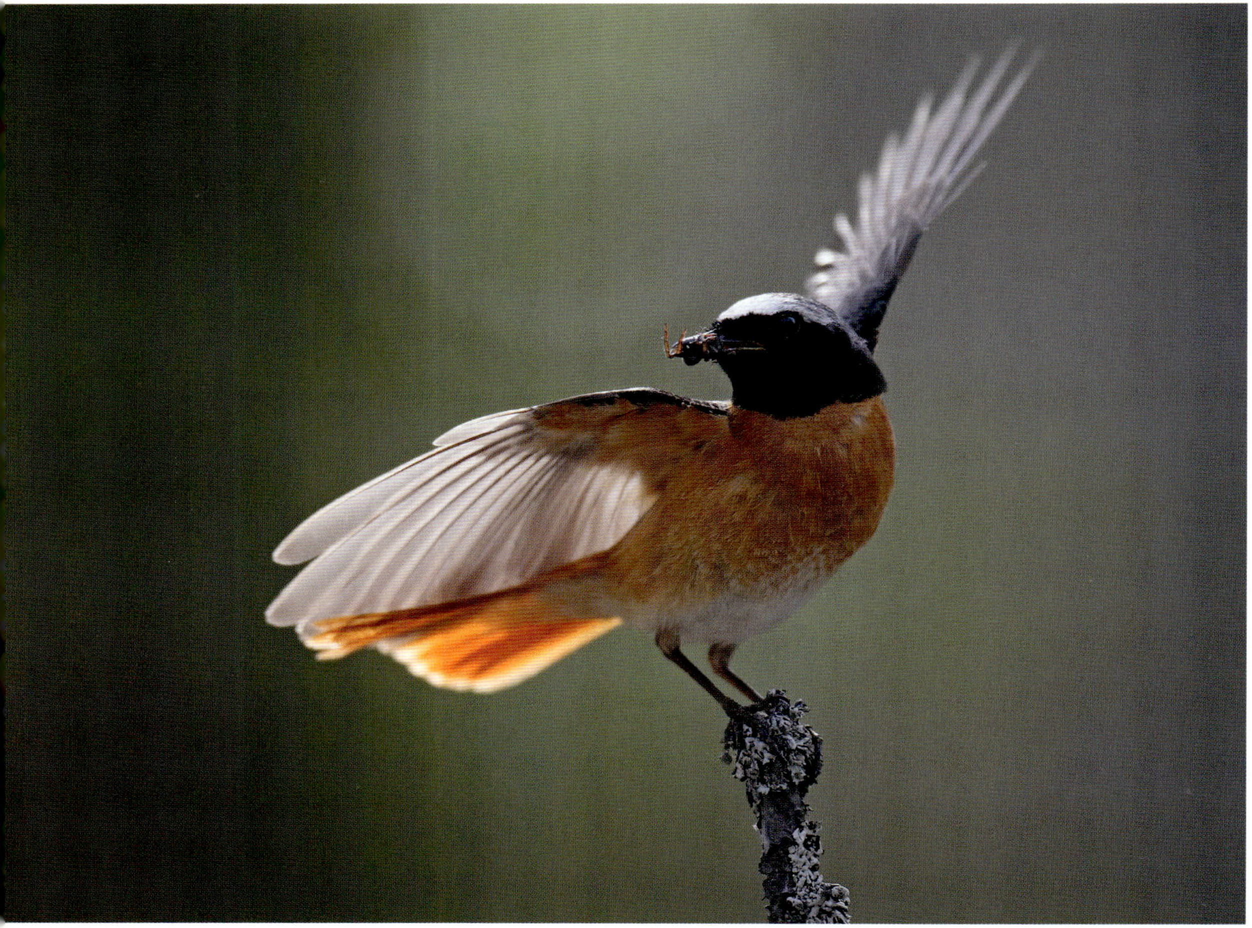

A Common Redstart bursting into flight *(Phoenicurus phoenicurus)*
Canon EOS-1D Mark III, 500mm f/4.0, 1/2500 second, f/4.5, ISO 2000, one-shot focus with a central focusing point, Gitzo tripod, Manfrotto 501 video head, blind. Vaala, Finland, June 2007.

head—the focus was probably deceived by the quick opening of the wings as the bird took off. I needed a new strategy, so I started using one-shot focus, which I aimed at the bird's head the second it landed on the perch. Then I pressed the shutter release to fire a series of images until the buffer was full or until the bird was out of the frame. A few days later I had many decent images.

Use manual focus when the autofocus isn't working for some reason, such as the following:

- There isn't enough light for autofocus, but you can still see well enough to focus manually
- The combined speed of your lens and extender is slower than f/8.0
- The available light is so low, or the air is so foggy, that autofocus struggles to find a bird that is low in contrast, such as a raven
- The subject is behind branches and the autofocus keeps locking on them
- It's snowing so heavily that the autofocus keeps locking on the flakes
- The subject is very small

JARI PELTOMÄKI

EXPOSURE IN BIRD PHOTOGRAPHY

It's essential to know the selected method of exposure inside out and expose images correctly.

This chapter takes a closer look at exposure basics, and I will also talk about how I expose in different situations. Exposure is all about the amount of light that hits the sensor, which you can control by changing the size of the aperture or the exposure time, or both. For example, if you change the aperture from f/4.0 to f/5.6, or change the exposure time from 1/125 second to 1/250 second, you halve the amount of light that reaches the sensor. The smaller the aperture (which is indicated by a growing number), the greater the depth of field (range of sharpness). Where aperture has an impact on the depth of field, exposure time dictates, first and foremost, how well you can freeze movement in your image, and it also plays a role in preventing camera shake. As a guideline, when you are photographing with a handheld camera and a 500mm lens without a stabilizer, the exposure time should be at least 1/500 second to avoid the effects of camera shake in your image. The latest stabilizers let you stop down remarkably and set the exposure time at 1/125 second, for example, and still get sharp images. The light metering mode influences exposure as well.

Metering Light

DSLRs offer a range of light metering modes, which determine the region in the frame where the camera meters light and how it is weighted. Nikon and Canon have the following light metering options:

- Spot: The camera obtains a meter reading from the center of the frame or a specific selected focusing point that is off center. You can use Automatic Exposure lock (AE lock) with this mode and reframe the image. If the meter is reading a spot that is either too dark or too light, the exposure can fail completely.
- Center weighted: The camera uses the whole frame and weights the center of the viewfinder. This mode is especially good for photographing flying birds. You can use AE lock with this mode and reframe the image.
- Evaluative/matrix: This metering method is called color matrix in Nikon cameras and through-the-lens (TTL) full-aperture metering in Canon cameras. This is the recommended setting for most situations, and it works well in bird photography.

When photographing flying birds, I suggest using center-weighted metering because it leads to a more accurate exposure than metering the entire frame. Also, you need to apply less exposure compensation—overexposure and underexposure—than evaluative/matrix metering. In some extreme lighting conditions, when the difference between light on the subject and light in the background is considerable, spot metering is justifiable. Nonetheless, I mostly use the evaluative/matrix metering modes. It might be easiest to learn one mode like the back of your

Jari Peltomäki

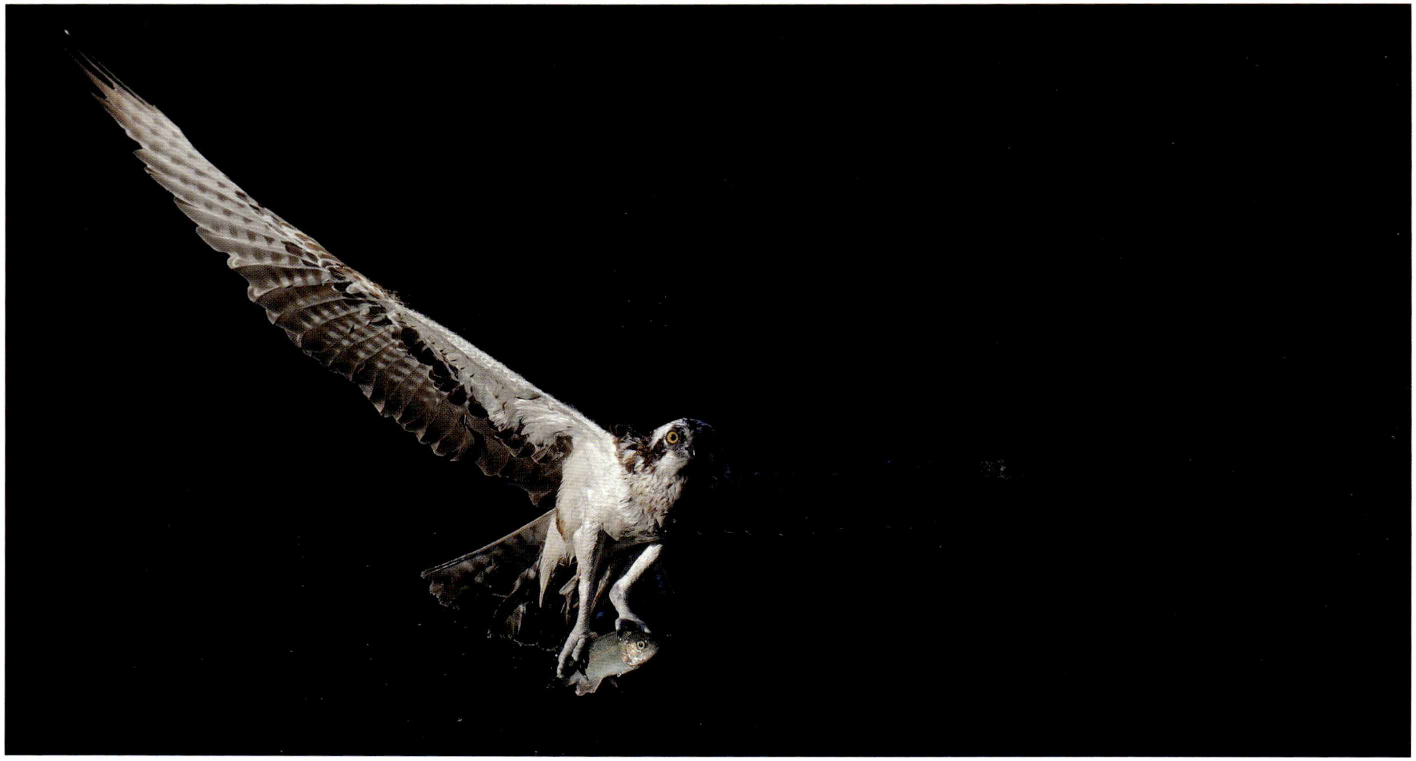

An Osprey in full sunlight against a black background, which is difficult to expose correctly *(Pandion haliaetus)*
Nikon D3S, 500mm f/4.0, 1/2500 second, f/8.0, ISO 1600, continuous focus with 51 focusing points, Gitzo tripod, Manfrotto 501 video head. Kangasala, Finland, September 2010.

hand—experience will teach you to judge how much you need to correct the exposure that the camera calculated for you in any given situation. If you want to momentarily change the mode in the middle of a session, you need to remember to change it back right away, or you will probably get some bad exposures.

Checking the exposure is easy with a digital camera; you can check the brightness histogram on the LCD monitor immediately after taking the picture to see if the frame is exposed properly. It's very important to get the exposure right, and preferably have the histogram reach all the way to the right edge because then you know you have the maximum amount of tonal values in the image. This is called exposing to the right (ETTR). Most cameras have a setting that makes the overexposed areas flash on the LCD monitor, and it marks them with a different color in the preview. State-of-the-art cameras tolerate some level of overexposure without undue data loss, but it's smart to keep an eye on the histogram and tweak the exposure if the histogram seems to lean too heavily to the right edge. When it is skillfully applied, moderate overexposure can often be recommended because it allows the sensor to capture the maximum amount of information and therefore, particularly with high ISO values, it gives you the best results.

In September 2010 I was photographing Ospreys at the Osprey Foundation in Kangasala, Finland. It was early in the morning, the sun was shining on the white Osprey, and the background was in the shade. I used evaluative/matrix metering and manual exposure. Compared to the reading in my camera, I had to underexpose by more than two stops to avoid clipped highlights on the white parts of the bird. During the same photo trip, I captured a Lesser Black-backed Gull flying against dark water. To avoid overexposing the gull's white head, I had to underexpose by one to two stops.

On another trip in April 2010 I was photographing Black-legged Kittiwakes on the Hornøya bird island in northeast Norway. They were set against a background that was in the shade. Here also, I had to underexpose more than two stops to make sure that their white heads wouldn't be overexposed.

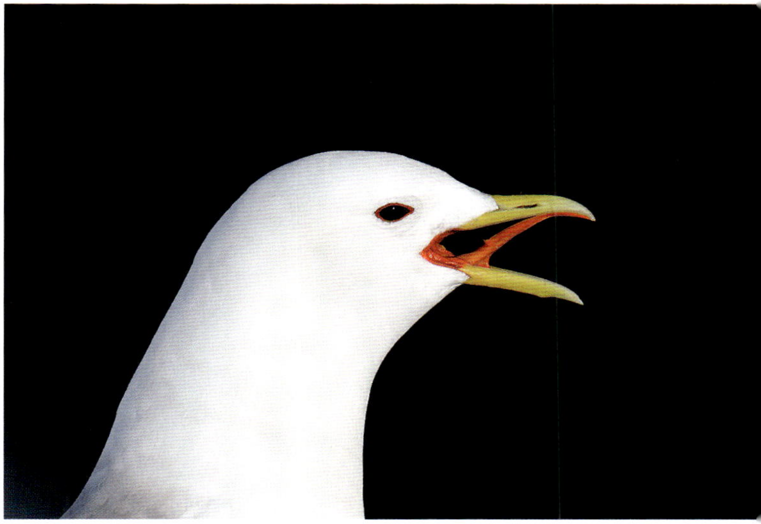

The white head of a Black-legged Kittiwake is easily overexposed when photographed against a dark background *(Rissa tridactyla)*
Nikon D3S, 500mm f/4.0 plus 1.4x extender, 1/2000 second, f/10.0, ISO 800, one-shot focus with one focusing point, Gitzo tripod, Manfrotto 501 video head. Hornøya, Norway, April 2010.

Jari Peltomäki

Exposure Modes

The photographer influences exposure by controlling the amount of light that hits the sensor. This is accomplished by changing either the aperture or the exposure time, or both. DSLRs allow manual adjustments of both the aperture and the exposure time. They also have preprogrammed exposure modes that let photographers control either the aperture or the shutter speed, while the camera controls the other one. You can also let your camera select both the aperture and the shutter speed.

More advanced DSLRs have exposure modes that are more or less suitable for bird photography:

- **P** (programmed): The camera determines the shutter speed and the aperture for the best possible exposure, incorporating the focal length to minimize camera shake. This is relatively foolproof, but it is better suited to a family trip or a casual day out than photographing birds.

- **A/Av** (aperture priority): You set the aperture, and the camera sets the shutter speed. This mode lets you control the depth of field. Setting the maximum aperture (smallest aperture number) that the lens allows gives you a shallow depth of field, which results in the fastest possible shutter speed. Many bird photographers use this mode.
- **S/Tv** (shutter priority): You set the shutter speed, and the camera sets the aperture. This is good for freezing and blurring movement. Experience gives you the knowledge to assess which shutter speeds freeze different-sized birds in flight. For example, a crane's wings are frozen at a mere 1/500 second, whereas a puffin requires a minimum of 1/1000 second.
- **M** (manual): You set both the aperture and the shutter speed. This gives you maximum control. This mode can be a bit slower to use in the field, but is excellent in situations where the background behind a flying bird alternates between a lighter sky and a darker forest. I use this mode in Nikon cameras. Manual exposure compensation is also easy.

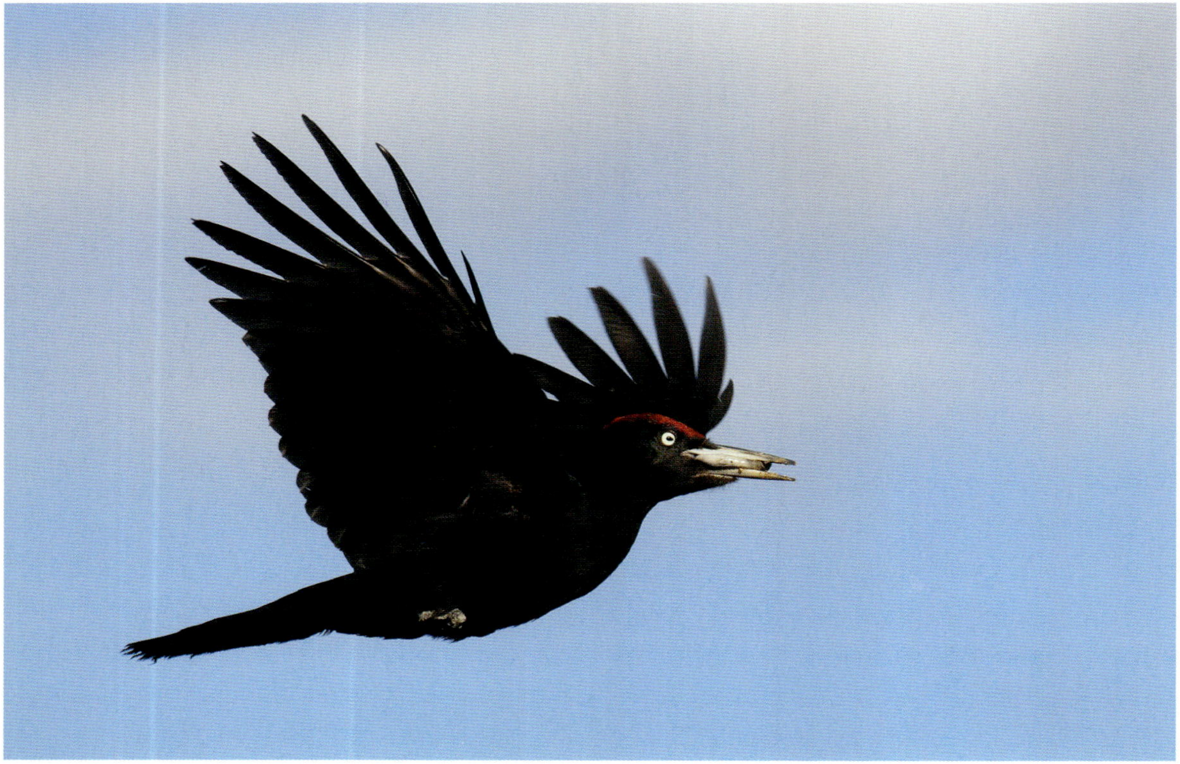

Jari Peltomäki

A Black Woodpecker flying against a blue sky *(Dryocopus martius)*. A typical example of a situation that requires overexposure by one f-stop.
Canon EOS-1D Mark III, 500mm f/4.0 plus 1.4x extender, 1/2000 second, f/10.0, ISO 800, continuous focus with an extended central focusing point, handheld camera. Kuusamo, Finland, June 2009.

Exposure Compensation

Regardless of the metering mode, or the exposure mode, you can be faced with the need to either overexpose or underexpose against the metering result that your camera has calculated. It's down to experience again; you will learn when to stop down and when to open up.

A typical situation for overexposure is when you're photographing a bird flying in the sky. The lighter the sky, the more you need to open up. When you photograph against snow, you usually need to give more light to the sensor than what your camera meter says.

In situations where a light-colored bird is set against a very dark background, you may have to stop down the exposure compensation—sometimes a lot. Otherwise you risk overexposing your subject.

Some cameras let you set an automatic ISO mode, which means the camera will automatically raise the ISO sensitivity if there is not enough light for the exposure you set. This can be a useful feature with new camera sensors, which tolerate extremely high ISO values.

Safety shift is an automatic setting that either increases the exposure time or opens the aperture, until the exposure is correct, if there isn't enough light for the aperture and shutter speed that you selected.

Bracketing

Your camera may have an option for automatic exposure bracketing. This means that your camera can automatically bracket exposures for multiple frames so they differ by 1/3 stop increments, for example. I try to always set the exposure as accurately as possible, but lately I have been experimenting with bracketing. Combining frames with different exposures by using the high dynamic range (HDR) technique can open new frontiers in bird photography.

It's vital that you practice changing your camera settings so you can change the aperture, shutter speed, and ISO value, in particular, without having to raise your eye from the viewfinder. You need to be able to make the necessary adjustments by feel to avoid missing great opportunities. To a photographer, this is just as important as being able to drive without having to look at the pedals and gear shift!

As a rule, especially when I'm photographing from a blind, I take test frames to make sure that my exposure is as good as possible. I try to get the image as bright as possible without any clipped highlights.

The brightness histogram on the camera's LCD monitor is a great tool for checking that you got your exposure right. Normally I stop down one to two f-stops and adjust the exposure time to get the right exposure.

Professional cameras have a button that you can press to see the depth of field in the viewfinder. If it's not deep enough, you can stop down more.

Depending on the selected metering mode, a Cinereous Vulture against a white sky requires overexposure by zero to two f-stops *(Aegypius monachus)*
Canon EOS-1D Mark II N, 500mm f/4.0, 1/2000 second, f/5.6, ISO 400, continuous focus with an extended central focusing point, handheld camera. Mongolia, June 2007. →

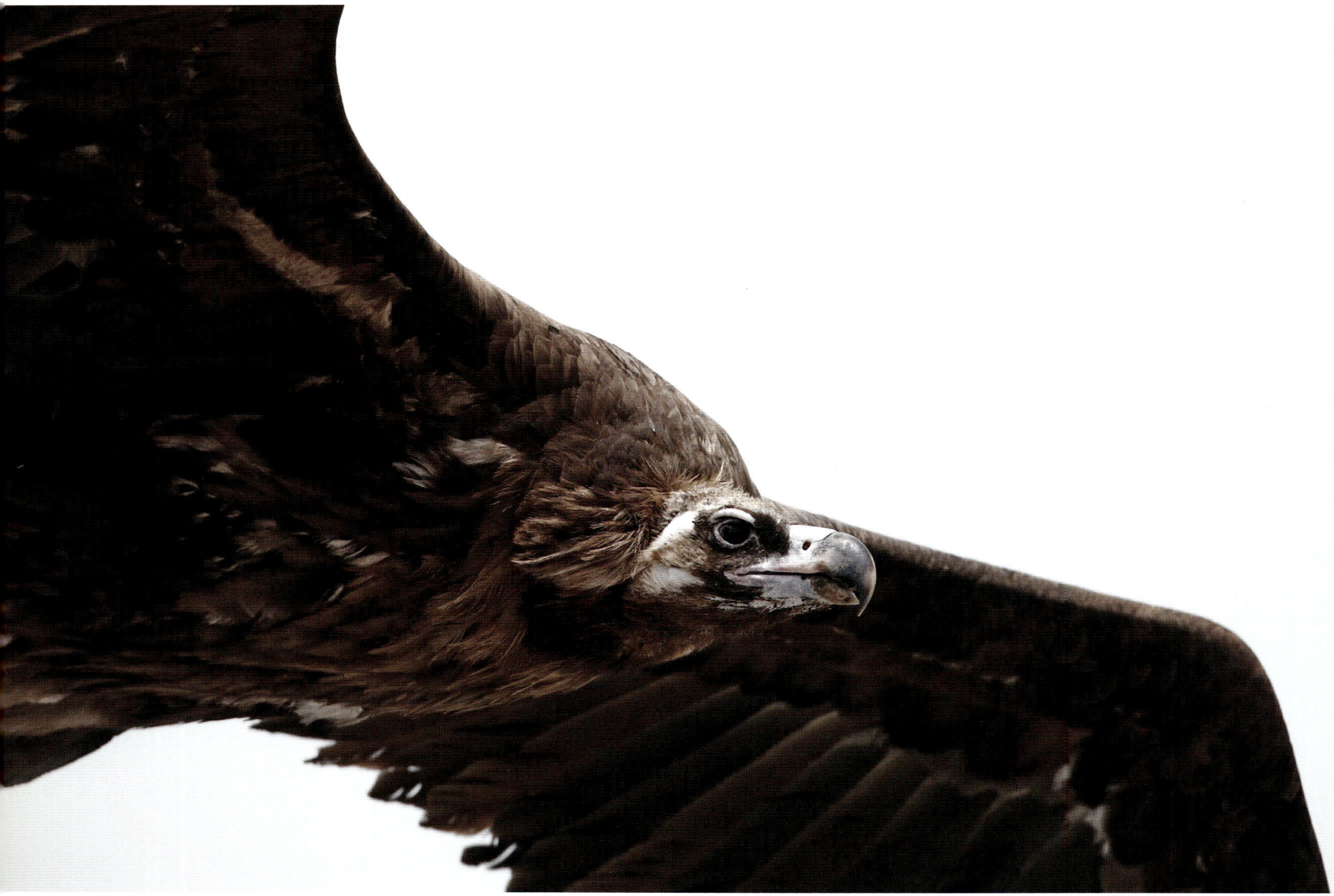

Jari Peltomäki

MARKUS VARESVUO

FREEZING MOVEMENT

This chapter looks at freezing movement, fully or partially, in existing light.

Movement is probably easiest to freeze when photographing waterfowl that are calmly swimming. It gets more difficult with flying falcons, and the biggest challenges come with small birds that are flying fast and erratically.

The rule of thumb is that the bigger the bird, the slower its movements, which makes taking sharp action shots easier. So where a shutter speed of 1/500 second is fast enough for capturing a raptor calmly gliding in the sky, catching a small bird in the middle of its flight requires at least 1/3200 second if you want to freeze the bird all the way to its wing tips.

When focusing on feeding waders, I have found that the shutter speed needs to be surprisingly high, at least 1/1000 second to freeze any movement of the head and bill.

The focal length also plays a role when setting the shutter speed. Longer lenses need faster shutter speeds to eliminate the camera shake caused by longer focal lengths. Advanced telephoto lenses (300–800mm) have sophisticated stabilizers that effectively reduce camera shake, producing remarkably sharp images even when shooting handheld with low shutter speeds.

Another factor affecting the shutter speed is that the closer the bird is to the photographer, the greater its angular velocity, which requires a faster shutter speed.

The King Eider taking off was captured with a handheld camera while standing in a small boat in rolling seas. Almost without exception, bigger ducks will take off into a headwind, which reduces their speed, and therefore the shutter speed can be slower than when photographing a bird flying close by with the wind at its tail. I used a 500mm f/4.0 telephoto lens with the stabilizer on. Even though the day was overcast, I had enough light to take flight shots. I set the shutter speed at 1/2000 second knowing that it would freeze the bird's head and body completely at takeoff. With this speed, there is some blurring of the wing tips, foot, and splashing water, but it is so minimal that you can say the action is frozen.

Action shots in general, and flight shots in particular, have been close to my heart all through my career as a photographer. For action photography, changing from film to digital was like changing from a horse cart to a jet. The mere fact that photographers are now able to take thousands of shots of any given situation without spending a fortune on film is a true revolution. Access to ISO values that would have been beyond our wildest dreams with film cameras is another major improvement with digital technology.

The image of the flying White-throated Dipper was taken in southern Finland during a week of clear skies and very low temperatures in March. The bright sunshine, and the way it was softened by reflecting off the snow, made the conditions optimal for taking flight shots. I took thousands of frames, and nearly a thousand of them are flight shots.

A King Eider taking off *(Somateria spectabilis)*
Canon EOS-1D Mark II, 500mm f/4.0, 1/2000 second, f/5.0, ISO 500, continuous focus with 45 focusing points, handheld camera. Vardø, Norway, April 2006.

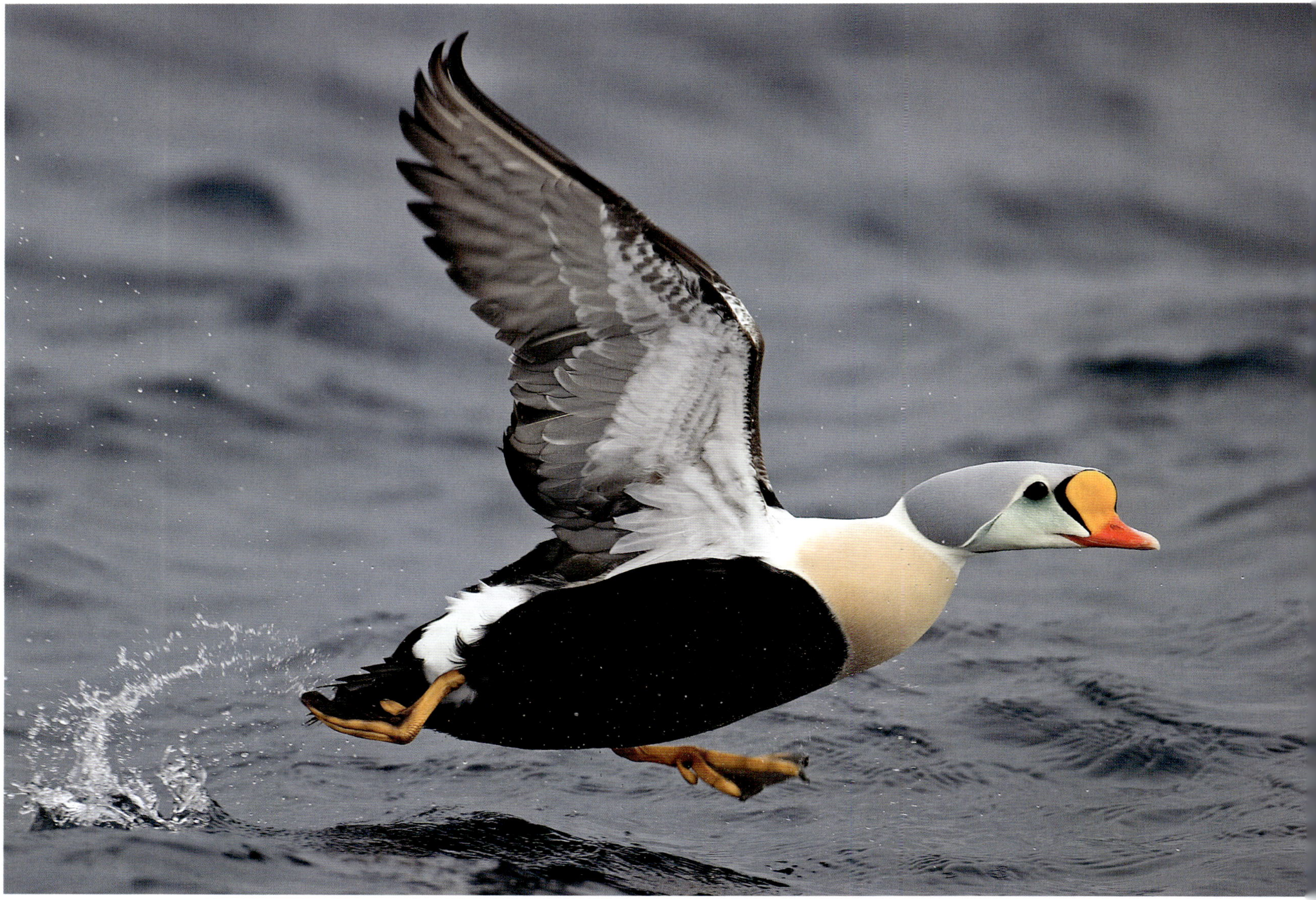

Markus Varesvuo

When I took this image, I wanted to freeze movement completely. After many attempts I came to realize that the shutter speed should be at least 1/3200 second. The White-throated Dippers soon got used to me, and I was able to get close enough to use my 300mm f/2.8 lens, which focuses very quickly. The only way to follow the White-throated Dippers in the viewfinder as they were speeding along the narrow river was by photographing handheld, not on a tripod.

Red-throated Loons nest on small marsh ponds that have no fish. The parents fly to the nearby lakes to fish, and they carry their catch in their bills back to the nesting pond to feed the chicks. The birds approach and descend very quickly, always into a headwind, and land on the pond with water splashing. It is a spectacular sight but rather difficult to capture. Photographing in the beautiful late evening light is a balancing act between using the fastest possible shutter speed and keeping the ISO value at a reasonable level to not lose image quality.

When they cover longer distances, Red-throated Loons fly in a steady pattern at an even pace, making it easy to get sharp images using shutter speeds as slow as 1/1000–1/1600 second, but to freeze a landing bird at close range requires the shutter speed to be at least 1/2500 second. Before it lands, one major challenge is to spot the approaching bird in time and to keep it inside the focusing area during the short time it's in landing mode. You don't want to start shooting too early because the buffer will easily fill up before the best part of the action.

A shutter speed of 1/1000–1/1600 second is enough to capture a cruising White-tailed Eagle with a 500mm lens. However, the situation captured in the photo on page 91 needed a much faster shutter speed. A frantic Common Gull was trying to chase the eagle away from its nesting rock. It kept diving down on the eagle from above, again and again.

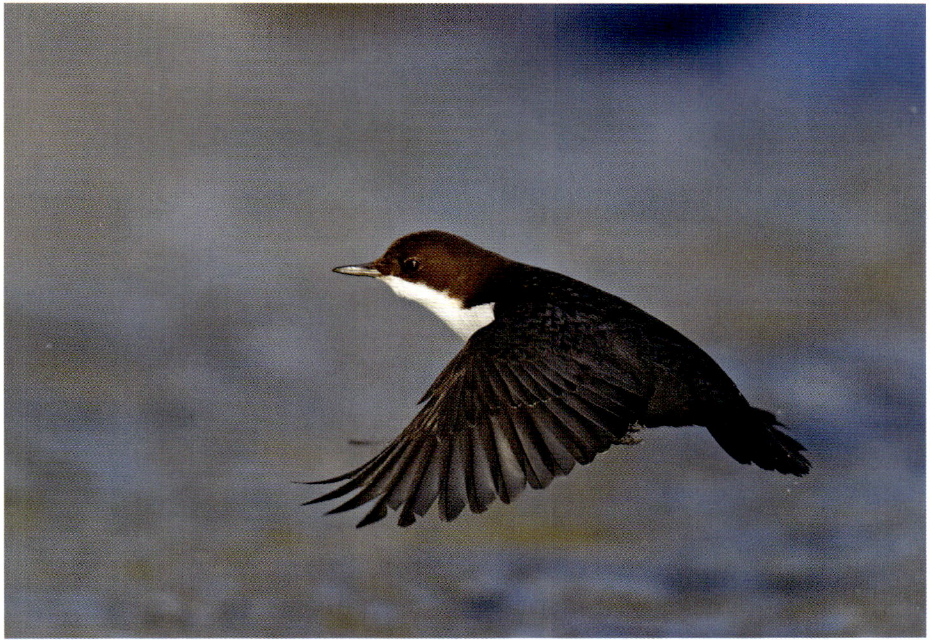

Markus Varesvuo

A White-throated Dipper *(Cinclus cinclus)*
Canon EOS-1D Mark II, 300mm f/2.8, 1/3200 second, f/2.8, ISO 500, continuous focus with 45 focusing points, handheld camera. Liljendahl, Finland, March 2005.

A Red-throated Loon *(Gavia stellata)*
Canon EOS-1D Mark III, 500mm f/4.0, 1/2500 second, f/9.0, ISO 1600, continuous focus with extended central focusing point, Gitzo tripod, Manfrotto 501 video head, blind. Vaala, Finland, June 2009.

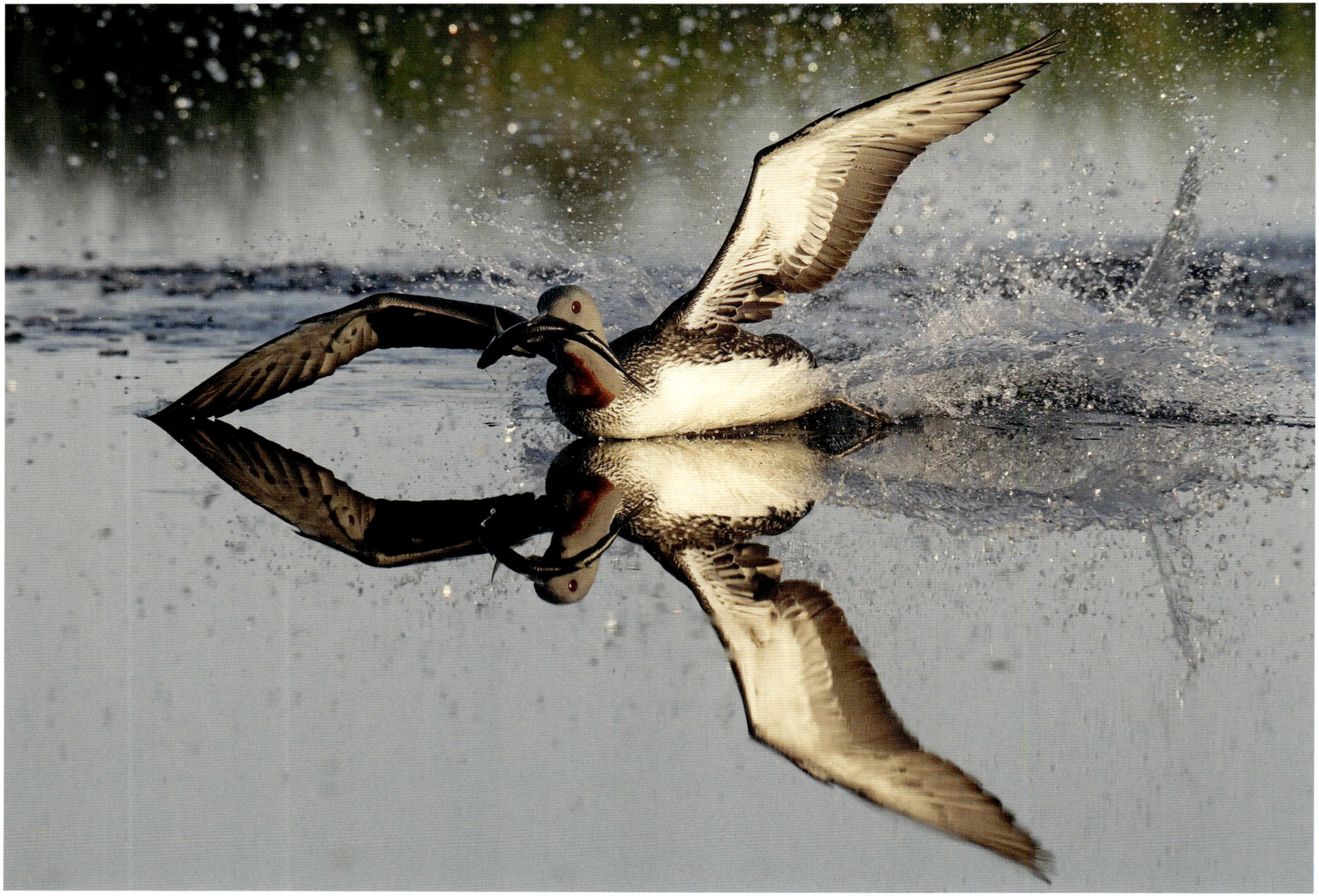

Markus Varesvuo

I noticed the situation developing in time and was able to increase the ISO value to 1000 and set the shutter speed to 1/2500 second, which I estimated would be enough to freeze the Common Gull in its nosedive.

To illustrate how fast the situation was, note that I was using my camera at maximum shooting speed, which is 9 fps. Even so, the frame before the action shot shows the Common Gull clearly above the White-tailed Eagle, and in the frame after the action the gull is again a foot or so above the eagle. Skill alone is not enough to capture the perfect shot—luck is needed, too. The gull was straddling the eagle's neck and pecking its head for a few hundredths of a second, and the last frame was exposed at the exact right moment.

Guidelines for completely freezing movement with a 500mm lens	
Target	**Shutter speed (minimum)**
Circling eagle	1/640 second
Flying goose	1/1000 second
Fighting Black Grouse	1/1600 second
Flying swift	1/2000 second
Flying small bird	1/3200 second

Markus Varesvuo

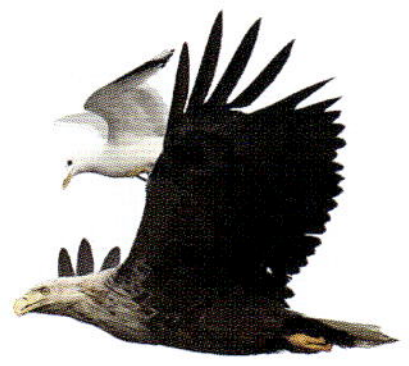

Frame before the action of a White-tailed Eagle and Common Gull *(Haliaeetus albicilla, Larus canus)*

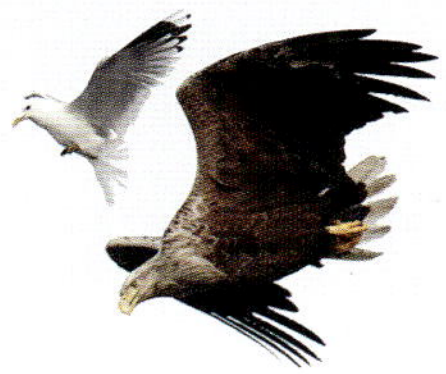

Frame after the action of a White-tailed Eagle mobbed by a Common Gull

Canon EOS-1D Mark IV, 500mm f/4.0, 1/2500 second, f/9.0, ISO 1000, continuous focus with an extended central focusing point, hand-held camera, boat. Flatanger, Norway, July 2010.

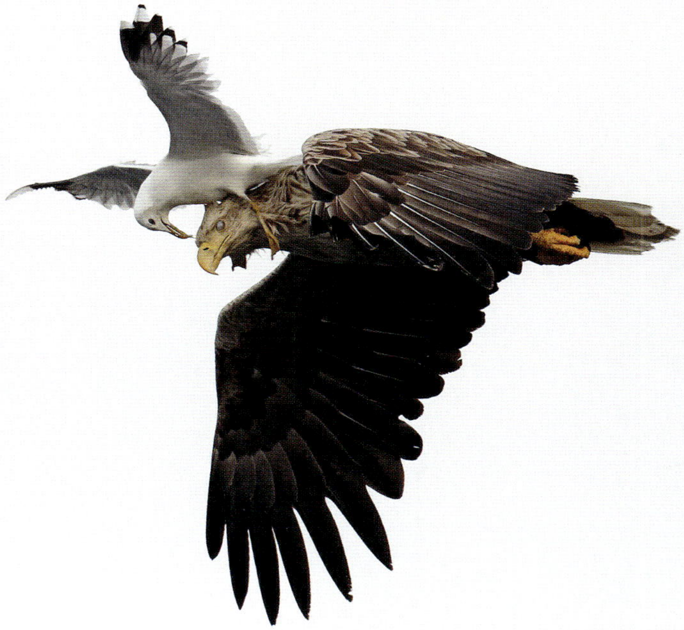

The action: A White-tailed Eagle mobbed by a Common Gull

JARI PELTOMÄKI

MOTION BLUR

Motion in the image makes a bird look more lifelike.

In normal light conditions you can quite easily freeze the movement of a flying bird with a modern digital camera. Yet I feel that an image of a flying bird is more natural looking when there is some movement, at least in the wings. Wildlife photographer Hannu Hautala maintains that birds become plastic when they are frozen in flight with a fast shutter speed. I try to completely freeze movement at times, but on the whole I prefer images that show movement and am therefore more likely to choose a slower shutter speed.

To get motion blur in the image, you need to consider the size of the bird and the rate of its wing beats when selecting a shutter speed. The larger the bird, the slower the shutter speed. A bird image can have motion blur from multiple sources; it doesn't necessarily have to be flying for the image to have motion blur. Let's take a closer look at a couple of examples of how to get motion blur in a bird image.

Motion in the Wings

Images such as the one of the Bank Swallows can be taken with or without a tripod. The shutter speeds are often so fast that it's possible to handhold the camera, which is easier when photographing flying birds. For this image I wanted motion blur in an otherwise sharp flight shot, so I chose a shutter speed that would freeze more of the bird's movement than just its wing tips.

Larger birds that are flying at a slower pace, such as cranes, swans, and large raptors, require shutter speeds at or faster than 1/125 second to bring out motion in their wings. To show some motion in the wings of medium-sized birds with fast strokes, use a 1/1000 second shutter speed, and if you want the wings totally blurred, use 1/500 second. With smaller passerines, there is movement in the wings even at 1/2000 second.

Motion in the Bird and the Background

In the image of the Golden Eagle on page 94, the bird's head is sharp, but there is motion in the wings and the background. The latter is made by using a slow shutter speed while following the bird. Use a tripod and a good video head or side mount to make sure you can follow the flying bird steadily for as long as possible. The shutter speed really needs to be slow to get motion in the background. I have found that shutter speeds ranging from 1/60–1/125 second work well. Sometimes it takes slower or faster shutter speeds to get the best results.

A Bank Swallow feeding its young, with motion blur in the wings *(Riparia riparia)*
Nikon D3S, 500mm f/4.0 plus 1.4x extender, 1/500 second, f/8.0, ISO 800, one-shot focus with a central focusing point, beanbag, car as a blind. Liminka, Finland, July 2010.

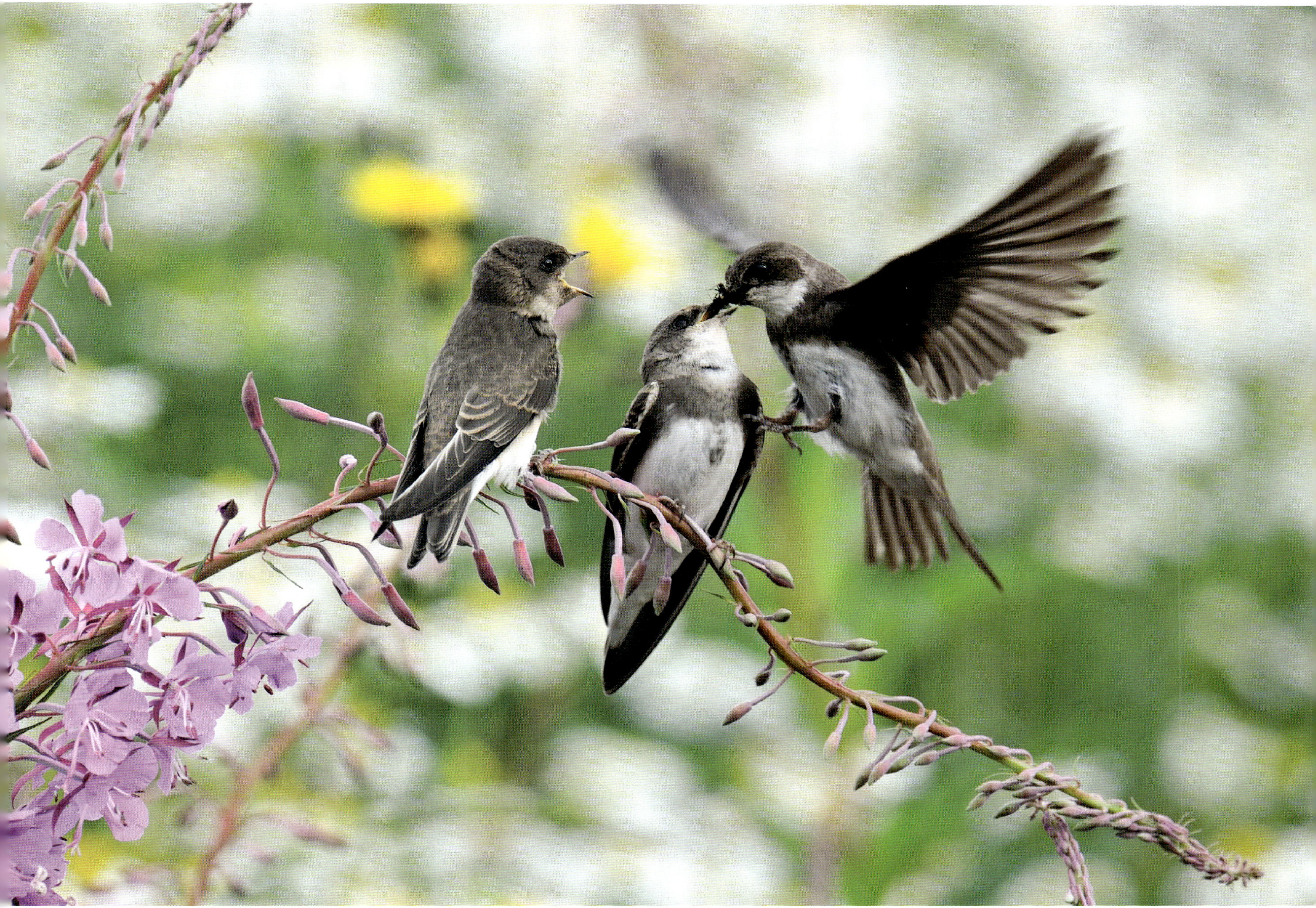

Jari Peltomäki

Jari Peltomäki

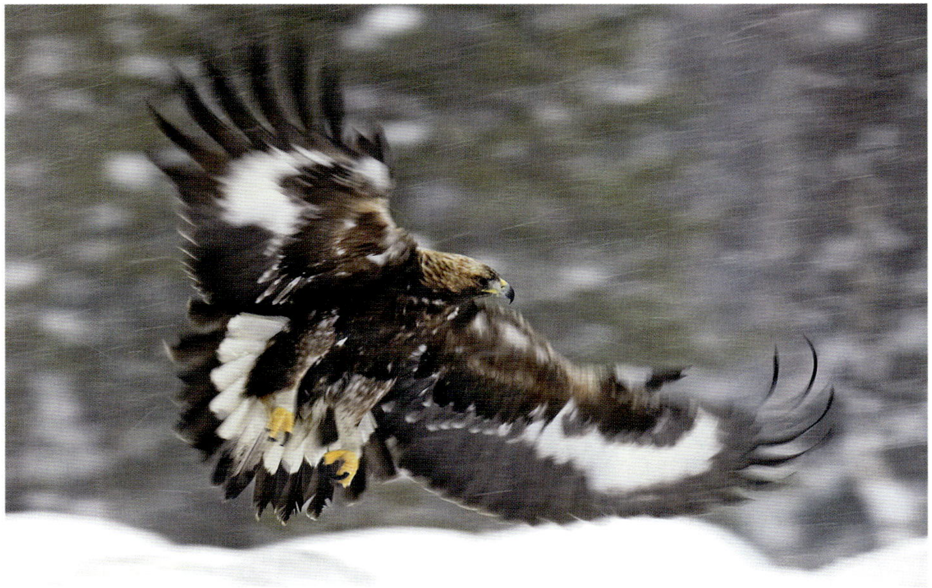

A Golden Eagle about to land *(Aquila chrysaetos)*
Canon EOS-1D Mark II, 300mm f/2.8, 1/60 second, f/4.5, ISO 400, continuous focus with 45 focusing points, Manfrotto 501 video head, blind. Utajärvi, Finland, January 2008.

The Whooper Swan's head is sharp even though I was handholding the camera. I took the image when the swan took off against a background glowing in autumn colors. But when I got the Red-throated Loon image on page 96, I was onshore with my camera firmly attached to a tripod where I was photographing the birds taking off, and I was able to pan for long stretches. The success rate in taking this kind of motion blur image is directly related to the amount of repetitions—the more you try, the better your chances that at least one image will be good.

Motion in the Background

You need a slow shutter speed to get motion blur in the background, so you will almost always need to support your camera firmly. With very slow shutter speeds you should consider using mirror lockup because it helps eliminate any camera shake caused by the mirror moving inside your camera. Your finger may also cause vibration and undesired photo blur when using a slow shutter speed. This can be avoided by using a remote or a cable release.

Your image can show motion even if the subject is not moving—maybe the bird is asleep or still on a shore, but waves lapping up against the shore can add interesting motion to your image. Or if you have a chance to photograph a bird perching on a rock by a rapid, try taking motion blur images. Water motion blurs at 1/60 second. The slower the shutter speed, the softer the water will look, but don't forget that your risk of getting motion blur of the bird increases as well. Lucky for us, digital technology lets us play with the possibilities and

A Whooper Swan against autumn foliage *(Cygnus cygnus)*
Canon EOS-1D Mark II, 300mm f/2.8 plus 2x extender, 1/60 second, f/13.0, ISO 200, continuous focus with 45 focusing points, handheld camera. Siikajoki, Finland, September 2004.

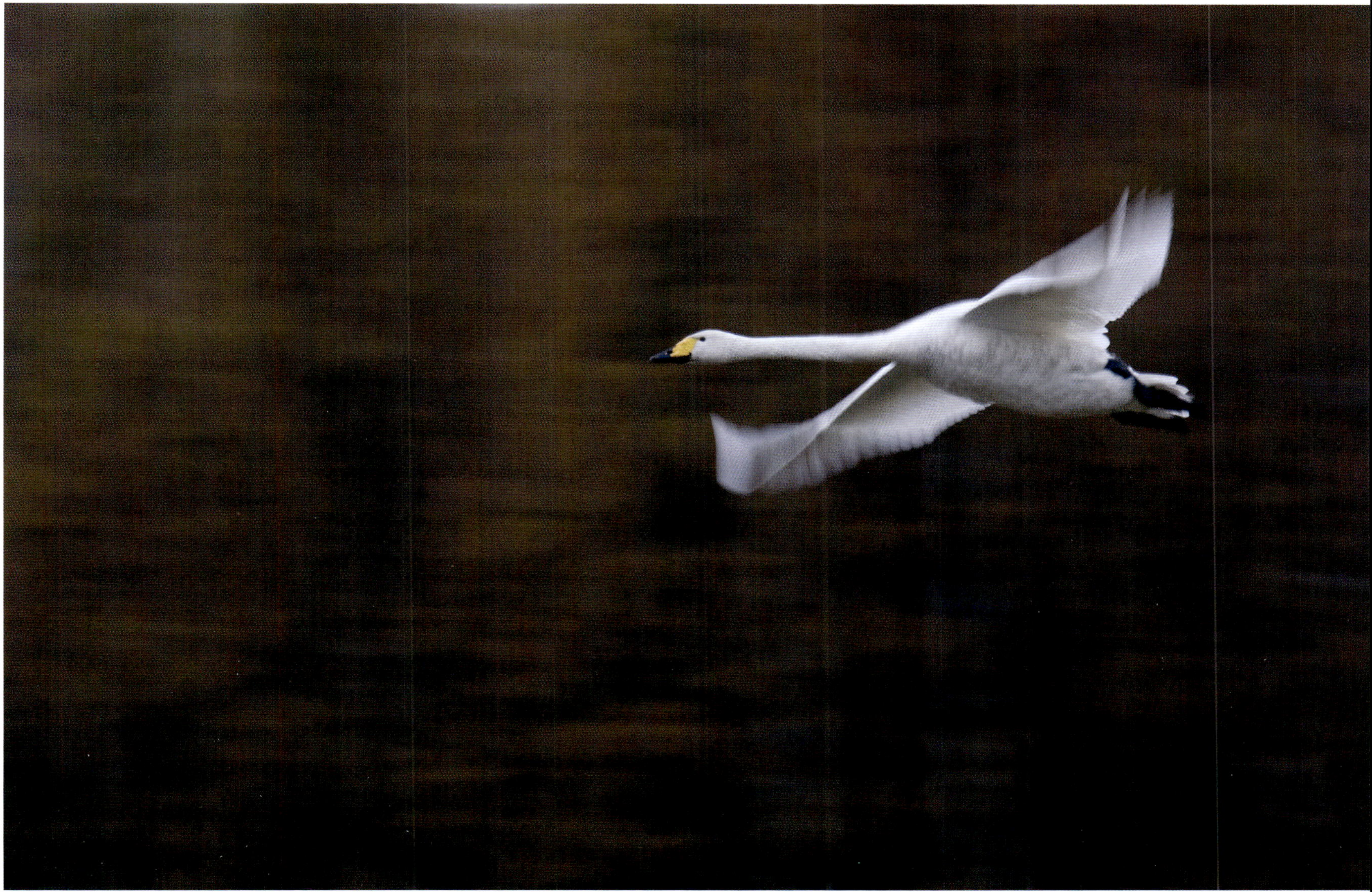

Jari Peltomäki

A Red-throated Loon taking off *(Gavia stellata)*
Canon EOS-1D Mark II, 300mm f/2.8 plus 2x extender, 1/125 second, f/9.0, ISO 500, continuous focus with 45 focusing points, Gitzo tripod, Manfrotto 501 video head. Valkeala, Finland, August 2004.

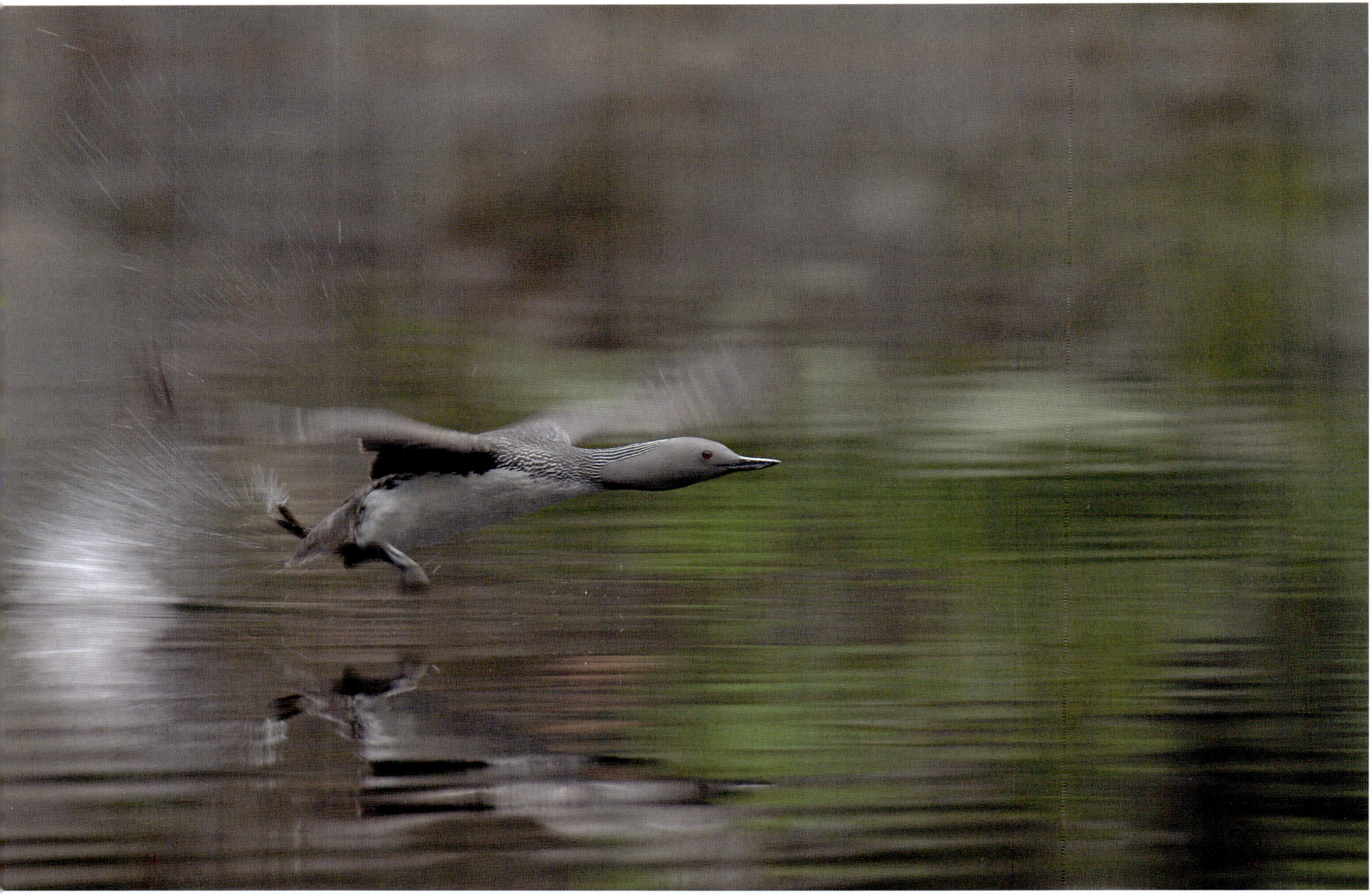

Jari Peltomäki

Jari Peltomäki

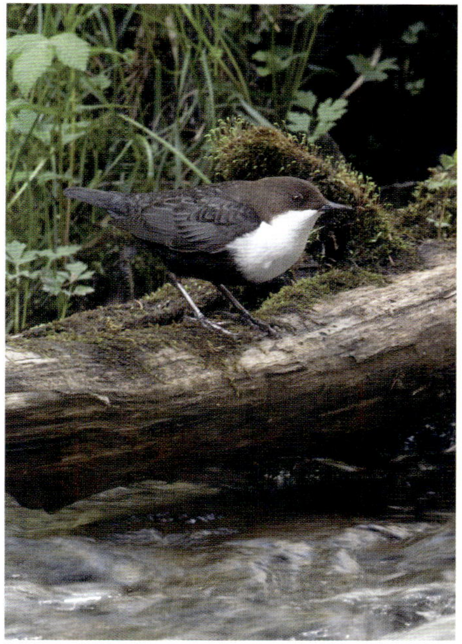

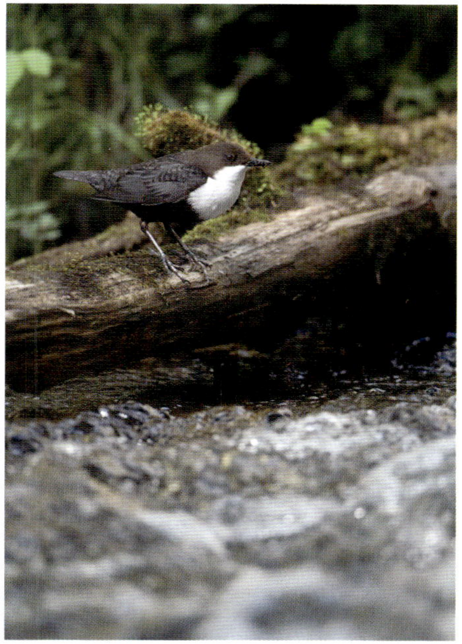

A White-throated Dipper and motion blur in the flowing water, with different shutter speeds *(Cinclus cinclus)*
Canon EOS-1D Mark III, 500mm f/4.0, ISO 800, one-shot focus with a central focusing point, Gitzo tripod, Manfrotto 501 video head. Kuusamo, Finland, June 2009.

freely experiment with as many shots as we want.

In heavy wind the swaying grasses and branches can add motion to the image, but the bird needs to be perched on something solid, like a still branch, the ground, or a rock. If the bird is perched on a branch that is swaying in the wind, your chances of getting anything sharp are slim at best.

With roosting birds you can try to get star trails in your image. I have seen some great images of this but have yet to try it myself. The shutter speed needs to be several minutes, or even longer, to create star trails in the dark sky. You could, in theory, take a spectacular bird image set against the blazing aurora borealis, but I haven't seen it yet!

I was photographing a White-throated Dipper at its breeding grounds by a small stream in Kuusamo, north-east Finland. It kept returning to the same log time after time, and I was able to get fast-flowing water into the frame. It was rather dim in the hollow of the stream, making it easy to use slow shutter speeds. I tested many speeds—1/30 second made the water nice and soft, whereas 1/500 second froze the motion. Note the difference in the depth of field in the images, caused by different apertures.

Everything Out of Focus

Sometimes an accidentally blurred image turns out well, but you can also aim for out-of-focus images on purpose when you photograph flying birds and use slow shutter speeds. If you're going for full-out blurred images, there's really no need for a tripod. So what makes an out-of-focus image good? With beauty famously in the eye of the beholder, the answer is somewhere between relative and subjective. Whatever the answer, experimenting with out-of-focus photography can be fun—and bird

Red-crowned Cranes heading for their roosts *(Grus japonensis)*
Canon EOS-1D Mark III, 500mm f/4.0, 1/15 second, f/10.0, ISO 500, continuous focus with 45 focusing points, handheld camera. Hokkaidō, Japan, February 2008.

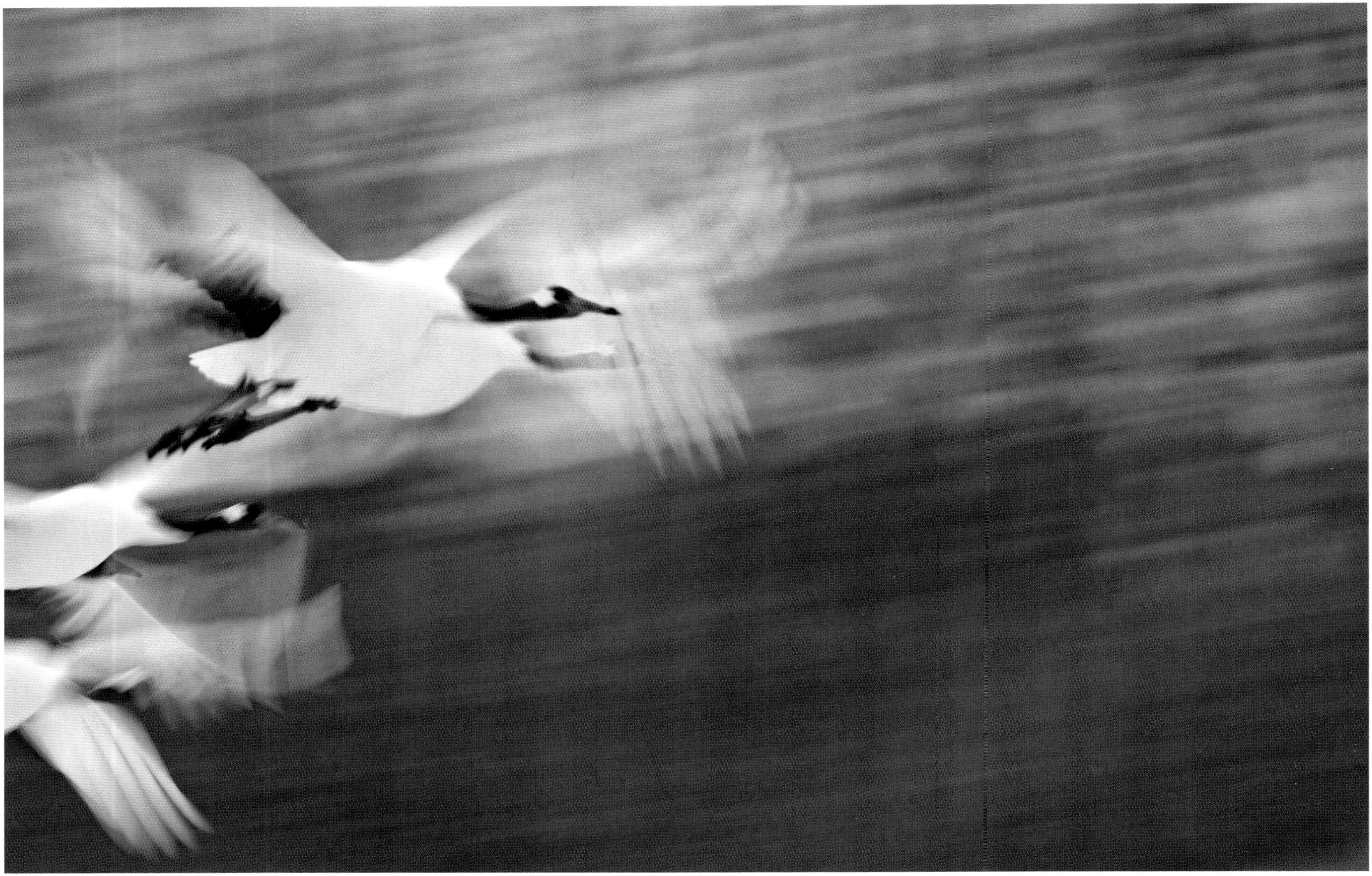

Jari Peltomäki

photography should definitely not be too serious. If you have flying birds but not enough light, it is time to make art! After all, there are books made entirely with blurred images.

I was photographing Red-crowned Cranes on the Japanese island of Hokkaidō, just after sunset, as the birds started to head toward their roosts. I wanted to emphasize the motion, so I photographed the cranes with a handheld camera and hoped that at least some frames would show the birds in aesthetically pleasant formations. I used shutter speeds from 1/15 second to 1/30 second, and the image shown here is pretty close to what I had in mind.

Zoom Effect

In a zoom effect image, the bird can be completely still; the motion is created by zooming the lens (also called racking the lens). You can apply the technique on flying birds too. I recommend using a tripod because zooming the lens is easier with the camera held steadily in place, but you can also get great zoom effect images with a handheld camera. The shutter speed needs to be slow, and the zoom needs to be racked fast enough to create the desired effect. A 70–200mm zoom lens works well for this, provided that the target is close enough. Try using shutter speeds of 1/5–1/30 second, and remember to rack the zoom with a quick and snappy motion.

Jari Peltomäki

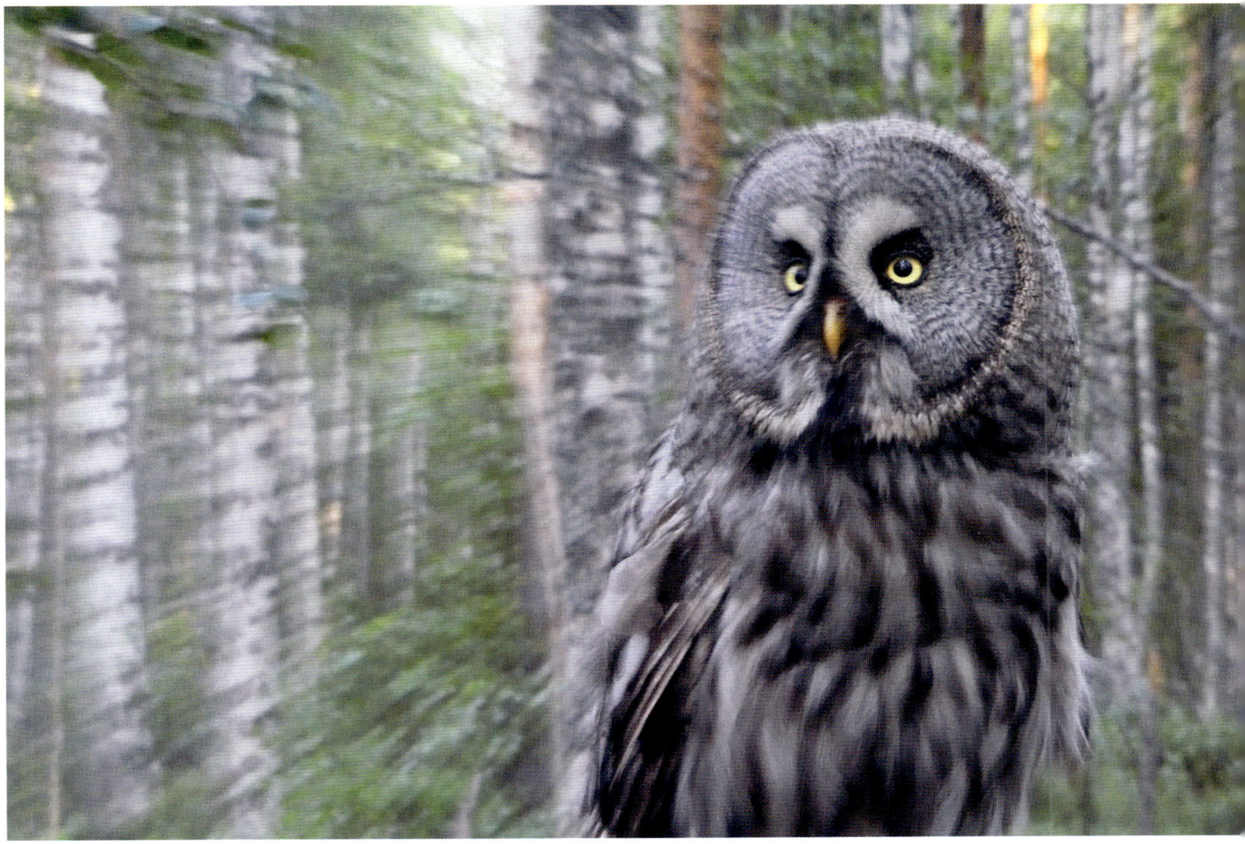

A zoom effect portrait of a Great Gray Owl *(Strix nebulosa)*
Canon EOS-1D Mark III, 70–200mm f/2.8, 1/10 second, 125mm, f/23.0, ISO 2500, one-shot focus with a central focusing point, Gitzo tripod, Manfrotto 501 video head. Oulu, Finland, July 2008.

JARI PELTOMÄKI

SEASONAL VARIATION

What species you photograph, and what kind of circumstances you need to prepare for, are greatly influenced by the time of year.

Probably everywhere in the world, the time of year has an influence on what bird species you can photograph and what the circumstances are. As a rule, high season in the northern hemisphere is during the lighter months from March or April to October, whereas in the southern hemisphere there is more to photograph from November to March. This doesn't mean that you can't photograph birds outside the high seasons—on the contrary, annual migrations and winter can be the best times to photograph certain species.

In this chapter, I focus on opportunities in Finland in all four seasons. Finland is so far north that the same latitudes in Siberia are all tundra, but the beneficial effects of the Gulf Stream that help keep temperatures warmer in Scandinavia influence our climate, too. The most northerly conifer forests grow in Finland. The country's far-north location gives photographers an advantage in bird photography because Finland has four distinct seasons, and each season yields different types of subjects.

Another advantage in a northerly location is that because the sun rises and sets slowly, the golden light lasts much longer than farther south. In winter you can work throughout the short days because the sun stays low, and in summer you can photograph birds throughout the night in great light, especially in northern Finland. And when it is at its darkest in November and December, a bird photographer in Finland can travel to sunnier climates or put some time and effort into browsing photos and archiving and handling selected image files.

Here is a review of what Finland has to offer bird photographers in different seasons.

Winter: December to February

From December to February, the weather in Finland is very wintery. At best, snow lasts from November well into March. A few years ago, everyone was talking about Finland having warm continental winters with very little snow, or even no snow, as was the case in southern Finland. But the past two winters have been very cold with record-breaking amounts of snow. Bird photographers around the country have been able to photograph in very snowy circumstances.

Golden Eagles and White-tailed Eagles, as well as Northern Goshawks, are popular subjects for bird photography in the Finnish winter. They are photographed at carcasses that are provided for the birds in specific spots in the woods throughout the winter. Gray-headed Woodpeckers and White-backed Woodpeckers are frequent visitors at other winter feeding spots, as are Black Woodpeckers and, in the north especially, Siberian Jays and Gray-headed Chickadees. In most years, Great Gray Owls and Northern Hawk Owls come out of the woods to more open areas to hunt, and every once in a while even rare Snowy Owls come to hunt on the open fields. Near the winter feedings that have been set for small birds, Eurasian Pygmy-Owls are often spotted preying on the feeding birds and small rodents.

Other good opportunities you should not miss, if they're available, are grouses and partridges. One winter's day I had the chance to work with a Western Capercaillie, and the temperature stayed at −30°C (−22°F) all day. The bird had settled at a location relatively close to people and was used to them. Every so often it would leave its snow burrow to eat needles in the pine trees nearby, eventually returning to snuggle deep inside the snow again. This way I got to shoot material that has rarely been photographed before: a Western Capercaillie peeking out of the snow.

People like to feed birds in the winter. Bird photographers set up feeding stations for the birds, but many people feed birds in their gardens for their own enjoyment. Birds have learned to come to the feeders, where they are easily photographed. Often birds that frequent the feeders get relatively used to people, and photography doesn't always require the use of a blind.

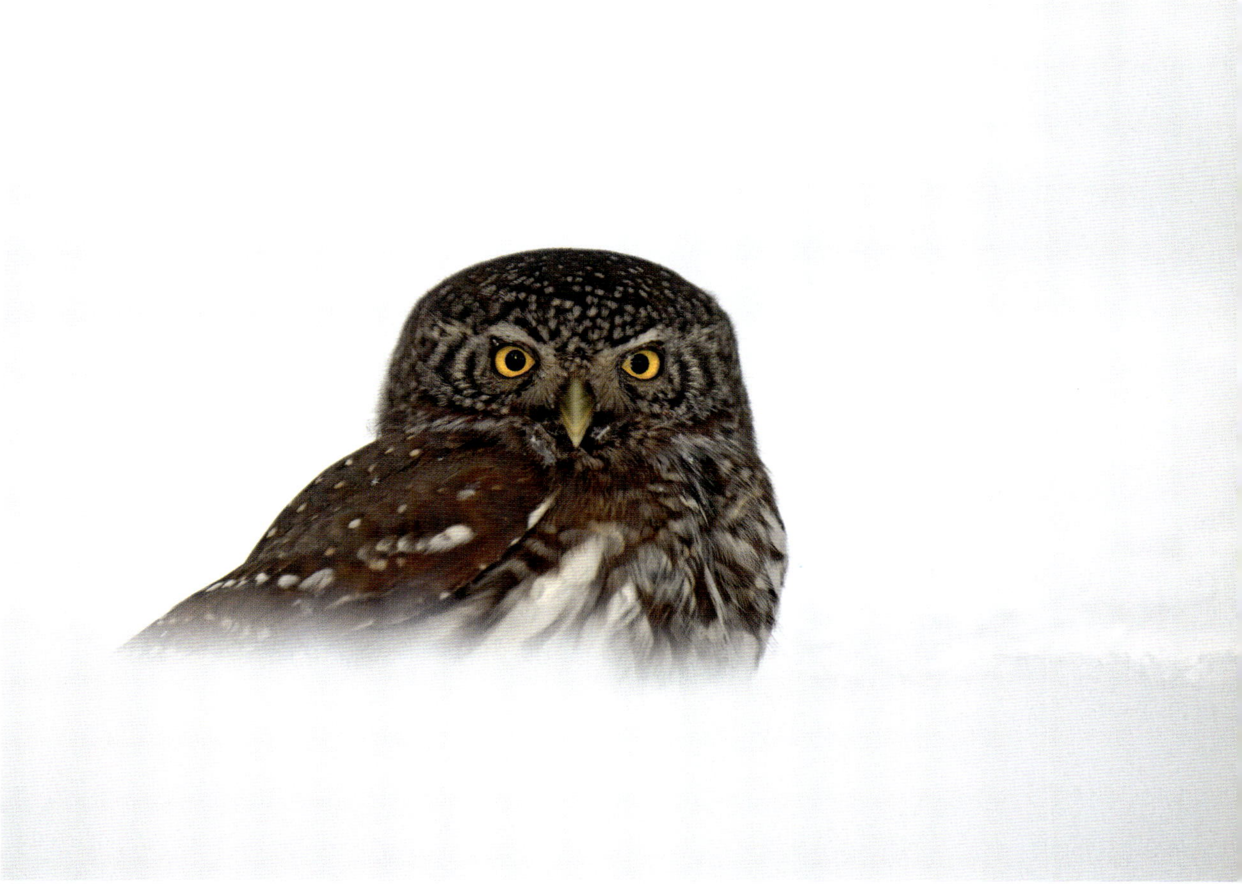

Jari Peltomäki

In winter Eurasian Pygmy-Owls can be photographed in the vicinity of bird feeders in gardens *(Glaucidium passerinum)*
Canon EOS 5D, 100–400mm f/4.6–5.6, 1/320 second, 340mm, f/6.3, ISO 400, continuous focus with an extended central focusing point, handheld camera. Vaala, Finland, March 2006.

Jari Peltomäki

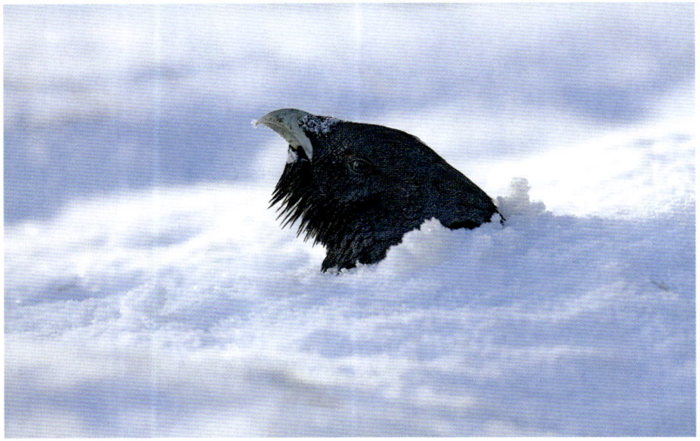

A Western Capercaillie in a snow burrow *(Tetrao urogallus)*
Canon EOS-1D Mark II, 300mm f/2.8, 1/800 second, f/4.0, ISO 400, one-shot focus with one focusing point, handheld camera. Vaala, Finland, January 2006.

Many nature photographers feed eagles and goshawks in winter with carcasses. In Finland, carcass feeding requires permission from the landowner, and it needs to be registered with the local veterinary authorities. At present, livestock carcasses that can be used for feeding include pigs and reindeer, and wild game animals that have been killed by vehicles on the road can be used, too. Many pig farms give their dead pigs to be used at bird feeding stations. Remember to check the local laws to find out about using dead animals for feeding; for instance, in the European Union all dead farm animals have to be recorded and reported to the relevant authorities.

November and December are usually bleak and gloomy, but if the snow comes early, and especially if the rowanberry crops are good, a bird photographer can have lots to photograph. Swans are still migrating in November, and some other birds might have delayed migrations, offering year-end opportunities to photographers.

In December the daylight is very short, but when the sun shines the light is gloriously beautiful all day. The best subjects for photography are normally found at feeders. In January the daylight hours start to lengthen, but winter usually tightens its grip. For me, January has often been the best time to photograph Golden Eagles, and at the end of the month Great Gray Owls start to appear at the edges of fields to hunt.

Even though the days are getting noticeably longer by February, it is still a true winter month, and in the north -30°C (-22°F) is more the rule than an exception. If a large high-pressure area reaches far into Siberia and settles over Finland, extremely cold and clear weather can last for several weeks. This is a good time for a bird photographer to

Markus Varesvuo

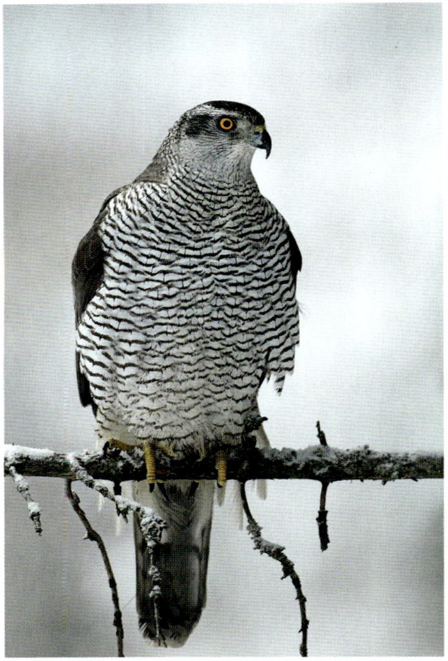

A Northern Goshawk near a feeding *(Accipiter gentilis)*
Canon EOS-1Ds 500mm f/4.0, 1/80 second, f/4.0, ISO 200, one-shot focus with a central focusing point, Manfrotto 501 video head attached to a plank in a blind. Ajalankoski, Finland, January 2004.

Jari Peltomäki

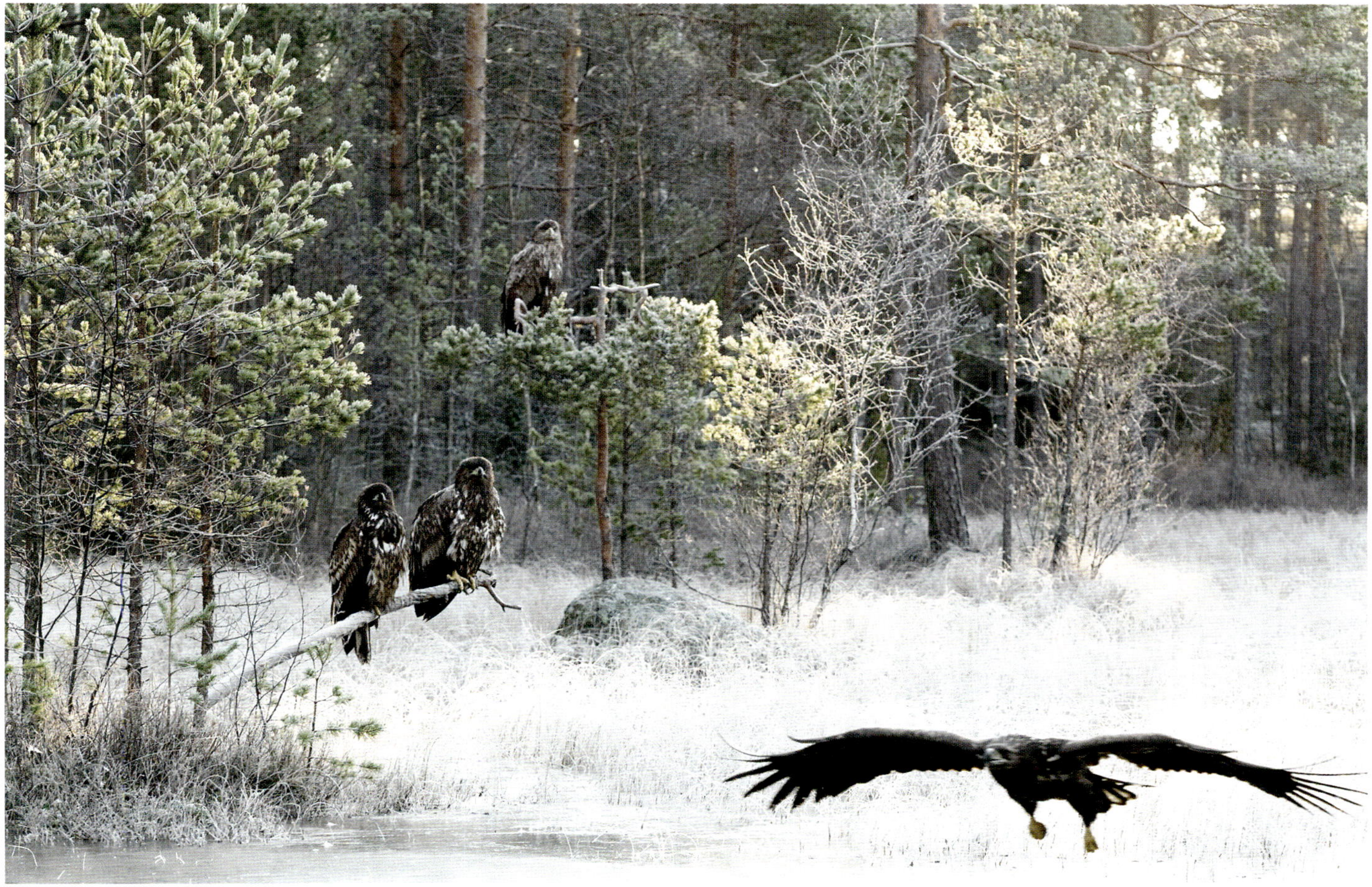

work from a heated eagle blind. On the other hand, with the daytime lengthening steadily, there starts to be enough light for photographing at feedings in the woods or targeting dippers by flowing rivers. February is normally the best time to photograph owls in winter.

Winter has a firm grip on northern Finland long into March and even into April.

White-tailed Eagles at a carcass feeding *(Haliaeetus albicilla)*
Canon EOS-1D Mark III, 70–200mm f/2.8, 1/250 second, 135mm, f/6.3, ISO 1600, manual focus, Manfrotto 501 video head attached to a plank in a blind. Vehmaa, Finland, November 2008.

Snow Buntings on spring migration often gather in large flocks *(Plectrophenax nivalis)*
Canon EOS-1D Mark III, 300mm f/2.8, 1/1600 second, f/7.1, ISO 400,
continuous focus with an extended central focusing point, handheld camera.
Tyrnävä, Finland, April 2008.

Spring: March to May

Spring comes in March, and the days start to get longer faster. The snowy landscapes abound with light, which reflects off the snow and back into the air, casting the most beautiful light on the flying birds from below. March sees the arrival of the first migrators, such as Whooper Swans, White-tailed Eagles, gulls, Rooks, and Snow Buntings.

In April spring takes charge with a vengeance, and most of the migrating birds arrive in Finland. April is by far the busiest month in a bird photographer's calendar. You need to be in many places at the same time. Luckily the day is almost long enough to do so. For example, you can use the early morning light at a Black Grouse lek and still make it to the ice-covered sea bay to photograph geese and other migrating birds flying in the fabulous midmorning light. In the afternoon you can settle in a blind that you have strategically set up near the first open patch in the frozen water and wait for the waterbirds to arrive so you can photograph them in the attractive evening light. For a bird photographer, spring is very hectic, and sleep deprivation is inevitable—the most you get is a few hours here and there. But having to get up after just a few hours of sleep to start photographing again has never

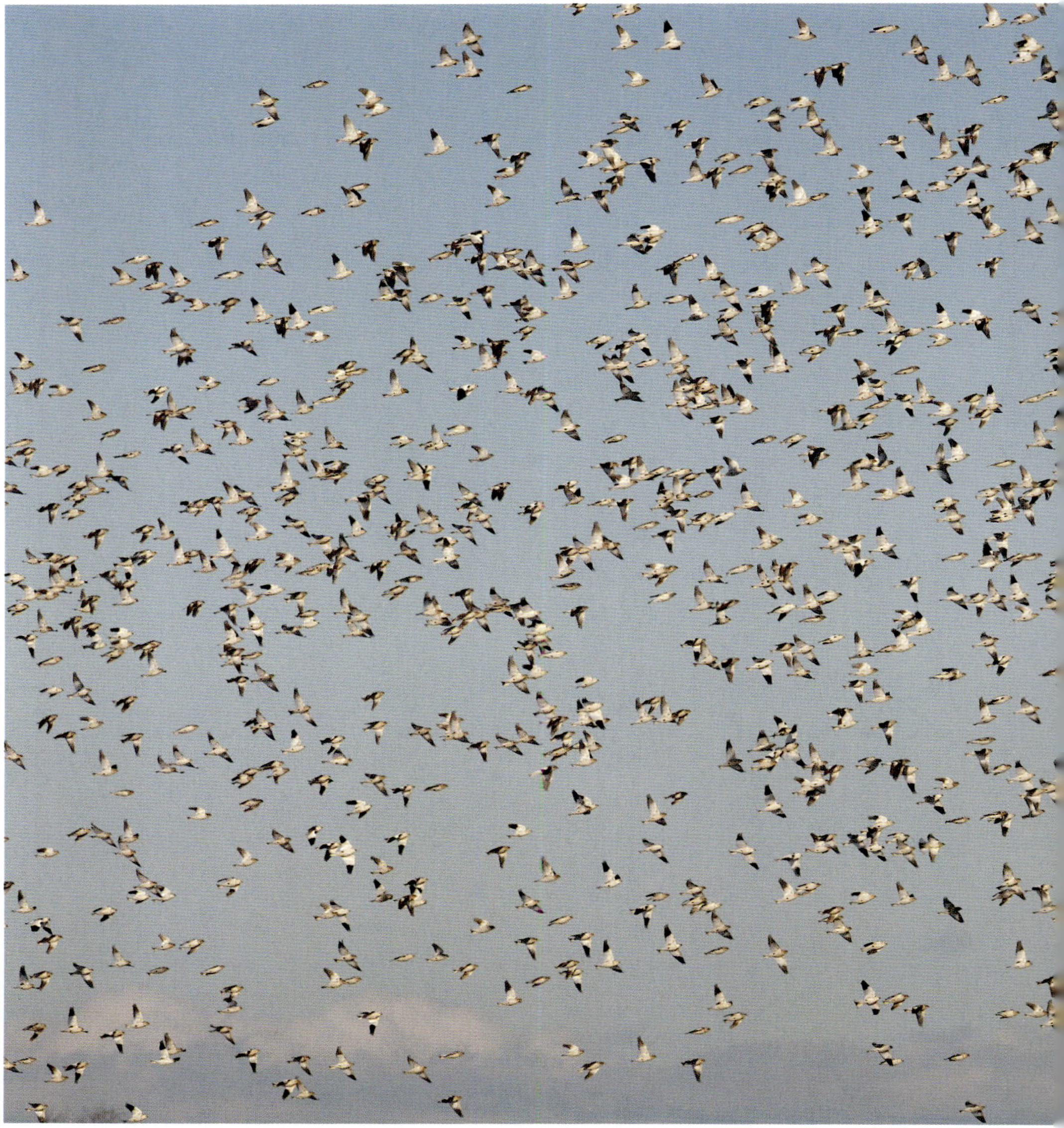

Jari Peltomäki

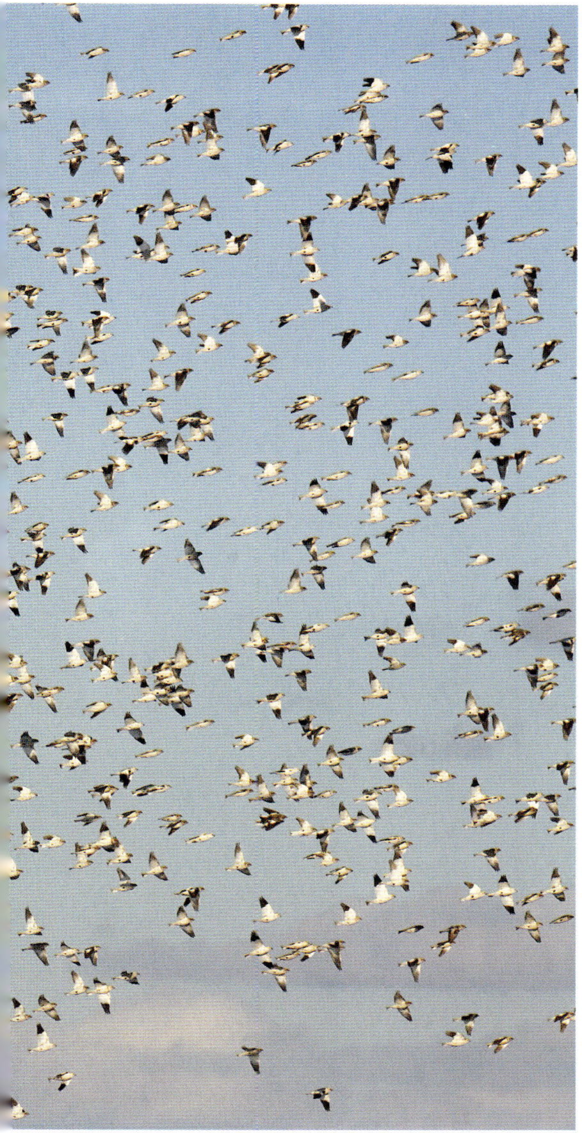

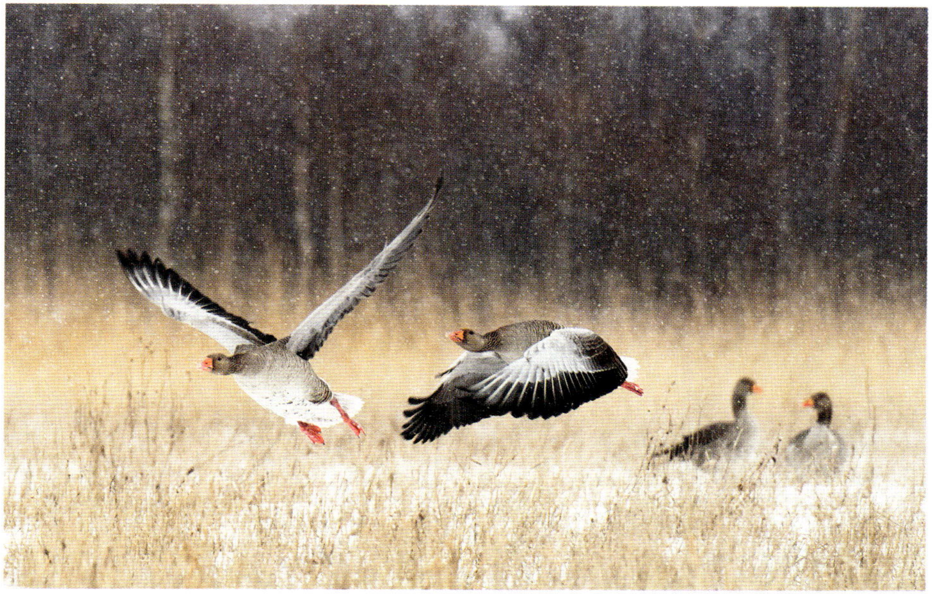

Jari Peltomäki

Graylag Geese in the grips of a late winter storm *(Anser anser)*
Canon EOS-1D Mark III, 500mm f/4.0, 1/1600 second, f/9.0, ISO 800, continuous focus with an extended central focusing point, Manfrotto 501 video head attached to a plank in a blind. Liminka, Finland, April 2008.

bothered me in the least. Also, the short catnaps you catch while waiting in your sleeping bag for the Black Grouse to arrive at the lek are memorable. Whenever possible, I try to stay overnight in the blind because mornings come so early. Besides, the sounds during spring nights are beyond description.

Spring is notoriously fickle, and April can see winter striking back. Such backlashes are cues for bird photographers to get out into the field because the conditions can become very photogenic. The snowfall in April can be remarkably heavy, with big flakes that stand out well in images. Birds tend to gather

Jari Peltomäki

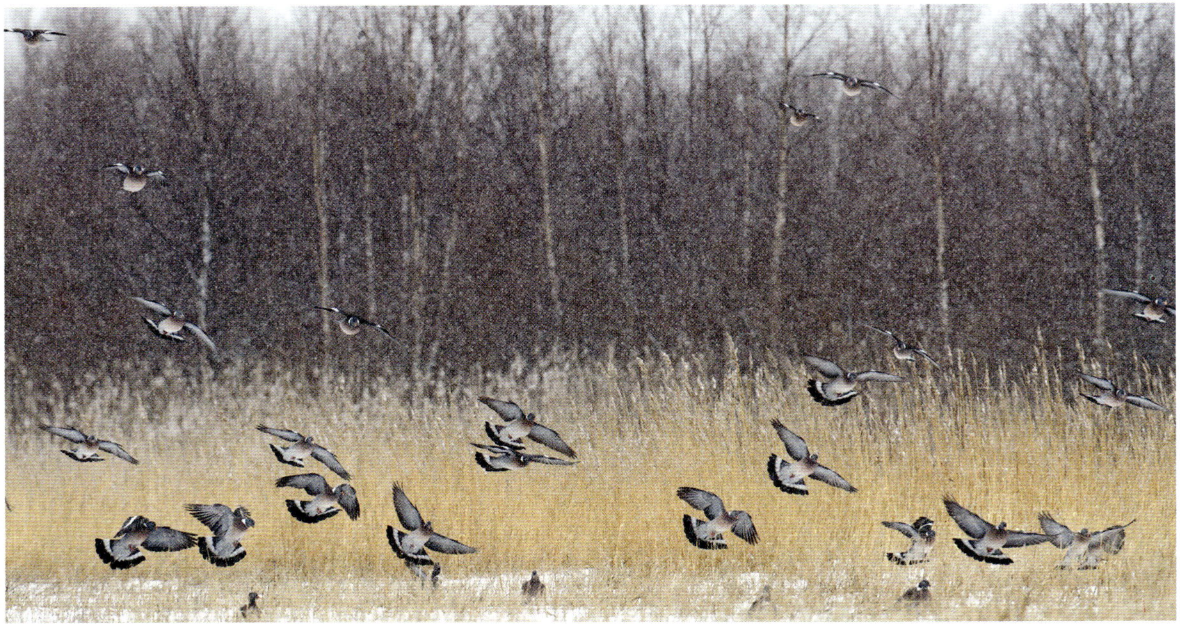

When winter strikes in April, Common Wood-Pigeons gather together in large flocks *(Columba palumbus)*
Canon EOS-1D Mark III, 500mm f/4.0, 1/1000 second, f/9.0, ISO 400, continuous focus with an extended central focusing point, Manfrotto 501 video head attached to a plank in a blind. Liminka, Finland, April 2008.

into big flocks, and even migrating birds start to gather around feeding stations.

I specifically remember one April day spent in a blind on the shore of Bothnian Bay, in Liminka, when it snowed all day. The field in front of my blind was full of birds in spectacular late winter storm settings: hundreds of Common Wood-Pigeons, dozens of Graylag Geese and cranes. The Graylag Goose and Common Wood-Pigeon flock images were taken on that day. The falling snow further enhances the wintery atmosphere.

Spring migration continues long into May. Waterbirds and waders are the main species at the start of the month, and the bulk of the insectivorous species also arrive throughout May. Most birds start nesting in May, and courting, mating, and nest building are popular themes among bird photographers.

Summer: June to August

The bird photography high season continues throughout the summer because the breeding season of most birds extends long into June, and even into July. Many species become more furtive and secretive compared to their behavior in spring, yet the birds are very active—after all, they have mouths to feed. You can read more about nest photography in the chapter "Photographing at Nests."

Just how short the northern summer is becomes evident in June, as the first female Eurasian Curlews and Spotted Redshanks start their journeys back already before midsummer! The last bird species to arrive north on spring migration, the Arctic Warblers, have not even reached their northern breeding grounds yet, when some birds are already going back south.

The long summer nights are an especially productive time for bird photographers. The sun does not set at all in the far north, and as long as the sky is clear you can photograph all through the night in fantastic light. On sunny days, with the light at its harshest, you can catch up on some of that lost sleep. At the end of summer, especially in July and August, the misty mornings and late evenings frequently offer good opportunities for creativity. One July night

Jari Peltomäki

I was returning from a successful photo session on Hailuoto, which is a great bird island on the Bothnian Bay just outside Oulu. I was driving along a road in the countryside, with mist swirling over the fields, when I spotted a Short-eared Owl mobbing something. The light was low, and with a film camera I wouldn't even have tried, but I adjusted my DSLR to ISO 2500 and spent 30 minutes photographing handheld as the owl darted and glided over the fields while mosquitos drilled into my arms. The resulting images are scenic shots, and I love the way they reflect that beautiful summer night feeling. I never found out what the owl was mobbing out in the field.

A Short-eared Owl on a summer night *(Asio flammeus)*
Canon EOS-1D Mark III, 300mm f/2.8, 1/500 second, f/4.5, ISO 2500, manual focus, handheld camera. Kempele, Finland, July 2009.

With some birds, such as raptors, swans, Red-throated Loons, and Arctic Loons, breeding season lasts well into July. Meanwhile, the insectivorous species are already inconspicuously preparing for their autumn migration, gathering together at the end of the summer to forage in mixed flocks. If you find a flock of small birds flitting about in low bushes, park yourself near some suitable perching branches and you can photograph quite a few species.

Many birds leave Finland in July; for instance, the majority of Black-headed Gulls head off toward their wintering grounds. Then again, July often offers the best opportunities for photographing arctic waders in their summer plumage. In spring they are normally in a hurry to get to their breeding grounds on the tundra, but in July they return to their wintering territories at a more unhurried pace. After a bout of low pressure you can find them at good feeding shores, where they are easy to photograph.

August is still a summer month, albeit the last one, yet the birds are already in the middle of their autumn migration. The wader migration is accelerating, and even some of the young ones are getting ready to go. Cranes are gathering on the traditional fields, and young raptors are heading south.

Autumn: September to November

Compared to spring, bird numbers in autumn are augmented by the new generation. Birds on autumn migration tend to stop for longer times on good feeding grounds than they did in the spring, when they were anxious to get to the breeding grounds. Wetlands, especially the protected ones where hunting is banned, such as Liminka Bay, draw large numbers of waterbirds. Cranes regularly flock to specific fields to feed. Söderfjärd in Vaasa and Soho fields in Muhos are the best-known crane fields in the Finnish autumn.

The autumn light can be truly beautiful, and the deep, rich colors in the autumn foliage further boost the atmosphere in your images. In autumn it is a good idea to station yourself somewhere along the migration routes, which we'll talk about more in the chapter "Photographing at Migration Flyways." Photographing berry-eating birds, especially when the berry crops are good, was covered in more detail in the chapter "Years Vary and Circumstances Change."

Common Cranes gather in fields during autumn *(Grus grus)*
Canon EOS-1D Mark III, 500mm f/4.0, 1/1000 second, f/16.0, ISO 800, continuous focus with an extended central focusing point, handheld camera. Liminka, Finland, September 2008.

Jari Peltomäki

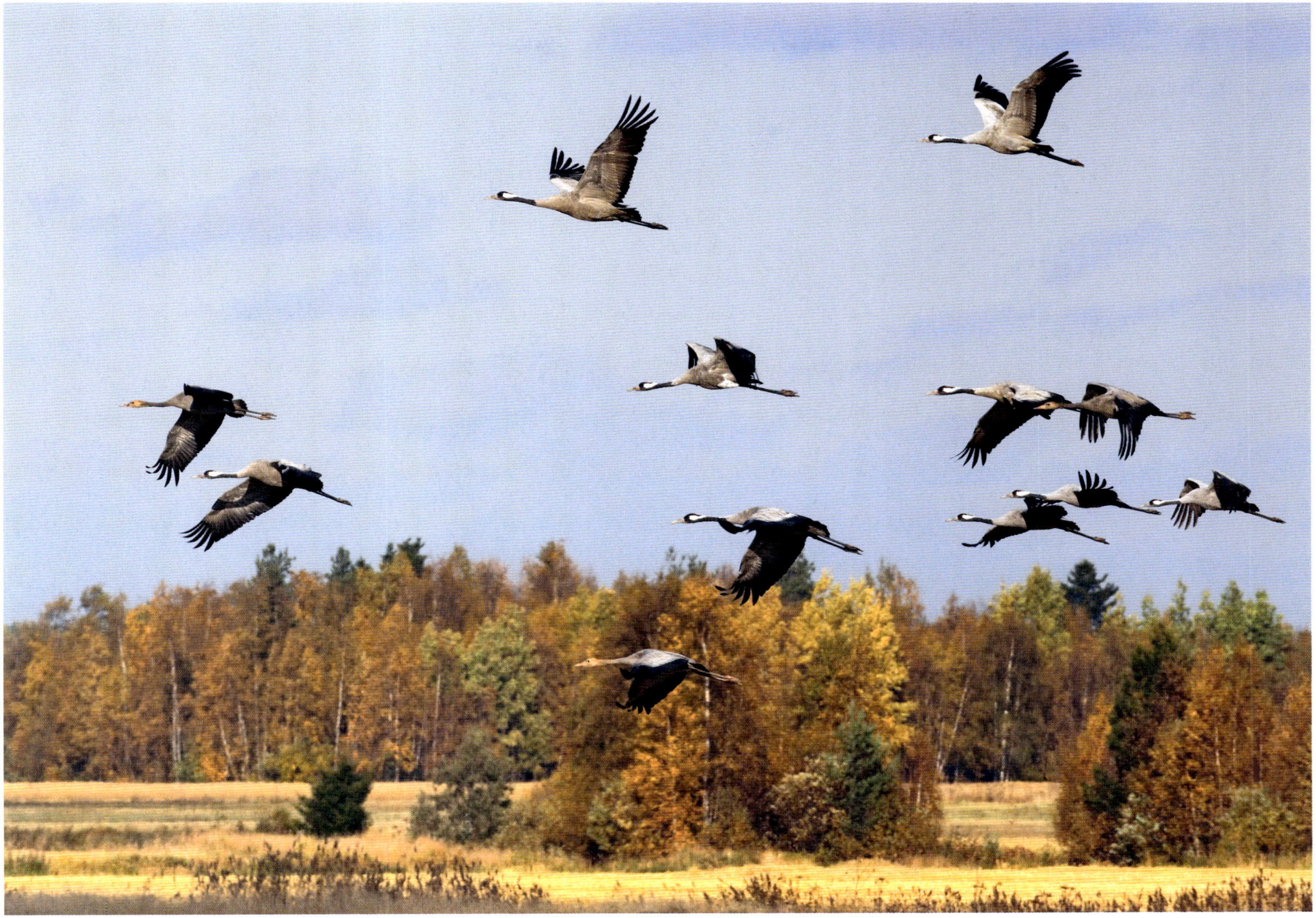

JARI PELTOMÄKI

ARRANGED SETUPS OR SPONTANEOUS SHOTS?

What is more rewarding: an image that required a lot of hard work and preparation, or a surprise opportunity?

For some, planning and preparations equal manipulation. Yet, when it is executed in moderation, preparatory work is a natural part of photography, and there is nothing to disapprove of. Well-made preparations can multiply your chances of getting good images. I would say that a large number of famous wildlife photos are taken in arranged setups. For example, with no feeding or other preparations there would not be many great shots of wild Golden Eagles.

Take, for example, my award-winning image of Dalmatian Pelicans on Lake Kerkini in Greece—it required more than sheer luck. The pelicans seem to perform a group dance with majestic mountains in the background. Luck did play a part in getting this image, because the clouds parted and revealed the mountains while I photographed, but there is human influence in this image. The fishermen on Lake Kerkini feed the pelicans with leftover fish, and the pelicans in my image are reaching for fish that has been thrown to them. I always say what is actually going on in the image instead of making up some idyllic story, like a yarn about rarely seen pelican display dances. My image shows what really happens on Lake Kerkini, which is that fishermen feed pelicans. This image has been used in many magazines, calendars, and books. It also opens discussions about what is an authentic nature photo and what is not. To me, this is a successful and visually interesting image of Dalmatian Pelicans.

I have also taken documentary images on Lake Kerkini that show fishermen with the pelicans, because there is a fascinating symbiosis between the fishermen and the pelicans. The fishermen hate Great Cormorants because they eat fish, but apparently they do not mind giving extra fish to the Dalmatian Pelicans because photographers are interested in the pelicans and bring extra income to the fishermen. The Dalmatian Pelicans follow the fishermen's boats eagerly, offering people good opportunities to photograph them.

Feeding

Feeding is a good example of arranged photography sessions. I feed birds in many different places throughout the winter because I want to both help them and photograph them. I may not have time to photograph at all the feeding sites, but at least the birds get food that helps them survive the winter. I use some of the feedings many times, and I normally have some props with me, such as a branch with lichens on it, or a

Dalmatian Pelicans reaching for fish thrown by a fisherman *(Pelecanus crispus)*
Canon EOS-1D Mark III, 70–200mm f/2.8, 1/2000 second, 95mm, f/10.0, ISO 800, continuous focus with an extended central focusing point, ground pod, Manfrotto 501 video head, angle finder. Lake Kerkini, Greece, February 2009.

Jari Peltomäki/Wild Wonders of Europe

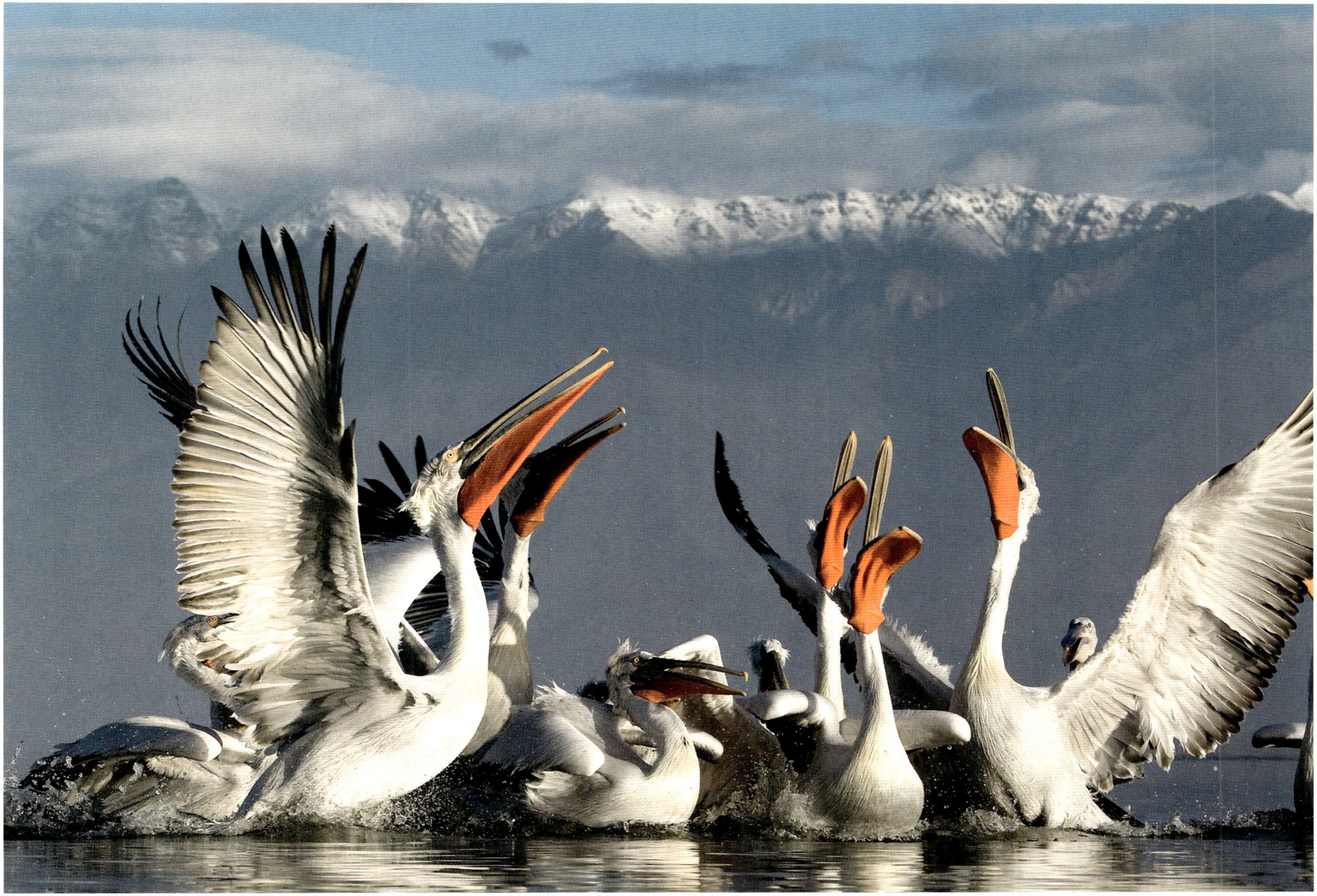

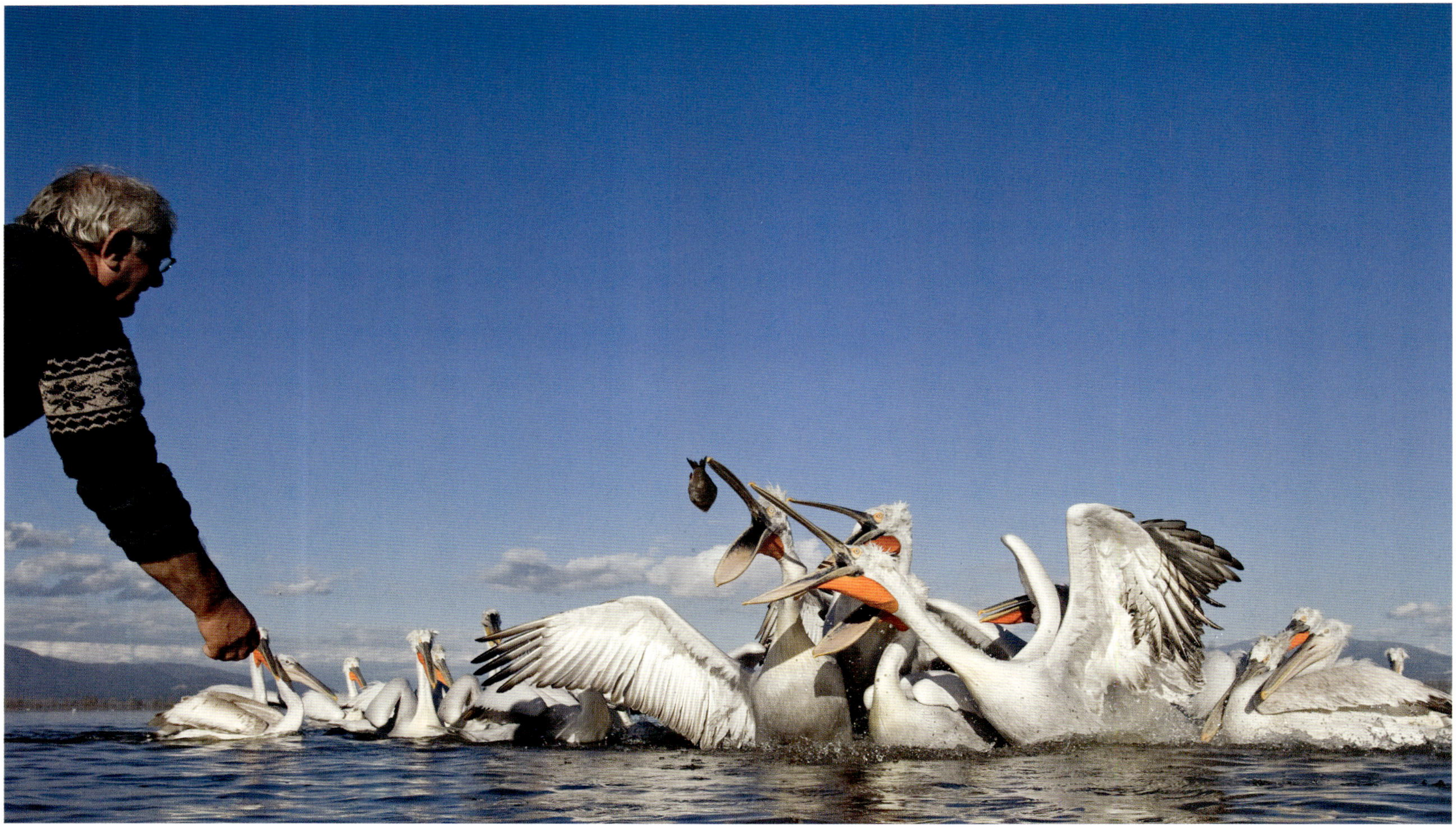

Jari Peltomäki/Wild Wonders of Europe

Fisherman Tom feeding Dalmatian Pelicans on Lake Kerkini *(Pelecanus crispus)*
Canon EOS-1D Mark III, 16–35mm f/2.8, 1/2000 second, 20mm, f/11.0, ISO 800, one-shot focus with one focusing point, ground pod, Manfrotto 501 video head, angle finder. Lake Kerkini, Greece, February 2009.

Jari Peltomäki

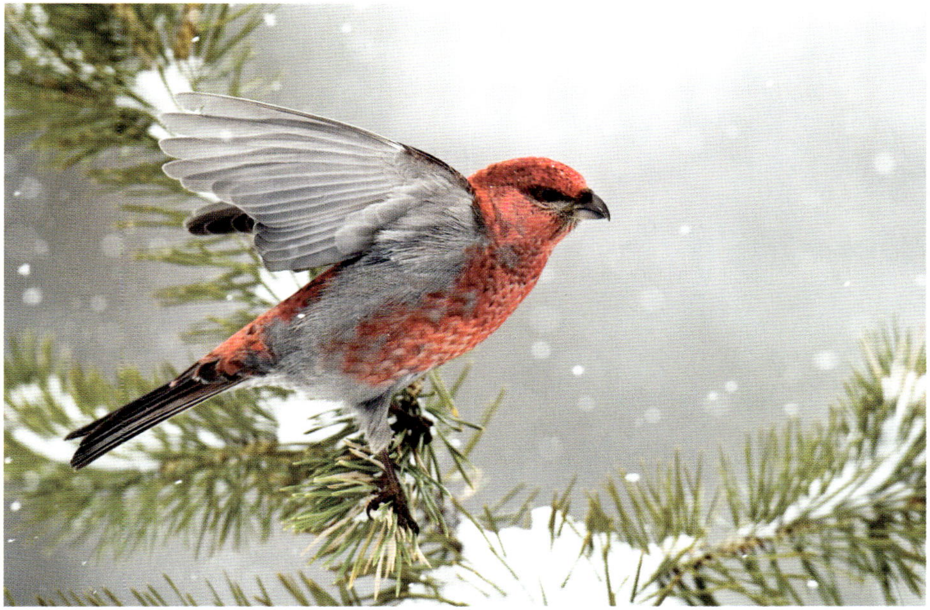

A Pine Grosbeak on an aesthetically pleasing perch erected for photographing at a bird feeder *(Pinicola enucleator)*
Canon EOS-1D Mark III, 500mm f/4.0, 1/3200 second, f/5.6, ISO 1600, continuous focus with an extended central focusing point, Gitzo tripod, Manfrotto 501 video head. Kaamanen, Finland, April 2008.

tree with some aesthetic value, which helps raise the visual interest of the image. Staging should be employed moderately, however, because trying too much will backfire and could make your image look phony. It is also good to change the perches regularly because you don't want to capture too many species on the same perch, plus the birds' droppings quickly soil the perches if there is much traffic on them.

Building Nests

Nests help many species of birds, and building nest boxes for cavity-nesting birds is probably the most common way to help them. The sizes of the nests vary, and you can try to make them look authentic; it's nice to photograph birds nesting in them if the boxes look like the real thing. When you go out to hang the nests, pay attention to the direction of light and to how open the area is in anticipation of your future photo projects. Take a moment to check out the place as if you were a bird, and make sure the nest is positioned along good flight paths. A couple of stronger branches would also be good, especially for bigger birds to perch on. The more you know about the nesting habits of the birds, the better. Your chances of getting the intended species to claim the box are much improved if you take the right kind of box to the right spot.

A dead tree that is still standing and has its top broken off can be leveled to better suit a nest. If you're lucky and have a big enough snag, you might get a Great Gray Owl, Ural Owl, or Northern Hawk Owl to nest there. If the cavity is too deep, fill it a little to make it a better nest and make the breeding parent more visible. You should also level smaller snags because Spotted Flycatchers or Mistle Thrushes might set up nests there. If you find a snag that is rotten inside, you can peel off a piece of the hard bark to help a Willow Tit dig a hole in the softer layers of the tree.

Jari Peltomäki

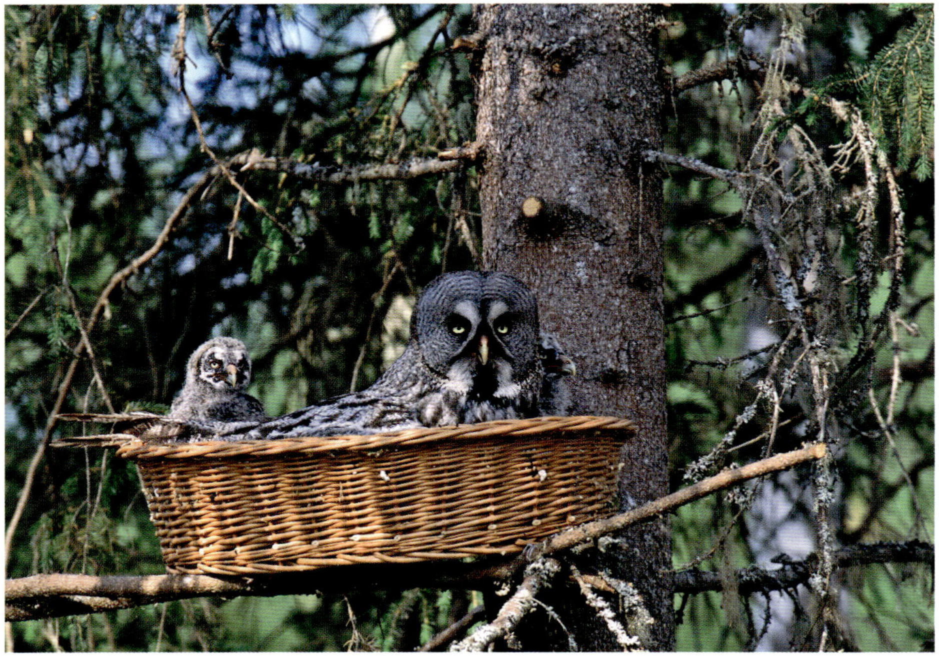

Great Gray Owls nesting in a willow basket taken into the forest
(Strix nebulosa)
Nikon F5, Nikkor 300mm f/2.8, Fuji Provia ISO 100, 1/500 second, f/8.0, manual focus, Manfrotto tripod, Manfrotto 501 video head. Pyhäjoki, Finland, June 2002.

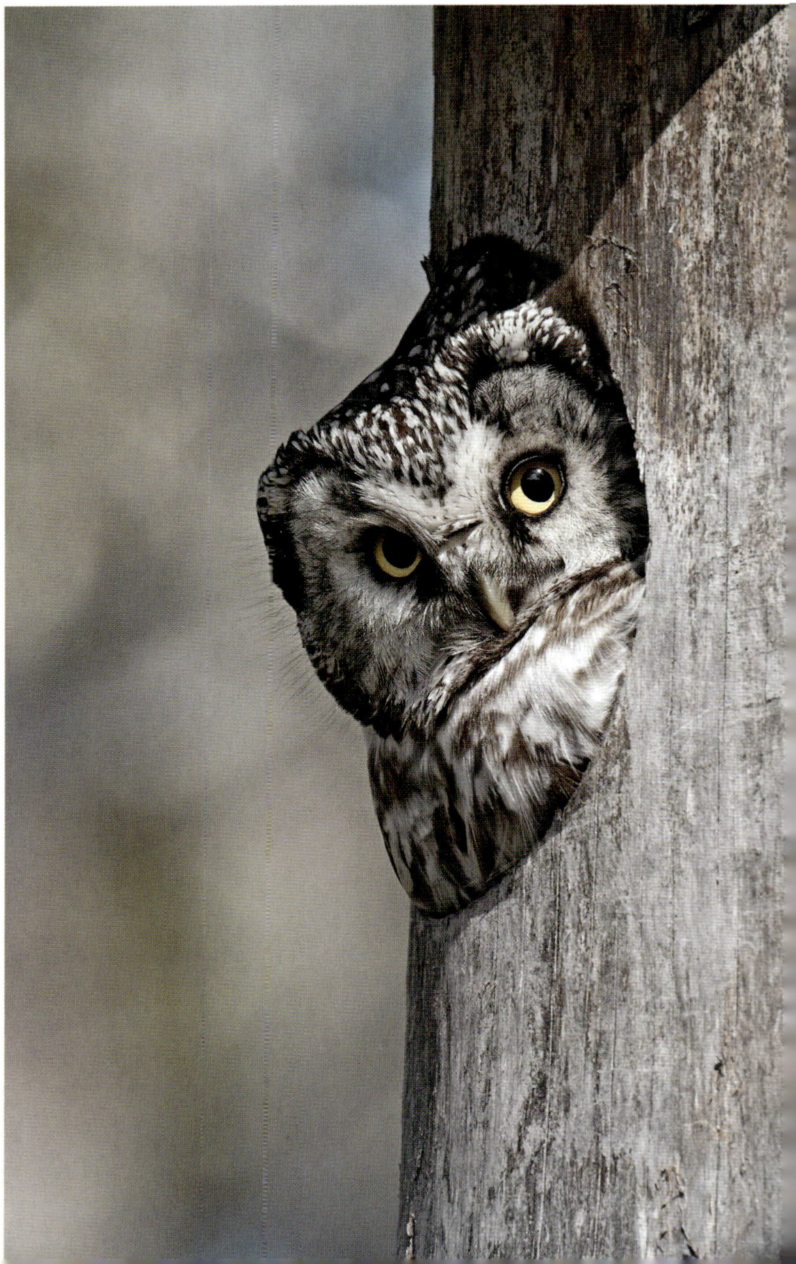

Jari Peltomäki

A Boreal Owl nesting in a natural-looking, manmade nest hole
(Aegolius funereus)
Canon EOS-1D Mark II N, 500mm f/4.0, 1/160 second, f/14.0, ISO 400, one-shot focus with one focusing point, Gitzo tripod, Manfrotto 501 video head. Siikajoki, Finland, May 2005.

Sometimes you may have to spring into action with not much advance warning and take nests into the forest. One spring we had a lot of sightings of Great Gray Owls, together with other owls, south of Oulu in an area with a very good vole population. The Great Gray Owl uses a Northern Goshawk's twig nest as a foundation for its own nest. I was sure that the number of Goshawk nests in the area would not be enough for this large owl population, so I rounded up a group of friends and colleagues. Together we took about 10 willow baskets and hung them up in trees in just one day. Great Gray Owls have nested in these baskets for at least two years, like the happy owl and its brood in the image here. I have yet to show this in a presentation and not raise a laugh.

We have, of course, built bigger, more natural-looking, and more sturdy twig nests for raptors, but it takes hours to build one. If you plan to take any bigger nest boxes into the forest or build big twig fortresses, you need to check with the landowners and get their permission. Contact your local raptor center as well, to avoid rival nests.

I won't photograph at all of the nests I built for birds, but I like to know I've done a bit to help them in their breeding efforts.

To Succeed without a Script You Need Luck

A spontaneous bird sighting never ceases to warm a birder's heart. An opportunity that presents itself to you totally out of the blue can be more satisfying than a prepared and arranged image, but you won't come by great, spontaneous opportunities that many times in any given year.

I was following a Short-eared Owl one spring evening as it was hunting over a small patch of land, and I saw it land on a fence post. It was getting dark already, but I knew I wouldn't find anything else to photograph that late anyway, so I decided to wait and see if something would happen. Soon after, another Short-eared Owl appeared, and the one that had been sitting on the post took off to chase the intruder away. I got an image of the owls fighting in the evening's dying daylight, set against a dark cloud. Every once in a while, patience is rewarded.

You can increase your chances of spontaneous, good photo opportunities by going to good locations, as mentioned in a few places in this book, and hanging around waiting for the birds to arrive. Places like these offer far better chances of taking good images than walking around randomly in the woods.

Short-eared Owls in an air battle in the last light of the day *(Asio flammeus)*
Canon EOS-1D Mark II, 500mm f/4.0, 1/320 second, f/4.0, ISO 800, continuous focus with 45 focusing points, hand-held camera. Tyrnävä, Finland, May 2005.

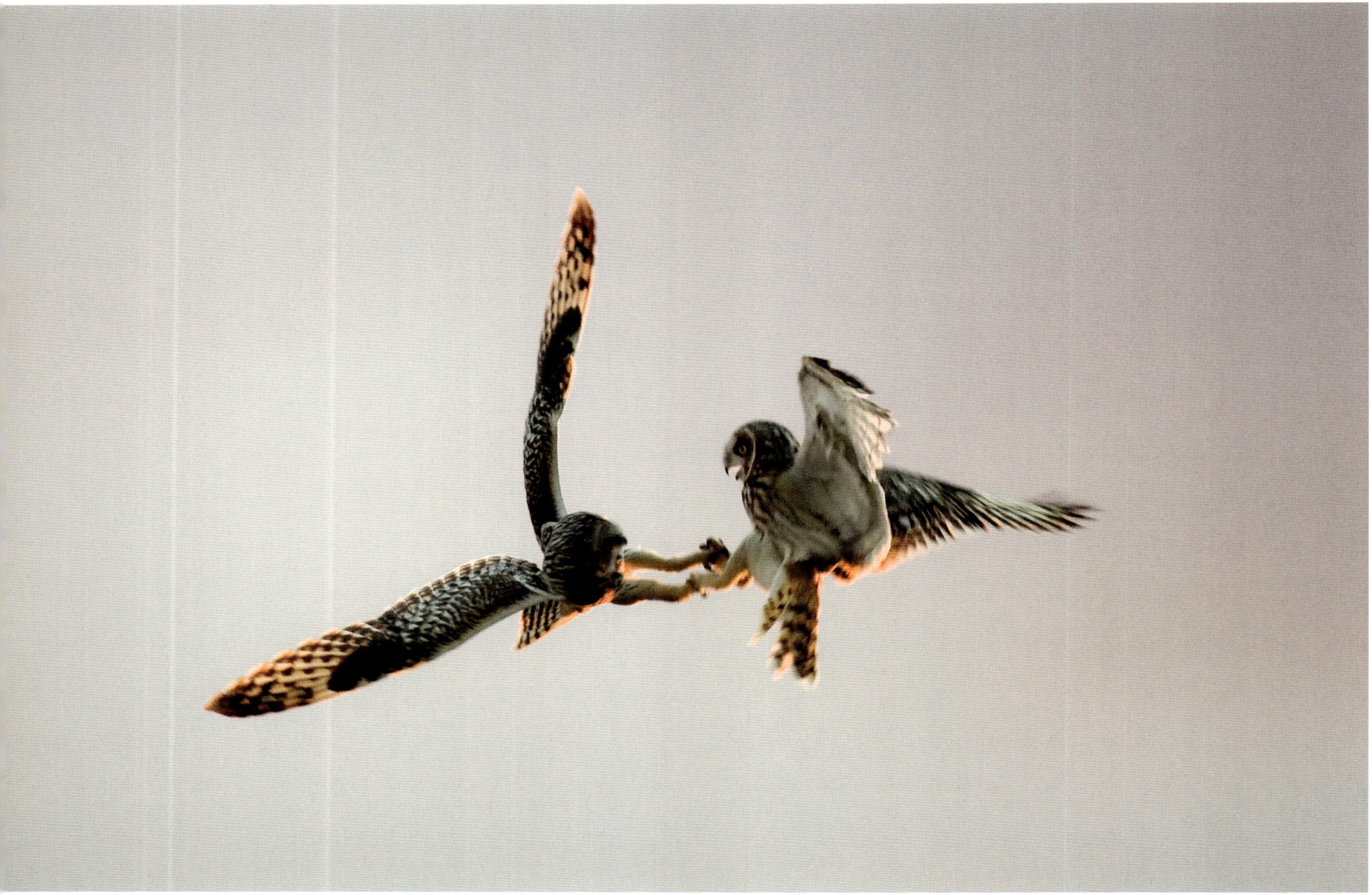

Jari Peltomäki

Jari Peltomäki

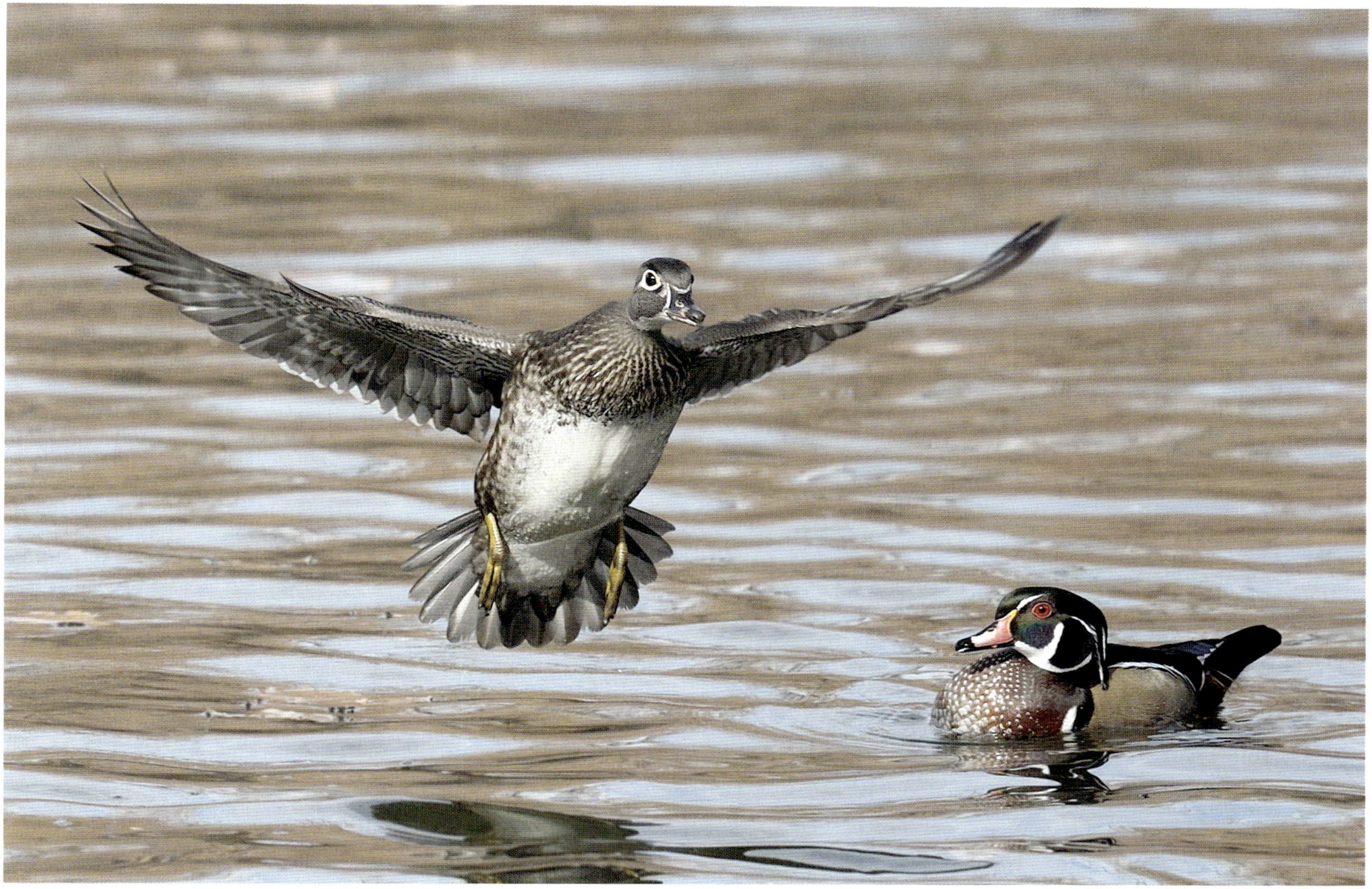

Wild and free Wood Ducks at a feeding pond in a zoo *(Aix sponsa)*
Nikon D3S, 200–400mm f/5.6, 1/2500 second, 400mm, f/8.0, ISO 1600, continuous focus with 51 focusing points, handheld camera. Albuquerque Zoo, New Mexico, December 2010.

Jari Peltomäki

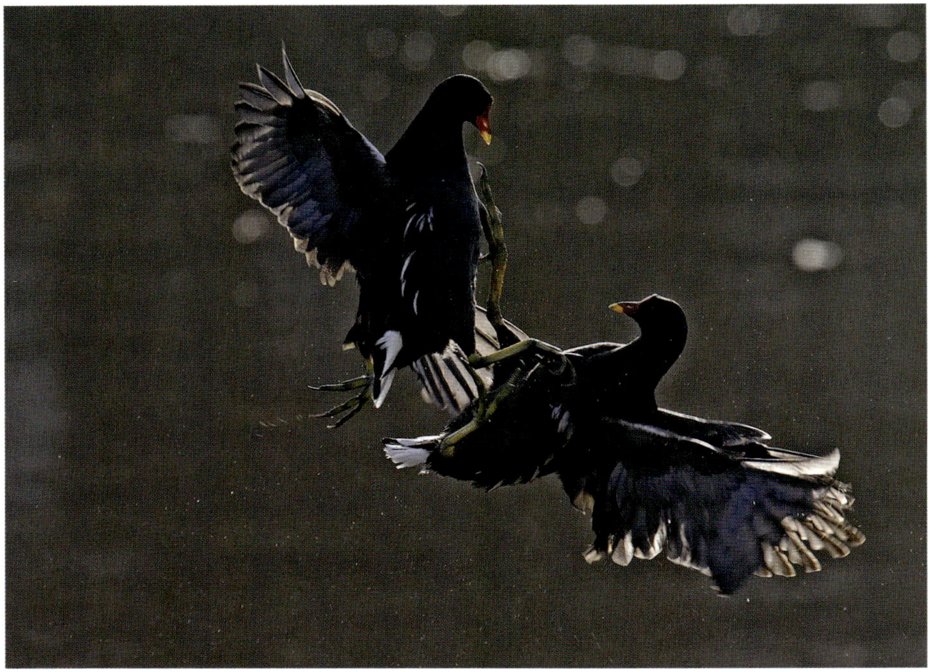

Eurasian Moorhens fighting in a park in London *(Gallinula chloropus)*
Canon EOS-1D Mark II, 300mm f/2.8, 1/1250 second, f/7.1, ISO 500, continuous focus with 45 focusing points, handheld camera. St James's Park, London, UK, January 2005.

Photographing from a car can offer pleasant surprises to a photographer seeking spontaneous opportunities. You can read more in the chapter "Photographing from a Car or a Boat."

A photographer walking openly in a field has the worst chances of taking good bird photos. Birds are mainly shy and will avoid an advancing photographer. The easiest way to get them close is to hide from them and wait quietly in the cover of the foliage in a camouflage outfit or net or in a blind. This applies especially to countries where birds are hunted. There are a lot of exceptions, though; in some countries birds are a lot more approachable, and when photographing such birds you should move as much as possible and seek different angles and backgrounds. There are also places where birds have become more used to people, such as city parks, and you should use the opportunities there to photograph birds at closer ranges.

There is no one right way to photograph birds. What works for one photographer is not necessarily good for another. I try to be as diversified as possible in photographing birds and vary my styles and locations widely. It makes bird photography all the more interesting to me and yields an extensive archive of photos.

MARKUS VARESVUO

KEEP YOUR EQUIPMENT READY

Your camera equipment should always be ready, and the camera and lens adjustments should be set for action photography.

One painful example of why I need to keep repeating this piece of wisdom to myself is when I took a photo trip to Ordesa National Park in northern Spain. We got back to our transport at the end of a particularly long day in the blind. Having walked through heavy snowfall in the darkening afternoon, I thought I was done photographing for the day so I packed my gear in my backpack. We started driving slowly down a winding mountain road, and just five minutes later I spotted a group of Gray Partridges on the side of the road. We stopped, and the partridges hurried away from us on the snow, but they went only a couple of yards before stopping under a small bush. I started to grab my camera and lens out of my backpack on the backseat, but by the time I got them out, the birds had moved deeper inside the bush. An absolutely beautiful opportunity was missed, and I had nobody to blame but myself.

When I am out in the field, I usually carry a camera and a 500mm telephoto lens, with a strap attached to the lens. My camera is set to continuous focus with 61 focusing points, and the ISO is set to give me at least 1/3200 second shutter speed. I set the focusing range of the lens to the value with the largest available distance to infinity.

Bird photography is full of surprises and fast action. Your chances of capturing these fleeting moments are greatly improved if you have your camera and its settings ready for action. If you find yourself photographing a calm, long-lasting situation, you have time to make the necessary changes to the adjustments, but in a fast situation you have no time to fiddle around with the controls.

When I drive along back roads, I keep my gear ready and available. Cars are good blinds, and some birds stay by the road when you stop your car. I have taken many good images from a half-open car window using a beanbag to support my camera.

The Black Grouse image is a typical example of how you can take a good photograph of a situation that presents itself to you suddenly, as long as you and your gear are prepared for the eventuality. Driving on a small road in the Kuusamo area in northeast Finland, I spotted a Black Grouse perching in the top of a pine within good range. The setting sun was hitting the bird, and the rising moon looked like I might be able to get it in the image. Lifting my camera out the window, I settled it into a good angle on the beanbag and drove on slowly. When I was within photographing range, I realized I would indeed get the bird and the moon in the same frame. I shot the first frames, with my camera set for action, as soon I stopped the car because Black Grouses often fly away as soon as you stop. This bird gave me time to change the adjustments on my camera to better suit the situation. One of the changes I made was setting the aperture at f/20.0 for improved depth of field, which helped emphasize the moon.

A Black Grouse and the moon *(Tetrao tetrix)*
Canon EOS-1D Mark II, 500mm f/4.0 plus 1.4x extender, 1/60 second, f/20.0, ISO 1000, one-shot focus with a central focusing point, beanbag, car as a blind. Kuusamo, Finland, June 2006.

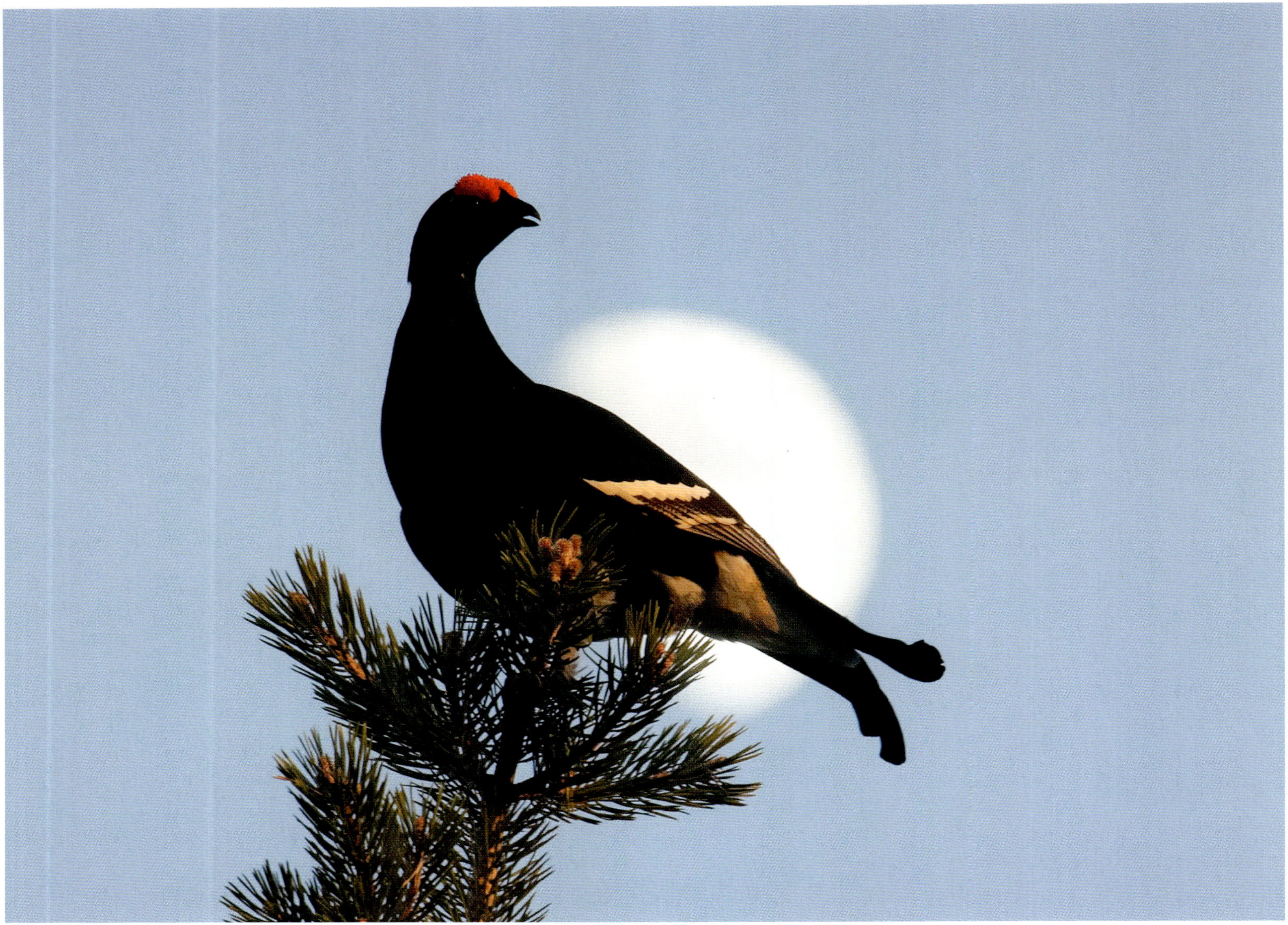

Markus Varesvuo

MARKUS VARESVUO

OPEN YOUR SENSES AND USE YOUR IMAGINATION

Every situation is full of opportunities.

The first chapters described how the foundation for good images is built on a well thought-out idea and patience and perseverance in working toward realizing the idea. This chapter aims to demonstrate that even an ordinary situation can be turned into an interesting image if you give yourself time to see all its potential and use your gray matter to come up with an original solution.

I was photographing a flock of Common Ringed Plovers one early autumn as they were resting on a small rock in shallow water close to the shore. Nothing special was going on. Moving right or left revealed nothing interesting in the background, and the light conditions were not likely to change for some time. It looked like the only thing coming out of this situation was a documentary image of a flock of Common Ringed Plovers resting on a rock, with both young and old birds.

Then I noticed that a rising wind was pushing the waves higher so the surf was breaking against the rock they were

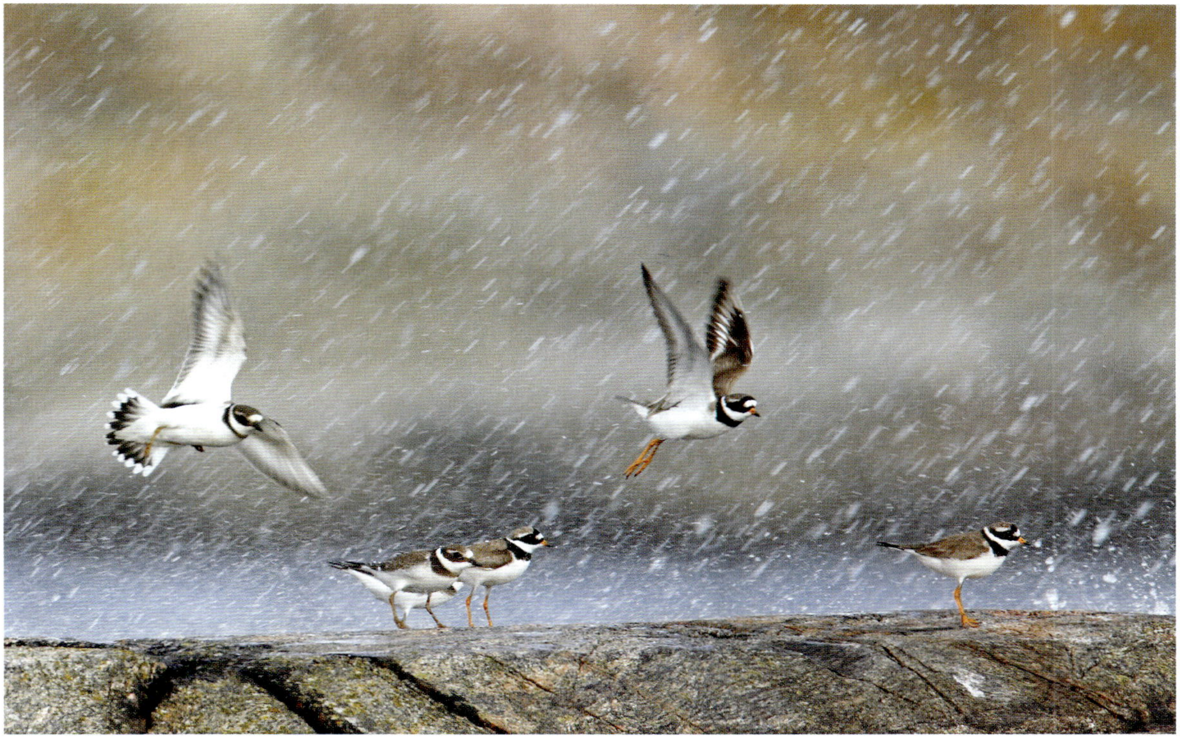
Markus Varesvuo

A flock of Common Ringed Plovers with breaking surf *(Charadrius hiaticula)*
Canon EOS-1Ds Mark III, 800mm f/5.6 plus 1.4x extender, 1/400 second, f/10.0, ISO 500, one-shot focus with a central focusing point, Gitzo tripod, Manfrotto 501 video head, blind.
Länsi-Turunmaa, Finland, September 2009.

A Bohemian Waxwing *(Bombycilla garrulus)*
Canon EOS-1D Mark III, 800mm f/5.6, 1/400 second, f/5.6, ISO 1600, one-shot focus with a central focusing point, beanbag, car as a blind. Porvoo, Finland, October 2008.

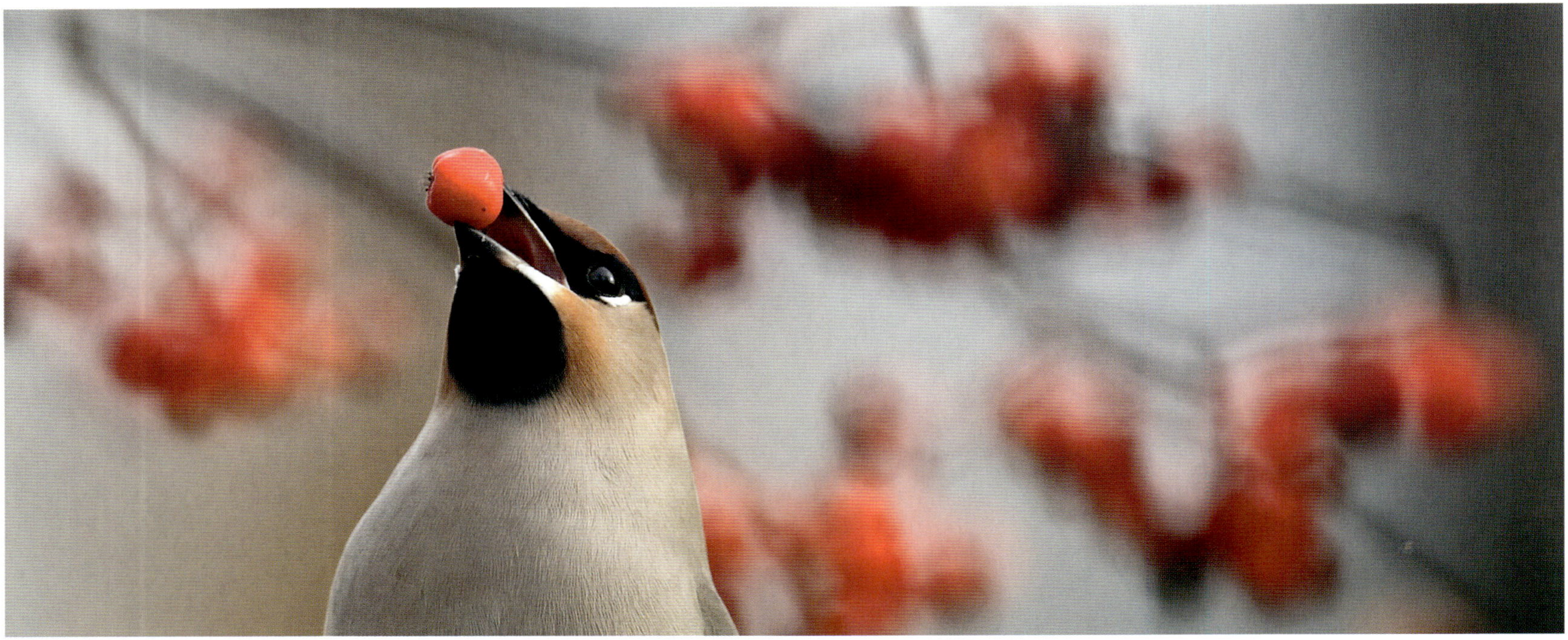

Markus Varesvuo

resting on. I decided to wait and see how the situation developed. In about 15 minutes the waves started to occasionally hit over the rock, causing the birds to start moving restlessly. I got several frames of waves splashing over the rock, and the best image shows the birds taking off as they apparently decided to go look for a calmer place to rest.

Bohemian Waxwings might be the species I have photographed the most. Despite having thousands of Bohemian Waxwing images, I don't get tired of photographing them, and finding new approaches and styles seems to be relatively easy. Their incredibly beautiful plumage and confident, trusting behavior around people make them an ideal subject.

In 2008 Bohemian Waxwings migrated southward from their northern breeding grounds earlier than normal to feast on a bumper rowanberry harvest. In early October some of the trees were still glowing with autumn colors, but the rowans had already lost all their leaves, and the bright red, juicy berries were left to blaze charmingly.

One day-long session with a long telephoto lens produced images with the glowing yellows and oranges of the autumn foliage blending into an even background for the Bohemian Waxwings. I was also after some less conventional super closeups, so I used a mix of compositions with dark backgrounds,

Markus Varesvuo

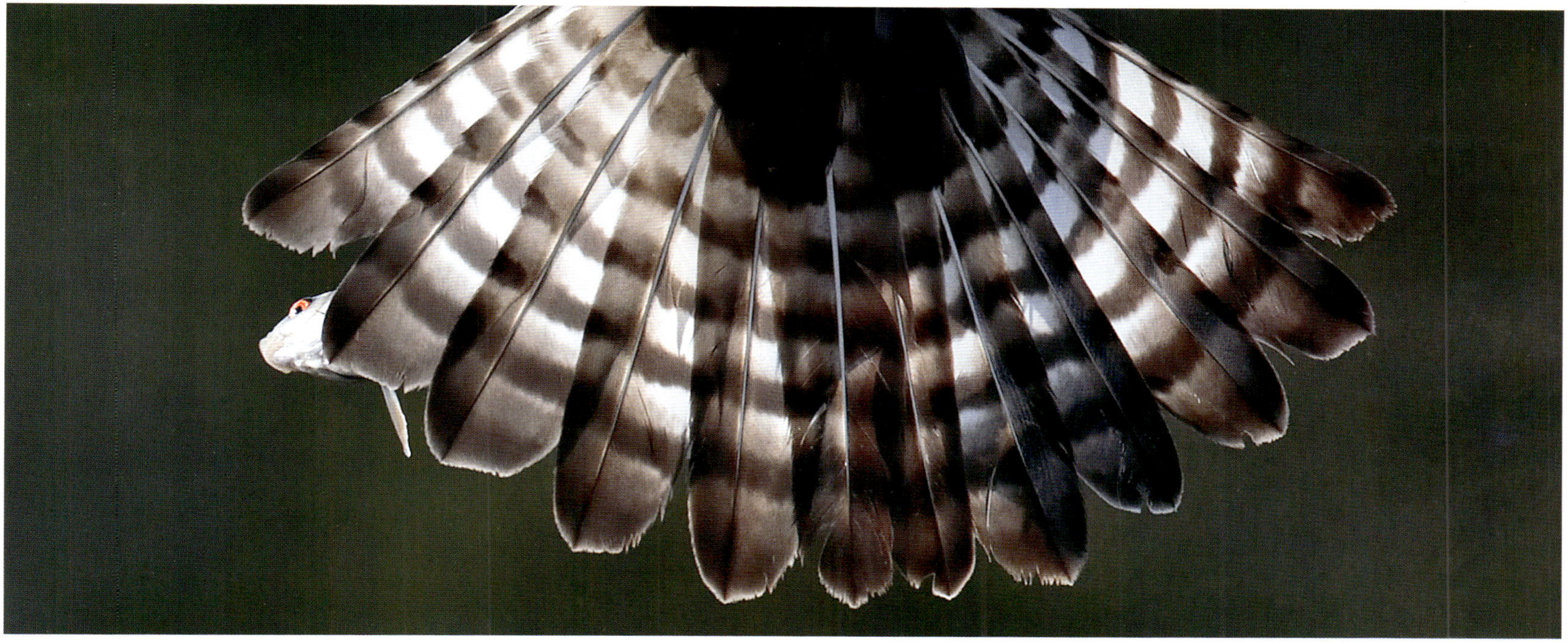

berries, and birds, knowing that I would be selecting the final framing on the computer.

A permanent blind has few disadvantages, but one clear drawback comes from not being able to adjust its position relative to the wind, a fact that I had to accept when I photographed the breeding activity of an Osprey pair from a blind. The male went off to fish in a nearby lake about five times during the day, but because of the direction of the wind, it always approached and landed on the nest with its back toward me. I decided to concentrate on photographing the female because it was dicing the fish for the young.

But then, as the male Osprey was once again coming to the nest with fish and presenting its back to me, it dawned on me that the challenging angle of its arrival was an opportunity to try a novel approach to Osprey flight shots.

An Osprey with a catch *(Pandion haliaetus)*
Canon EOS-1D Mark III, 500mm f/4.0, 1/1600 second, f/7.1, ISO 1600, continuous focus with an extended central focusing point, Gitzo tripod, Manfrotto 501 video head, blind. Vaala, Finland, June 2008.

JARI PELTOMÄKI

GET TO KNOW YOUR AREA

Local knowledge is important.

Find out where the best spots for bird photography are in your area. Through experience you will learn which species to photograph in each time of the year, and especially where to photograph them.

This is elementary information, but it's easy to forget unless you write it down. I plan photo projects in my annual calendar, trying to reserve several days for each species that I am targeting, at the best possible time, based partly on notes I have taken. I write notes on maps for future use, paying special attention to any observations I have made in the field. You can also find good locations for photographing birds by studying maps.

I record the GPS coordinates of most of my photo locations because they help me find my way in the dark and through thick fog. You might want to record GPS coordinates for any raptor nests and boxes because they may help in research and conservation efforts.

Bird guidebooks and the Internet are good sources for information about bird locations. You can find fairly exact maps on the Internet, which help you search for potentially good sites for photographing birds.

Keep in mind, though, that good birding spots are not necessarily the best bird photography sites. Most good birding spots are normally teaming with birders, increasing the risk of conflicting interests between the groups; birders like to study their subjects from afar with telescopes, whereas bird photographers need to get much closer, despite having long telephoto lenses. This can cause some criticism from birders, but photographers also suffer if they scare the birds away because they are left empty handed.

It is fair to say that often a site that is less spectacular and popular than the so-called hot spots suits bird photography better. And as a photographer, you will find that it's easier to manage a smaller site than a larger area.

Potential Sites for Photography

Black Grouse and Western Capercaillies tend to return to the same lek site every year, and once a good site has been discovered, it can offer great photo opportunities for decades. Old forests have lots of great species, not just owls and Western Capercaillies; look for breeding Northern Goshawks or Eurasian Three-toed Woodpeckers, which often nest in the same areas. These species are loyal to their territories, and they return each year—assuming the forest is still there.

You can also chart your area for small-scale key biotopes. You can find, for example, that a Rustic Bunting claims a patch every year on a swamp by a small stream, where a pair can be photographed in both the singing season and the short breeding season while the parents are busy feeding the young. If you discover a nice bog you may find a crane's nest, where the birds may come several years in a row. Set up your blind well in advance of the birds' arrival in spring.

Many manmade environments can be good bird photography locations, such as any wetlands that have been created

Jari Peltomäki

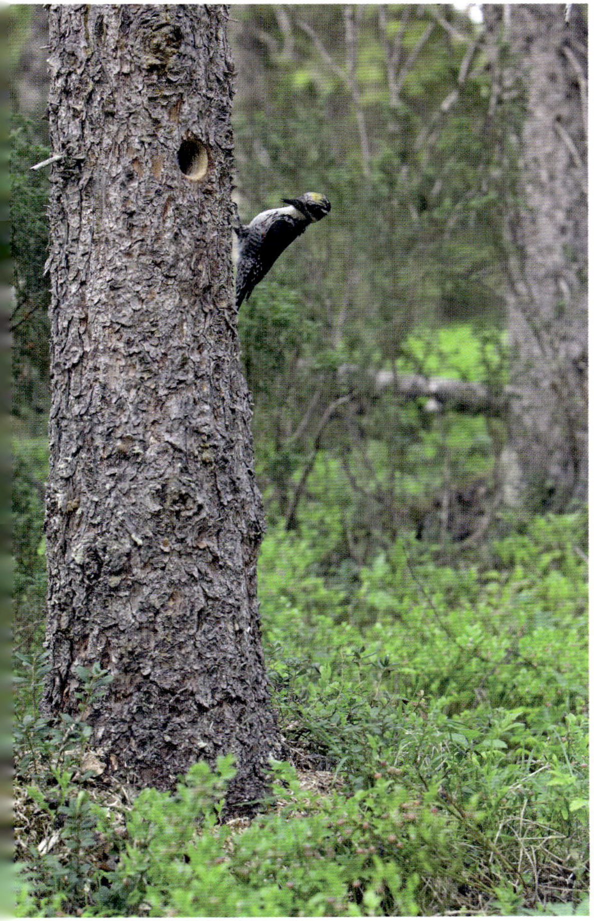

Eurasian Three-toed Woodpeckers often dig their nest holes quite low *(Picoides tridactylus)*
Canon EOS-1D Mark II, 70–200mm f/2.8, 1/125 second, 70mm, f/5.0, ISO 400, one-shot focus with one focusing point, Gitzo tripod, Manfrotto 501 video head. Kuusamo, Finland, June 2005.

through dredging, or around wastewater treatment plants or other structures. Landfills draw birds in great numbers, and some species can be easily photographed there. Most waste management sites require permission to enter.

There are ways bird photographers can assist nature in providing good bird sites and thus promote their own bird photography projects. It's relatively easy to create artificial flood ponds on fields close to shores, which help maintain spring flooding conditions for longer than normal and where you can feed migrating birds. This must, of course, be done in cooperation with the landowner. Scythes and brush cutters are great tools for clearing overgrown photo sites. As an example, I use a Black Grouse lek in a sand quarry, where the birds had been coming for years and where it was easy to photograph from a car. Eventually, though, the brush took over the site and made it difficult for the Black Grouse to perform their courting rituals, and for me to photograph them. A local bird photographer worked some magic with his scythe, and we are now anxiously waiting for next spring to see if the birds come back to their familiar courting grounds!

Find out where the migrating birds' staging areas are and if it's okay to set up blinds in the area. If it is, survey the grounds to determine the best location for your blind. In practice this means you need to do your preparatory work at least a year in advance. Wherever ground is first exposed from under the snow and ice is where the birds tend to gather, often on ponds formed by spring floods on the fields or in the mouths of ditches where the streaming water breaks through the melting snow and ice. These are good sites for bird photography.

Birds on spring and autumn migration often follow so-called main lines, which are land shapes formed by capes and barriers between large bodies of

Marja Kuosa

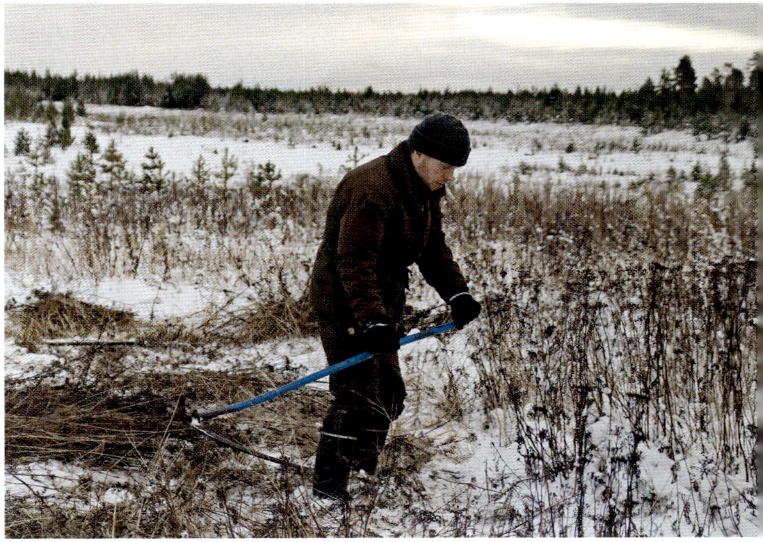

Bird photographer Harri Taavetti is using a scythe to clear an overgrown Black Grouse lek

Jari Peltomäki

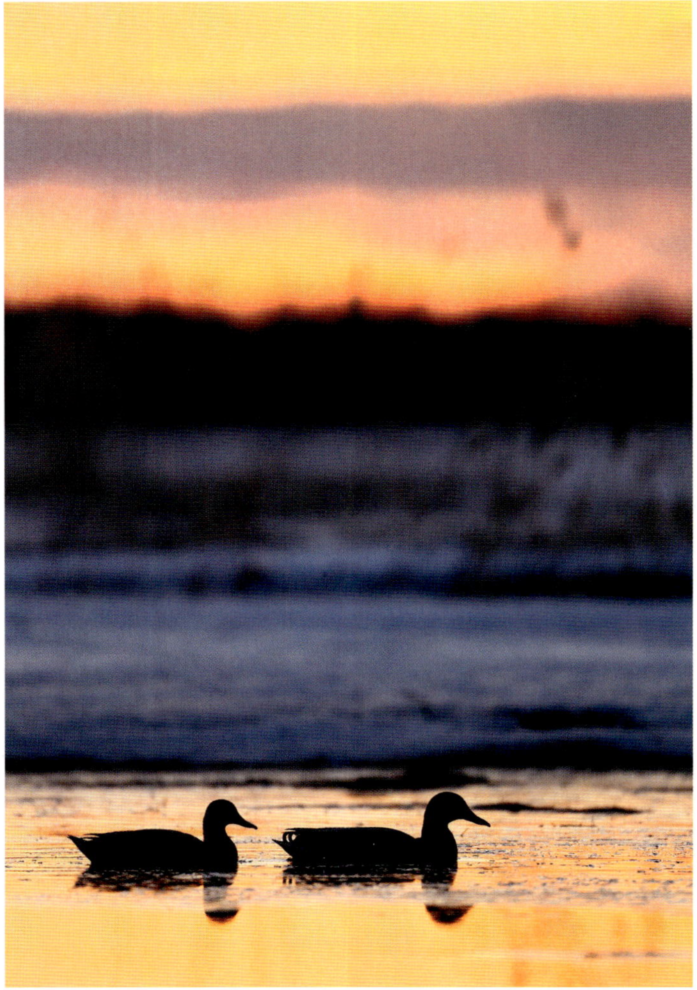

Mallards against the setting sun on Liminka Bay *(Anas platyrhynchos)*
Canon EOS-1D Mark III, 500mm f/4.0, 1/1250 second, f/4.0, ISO 800, one-shot focus with one focusing point, ground pod, Manfrotto 501 video head, blind. Liminganlahti, Finland, April 2008.

water. Other clear land formations can also become main lines that the birds follow. Birds on migration tend to fly along shores, river valleys, and arable fields. Find out if your area is along any migration flyways.

Weather Matters When Choosing Your Location

When you are deciding where to go, pay attention to the weather. Detailed weather forecasts will help you make the right decisions about where and what to photograph, and it's especially crucial to know whether the day is going to be sunny or cloudy. Cloud cover has a lot to do with how much light you are going to have. I like to photograph in a forest in the even light of a cloudy day because in full sunshine the intensity of light varies greatly between sunny and shady areas. The direction of light also plays an important role, especially in bright sunshine. When you plan your day or think about where to set up your blind, remember that backlight is at its best just after sunset or just before sunrise. If snowfall is expected, find a place where you can get a nice dark background behind the birds you're about to photograph. Snowflakes stand out well against a dark background!

Water level determines if, from a bird photographer's point of view, there is too much, not enough, or just the right amount of shore exposed for the waders to forage. If you photograph on shores with tidal waters, get a tide table so you will know the times and heights for the ebb and flow peaks. The Baltic Sea has very little or no tides, but the direction of the wind can alter the water level significantly, particularly on the low shores of the Gulf of Bothnia. The water level can fluctuate several inches between rapidly receding shorelines, taking the birds too far out from the blind or suddenly raising water that threatens to flood your blind. That's why it's good to have a waterproof floor in your tent. Weather websites often provide information about the tides and water levels.

A fledgling photographer should hook up with a more seasoned bird photographer, if possible, to learn new things about photo techniques and locations. But not everybody likes to share hard-earned knowledge and experience.

A Temminck's Stint onshore with the water at an ideal level *(Calidris temminckii)*
Nikon D3S, 500mm f/4.0 plus 2x extender, 1/1250 second, f/11.0, ISO 1600, continuous focus with an extended central focusing point, ground pod, Manfrotto 501 video head, blind. Siikajoki, Finland, August 2010.

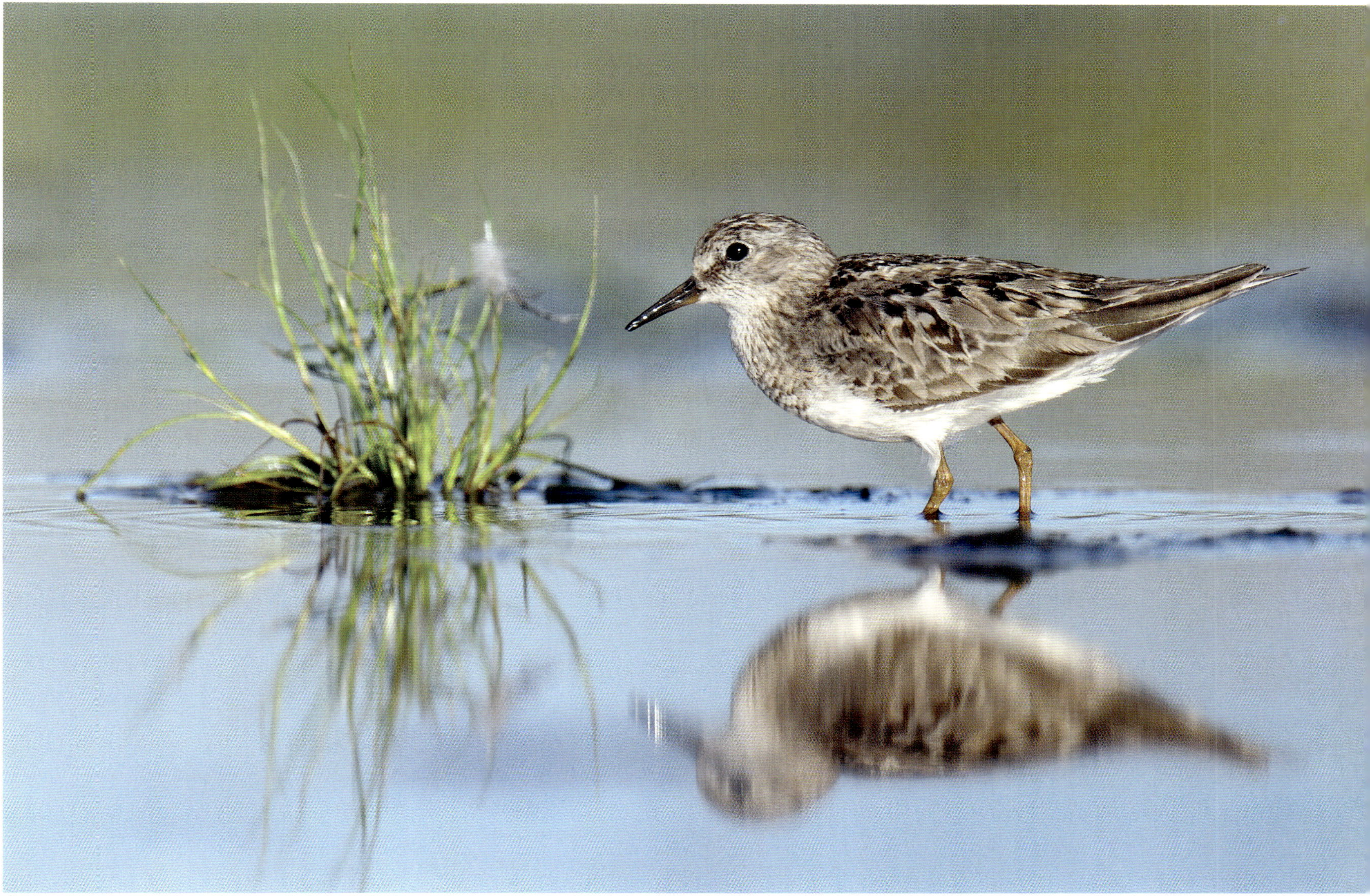

Jari Peltomäki

MARKUS VARESVUO AND BENCE MÁTÉ

CIRCUMSTANCES DICTATE

Modern camera technology lets you photograph in practically any weather. Just make sure you are prepared for all circumstances.

Freezing Cold (Markus)

My experience is that photographing in temperatures below −30°C (−22°F) is amazingly similar to photographing in more normal conditions. The only real drawback is that the camera battery life depletes dramatically, but that problem is easy to solve by taking spare batteries along. You should keep them under the many layers of clothing you are wearing, as close to your skin as possible, so they stay warm.

I was photographing a Eurasian Pygmy-Owl on a winter's day, when it was −37°C (−35°F). My Canon EOS-1D Mark IV battery lasted 50 minutes, after which I replaced it with a warm battery and put the cold battery in a pocket inside my clothes. After the next 50 minutes I swapped the batteries again. The first one had regained its power inside the warmth of my clothing. The cold does not make batteries discharge; instead, the cold makes them sluggish and weakens their capacity to release power to the camera. After they warm up, they work again.

Cold affects tripods, too. In extreme cold, especially, video heads become stiff. My Manfrotto 501 video head, for example, is useless for flight shots in temperatures below −25°C (−13°F). It is okay for still subjects even at −37°C (−35°F), but its performance is noticeably slower. A Wimberley gimbal works better than a video head in extreme cold (read more in the chapter "Bird Photographer's Tripods").

You should change lenses in the same temperature that you will be photographing in. If, for instance, you were to get into a warm car to change the lens, the difference between the temperatures would cause your camera and lens to fog up. When you change the lens outside, make sure no snow gets in your equipment. Remember that even if it's not snowing, wind may blow snow from the trees or snowbanks.

When you take your equipment outside and then bring it back in, and if the temperature outside is much colder than the air inside, keep the equipment in your camera bag so the temperature changes gradually. This helps prevent condensation inside the lenses.

If you're photographing from a heated blind in the winter and it's very cold outside, place your lens through the lens openings and firmly tighten the pouches around it before you turn the heater on. And don't change the lens at

A Eurasian Pygmy-Owl is on the lookout for prey in extreme cold weather *(Glaucidium passerinum)*
Canon EOS-1D Mark IV, 800mm f/5.6 plus 1.4x extender, 1/50 second, f/13.0, ISO 1000, one-shot focus with a central focusing point, mirror lockup and 2 second self-timer, Gitzo tripod, Manfrotto 501 video head. Kuusamo, Finland, January 2010.

Markus Varesvuo

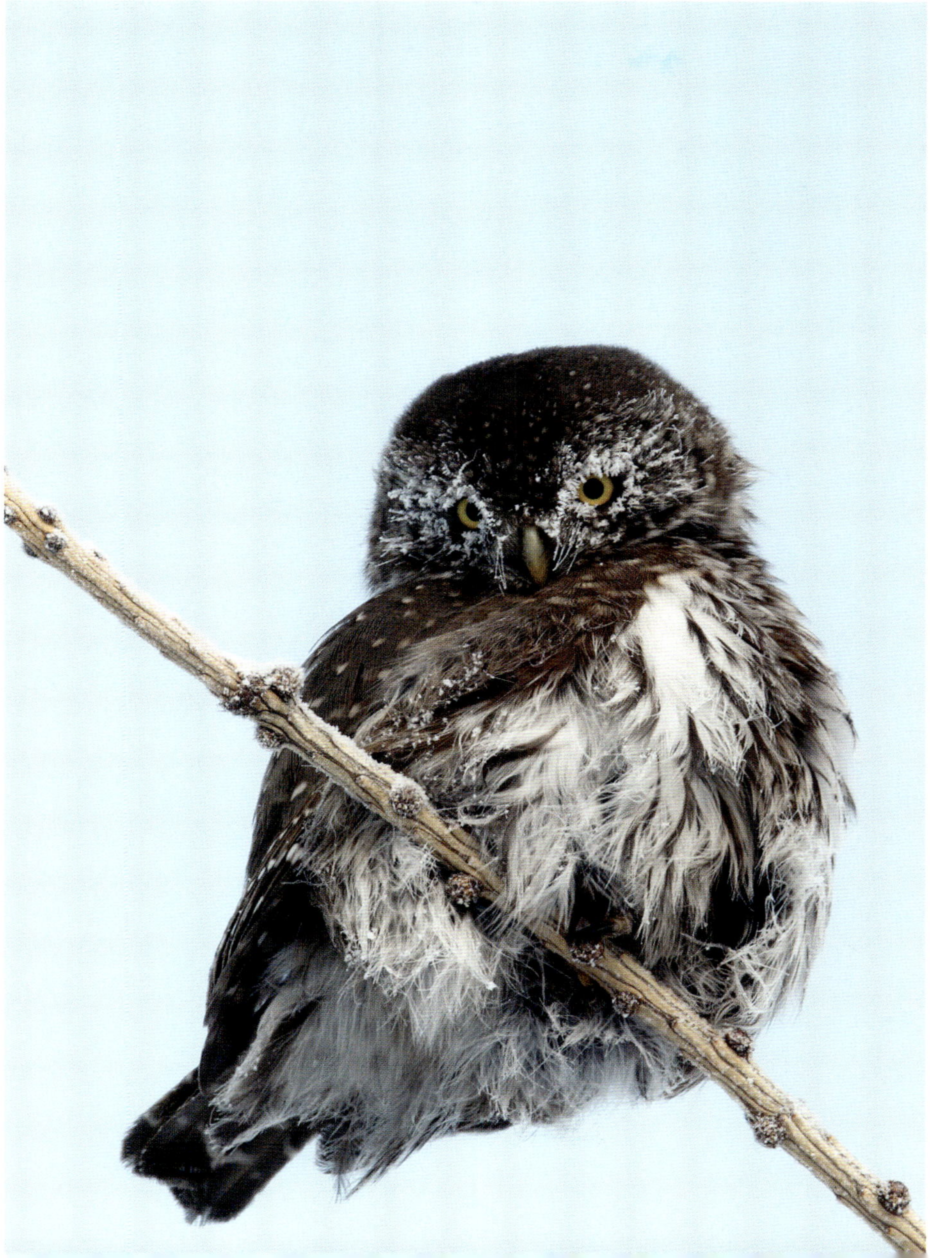

any time throughout the day, because it will instantly fog up.

Last, but definitely not least, do not underestimate the need for warm clothing and footwear. Photography often means staying put for long periods of time, which heightens the risk of frostbite. When you have the proper gear to stay warm, you can concentrate on the main task.

Dust (Markus)

Dust is rarely a big problem in Europe. Granted, during normal use, dust accumulates on a digital camera's sensor, but modern cameras have automatic dust removal systems that can take care of the problem. Some dust particles are more persistent, and the camera has to be cleaned professionally. I take my cameras to a service center about twice a year to get properly cleaned.

Obviously you could have problems with dust in Europe, for instance if you change lenses in windy weather anywhere near fine sand. You might get so much sand on the sensor that the camera's automatic dust removal system cannot remove it.

But in many other places around the world, dust is a real problem. To fight sand and dust whenever you're not using your camera, or while you're moving from one place to another, keep your equipment in a sealed pouch that won't let dust inside. Over any length of time, the extremely fine dust can collect inside your camera and lenses and do serious damage. The best professional cameras and lenses fare better in the fight against dust and humidity than more economical models.

My own experiences in seriously dusty areas are limited to the sand plains in Morocco and in Oman. There is always a lot of dust in the air when it is windy, and it's definitely smart to avoid changing lenses anywhere except inside, such as in a car.

Humidity (Bence)

High humidity is not only a strain on the photographer, it's hard on the equipment, too, for several reasons. Most camera manuals say that the operating humidity is a maximum of 80 percent, even though manufacturers know their cameras work even in higher humidity. The risks for malfunction or damage grow, though; humidity can spell trouble just like rain or extreme cold.

The temperature is significant when weighing the risks of humidity because relative humidity is not the whole truth.

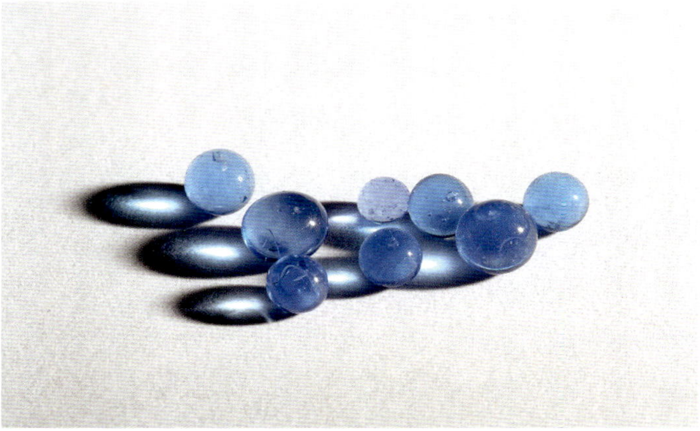

Ferenc Fodor

Dry silica gel

The warmer the air, the more water it can hold, and increased humidity causes decreased sharpness in the image.

In Europe humidity has caused me the most trouble when photographing birds at night in starlight; with the temperature at around 10°C (50°F), my equipment was wet with dew. I used a small electric fan to keep the lens dry so I could keep photographing.

But when I was photographing in Costa Rica, my troubles were not so easily solved. In the tropics, the temperature stayed at 25°C (77°F), but rain and sunshine alternated about once an hour. I quickly realized that it would not be as easy to get sharp images with long lenses from a low angle, as was the case at home in Hungary during the summer. How could I get a distant subject in sharp focus when the heat haze was clear to the naked eye and the humidity was so thick you could have leaned against it?

I started photographing closer to my subjects, at a higher camera angle and with a 300mm f/4.0 lens instead of an f/2.8 lens, because its outer lens diameter is smaller.

It rained regularly, but silica gel helped keep my gear dry. Silica gel absorbs moisture, and when it has reached full capacity it changes color, telling you that it is time to swap it with dry silica gel. You can dry the wet gel in an oven—about 120°C (250°F) for about two hours—and then reuse it. Pack your equipment and the gel into an airtight bag, such as plastic bags with zipper locks, and your gear dries nicely.

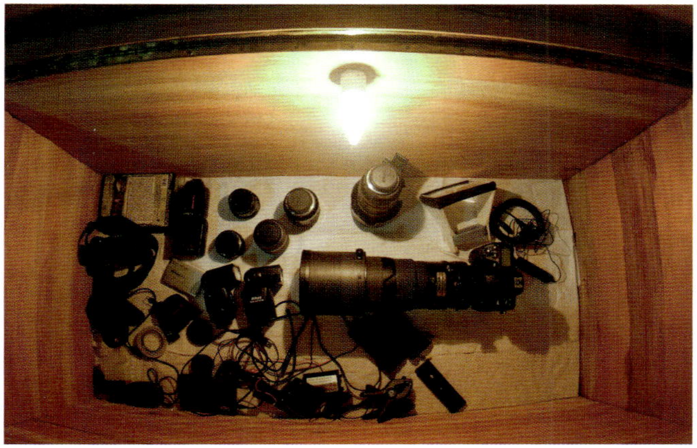

Bence Máté

A wooden box for the camera gear with a light bulb inside to ward off moisture

I stayed in Costa Rica for several months. In the beginning I diligently packed my gear in airtight bags with silica gel, but eventually I grew tired of the constant packing and repacking, so I gave up. As a consequence, my equipment started to develop fungus, even deep inside some of the lenses. This natural-made filter made my images so opalescent that I could not stop down more than f/8.0.

I tried unscrewing and opening the lenses to clean them, but without the right tools it was a waste of time. I needed to find a solution fast because I couldn't let the problem escalate any further. So I built a wooden box and placed a regular light bulb inside it, which I left on all the time so it would produce enough heat to keep the box nice and dry.

This solution served me for the rest of my time in Costa Rica, but if your stay is shorter than two weeks, silica gel is an ideal solution. Your equipment will probably be okay without any protection if you stay for less than a week.

MARKUS VARESVUO

USE WEATHER TO YOUR ADVANTAGE

Some weather conditions and phenomena can add interest to your photographs.

Rain and Snowfall

Rain and snowfall stand out best when they are staged against a dark background. The end result depends greatly on the rate of precipitation, the distance between the background and the subject, and the exposure time.

If you're aiming to take rain pictures from a blind, face your blind toward a dark background. If you're out in the field photographing in the rain, try to get to a place where you can get as dark a background as possible. If your subject is in water, try to find an angle where a forest or some other equally dark surface is reflected on the water instead of the cloudy sky. This will help bring out rain in your images.

You can emphasize the rain effect by using a slow shutter speed (for example, 1/80 second), which stretches the raindrops into streaks.

In the Common Crane image, neither the blind nor the camera angle were originally planned with rain in mind. A slow shutter speed makes the rain visible against the dark forest, but it is invisible against the light water. Had the camera been at a lower angle, there would have been more dark forest and less light water in the image. In calmer weather the dark forest was reflected on the water, but with the rain came wind, which broke the surface and then mainly mirrored the cloudy sky above.

Your ideal kit for rainy weather should include a fast lens with a focal length of at least 200mm. Use a shallow depth of field to bring out the raindrops and snowflakes instead of blurring them into the background. Backlight is good for highlighting raindrops, but rain and sun at the same time is not very common, so it's better to use a flash. Of course, using a flash requires at least some level of predictability from the situation and the subject (more in the chapter "Sources of Light").

For taking the White-throated Dipper image, I positioned myself on a spot where the dark forest on the other side of the narrow river was reflected on the water. I used a 1/60 second shutter speed to highlight the small, dense snowflakes as they fell.

If the snowfall is extremely heavy and the distance to the dark background is great, it might be better to use a faster shutter speed, otherwise the motion blur created by the snowfall becomes a white blanket in front of the dark background, with individual flakes lost in the whiteness.

With snowfall, you can evoke powerful moods in images. Remember to overexpose by one or two f-stops over the light meter reading.

Sometimes snowfall can be shown against a light background, at least indirectly, as in the Eurasian Griffon image, where snow that had been falling for quite some time was piling up on the bird's back. The image tells of the incredible ability of the feathers to insulate—to keep the warmth in and the cold out.

A Common Crane incubating its eggs *(Grus grus)*
Canon EOS-1Ds Mark II, 300mm f/2.8, 1/80 second, f/4.5, ISO 400, one-shot focus with a central focusing point, Gitzo tripod, Manfrotto 501 video head, blind. Pernaja, Finland, May 2005.

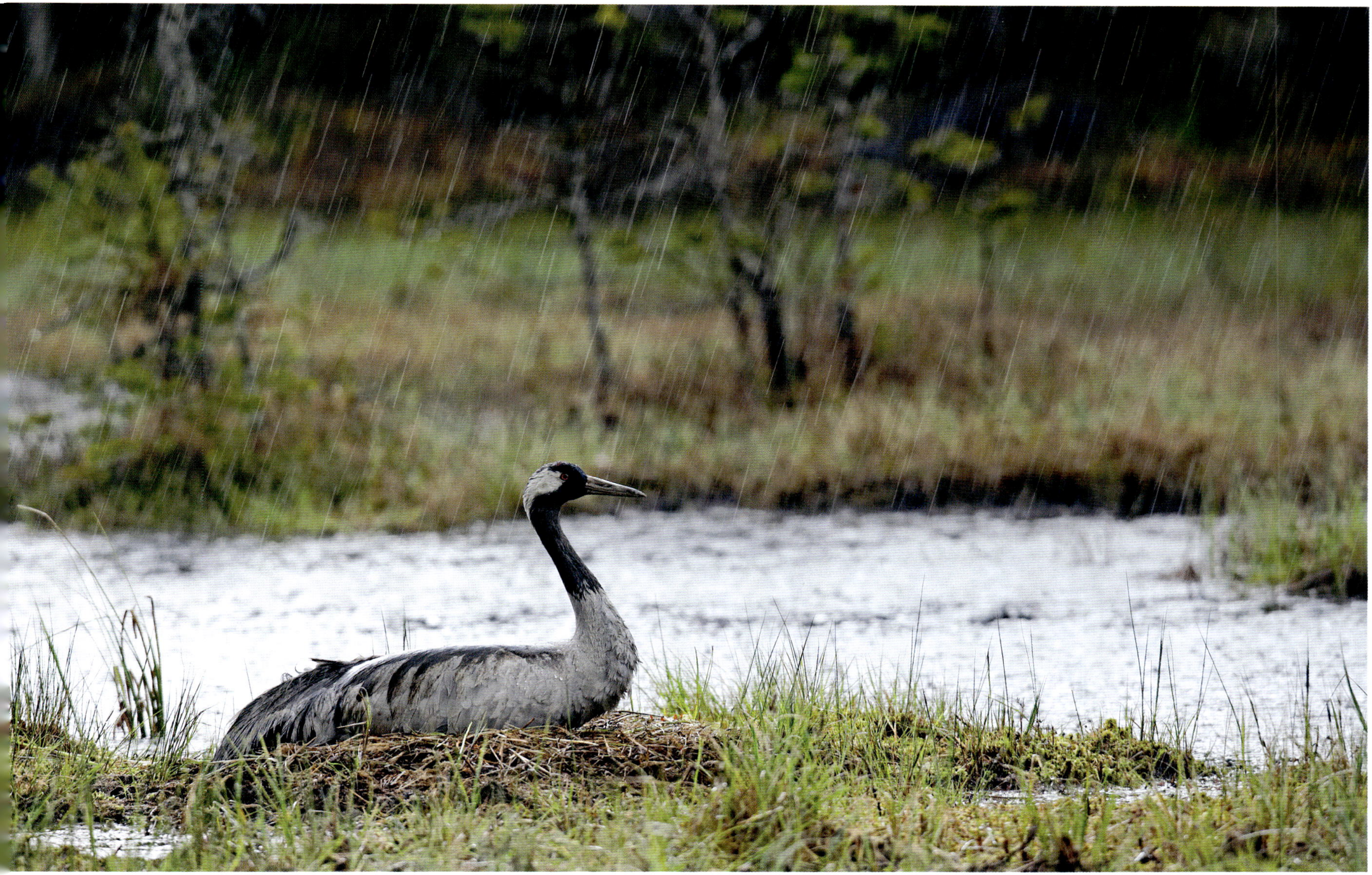

Markus Varesvuo

Bence Máté

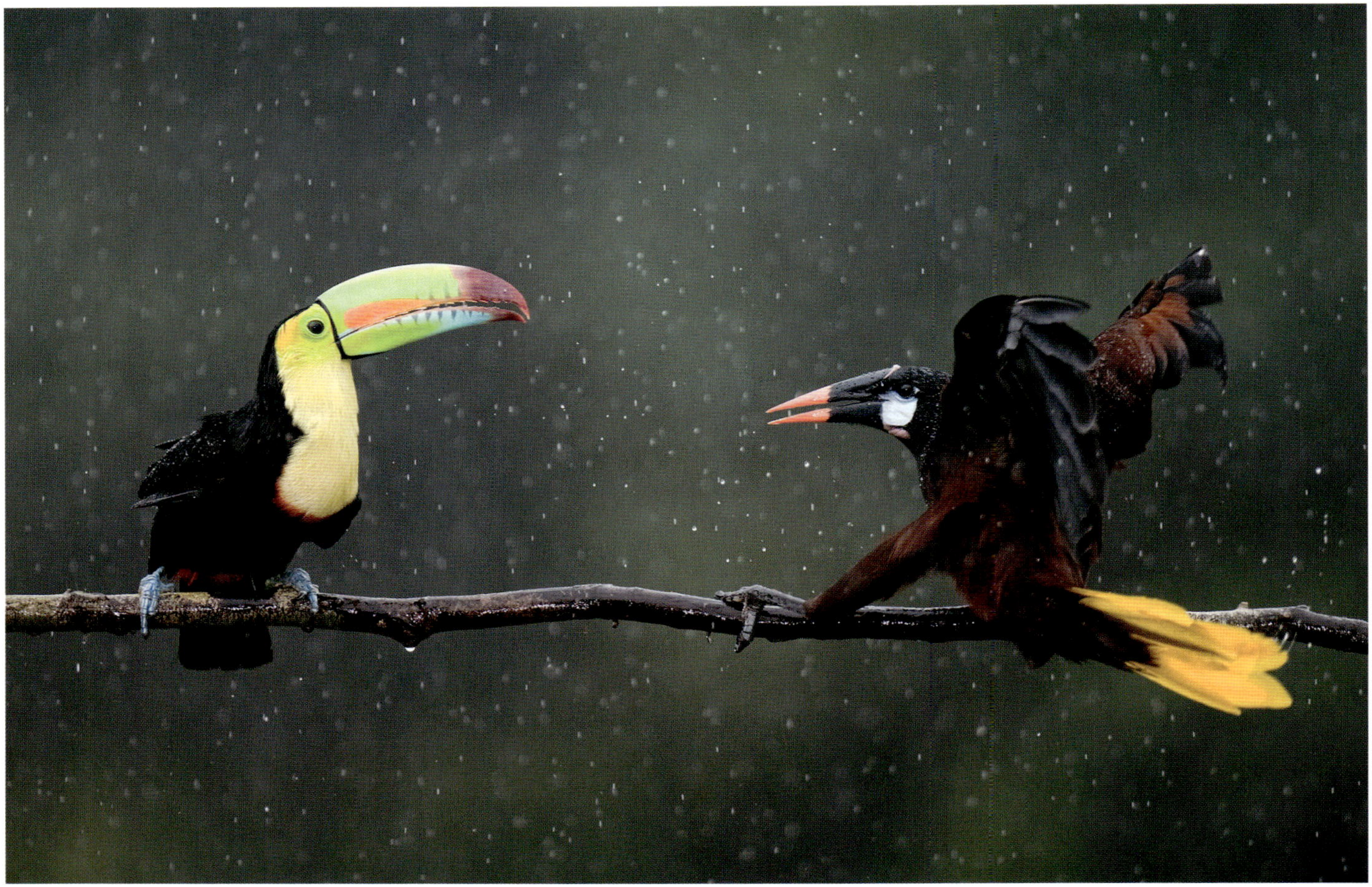

A flash provides backlight and emphasizes the water drops in this photo of a Keel-billed Toucan and a Montezuma Oropendola *(Ramphastos sulfuratus, Psarocolius montezuma)*
Nikon D700, 300mm f/2.8, 1/1600 second, f/2.8, ISO 1000, three Nikon SB-800 flashes, manual focus, Gitzo tripod, video head. Costa Rica, January 2010.

A White-throated Dipper in snowfall *(Cinclus cinclus)*
Canon EOS-1Ds Mark III, 800mm f/5.6, 1/60 second, f/8.0, ISO 500, one-shot focus with central focusing point, Gitzo tripod, Manfrotto 501 video head. Kuusamo, Finland, February 2010.

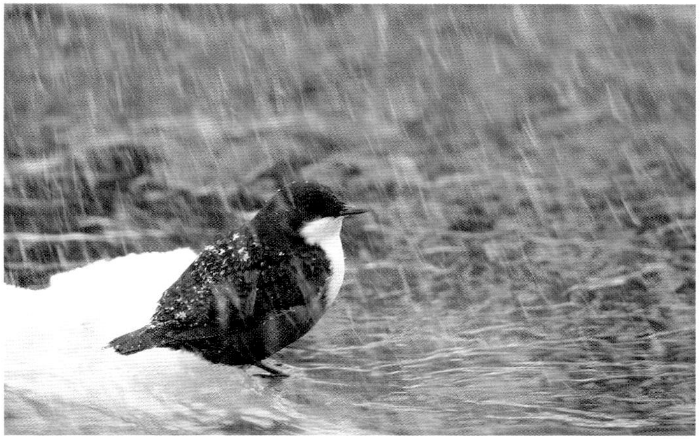

Markus Varesvuo

A Black-legged Kittiwake in heavy snowfall about 70 m (230 ft) from the dark backdrop of the sea *(Rissa tridactyla)*
Canon EOS-1D Mark III, 70–200mm f/2.8, 1/640 second, 185mm, f/3.5, ISO 1600, continuous focus with an extended central focusing point, handheld camera. Norway, April 2009.

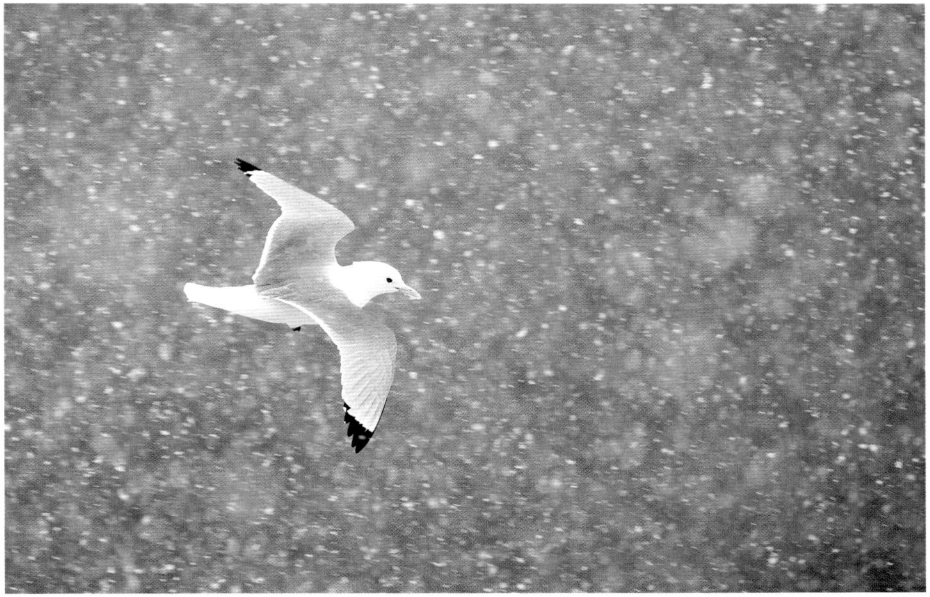

Markus Varesvuo

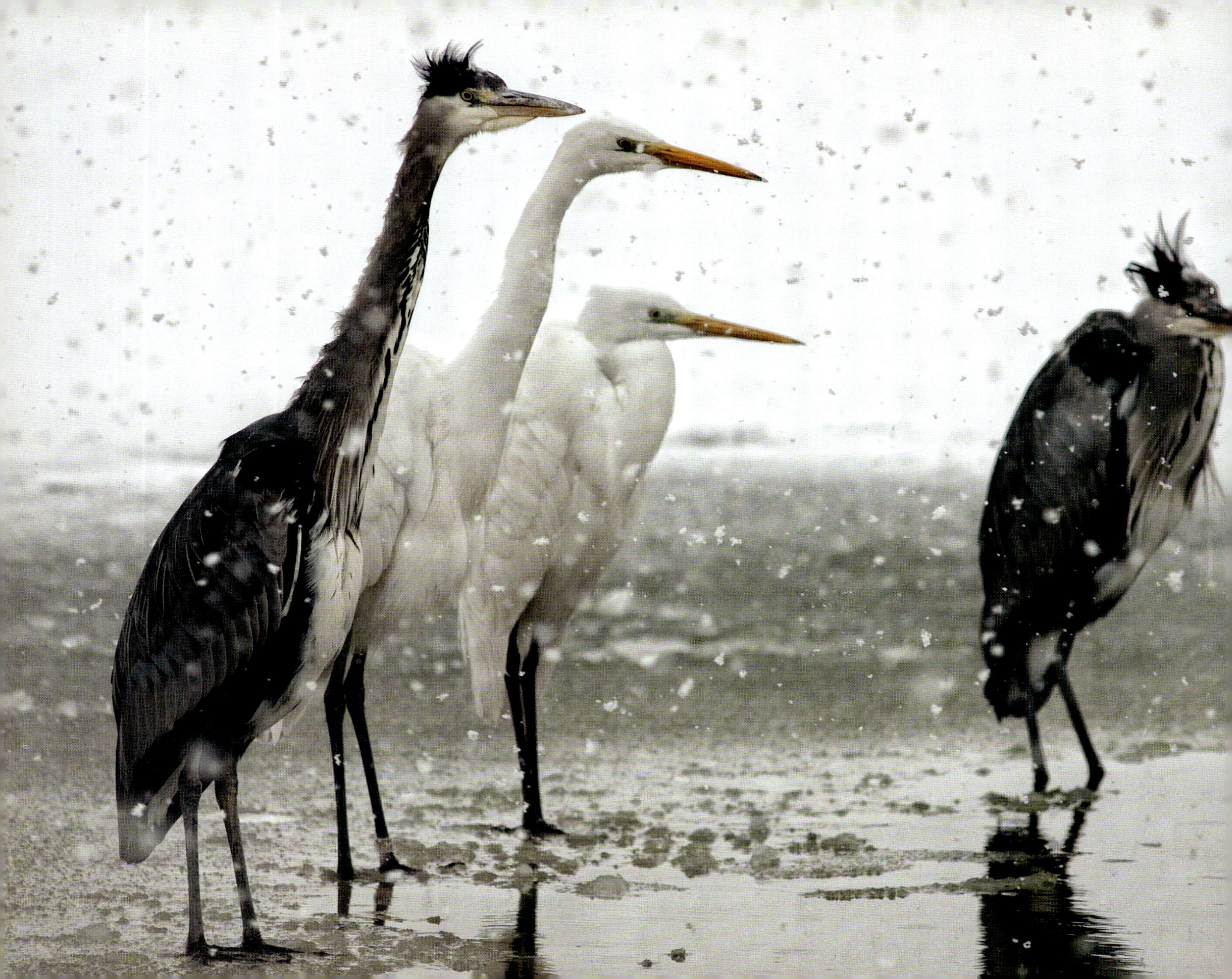

Bence Máté

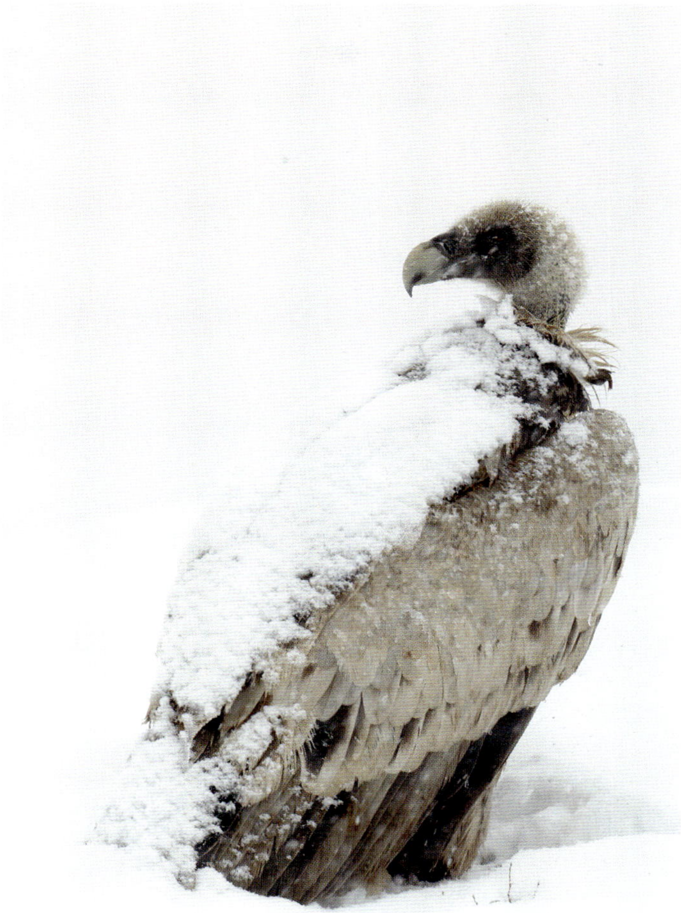

Markus Varesvuo

A Eurasian Griffon covered in snow *(Gyps fulvus)*
Canon EOS-1D Mark IV, 500mm f/4.0, 1/200 second, f/7.1, ISO 400, one-shot focus with a central focusing point, Gitzo tripod, Manfrotto 501 video head, blind. Spain, November 2010.

When photographed against a light background, snowfall is not easy to spot unless the flakes are really big, as in this photo of Great Egrets and Gray Herons *(Ardea cinerea, Ardea alba)*
Canon EOS 300D, 300mm f/2.8, 1/1000 second, f/4.0, ISO 100, manual focus, Gitzo tripod, video head, blind. Hungary, February 2005.

Jari Peltomäki

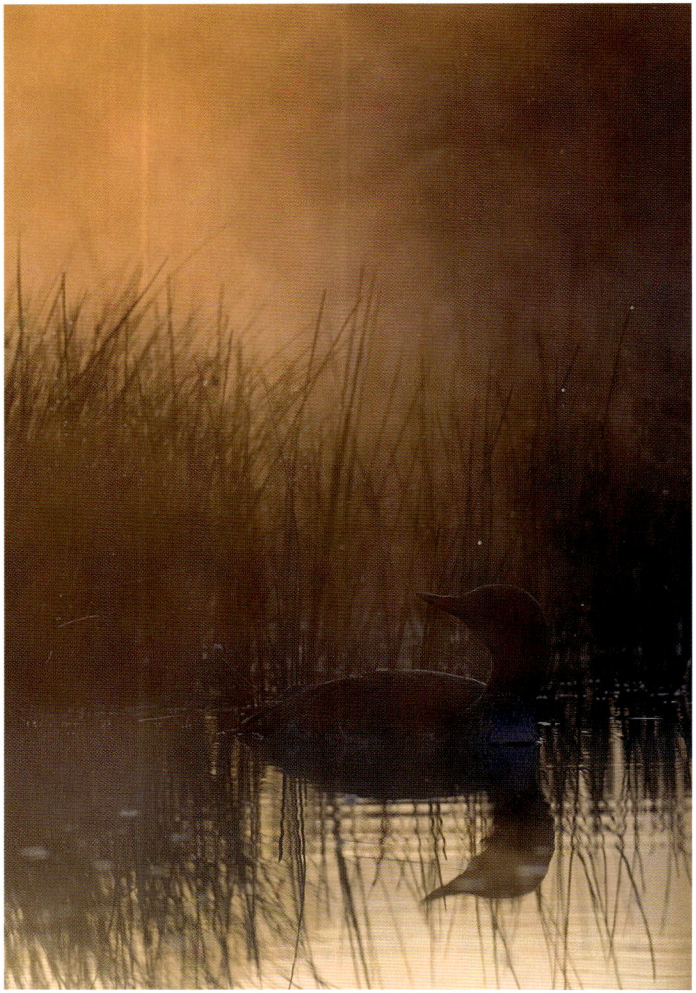

A Red-throated Loon on its nesting pond in the morning fog *(Gavia stellata)*
Canon EOS-1D Mark II N, 500mm f/4.0, 1/500 second, f/6.3, ISO 320, one-shot focus with a central focusing point, Gitzo tripod, Manfrotto 501 video head, blind. Vaala, Finland, July 2010.

A Lammergeir in the fog *(Gypaetus barbatus)*
Canon EOS-1D Mark IV, 500mm f/4.0, 1/2000 second, f/7.0. ISO 800, one-shot focus with a central focusing point, Gitzo tripod, Manfrotto 501 video head, blind. Spain, November 2010.

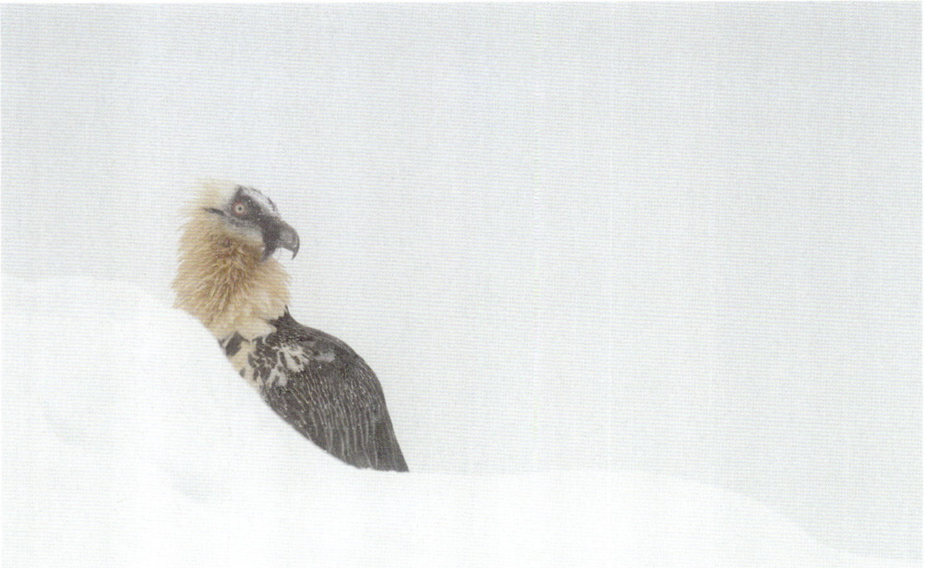

Markus Varesvuo

Fog and Mist

At worst, fog can totally ruin any notions of photography for a full day, or days even, but at best it's a great element in an image. A thick blanket of fog on a cloudy day doesn't offer many photo opportunities because finding and seeing birds can be difficult. But you can try taking minimalist pictures, where the background is a subdued gray and the smooth diffuse light softens the lines, edges, and colors.

As a supporting element in an image, mist is at its best in early morning and late evening, when the sun is tinting the misty tendrils with its rays, or in landscape shots, where blankets of fog, floating like magic carpets over the silent land, add interest and atmosphere to an image.

The best times for fog on Red-throated Loons' breeding ponds are the clear and calm late summer mornings, when fog after a cold night condenses over a still relatively warm pond and watery bog.

In the Lammergeier flight shot, the clouds break up just enough to let the sun shine on the mountains, which

A Lammergeier and the mountains in fog *(Gypaetus barbatus)*
Canon EOS-1D Mark IV, 500mm f/4.0, 1/2000 second, f/10.0, ISO 800, continuous focus with an extended central focusing point, Gitzo tripod, Manfrotto 501 video head, blind. Spain, November 2010.

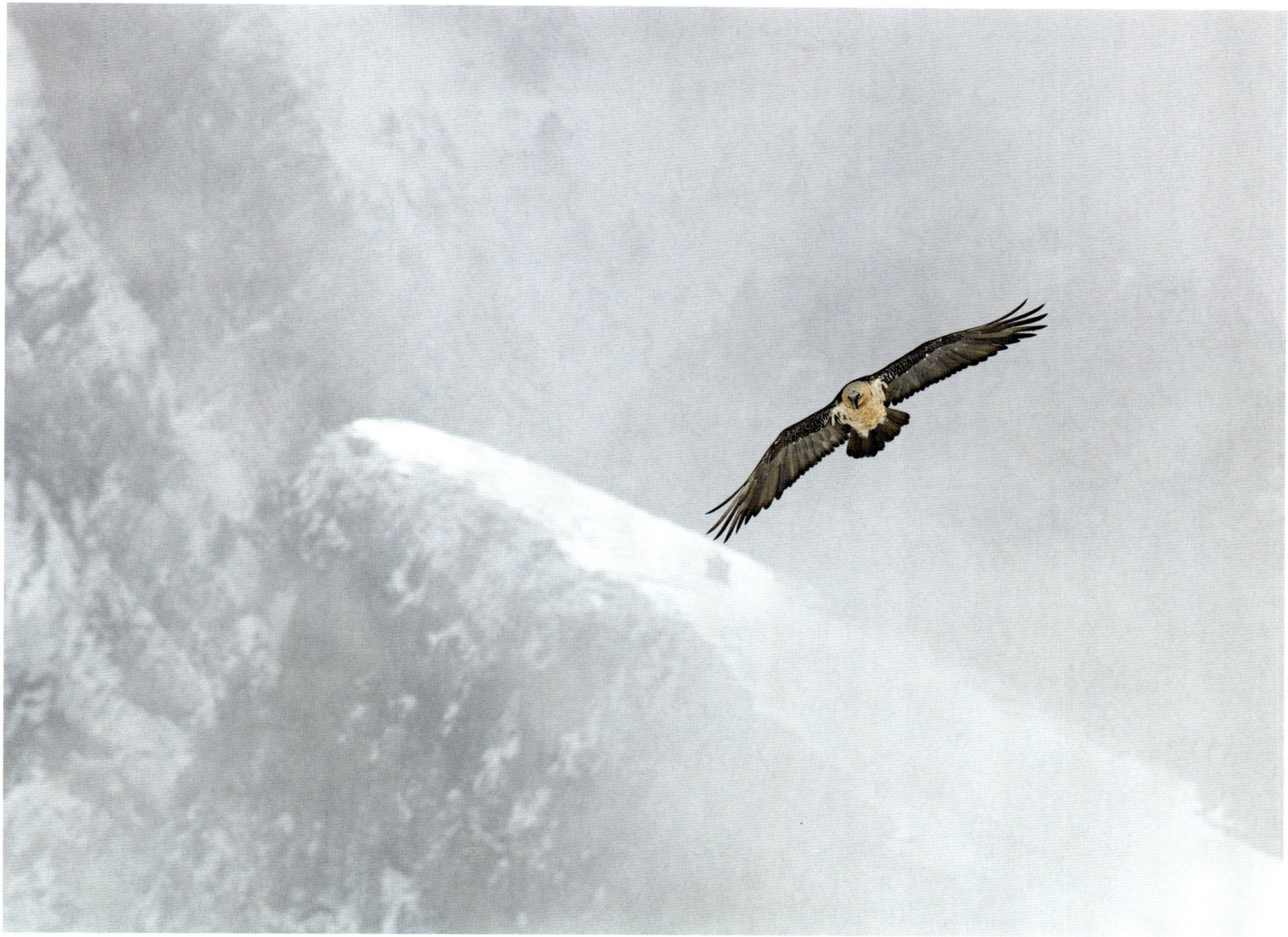

Markus Varesvuo

are partially in the fog. There is no fog between the photographer and the subject, and the Lammergeier is lit by diffuse reflection off the snow and a touch of direct sunlight.

Frost

In extreme cold weather, the birds' breath steams up and the moisture clings to their feathers and creates frost in the cold air. Most often this is visible around the head, but it can also be seen on their backs because birds often bury their bills in the feathers on their backs for warmth while they rest.

Also, when the dew point is very close to the temperature, vapor begins to condense and create frost on branches and trees. Frosty branches are a lovely setting for bird photographs.

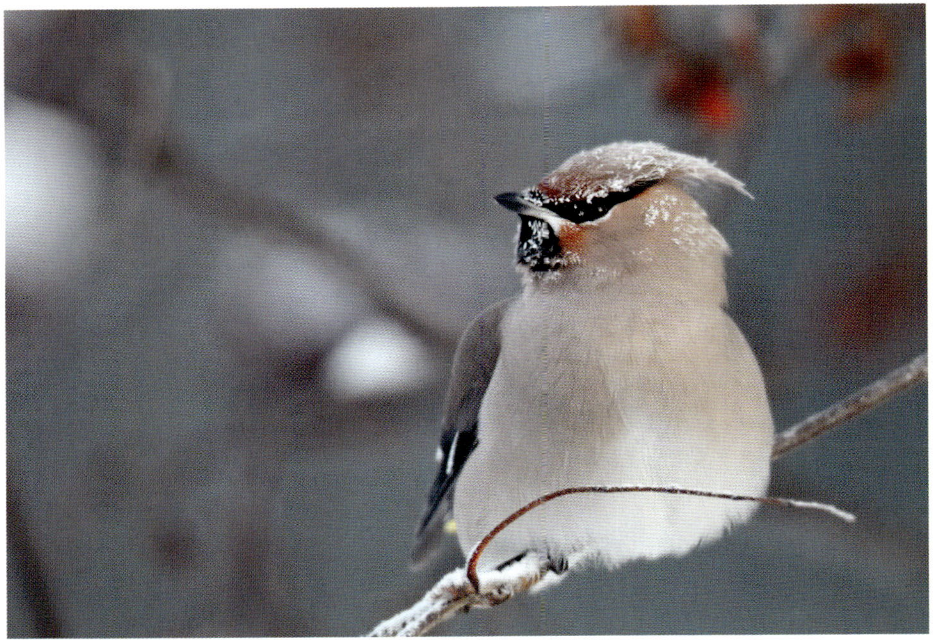

Markus Varesvuo

A frosty-faced Bohemian Waxwing *(Bombycilla garrulus)*
Canon EOS-1D Mark IV, 800mm f/5.6, 1/125 second, f/7.0, ISO 1600, one-shot focus with a central focusing point, Gitzo tripod, Manfrotto 501 video head. Kuusamo, Finland, January 2010.

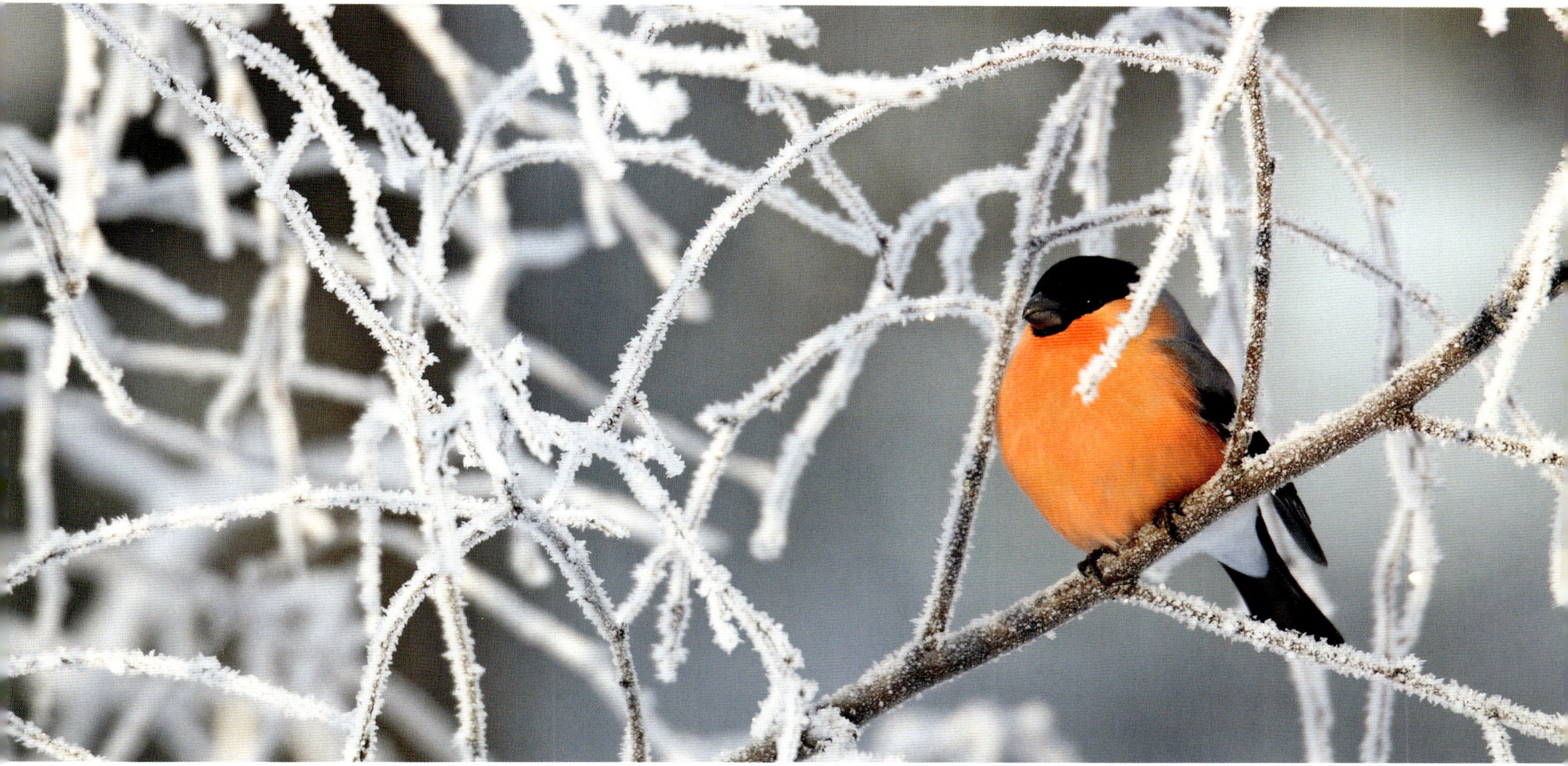

Markus Varesvuo

A Eurasian Bullfinch among frosty branches *(Pyrrhula pyrrhula)*

Canon EOS-1Ds Mark III, 500mm f/4.0 plus 1.4x extender, 1/500 second, f/6.3, ISO 800, one-shot focus with a central focusing point, Gitzo tripod, Manfrotto 501 video head. Kuusamo, Finland, January 2008.

BENCE MÁTÉ

LIGHT

A good image is made with good light.

Light is probably the most important element in a photo. Its direction, intensity, and diffusion have a huge impact on your image. If you photograph a rabbit mating with a fox but the light isn't good, you have a document of an interesting event, but you don't have a great photograph. This chapter looks at light in nature.

Front Light

Photographing animals is easiest when light hits them from behind the camera. The light metering is simple, the subject's colors come out nicely, the shadows are soft, and with the sunlight behind you there is no lens flare. Front light is comfortable, which explains why about 80 percent of nature photos are taken in it.

Backlight

Backlight causes a number of difficulties, which may be why it's not very popular among photographers. But it can give an image a special atmosphere and enhance shapes and forms. I always try to imagine the ideal light before starting a photo project. Sometimes I can see in advance that the effects of backlighting are more important than the colors of the subject, so I face my camera toward the source of light. The Black Grouse and the Pygmy Cormorants are excellent examples of the power of backlight. Neither image would have been as compelling had they been shot in basic front light. Anything that lets light shine through, such as water drops, fog, ice, feathers, fine sand, or dust, are especially good for backlight.

Basic front light situations often last for quite a long time, whereas great backlight opportunities quickly end. Sunrises and sunsets are fast, and the angle of light keeps changing. The wider the angle, the harsher the light; it creates stark contrasts between light and shadow, and it does not contour the subject evenly and softly.

Automatic light metering is not helpful in backlight conditions because the light is so uneven that the brightness among different parts of the picture may differ by up to 10 f-stops. No automatic system can compute what kind of exposure you need in a situation like backlight. Manual mode yields better results.

The closer the source of light (for example, the sun) is to the optical axis, the stronger and more extensive the effect created by backlight. With light

The sun shining straight toward the blind helps bring out the Black Grouse's breath, steaming in the cold air *(Tetrao tetrix)*
Nikon D200, Sigma 300–800mm f/5.6, 1/640 second, 650mm, f/7.1, ISO 400, continuous focus with a central focusing point, beanbag. Pernaja, Finland, April 2007.

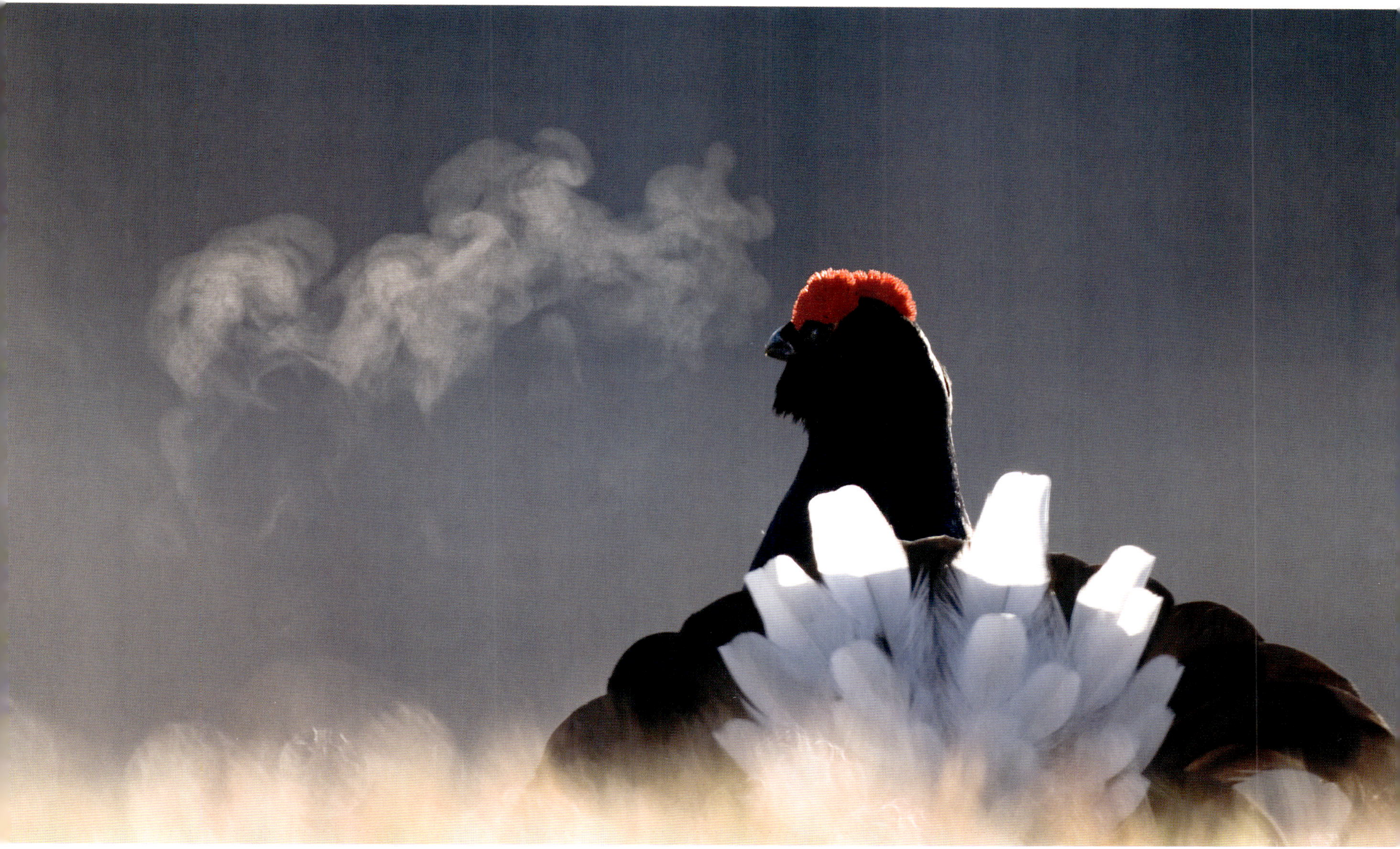

Bence Máté

Bence Máté

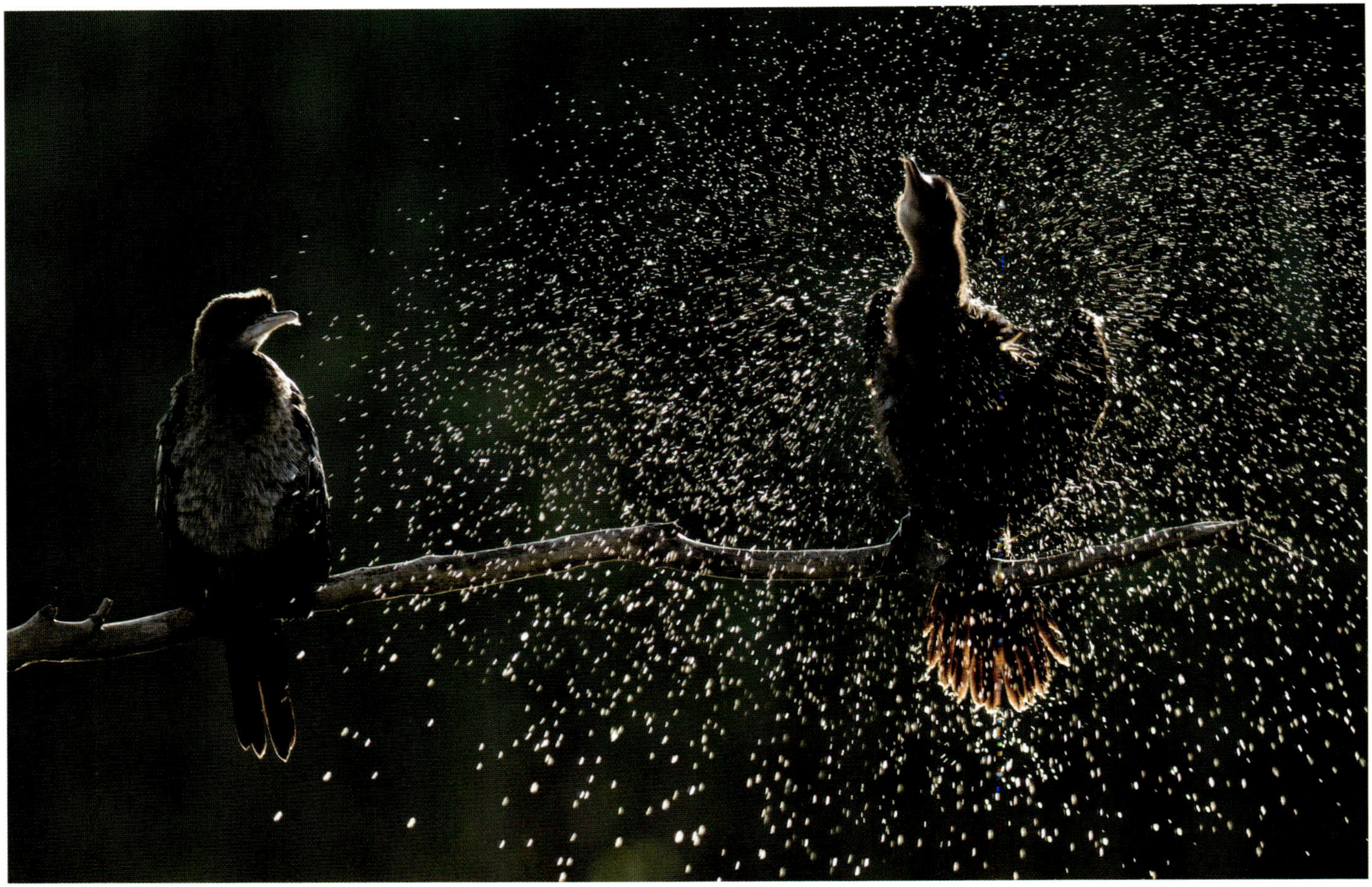

The backlit water drops stand out clearly against the dark background as these Pygmy Cormorants dry their feathers *(Phalacrocorax pygmaeus)*

Nikon D300, 300mm f/2.8, 1/640 second, f/2.8, ISO 200, continuous focus with a central focusing point, Gitzo tripod and video head, blind. Hortobágy, Hungary, August 2008.

coming straight toward the camera, the unusual angle of light easily creates lens flare. You can work around this by using a lens shade, preferably one that is longer than those that are commercially available. In permanent blinds this is solved with an overhang. The farther it protrudes, the better the shade. Ideally it can jut out 2–3 m (6.5–10 ft) without bothering the birds or blocking your field of vision.

When you photograph toward light, the background is usually in shade, but there may be details that could reflect light and thus create unwanted sparkling in the image. Sometimes this can be good, as the Great Reed-Warbler image beautifully demonstrates. The sparkling sunshine reflecting off the dark water in the background is what makes this image.

Bence Máté

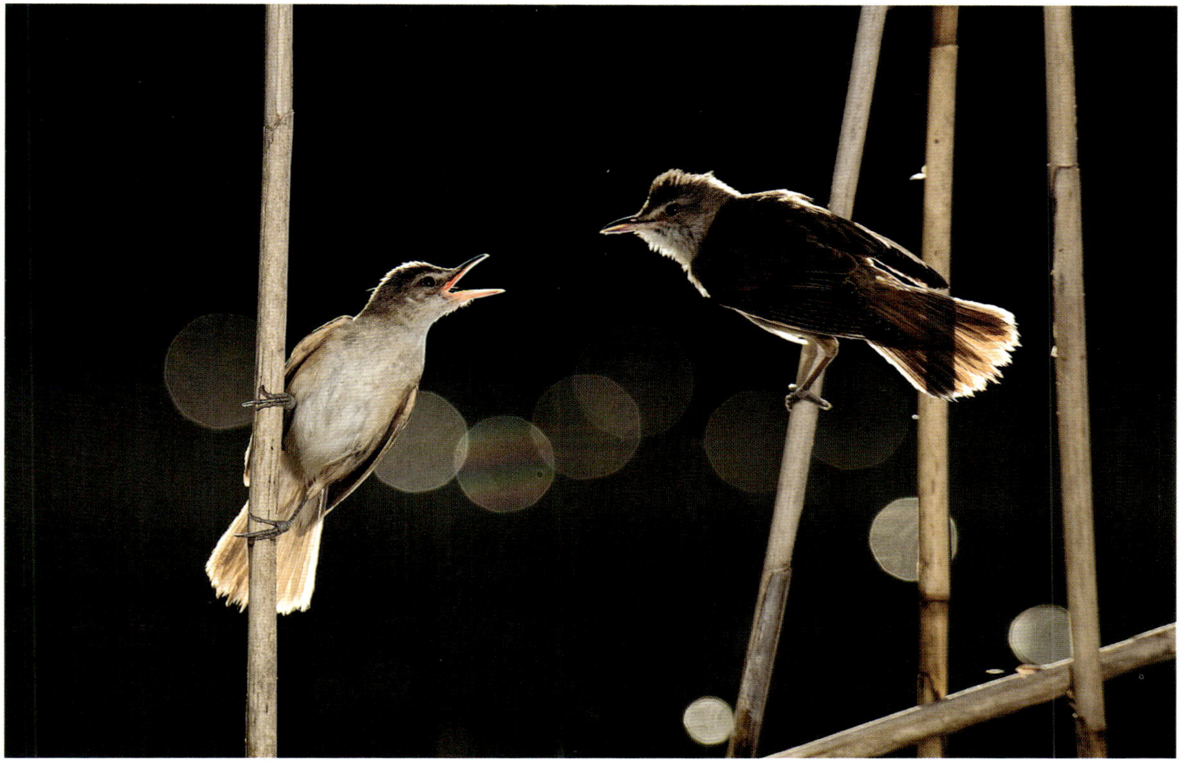

Light coming from behind the subject hits the rippling water and reflects the colors of the reeds, creating a nice background for the Great Reed-Warbler *(Acrocephalus arundinaceus)*
Nikon D700, 300mm f/2.8, 1/6400 second, f/5.0, ISO 1000, two Nikon SB-800 flashes, manual focus, Gitzo tripod and video head, floating blind. Pusztaszer, Hungary, June 2010.

Diffused Light

Good weather for photography seldom means full sunshine from sunrise to sunset. Cloudless, blue sky is good for about two hours after sunrise and before sunset, but in the middle of the day and in the afternoon cloudy weather is ideal because it offers softer, more even light that suits photography better, and the contrasts between light and shadow are softer. Midday light comes from one source that creates strong shadows.

Bird Photography at Night

Artificial light makes it possible to photograph in situations where digital sensors are not sensitive enough. However, it is difficult to light the whole image

Bence Máté

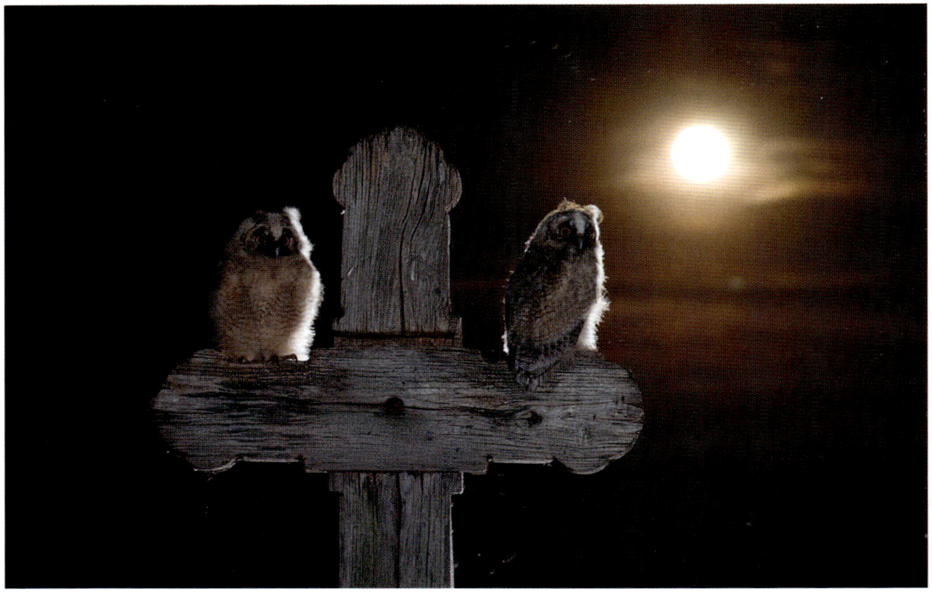

The backlight effect comes from photographing against the moon, and a stroboscopic flash behind the Long-eared Owls further enhances the effect, while also exposing the insects flying in the air around the birds *(Asio otus)*
Nikon D300, 300mm f/2.8, 5 seconds, f/7.1, ISO 200, Canon Speedlite 550EX flash, manual focus, Gitzo tripod and video head. Pusztaszer, Hungary, June 2008.

with a flash and get natural-looking results. Moreover, even if it resembles lightning, a flash can frighten birds as they are roosting or hunting, so be extremely cautious. Pushing the existing, natural light as far as possible and using flash to give some extra light can yield good results. You can read more in the chapter "Sources of Light."

Lightning

Lightning is one of nature's greatest shows, and it has always fascinated people. I try to go out every time there is thunder and lightning to photograph my favorite subjects in its light. Being able to get the lightning in the image is great, but even if I don't, strong lightning is a good source of light for taking pictures.

Sunlight weakens the dramatic effect, so photographing lightning or in its light is best done when there is very little light or full darkness. Exposing is relatively simple: use bulb exposure (the shutter stays open until the shutter release button is pressed again), mount your camera on a tripod, and use a low ISO value to ensure good technical quality. The right aperture is found through trial and error—depending on the intensity of the lightning I set the aperture somewhere between maximum and f/22.0. Note that many lenses do not have infinity at the end of their range of focus; instead, you focus the lens manually while it is still light outside, and then you lock the focus ring with tape so it doesn't move. I learned this the hard way during a couple of thunderstorms when I fumbled in the darkness and had only blurry, useless images to take home.

During exposure I try to anticipate the lightning and figure out where it is likely to strike and how I can get it in my image. At some point I decide that the lens has collected enough light, so I press the shutter and start a new bulb exposure. This is a very exciting game—be careful because it can be addictive.

Bence Máté

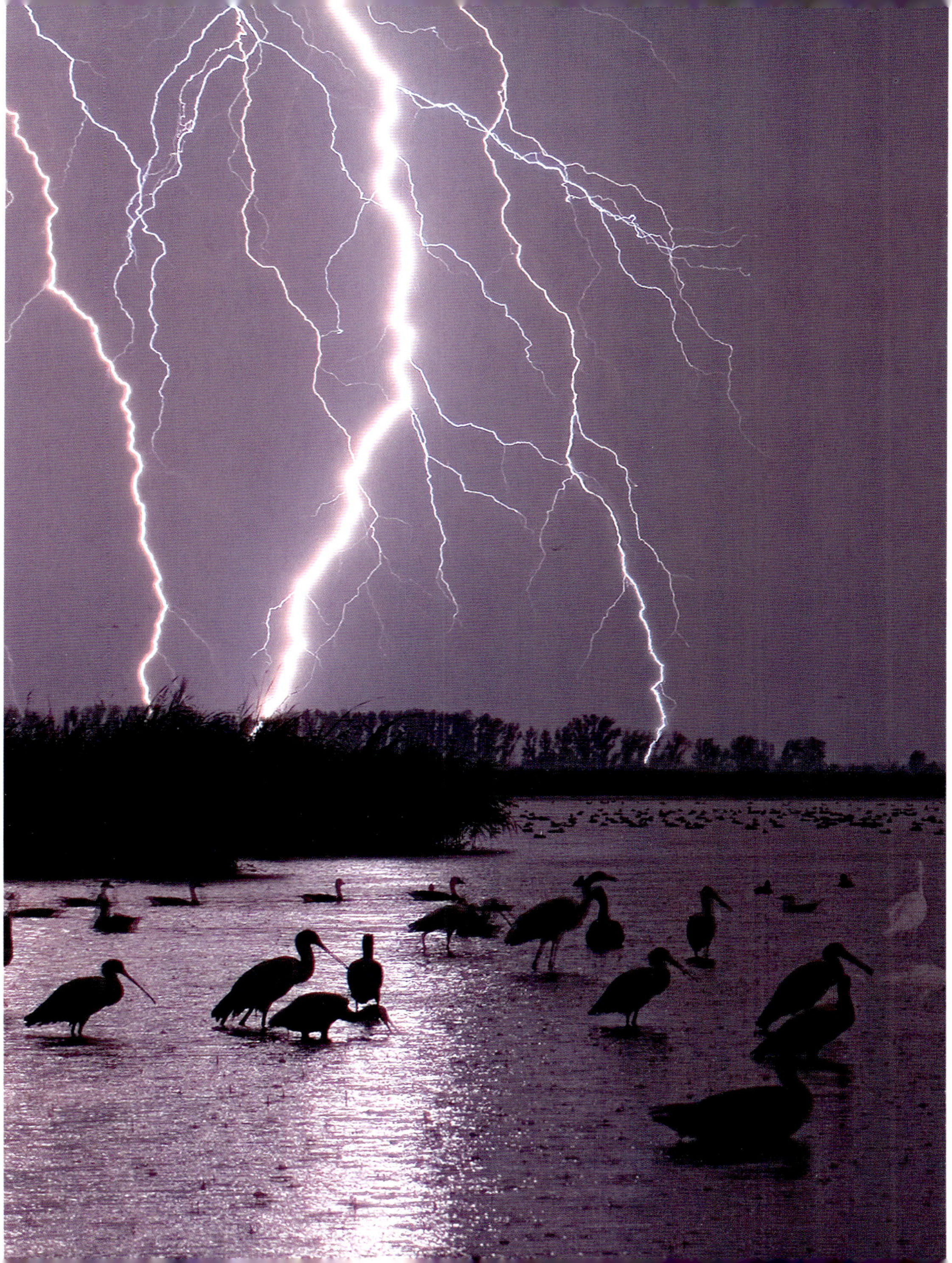

Lightning illuminates Eurasian Spoonbills and Graylag Geese roosting in nocturnal darkness *(Platalea leucorodia, Anser anser)*
Canon 300D, 28–80mm f/4.0, 30 seconds, 69mm, f/8.0, ISO 100, manual focus, Gitzo tripod and video head, blind. Pusztaszer, Hungary, July 2006.

Aurora Borealis

Photographers near the polar regions should follow websites that track and forecast the aurora borealis. In addition to being a spectacular natural phenomenon, the aurora lights the night sky and creates very interesting lighting conditions. For a photographer they are very much like lightning strikes but are weaker in intensity. As digital camera sensor technology advances, there are likely to be new opportunities to photograph birds in the light of the aurora borealis. I have not yet seen a nice image of a bird glowing in the aurora borealis; it is high time someone took it.

Moonlight

Photographing birds in moonlight—or, to be precise, sunlight reflected off the moon—is a technique where you can come up with something new relatively easily. As a rule, people are not nocturnal creatures. We are usually fast asleep at night instead of out taking great new images. Even if you don't get the moon in the image, with long exposure times you can get some spectacular shots revealing a world that is normally hidden from us. I strongly recommend magical nighttime excursions to all nature photographers!

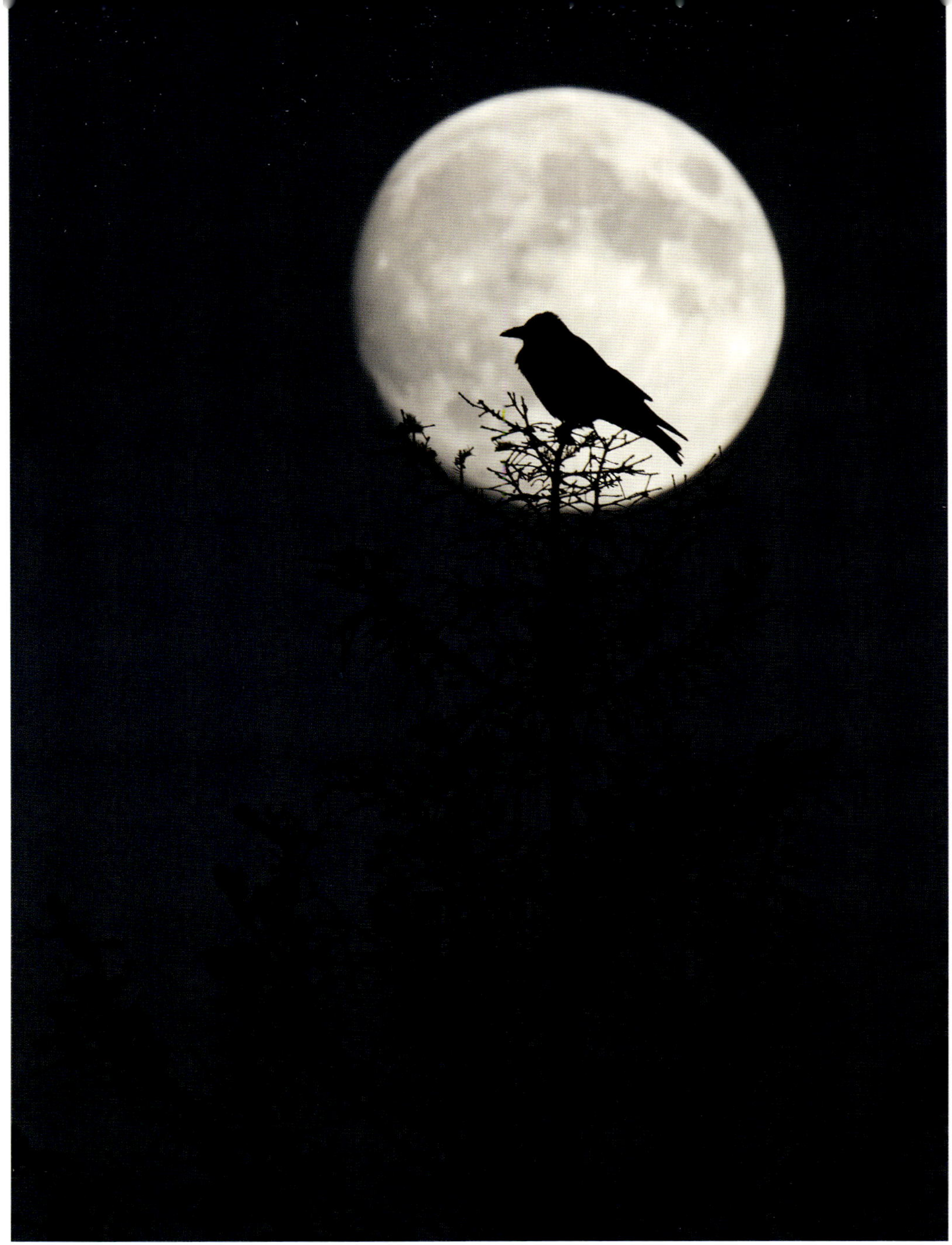

Markus Varesvuo

A Common Buzzard *(Buteo buteo)*
Nikon D300, 300mm f/2.8, 1/1000 second, f/2.8, ISO 1000, continuous focus with a central focusing point, Gitzo tripod and video head, blind. Pusztaszer, Hungary, January 2008.

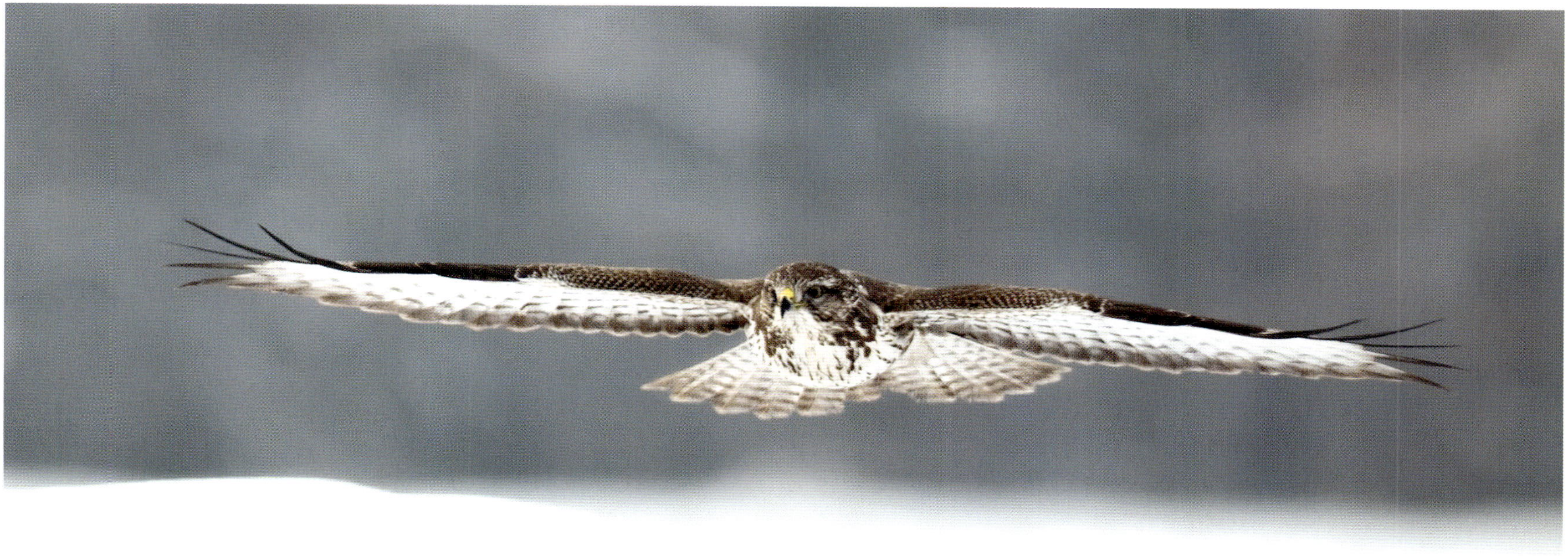

Bence Máté

A Hooded Crow photographed against the moonlight *(Corvus corone cornix)*
Canon EOS-1Ds Mark III, 500mm f/4.0 plus 1.4x extender, 1/20 second, f/45, ISO 800, one-shot focus with a central focusing point, mirror lockup and 2-second self-timer mode, Gitzo tripod, Manfrotto 501 video head. Helsinki, Finland, December 2007.

Reflected Light Is the Best Light

Even natural light often comes from several directions, for example on shores or in snow-covered landscapes. Reflected light can be very useful because it helps reduce shadows in the image. It is hard to think of another situation as ideal for photography as a snowy landscape that reflects light back into the air; your subject is lit practically from every direction, as if it were in a studio.

Moreover, while it beautifully lights the underparts of a flying bird, diffuse reflection off snow also has an effect on the shadowy parts in the image. In sunny weather, if the light reflecting off a snowy bank hits a forest in the shadow, the shade turns bluish. The effect is emphasized in photos.

In the Black Woodpecker image, light is hitting the wings directly from

A Black Woodpecker in flight against the taiga *(Dryocopus martius)*
Canon EOS-1D Mark III, 70–200mm f/2.8, 1/2500 second, 85mm, f/7.1, ISO 1600, continuous focus with 45 focusing points, Manfrotto 501 video head attached to a plank in a blind. Posio, Finland, February 2008.

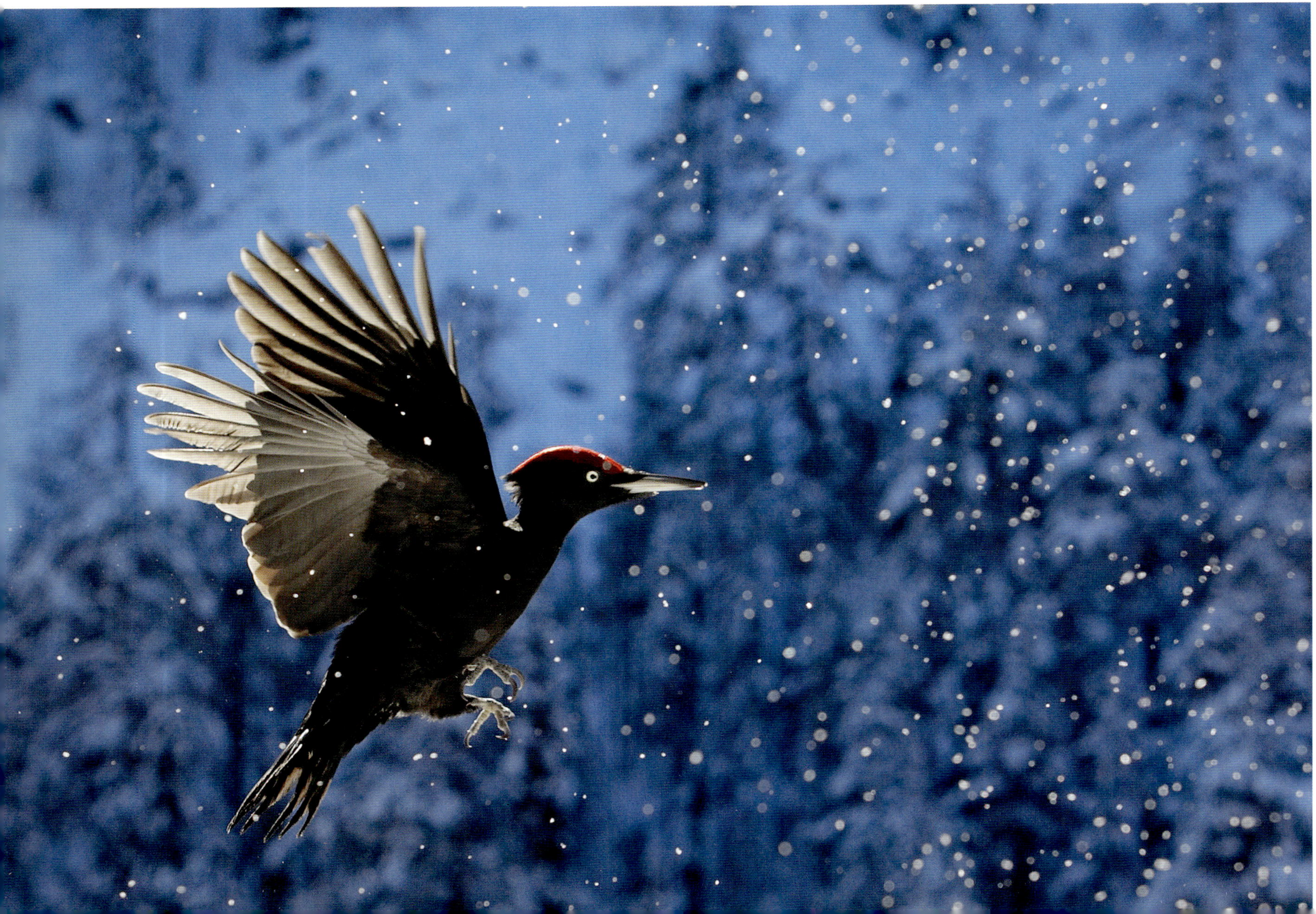

Markus Varesvuo

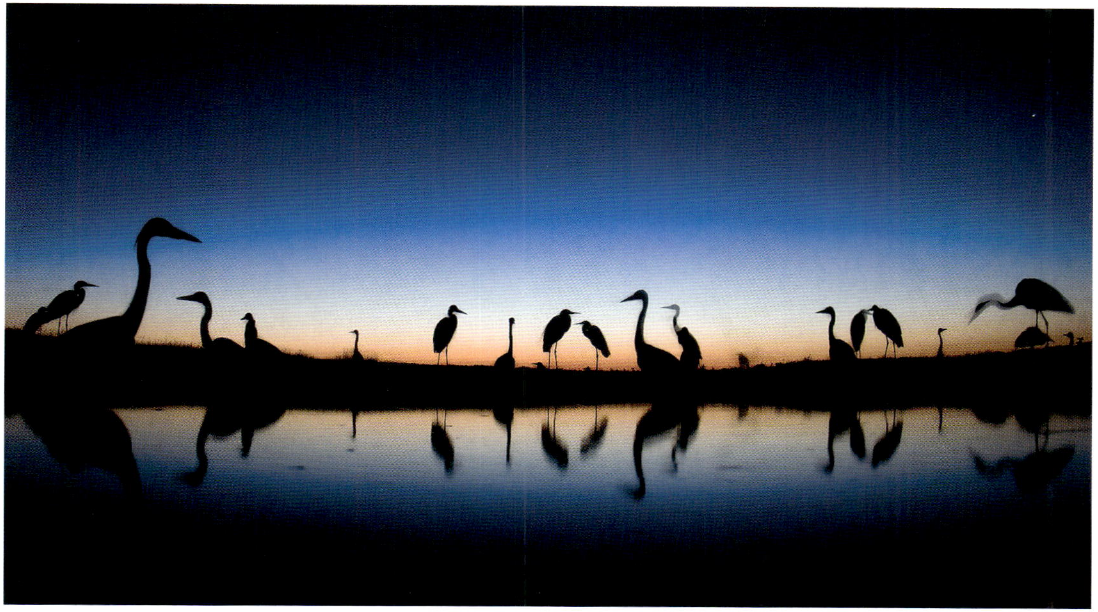

Bence Máté

Gray Herons at dawn *(Ardea cinerea)*
Nikon D300, Tokina 10–17mm f/3.5–4.5, 4 seconds, 13mm, f/9.0, ISO 200, manual focus, remote controlled head, blind. Hungary, Pusztaszer, July 2009.

behind but also by reflecting off the snow. What's more, the diffuse reflection off the snow is turning the snowy forest blue in the shadows. There is also an added effect of falling snow because wind was blowing snow off the trees.

Where there are wide expanses of light sand, like on shores or in the desert, there is the same diffuse reflection off sand as there is off snow, which casts light on the underparts of flying birds. Water reflects light too, which is discussed in the chapter "Water as an Element in a Bird Photo."

Indirect light can create great lighting, for instance after sunset or before sunrise, when the rays color the horizon with splendid hues of red and yellow—the effects can be stunning. The image of the Gray Herons standing in the water, with the light blue horizon in the background, was taken more than an hour after sunset. The sun is not visible in the image, but its light hit the dust particles floating in the air and painted the landscape in an array of rosy hues.

BENCE MÁTÉ

ISO SETTINGS IN DIFFERENT SITUATIONS

Always use the lowest possible ISO value.

I'm in the last wave of photographers who learned to photograph with film cameras, and I can fully appreciate the fact that I can change my camera's sensitivity to light, on the run, with one button. I've been photographing for about 13 years—almost half of it with a film camera. Slow film speed was the biggest challenge in bird photography. Nobody in their right mind used film speed over ISO 400. If you wanted beautifully reproduced colors with no grain, you had to use Fuji Velvia, a very slow film with an ISO of 50. Digital cameras today produce the same image quality at ISO 1000 as Velvia does at ISO 50, which is the biggest single reason behind the revolution that took place in bird photography in the few years during the change from film to digital.

How should you use your digital camera? What are its technical limits, and what ISO values should you use in different situations? Never mind the leaps taken in technology—you can't bend the laws of physics. The rule still applies that the lower the ISO value, the better the quality of your image. So when you do not need a fast shutter speed, stop down one or two f-stops and lower the ISO as much as possible to result in less noise, better colors, and better overall picture quality. Low ISO values will also give you more range for sharpening the image with little to no loss of quality.

One option is to use auto ISO, which automatically alters the ISO setting to get the right exposure for the given aperture and shutter speed combination, but I don't use it. In bird photography, I prefer to adjust the aperture, shutter speed, and ISO myself to suit each situation.

I set the shutter speed based on my subject, normally either to 1/2 second to 1/100 second, or faster than 1/1000 second. Other values are either too fast for motion blur or too slow to freeze movement.

When I want to emphasize motion in an image, I go for a low ISO to guarantee the best possible image quality. Then I set the shutter speed as described earlier, and then I adjust the aperture according to the exposure meter. Don't worry if your background is busy or ugly because the movement will blend the elements together as the camera tracks the subject. Watch out for diffraction, though, because it will weaken the image quality when the aperture is smaller than f/11.0—I don't use a smaller aperture unless I absolutely have to.

When you want to use the fastest shutter speed possible, use the largest aperture and raise the ISO as high as you can without getting too much noise in the image. If I can get shutter speeds of 1/1000 second to 1/2000 second, I will use these settings, but if they produce a faster shutter speed than I deem necessary based on experience, I lower the ISO or stop down 0.5 to 2.0 f-stops, which helps improve the image quality.

The highest possible ISO varies from one camera to another; it is also one of the fastest developing areas in digital camera technology. As of this writing, photographing birds with ISO 12800 produced good-quality images; for

Bence Máté

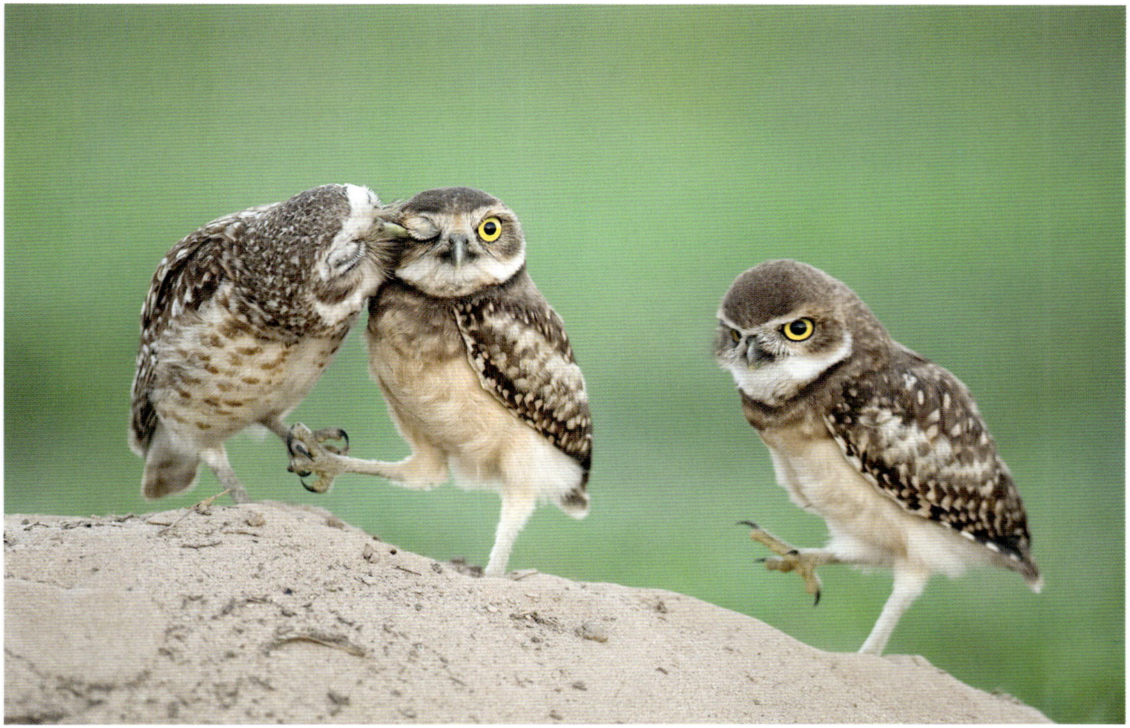

Burrowing Owls in the low light of twilight just after sunset *(Athene cunicularia)*
Nikon D700, 300mm f/2.8, 1/320 second, f/2.8, ISO 1600, manual focus, Gitzo tripod and video head, blind. Pantanal, Brazil, November 2009.

Bence Máté

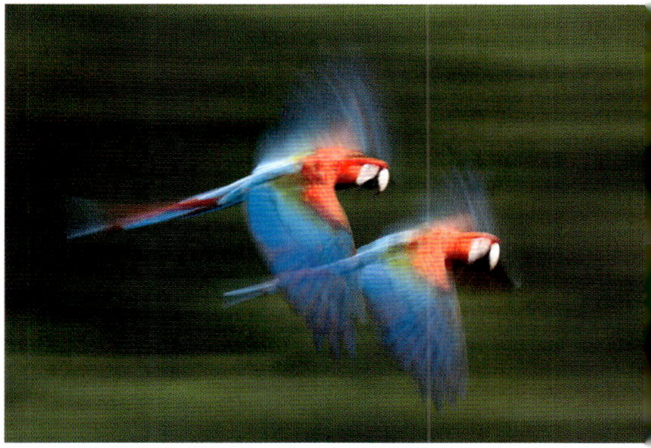

A shutter speed of 1/13 second was just slow enough to create motion blur with the movement of the Red-and-green Macaws and the background *(Ara chloropterus)*
Nikon D700, Sigma 300–800mm f/5.6, 1/13 second, 650mm, f/16.0, ISO 100, continuous focus, Gitzo tripod and video head. Buraco das Araras, Brazil, February 2010.

example, see the Golden Eagles in the chapter "Bird Photographer's Camera."

These settings aren't absolute, they are just settings that I use most often in the field. In bird photography, sometimes even 1/4000 second is not enough to freeze movement, so I improvise all the time, adjusting to the situation and the circumstances. A photographer has to evaluate each situation and decide how to prioritize shutter speed, image quality, and depth of field to get the best results.

BENCE MÁTÉ

COMPOSITION AND CROPPING

In a well-composed image every element supports the composition.

In the Field and at the Computer

There are no hard-and-fast rules on how to compose a perfect image; there are many contributing factors that cannot easily be listed in any order of importance. Composition is successful when the elements in the image are in balance and are connected to one another, and nothing seems disjointed.

In a good image, each element supports the composition and has a role to play. Small details—such as a distracting blade of grass, the cut-off tip of a bill, or a half length of a leg—can ruin an image just the same as a missing detail, something that obviously should have been captured in the image but wasn't. It's not enough to have your subject fully inside the frame, it should have free space around it so it doesn't appear cramped. As a general rule, for a profile shot, the subject should be placed off center so there is more space in the direction the subject is facing (or the direction of motion).

The European Roller image was captured in one of the most memorable moments of my photography career so far. I was photographing European Rollers as they were emptying a nest box in which Starlings, to their misfortune, had already started breeding. I caught the European Roller as it was dragging a Starling chick out of the box, but I was just late enough to miss any chance of getting the composition right. In the image the European Roller is just about to fly head-on into the left side of the frame, severely handicapping the composition.

It's often easiest to place the subject in the center of the frame, but this can be the worst composition. Sometimes it's okay, for example if your subject is flying directly toward the camera and the image requires no extra space on the sides, either vertically or horizontally. Yet we are inundated with center-staged images, especially when there are no good reasons to place the subject in the center. The reason for this is autofocus, which has made it much easier to take sharp images, but you could say that it has been at the expense of good composition.

Autofocus technology has a way to go before it can follow birds accurately. Autofocus is at its fastest when it is used with one central focusing point. When a photographer is shooting a moving subject, it's a struggle to keep the subject within the chosen focusing area. This puts focusing at the top of the list of priorities, and composition takes second place.

An aspect ratio of 3:2 is near perfect for bird photography, but there are quite a few occasions when good composition requires some other ratio. Luckily you can crop afterwards, on a computer.

Quite often it is obvious that photographers did not realize that another format could have been better for a picture

Bence Máté

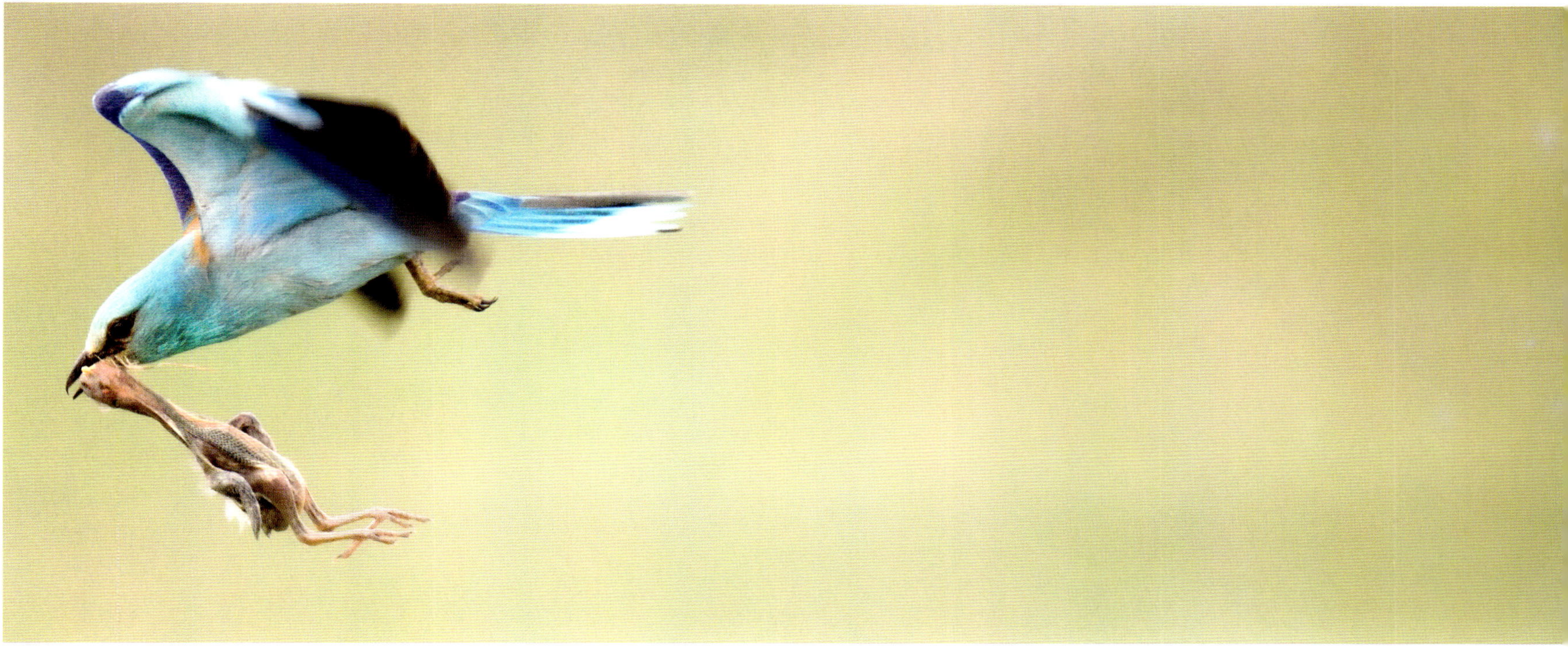

they took. Horizontal is the favored format, but you should teach yourself to recognize situations that would benefit from a vertical composition. A fledgling photographer typically takes only horizontal pictures.

If you're photographing birds by water, always remember to get the subject's reflection in the water. If you cut it off, it can ruin the image almost as much as if the subject itself had been cut off. If you can't photograph the full reflection, try to crop it out as completely as possible. Photographing a reflection is challenging; the bird's smallest movement causes ripples and distorts or breaks the reflection, which you might not notice as you focus in on the subject.

Producing the final image from the digital RAW file is quite a lengthy process, and you may lose sight of the

A European Roller just about to collide with the edge of the frame *(Coracias garrulus)*
Nikon D200, 300mm f/2.8, 1/1000 second, f/2.8, ISO 800, continuous focus with a central focusing point, Gitzo tripod and video head, blind. Pusztaszer, Hungary, May 2007.

compositional aspects of your image and hence fail to recognize its shortcomings, which might stick out like a sore thumb to somebody who sees the image for the first time. If I've been looking at an image for too long, I can flip it horizontally and spot faults that I missed in the original. If the mirror image is just as good as the original, then it passes my composition test.

Cropping an image after capture is necessary, especially in bird photography, regardless of your photographic skills, reaction speed, or painstaking composition in the field. I crop about 90 percent of my images on the computer. I would even say that you can almost never perfectly compose a bird photo in the field. By cropping it on your computer you will most likely enhance its artistic merit.

There is no shame in cropping, because nature photos are not taken in studios where you can control every aspect of your photography. Composition is mainly determined by nature; what the photographer can do is make sure that the opportunities are optimized.

Here are a few examples of composition. The fighting Gray Herons fill the image area from side to side; in fact, they are partly cut off. Part of the left heron's wing is cut off by the left edge of the frame, causing the image to look as if it is tilting toward the left. To make it look better, I cropped the image on the top, bottom, and right edges, which makes the wing of the heron on the right point to the right top corner. A 15 percent crop helped give the image better balance.

The Red-legged Honeycreeper image works best in a horizontal orientation, but the aspect ratio of the camera does not always yield the best possible composition. Luckily, the computer does. Cropping the top and bottom of the image improved the result remarkably.

Ideally, every important element should be included in the image. Sometimes a missing tip of a wing or leg, or even a drop of water that has been split in half by the frame edge, can break the harmony.

All the same, there's no absolute rule saying a bird must always be full in the frame, captured from the tip of its bill to the end of its tail feathers. When you're photographing action at close range, especially if you think the action will not fit in the frame, your instinctive reaction is to back down or grab a wider lens, but sometimes the right thing to do is get even closer and take super closeups.

An image is not balanced if it has empty areas that serve no purpose, or if it is disproportionate or unevenly centered. Almost without exception, cropping improves the result.

Fighting Gray Herons *(Ardea cinerea)*
Canon 300D, Nikon 300mm f/2.8, 1/1000 second, f/5.6, ISO 200, manual focus, Gitzo tripod and video head, blind. Pusztaszer, Hungary, February 2005.

Bence Máté

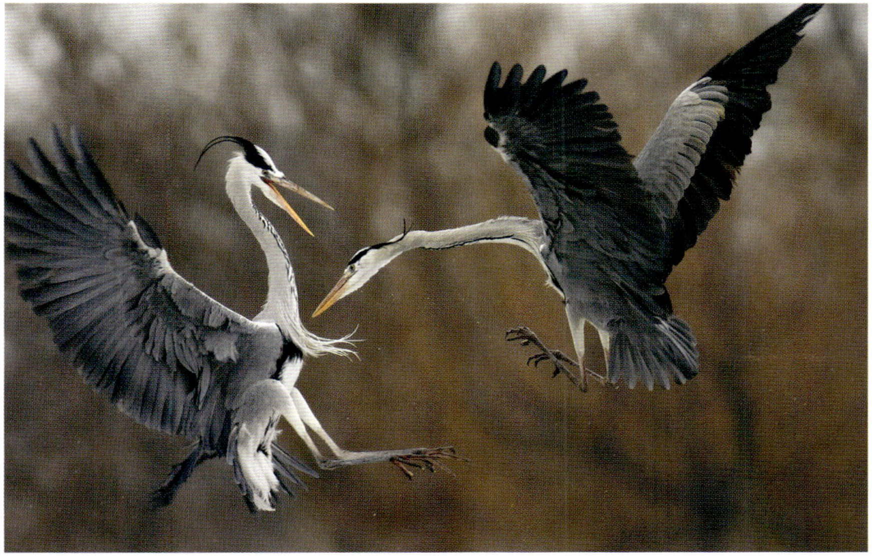

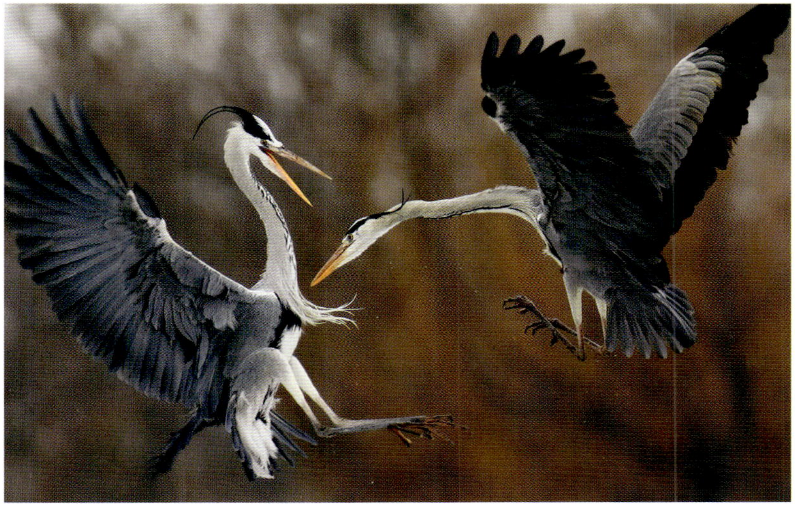

Bence Máté

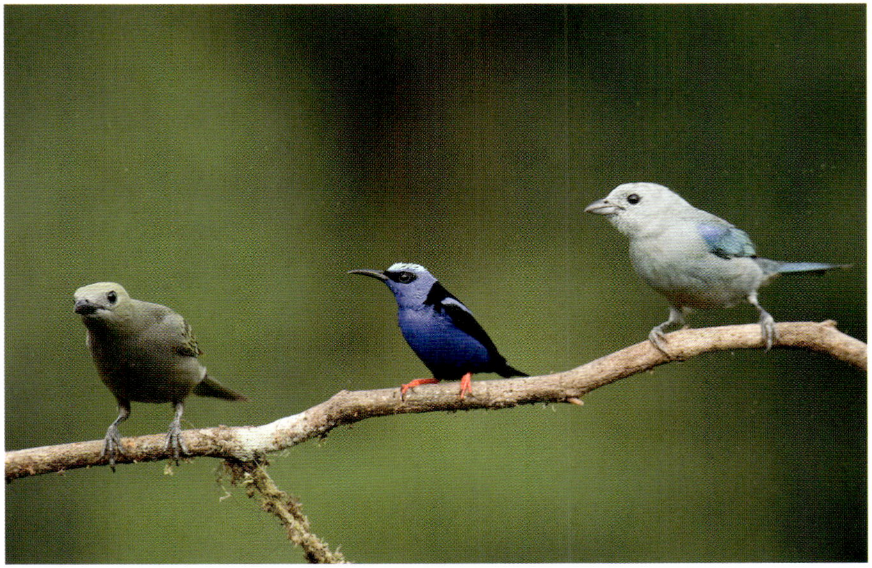

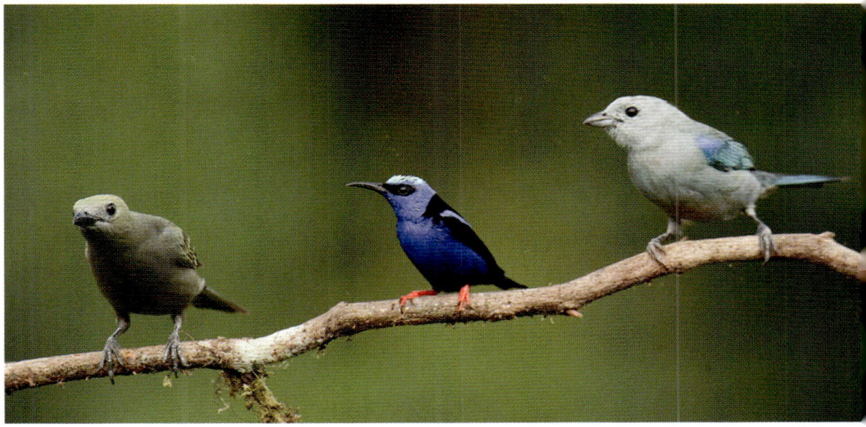

Panorama of Red-legged Honeycreeper *(middle)* and Blue-gray Tanagers *(Cyanerpes cyaneus, Thraupis episcopus)*
Nikon D700, 500mm f/4.0, 1/500 second, f/10.0, ISO 800, Gitzo tripod and video head, blind. Costa Rica, January 2010.

Dalmatian Pelicans *(Pelecanus Crispus)*. Intense cropping, with the subjects filling the entire image area from edge to edge, can sometimes improve the result.
Nikon D200, Sigma 300–800mm f/5.6, 1/400 second, 600mm, f/8.0, ISO 400, continuous focus with a central focusing point, Gitzo tripod and video head, blind. Romania, April 2007.

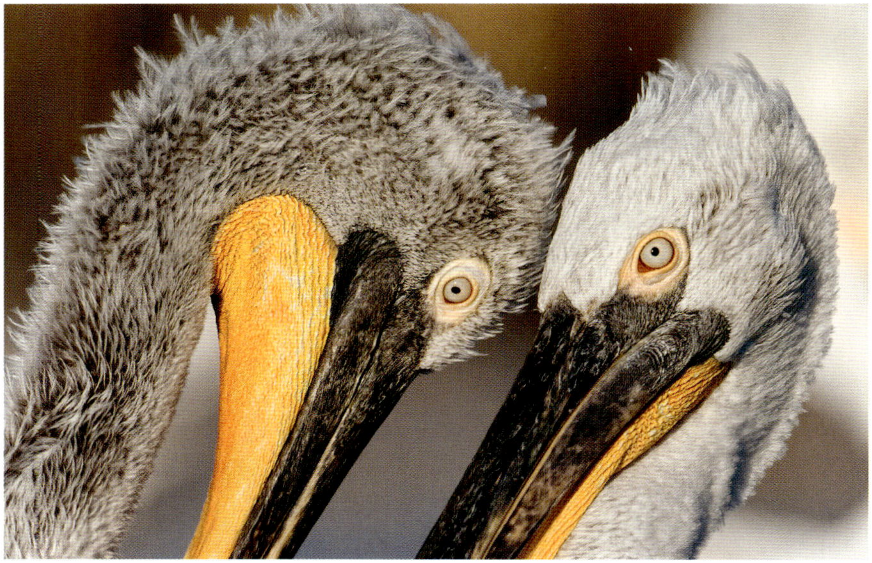

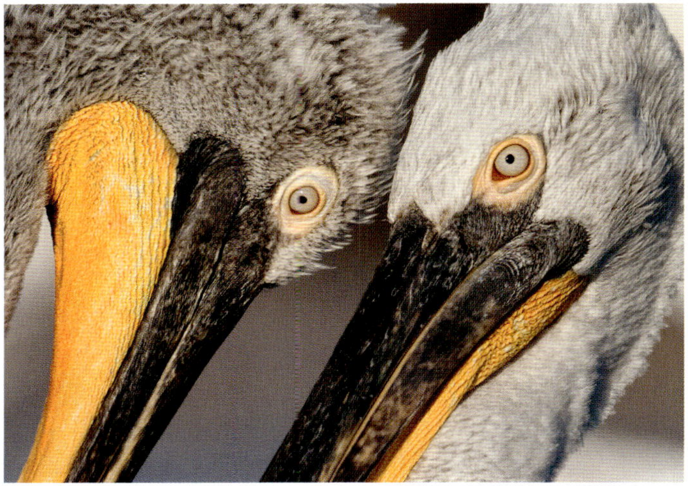

Bence Máté

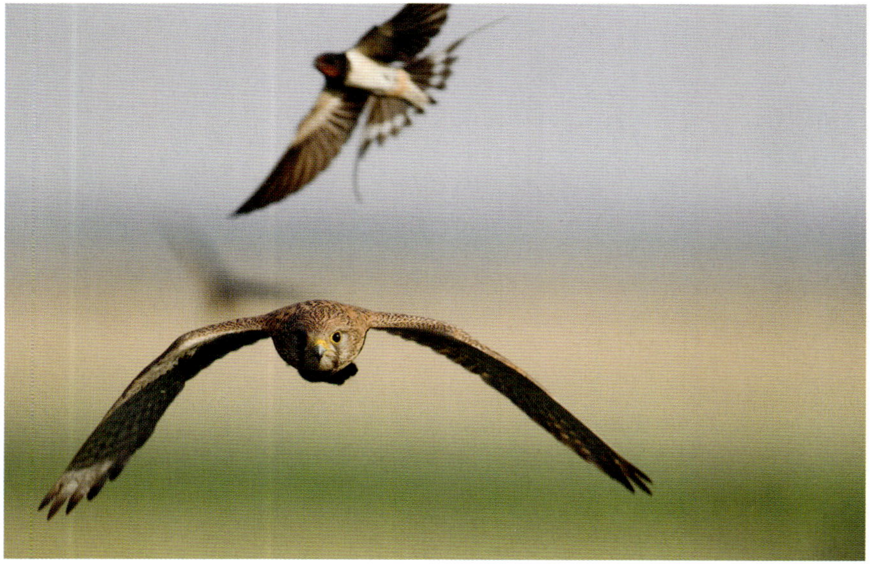

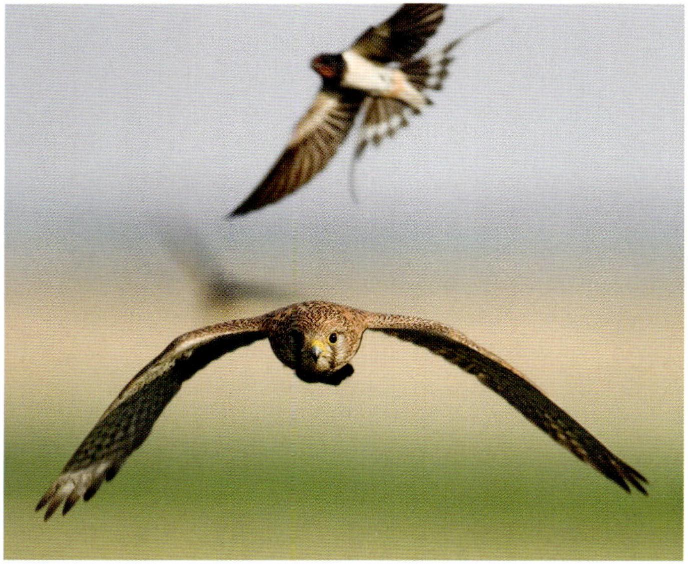

Bence Máté

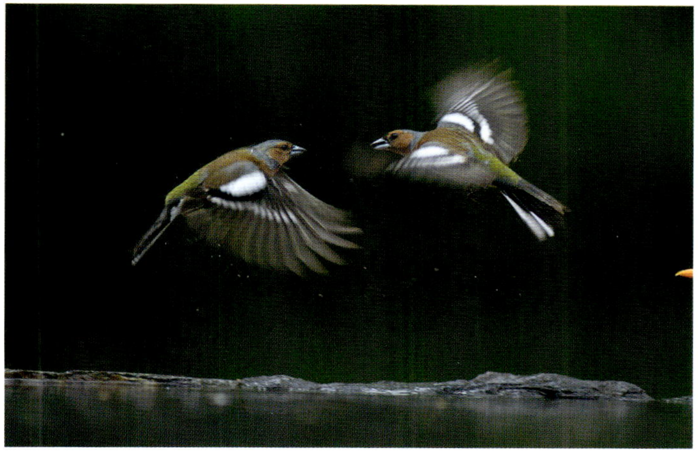

Common Chaffinches fighting *(Fringilla coelebs)*. The image is remarkably better after the rocks at the bottom and the tip of a Blackbird's bill on the right have been trimmed out.
Nikon D200, 300mm f/2.8, 1/640 second, f/2.8, ISO 320, manual focus, Gitzo tripod and video head, blind. Pusztaszer, Hungary, May 2006.

Even in ideal circumstances it is probably impossible to follow a moving subject and not lose control of the composition. There is rarely time in the field to compose every image perfectly, and when you're following a subject with your camera and concentrating on focusing and exposure, you'll undoubtedly capture elements in the image that you don't want. If you're lucky, those elements can be cropped out on the computer. If you are less lucky, they will ruin your image.

Keeping the horizon straight is not always easy, especially in action photography. Always adjust the horizon afterwards, either by cropping or straightening in your image editing software.

Regardless of what you can accomplish on the computer, it is important to do as good a job as possible in the field. Great composition usually means taking advantage of the entire image area, which means the need for cropping is minimized and the image file will stay big.

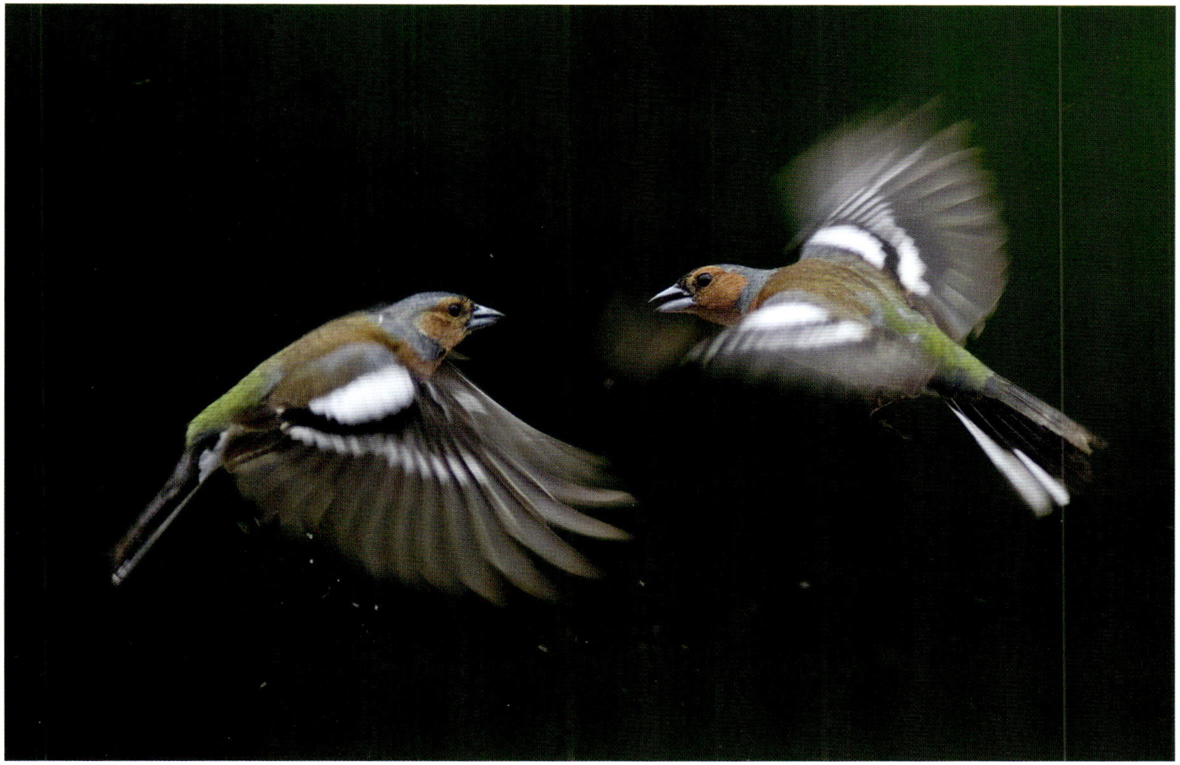

Bence Máté

← **A Barn Swallow mobbing a Eurasian Kestrel *(Falco tinnunculus, Hirundo rustica)*. By cropping the empty space on the right, the image became more balanced.**
Nikon D300, 300mm f/2.8, 1/1600 second, f/2.8, ISO 400, continuous focus, Gitzo tripod and video head, blind. Pusztaszer, Hungary, June 2008.

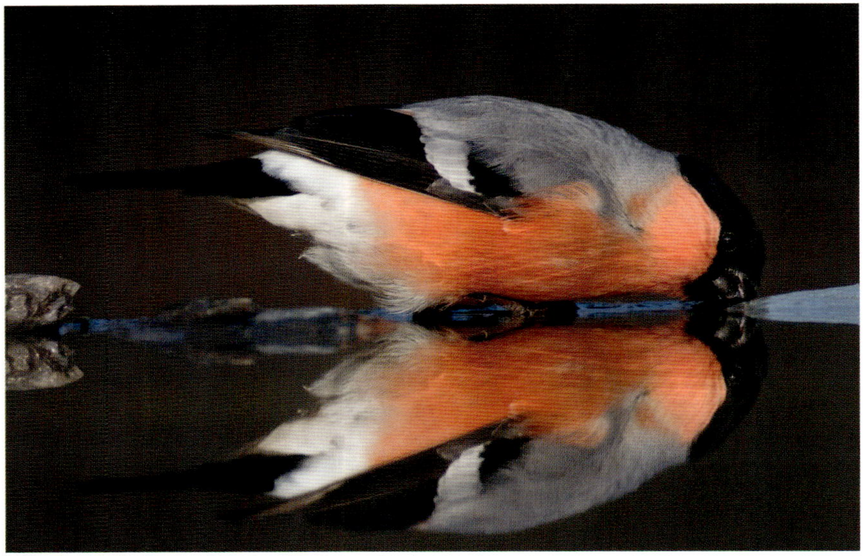

Bence Máté

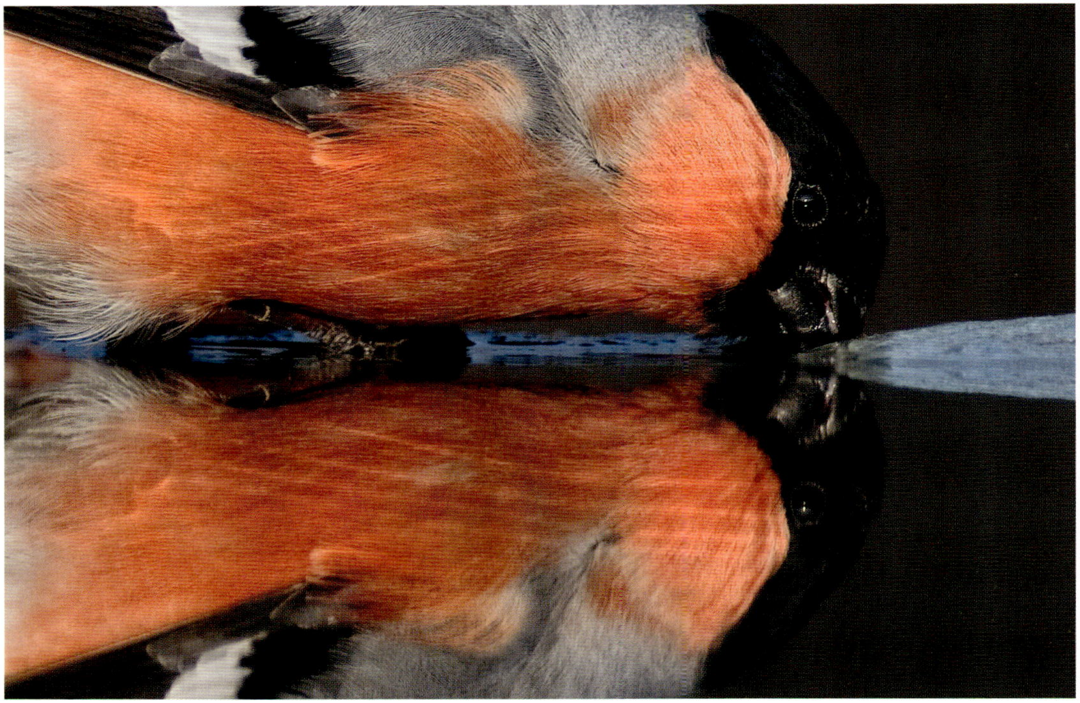

Here the crooked horizon is easily fixed by more tightly cropping the drinking Eurasian Bullfinch *(Pyrrhula pyrrhula)*
Canon 300D, Nikon 300mm f/2.8 plus 1.4x extender, 1/800 second, f/5.6, ISO 200, manual focus, Gitzo tripod and video head, blind. Pusztaszer, Hungary, February 2005.

BENCE MÁTÉ

BACKGROUND AND FOREGROUND

The background is a combination of what nature gives you, how you compose it, the focal length, and the aperture.

The background plays a big role in a nature photo, just as light does. If you're out photographing for a couple of days, you will probably get material that is 90 percent okay, but to win the last 10 percent is much more difficult. It's not enough to have captivating action, perfect light, and interesting perspective; a spot-on photograph requires a perfect background. You need to have figured out the best angle and direction to get a good background before you aim your lens.

The background can bring extra information to the image, something that relates directly to the main subject, such as another bird or a detail that reveals something about the subject's habitat. These extra elements should be soft and out of focus so they don't steal attention from the main subject, yet they should be sharp enough to convey information to the viewer.

Sometimes it's good to stop down far enough to capture every detail sharply in the background to reveal the bird's environment. I aim to include the background in the image whenever it's especially beautiful or when there are so many birds that the world around the main subject adds interest to the image. To get this you need a large depth of field. This requires a wider lens, which leads to a remarkably shorter shooting distance than a telephoto lens. Creating a good composition gets even more difficult because you now need to control all the details in the background, not just the main subject.

Telephoto Lenses Blend Background Elements into a Uniform Backdrop

One option is to have one color in the background, or a mixture of the colors

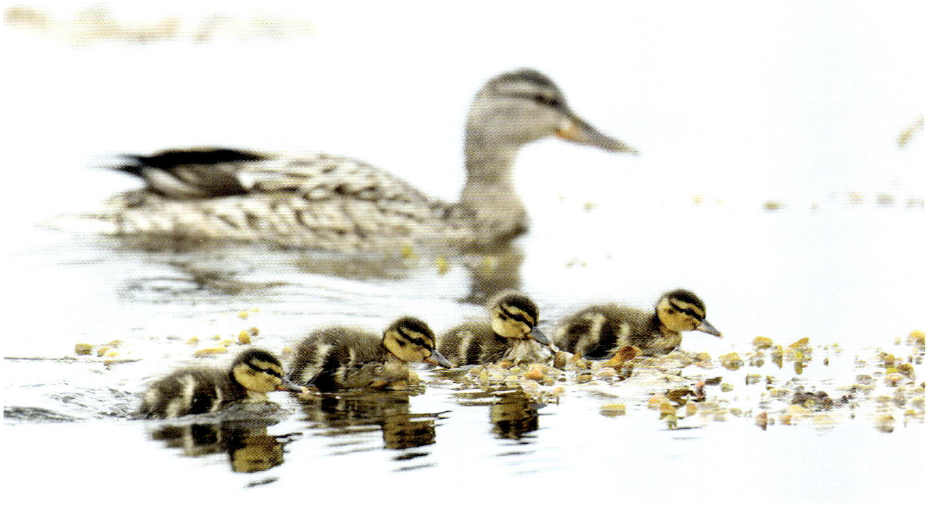

Markus Varesvuo

Mallard brood with parent *(Anas platyrhynchos)*. Left outside the depth of field, the blurred parent provides additional information in the image but lets the young claim the main stage. Canon EOS-1D Mark III, 500mm f/4.0, 1/1600 second, f/5.0, ISO 1600, Gitzo tripod, Manfrotto 501 video head, blind. Parainen, Finland, May 2009.

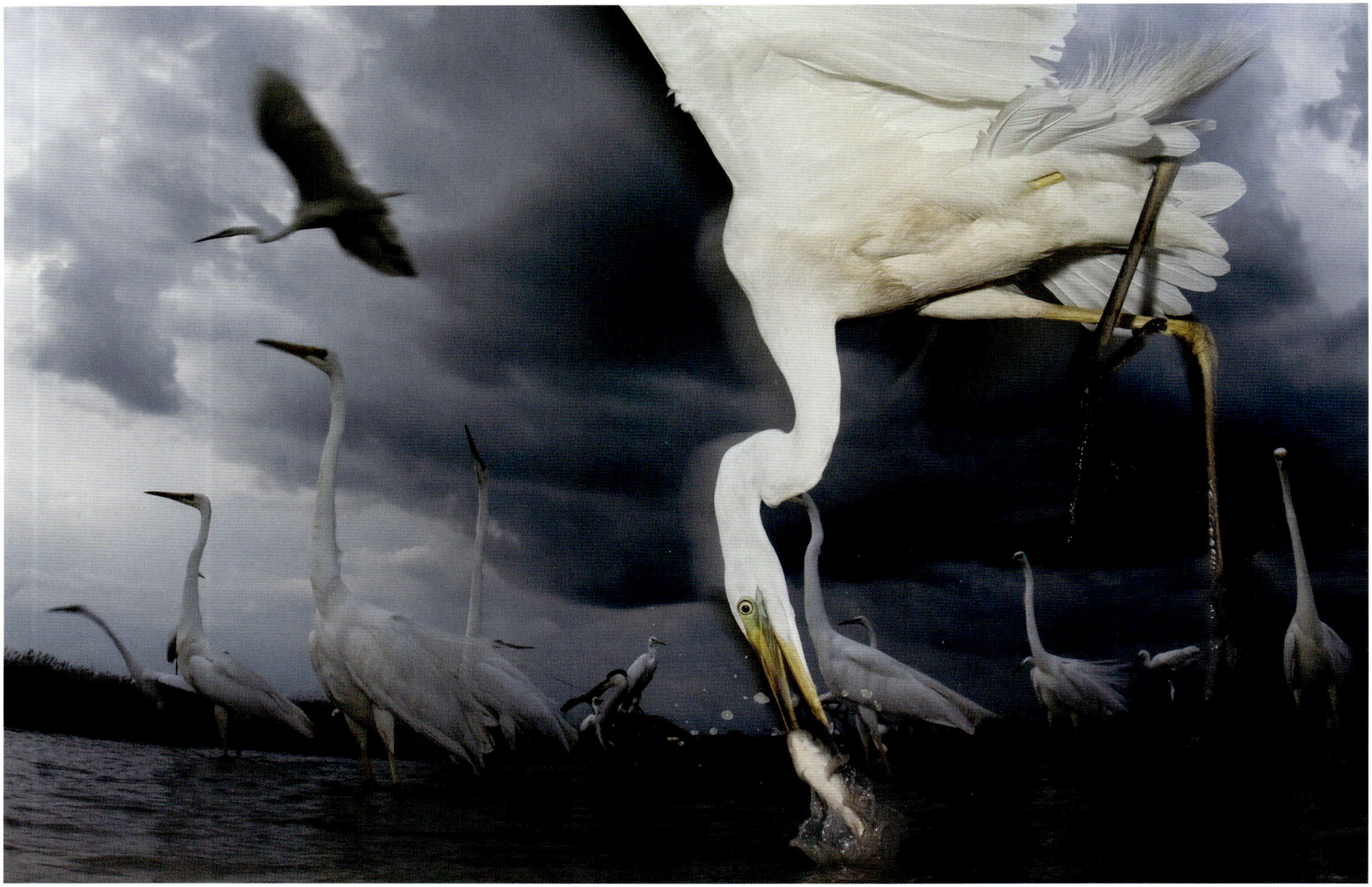

Bence Máté

Great Egrets fishing *(Ardea alba)*. Neither the number of birds nor their environment is the main theme in this image, but both play a valuable role in creating the general atmosphere.
Nikon D300, Tokina 10–17mm f/3.5–4.5, 1/50 second, 16mm, f/11.0, ISO 400, two Nikon SB-800 flashes, manual focus, remote control head, blind. Pusztaszer, Hungary, June 2009.

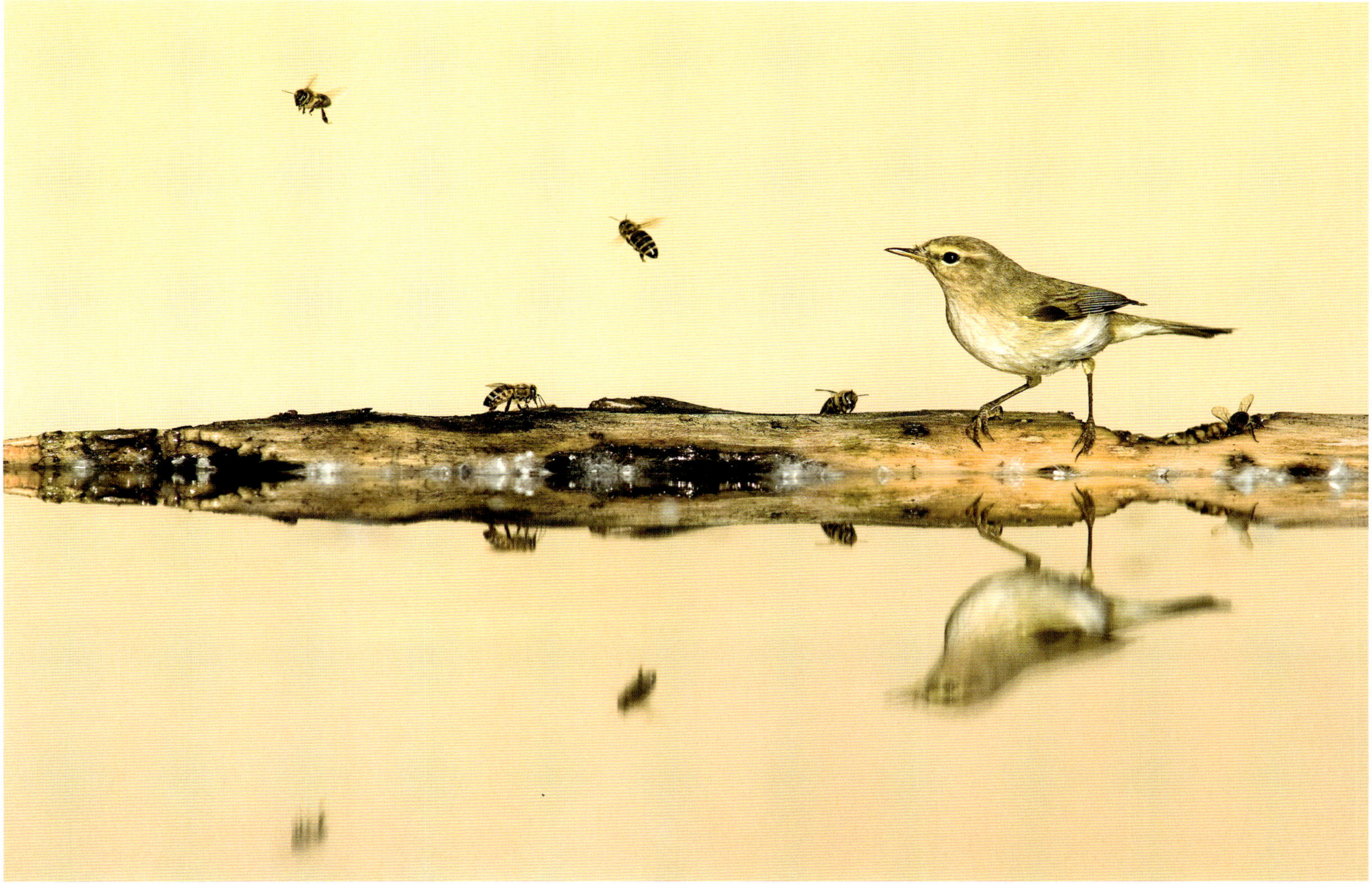

Bence Máté

Common Chiffchaff at a drinking pool *(Phylloscopus collybita)*. A sand dune in the background is blurred and blends in to a completely harmonious background, allowing the small bees to be clearly projected against it.
Nikon D300, 300mm f/2.8, 1/1250 second, f/5.6, ISO 640, manual focus, Gitzo tripod and video head, blind.
Pusztaszer, Hungary, May 2008.

Bence Máté

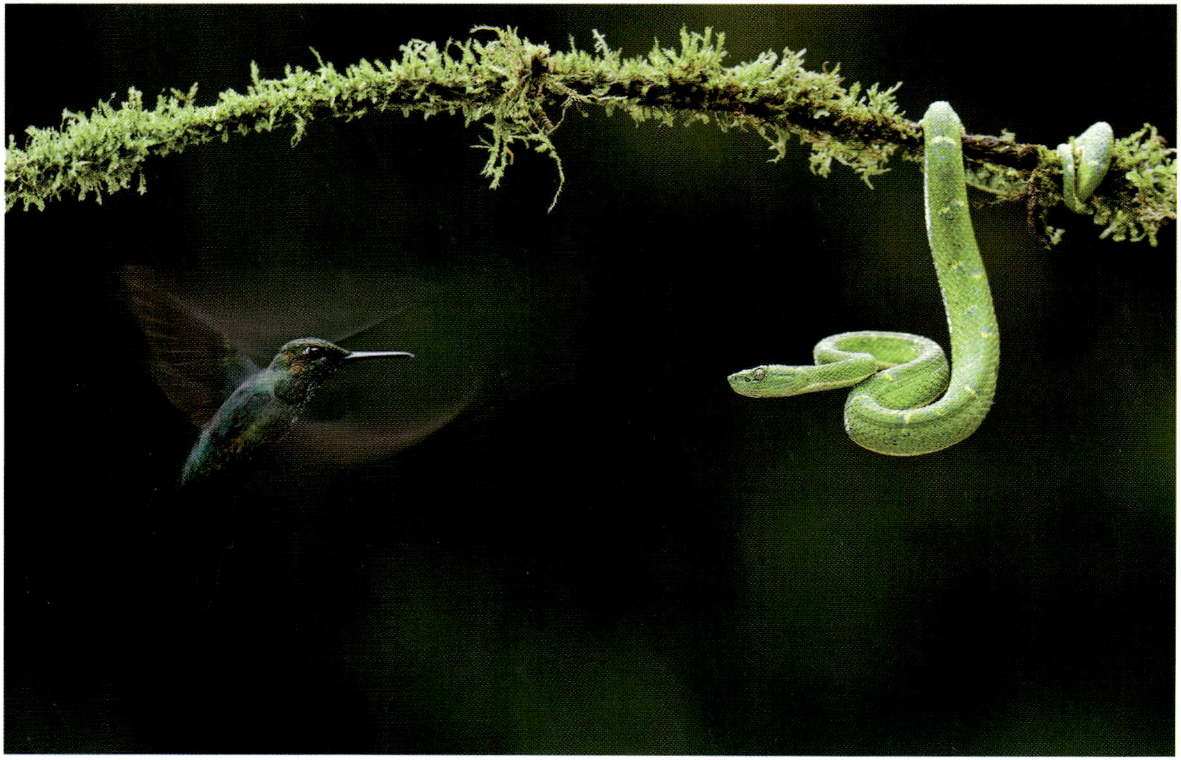

A Green-crowned Brilliant and a snake *(Heliodoxa jacula)*. The almost homogeneous background has nuances that hint at the animals' habitat but does not steal from the main attraction. Nikon D300, 300mm f/2.8, 1/100 second, f/4.0, ISO 200, Canon Speedlite 550EX and 540EZ flashes, manual focus, Gitzo tripod and video head, blind. Costa Rica, February 2009.

that nature gives you. Telephoto lenses have a shallow depth of field, and if you can find an even color combination to serve as your background, and keep an adequate distance that lets the colors blend together, it's easy to create uniform backgrounds. What is not so easy is to find a big enough area in the field that does not have great contrast between shapes, light, or colors, such as the line between sky and ground, or water and reeds.

Forests and hillsides are good backgrounds, but they aren't always available. If your background is less than ideal, you can try photographing from a higher angle. The ground then becomes your background. Try to attract the bird to a higher level, otherwise you won't have enough distance between your subject and your background; the background should be twice the distance between the subject and the lens, preferably even more.

With a few exceptions, the greater the distance to your background, the better the result. One exception is precipitation. When you have snowfall and rain, you should photograph against a dark background and keep the distance at less than 100 m (328 ft). When the distance is greater, there is more precipitation between the subject and the background, which causes the drops or flakes to merge into a uniform, pale mass instead of standing out individually.

What should you do if the background is too close? The best way to blur the background is to find an angle where you have three to four times more light on the subject than on the background, which becomes blurred and doesn't attract the viewer's eye when it is underexposed. A general rule

Bence Máté

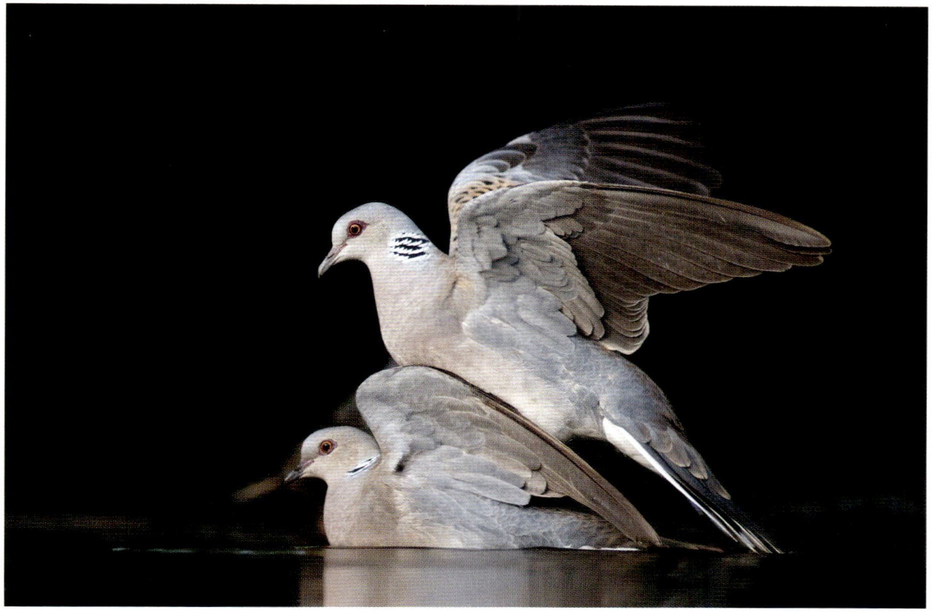

European Turtle-Doves mating *(Streptopelia turtur)*. When the light intensity varies greatly between the subject and the background, even the most restless background becomes a harmonious backdrop.
Nikon D200, 300mm f/2.8, 1/1000 second, f/2.8, ISO 400, manual focus, Gitzo tripod and video head, blind. Pusztaszer, Hungary, May 2006.

for sunny weather is to keep the background in the shade and the subject in sunlight. If that's not possible, a blue sky is a good uniform background in almost all light conditions and with every focal length.

When you want to bring out details in the background, use a wide lens and stop down. When you are photographing with a telephoto lens, use the biggest possible aperture to blur the background into a uniform color. Stopping down even just one f-stop with a telephoto lens has a surprisingly big impact on the amount of information in the background.

Foreground

Do not overlook the foreground. You can create exciting effects in your image by using the elements between your camera and the subject. For example, if a bird is partially concealed behind a rock or a snowbank, include the obstructing element in your image. This way it doesn't truncate your subject, and the viewer can see why only part of the bird is visible.

The distance between the element in the foreground and your camera should be about half of your distance to the subject. If it's less, the element is too sharply focused and steals the attention; if it's more, the connection between the element and the subject can be lost.

You might think that composing a good background and an interesting foreground is not that difficult, but in reality, getting them right requires time, consideration, and planning. Well-composed backgrounds and foregrounds will reward your efforts many times over, so it's smart to put effort into them.

A Great Egret preening *(Ardea alba)*. Softly blurred snow ties the separate elements together, and the result is a balanced image.
Canon 300D, Nikon 300mm f/2.8, 1/1600 second, f/5.6, ISO 200, manual focus, self-made tripod, Gitzo video head, blind. Pusztaszer, Hungary, March 2005.

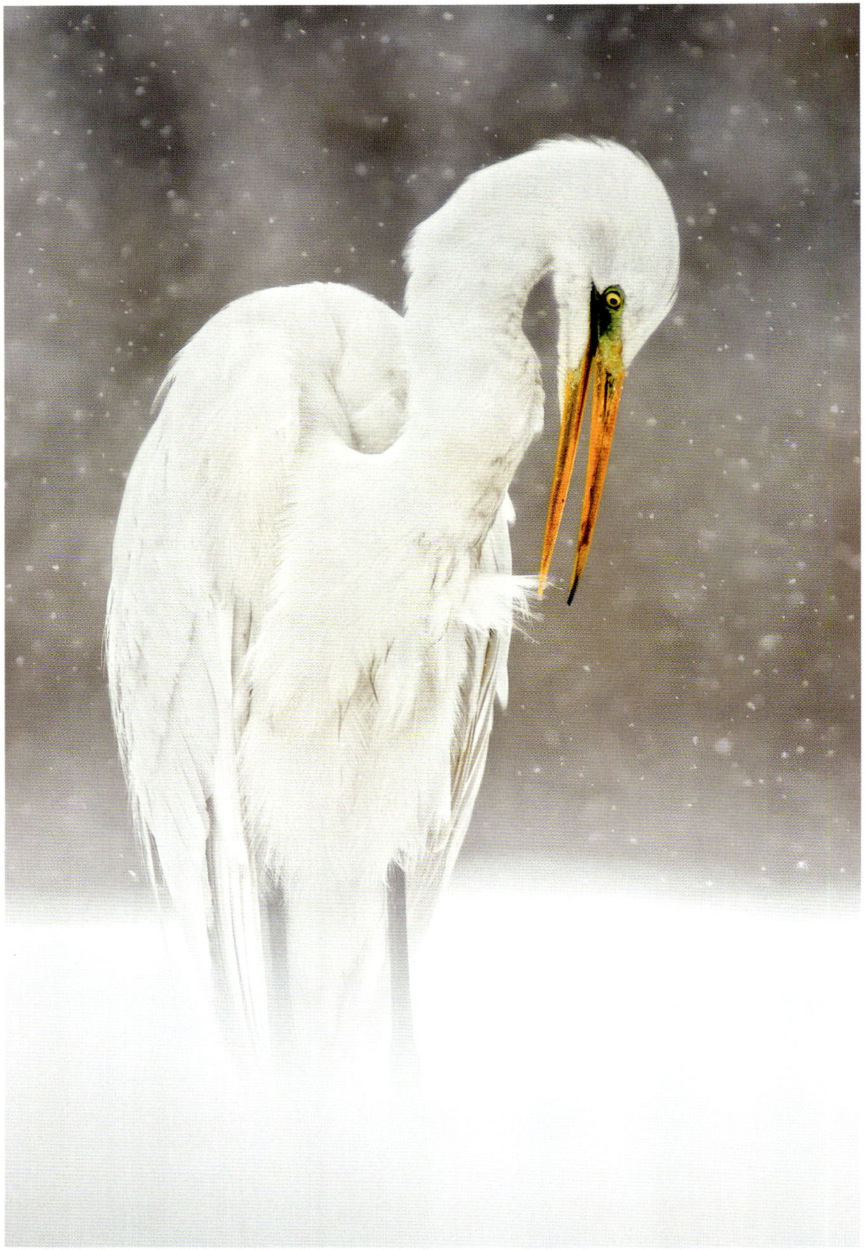

Bence Máté

BENCE MÁTÉ

ANGLE MATTERS

Take time to find the ideal camera angle for your image. Often, angle doesn't get the attention it deserves, considering the role it plays in a successful image.

The sentence above is a bit of a generalization, but considering how even tripod manufacturers spend more time designing a tripod that can easily be raised to eye level for maximum comfort than designing a tripod that adapts perfectly to photography on ground level, the statement isn't that big of a leap.

A tripod's primary job is to help you to take great photos; helping you do so with maximum comfort should come second. After all, it's no secret that the best angle is seldom at human eye level.

If you've captured a moment in a bird's life as seen through the eyes of another bird, instead of an external observer, the dynamics in the image are way more interesting. The easiest way to create a feeling of peer perspective is to photograph at your subject's level. It's not as difficult as photographing a flying bird or birds flitting about the trees, but your equipment will pose some limitations when shooting from ground level. Watching through the viewfinder is awkward, your sense of the horizon is distorted, and aiming can be difficult.

Using an angle finder helps by allowing you to look through your viewfinder from the top, but even so, your position is far from ideal for observing birds and your surroundings. Sometimes you can improve the conditions; you can dig a hole in the ground to get lower than your camera and shoot from a more normal position; or wear clothing that protects you against wet, muck, and cold and lie down to photograph; or use a mat.

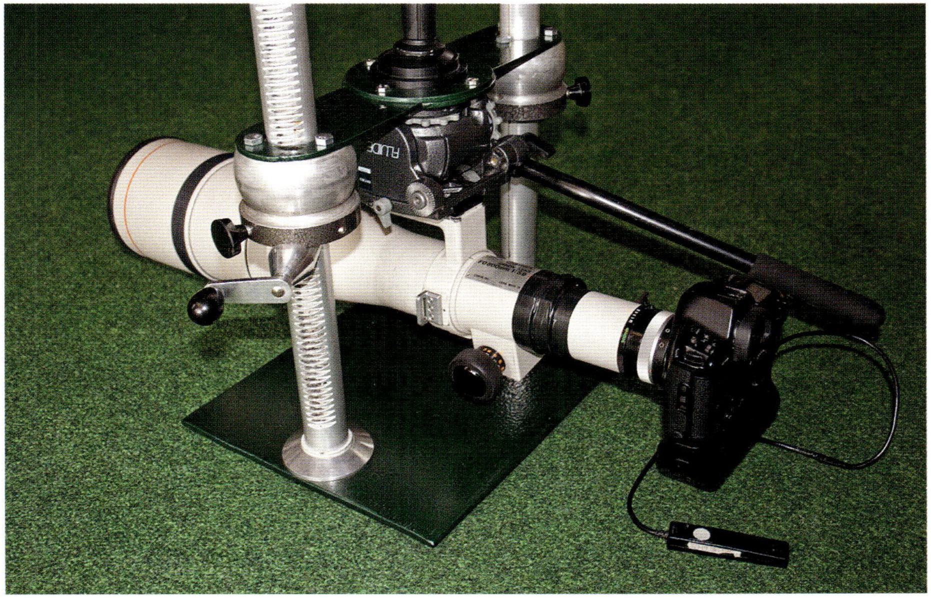

Bence Máté

This is a self-made ground pod for photographing at 0–30 cm (0–11.8 in) height. I have yet to find these commercially made.

Egrets and herons fishing, with a Black-crowned Night-Heron in the foreground *(Nycticorax nycticorax)*. The reflection is the strongest when photographing at water level and the surface is dead calm with nothing to break it—no leaves, twigs, or small insects, for example.
Nikon D300, Tokina 10–17mm f/3.5–4.5, 1/250 second, 13mm, f/9.0, ISO 400, manual focus, remote control head, blind. Pusztaszer, Hungary, August 2010.

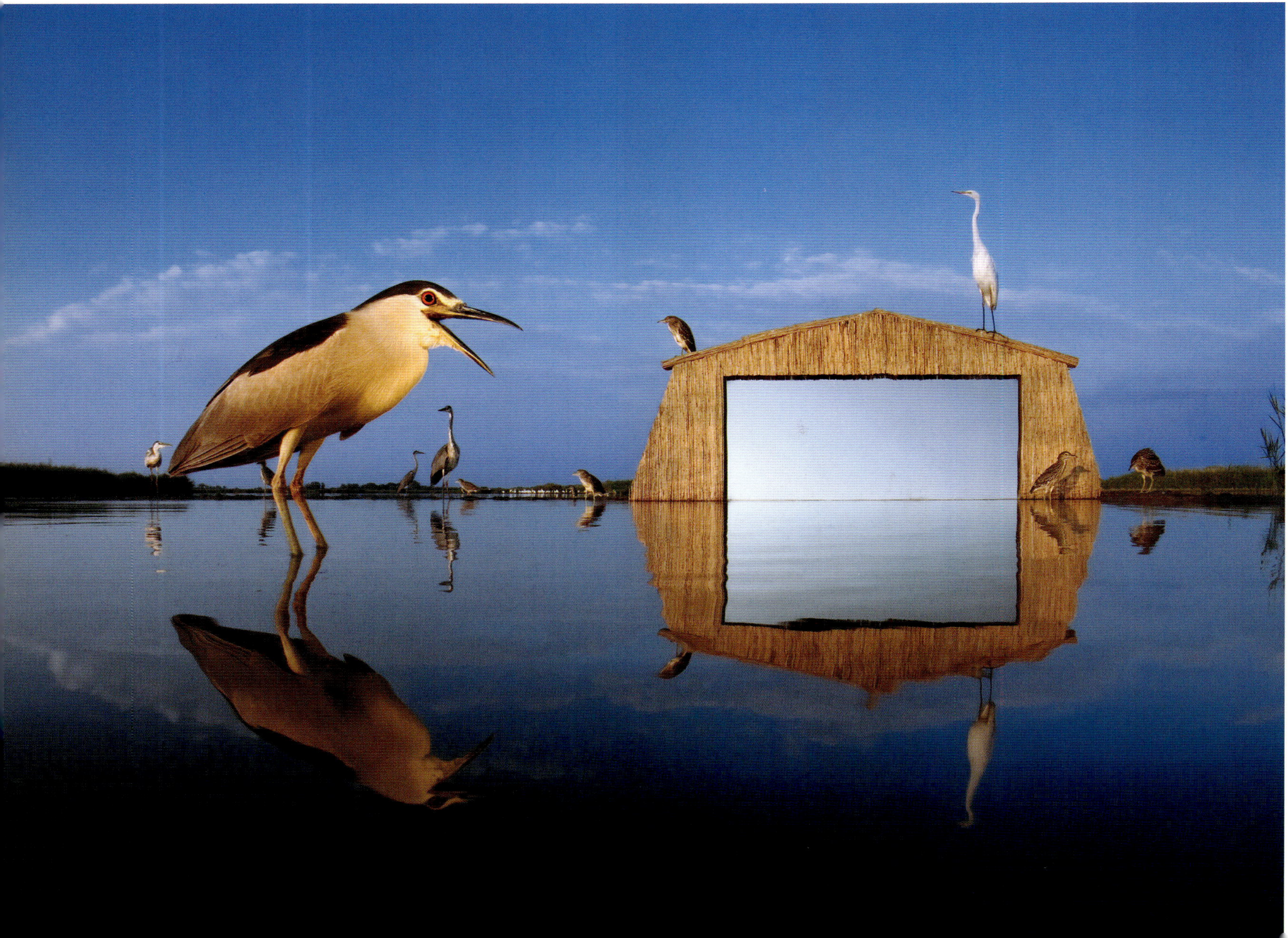

Bence Máté

Common Cuckoos fighting *(Cuculus canorus)*. Taken from a tower blind in a diagonal slant downward to get the green lawn in the background.
Nikon D300, 300mm f/2.8, 1/1000 second, f/2.8, ISO 640, manual focus, Gitzo tripod and video head, blind. Pusztaszer, Hungary, May 2008.

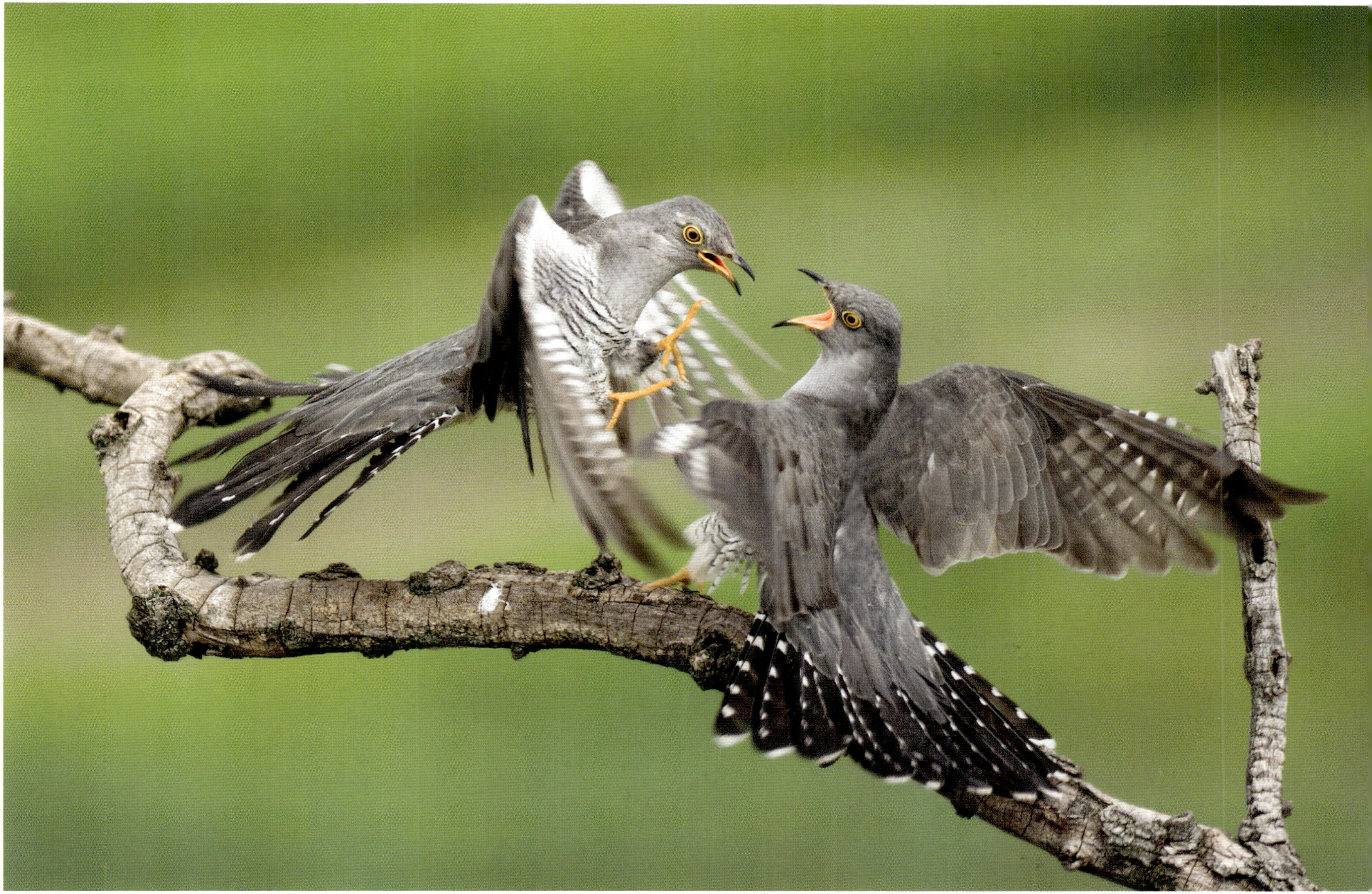

Bence Máté

Dalmatian Pelicans and Yellow-legged Gulls fighting over nesting sites *(Larus michahellis, Pelecanus crispus)*. I photographed at ground level to get the blue sky into the background and to avoid having the horizontal line split the image in half.
Nikon D200, 14mm f/2.8, 1/640 second, f/7.0, ISO 400, manual focus, handheld camera, blind. Romania, April 2007.

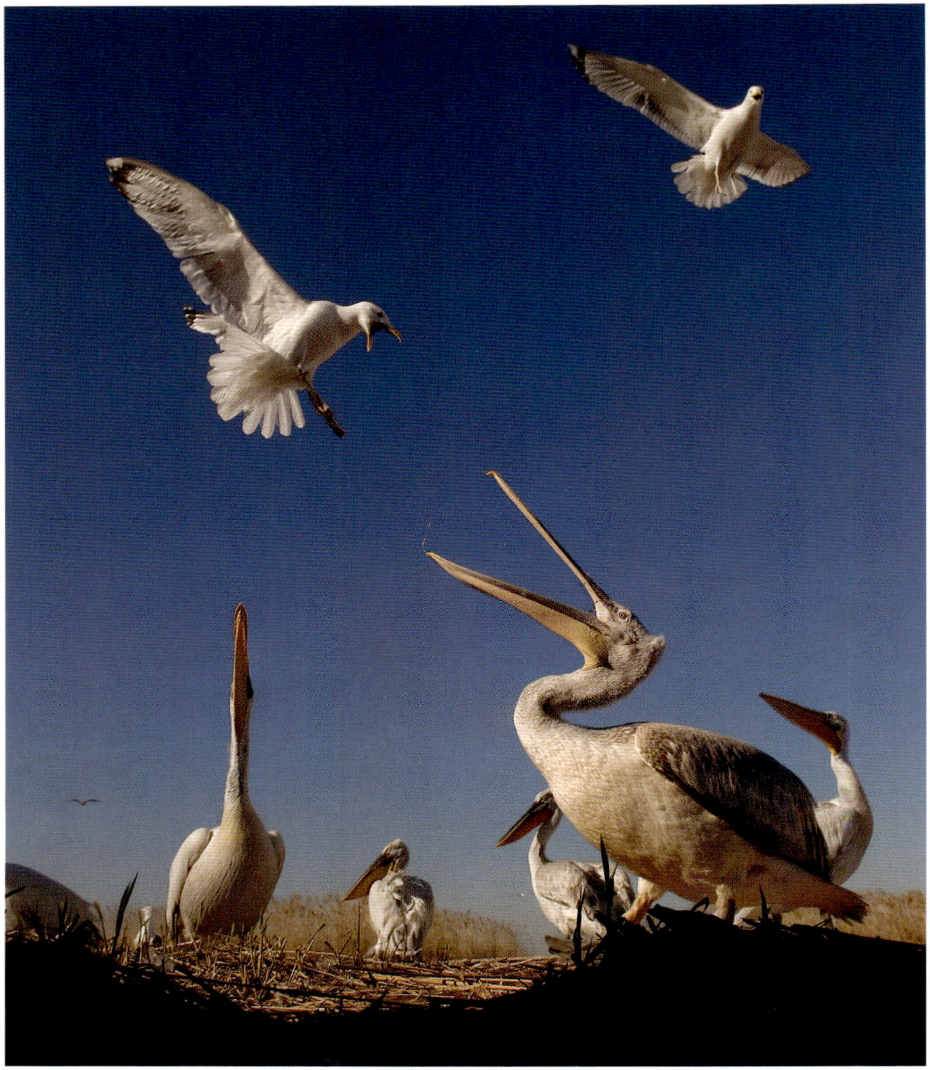

Bence Máté

Viewers are instinctively drawn to an image that is taken from an unusual angle, and that makes them wonder how the image was taken in the first place. We like to see images where we can marvel at the photographer's skill and ingenuity in beating the difficulties posed by equipment, angle, and distance.

You can approach your subject from many angles, and in my opinion you are indeed justified to take time to consider all the options—and even try them. What would the outcome be if the subject were photographed from below, above, far away, close up, with a wide lens, or with a telephoto lens?

Birds are usually wary, which means you don't always get a chance to test the angles. But some locations have a lot of birds on a regular basis, offering you valuable opportunities to test angles. Testing is recommended for beginning and advanced photographers alike because the best camera angle is usually a sum of many variants, and experience helps you make good decisions quickly, when it matters. It's not just the angle that needs to be decided, but how you're going to get that angle in field conditions.

Here are a few hypothetical examples to demonstrate how a situation affects your camera angle.

A Black-winged Stilt pair is wading in shallow water and looking for food.
The ideal angle is 30 cm (11.8 in) above water, which would accommodate the birds, their reflections, and the sedges in the background.

A Black-winged Stilt pair is wading in shallow water and looking for food; the wind is rising.
I would photograph at water level because the bright sky is now reflecting on the waves. I would lower the camera as much as possible so the horizontal line between the water and the reeds wouldn't split the image at the halfway point.

A Black-winged Stilt pair that had been wading in the shallow water and looking for food begins to copulate.
The ideal height from water is 80 cm (31.5 in) because the combination of the male on top of the female, with the male's open wings, is so high that if I were to photograph from a lower level, the horizontal line would split the male in half and make the image half green, half white. But because I am photographing from a greater height, the blue sky reflecting on the water makes a good background for the mating birds.

A Black-winged Stilt pair with a brood is wading in shallow water near the blind; the water is still and the surface is completely flat.
I would photograph from a height of 120 cm (47.2 in) from the water because this would capture the chicks' and the parents' reflections, without actually showing the parents, which would make the image less mainstream.

Even though you're photographing nature's creatures, whose movements and actions are just as hard to predict as the weather and the conditions around your location, it's still hugely beneficial to make field trips so you can plan all kinds of photography projects and visualize scenarios you might come across and want to photograph. The only thing you can count on when you are actually out there photographing is the element of surprise and the unexpected. The best way to arm yourself is to gain experience, to be open to sudden changes, and to respond fast to the opportunities they offer.

Markus Varesvuo

BENCE MÁTÉ

WATER AS AN ELEMENT IN A BIRD PHOTO

Water is a source of life for birds; it is also an interesting element in a photograph.

Like most living things, birds consist mostly of water and need to replenish regularly. Birds get water by drinking and from the food they eat. To regulate their body temperature, they lose water through their skin and respiration; the more they lose, the more they need to consume. The loss of water does not necessarily occur the most in hot weather; more is lost with physical exertion, which is higher than normal during courtship, breeding time, and migration—hectic times in a bird's life. These are the times when activity around the drinking pond is at its most feverish. Birds arrive to drink and bathe because maintaining healthy plumage is very important.

Water is a very good way to attract birds. Water also looks good in photographs, unlike most other methods of attraction, which you would, for the most part, rather not have in your images. Water can be composed in the image in so many ways and is often an essential part of the theme. Read more about rain, snowfall, and fog, in the chapter "Use Weather to Your Advantage."

When it's cold enough, a bird's breath steams up and adds a small but dramatic detail to your image. Try to compose the steaming breath against a dark background, and preferably against light, which will bring it out even better. Black Grouse leks offer good opportunities with cold mornings and the rising sun at a low angle. Note that the breath can be captured only in calm weather because wind quickly disperses the steam.

Reflections

Even if you work with a subject or a theme that has been photographed extensively, you can get a touch of something new or unexpected if you add water to the image. A reflection on water can help make an image unique. With low camera angles, the intensity and quality of light on the subject often matches the light on the reflection. A good reflection requires, of course, a calm water surface with no floating matter. Even the smallest bubble or ripple can distort the pin-sharp reflection and ruin the illusion.

Late evening backlight gilds the droplets around a bathing European Robin *(Erithacus rubecula)*. The long exposure time turns the drops into arcs.
Canon EOS-1D Mark II, 500mm f/4.0, 1/10 second, f/22.0, ISO 500, Gitzo tripod, Manfrotto 501 video head, blind. Pusztaszer, Hungary, July 2006.

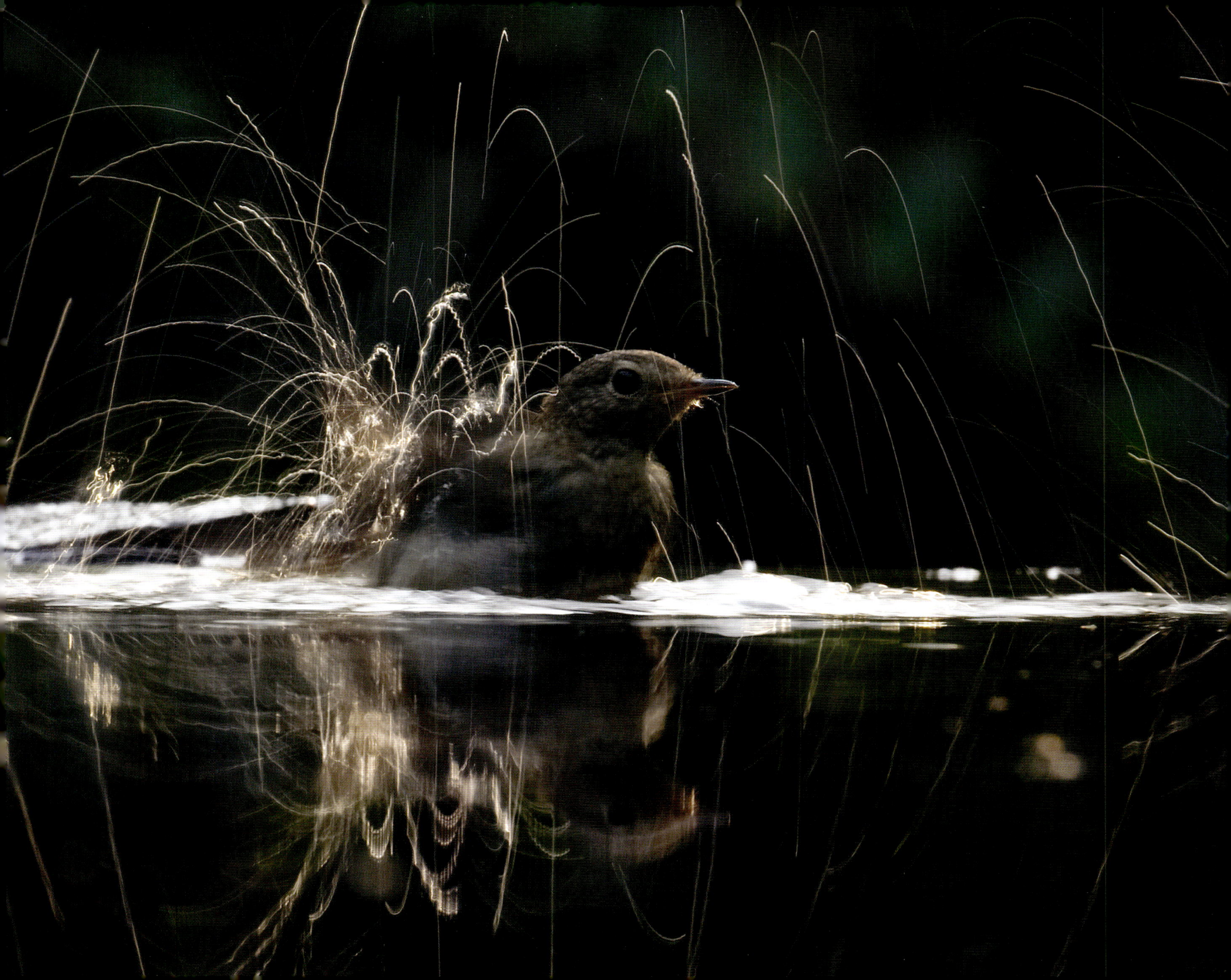

Jari Peltomäki

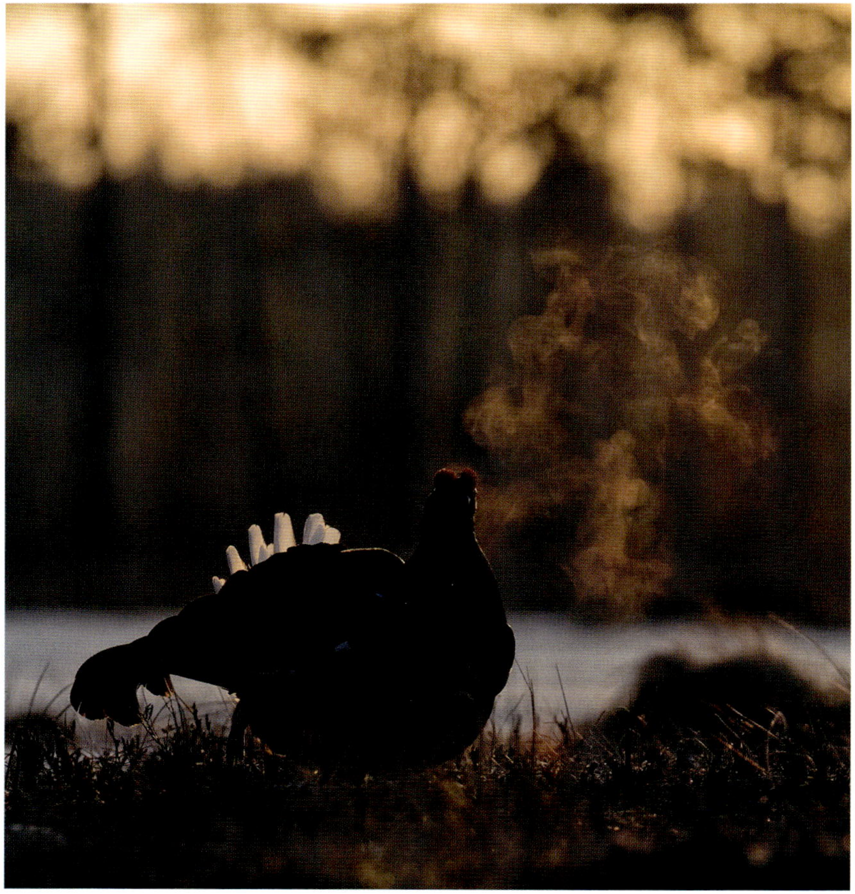

A few examples of how to use water as an element in your images include reflections of shapes and colors in the background; waves; surf spray; streaming water; or splashes caused by birds landing, taking off, or fighting.

Twigs and stalks often make an image appear restless, but the fascinating geometry of ice formations seems to please the human eye, maybe because ice is light and translucent, making the chaotic details appear as a harmonious whole. Frozen water, chunks of ice, and frosted branches push a photographer's imagination.

With backlight, the Black Grouse's steaming breath is etched against the dark background *(Tetrao tetrix)*
Canon EOS-1D Mark II N, 300mm f/2.8, 1/500 second, f/7.1, ISO 500, manual focus, ground pod, Manfrotto 501 video head, blind. Liminka, Finland, March 2007.

A Common Chaffinch with its reflection *(Fringilla coelebs)*. You need a low camera angle and a flat water surface to get a perfect reflection.
Nikon F100, 300mm f/2.8 plus 1.6x extender, 1/60 second, f/2.8, Fuji Velvia ISO 50, manual focus, Gitzo tripod and video head, blind. Pusztaszer, Hungary, 2001.

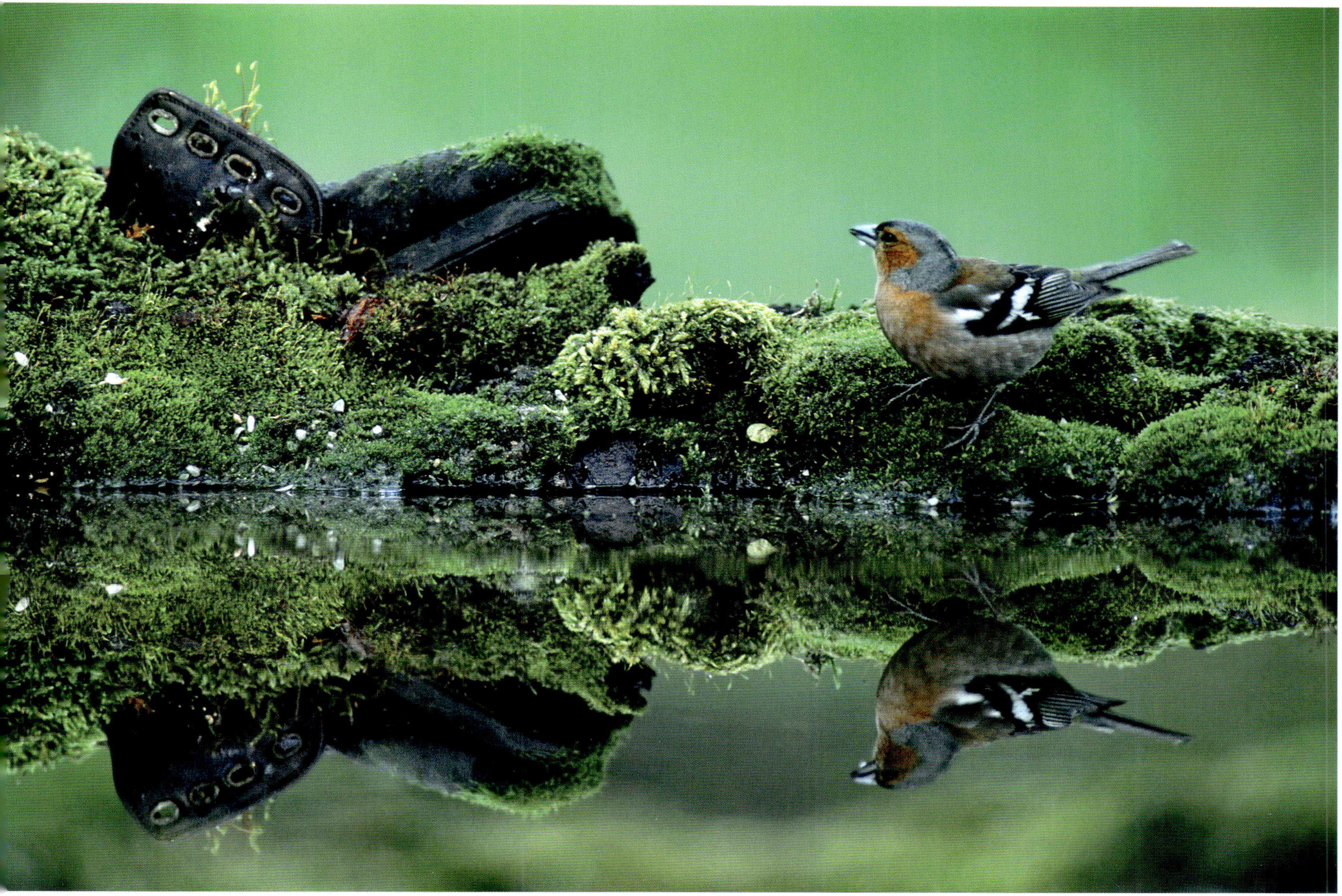

Bence Máté

Markus Varesvuo

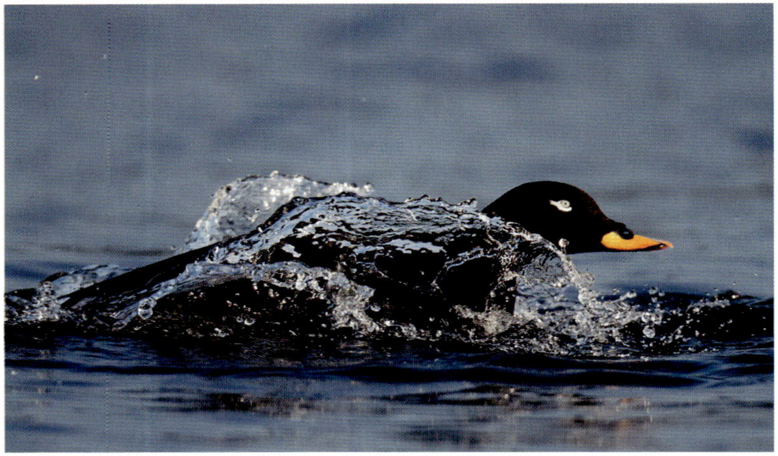

Mallards *(Anas platyrhynchos)*
Canon EOS-1Ds Mark II, 70–200mm f/2.8, 1/160 second, 200 mm, f/13.0, ISO 400, Gitzo tripod, Manfrotto 501 video head. Helsinki, Finland, December 2007.

A Velvet Scoter charging ahead in a courtship frenzy *(Melanitta fusca)*
Canon EOS-1D Mark IV, 800mm f/5.6, 1/2000 second, f/5.6, ISO 800, continuous focus with a central focusing point, Gitzo tripod, Manfrotto 501 video head, blind. Parainen, Finland, May 2010.

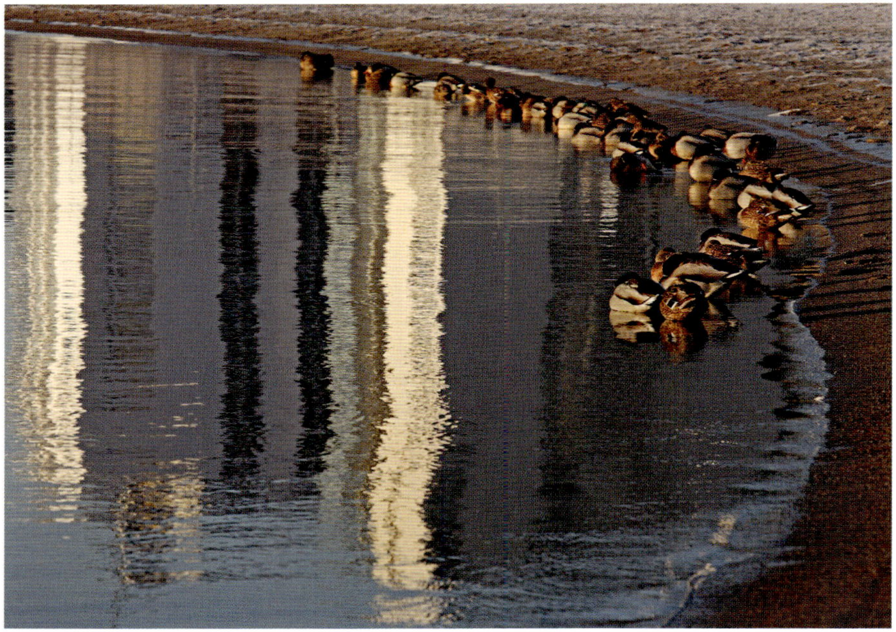

Markus Varesvuo

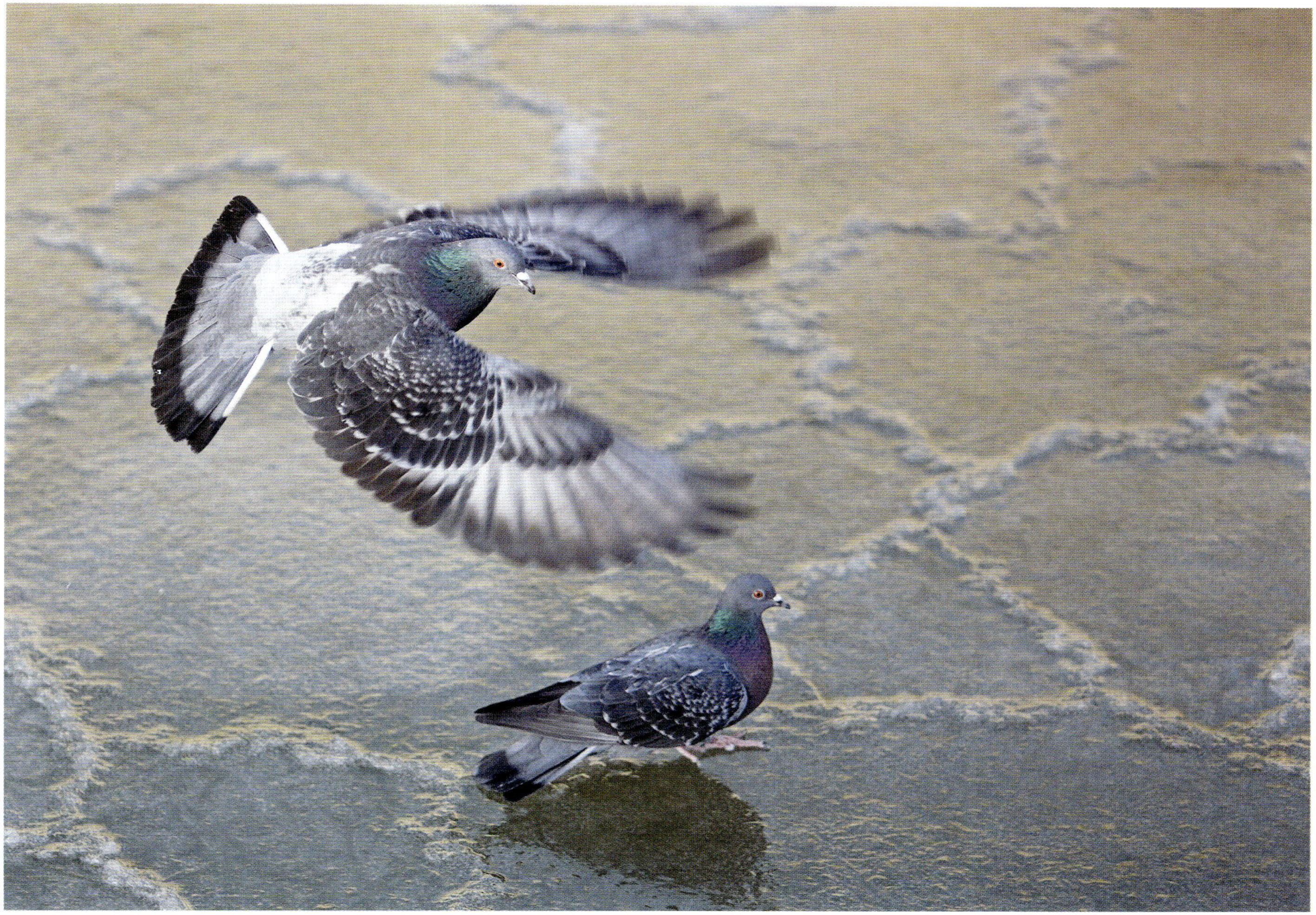

Markus Varesvuo

Rock Pigeons against ice *(Columba livia)*
Canon EOS-1Ds Mark III, 70–200mm f/2.8, 1/800 second, 110 mm, ISO 1000, continuous focus with 45 focusing points, handheld camera. Helsinki, Finland, February 2008.

Markus Varesvuo

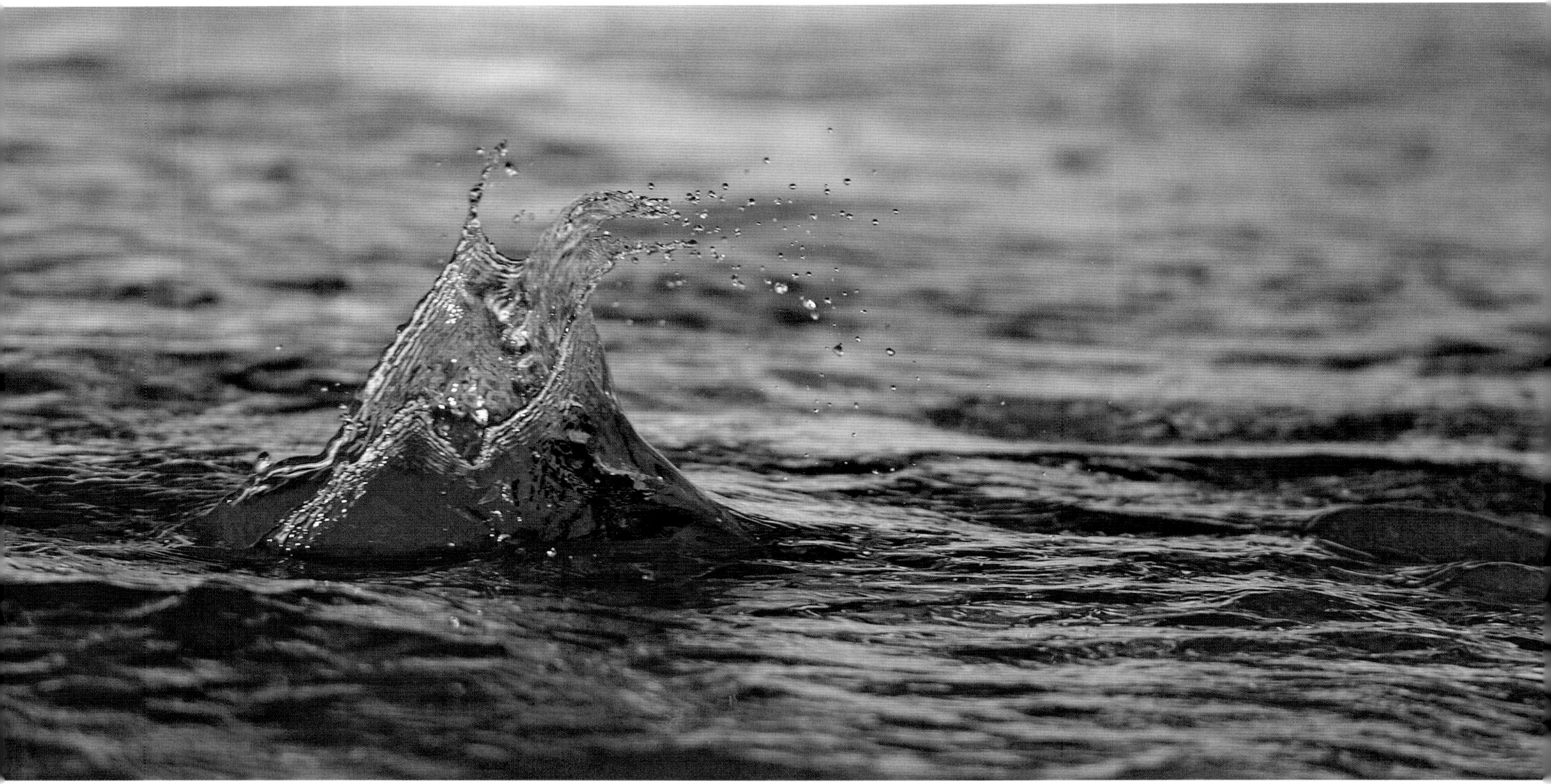

Water is a habitat to many bird species, and the underwater world is as familiar to them as life on land, if not more so. Yet there are few images taken of birds underwater. This is clearly an area for a photographer to venture into.

A White-throated Dipper plunging into the underwater world *(Cinclus cinclus)*
Canon EOS-1D Mark II, 300mm f/2.8, 1/3200 second, ISO 500, Gitzo tripod, Manfrotto 501 video head. Lapinjärvi, Finland, February 2006.

BENCE MÁTÉ

ATTRACTING BIRDS

Good bird photos require getting close to birds. How can you get close without causing harm?

Exploring nature, especially with a pair of binoculars, can result in many nice experiences in a single day. The combination of distances, light conditions, backgrounds, surroundings, and the surprise of the unexpected usually prevents you from recording what you've experienced and sharing it with others.

If you want to produce technically flawless and visually appealing images of the phenomena and events you witness, you should try to predict what is going to happen in front of your lens. Predicting gets easier when you can attract your subjects to within a good range and also to a location of your choice. There are some ways to accomplish those goals, but attracting birds must not harm them, nor should it cause action that would not have happened in an unstimulated situation.

> Bird photographers can promote nature awareness by letting the wider audience see images of the nature around us and by spreading information about our natural heritage.

Study your subjects well before going out into the field with you camera, and learn about their biology and behavior so you don't harm the environment or the animals in it. Understanding bird behavior gives you an indispensable edge in the field when you are trying to predict birds' reactions to your attempts to attract them, and especially when you evaluate if your actions pose any risks to them.

Perching Branches

Birds like to perch on branches. Place a good perch in an area where birds would come anyway. Waterbirds, for example, are fond of snags or tree trunks sticking out of the water or floating along where they can sit in relative safety and preen their plumage. In steppes or other vast, open areas, where there is a shortage of prominent vantage points, even a small twig stuck in the ground may soon become a favorite perch for birds. Branches jutting out of bushes or reed beds are also frequented for perching purposes. Birds use them as vantage points to keep watch on their environment and to make their calls heard as far as possible.

Islands

You can build a small island on a pond or a lake, near a blind that you have placed on the shore. Birds may discover that your island is a good place to rest, or if it is large enough they may even nest on it. An island provides safety against most terrestrial predators and offers birds an excellent opportunity to keep an eye on their surroundings.

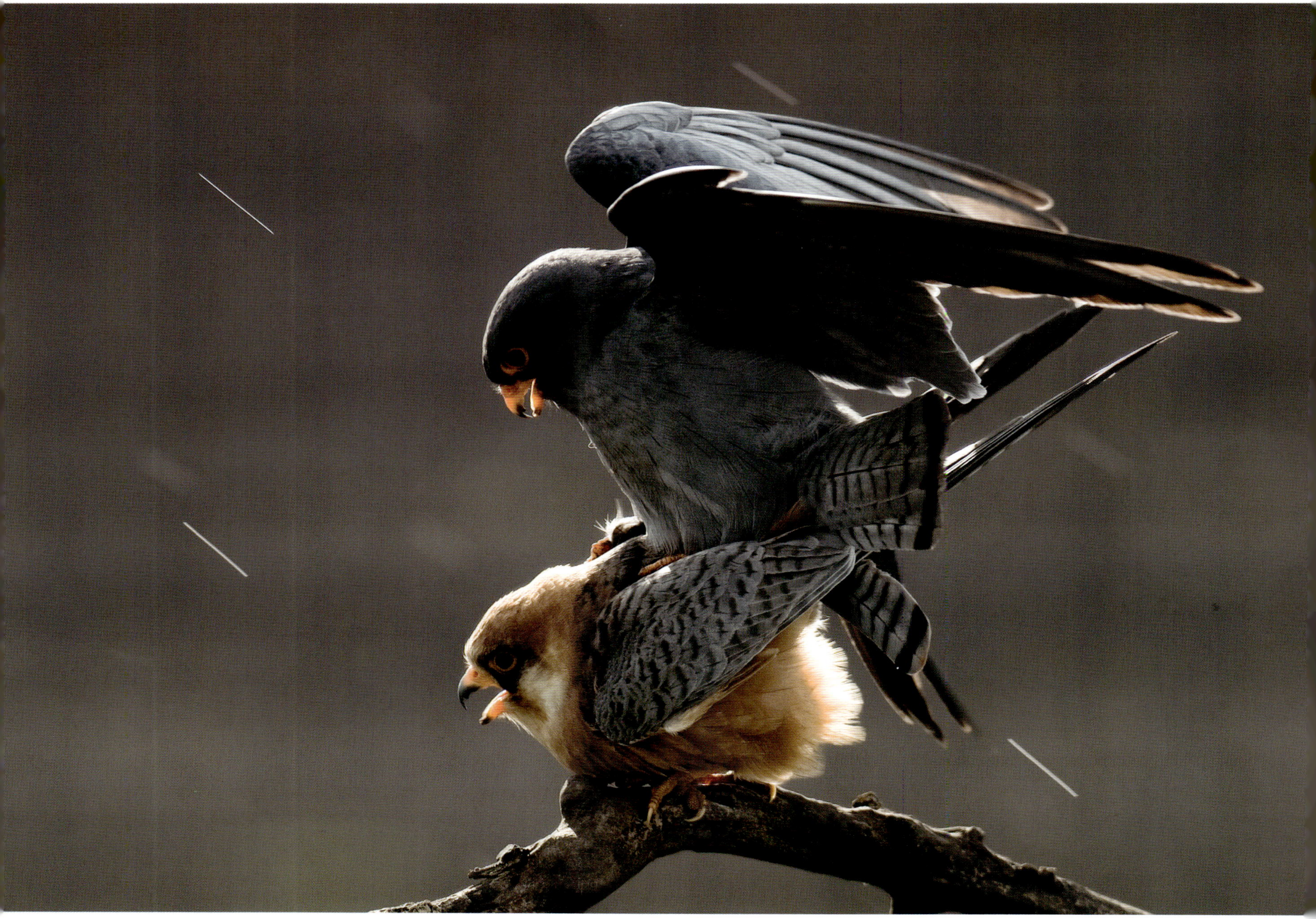

Bence Máté

Nests

Some species build their own nest holes, but mostly birds nest in existing holes and crevices, and housing shortage is a constant problem in the bird world. Most birds are happy to nest in human-made nest boxes, which benefits both birds and bird photographers. Hundreds of bird species ranging from small sparrows to large owls breed in artificial boxes worldwide. Instructions on how to build the many different types of nest boxes can be found on the Internet. Take every possible precaution when photographing near nests after the birds have started breeding because they are extremely vulnerable to disturbances during the breeding season. The use of a blind is always recommended. You can read more about the topic in the chapter "Photographing at Nests."

Disturbances at the nest can be very harmful to birds, so any activity in the vicinity of the nest must be carried out with extreme precaution.

Bence Máté

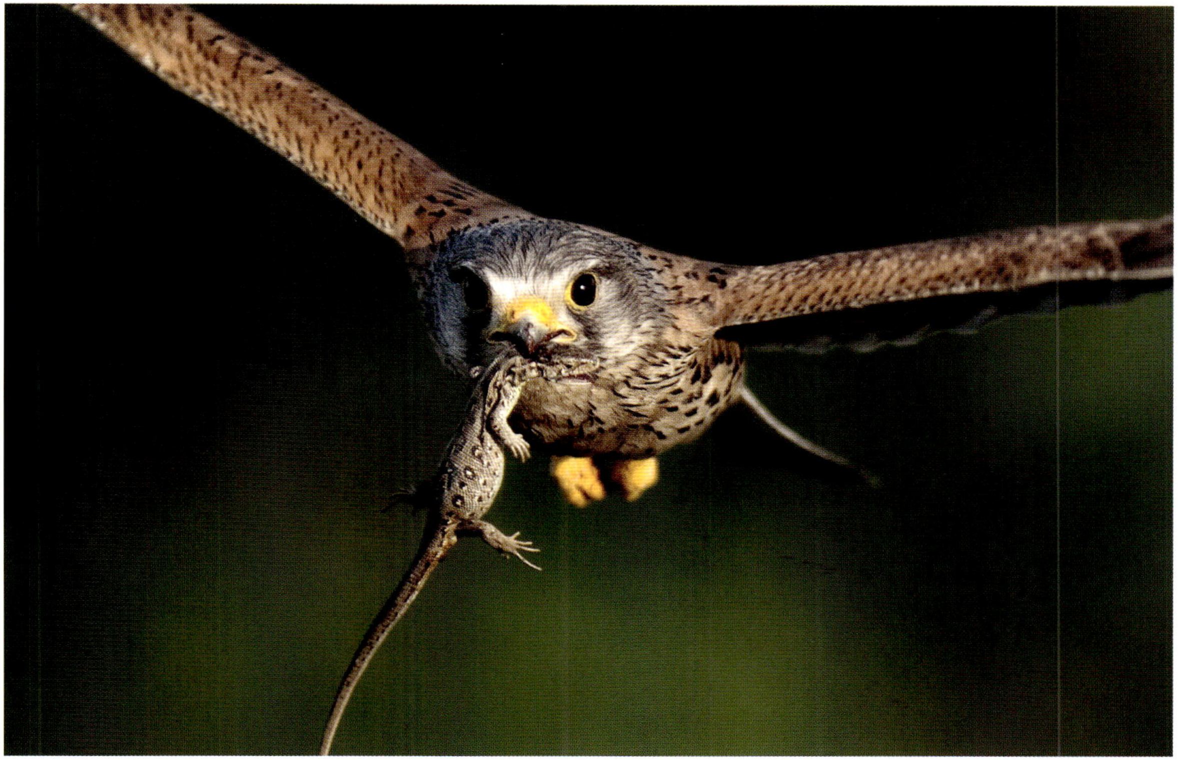

Eurasian Kestrel arriving to a nest box fitted to the side of a tower blind *(Falco tinnunculus)*. It's bringing a Sand Lizard to its young.
Nikon D200, 300mm f/2.8, 1/1250 second, f/2.8, ISO 400, continuous focus, Gitzo tripod and video head, blind. Pusztaszer, Hungary, June 2007.

Red-footed Falcons mating on a perch placed above their nest box that was erected just two weeks before their arrival *(Falco vespertinus)*
Nikon D300, 300mm f/2.8, 1/1000 second, f/2.8, ISO 640, manual focus, Gitzo tripod and video head, blind. Hungary, May 2008.

Bence Máté

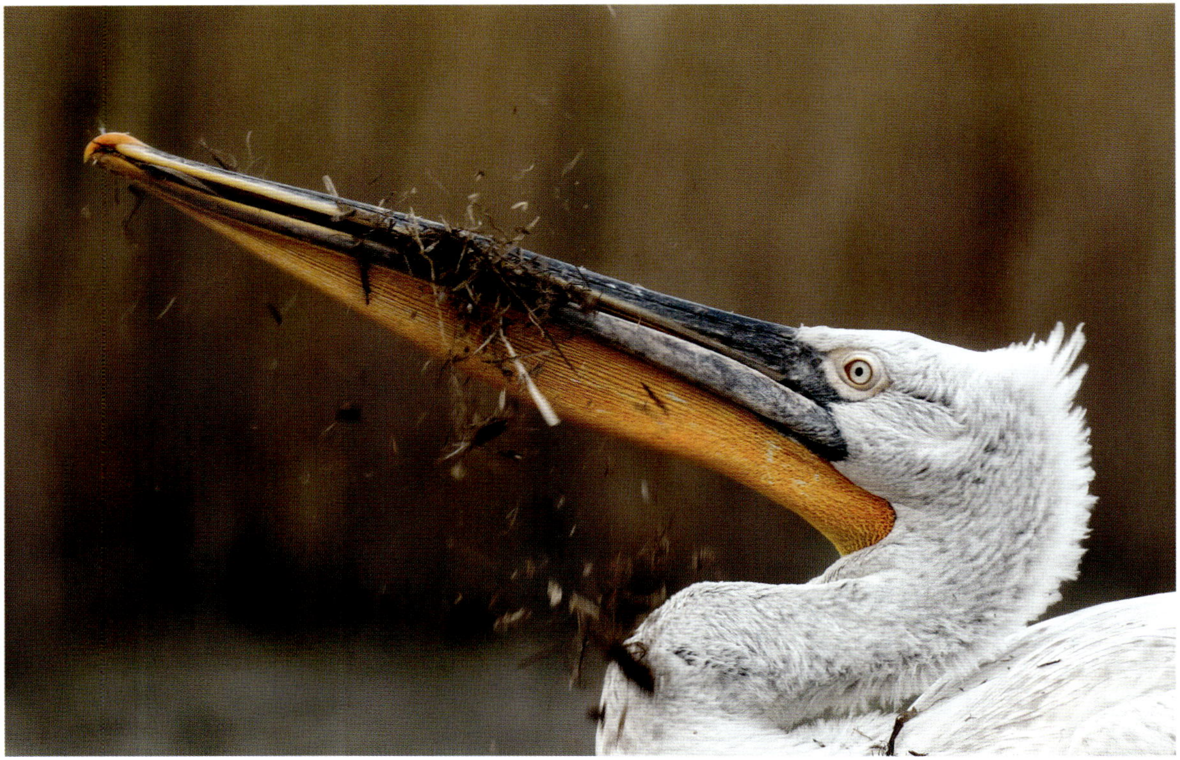

A Dalmatian Pelican scoops a pouchful of vegetation for nest building purposes *(Pelecanus crispus)*
Nikon D200, Sigma 300–800mm f/5.6, 1/400 second, 440mm, f/7.1, ISO 400, manual focus, Gitzo tripod and video head, blind. Romania, April 2007

Nest Material

If you know when different bird species start gathering nest material and what they're looking for, you can attract them by bringing suitable material to a spot you think is good for photographing them. When the birds come, they reward your efforts with good photo opportunities. Small downy feathers are especially sought after among many species; starlings and tits are quick to spot light and colorful feathers. Golden Orioles like pieces of hemp string, which you can coil on branches. Any pile of dry reed stems on a rock jutting out of the water can cause skirmishes among waterbirds as they fight over who gets to take them to their nest.

Decoys

Waterbirds tend to find safety in numbers, and sometimes you can use this instinct to attract a wary waterbird closer to your blind by placing a decoy near it. Your decoy does not have to be an exact replica as long as the main features are right. Decoys can be purchased, or you can make one from wood or plastic. I have used decoys successfully in photographing shy geese, ducks, European Green Woodpeckers, Bluethroats, Common Cuckoos, egrets, and herons. I have heard that decoys also work well with cranes and bustards.

Markus Varesvuo

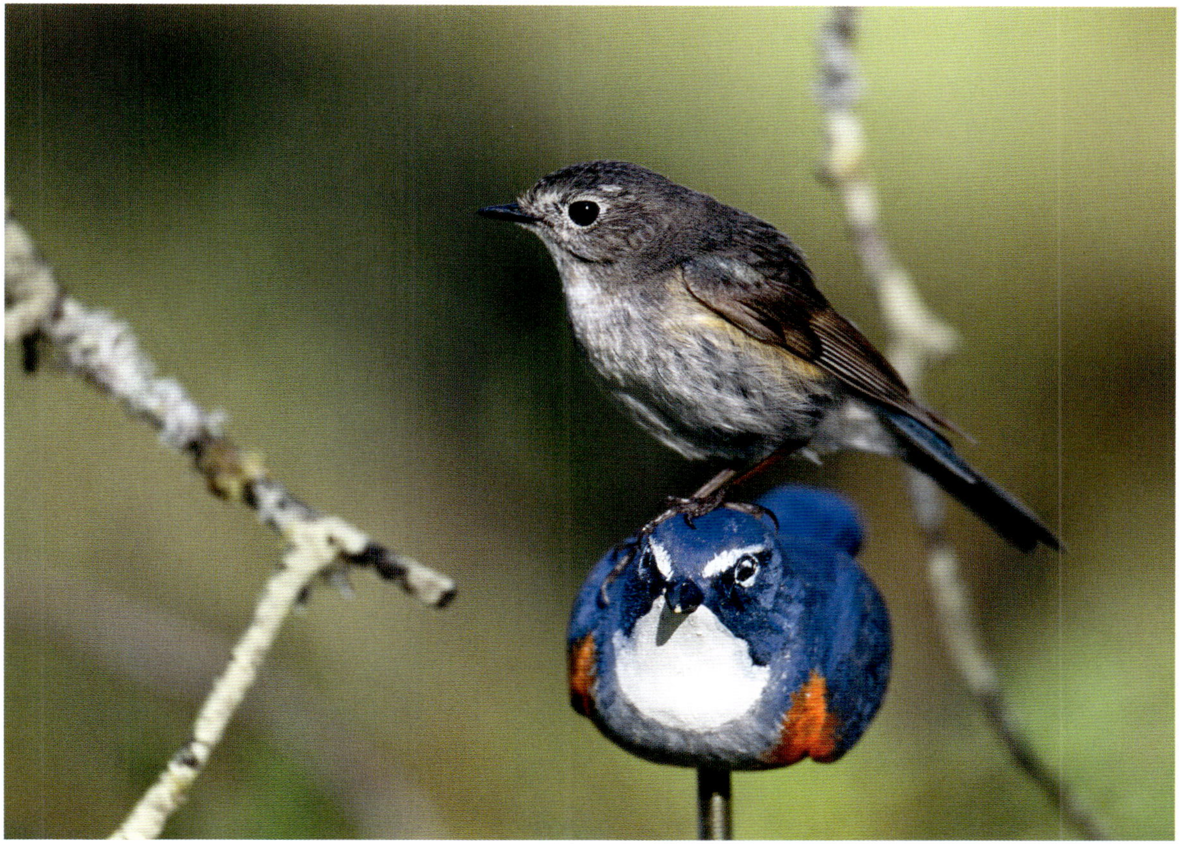

Decoys sometimes work surprisingly well. Here a young Red-flanked Bluetail male is observing a wooden imitation of an old male *(Tarsiger cyanurus)*. Decoys can also be made of plastic.
Canon EOS-1v, 500mm f/4.0 plus 1.4x extender, 1/200 second, f/8.0, Fuji Provia ISO 100, Manfrotto tripod, Manfrotto 501 video head. Kuusamo, Finland, June 2000.

Markus Varesvuo

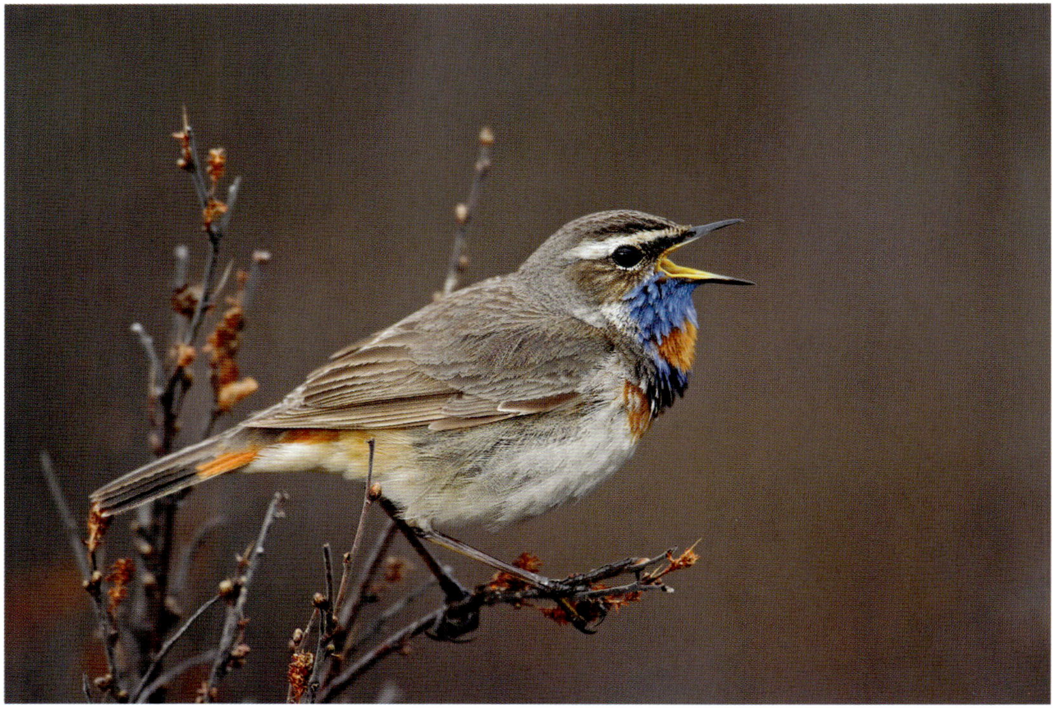

This image of a singing Bluethroat was taken from a car *(Luscinia svecica)*. A recording of its song was used to attract it.
Canon EOS-1Ds Mark II, 500mm f/4.0 plus 1.4x extender, 1/320 second, f/5.6, ISO 320, one-shot focus with a central focusing point, beanbag, car as a blind. Utsjoki, Finland, June 2006.

Playback of Bird Calls

Almost every bird species will react to luring with bird songs and calls, provided that the right sound is played at the right time, in the right place, and at the right volume. The birds' interest is often piqued by playback because they assume a sexually aroused mate has turned up and they don't want to refuse it, or because they want to drive out an intruder from their territory. Bird calls should be played in moderation because overuse can have the opposite result—your subject grows bored and disappears. Turn off your device when your subject arrives, and never play the same bird call more than two or three times.

You can also use a bird whistle or mimic their calls. A partridge whistle, for example, works better than a recorded voice, and a Black Woodpecker can be attracted quite easily by whistling its contact call. And most small birds come to take a closer look at a hissing photographer. It's up to you to practice and experiment! A small MP3 player and a loudspeaker work best, but you can use a CD player, too.

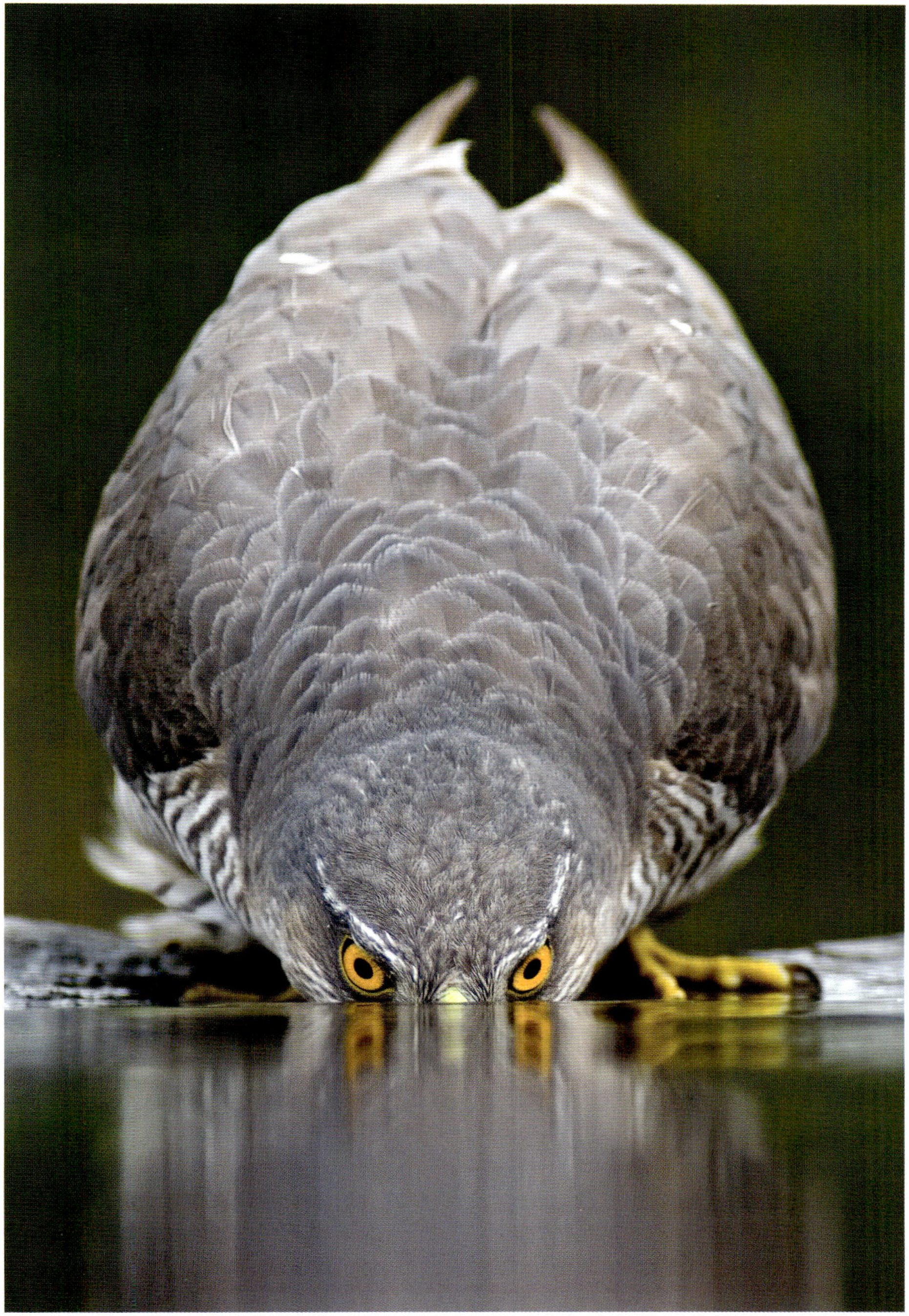

Bence Máté

Drinking and Bathing Ponds

Building a drinking pond for the birds in a dry area is one of the simplest and most productive and low-maintenance ways of attracting birds. Drinking ponds don't create dependence or otherwise confuse their natural behavior. It's good to choose a site with no other source of water within a few hundred yards, but it's important to have a thicket nearby where small birds can find shelter. Birds come to drinking ponds to bathe in the water more often than to drink, so make sure the pond has places that are shallow enough so even the smallest birds can stand in the water. Don't expect to see any waterbirds, though.

Eurasian Sparrowhawk at a bird pond that has attracted more than 50 species *(Accipiter nisus)*
Nikon D200, 300mm f/2.8 plus 1.4x extender, 1/350 second, f/5.6, ISO 320, manual focus, Gitzo tripod and video head, blind. Pusztaszer, Hungary, April 2005.

Erkki Toppinen

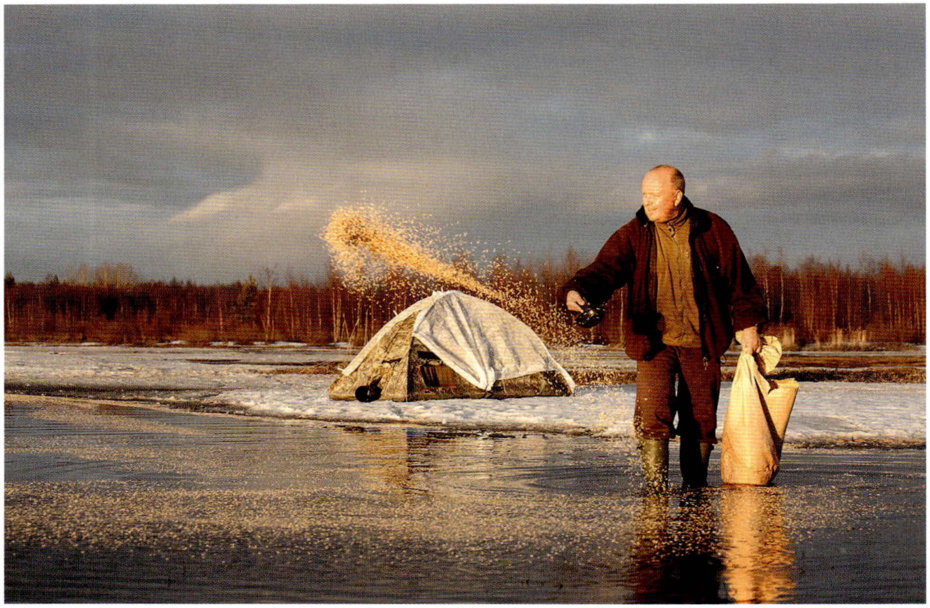

Putting out grain for waterbirds

Feeding

Feeding is the most obvious method to attract birds because they need to eat every day of the year. Attracting birds with food is especially easy when it is hard for them to find food in nature by themselves or when they have nestlings, when the weather is extremely cold, when everything is covered in deep snow, or when the days are short. Feeding is an action that interferes with birds' lives rather drastically and requires caution. Regular feeding teaches birds to come to the feeding on a daily basis, but if the feeding comes to an abrupt stop, the birds may not find another source of food in the area.

Another drawback is that feeding provides food even to individuals that would otherwise die by natural selection. These birds wouldn't normally reproduce and pass down their defective genes. Therefore, feeding wild animals needs to be undertaken with due caution and should be done only after a thorough assessment of the potential consequences. To get good advice, ask a local expert and follow up with the latest bird research and science.

There are a few tried and tested feeding methods. Birds around the world eat grain. Geese and ducks on shores can be fed corn or other cereal that is cheap and easy to get. Pour grain on the shore or in the shallow water, or even deeper out into the water; diving ducks and coots have no problem diving several yards if they know there is food to be found.

In cold weather birds favor fatty foods such as sunflower seeds, walnuts,

Bence Máté

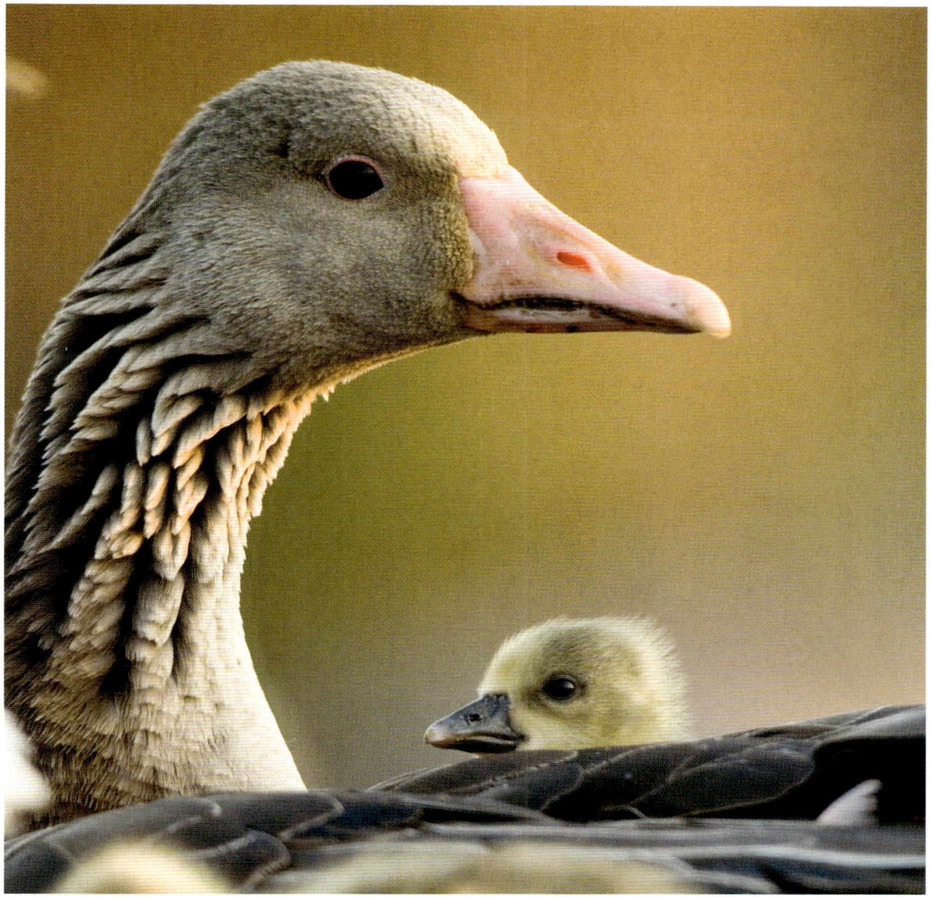

A Graylag gosling rests under a parent's wing after both have feasted on corn scattered in front of the blind *(Anser anser)*
Nikon D300, Sigma 300–800mm f/5.6, 1/100 second, 600mm, f/5.6, ISO 800, manual focus, self-made tripod, Gitzo video head, blind. Pusztaszer, Hungary.

and hazelnuts. Tits, like many other insectivorous species, will eat grain when their normal food is not available. As soon as the weather warms up, they will leave the feeders and look for their own food, but until that happens it's very important that the feeding is continuous and regular. It if is stopped abruptly it can cause the birds to starve and die because they learned to depend on the feeding. There are other perils to take into consideration too, namely the local cats that may start frequenting your bird feeders. Cats can be prevented from getting to the birds, but you should make sure that the birds can't bathe in the grain or otherwise cause food to fall on the ground, where they will then land to feed and the cats can prey on them.

Cold weather or shortage of food is not so much a problem to tropical birds, but they too like to come to feeders and supplement their diet of wild seeds with some grain.

In temperate climates, where fruiting is limited to a relatively short season, there are no real frugivorous species, whereas in the tropics, where the fruiting season is much longer and ripe fruits are available almost all year, many species can be attracted with fruits. In Costa Rica I had 26 different bird species responding to fruit baits.

Brown-hooded Parrots squabbling over fruits that were tied to a tree to attract them *(Pyrilia haematotis)*

Nikon D700, 300mm f/2.8, 1/1000 second, f/2.8, ISO 1000, two Nikon SB-800 flashes, manual focus, Gitzo tripod and video head. Costa Rica, January 2010.

Bence Máté

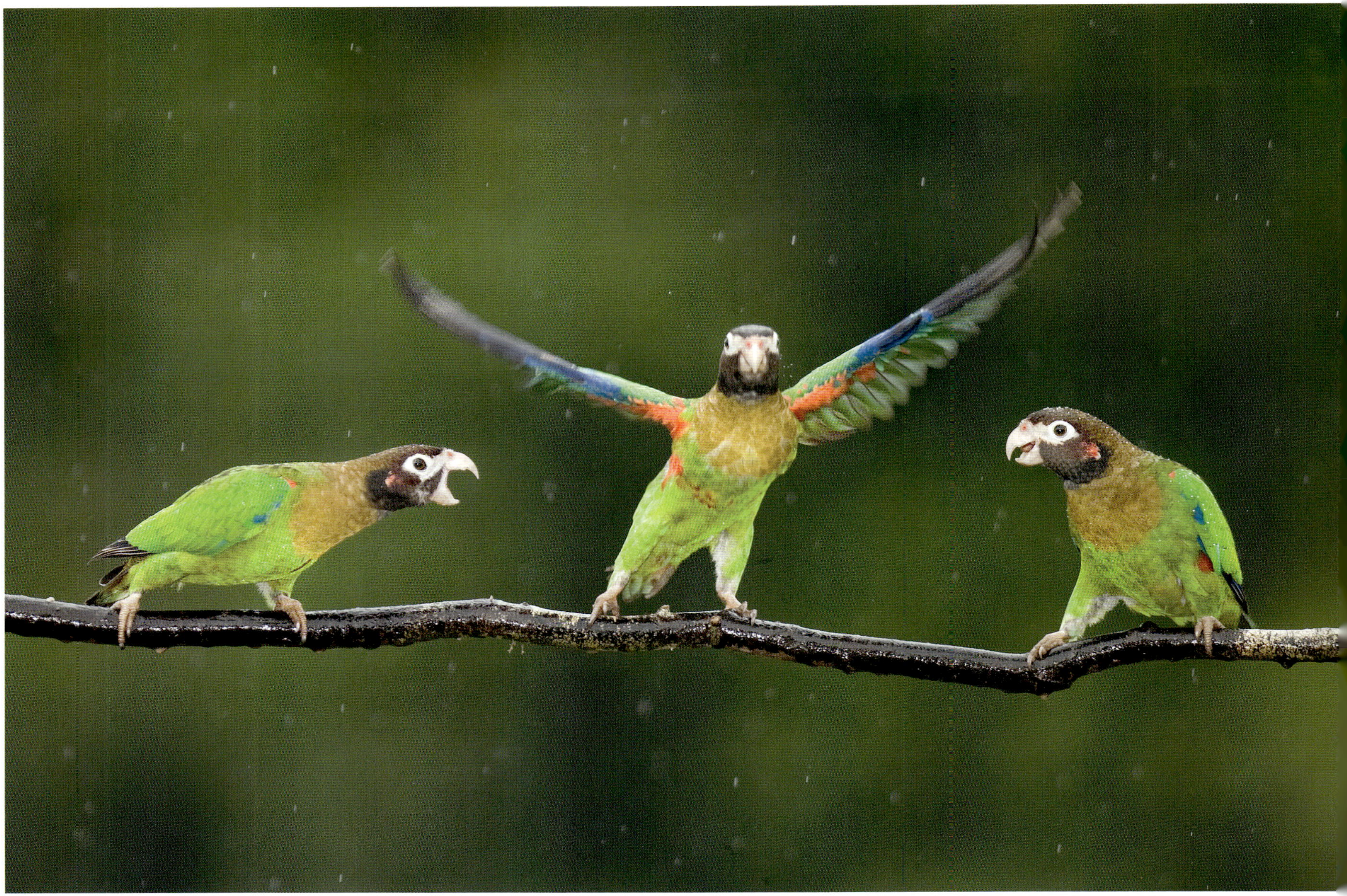

In the Americas, hummingbirds are commonly fed with commercially made feeders. Wherever I asked about the recipe for the nectar used as bait in the feeders, everybody recommended a ratio of three to four parts water to one part sugar. Hummingbirds are not shy, so a blind is not normally needed, but an image of a bird feeding from a plastic bottle isn't exactly the same as a hummingbird sipping nectar from a wild flower.

Bence Máté

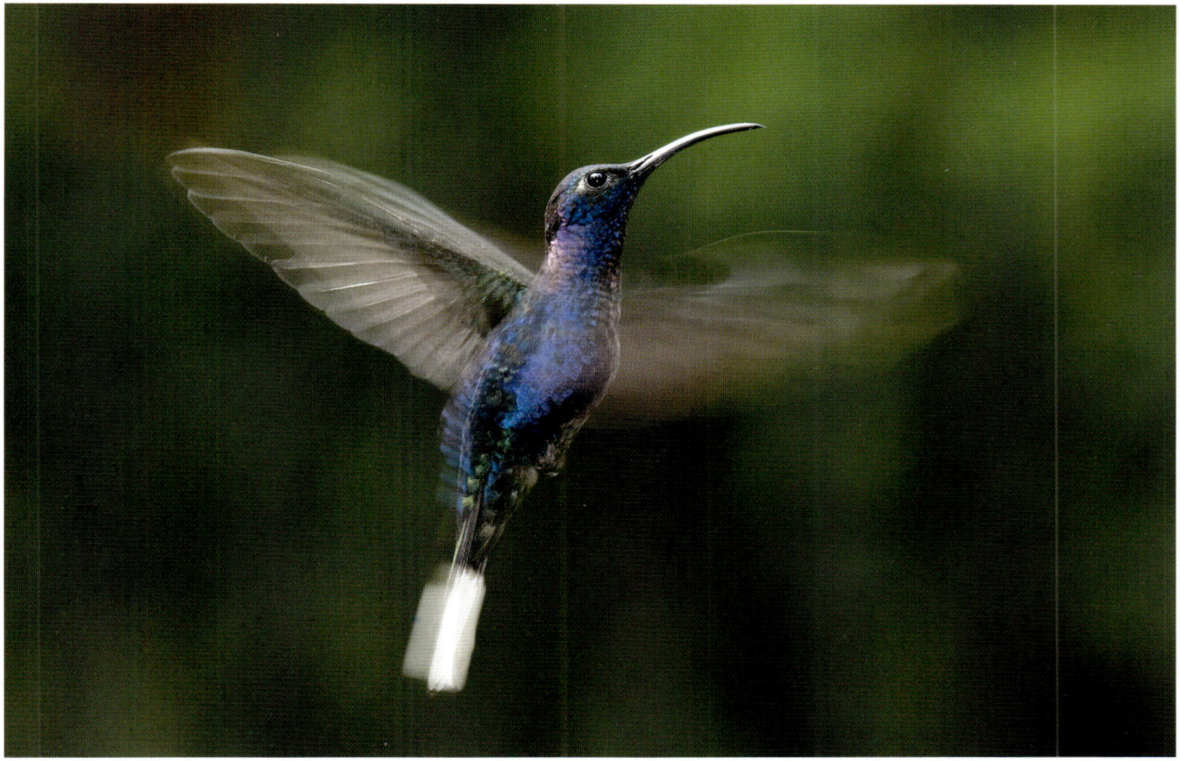

Violet Sabrewing hovering in front of a hummingbird feeder in a Monte Verde cloud forest *(Campylopterus hemileucurus)*
Nikon D300, 300mm f/2.8, 1/40 second, f/6.3, ISO 200, Nikon SB-800 flashes, manual focus, Gitzo tripod and video head. Costa Rica, February 2009.

A cow's head attracted Black Vultures and King Vultures to a photo blind
(Coragyps atratus, Sarcoramphus papa)
Nikon D300, Sigma 300–800mm f/5.6, 1/400 second, 500mm, f/8.0, ISO 800, manual focus, Gitzo tripod and video head, blind. Costa Rica, January 2009.

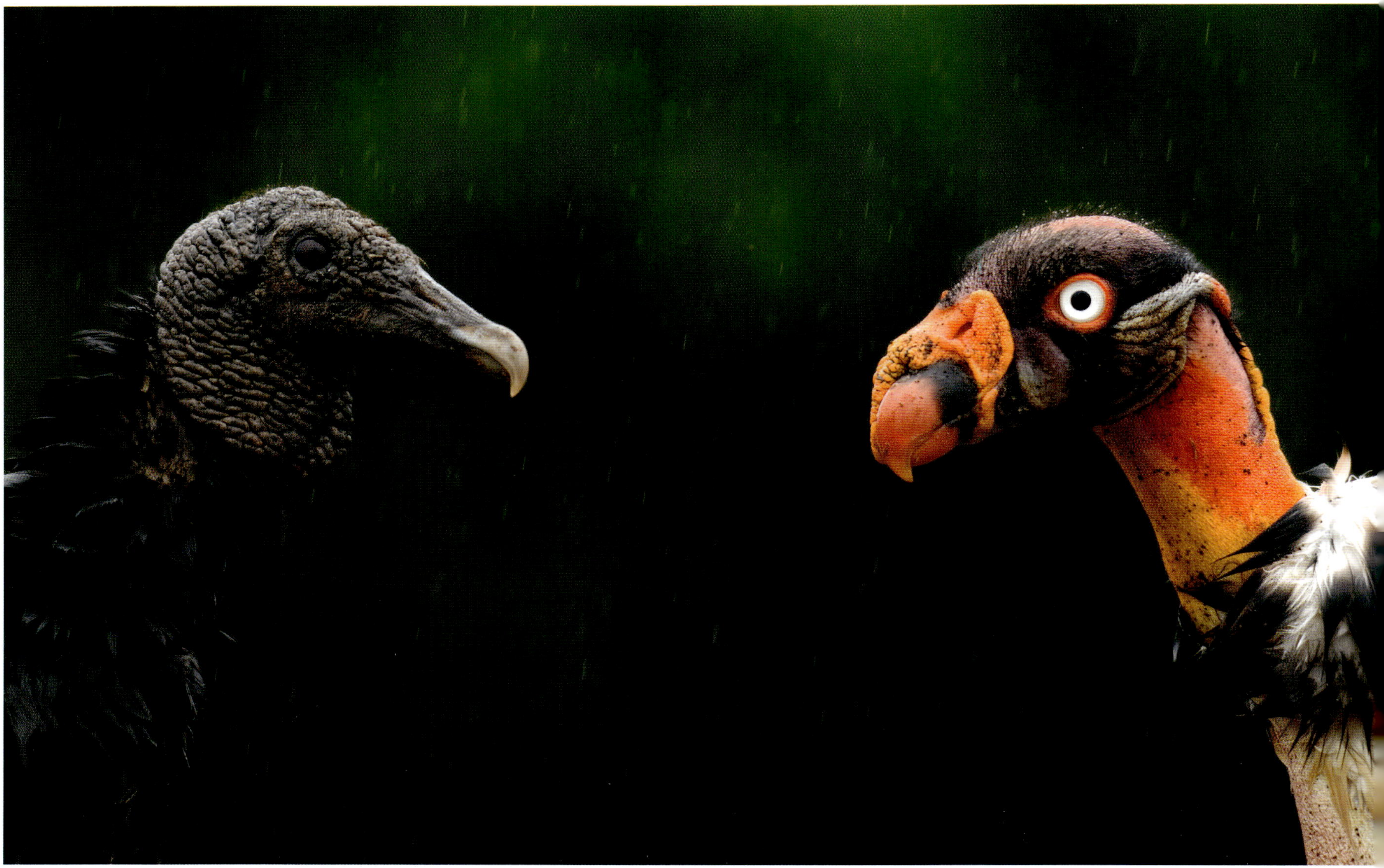

Bence Máté

Bence Máté

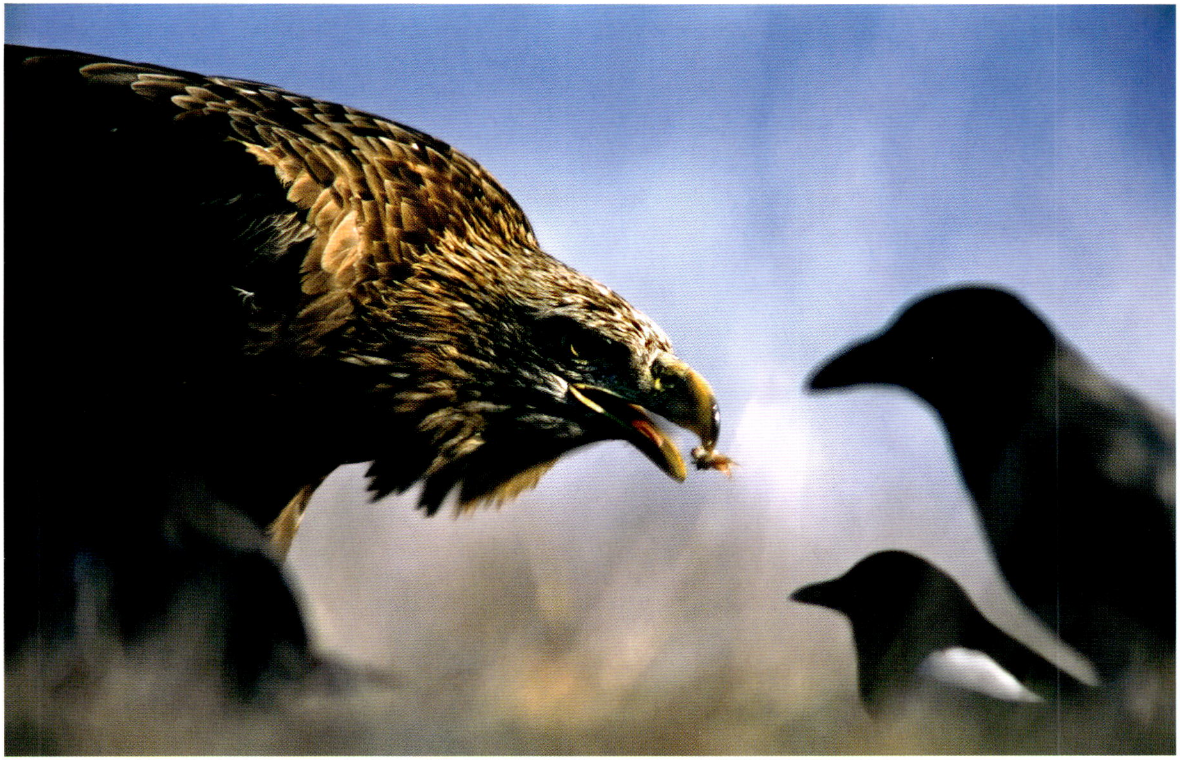

A Hooded Crow and a Eurasian Magpie wait impatiently for a White-tailed Eagle to finish eating *(Haliaeetus albicilla, Pica pica, Corvus cornix)*
Canon EOS-1N RS, FD 800mm f/5.6 plus FD-EOS extender, 1/80 second, f/7.1, Fuji Velvia ISO 50, manual focus, beanbag, blind. Pusztaszer, Hungary 2004.

Carcasses draw vultures year round, and they draw other raptors in the coldest weeks of winter. In Europe, the species I've seen feeding on carcasses include White-tailed Eagle, Golden Eagle, Imperial Eagle, Spotted Eagle, Northern Harrier, Northern Goshawk, Common Buzzard, Common Raven, Jackdaw, Hooded Crow, Rook, Eurasian Magpie, Gray Heron, and even Water Rail. Because handling carcasses carries an increased risk of infection, take every necessary hygienic precaution not to harm yourself or the environment. Always make sure the carcasses used are not victims of poisoning. Safe options include carcasses from hunters and ranchers. You can pick up animals that have been killed by vehicles and take them into the forest. Remember to find out what the local laws say about carcass feeding birds.

Using live bait is not very popular nowadays. If I skipped this subject, or wrote what some people would like to read, I would probably save myself a lot of trouble, but I prefer to state my view on the matter. I condemn any activity that causes animal suffering, be it at any level of the food chain, wild or feral animal alike. But like it or not, carnivorous animals do not eat grain.

Live bait is justifiable provided that the bait animal belongs to the predator's natural diet and the bait species is not an endangered or protected species. Everybody who eats meat takes part in killing, even if they themselves don't pull the trigger. Even vegetarians shouldn't think that crops are grown without destruction of whole habitats. I endorse all efforts to promote and ensure animal welfare, and at the same time I call for a more broad-based

Gray Heron catching fish on a bird feeding pond, just a few inches from a fish-eye lens *(Ardea cinerea)*
Nikon D300, Tokina 10–17mm f/3.5–4.5, 1/100 second, 17mm, f/7.1, ISO 400, two Nikon SB-800 flashes, manual focus, remote control head, blind. Pusztaszer, Hungary, June 2009.

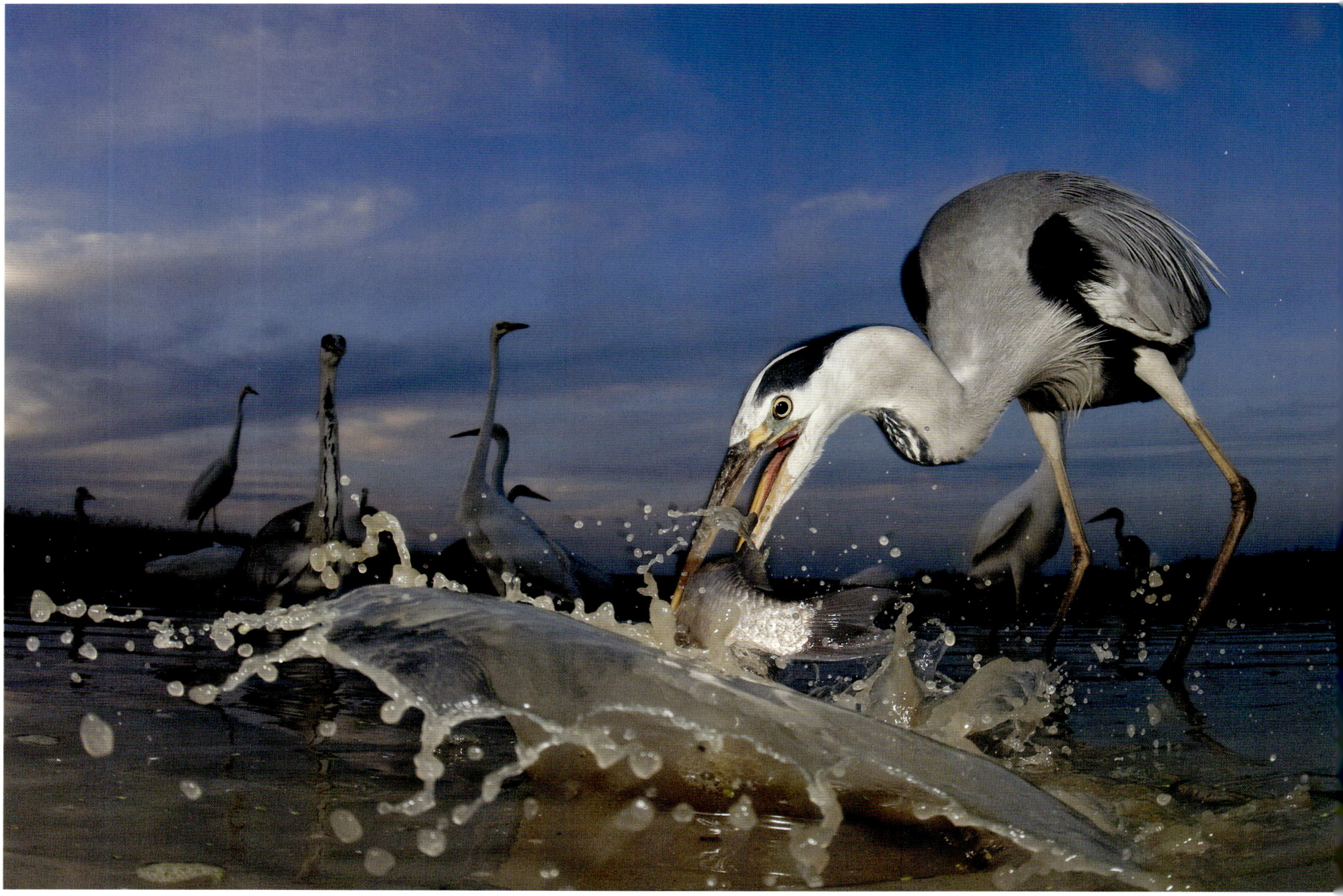

Bence Máté

Jari Peltomäki

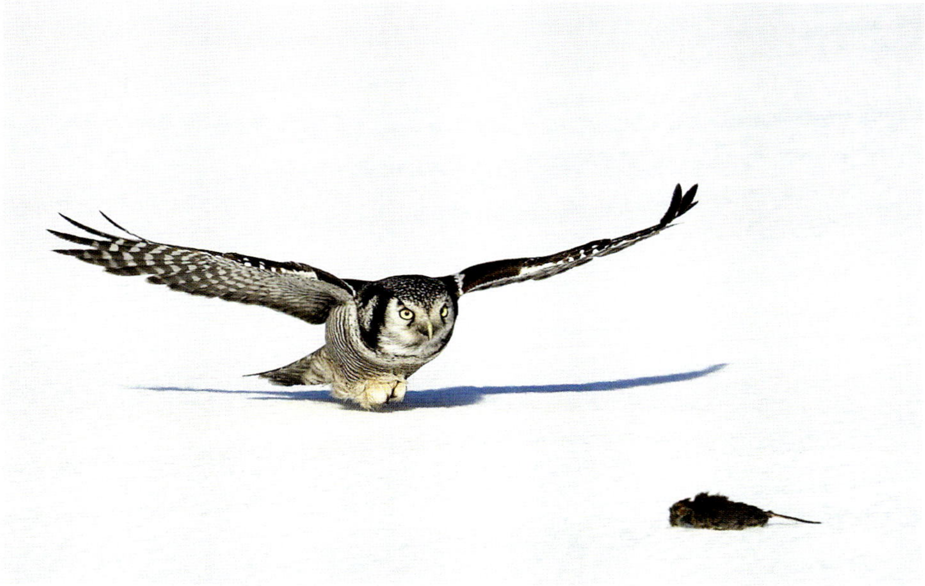

A Northern Hawk Owl catching a mouse *(Surnia ulula)*
Canon EOS-1D Mark III, 70–200mm f/2.8, 1/3200 second, 105mm, f/7.1, ISO 800, continuous focus with an extended central focusing point, handheld camera. Liminka, Finland, March 2009.

discussion that aims for real and practical solutions and comprehensive protection of nature and wildlife.

Here are a few feeding techniques with live bait. Maggots, earthworms, and mealworms are widely available in angler shops, and most woodland birds are mad about them. In the breeding season, when birds are feeding their young, a tray of mealworms in the forest will be found quickly.

Fish farms and fishermen can have surplus fish that for various reasons isn't saleable. In some places this fish is taken to feed animals in a zoo, but it has to be disposed of one way or another. Find out if you can get this type of fish locally.

Mice and rats are included in the diet of many raptors, and baiting these birds with rodents is easy. I find it strange to talk of animal suffering in this context; a raptor eating a rodent is a perfectly natural, everyday occurrence, right there in nature's food chain.

When you've figured out your own position on live bait, find out what the local laws say about it. In Finland, for instance, the various laws are presently interpreted to ban the use of live bait in attracting or feeding birds, even if the bait species is not protected. Luckily, the use of dead rodents in bird photography is not illegal—which has saved quite a few owls from certain death.

A European Roller that caught a small rodent *(Coracias garrulus)*
Nikon D300, 300mm f/2.8, 1/2500 second, f/5.6, ISO 640, continuous focus, Gitzo tripod and video head, blind. Pusztaszer, Hungary, June 2008. →

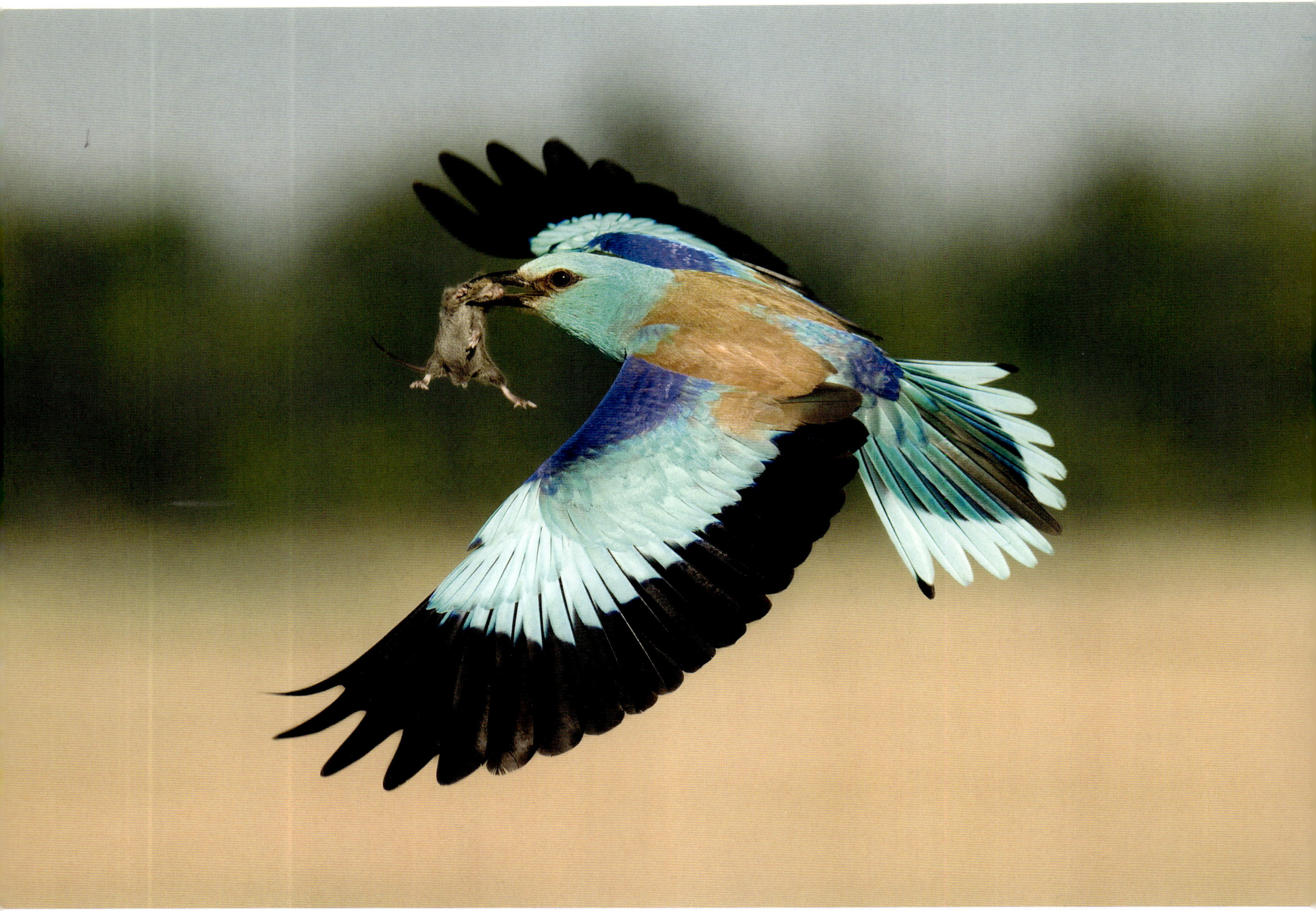

Bence Máté

BENCE MÁTÉ

HOW TO BUILD AND USE A BLIND

Find out where the birds go and when they show up, and hide well.

Over the past 10 years I have built more than 100 blinds, and no two are identical. Every site has its own surprise to figure out. In the following paragraphs I will outline some essential factors to consider when you design a blind.

Invisibility

A blind has to completely conceal you from the surrounding world—sometimes not only visually, but also by cutting off sounds and smells. Most animals rely on their vision for safety, and as soon as they become suspicious of unusual movements, your chances of wearing out your shutter are lost. Sounds, especially snapping noises, can also cause animals to leave the area, so build a blind that keeps most of the noise inside. When you are photographing mammals with a keen sense of smell, you need to stay downwind or in an airtight blind with a vent that keeps the smells several yards high.

Good Visibility

It's crucial to be able to see and photograph in all directions without obstructions, but the better you hide yourself, the more difficult this becomes. Most photographers use traditional fabric blinds, but the field of view in them is very restricted. If you're not always a

Canvas tents are good for many purposes, but they are no use against the cold. Here is one of my earliest tents, which I used for photographing egrets one winter. I had cardboard as insulation, but without a sleeping bag to keep me warm, I wouldn't have endured the day-long sessions in −10ºC (14ºF) temperatures.

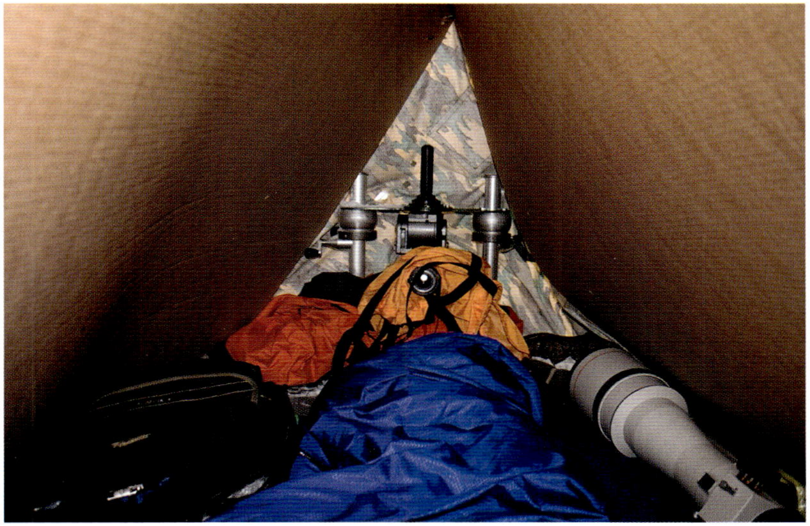

Bence Máté

A tent on the ice of a frozen lake is a great place to observe birds, but it has its dangers. The ice was slowly melting under the legs of my tent frame, which I didn't notice before the end of the five-day project.

Csaba Daróczi

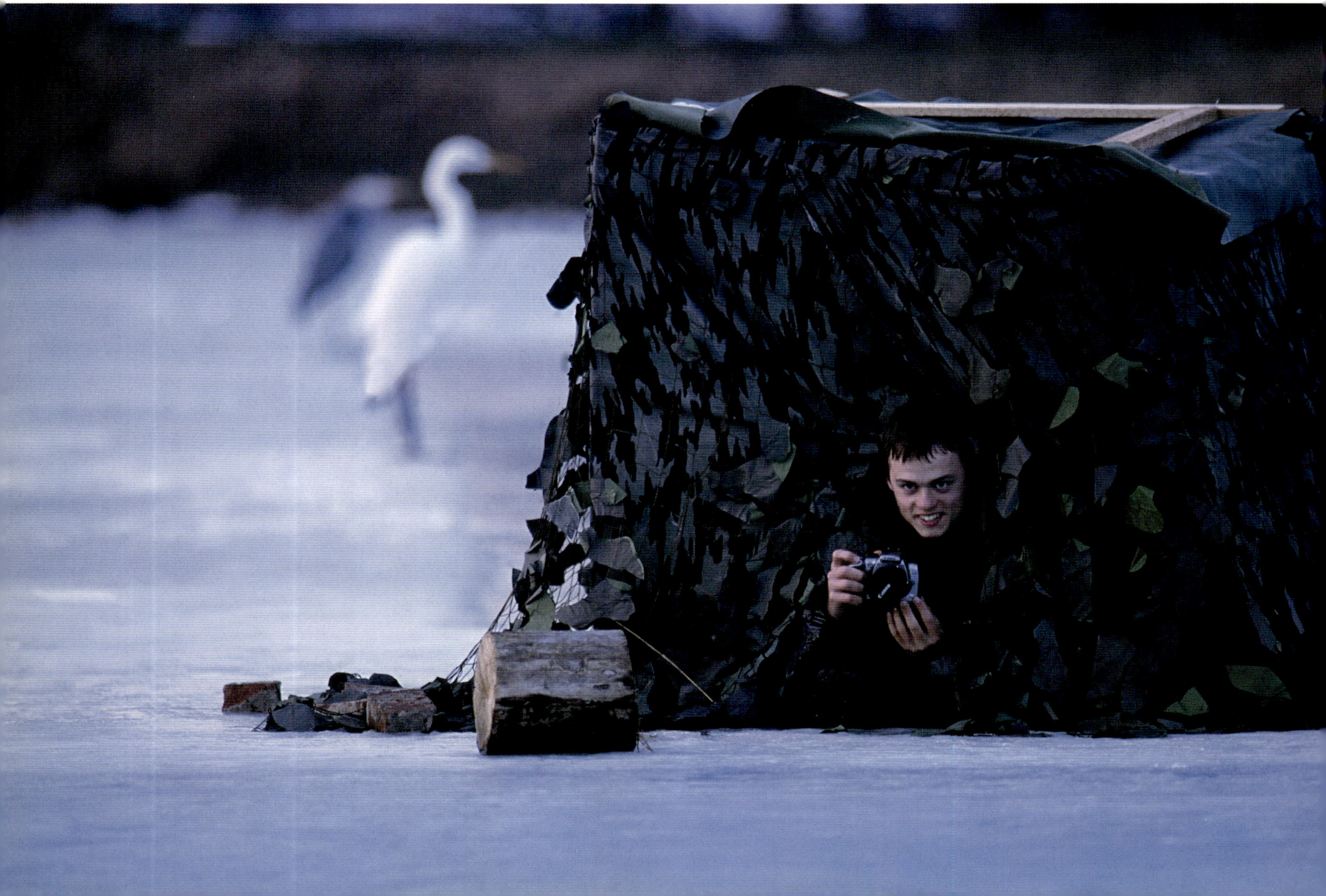

step ahead of your subjects, and you have no idea what to expect and what direction the action will come from, then unfortunately you'll miss most of the action.

This problem was always at the back of my mind, until about six years ago I was struck with the idea to experiment with semitransparent glass. Since then, I have incorporated 4mm (0.2 in) Stopsol Classic Clear glass in my blinds when possible. In optimal conditions it blocks all movement from inside the blind, plus it improves soundproofing. Photographing through glass makes you lose one f-stop, but in my opinion this is a small price to pay for increased freedom of movement and field of vision. Its effect on image quality is minor if the lens is as close to perpendicular as possible. It's essential that light enters the blind only through the window and that the slope of the window reflects the brightest surface in the surroundings—usually the sky—toward the birds. The glass is see-through from the inside and has a reflective coating on the outside. The window must always be covered when the blind is not being used.

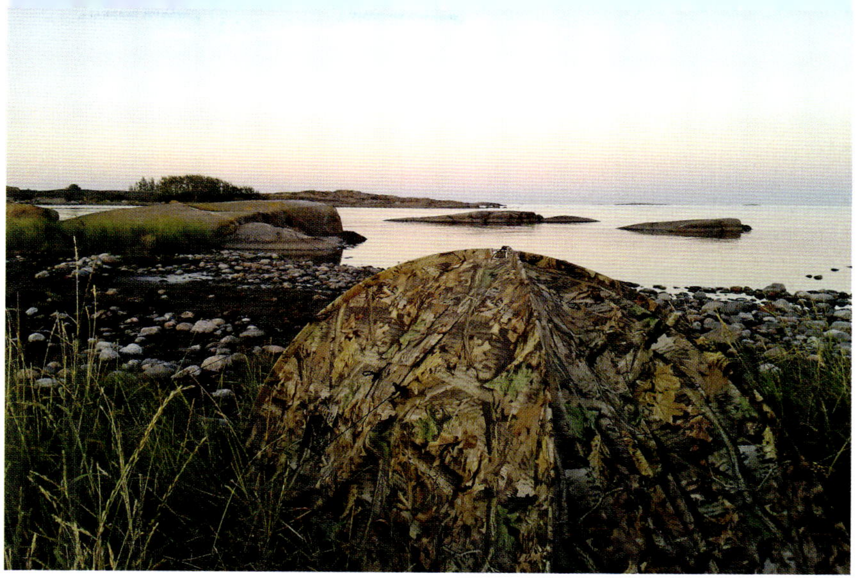

Minna Lindroth

Most camera equipment retailers stock tent blinds specifically designed for field photography. Low, camouflaged blinds are the best option for short-term use. Here a blind is placed at the base of a shoal with a range that covers both the waders that favor the strip and the ducks that come to feed at the shallow water. The blind is strategically positioned with the evening light falling on the birds over the back of the blind.

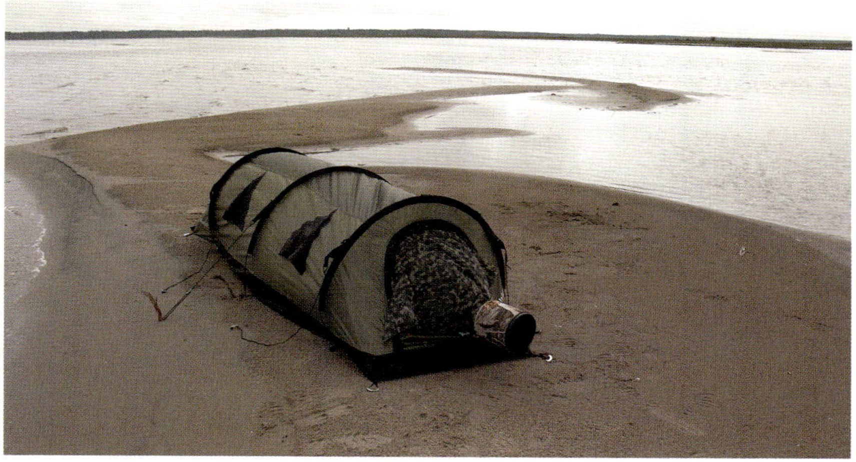

Jari Peltomäki

Tent blinds are the most popular choice in bird photography. Manufactured blinds offer ready-made solutions, but it's easy to modify regular tents for a custom-built blind. A fully waterproof tunnel tent is excellent for photographing on beaches where the ground is wet. The tent is open at both ends, and the end protruding out is covered with a tightly woven camouflage netting. The tent has good visibility and allows a camera angle as wide as 180 degrees.

Bence Máté

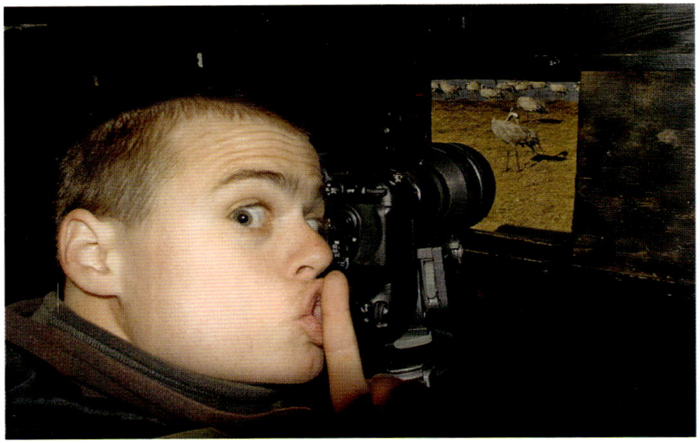

Cranes were feeding in front of this blind in Hornborga, Sweden, within just a couple of yards from the blind's window. It is exciting to see how at ease and confident the birds are here, where they are used to being fed and the conditions are familiar every year, compared to cranes almost anywhere else.

Minna Rautio

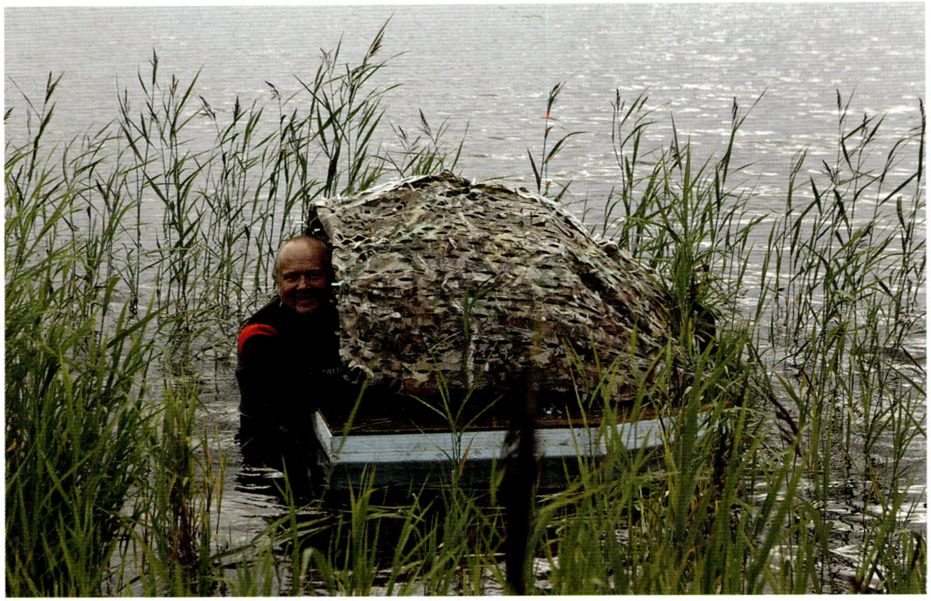

A floating blind gives you the freedom to move about in water, letting you get surprisingly close to birds and try different shooting angles. Ready-made solutions are hard to find, and do-it-yourself is often the best solution. Some floating blinds are built to hold the photographer and the camera on top of the water, but this version has the photographer submerged in water. A wet suit offers sufficient protection against milder conditions, but in colder water a more expensive dry suit is better.

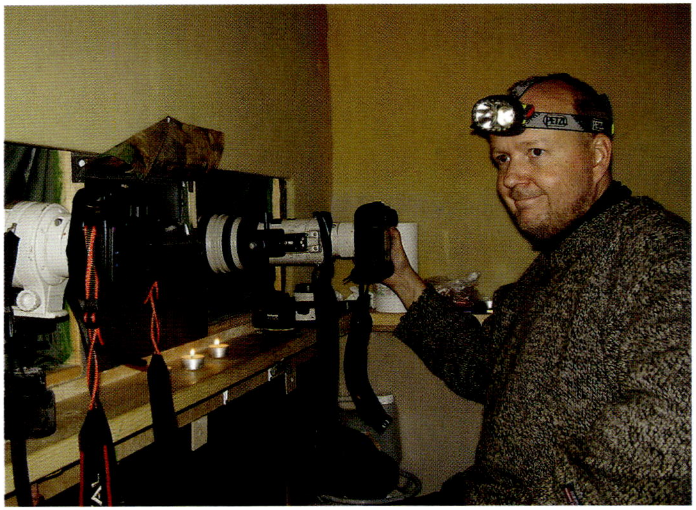

Erkki Toppinen

Ideal Angle

You might be sitting in the middle of the world's biggest bird paradise, but if you can't take your pictures from an ideal camera angle, you're really just wasting your time. The best angle is often found low near water or ground level, where you would normally use an angle finder. The working position is very uncomfortable. On land, it's easy to dig the blind partially underground, where you can sit in a comfortable position and photograph at ground level. In water you can cloak your head with a blind and stand neck-deep in water, which is a relatively simple but somewhat uncomfortable solution.

Or you can go for a comfortable but extremely complicated solution and build a half-submerged photo blind, where you can sit inside and stay dry while you photograph at water level. The blind must be waterproof and very heavy to counter the uplift that equals the weight of water that is displaced by the blind. A single-person blind displaces at least 700 L (185 gal) of water, which means that if you choose this option rather than risk becoming hypothermic after hours in a cloak blind, your blind, your equipment, and you must weigh more than 700 kg (1,543 lb).

If either solution sounds intimidating, you should find a good spot on the shore, place your camera on a beanbag, and lie down. The result is the same, although the position is not quite so comfortable. Read more about angle in the chapter "Angle Matters."

Working Conditions

In the long run, a comfortable blind will contribute to better photos. It's hard to concentrate on photography if your feet are freezing or if you run the risk of heat stroke. If you decide to build a blind, remember to include comfort and good working conditions in your plans.

In Finland Eagles are photographed in winter from heated, insulated blinds. Even with outside temperatures dropping to below −30°C (−22°F), it's possible to sit inside wearing just a T-shirt. Normally the tripod head is bolted onto a sturdy plank inside the blind. The lens hole has a pouch made of thick insulating material that fits snugly around the telephoto lens to keep the cold out and the heat in. The thermal windows have a reflective coating on the outside so the photographers remain invisible but have a good view. But remember to move your telephoto lenses extremely carefully to avoid spooking the keen-sighted ravens and eagles!

A Low-Budget Tent or a Permanent Blind?

Before you build a permanent blind, it's not a bad idea to sit at the location, put aside all grand visions, and ask yourself how long you will really use the blind. If it's only for two weeks, you can unfold the fabric blind you decided was unsuitable and give it another try.

But if you're certain you would use the blind for several years, tell the landowner your plans, and if you get permission then proceed. Even then I recommend spending a few weeks in a mobile tent on your chosen spot before building a permanent blind to really learn the site well.

There is no standard way to build a blind because every site has individual characteristics. What's important, though, is to figure out the light conditions, the blind's position relative to the sun, the wind directions, the backgrounds, and possible human presence.

Before building a permanent blind it's good to spend a few days on the location in a tent blind. Gathering information about the behavior of the animals around a particular spot, studying the light conditions, and generally getting the feel of the place are handy details for designing the blind and planning its optimal positioning.

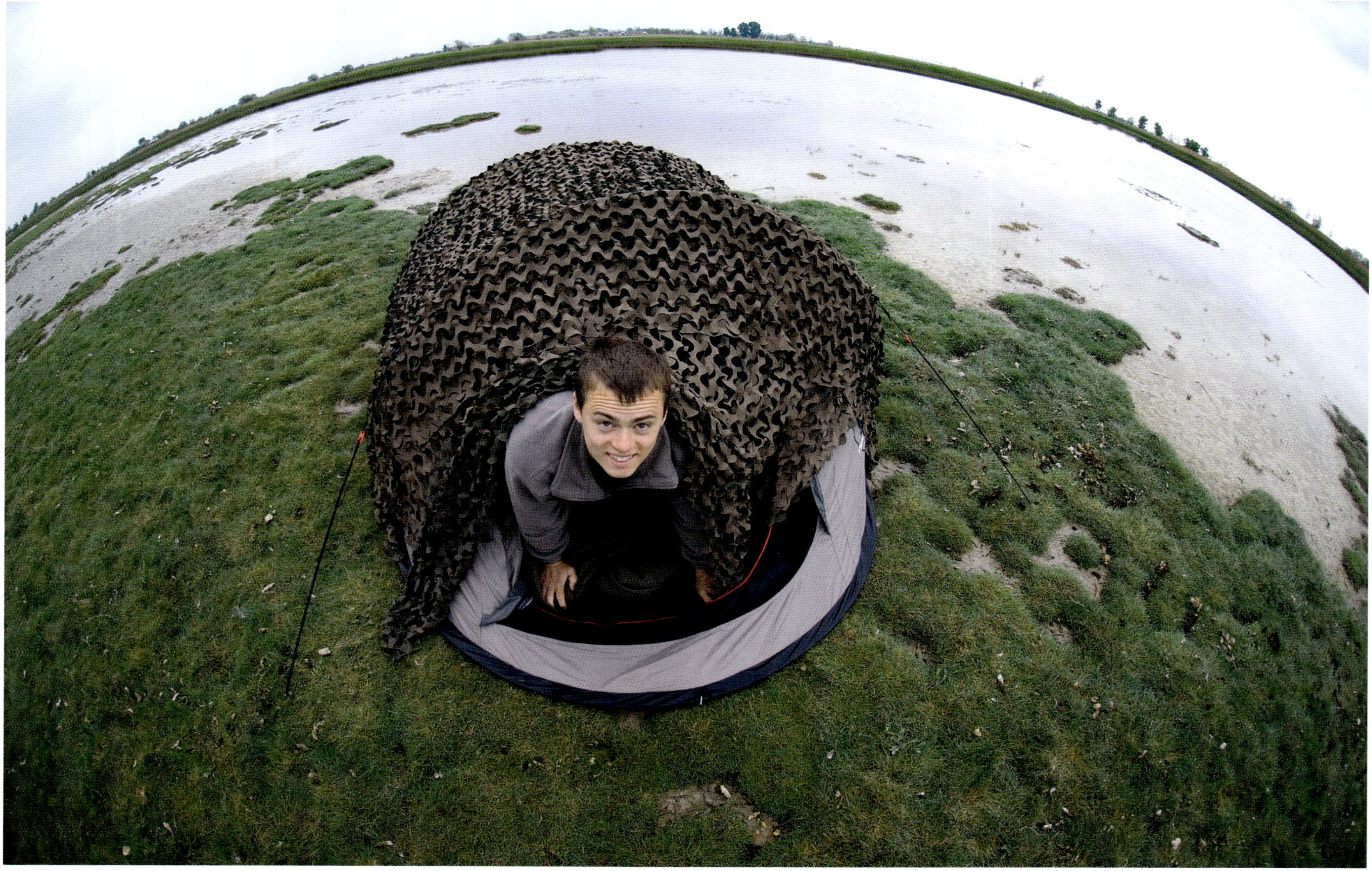

László Nehézy

Csaba Daróczi

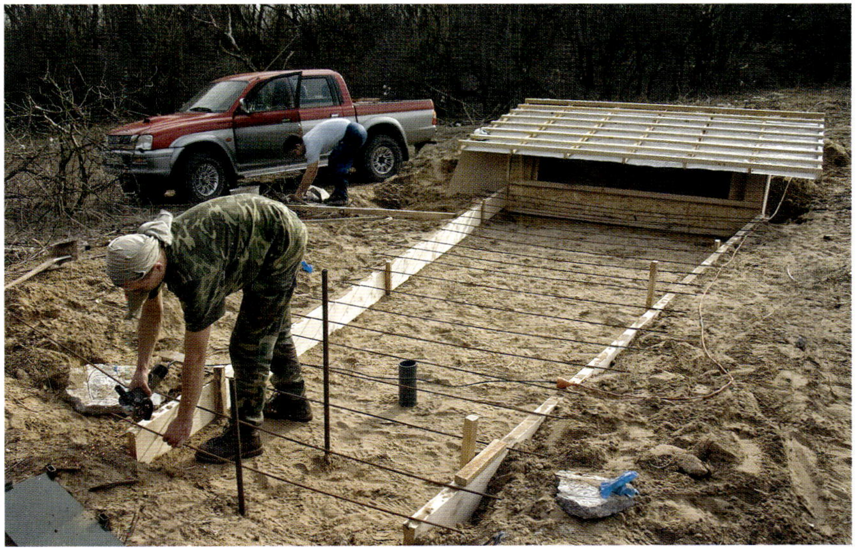

The blind should be placed in an optimal position to the birds so that it faces them with light coming from the best possible direction.

Bence Máté

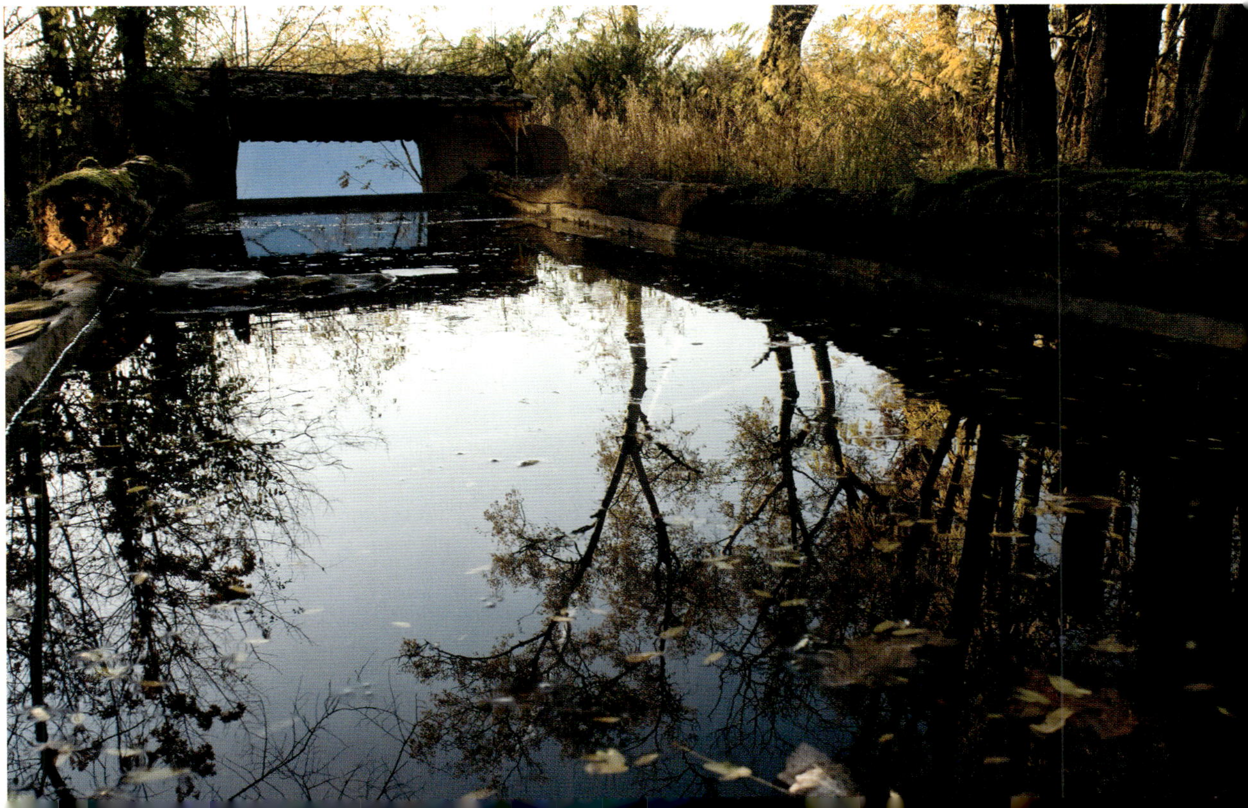

When the water in the pond comes all the way to the blind window, even the big birds' reflections fit in the frame.

Nesting boxes have been rigged onto and around this tower blind to attract many birds. A Eurasian Kestrel pair, a European Roller pair, and 20 or so European Starling pairs nest here on a yearly basis, together with the occasional Long-eared Owl and Little Owl.

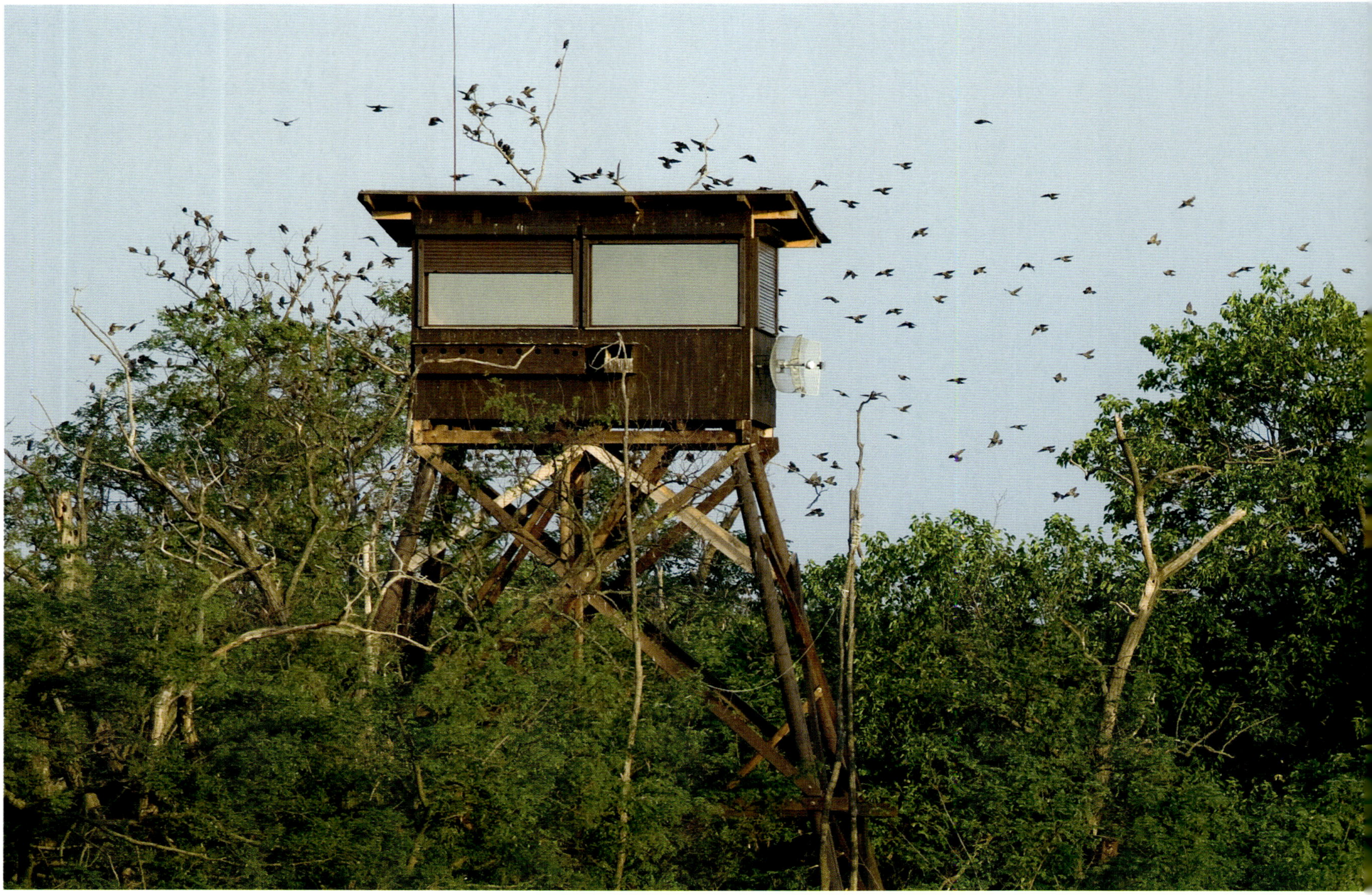

Bence Máté

Blending in with the Surroundings

Few animals can distinguish between a brightly colored and a camouflaged blind, especially if they have time to grow accustomed to the color. Shape is important only in mobile blinds, which shouldn't stand out from the surroundings; they should blend in with a bush, for example. Blending permanent blinds into the surroundings is important. When you build in the wild, avoid spoiling the landscape, and when the blind is no longer needed, demolish it and restore the site to its natural condition!

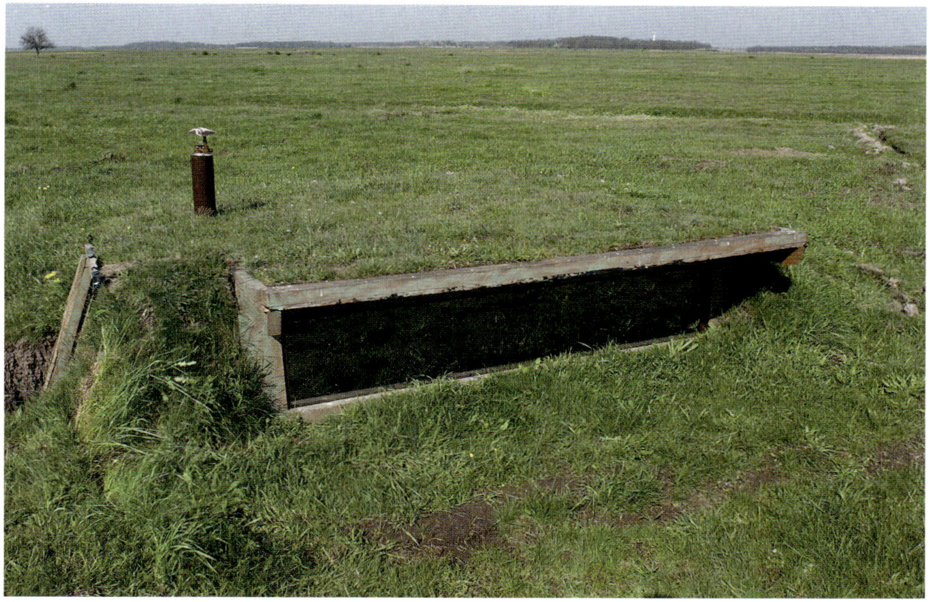

Bence Máté

Disguising the blind as a natural land formation is important because the eagles are extremely cautious, nearly paranoid.

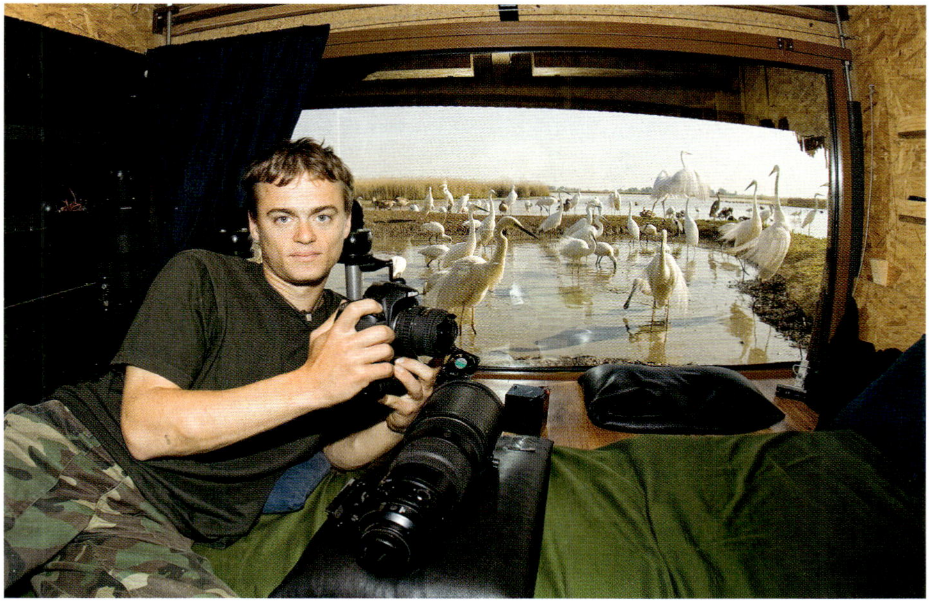

Agnes Kiss

Stopsol Classic Clear reflective glass provides the opportunity to observe and photograph even the shy bird species within very close range.

JARI PELTOMÄKI AND MARKUS VARESVUO

PHOTOGRAPHING FROM A CAR OR A BOAT

A car makes a good mobile blind, and a boat takes you to the waterbirds.

Car (Jari)

A car is an excellent mobile blind, especially where the birds are few and far between and pitching a tent blind isn't possible. Also when time is limited, like on photo trips abroad, a lot of photographs tend to be taken from a car. Many small birds aren't afraid of a moving car, often allowing you to get surprisingly close to your subjects. Overall, smaller back roads are more rewarding than bigger and busier main roads. Remember that many countries have banned off-road driving.

I had a box made for my car that fits between the two front seats. It holds two cameras and two different-sized lenses. When I'm out driving, I always have my gear ready for action. Over the years I've come across a great many opportunities that I would have missed without my camera box. Plus, the gear is out of sight when it's in the box.

Another option is to have your gear in a camera bag somewhere close to you so you can reach it without getting out of the car. Keeping the camera on the other seat is not a good option because if you need to brake abruptly, it would probably catapult off the seat and onto the floor.

If there are two photographers in the car, a good tactic is for one to drive and the other to sit in the backseat behind the driver. This way both photographers get a fair chance at fast-action situations. It doesn't matter so much which side of the car the bird is on because both photographers can shoot from either side.

Beanbags are excellent for photographing from a car through an open window. You can read more about this in the chapter "Bird Photographer's Tripods." Sometimes I use camouflage netting to hide my face and movement, especially when photographing wary birds from a car.

When you are driving, keep your bird sounds ready. For example, in winter you may find a Gray Partridge feeding in deep snow by the road, and by briefly playing its call you can make it peek out of the snowpack. Sound luring should be used in moderation to avoid disturbing the birds.

Particularly in winter, when it's very cold outside, keep the temperature inside the car as low as you can, otherwise the heat you're letting out through the open window creates heat haze, which may cause blurry images.

The Eurasian Collared-Dove image was taken as I was coming home from getting my groceries one day. When I turned in to my front yard I spotted a backlit dove perching in a maple that still had its autumn-colored leaves and was daintily covered with fresh snow. Luckily I had my camera handy and was able to capture a nice early winter moment.

Tomi Muukkonen

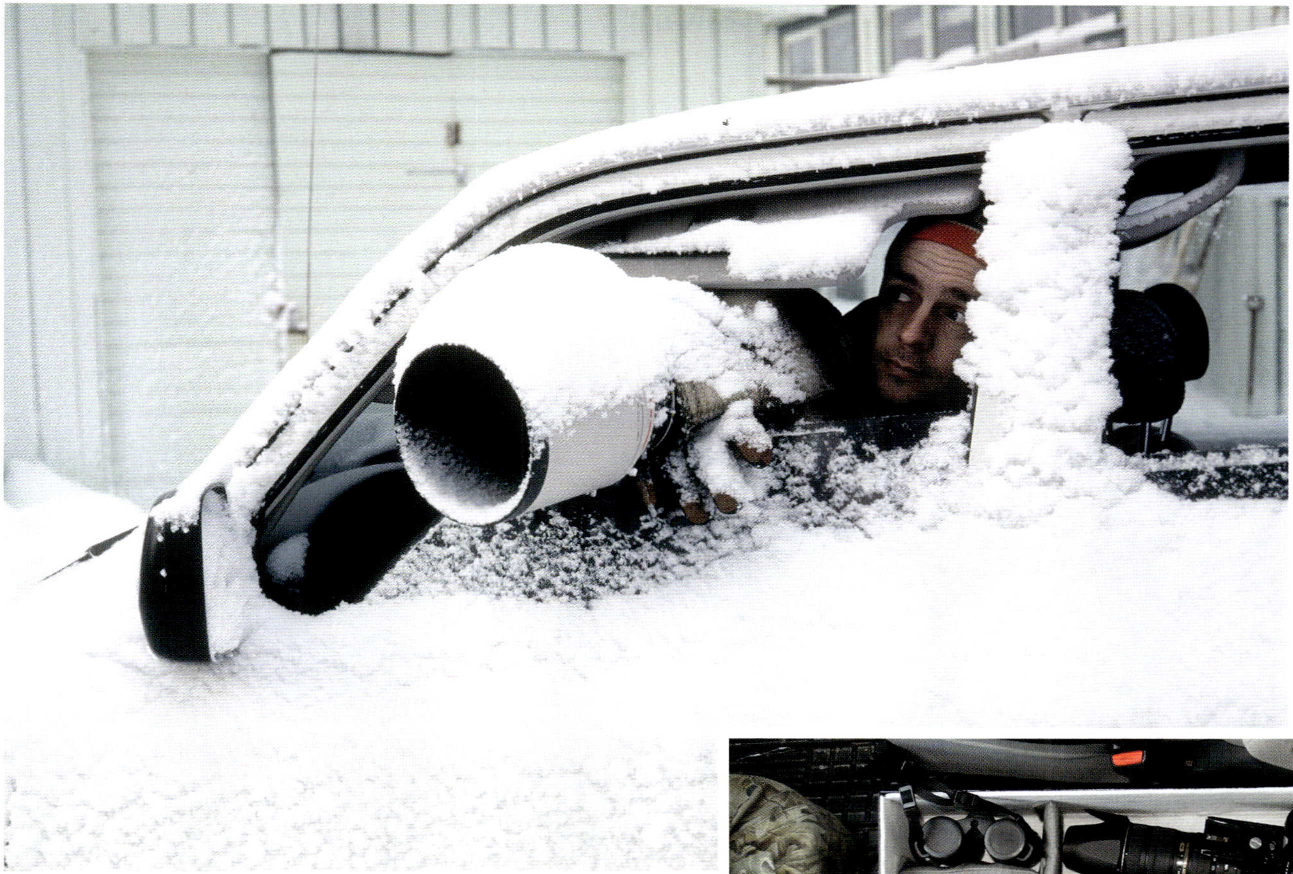

A car functions well as a blind. This photograph was taken during a two-hour stint photographing Glaucous Gulls on a harbor pier in Vardø, North Norway, in heavy snow.

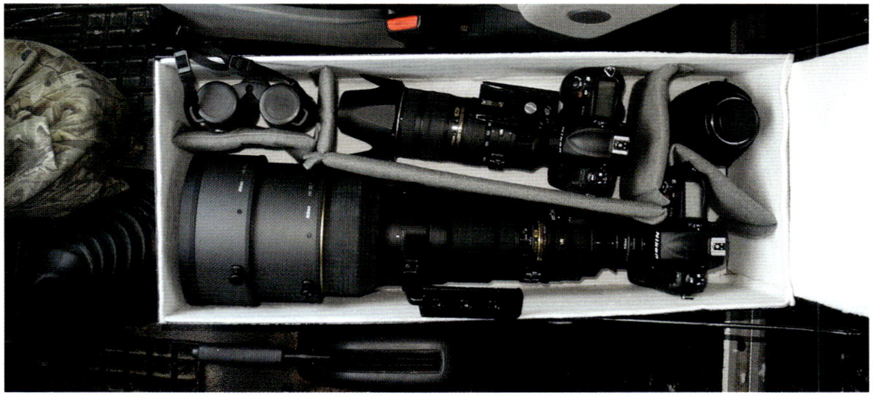

Camera gear in a box that was designed for a car

Jari Peltomäki

Jari Peltomäki

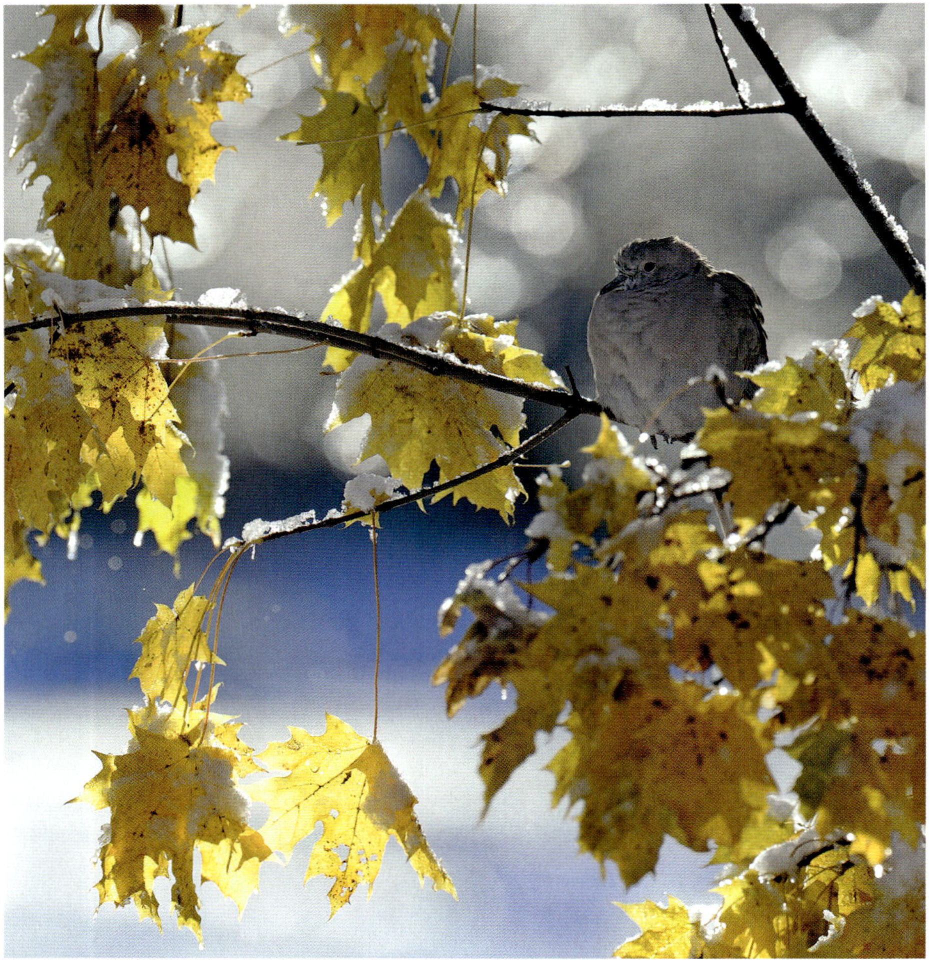

A Eurasian Collared-Dove in a maple on my front lawn *(Streptopelia decaocto)*
Nikon D3S, 500mm f/4.0, 1/1600 second, f/7.1, ISO 800, one-shot focus with a central focusing point, beanbag, car as a blind. Liminka, Finland, October 2010.

The image of a Green Sandpiper sounding its alarm is the result of one midsummer tour in the neighboring woods. The bird had brought its chicks to the side of the road and was warning them of an approaching car. Seeing that the chicks were safe in the ditch by the road, I took a few quick frames of the Green Sandpiper parent before driving off.

One November, when winter had come early, I was out with a fellow photographer when we found a Gray Partridge flock foraging in a field. We had been photographing them from the car for about an hour, when suddenly they all took cover beneath the snow. Just a few seconds later a Northern Goshawk struck about 10 m (32.8 ft) out in front of us. I don't know who was more dumbfounded, us or the Northern Goshawk, but some seconds later it took off clutching a Gray Partridge that was still alive. Our camera settings were all wrong, of course, because we had been photographing slowly moving, feeding birds, but luckily the Northern Goshawk was struggling with the weight of its prey and had to land to get a better hold. Now we were ready for the action. Something like this can be a once-in-a-lifetime opportunity.

I was in Lithuania one spring on a photo trip and managed to drive to a

A Green Sandpiper sounding an alarm call by the side of a road *(Tringa ochropus)*
Canon EOS-1D Mark III, 500mm f/4.0, 1/200 second, f/7.0, ISO 800, one-shot focus with a central focusing point, beanbag, car as a blind. Lumijoki, Finland, June 2007.

Jari Peltomäki

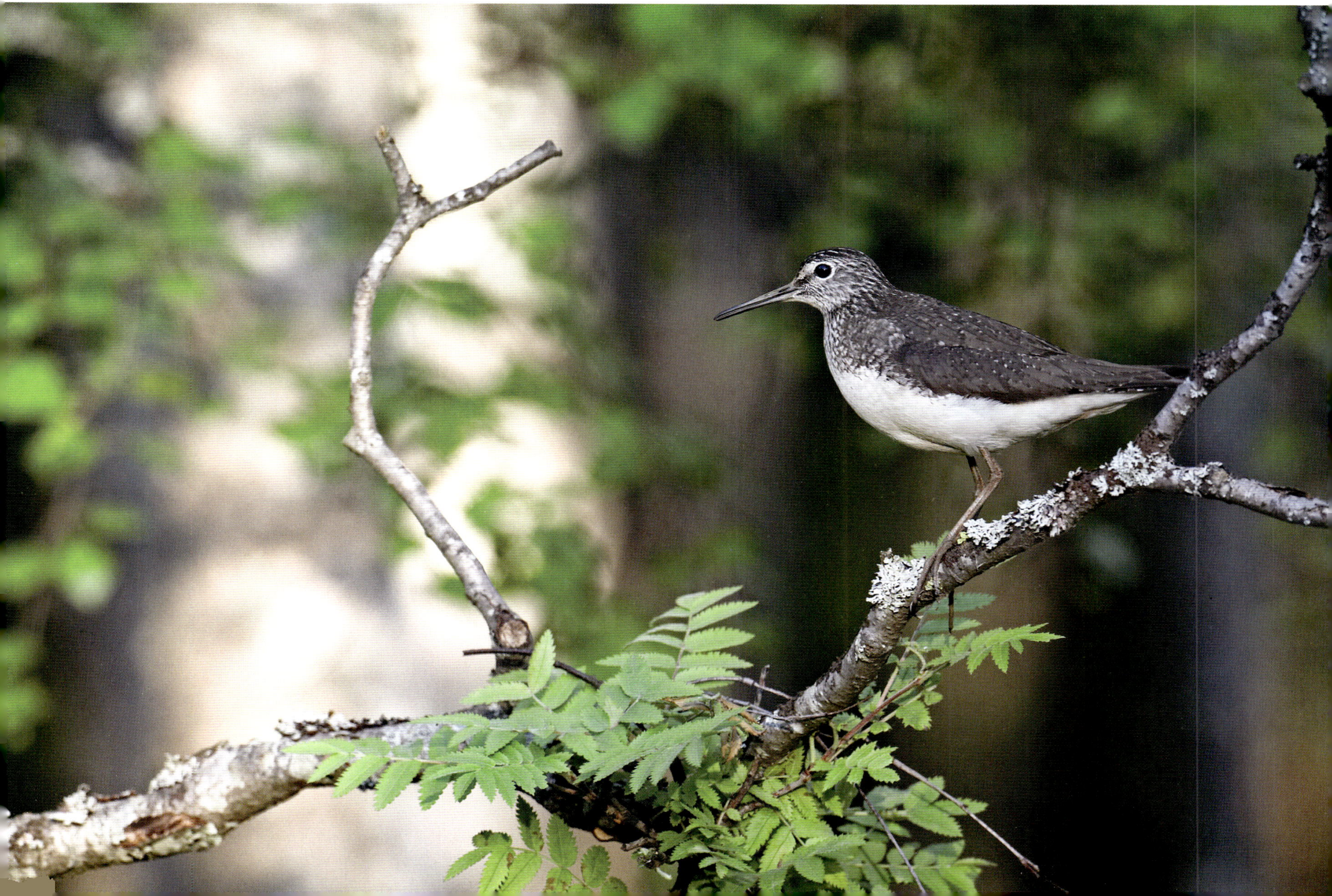

A Gray Partridge caught by a Northern Goshawk *(Perdix perdix, Accipiter gentilis)*
Canon EOS-1D Mark II, 500mm f/4.0 plus 1.4x extender, 1/2500 second, f/6.3, ISO 1600, continuous focus with 45 focusing points, handheld camera, car as a blind. Liminka, Finland, November 2006.

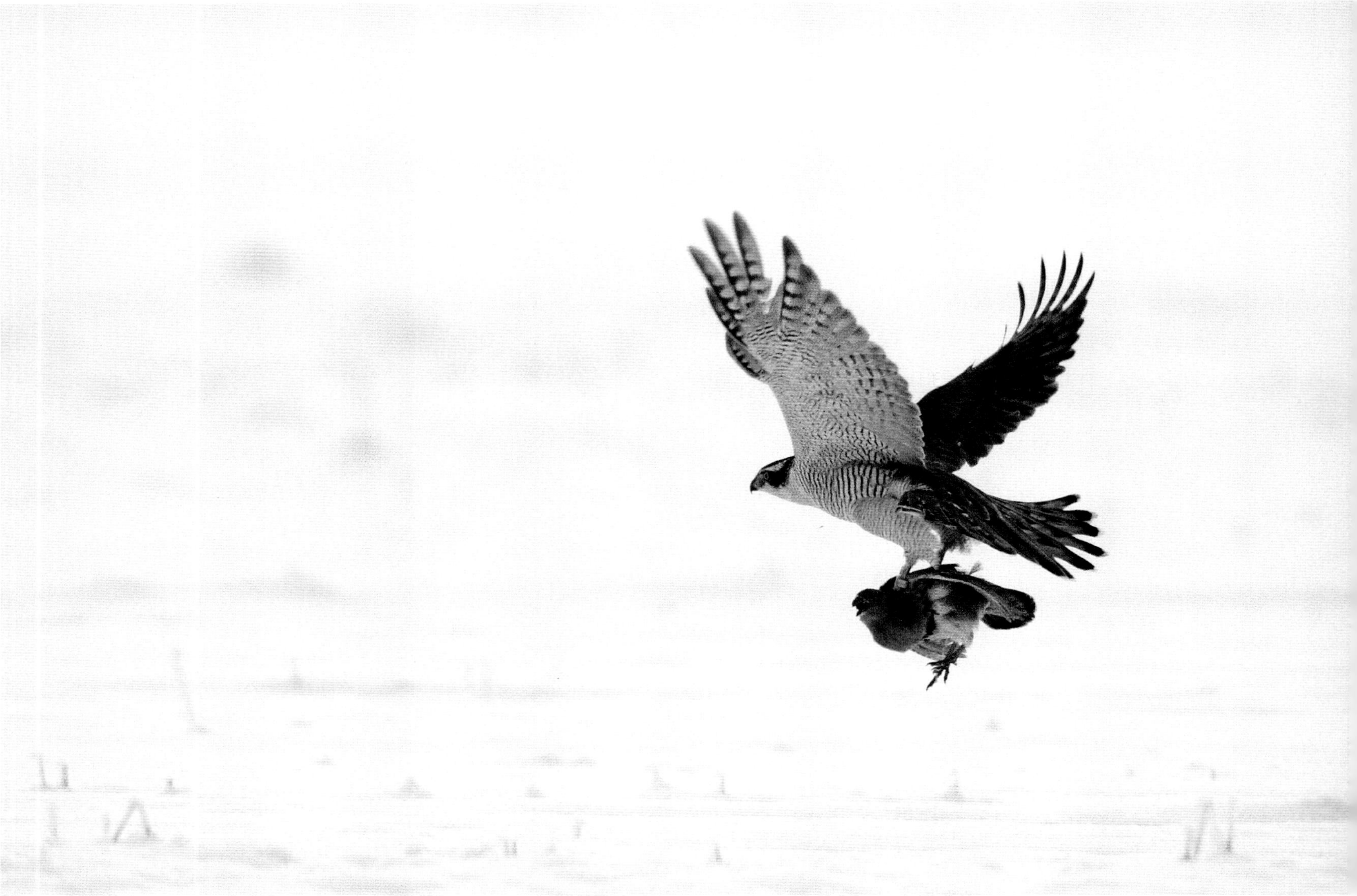

Markus Varesvuo

Jari Peltomäki

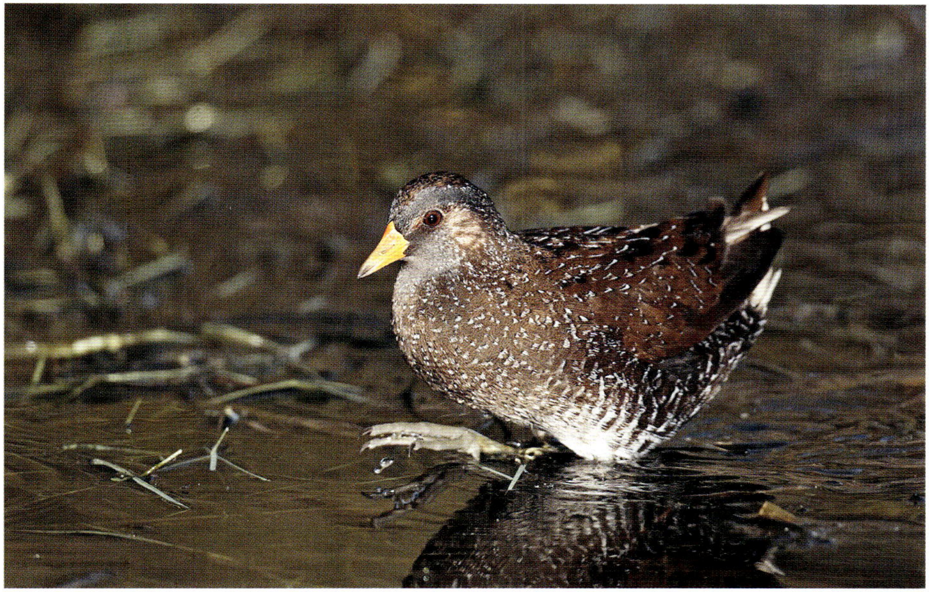

A Spotted Crake photographed from a car *(Porzana porzana)*
Canon EOS-1D Mark II N, 500mm f/4.0, 1/2000 second, f/5, ISO 500, continuous focus with an extended central focusing point, beanbag, car as a blind. Lithuania, May 2006.

great location in the middle of a wetland that had been flooded. Driving the mother of all off-road vehicles—the Land Rover Defender—I was able to follow the road, even though it was covered in half a yard of water, and access the flooded area. I spent a morning photographing Red-necked and Eared Grebes and Spotted Crakes. Spring was just around the corner, and the birds were in full courting mode, so sound luring them tc within a good photographing distance was easy.

Boat (Markus)

A boat is great for bird photography. Many times it's the only way to get close enough to birds that are out in the middle of a large body of water or on rivers that wind over rough terrain. The principles of photographing from cars apply to boats—birds are less bothered by a boat than by people moving openly on the shores. Birds are often used to fishing boats and seem to not be bothered by photographers, either.

I use a boat to photograph arctic geese and ducks during spring migration as they fly north along the Gulf of Finland. For years I tried photographing them from little skerries out in the open sea, but with poor results. The birds seem to avoid the skerries, and their migratory paths vary with changes in the weather. I was always either in the wrong place or out at the wrong time.

I started getting much better results when I began to photograph the migration from a boat. I live in Helsinki, right on the coast. On a good migration day, I check where the main migratory path is, which is somewhere out on the open

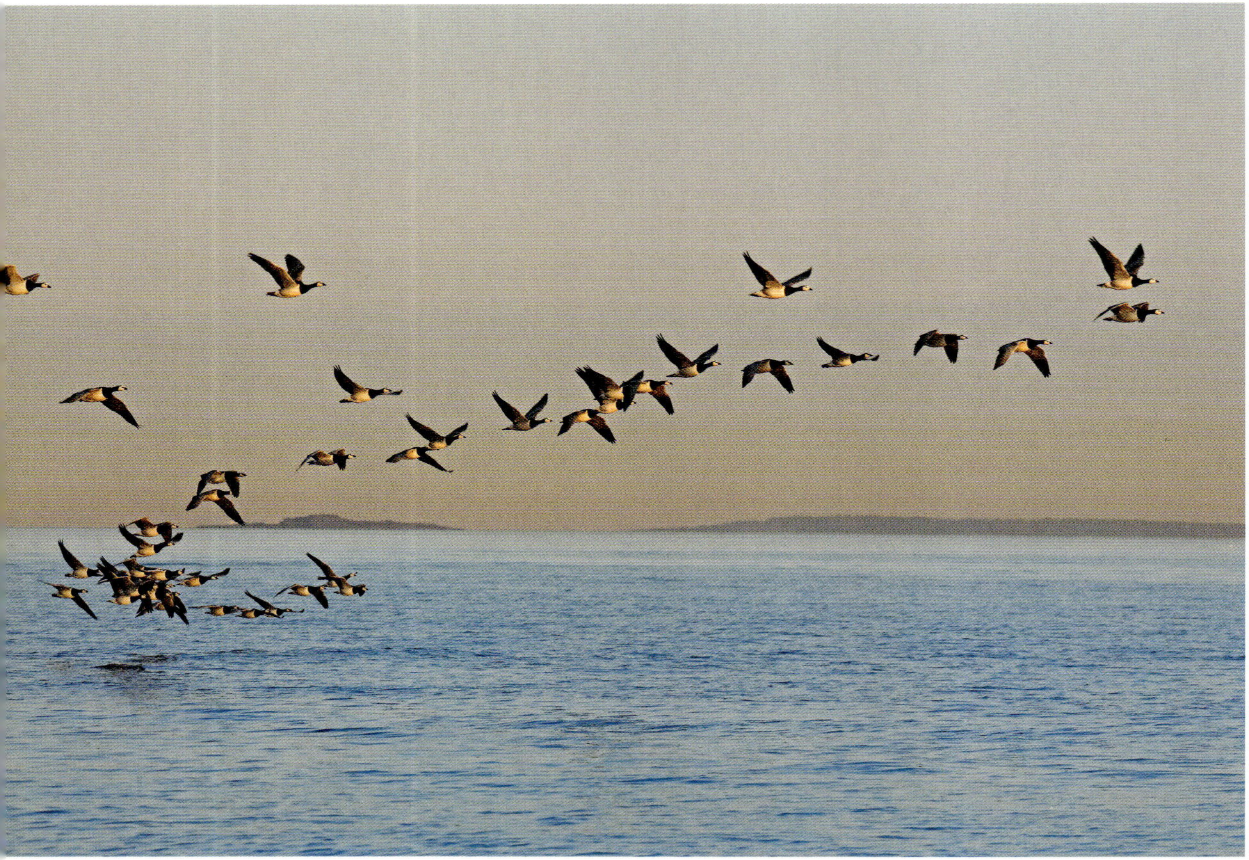

Markus Varesvuo

A migrating flock of Barnacle Geese, photographed from a boat on the open sea *(Branta leucopsis)*
Canon EOS-1D Mark II, 300mm f/2.8, 1/500 second, f/10.0, ISO 800, continuous focus with 45 focusing points, handheld camera. Porvoo, Finland, May 2007.

sea outside Helsinki. I drive my boat there, kill the engine, and let it drift. The migrating birds are not unnerved by a little boat standing still in the sea, and the flocks often fly at close range right by the boat. When the migratory path seems to move and settle along a new route, I navigate closer to a new vantage point and wait again.

Photographing from a boat has some special characteristics. At sea the wind is rarely weak enough to allow a tripod to be used, so I mainly photograph handheld, which in a rough sea is very difficult, even if it's still safe enough to be out there. For photographing from a boat, the ideal weather is after a couple of days of light breezes so that even the swells have calmed down.

Bigger boats and ships are steadier, making the use of a tripod possible, but normally vibration from the engines tends to make photography impossible. A monopod can be a viable option for photographing from a boat.

MARKUS VARESVUO

PHOTOGRAPHING AT MIGRATION FLYWAYS

Many species are easier to photograph while they are migrating than in their breeding grounds.

It's been said a few times in this book, but it's worth repeating: it's better to have the birds approach you than for you to approach them. Blind photography probably conforms to this principle in its purest form, and it is well suited to photographing migrating birds at staging sites as the birds stop to rest and feed. You can also get good results without a blind by waiting calmly in the right spot. Photographing migrating birds is based not only on knowledge about staging sites and ideal weather conditions, but also on tenaciously waiting for good opportunities.

Photographing Resting Birds on Migration

Over the years I have photographed feeding and resting birds along their migration paths on numerous occasions both in my native Finland and abroad. In Finland my favorite staging sites are two islands on the Gulf of Finland, Utö in the Archipelago Sea and Långskär in the Åland Islands archipelago. Both islands are out on the open sea and offer the first opportunity for rest after a long flight over the sea for the migrating birds as they are heading north. There are also many sources of food for a variety of bird species. While the spring and autumn migrations are in full swing, the islands see a wide range of bird species, offering something new to photograph on a daily basis. You can read more about Utö in the chapter "Utö Island on the Baltic Sea."

Wetlands draw a lot of birds at migration season, too, and are good places for bird photography.

When you're photographing at staging sites, remember that the sites are vital for the birds' welfare as places of rest and refueling before continuing their journeys. Especially when photographing the more shy and wary species, it's best to use a blind and stay hidden there for long periods. This way you get close to the birds, and they get to rest and feed in peace.

Many small birds, such as Red-breasted Flycatchers, are easier to photograph at staging sites than in their breeding biotopes in the murky forests.

A great place for photographing resting birds on spring migration is Eilat in Israel, which is covered in more detail in its own chapter. The area offers many types of feeding biotopes for different species within a relatively small area, and in spring it's the first green oasis after crossing a big desert as the birds are heading north from their winter grounds in Africa. There is no legal bird hunting in Israel, which has made the birds quite trusting, and they are easy enough to approach within photographing range.

Many islands in the eastern Mediterranean, such as the Greek island of Lesbos, are excellent stopovers for birds on spring migration.

A migrating Red-breasted Flycatcher on an island in the Baltic Sea *(Ficedula parva)*
Canon EOS-1D Mark IV, 800mm f/5.6 plus 1.4x extender, 1/250 second, f/11.0, ISO 500, one-shot focus with a central focusing point, Gitzo tripod, Manfrotto 501 video head.
Parainen, Finland, May 2010.

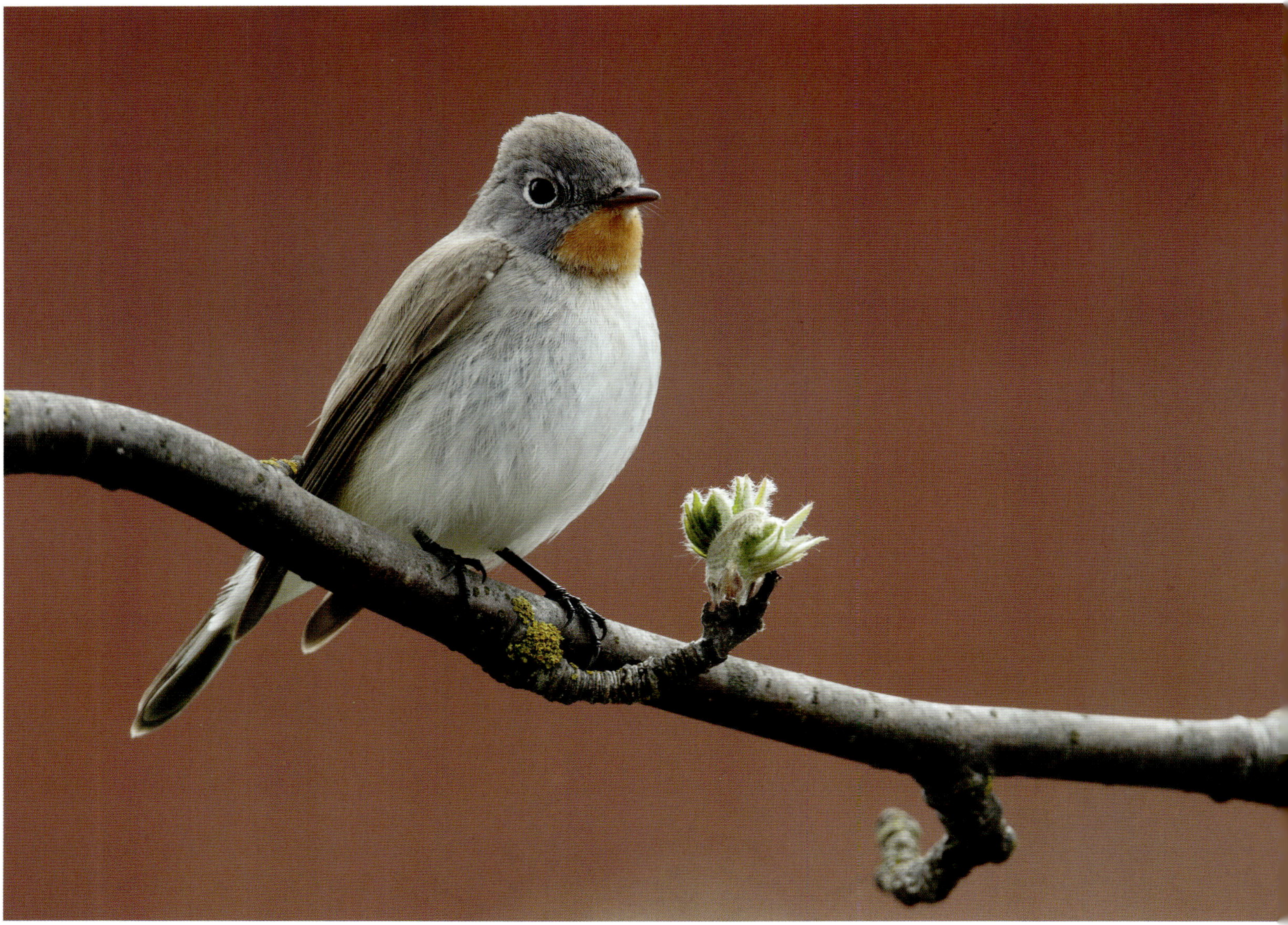

Markus Varesvuo

Markus Varesvuo

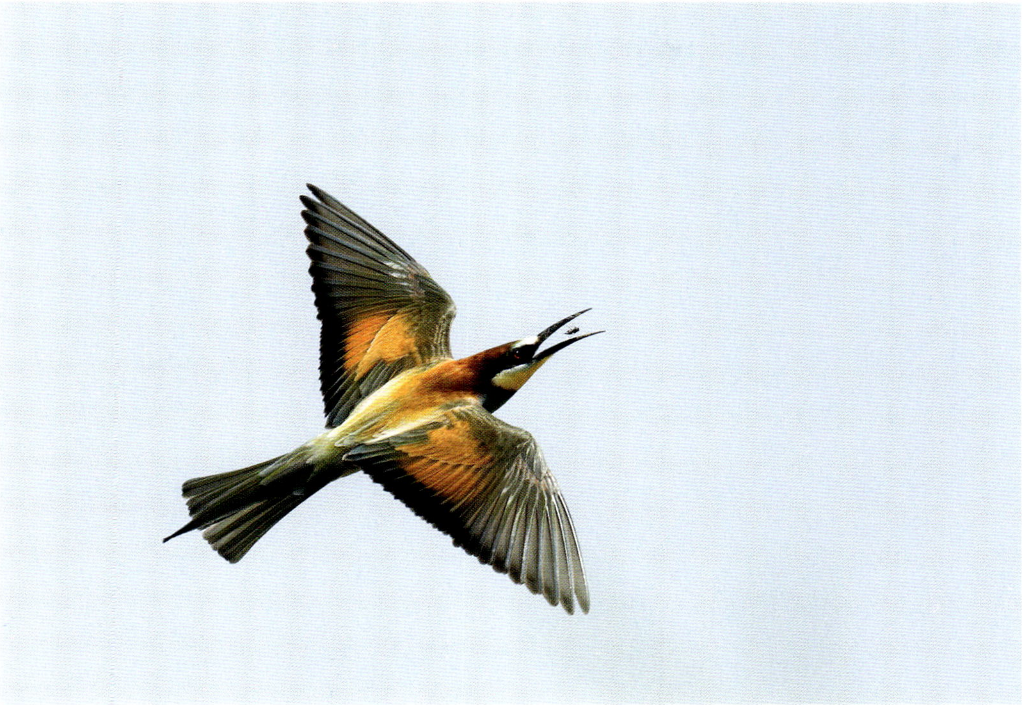

European Bee-eaters stop in Eilat to refuel on migration *(Merops apiaster)*
Canon EOS-1D Mark III, 800mm f/5.6, 1/2000 second, f/9.0, ISO 1250, continuous focus with an extended central focusing point, handheld camera. Eilat, Israel, May 2009.

Photographing Flying Birds on Migration

Many well-known sites for migration observation can be very good photo sites. What is decisive for a photographer, though, is not how many birds pass the site on their migration, but how often they pass close enough to be within a good photographing distance. Ten migrating Common Buzzards that fly close to the photographer is better than 20,000 migrating birds high up in the sky.

As a rule of thumb, birds flying into a headwind are better for photographers than birds flying with a tailwind, because a headwind forces the birds to fly closer to the earth's surface. When the birds are flying with a tailwind, the best time for photography is in the early morning, before the birds have gained their cruising altitudes. Other key factors in migration behavior are visibility, cloud cover, and precipitation.

Species that are otherwise hard to photograph, such as many raptors, can be quite easy to photograph on migration. Birds often flock during migration, even if they disperse into pairs upon reaching their breeding grounds. In Finland, a flock of Common Wood-Pigeons or cranes, for instance, is easiest to

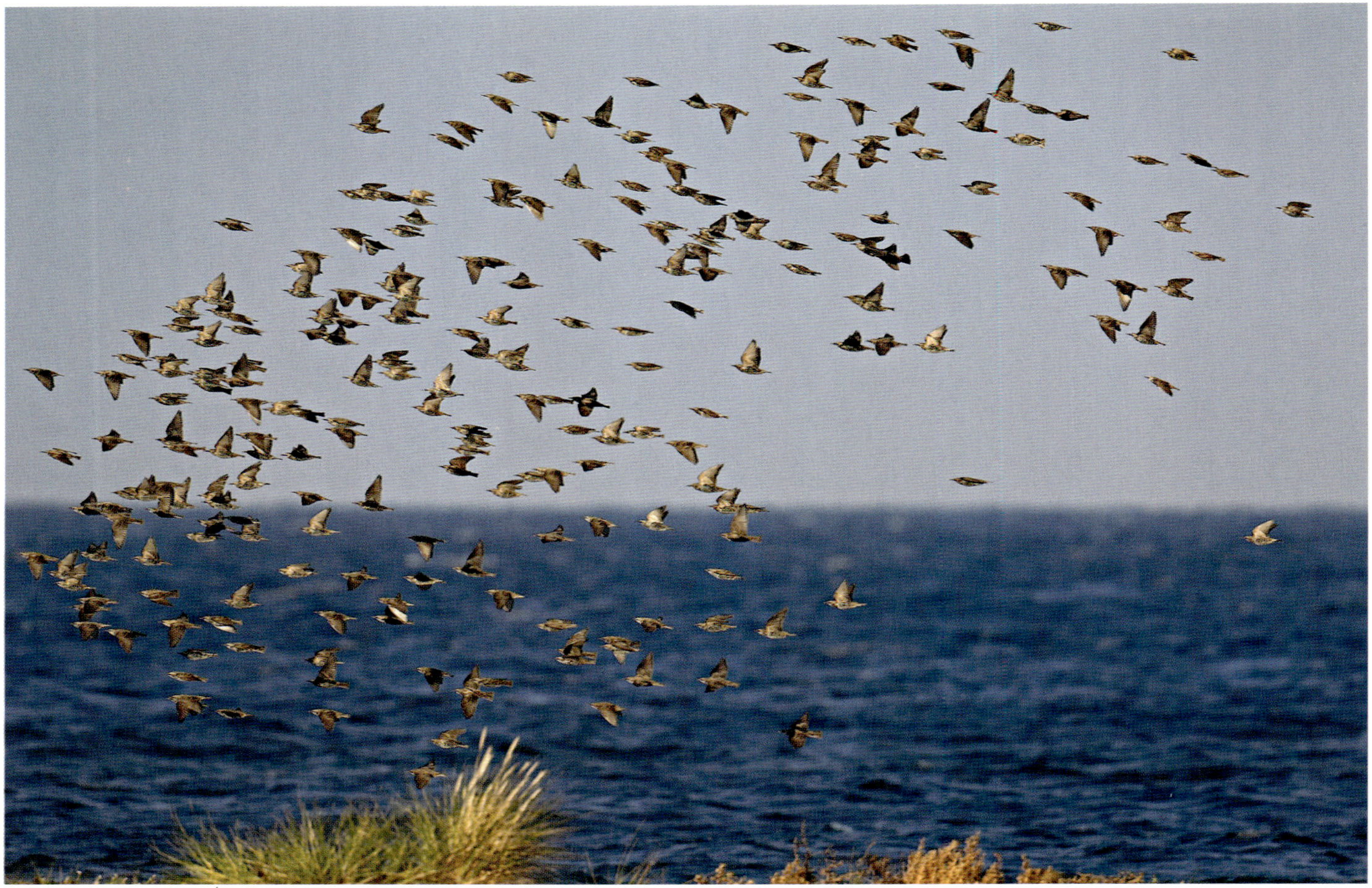

Markus Varesvuo

Migrating European Starlings in Falsterbo *(Sturnus vulgaris)*
Canon EOS-1D Mark II, 500mm f/4.0, 1/2500 second, f/5.6, ISO 400, continuous focus with 45 focusing points, Gitzo tripod, Manfrotto 501 video head. Falsterbo, Sweden, October 2004.

photograph at a staging site or after the breeding season because they gather in communal feeding flocks before starting on their autumn migrations.

Breeding successes and failures cause some species' numbers to fluctuate greatly, and with certain nomadic birds, for example, you may have to wait several years before there is any chance of good photo opportunities.

Birds tend to use different routes for their spring and autumn migrations. In Finland, good spots for spring migration include the Porkkala Spit in Kirkkonummi, the archipelago on the eastern Gulf of Finland, the archipelago outside Kristiinankaupunki, and the Parhalahti fishing harbor in Pyhäjoki. In autumn the premier place for migration is the tip of the Hanko Peninsula, which is covered in more detail in the chapter "Hanko Peninsula, Finland."

Other great locations near Finland for spring migration include the Curonian Spit in Lithuania, Cape Kolka in Latvia, and Põõsaspea Spit in Estonia. Autumn migration, from a photographer's perspective, is good in Estonia in Põõsaspea, Sõrve on Saaremaa Island, Puise in the Matsalu Bay, and Falsterbo in Sweden.

Falsterbo, at the southernmost tip of Sweden, is the best place in Scandinavia for photographing birds on their autumn migration, and it is one of the best locations in Europe. Millions of birds pass through and over Falsterbo, including tens of thousands of raptors, a few hundred thousand Common Wood-Pigeons, and more than 100,000 European Starlings. There is no shortage of targets for your camera. For a photographer, the best time is probably from mid-September to mid-October. Winds

Markus Varesvuo

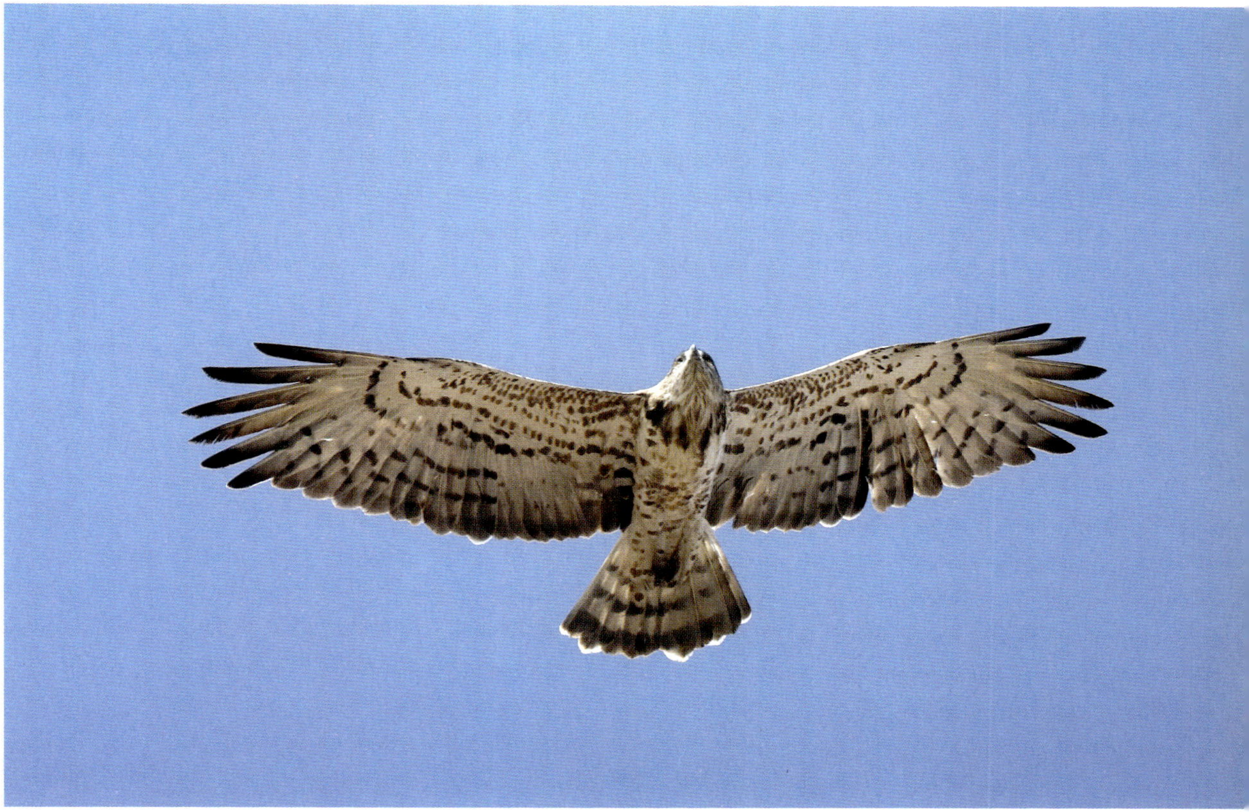

Tarifa offers good opportunities to photograph many raptors, such as Short-toed Eagles *(Circaetus gallicus)*
Canon EOS-1D Mark III, 800mm f/5.6, 1/1600 second, f/5.6, ISO 800, continuous focus with a central focusing point, Gitzo tripod, Manfrotto 501 video head. Tarifa, Spain, September 2008.

from the south and southwest and clear skies are on photographers' wish lists.

In addition to these locations, other proven areas include Tarifa in Spain and Eilat in Israel, both of which are especially good for raptor photography. Eilat is best in spring, and Tarifa works well in both spring and autumn.

Each location has its special features, but they all share one common denominator: many factors must fall into place to make a good day.

The main raptor migration in Tarifa is between the last week in August and the end of September. I've been in Tarifa at the end of August and in the first two weeks of September. On a good day, thousands, if not tens of thousands, of raptors pass Tarifa, but that doesn't automatically mean you get good opportunities to use your camera. The migratory paths vary from day to day and can even change during the day.

Tarifa is quite large, and there are remarkable variations in the local elevations. You can go many days without finding an ideal place for photography. There is a beautiful new roofed observation center at a watch point a few kilometers east of the town Tarifa, by the main road. Mornings and evenings tend to offer the best opportunities.

The ideal conditions for raptor photography develop when strong easterly winds, the Levante, blow for several days. Coming from the north, the raptors can drift too far west, and when they hit the coastline they turn back east toward Tarifa, where they cross the ocean to Africa. Flying into a headwind forces them to fly low and slow, which makes them very easy to photograph, and a dark mountainside in the background is often a nice bonus. The Levante can be so strong that it makes photography difficult. Try to find a good spot next to a building or a rock, where you can photograph without the worst of the wind hitting you.

Find out if there are good migration lines or staging sites in your area, and make field trips to determine how well they suit your photography.

Although the best migration paths tend to be found along the coasts and other clear flyways, anyone can find good spots in their area where birds come to rest. These spots often draw migrating birds and offer good opportunities for photographing them.

JARI PELTOMÄKI

PHOTOGRAPHING AT NESTS

Breeding season offers great chances for photographing birds, but expertise and extreme caution are required.

Especially when photographing at nests, the birds' needs come first. You need a thorough understanding of the species' behavior and ecology, and you need to minimize any potential disturbance to breeding. Species knowledge is essential because some species are more vulnerable than others, and there is also variation among individuals. Prerequisites for photographing at nests are knowledge of the birds' behavior, their alarm calls, and their natural feeding intervals so you can stop your project before any harm is done. If the parent is sounding alarm calls ceaselessly, or seems to not be feeding its young at a normal pace, or stays away from the nest, you must leave. Common sense is often helpful, and you must know when to quit before problems occur. If a parent is constantly calling out in apparent stress, it can attract predators and lead to the nest being revealed and destroyed. If you have any doubts, you should trust your instincts and stop your project. Some species show their distress clearly; others don't necessarily show it, but their fear may cause them to shun the nest as long as you're near.

In most countries, nest photography requires permission from environmental authorities. In Finland, all intentional disturbances of birds, especially during breeding, are forbidden by the Nature Conservation Act. Strictly speaking, this means that permission is needed to photograph the nests of all species, but the authorities probably don't want to be swamped by thousands of applications for photographing, say, a European Pied Flycatcher at nest. As a guiding principle, the less common the species, the more likely that permission is needed. Don't go to the nest unless you know for sure what the legal situation is. It's a good idea to contact the relevant authorities well in advance to find out if permission is needed for the species you are planning to photograph at nest.

There is at least one known case in Finland where a person photographed at a Golden Eagle's nest without a license and got fined afterwards based on his published photo. Nest photography, and other potential disturbances, will surely get even closer attention in the future. Therefore, if you have plans to photograph at a raptor's nest, for example, always find out about the permission policy and get a license when needed. Note that you need good justification for your project; where permissions are needed, they are rarely issued just for fun.

Disturbance

Does nest photography disturb birds, and if it does, how much? If you plan and execute the project with knowledge and caution, and always use an escort and monitor the parents' behavior to gauge that all is well, then it isn't a disturbance. Images of Snowy Owl parents feeding their young in the nest tell us that the birds have been conditioned to a blind and an escort has been used.

As a rule, photographing raptors at nest requires permission. A Northern Harrier feeding its young *(Circus cyaneus)*.
Canon EOS-1D Mark II, 70–200mm f/2.8, 1/800 second, 155mm, f/5.6, ISO 500, manual focus,
Gitzo tripod, Manfrotto 501 video head, blind. Oulu, Finland, June 2005.

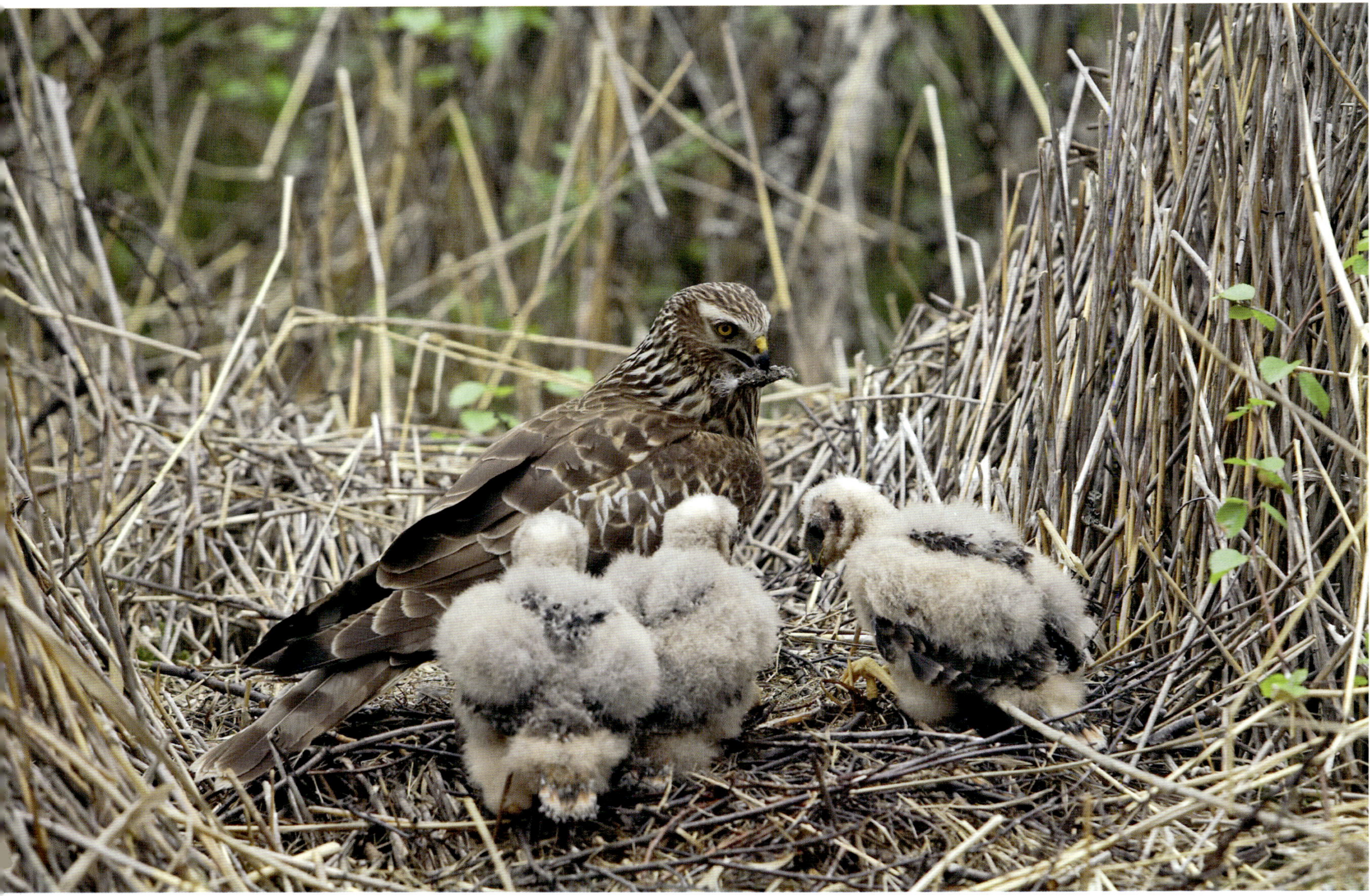

Jari Peltomäki

A male Great Gray Owl brings a vole to the female, who cuts it up for the chicks *(Strix nebulosa)*
Canon EOS-1D Mark II N, 500mm f/4.0, 1/250 second, f/7.1, ISO 1000, manual focus, Manfrotto 501 video head, blind in a tree. Siikajoki, Finland, May 2006.

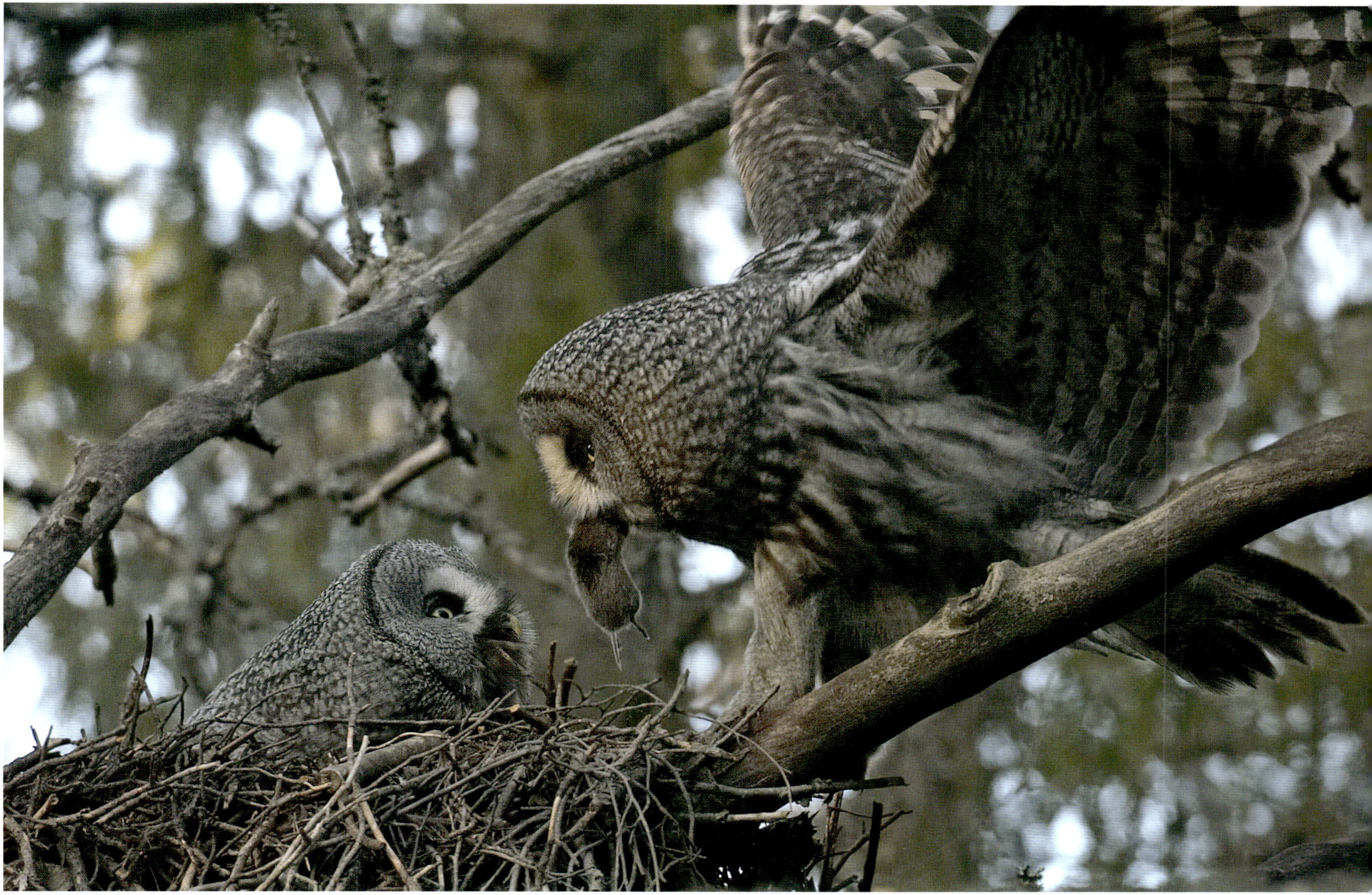

Jari Peltomäki

Jari Peltomäki

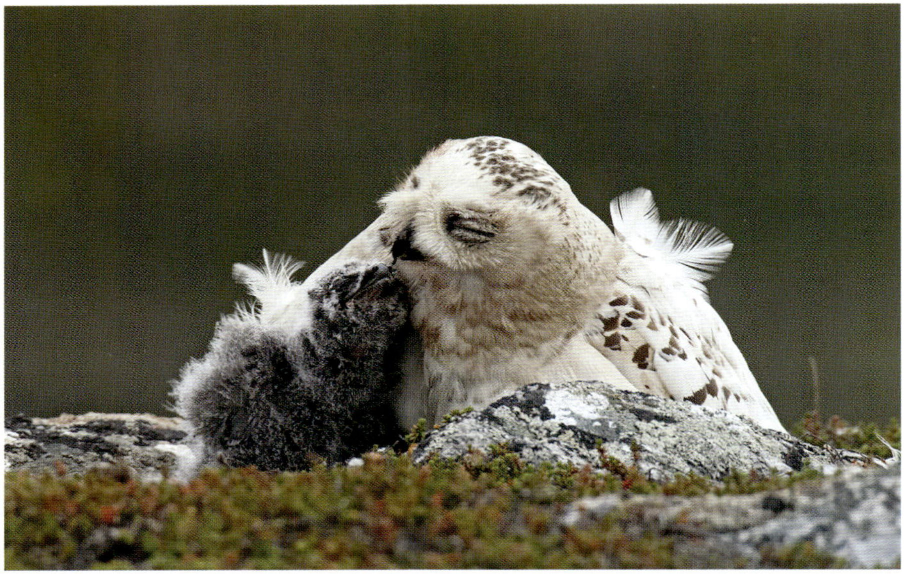

A female Snowy Owl feeding a chick *(Bubo scandiacus)*
Canon EOS-1D Mark III, 500mm f/4.0 plus 2x extender, 1/500 second, f/10.0, ISO 800, manual focus, Gitzo tripod, Manfrotto 501 video head, blind. Inari, Finland, July 2007.

Jari Peltomäki

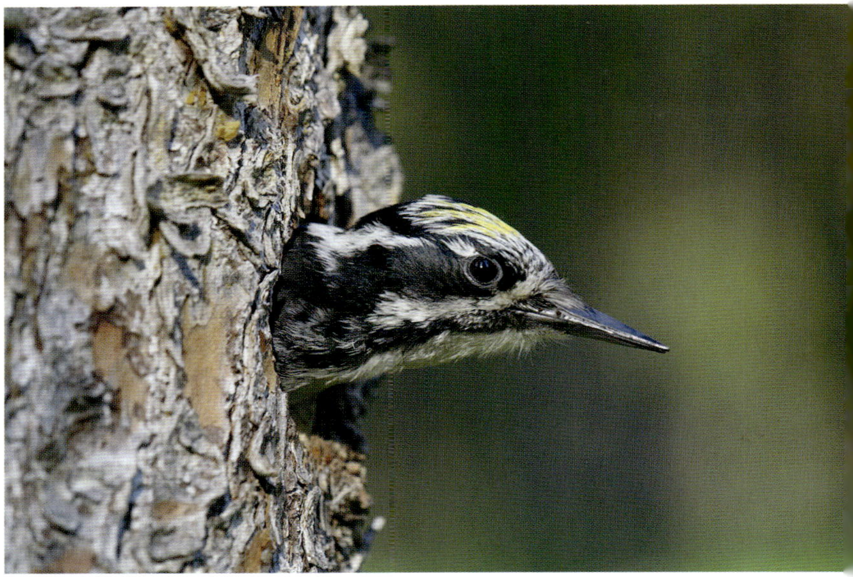

A Eurasian Three-toed Woodpecker peeks out from its nest hole *(Picoides tridactylus)*
Canon EOS-1D Mark II, 180mm f/3.5 macro, 1/100 second, f/5.0, ISO 200, manual focus, Gitzo tripod, Manfrotto 501 video head, remote control. Kuusamo, Finland, June 2005.

This minimizes any potential risk to breeding.

Breeding season is a vital and vulnerable time in birds' lives. Breeding can fail for many reasons. If, for example, one of the parents dies, the remaining parent struggles and often fails in getting the young out of the nest and onto their wings. Many raptors have clearly defined parental roles, with the male hunting and then giving the prey to the female, who cuts it up for the young.

In the summer of 2007 we were in Finnish Lapland photographing breeding Snowy Owls, with permission. We spotted a male Snowy Owl chasing a Golden Eagle high up in the sky over the open landscape of gently sloping arctic hills, and we came to the conclusion that a nest could be found in that direction—and it was. Unfortunately, what we found was eight dead chicks of different ages and three plump lemmings neatly laid out on the edge of the nest. The male Snowy Owl was observing us from a distance of about 50 m (164 ft), but we hadn't seen a glimpse of the female. The male had brought prey to the nest but didn't know how to cut it up for the chicks, who were still too young to swallow the lemmings

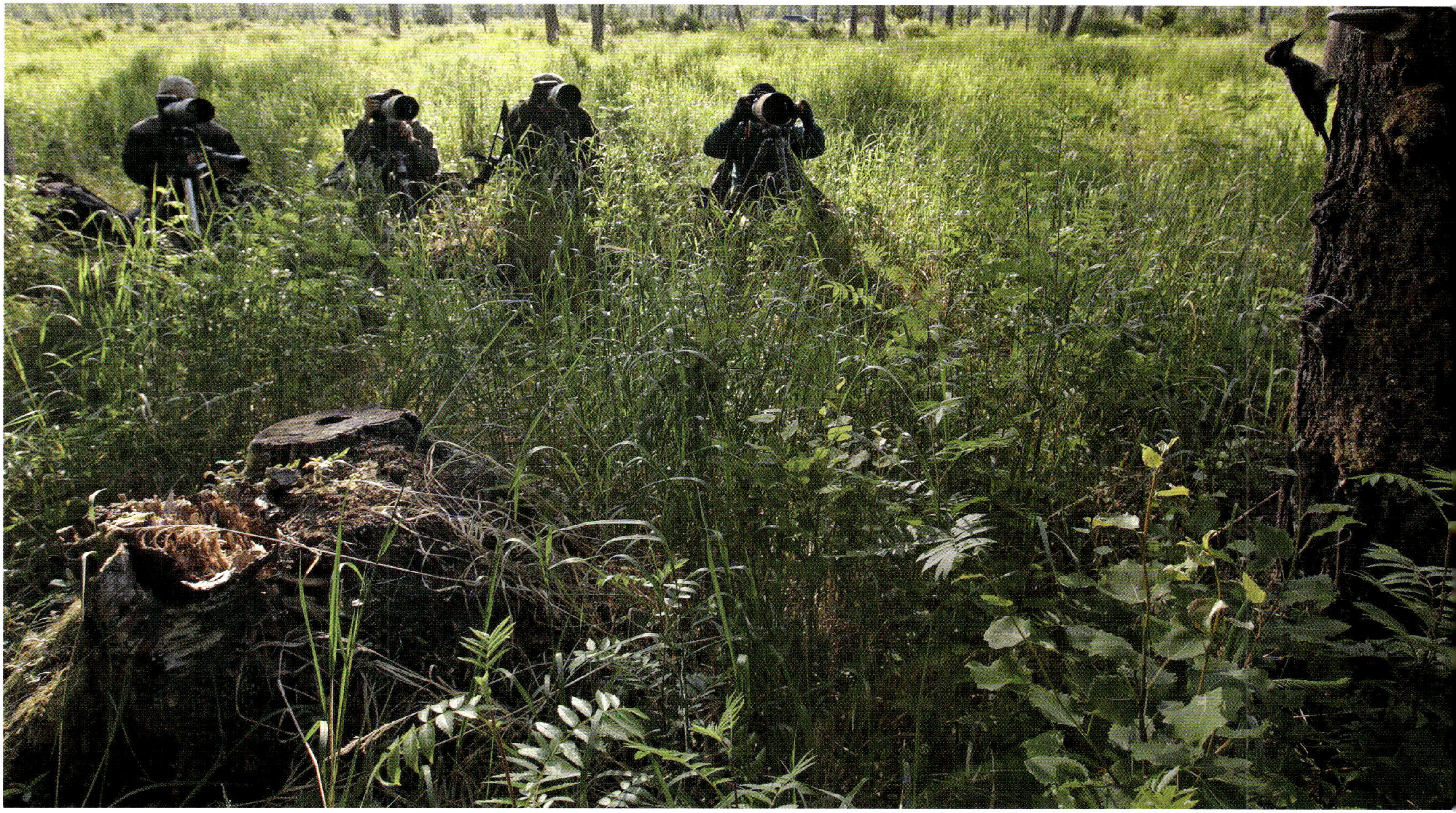

Jari Peltomäki

Photographers at a Eurasian Three-toed Woodpecker's nest *(Picoides tridactylus)*. The image was taken with a remote control.
Canon EOS 5D, 16–35mm f/2.8, 1/500 second, 17mm, f/8.0, ISO 800, manual focus, Gitzo tripod, Manfrotto 501 video head, remote control. Siikajoki, Finland, June 2009.

whole. The chicks had starved to death alongside their food because something had apparently happened to the female. Our bet was on the Golden Eagle we had seen earlier.

Conditioning

There are big differences among species regarding behavior in the nest, and there are also individual differences. Most species have a fear of the human shape and will not come to the nest if there are people in sight. With nest photography, the use of a blind is almost always the right method. The subjects of your project should be conditioned to the blind. With more timid species, the blind is first introduced at a distance, far from the nest but close enough so the birds can see it and get used to its shape and color. Move the blind forward about once a day. After you have moved the blind and walked away from it, stay for a while to follow the bird with your binoculars to see that it returns to the nest immediately after your departure. When your blind is close enough to the nest, you will always need an escort. This plays a major role in minimizing the disruption because seeing the human leave normally calms the birds down and makes them return to the nest quicker. Likewise, it would be good to have somebody come and pick you up from the blind, otherwise the nesting birds might be spooked by you emerging from the blind and they will start to fear it. Whenever you have more than one photographer involved in the same project, the next photographer functions as an escort—the switch causes minimal disruption. Each photographer should stay in the blind for long periods; if the switches are in a quick succession, they can be disruptive.

A remote control is a great option for nest photography because it allows you to operate your concealed camera from a distance. But note that some species won't tolerate a camera next to their nests!

Birds are very particular in selecting nesting sites, and a photographer must always respect the nest's privacy and protection. Many species build their nests in very secretive and safe places. If the nest is hidden, do not bring it out into the open or you might inadvertently seal the brood's fate. Predators will easily find nests that are out in the open. If a branch is hiding the nest, find a way around it instead of removing it. If you must, you can briefly turn it aside, but make sure it's back in the original place when you're done. A sheltered nest also keeps the brood out of direct sunshine.

Some species are very approachable in the breeding season. A good example of a trusting bird is the Eurasian Dotterel; it can be photographed with a wide lens even when it is sitting in the nest. Another carefree species during the breeding season is the Eurasian Three-toed Woodpecker; a human presence doesn't seem to bother it in the least.

Weather plays a role in nest photography, in more ways than you'd think. If it's cold and windy or raining, you shouldn't do anything that makes the parent leave the nest because it could expose the eggs or the small chicks to cold. The best conditions for nest photography are on a dry and warm, but not hot, day.

Photographs should not be taken at all costs. If you have even the slightest doubt that your photo project might harm the breeding, be prepared to quickly abort the project. Making birds and their breeding success a top priority should guide your actions. No photo is more important than the birds' lives.

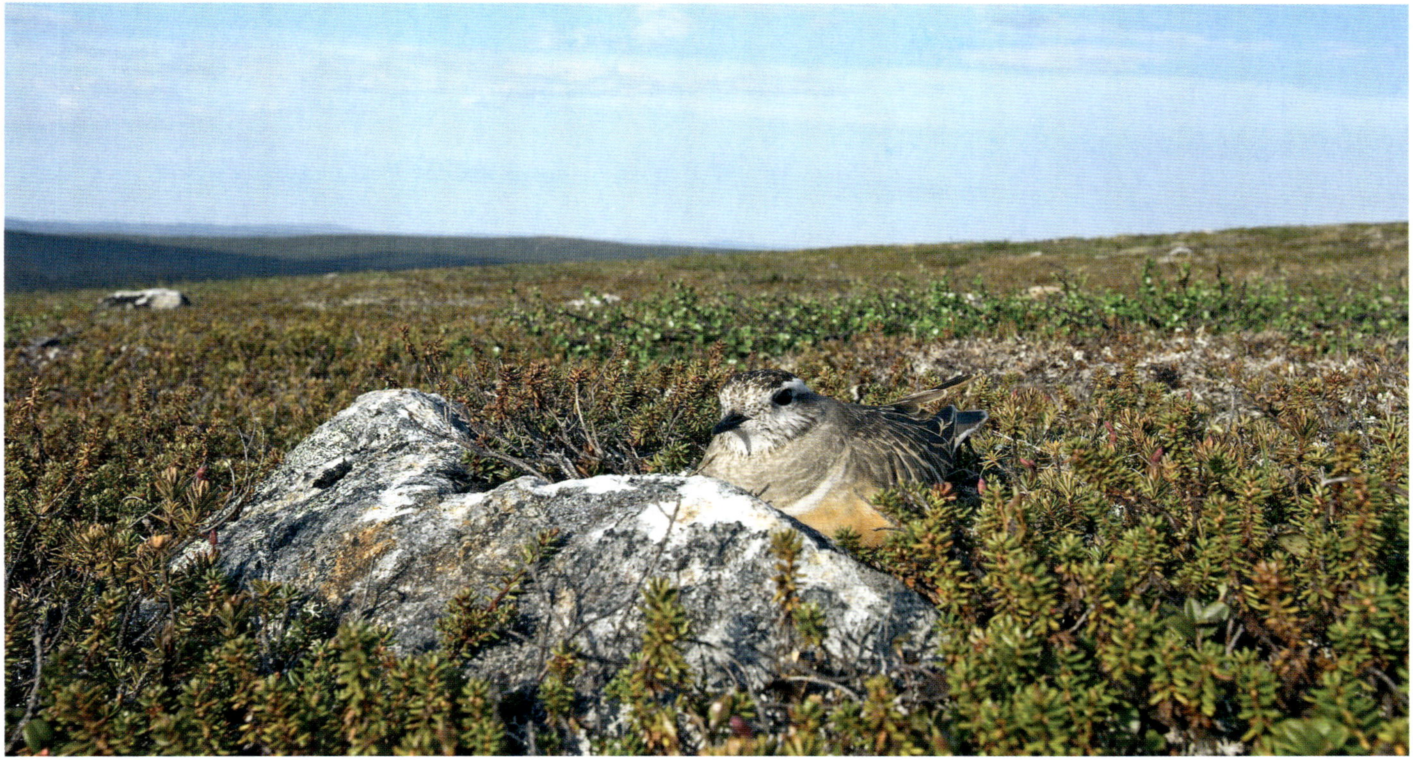

Jari Peltomäki

A Eurasian Dotterel captured at its nest with a wide lens *(Charadrius morinellus)*
Canon EOS 5D, 16–35mm f/2.8, 1/125 second, 35mm, f/16.0, ISO 200, one-shot focus with a central focusing point, handheld camera. Inari, Finland, June 2006.

MARKUS VARESVUO

HANKO PENINSULA, FINLAND

Hanko Peninsula offers a flight photography feast on the most southerly spot in mainland Finland.

The tip of Hanko Peninsula is a nature reserve, and it is the location of the Hanko Bird Observatory. Hundreds of thousands of birds move south along the lines of Hanko Peninsula. Many species won't start out to sea before they've reached the very tip of the narrow spit, which collects birds like a funnel, making this an excellent site for banding, observing, and photographing birds. In autumn this is the absolute best location for taking flight shots of migrating birds, excluding waders and seabirds. The tip draws masses of small birds, too, as they contemplate the task of crossing the water, so the trees and bushes are positively teeming with birds to photograph. Good opportunities for photographing resting waders are normally found on the rocky shores around the tip, especially on the southwestern sandbar.

Entry to the observation center is through a free port, but it requires permission from the center attendant. Contact details can be found at www.tringa.fi (Tringa is the ornithological society for the Uusimaa province in southern Finland). The center has lodging facilities for longer stays, but it's possible to make day trips too. The weekends in September and October are fairly busy, so it's good to book early.

The flying birds can be photographed from the roof of an old bunker, which is where the migration observers are stationed, or on the rocks at the very tip of the peninsula. The bunker is higher up than the rocks and offers better chances of getting trees and the sea into the background. However, space on the bunker roof is limited, and the long-term occupiers get preference, so at the busiest times in September and October, photographers tend to end up on the rocks.

The best time to photograph on Hanko Peninsula is from the last week in August to mid-October. Fair to strong winds from the south, and clear or partly clear skies, are the best weather for photography because the wind forces the birds to fly low as they approach the tip of the peninsula, offering ample opportunities for vigilant photographers. At Hanko Peninsula the most numerous migrating raptor is the Eurasian Sparrowhawk, with a few hundred individuals per day counted on several days during autumn. In ideal conditions, they fly just above the treetops, and at times they whiz by right next to the bunker.

The numbers of other raptors are noticeably lower, but over the years I've shot a lot of good photographs of species such as Rough-legged Hawk, Common Buzzard, European Honey-buzzard, Northern Harrier, Eurasian Hobby, Eurasian Kestrel, and Northern Goshawk.

The Hanko Bird Observatory is known for its nomadic birds and is a world-class photo location for many species. The nomadic birds' numbers fluctuate greatly from one year to another, and the years can peak at long intervals. In some years between the peaks, some nomads aren't seen at all, or there may be only a precious few. Depending on the year, at least the

A flock of Bohemian Waxwings and a view south from the bunker *(Bombycilla garrulus)*
Canon EOS-1Ds Mark III, 70–200mm f/2.8, 1/2000 second, 120mm, f/7.1, ISO 800, continuous focus with 45 focusing points, handheld camera. Hanko, Finland, October 2008.

Markus Varesvuo

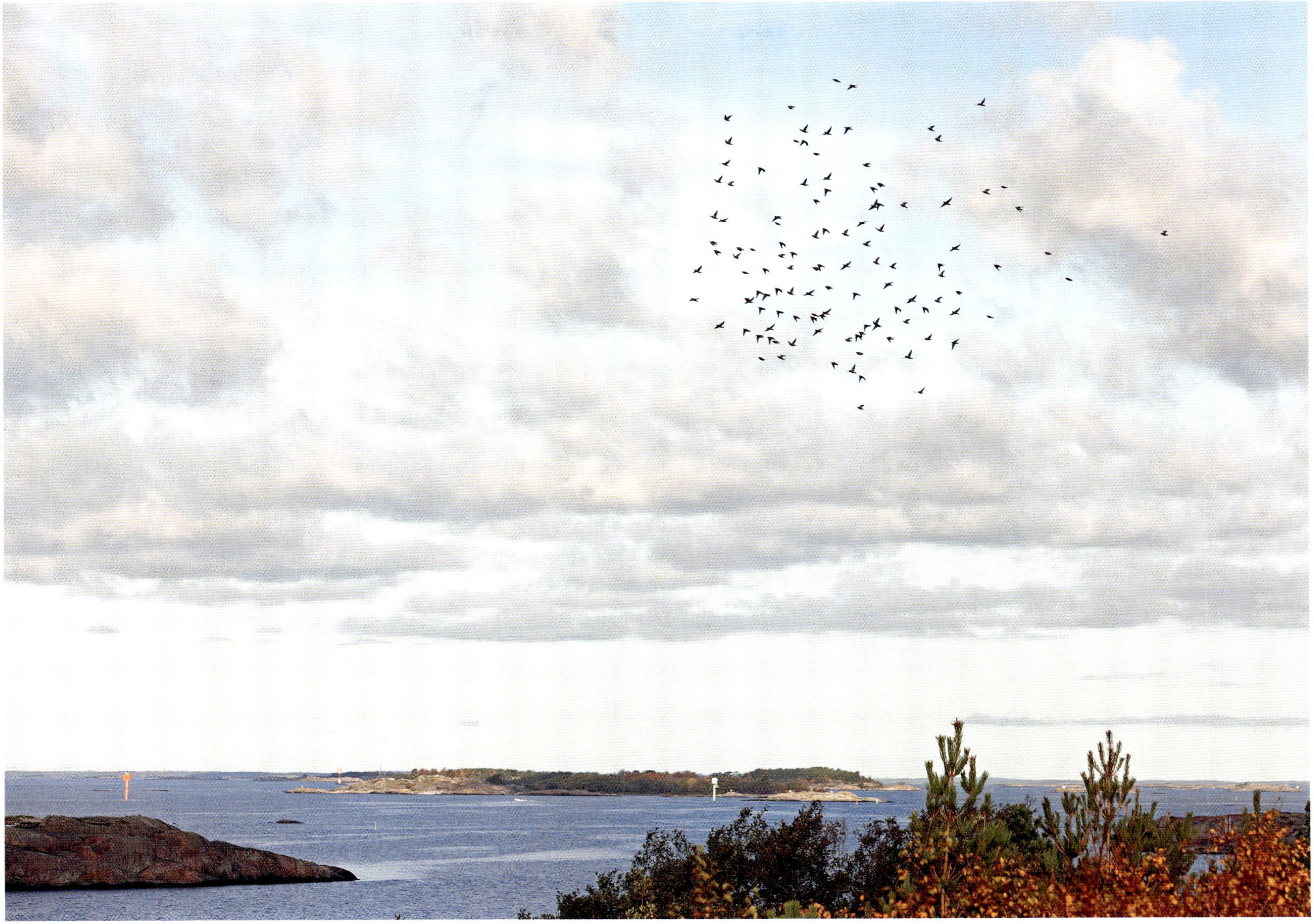

The Hanko Bird Observatory is the best place I know for photographing Eurasian Sparrowhawks in flight *(Accipiter nisus)*
Canon EOS-1Ds Mark II, 500mm f/4.0 plus 1.4x extender, 1/2000 second, f/9.0, ISO 400, continuous focus with a central focusing point, Gitzo tripod, Manfrotto 501 video head. Hanko, Finland, September 2005.

Markus Varesvuo

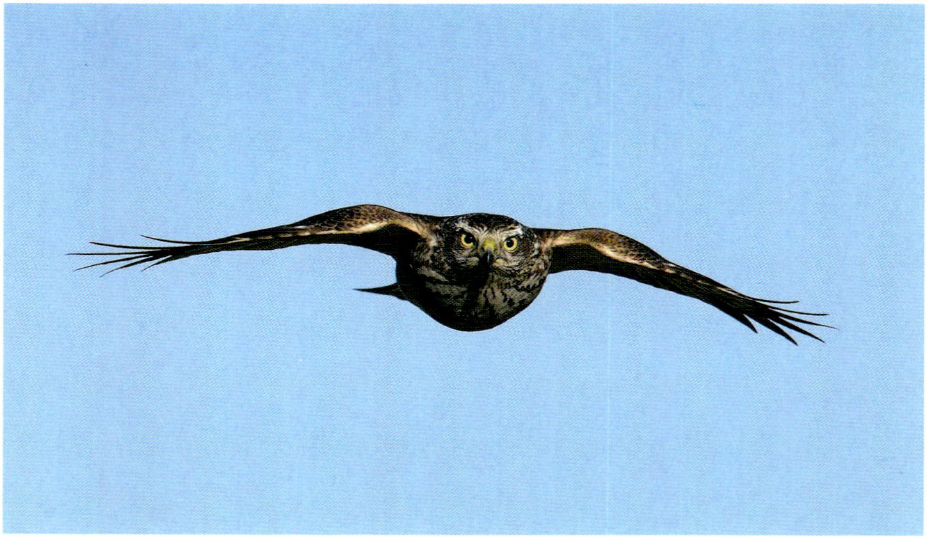

A young European Honey-buzzard flying very close to the photographer *(Pernis apivorus)*
Canon EOS-1D Mark II, 500mm f/4.0 plus 1.4x extender, 1/800 second, f/5.6, ISO 500, continuous focus with 45 focusing points, Gitzo tripod, Manfrotto 501 video head. Hanko, Finland, September 2006.

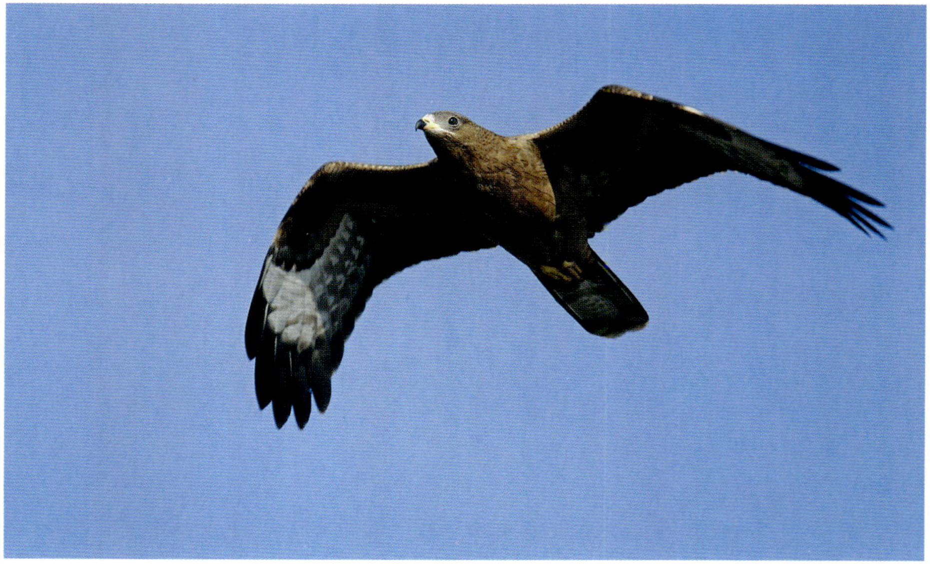

Markus Varesvuo

Black Woodpeckers are a daily sight at the Hanko Bird Observatory *(Dryocopus martius)*
Canon EOS-1D Mark II, 500mm f/4.0, 1/3200 second, f/4.5, ISO 500, continuous focus with 45 focusing points, handheld camera. Hanko, Finland, October 2005.

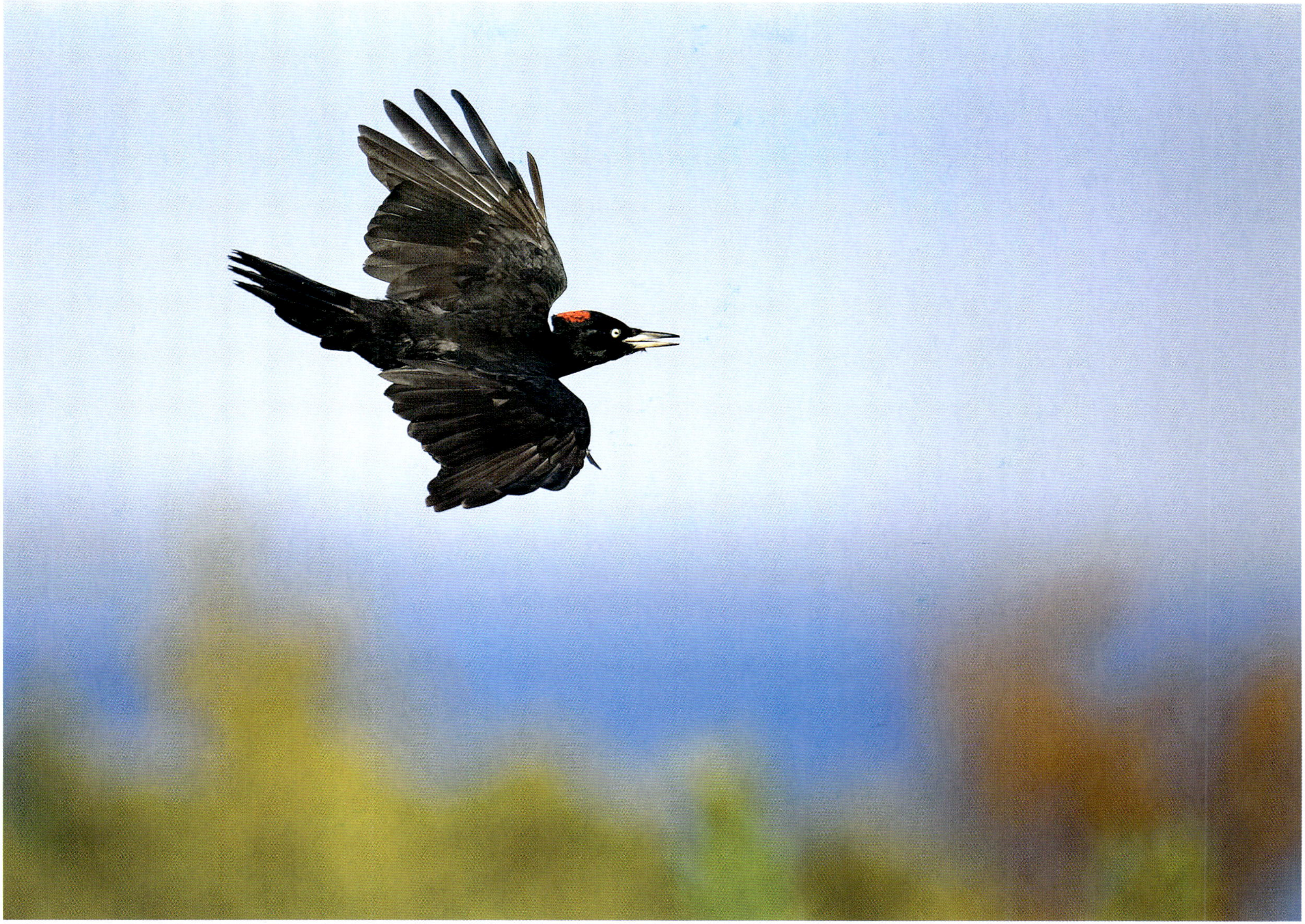

Markus Varesvuo

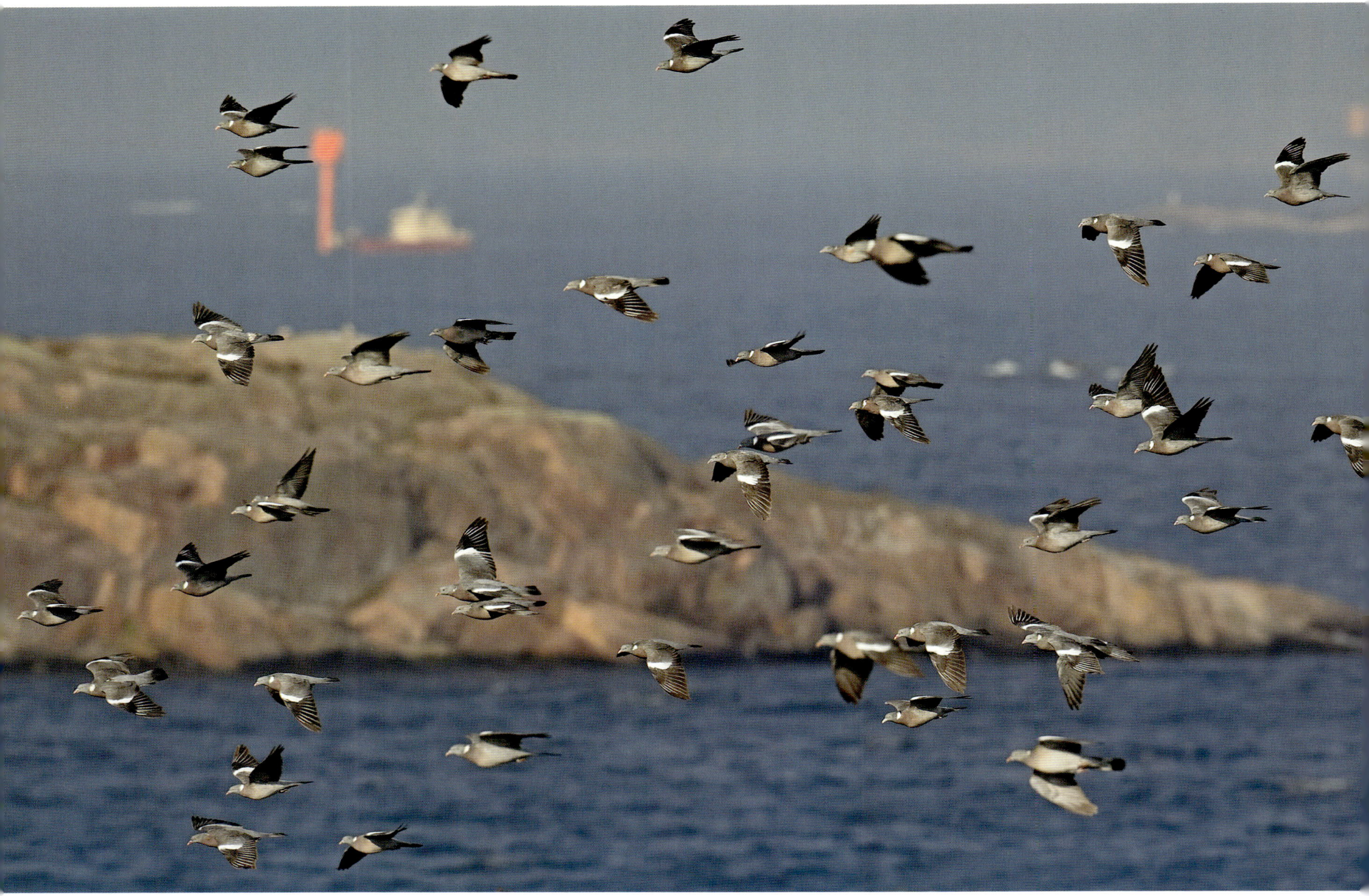

Markus Varesvuo

Migrating Common Wood-Pigeons flying into a headwind with the sea in the background *(Columba palumbus)*
Canon EOS-1D Mark III, 500mm f/4.0, 1/1600 second, f/8.0, ISO 800, continuous focus with an extended central focusing point, hand-held camera. Hanko, Finland, September 2007.

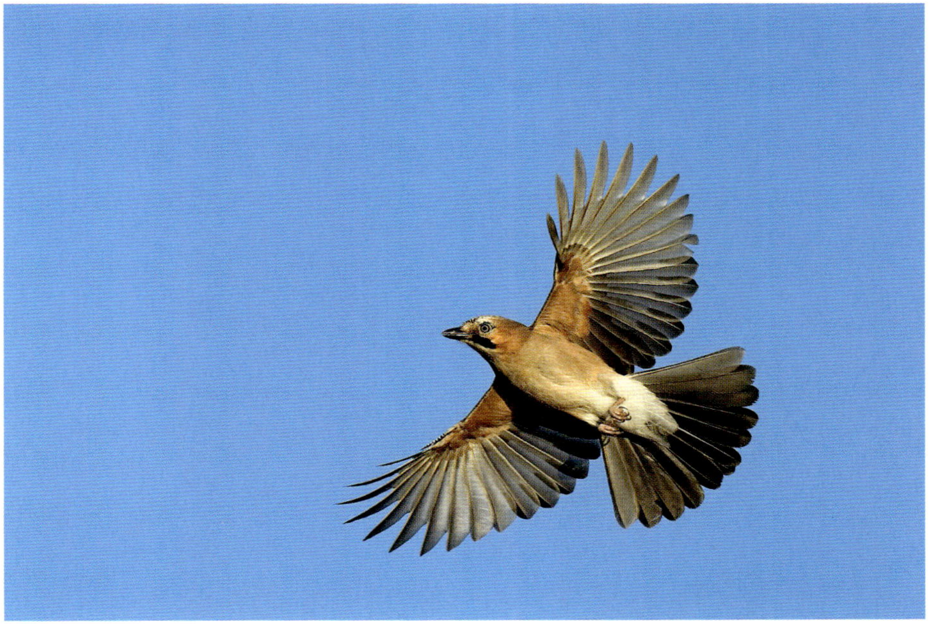

Markus Varesvuo

A Eurasian Jay on an eruption migration *(Garrulus glandarius)*
Canon EOS-1D Mark III, 800mm f/5.6, 1/3200 second, f/7.1, ISO 1600, continuous focus with an extended central focusing point, Gitzo tripod, Manfrotto 501 video head. Hanko, Finland, October 2008.

following species can be seen at the center: Black Woodpecker, Eurasian Three-toed Woodpecker, Lesser Spotted Woodpecker, Long-tailed Tit, Eurasian Nutcracker, and Eurasian Jay, plus many owls, including Eurasian Pygmy-Owl and Boreal Owl. Tits are the most common nomads (Great Tit, Eurasian Blue Tit, and Coal Tit), and sometimes in their midst are a few of the Eurasian Nuthatch's eastern subspecies *Sitta europaea asiatica*.

Eurasian Jay eruptions occur every few years, when they come to Hanko Peninsula in the thousands—a record-breaking day saw more than 3,200 migrating Eurasian Jays. When they fly in loose flocks they give photographers easy opportunities to practice taking flight shots.

Hanko Peninsula is along the migratory path for many thrushes, waxwings, jackdaws, and cranes. A good migration day prevents photographers from taking much time off.

MARKUS VARESVUO

KUUSAMO, FINLAND

Kuusamo attracts photographers with its many taiga species.

Kuusamo is a fascinating location for bird photographers because, from a European perspective, it's on the western edge of the taiga, in the northern part of the boreal forest, below the arctic tundra. This affects the avifauna of the region, and many species are found in the Kuusamo region that are difficult to see and photograph elsewhere in western Europe.

The second appealing factor for a bird photographer is that Kuusamo is covered with snow for more than half the year. In winter the temperatures dip extremely low, and almost every year the snowpack is nearly a meter (3.3 ft) deep. There's snow still in May, and during the months between February and May the light conditions are particularly exciting because of light reflecting off the snow (read more in the chapter "Light"). The severe winter conditions with deep snow, cold weather, and short daylight make the birds more likely to visit feeding stations, and the snowy forests are fine settings for your images.

As a bird photographer, I find that the best times in Kuusamo are winter, spring, and summer all the way to the end of the small birds' singing season at the beginning of July. This chapter highlights the photo opportunities in these seasons.

In the heart of winter from December to February the trees are covered in snow in the most photogenic manner, and January is often the best time for snow-capped trees. The length of daylight is only a couple of hours in December and much of January, setting certain limits to photography, and it's best not to schedule too many projects in one day. Because the light shines from a very low angle, it has a fabulous quality, but mostly it reaches only the tops of the trees. Any feeding stations should be set on hillsides where the sun shines for the full length of the short day. On cloudy days there is very little light, even at the brightest time of the day.

In deep winter there aren't many species in Kuusamo, and part of the resident species lead quiet lives deep inside the forests, making them quite hard to photograph. Feeding stations in the woods draw Siberian Jays, Gray-headed Chickadees, and Willow Tits. With good luck you can also see the Crested Tit, infrequent in Kuusamo, or a Eurasian Pygmy-Owl that's looking to get a juicy meal. White-throated Dippers are quite easily photographed in beautiful winter settings by the open water, which can be found where the streams are so powerful that the water doesn't freeze over, such as Käylä or Kiveskoski. While driving along the small back roads in Kuusamo, you may spot a group of Black Grouse feeding in the top of a handsome birch.

A Siberian Jay in a winter wonderland *(Perisoreus infaustus)*
Canon EOS-1Ds Mark III, 500mm f/4.0, 1/100 second, f/4.0, ISO 800, one-shot focus with a central focusing point, Gitzo tripod, Manfrotto 501 video head. Kuusamo, Finland, January 2010.

Markus Varesvuo

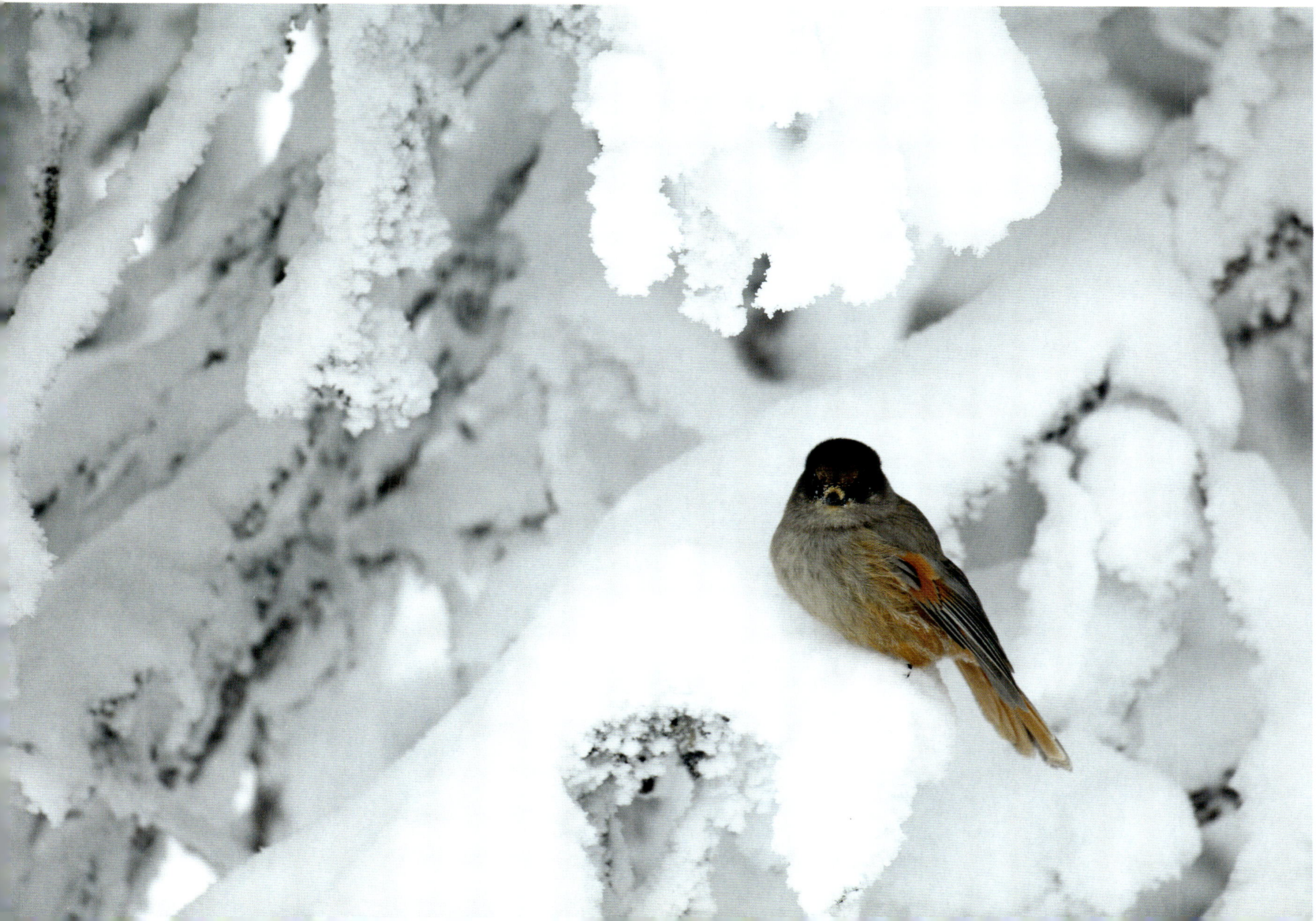

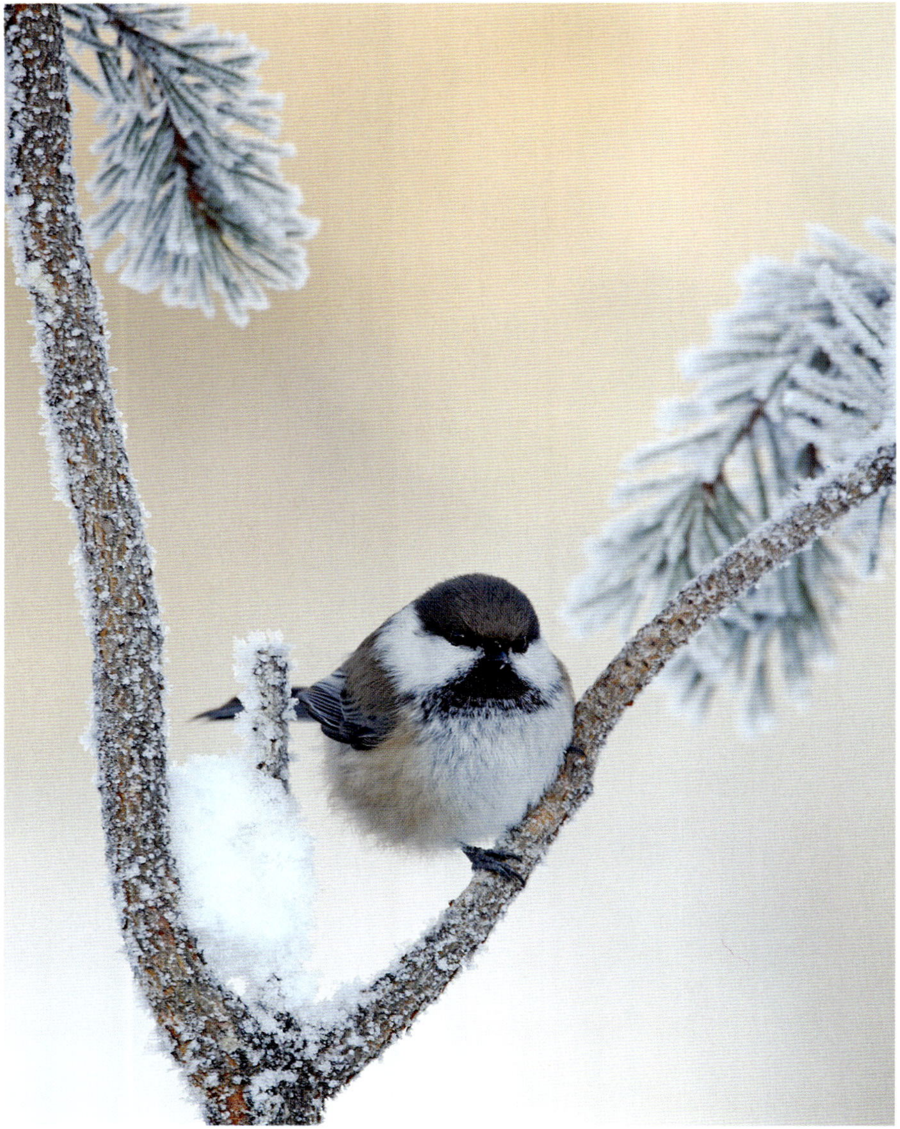

A Gray-headed Chickadee cast in the soft January light *(Poecile cinctus)* Canon EOS-1Ds Mark III, 500mm f/4.0 plus 1.4x extender, 1/200 second, f/7.1, ISO 800, one-shot focus with a central focusing point, Gitzo tripod, Manfrotto 501 video head. Kuusamo, Finland, January 2008.

Markus Varesvuo

Come February the daylight starts to get longer fast in Kuusamo. What was a mere couple of hours in early January creeps toward 10 hours by the end of February. A photographer's peak season in Kuusamo starts in mid-February.

The Kuusamo town center has a lot of rowan trees, and when they have a good berry crop Bohemian Waxwing flocks of several hundred birds feed on them daily throughout the winter, as long as there are berries to eat. Pine Grosbeaks eat rowanberries too, but far fewer of them winter in Kuusamo. They are probably easiest to photograph in November when their quantities are larger.

Toward the end of February there is already enough light to let you take flight shots of Siberian Jays, Bohemian Waxwings, and White-throated Dippers. February also sees the start of the eagle blind season. On short winter days, eagles visit feeding stations practically on a daily basis, and at the end of February and in early March there are good chances of complementing your stock of portraits and flight shots with pictures of mating eagles. Golden and White-tailed Eagle season continues well into early May.

A flock of Bohemian Waxwings in Kuusamo's winter *(Bombycilla garrulus)*
Canon EOS-1Ds Mark III, 70–200mm f/2.8, 1/250 second, 200mm, f/9.0, ISO 500, one-shot focus with a central focusing point, Gitzo tripod, Manfrotto 501 video head. Kuusamo, Finland, January 2010.

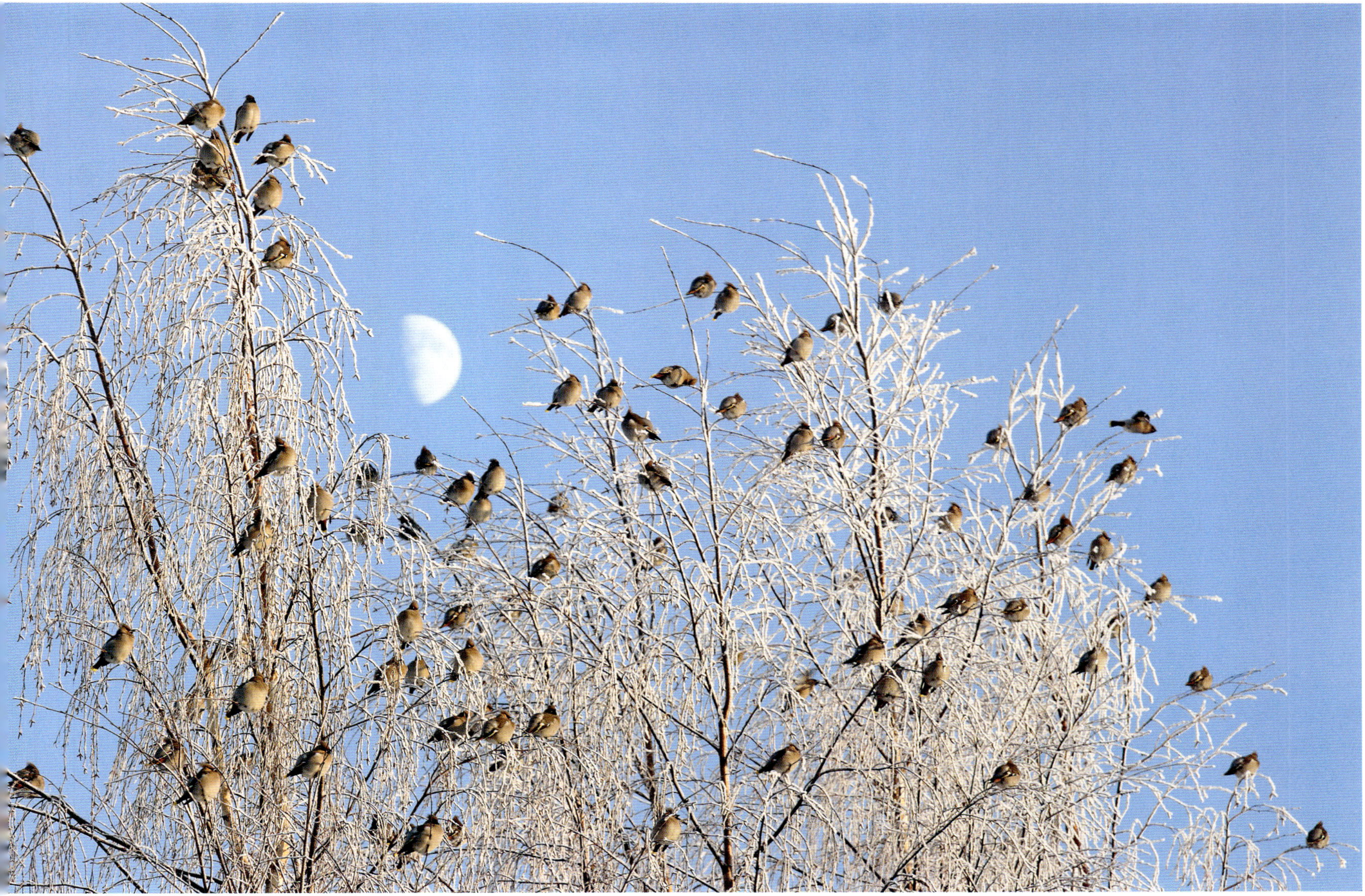

Markus Varesvuo

Markus Varesvuo

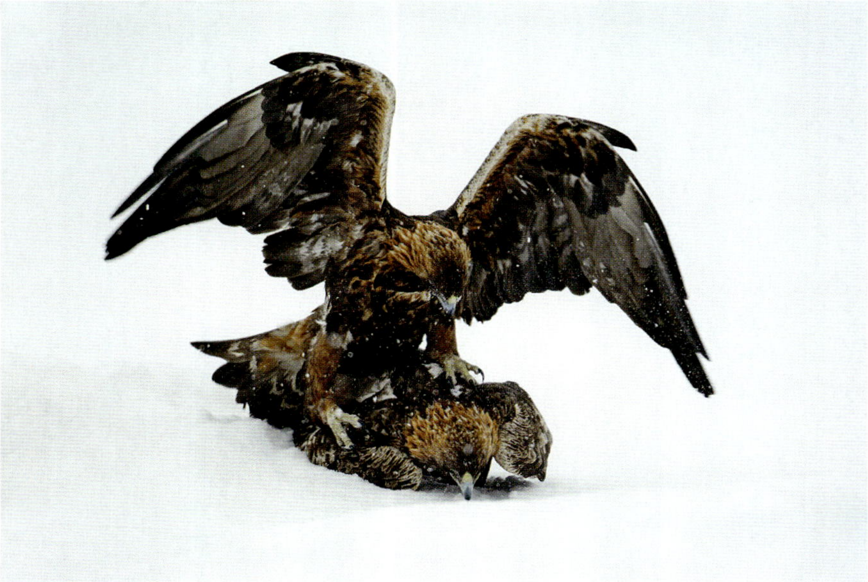

Golden Eagles mating *(Aquila chrysaetos)*
Canon EOS-1D Mark III, 500mm f/4.0, 1/500 second, f/4.0, ISO 1600, continuous focus with a central focusing point, Gitzo tripod, Manfrotto 501 video head, blind. Kuusamo, Finland, February 2008.

Markus Varesvuo

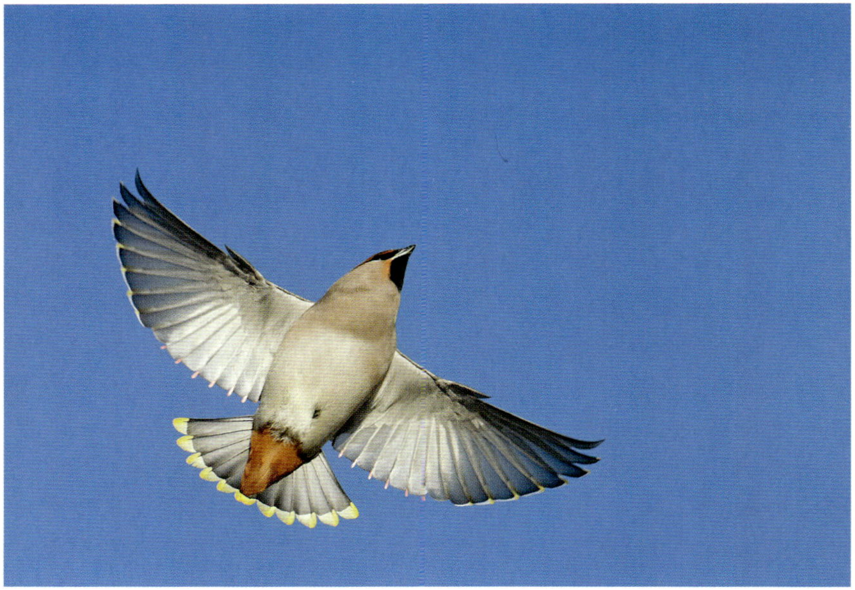

February starts to have enough light for freezing a Bohemian Waxwing in flight *(Bombycilla garrulus)*
Canon EOS-1D Mark IV, 500mm f/4.0, 1/3200 second, f/8.0, ISO 1250, continuous focus with 45 focusing points, handheld camera. Kuusamo, Finland, February 2010.

March is the best time for photographing the Great Gray Owl in Kuusamo. When there are no more voles in the woods, the owls come to hunt in the open fields. This makes them easier to spot, and photographing them is made possible by patiently waiting by the side of a field. You might catch the owls hunting, or you could offer them dead mice or voles. The hungry or starving owls eagerly come to food that is offered. Needless to say, these are great opportunities for taking flight shots and other types of shots.

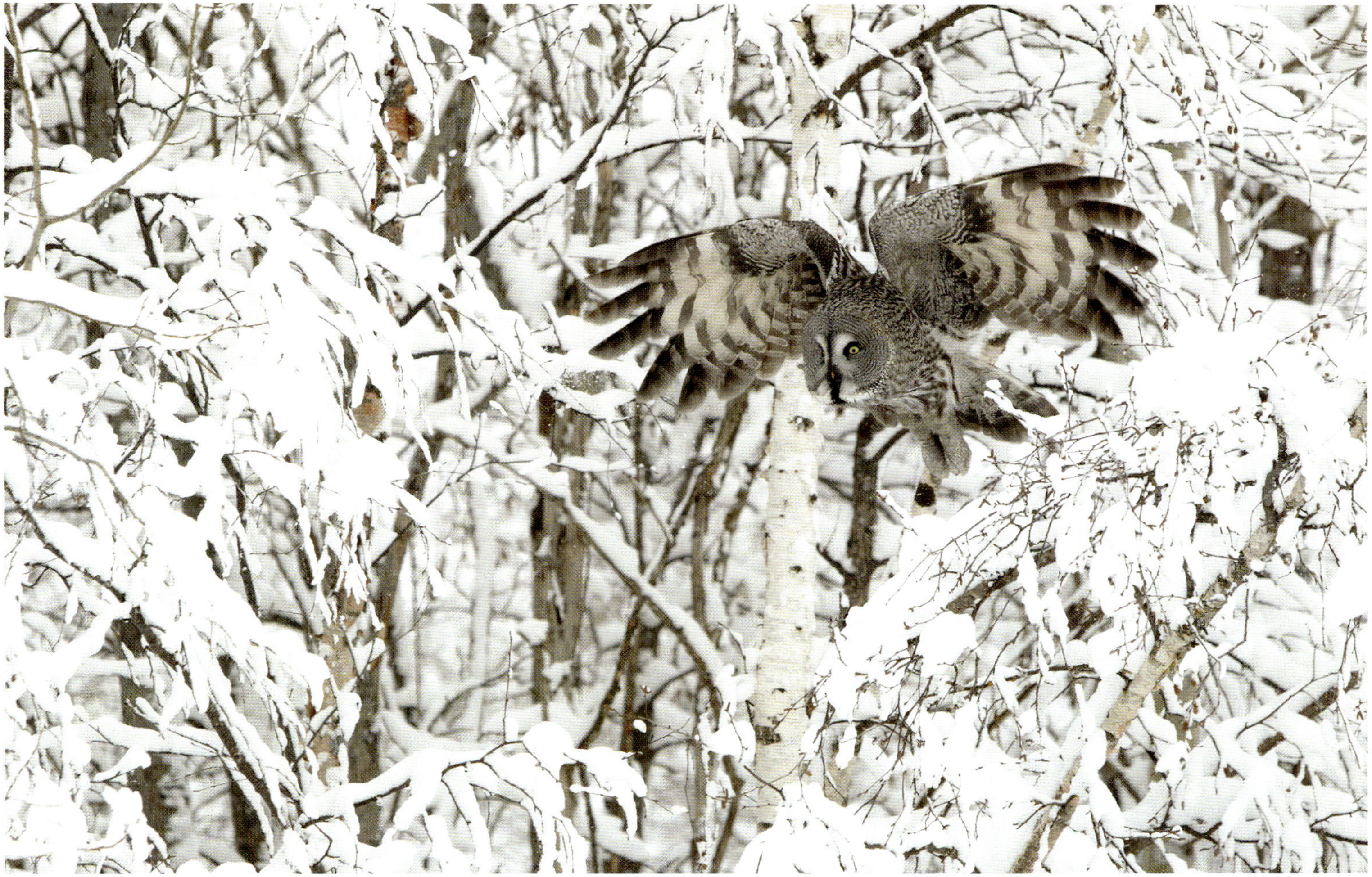

Markus Varesvuo

In March Great Gray Owls can be spotted hunting in fields *(Strix nebulosa)*
Canon EOS-1D Mark IV, 70–200mm f/2.8, 1/2000 second, 200mm, f/5.6, ISO 1250, continuous focus with 45 focusing points, handheld camera. Kuusamo, Finland, February 2010.

A female Black Grouse selecting a mating partner *(Tetrao tetrix)*
Canon EOS-1D Mark II, 500mm f/4.0, 1/50 second, f/4.0, ISO 200, one-shot focus with a central focusing point, Gitzo tripod, Manfrotto 501 video head, blind. Kuusamo, Finland, May 2004.

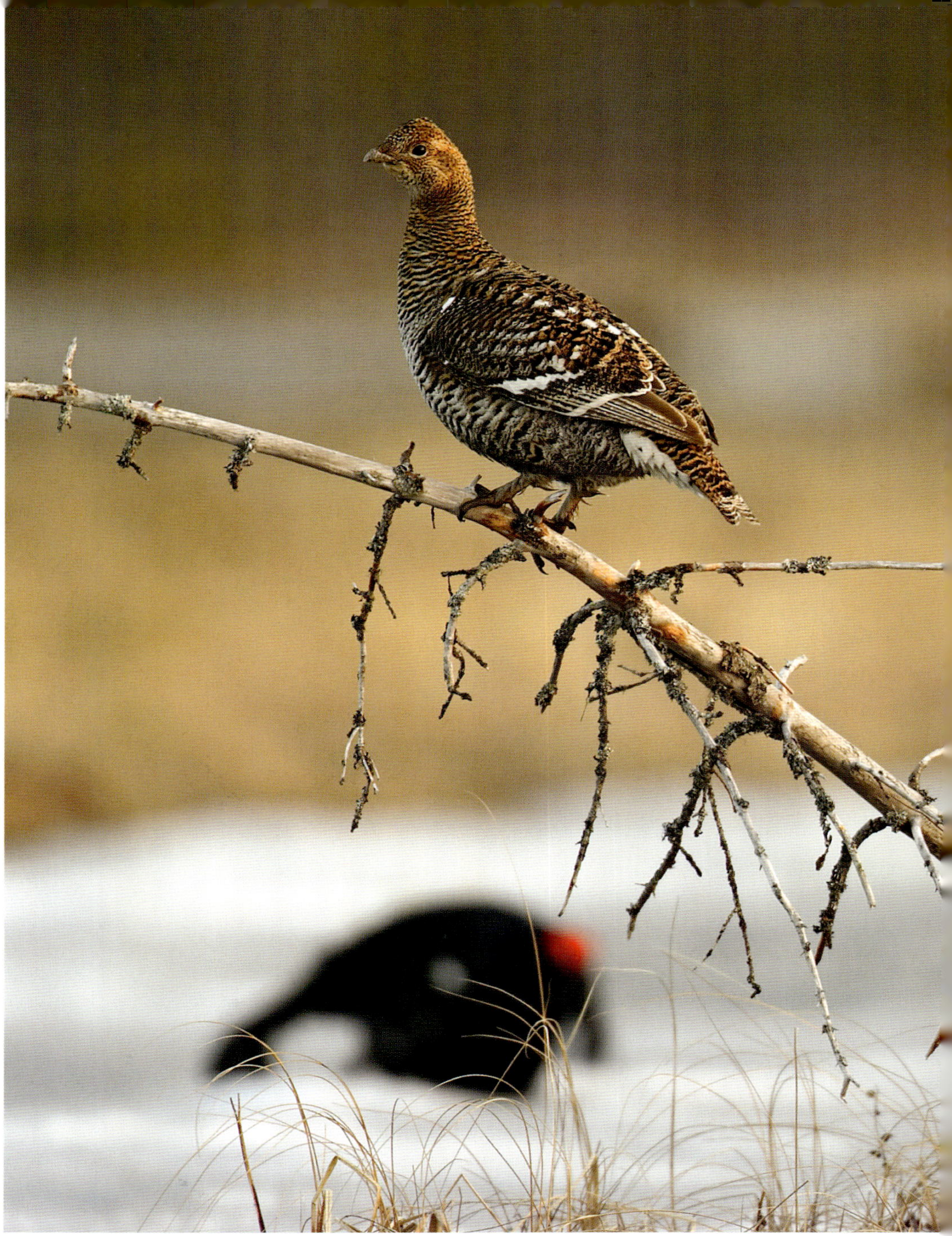

Markus Varesvuo

Markus Varesvuo

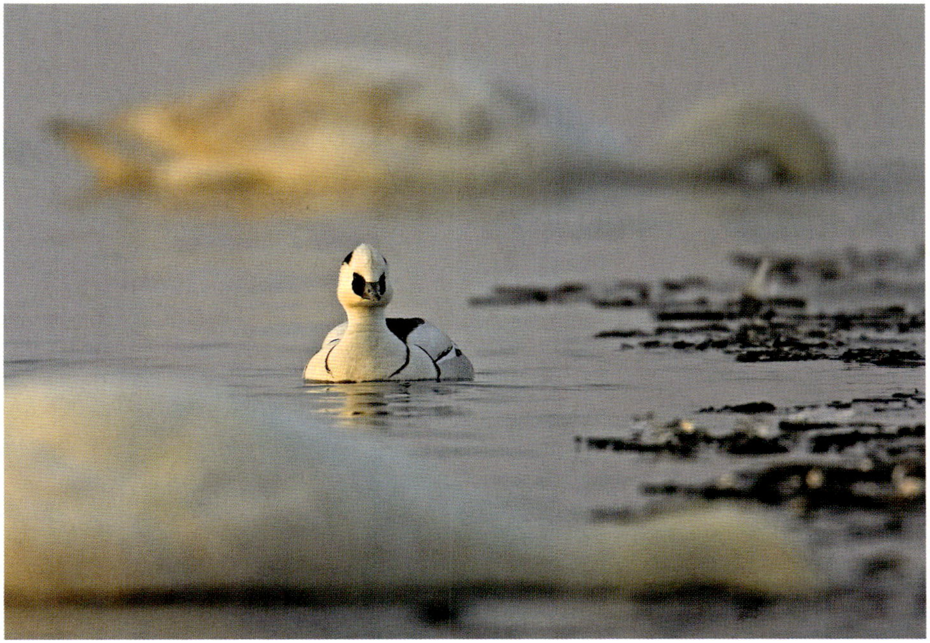

Two birds characteristic of Kuusamo: Smew between two Whooper Swans *(Mergellus albellus, Cygnus cygnus)*
Canon EOS-1D Mark II, 500mm f/4.0 plus 1.4x extender, 1/640 second, f/5.6, ISO 250, one-shot focus with a central focusing point, Gitzo tripod, Manfrotto 501 video head, blind. Kuusamo, Finland, May 2004.

The end of April and early May are good times for photographing game birds. Female Black Grouse arrive to the lek around the turn of the month, when the males have reached the high peak of their courtship tournaments. In May the snow vanishes from the roadsides, exposing the gravel for the game bird species to pick up as gizzard stones. Driving slowly along the back roads can take you to the right place at the right time to photograph Capercaillies and Black and Hazel Grouse on the shoulder of the road from your car.

May is also a busy time for bird photographers in Kuusamo. Many of the migratory birds arrive in May, and birds congregate on any patch of open water exposed from the snow and ice, such as geese, cranes, Whooper Swans, waders, and waterbirds. Photographing is done from a blind, and the best results come from fixed blinds that have been in the same place for quite some time. Mobile tent blinds are fine too, but it takes good local knowledge to find open patches that suit photography and perseverance to wait for the birds to get used to the appearance of a blind. Note that fixed structures require permission from the landowner.

Up-to-date information about birds and blinds in Kuusamo can be found online, such as at www.facebook.com/KuusamoNaturePhotography.

Throughout May and in the beginning of June, many interesting small bird species reach Kuusamo: Little and Rustic Buntings, Arctic and Greenish Warblers, plus Red-flanked Bluetails. The best time to see and photograph them is as soon as they arrive, which is their most active singing season. For locating the species mentioned, you must be able to recognize their calls and songs, plus you should know where to look for them.

The Red-flanked Bluetail is one of Kuusamo's specialties *(Tarsiger cyanurus)*
Canon EOS-1D Mark II, 500mm f/4.0 plus 1.4x extender, 1/160 second, f/5.6, ISO 500, one-shot focus with a central focusing point, Gitzo tripod, Manfrotto 501 video head. Kuusamo, Finland, June 2005.

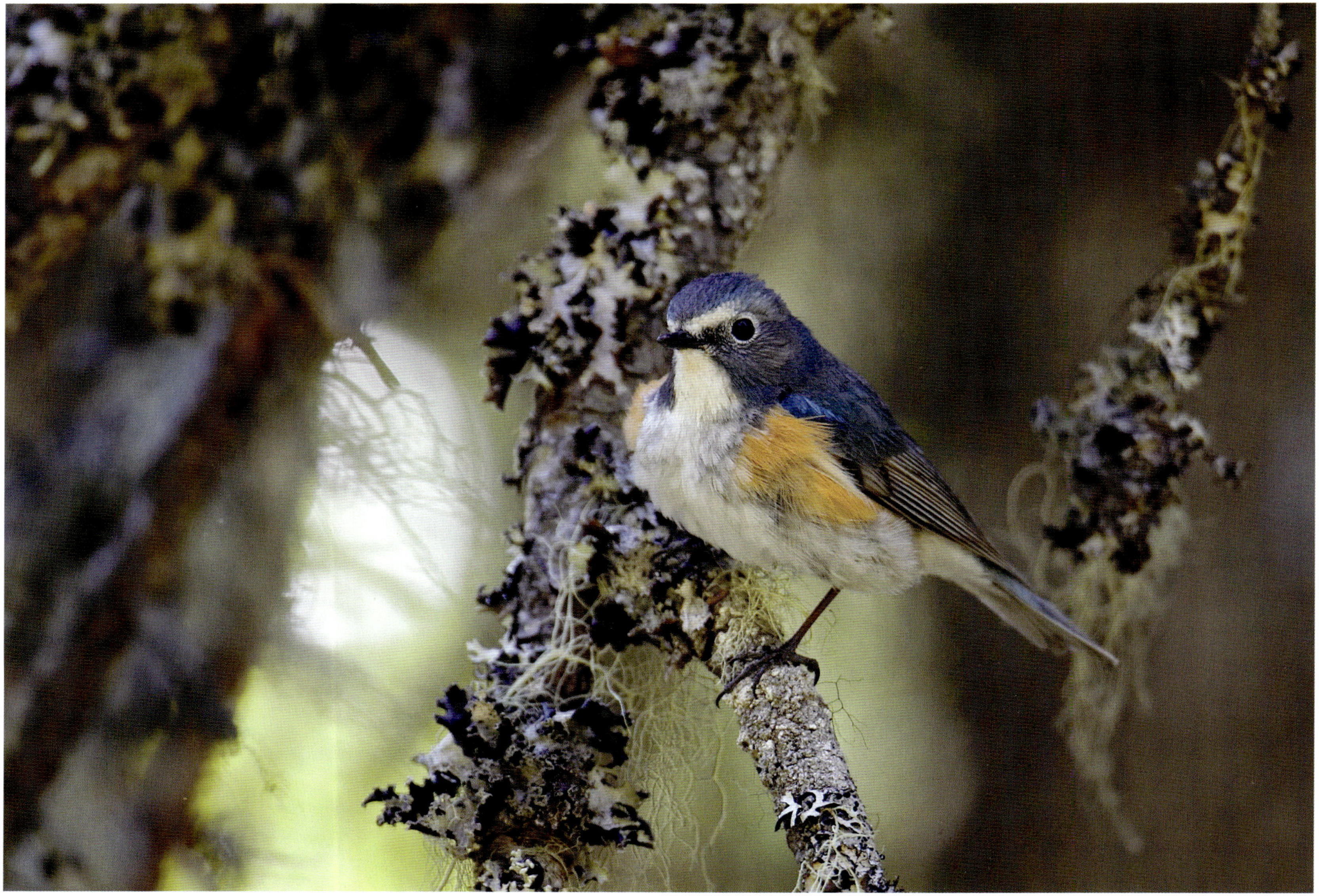

Markus Varesvuo

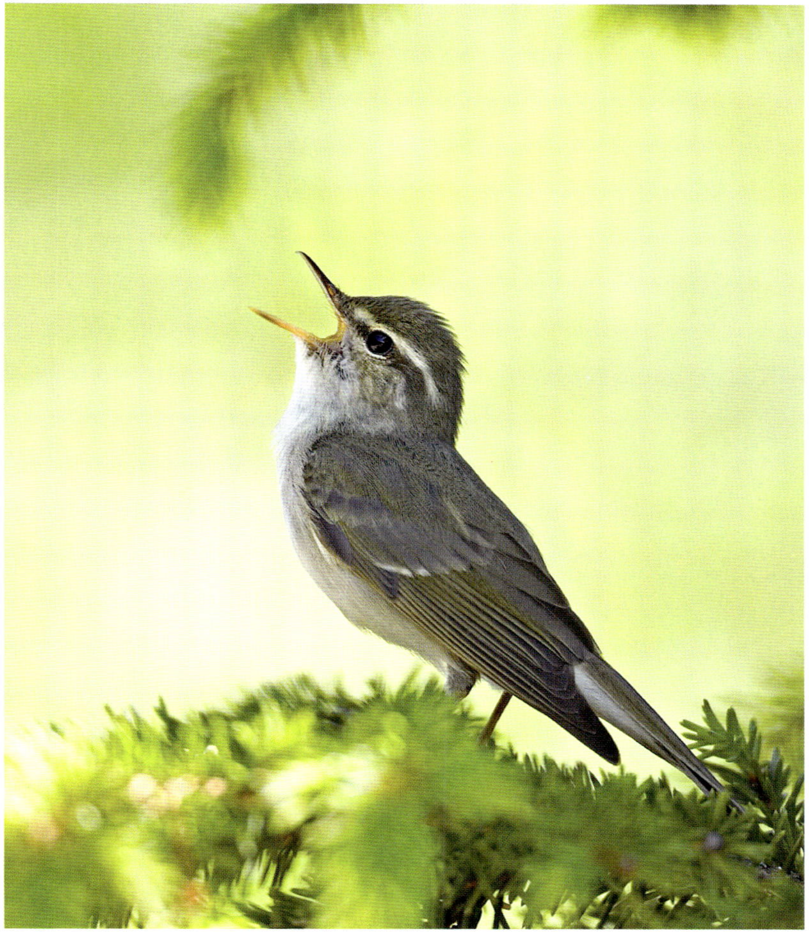
Markus Varesvuo

The Arctic Warbler doesn't normally reach Kuusamo before the middle of June *(Phylloscopus borealis)*

Canon EOS-1D Mark II, 500mm f/4.0, 1/500 second, f/4.0, ISO 320, one-shot focus with a central focusing point, Gitzo tripod, Manfrotto 501 video head. Kuusamo, Finland, June 2005.

Valtavaara Hill in Kuusamo is favored by the Red-flanked Bluetails and Greenish Warblers. Breeding species in the region include Siberian Jay, Eurasian Three-toed Woodpecker, Pine Grosbeak, and Boreal and Eurasian Pygmy-Owl, as well as White-winged Crossbill, if the cone crop has been good.

Kuusamo is a large area (5,800 km²/2,239 mi²), and finding the scattered birds is not so easy. Getting the help of a local guide speeds up things; however, if you can spend a couple of weeks there, you will get good material on your own, too.

MARKUS VARESVUO

UTÖ ISLAND ON THE BALTIC SEA

Utö Island is an absolute gem.

This remote little island in the Archipelago Sea is the most southerly piece of land in Finland with permanent habitation. It lies on the edge of the open sea, and as the first larger piece of land when crossing the sea northbound, it attracts birds on their spring migration. In autumn it offers birds a good place for refueling before they start their journey across the sea. At about 2 km (1.2 mi) long and just over 1 km (0.6 mi) at its widest, Utö sports a couple of little groves, a fair-sized meadow, some dry heath, a few sheltered coves, a shallow shore with seaweed, and a little village with gardens—many and varied locations for birds to rest and feed.

Part of the island still belongs to the Finnish Defence Forces, even though it's not manned. The military zones are off limits, and visitors should check the latest maps upon arrival. It's also important to respect the local people's gardens and boat houses with small docks. Use discretion when photographing around the houses and gardens. The island boasts Finland's oldest still-functioning lighthouse.

A ferry runs between the mainland and the island daily from June to August and five times a week in other seasons. Normally the journey takes about five hours, but in the winter, depending on the ice situation, it can take up to 10 hours. The island has a hotel with a good restaurant, cabins for rent and more economic hostel-type lodging, plus a small grocer. The island has a good Internet connection. You can read more at www.uto.fi, and firsthand and local information from an experienced birder and bird photographer is available at www.jtenovuo.com/blogi (in Finnish).

I would argue that a bird photographer finds spring to be the best time on Utö, although I wouldn't underrate the flurry of action on the wader shore at the end of summer or the semirarities seen in autumn.

In Finland the migration peaks in April and May, and a place like Utö gives you the chance to witness the progress of migration in miniature scale. In addition to passing migratory birds, Utö has its own avifauna, which also returns during this high season. The birds that land on the island—some for a short stay, others for the breeding season—are rather hungry after their trip across the sea, so they focus on eating, which makes them quite fearless and thus relatively easy to photograph.

Sometimes winter on Utö comes with lots of snow, and then it's possible for the snow to partly cover the island as late as March and even into April. The first birds to the island then have to find their food in the few open patches.

European Robins are among Utö's most numerous and common birds in April *(Erithacus rubecula)*
Canon EOS-1D Mark IV, 800mm f/5.6, 1/250 second, f/10.0, ISO 500, one-shot focus with a central focusing point, Gitzo tripod, Manfrotto 501 video head, blind. Utö, Finland, April 2010.

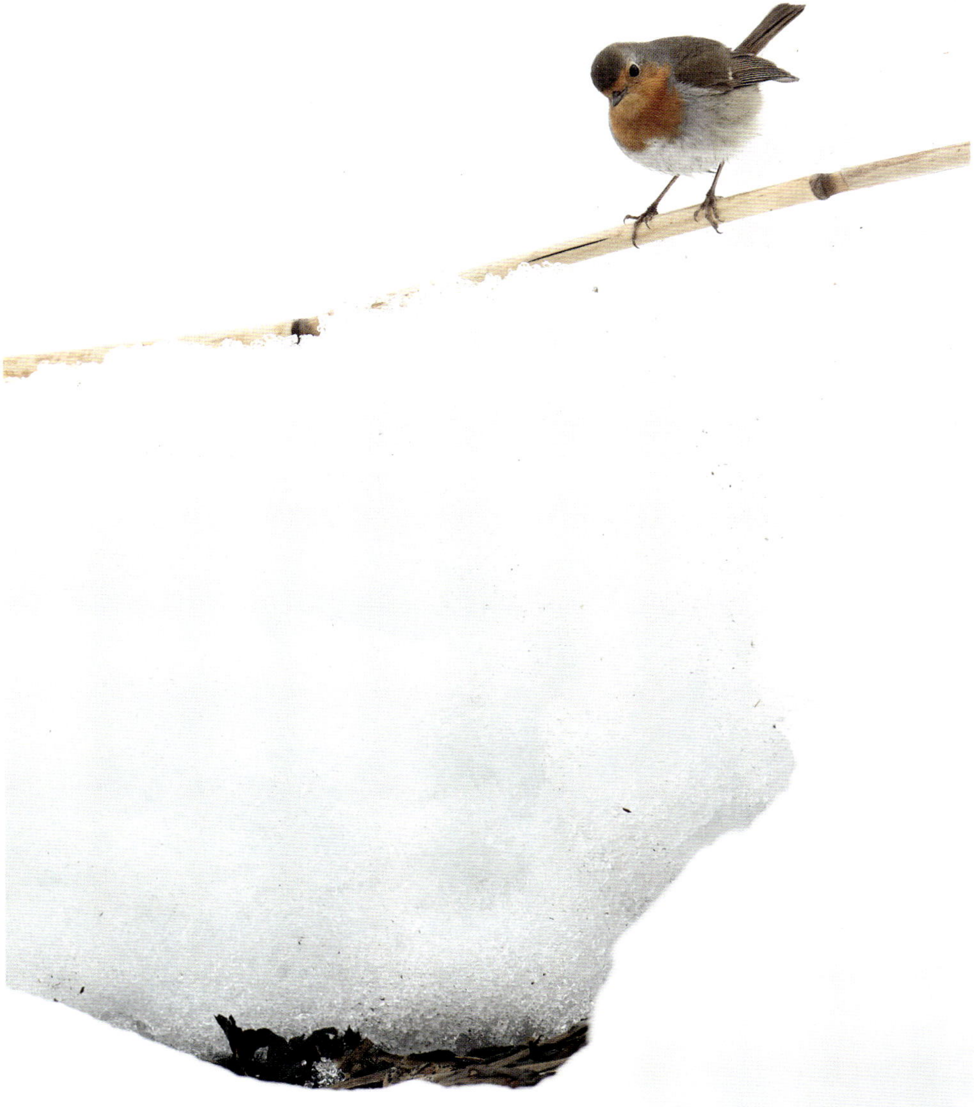

Markus Varesvuo

Markus Varesvuo

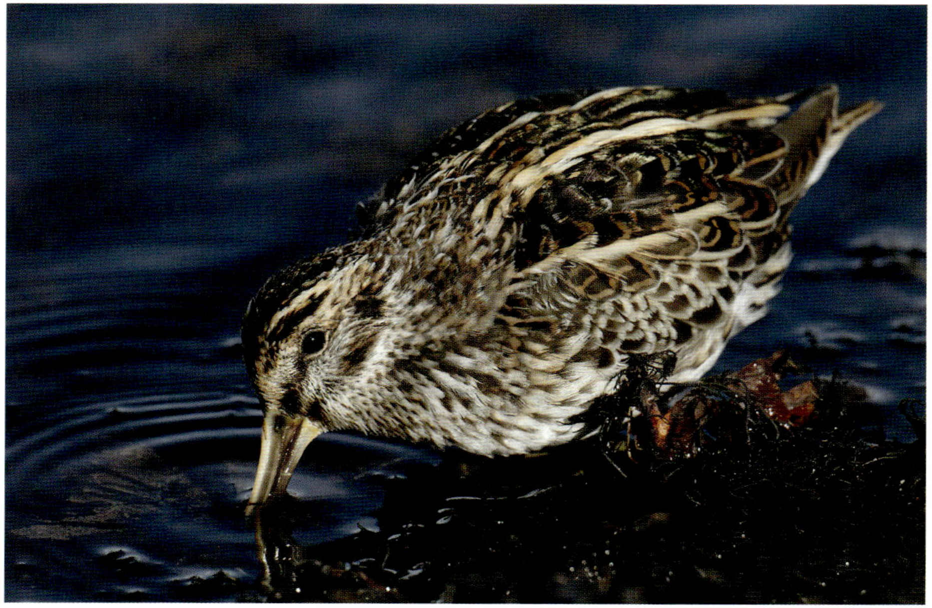

A Jack Snipe feeding on the east shore *(Lymnocryptes minimus)*
Canon EOS-1D Mark IV, 500mm f/4.0, 1/1000 second, f/9,0, ISO 800, one-shot focus with a central focusing point, Gitzo tripod, Manfrotto 501 video head, blind. Utö, Finland, April 2010.

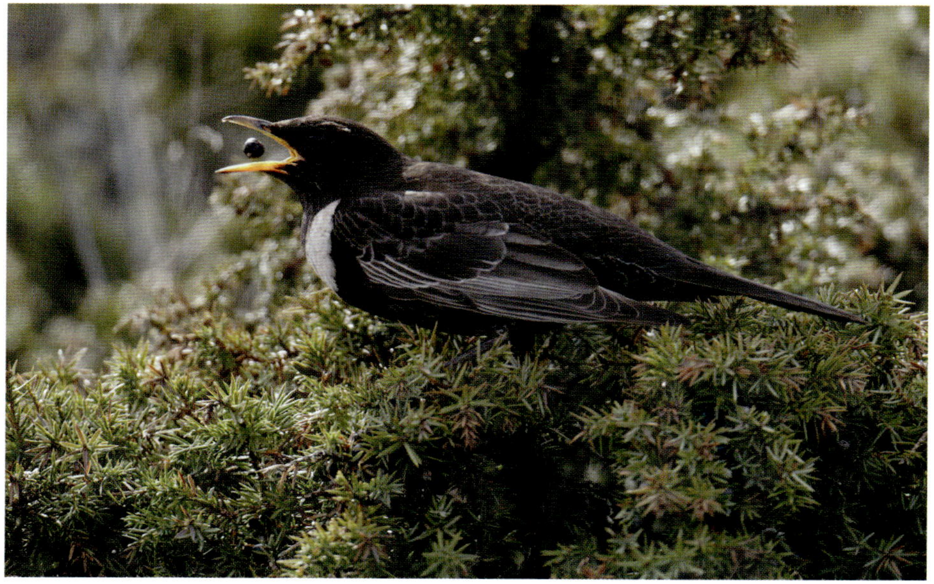

A Ring Ouzel feeding on juniper berries *(Turdus torquatus)*
Canon EOS-1D Mark IV, 800mm f/5.6, 1/1250 second, f/5.6, ISO 1600, one-shot focus with a central focusing point, Gitzo tripod, Manfrotto 501 video head. Utö, Finland, April 2010.

Markus Varesvuo

A sheltered cove on the eastern side of the island becomes very busy in early April with thrushes, Rock Pipits, Reed Buntings, Northern Wheatears, and many wader species looking for food among the seaweed on the shallow shore. The best chances to photograph the secretive Jack Snipe is in mid-April. On the shore, the best photos are taken from a blind.

In April and May a few Ring Ouzels are usually seen in the island's juniper bushes, as the birds are on their way to Lapland. They are mostly shy, but sometimes there are more trusting individuals. And occasionally some of them feed on the seaweeds on the eastern shore, where they can be photographed from a blind.

The numbers of insect-eating birds start to grow in the beginning of May. Common Redstarts, Bluethroats, Blackcaps, Lesser Whitethroats, and Chiffchaffs are everywhere. There are some good chances for Ortolan Buntings, and the Collared Flycatcher is one of the rare species that is spotted on Utö in May almost every year. A blind is not necessary for photographing small birds on Utö; instead, you get the best results by waiting patiently and quietly near where the birds come to feed.

For a bird photographer the most interesting of Utö's breeding species are probably the Barred Warbler, which is declining fast elsewhere in Finland, and the Common Shelduck, Horned Grebe, Velvet Scoter, and Eurasian Wryneck. The communal display rituals of the Velvet Scoter peak toward the end of May, with the birds flying above the island in small groups early in the morning. The dirt road leading to the southern tip of the island is the best place for photographing them in display flight, because you can stay out of sight in the rocks by the road.

The end of May sees lots of Common Whitethroats; Garden, Willow, and Wood Warblers; and European Pied and Spotted Flycatchers. Less numerous but regular enough are Icterine, Greenish, Marsh, and Blyth's Reed-Warblers, as well as Red-backed Shrikes.

In May on the east shore there can be a few Broad-billed Sandpipers, Spotted Redshanks, Common Greenshanks, Dunlins, and Curlew Sandpipers. Other regular visitors to the shore include Northern Shovelers, Gadwalls, Common Eiders, and Common Shelducks.

Adult waders start back on their autumn migration as early as mid-June. The first to return are handsome Spotted Redshanks, still in their elegant breeding plumage. Around the second half of July or early August the east shore sports Dunlins, Curlew

Markus Varesvuo

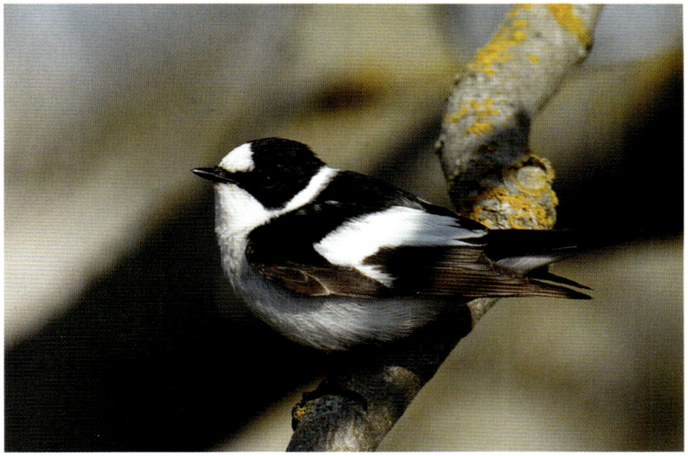

The Collared Flycatcher is an Utö specialty *(Ficedula albicollis)*
Canon EOS-1D Mark IV, 800mm f/5.6, 1/640 second, f/10.0, ISO 400, one-shot focus with a central focusing point, Gitzo tripod, Manfrotto 501 video head. Utö, Finland, May 2010.

Velvet Scoters in display flight make a lovely sight *(Melanitta fusca)*
Canon EOS-1D Mark III, 500mm f/5.6, 1/1000 second, f/4.0, ISO 2000, continuous focus with an extended central focusing point, handheld camera. Utö, Finland, May 2009.

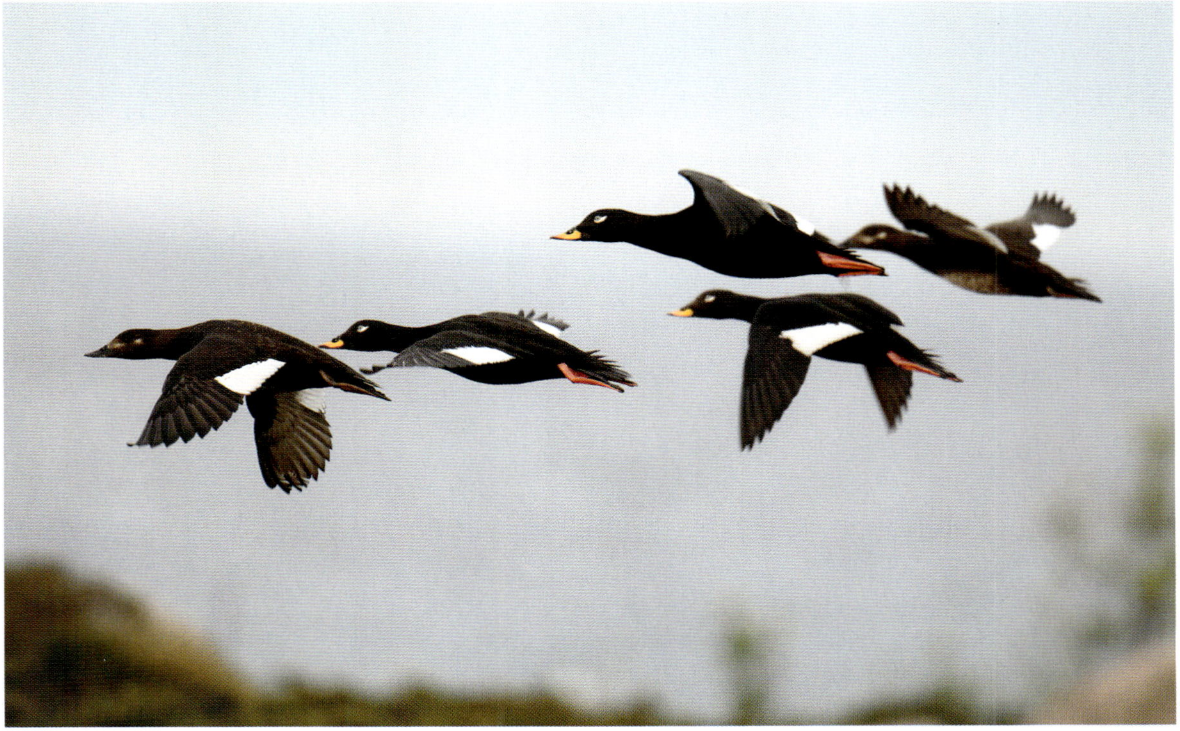

Markus Varesvuo

Markus Varesvuo

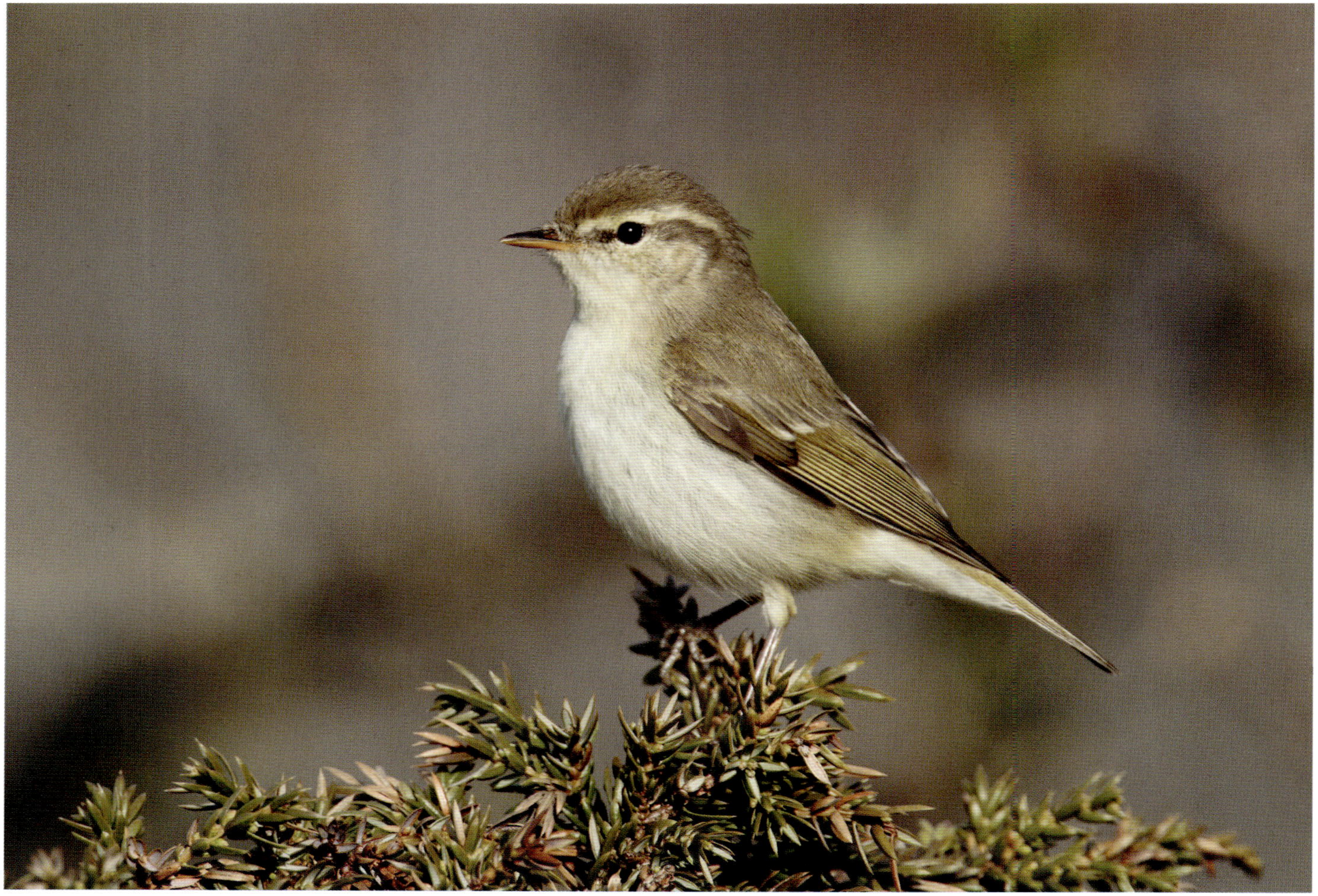

Greenish Warblers can be seen on Utö toward the end of May *(Phylloscopus trochiloides)*
Canon EOS-1D Mark IV, 800mm f/5.6 plus 1.4x extender, 1/500 second, f/11.0, ISO 400, one-shot focus with a central focusing point, Gitzo tripod, Manfrotto 501 video head. Utö, Finland, May 2010.

Sandpipers, and Little Stints returning from their breeding grounds in the Russian Arctic. Among the migrating birds, Utö's own breeding species, such as Common Ringed Plovers, Eurasian Oystercatchers, and Ruddy Turnstones, feed regularly on the east shore.

Most of the waders on Utö from early August to early October are young birds. In addition to those mentioned, there are Wood Sandpipers, Ruffs, Red Knots, Whimbrels, and European Golden Plovers.

The migration of small birds has already started in August, but it's most visible in September and October, with lots of Common Chaffinches, Bramblings, Winter Wrens, Goldcrests, tits, and European Robins, with some rarer eastern species among them, such as Pallas's Leaf-Warblers and Yellow-browed Warblers.

Short-eared and Long-eared Owls are the more common owls on Utö in autumn, with some less frequent visitors, such as Eurasian Pygmy and Boreal Owls. With quite a few rowan trees, Utö also draws berry-eating birds, and in a good berry year there can be hundreds of thrushes and waxwings swarming the trees.

When the vole populations are healthy, many raptors stop at the meadow to hunt. If you hide in the cover

Markus Varesvuo

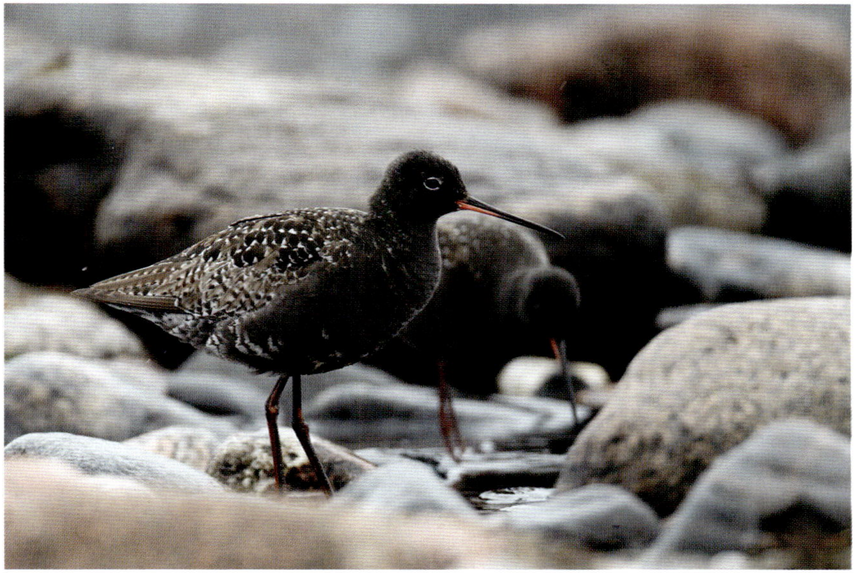

The appearance of the handsome Spotted Redshank on Utö is the first sign of the autumn migration *(Tringa erythropus)*
Canon EOS-1D Mark IV, 800mm f/5.6, 1/500 second, f/5.6, ISO 500, one-shot focus with a central focusing point, Gitzo tripod, Manfrotto 501 video head, blind. Utö, Finland, June 2010.

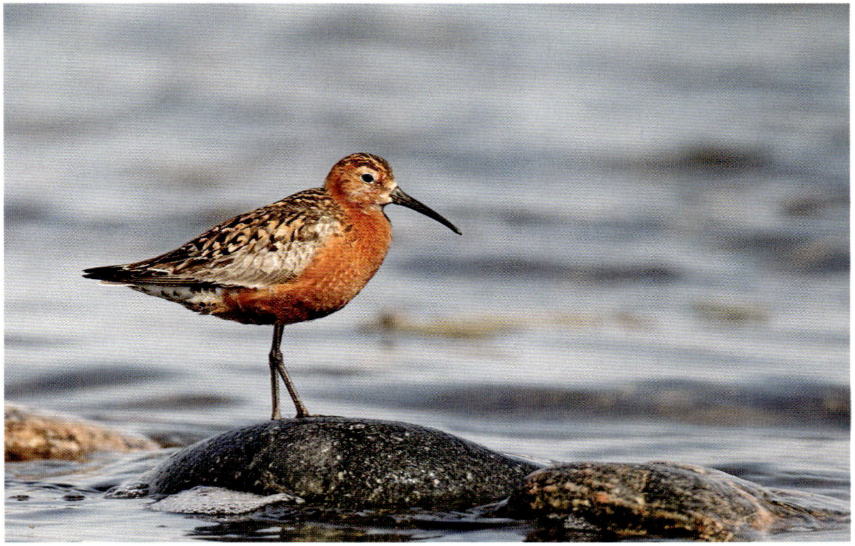

Markus Varesvuo

Curlew Sandpipers, in their summer plumage, come to Utö in mid-July *(Calidris ferruginea)*
Canon EOS-1D Mark IV, 800mm f/5.6, 1/3200 second, f/8.0, ISO 1250, one-shot focus with a central focusing point, Gitzo tripod, Manfrotto 501 video head, blind. Utö, Finland, July 2010.

Markus Varesvuo

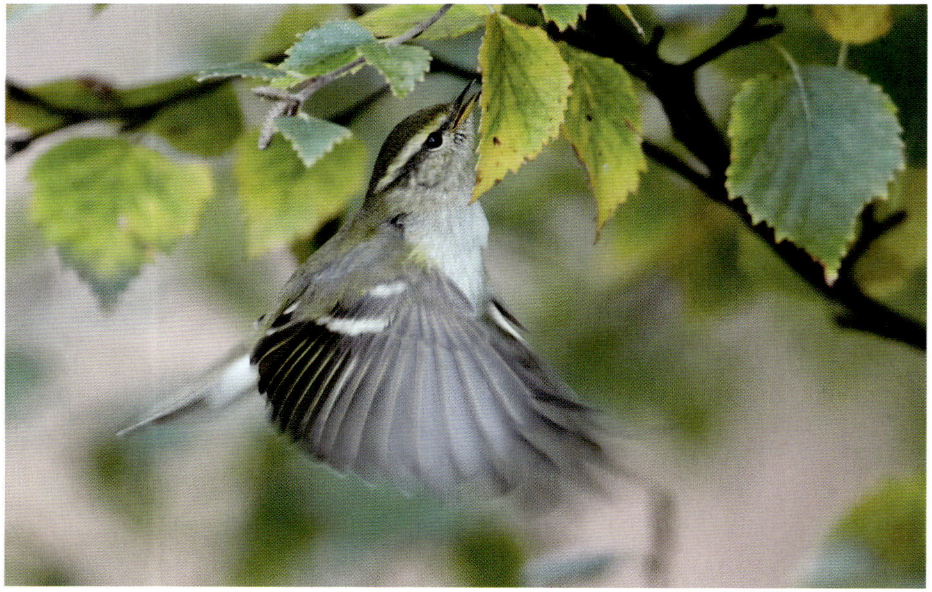

A Yellow-browed Warbler hunting insects *(Phylloscopus inornatus)*
Canon EOS-1D Mark IV, 800mm f/5.6, 1/400 second, f/5.6, ISO 2000, continuous focus with 45 focusing points, Gitzo tripod, Manfrotto 501 video head. Utö, Finland, October 2010.

of the trees and bushes, it's possible to photograph Western Marsh Harriers and Northern Harriers. Sparrowhawks and Kestrels are a common sight on Utö in autumn and are often quite easily photographed.

> It's good to keep in mind that the local hunting group has a license to hunt on the eastern meadow and shore in autumn.

As autumn turns to November, the birds fade from both the audio and the visual world. Even though the winter landscapes can be spectacular, especially those with more snow and in lower temperatures, a bird photographer would struggle to find birds to photograph. There are swans, waterbirds, cormorants, and White-tailed Eagles in the area, but they are usually not within easy reach.

In the outer archipelago the winds are often strong and the weather changes fast. In spring the strong north winds can bring migration to a screeching halt for days, and nothing much happens in the birding world. A short island trip may end without many photographs, but a week is often long enough to ensure that there is at least one good day.

A Rough-legged Hawk hunting over the east meadow *(Buteo lagopus)*
Canon EOS-1D Mark IV, 800mm f/5.6, 1/2000 second, f/9.0, ISO 1250, continuous focus with an extended central focusing point, Gitzo tripod, Manfrotto 501 video head. Utö, Finland, October 2010.

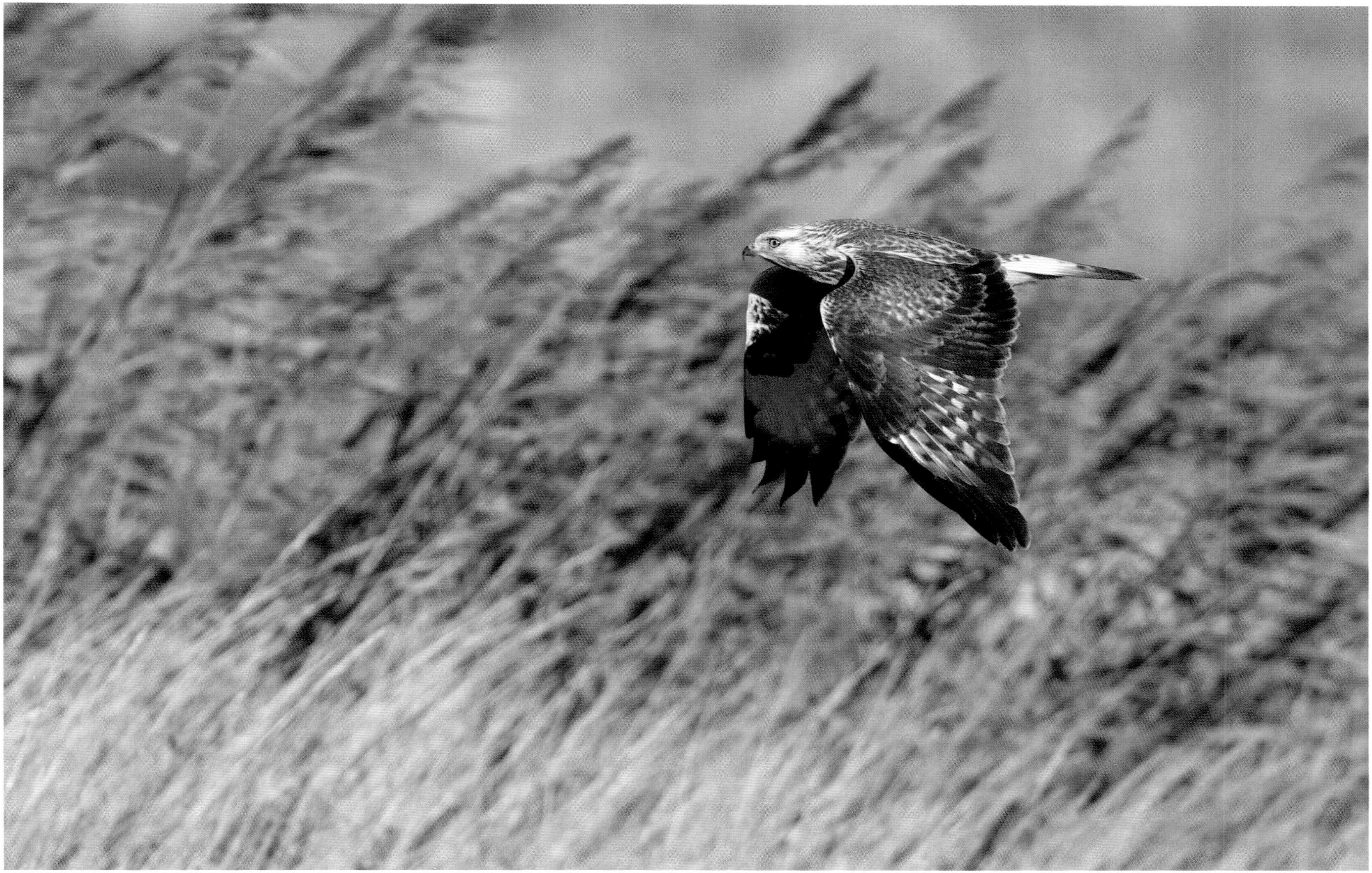

Markus Varesvuo

JARI PELTOMÄKI

OULU AND VAALA, FINLAND

Interesting species can be seen in the middle of Finland.

The region and city of Oulu in central Finland borders the northeast shore of the Gulf of Bothnia, and it's a meeting point of two different avifaunas: the birds of the shallow shores of the Baltic Sea and those of the northern coniferous zone. Open fields in flat landscapes are distinctive to this coastal area, where snow melts earlier than in the surrounding areas during spring. The open patches revealed by the spring sun draw geese, cranes, and swans. Graylag Geese breed in the area and are easiest to photograph in early April, just as they arrive but before they start breeding. Many other geese in the area are in transit, such as Bean, Pink-footed, Greater White-fronted, and the endangered Lesser White-fronted Geese.

In the beginning of May, many waterbird and wader species are busy feeding on the shores in the region, and the large network of surrounding bogs is rich in bird life. Most of the bogs have Black Grouse leks, with the males fighting for supremacy in spring, and cranes nest in these bogs.

The larger Oulu area has a wide range of habitats for birds: shore meadows, reed beds, fallow fields, logging clearances, and moist forest floors. There aren't many old forests in the Oulu area, but there is variation that forms an interesting mosaic of habitats that also benefit vole populations, which bring owls to the forests on the northeastern coasts of the Gulf of Bothnia. The Great Gray Owl, for example, breeds yearly in the area between Pyhäjoki and Kemi. Other breeding owl species include the Eurasian Pygmy, Boreal, Short-eared, Long-eared, Ural, and Eagle. In peak vole years, there's even the Hawk Owl.

Each of the four European harriers breeds in Oulu—the Western Marsh and Northern Harriers every year, and the rarer Pallid and Montagu's Harriers infrequently. In winter you can photograph Gray Partridges, and in some years even Snowy Owls, on the fallow fields in the Oulu region.

Oulu is also known for Liminganlahti (Liminka Bay), Finland's most valuable wetland. It's a large and shallow bay in the Gulf of Bothnia. The shores are rough and difficult to access for a bird photographer, and the best birding sites are nearly impossible from a photographer's perspective. Luckily there are a couple of good spots where a photographer can target some of the areas specialties from a blind.

The Oulu area offers the best opportunities in Finland for photographing the Pink-footed Goose *(Anser brachyrhynchus)*
Canon EOS-1D Mark II, 500mm f/4.0, 1/500 second, f/9.0, ISO 200, continuous focus with 45 focusing points, Manfrotto 501 video head attached to the blind's equipment plank. Liminka, Finland, April 2005.

Jari Peltomäki

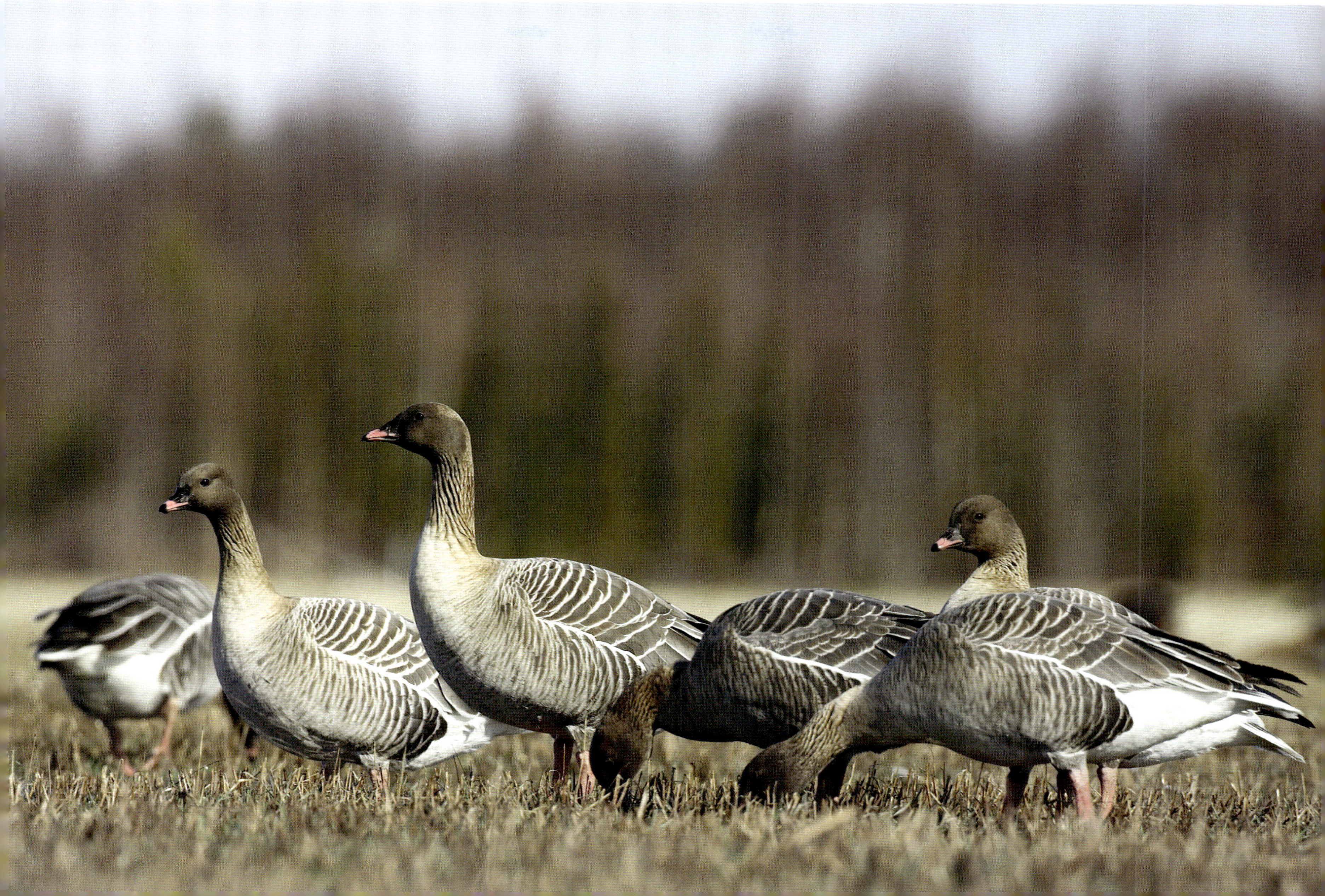

Great Gray Owl in the summer *(Strix nebulosa)*
Canon EOS-1D Mark III, 16–35mm f/2.8, 1/3200 second, 16mm, f/4.0, ISO 2500, continuous focus with an extended central focusing point, handheld camera. Siikajoki, Finland, July 2008.

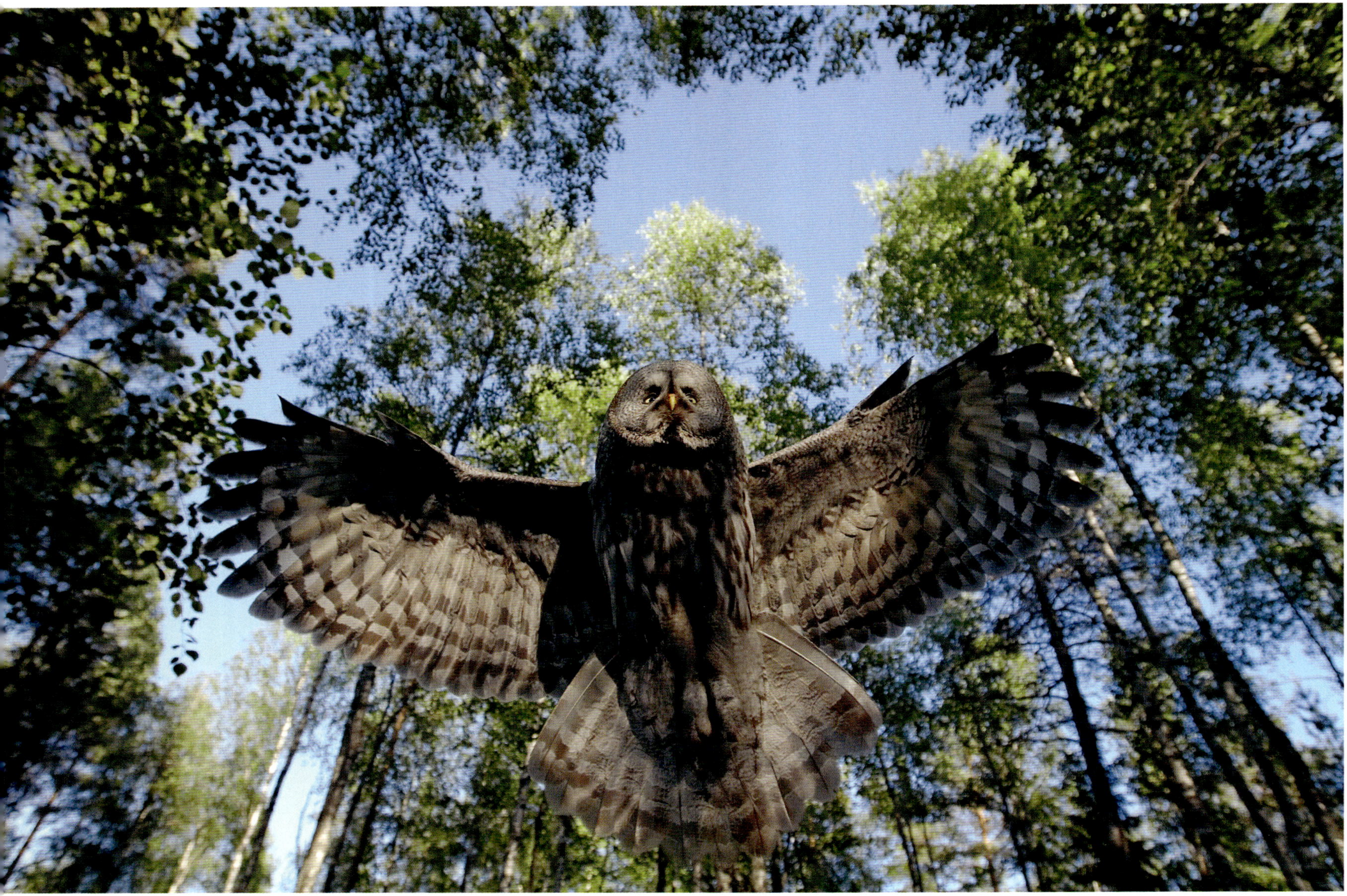

Jari Peltomäki

Jari Peltomäki

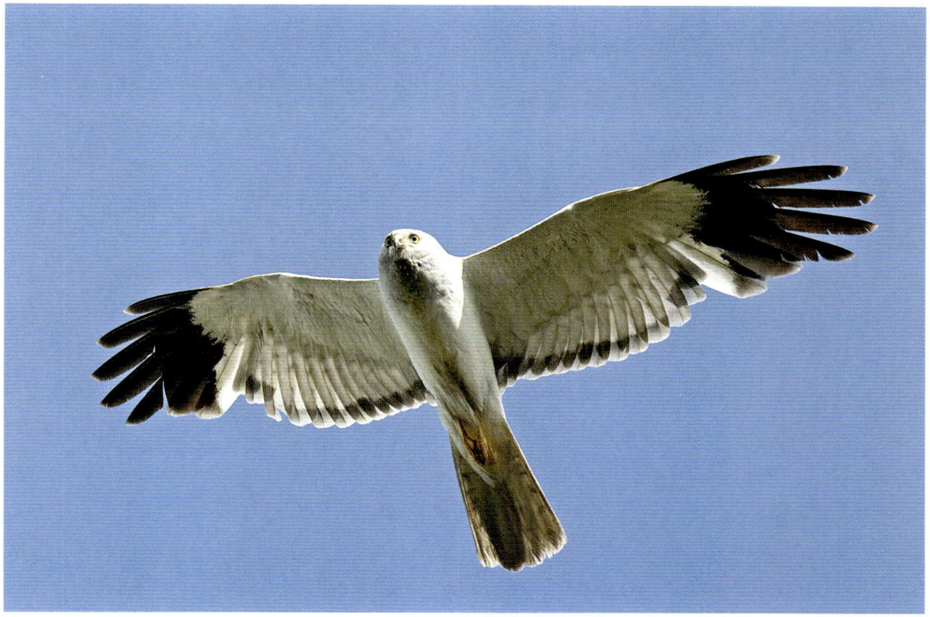

When the vole populations are high in the greater Oulu area, the numbers of breeding Northern Harriers increase *(Circus cyaneus)*
Canon EOS-1D Mark II, 300mm f/2.8, 1/2000 second, f/4.0, ISO 320, continuous focus with 45 focusing points, handheld camera. Liminka, Finland, July 2005.

The Black-tailed Godwit is a local specialty that is best photographed in June, when the precocial chicks are moving about and the parents guide them with alarm calls, at times right by the road. The best fields with Black-tailed Godwits are along the Selkämaantie road leading from Liminka to Oulunsalo. I took the image of the parent sounding alarm calls from a barn roof using my car as a blind. Unfortunately, the barn is long gone, so this shot would be hard to reproduce. Barns are part of a vanishing culture.

Ruffs have been noticeably declining in Finland in recent years, but Liminganlahti still has a few Ruff leks where it's possible to capture the fancy males

Jari Peltomäki

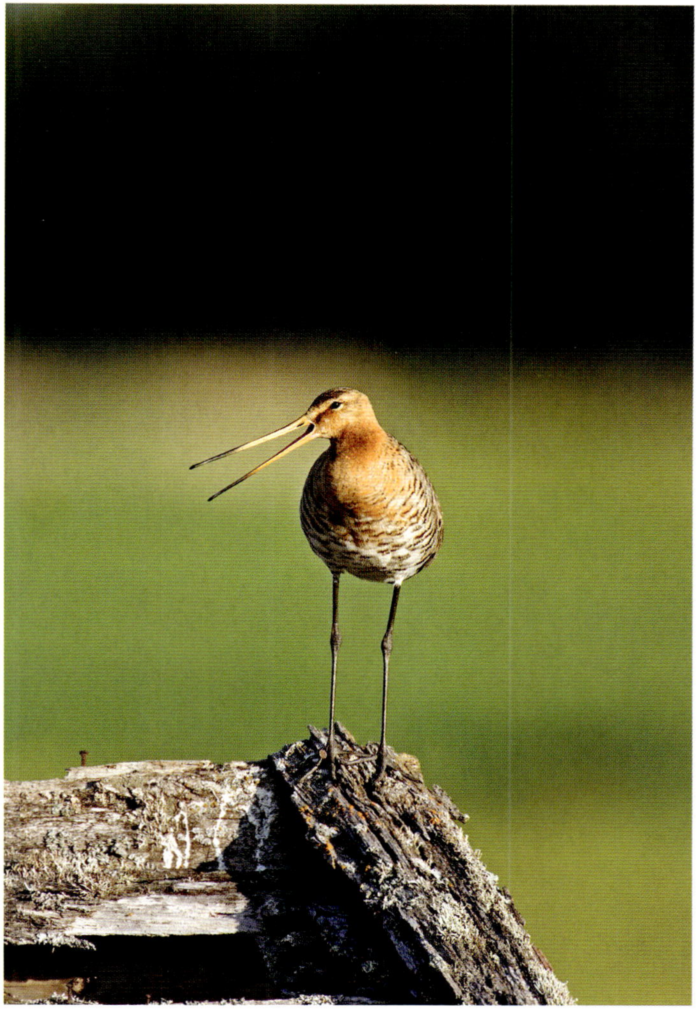

The only breeding Black-tailed Godwits are in the Liminganlahti area *(Limosa limosa)*
Canon EOS-1D Mark II, 500mm f/4.0 plus 2x extender, 1/500 second, f/8.0, ISO 400, one-shot focus with a central focusing point, beanbag, car as a blind. Liminka, Finland, June 2005.

A Ruff with battle wounds *(Philomachus pugnax)*
Nikon D3S, 500mm f/4.0 plus 1.4x extender, 1/1000 second, f/7 1, ISO 3200, continuous focus with 51 focusing points, ground pod, Manfrotto 501 video head, tent blind. Oulunsalo, Finland, May 2010.

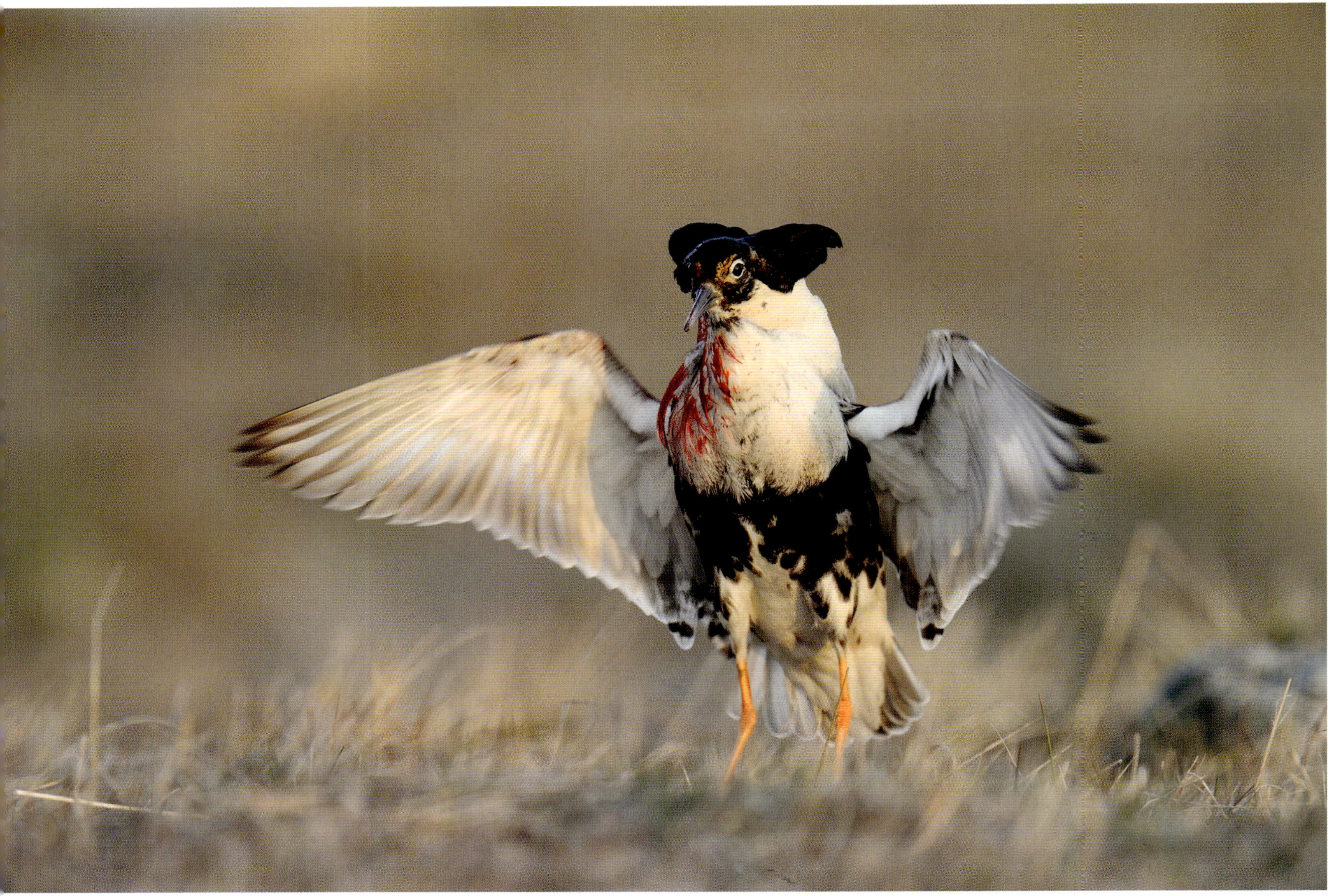

Jari Peltomäki

in the heat of their flamboyant tournaments. While photographing at a Ruff lek in May 2010, I caught this image of a male that just received a blow to the corner of its eye and is bleeding. It had been fighting with another male over the females' attention.

There are lots of waders to photograph on the shallow shores of sand and mud along Siikajoki and on Hailuoto Island, especially during autumn migration from July to September. The water level and the weather conditions have an impact on the occurrence of waders. The conditions are ideal when the water is low enough to expose the mud and silt for food, and when it is still high enough so the exposed area is not too large, because this would let the birds scatter over a wide area. The narrow stretch of shore helps photographers keep the birds close. The best weather conditions are unsettled because high pressure keeps the birds flying high and fast over the staging areas, whereas low pressure forces them to land and spend time feeding. Summer thunderstorms tend to bring birds to the ground, too. And while you're out there photographing the waders, you're likely to also photograph Common Shelducks feeding or Little Terns landing for some rest in front of your blind.

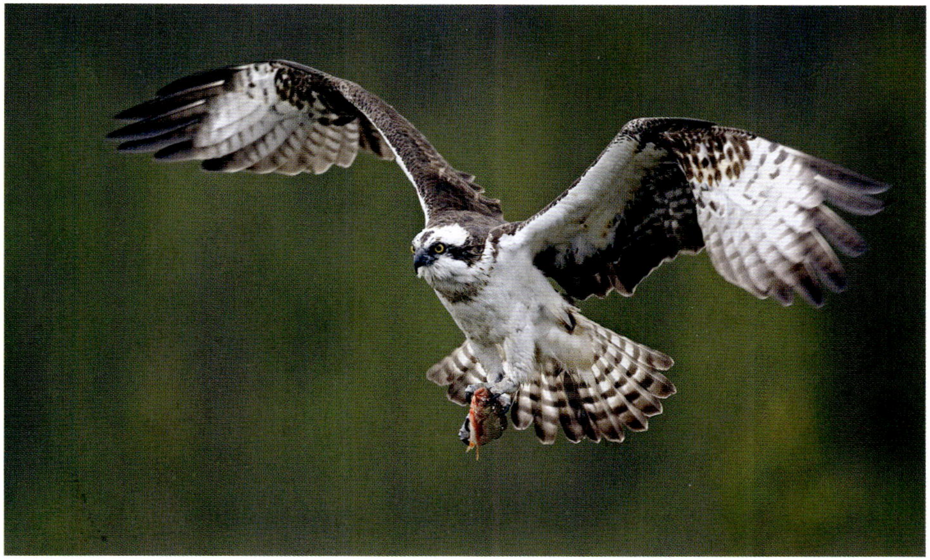

Markus Varesvuo

An Osprey with a catch *(Pandion haliaetus)*
Canon EOS-1D Mark III, 500mm f/4.0, 1/1000 second, f/4.0, ISO 1600, Gitzo tripod, Manfrotto 501 video head, blind. Vaala, Finland, June 2008.

The shallow shores around the Oulu area are good for wader photography.
Dunlins in rain *(Calidris alpina alpina)*.
Canon EOS-1D Mark III, 500mm f/4.0 plus 1.4x extender, 1/500 second, f/13.0, ISO 800, continuous focus with an extended central focusing point, ground pod, Manfrotto 501 video head.
Siikajoki, Finland, July 2007.

Jari Peltomäki

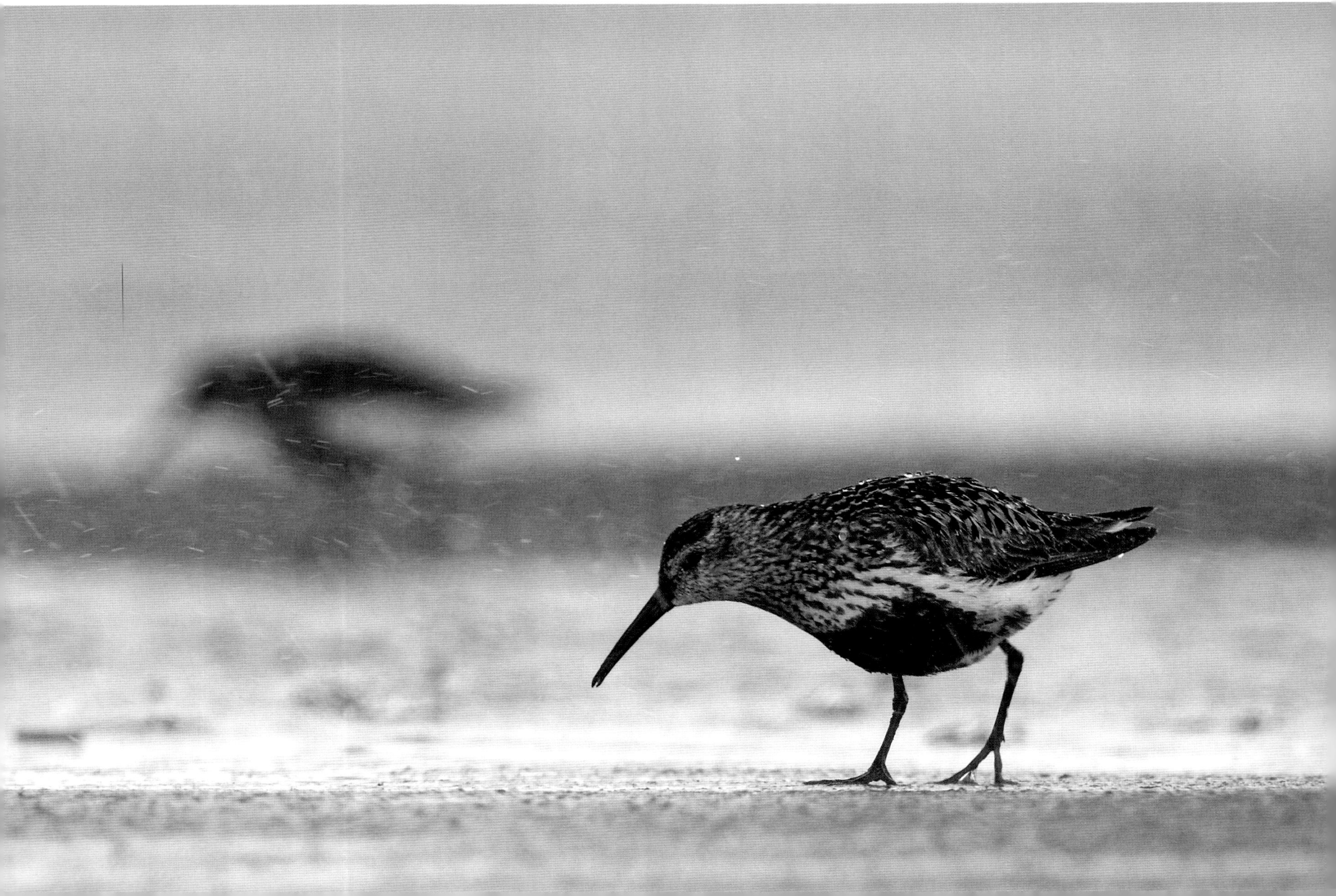

The Dunlin image was taken during a heavy thunderstorm on the shore of the river Siikajoki. It's not smart or advisable to wander around waders' breeding grounds in May and June! You might inadvertently disturb an endangered species' breeding time, such as Temminck's Stints, Dunlins, or Little Terns.

One of Europe's best winter feeding sites for the Golden Eagle is in Utajärvi between Oulu and Vaala. On good days it's possible to see 10 Golden Eagles at the feeding station, plus a couple of White-tailed Eagles; in some years there has even been a Gyrfalcon. What's special about the location is that you can photograph the eagles at their level. Out in front of the blinds is a mound where the eagles land to eat, providing great opportunities for taking flight shots. And when there is more than one eagle, it's likely that they will get into fights over whose turn it is on the carcass. The place has yielded many good eagle images over the years.

The typical scenery in the Vaala area is barren, lichenous pine heath forests and lakes with crystal-clear water. In April and May the forests echo with display rituals of Eurasian Capercaillies, and the lakes carry the Arctic Loon's hauntingly beautiful call far and wide. With the aid of a knowledgeable local guide it's possible to photograph the

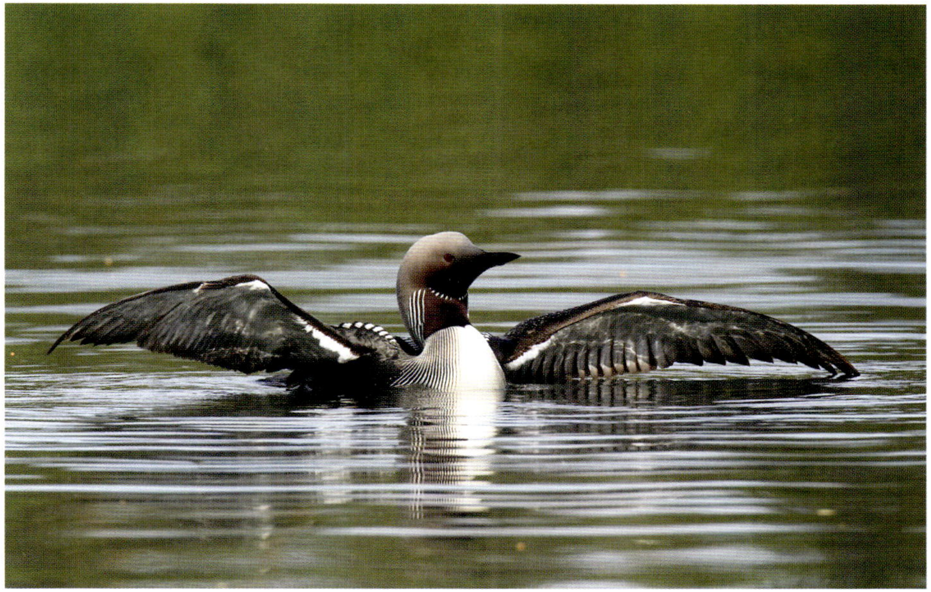

Jari Peltomäki

Arctic Loons breed on the clear lakes in the Vaala region *(Gavia arctica)*
Canon EOS-1D Mark III, 500mm f/4.0 plus 1.4x extender, 1/1000 second, f/13.0, ISO 800, continuous focus with an extended central focusing point, Gitzo tripod, Manfrotto 501 video head. Vaala, Finland, July 2009.

A Red-throated Loon parent feeding its chick *(Gavia stellata)*
Canon EOS-1D Mark II N, 500mm f/4.0, 1/2000 second, f/8.0 ISO 500, continuous focus with an extended central focusing point, Manfrotto 501 video head, blind. Vaala, Finland, July 2006.

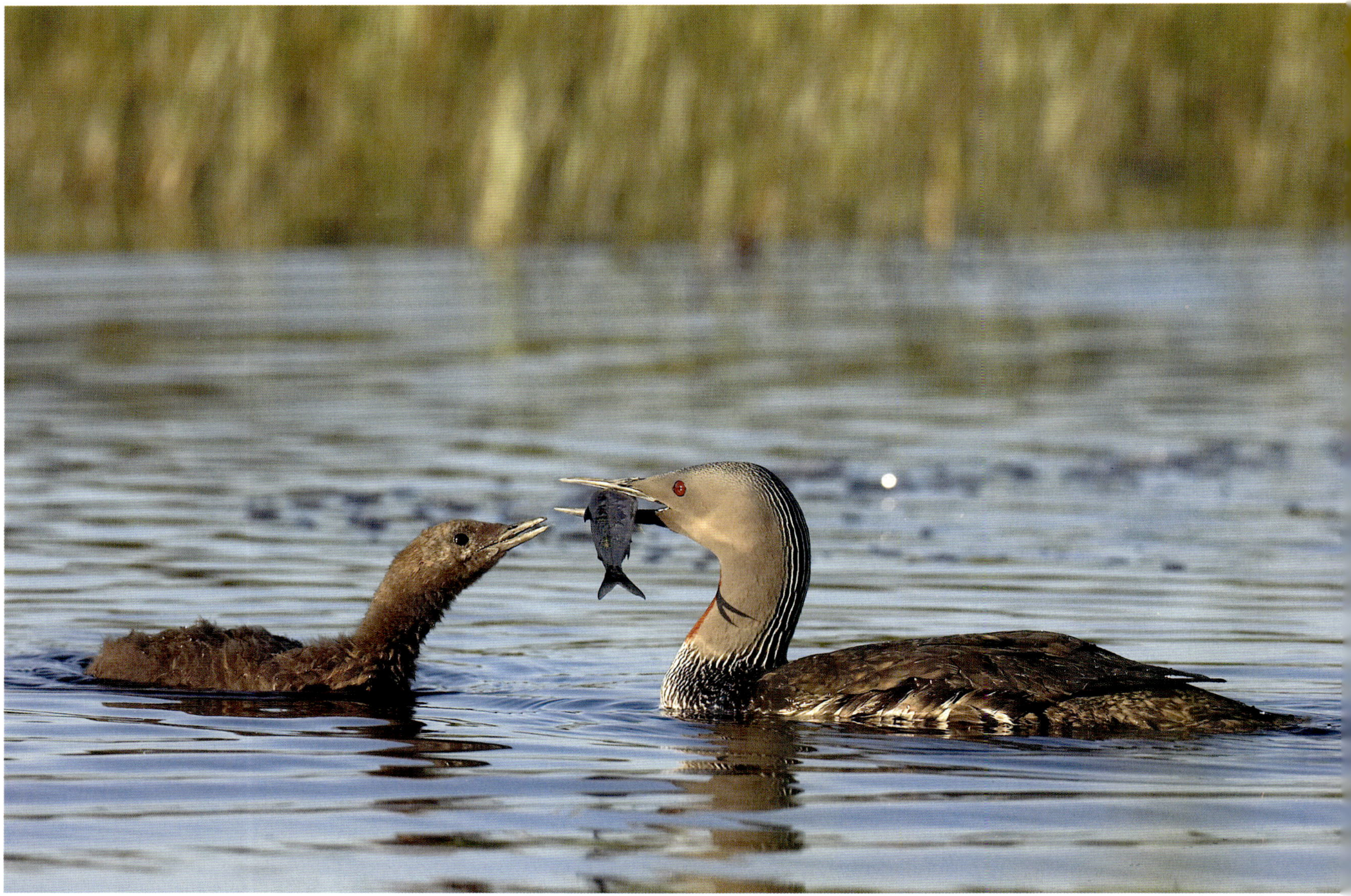

Jari Peltomäki

latter, especially in June or July. Vaala also has beautiful bogs with birds such as the Red-throated Loon, which nests in the small bog pools. It can be photographed from a blind in June and July as the parents are busy feeding the young with fish that they catch from bigger lakes nearby. Vaala also offers good chances with Osprey and common species in the pine forests, such as Mistle Thrush, Redstart, and Common Cuckoo.

Oulu Airport is the second busiest airport in Finland, making it easy to get into Oulu. Fast trains also go to Oulu many times a day. From Oulu to Vaala is about an hour's drive. The area has a wide range of accommodations, blinds for rent, and bird guide services. The newly extended Liminganlahti Visitor Centre organizes birding courses and the annual Liminganlahti Bird Photography Festival in April.

You can find more information at www.liminganlahti.fi and www.finnature.fi. More information about bird photography in Finland and globally is available from the following resources:

- Other photographers in the region (trading information is always a good strategy!)
- Birders
- Birdlife International Data Zone
- Online discussion sites related to nature photography
- Websites and Facebook pages related to bird photography
- Newsletters from bird touring companies
- Guidebooks
- Events related to birding, such as the Bird Fair (UK), Eilat Bird Festival (Israel), Dutch Bird Fair (Netherlands), and others
- Ornithological societies and bird observation centers, such as Hanko Bird Observatory (Finland), Falsterbo Bird Observatory (Sweden), and others
- Exploring the target area yourself

JARI PELTOMÄKI

KANGASALA OSPREY FOUNDATION, FINLAND

Discover the best place in the world to photograph Ospreys.

The Pohtiolampi pond in Kangasala, near Tampere, Finland, is the best place in the world to photograph Ospreys. Most of the images of Ospreys fishing have been taken there. The place is operated by the Osprey Foundation, which has run the fish pond for the Ospreys for more than two decades, and the locally breeding wild Ospreys have learned to use the pond for fishing regularly. On a good day there can be as many as 150 Osprey fishing dives!

The fish pond was originally built to serve Osprey protection and research. Likewise, the first blinds that were built around the pond were designated for researchers. Then photographers visiting the site wanted to rent the blinds for photography, and the foundation set up a carefully monitored and regulated schedule for photographers. Now the income from renting the blinds helps pay a large part of the costs incurred by the feeding activities.

Pohtiolampi has a big watchtower, roughly 40 m (131 ft) from the pool, that is open to everyone. The tower is good for observing the birds, but you can also rent one of six photographers' slots in the tower. Bookings can be made on-site or by calling the Osprey Center. A path takes you to the tower along a route that doesn't disturb the birds.

You can also rent the six photo blinds around the edge of the fish pond. The blinds are rented to just one photographer at a time, who can bring two other people. The limit of three photographers at any given time has been found to cause minimal disturbance to the Ospreys.

Bookings for the spring and summer season are made online starting in January, when the new booking calendar is published (it can be found on the website shown in the next paragraph). The Osprey Center is quite popular, and the best times are normally booked right after the calendar is published. The website also has instructions and guidelines for photographing at the center and for the use of the blinds. The center has modest on-site accommodations, and bookings are made at the same time as blind reservations. It is also possible to spend the night in some of the blinds.

You can find more information on the foundation's website *(www.saaksisaatio.fi/en/index.htm)* and their Facebook page *(https://www.facebook.com/saaksisaatio)*.

Eye of the Osprey *(Pandion haliaetus)*
Nikon D3S, 500mm f/4.0, 1/3200 second, f/7.1, ISO 800, continuous focus with 51 focusing points, beanbag, blind. Kangasala, Finland, September 2010.

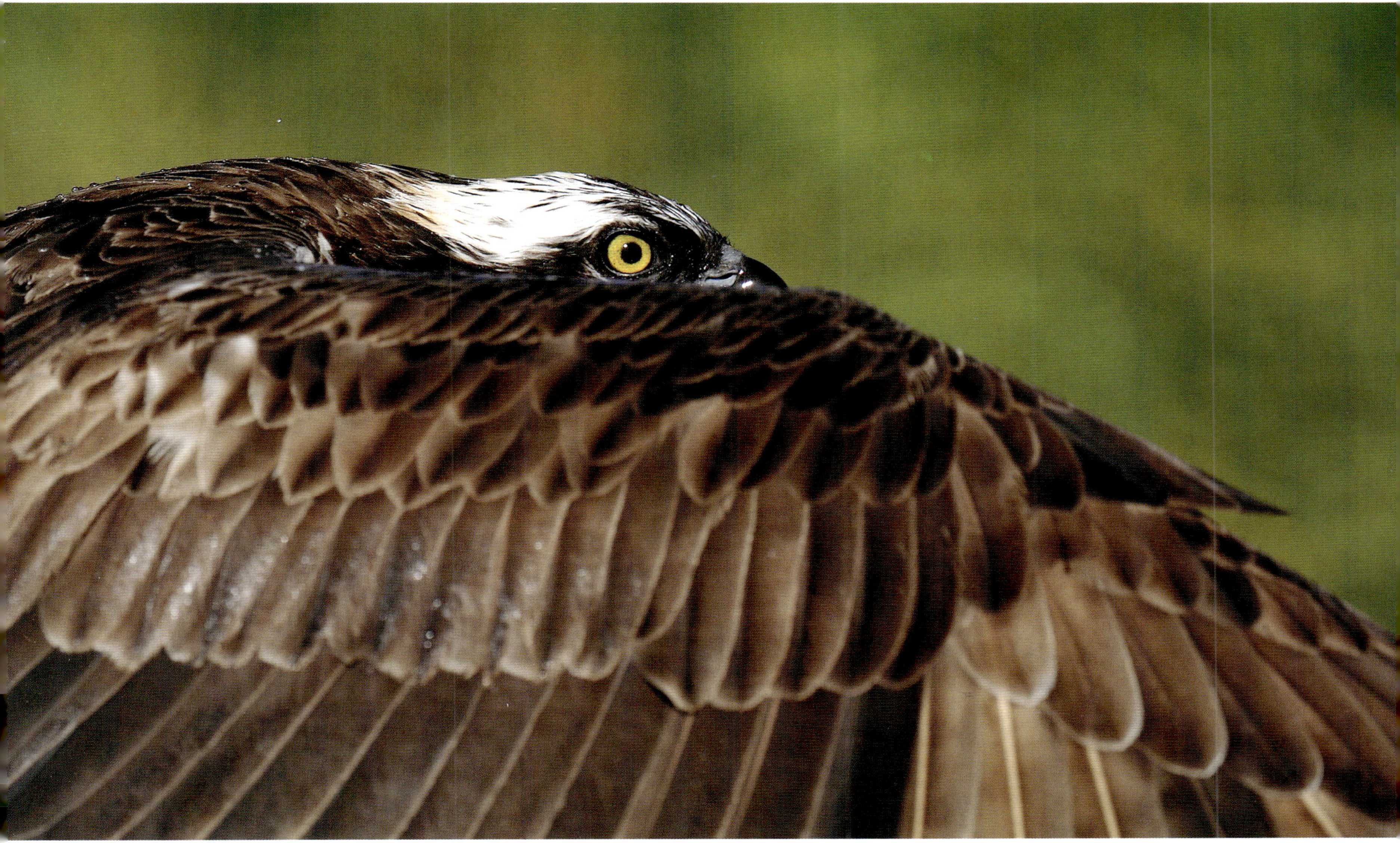

Jari Peltomäki

Jari Peltomäki

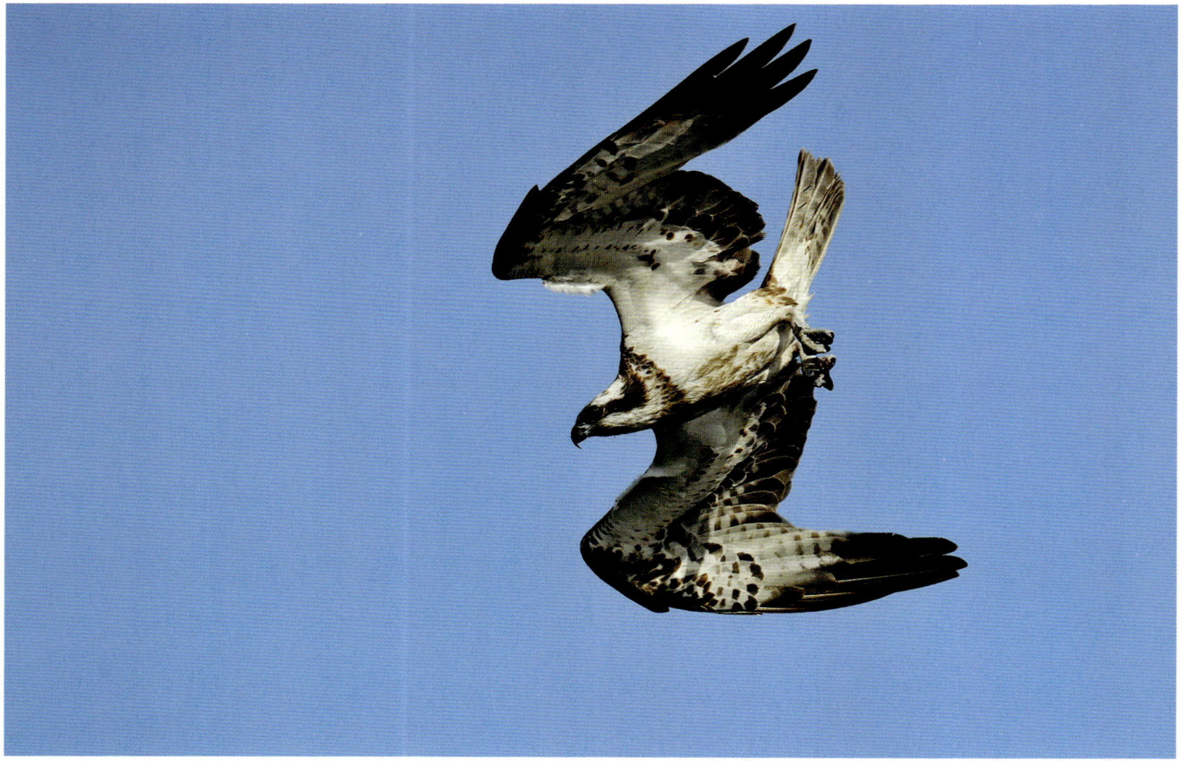

This image of an Osprey that has just launched into a dive was taken from the tower blind *(Pandion haliaetus)*
Nikon D3S, 500mm f/4.0, 1/3200 second, f/7.1, ISO 800, continuous focus with 51 focusing points, beanbag, blind. Kangasala, Finland, September 2010.

Times and Instructions for Photographing at the Center

The first Ospreys to return on spring migration come to fish in the pond around mid-April. In spring and summer, the Ospreys fish in the pond regularly, with one to three strikes per hour during daylight. In the middle of the summer, especially when the wind is strong and the local Ospreys struggle to fish in the lakes in the region, there can be many more visiting the pond.

The female Ospreys and the fledgling young join in the fishing crowd in August and September, doubling or even tripling the action at the pond, compared to early summer. The action peaks at the end of August; on August 28, 2010, there were 150 hits in the fish pond. With the young birds honing their fishing skills in early autumn, and at first missing quite often, there is plenty of action for photographers. The Ospreys fish in the pond until the middle of September.

Gray Herons fish in the pond, too. They arrive well before sunrise, so it's good to get in the blind the previous evening or in the wee hours of the morning at the latest. The Ospreys are most active just before midday, which is followed by a lull that is a good time to have lunch in the coffee shop. The

Catching a big fish can cause a long fight in the water *(Pandion haliaetus)*
Canon EOS-1D Mark III, 500mm f/4.0, 1/1250 second, f/4.0, ISO 1600, continuous focus with an extended central focusing point, beanbag, blind. Kangasala, Finland, September 2009.

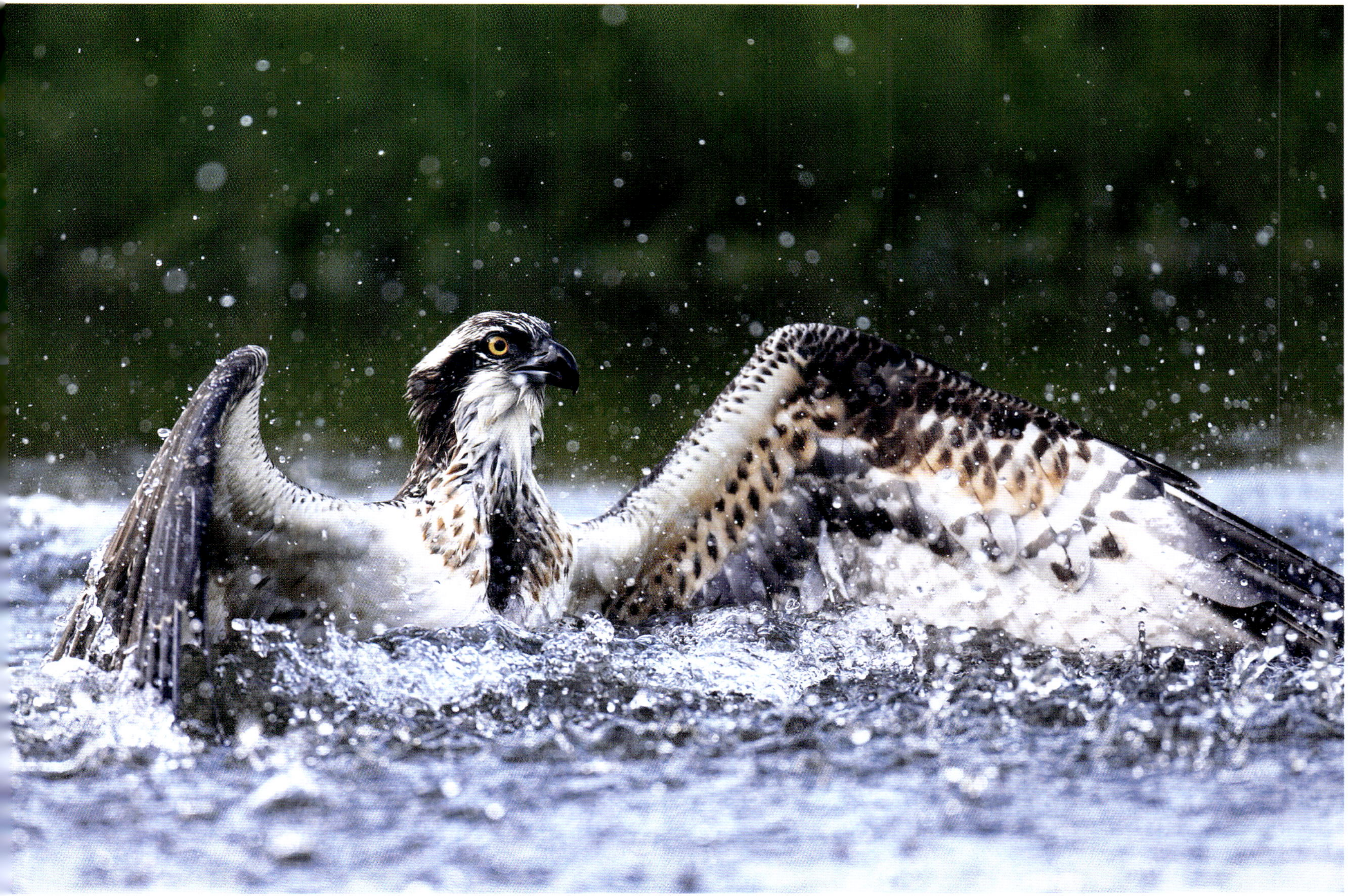

Jari Peltomäki

A Eurasian Magpie and an Osprey, taken from the tower blind ***(Pica pica, Pandion haliaetus)***
Canon EOS-1D Mark III, 500mm f/4.0, 1/2000 second, f/6.3, ISO 800, one-shot focus with one focusing point, beanbag, tower blind. Kangasala, Finland, September 2007.

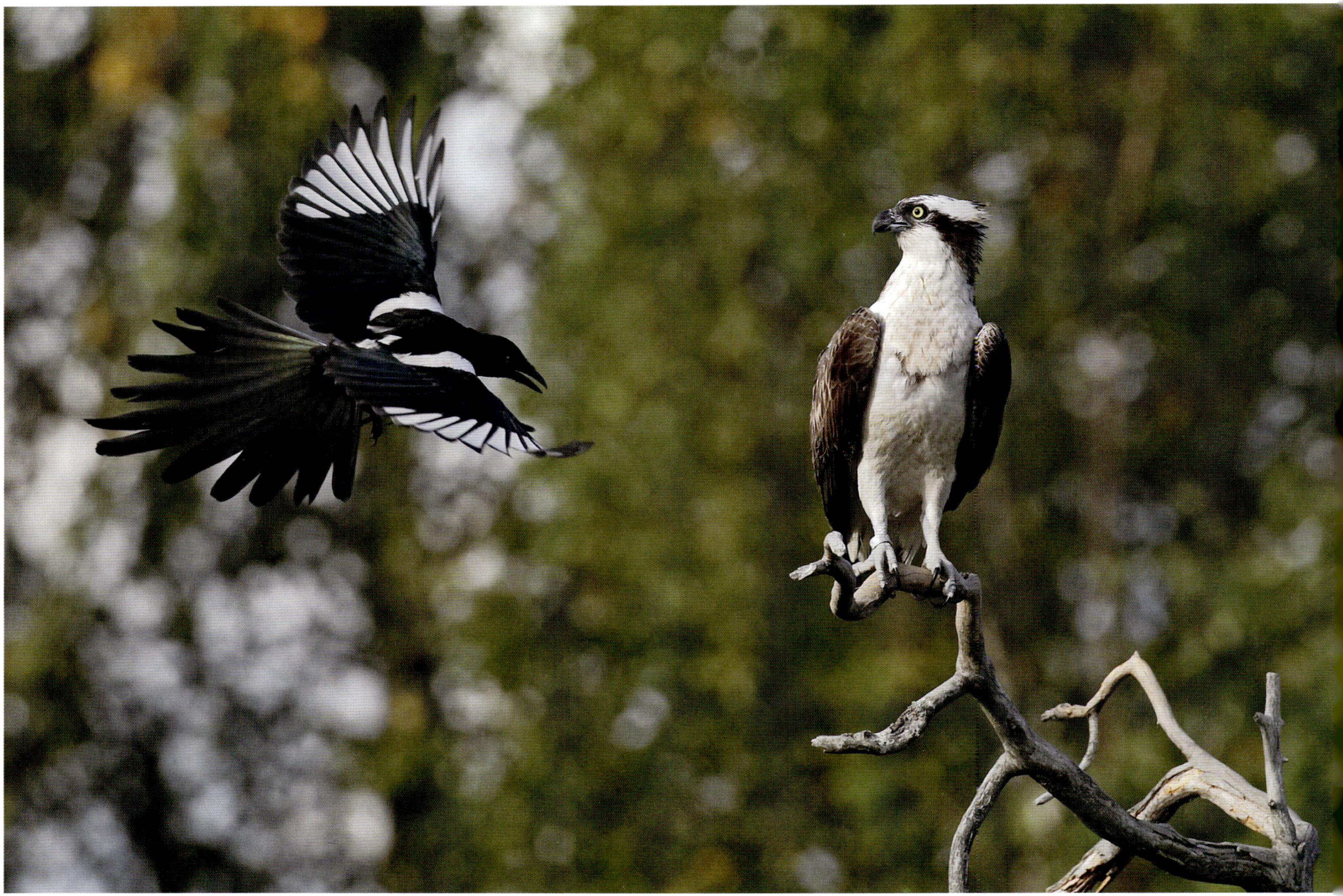

Jari Peltomäki

Ospreys hunt well into the darkness of the evening.

Normally I start my day in the main blinds, or in a blind to the right of them, depending on which way the wind is blowing. The wind determines the direction the Ospreys go because they lift from the water and take off with their catch. If the wind is blowing from the west or the north, the birds will usually head away from the two main blinds that are on the edge of the pond. This makes it very difficult to take any good images of the Ospreys, but it gets much easier from blinds that are on the sides of the pond. In sunny weather the tower blind is excellent for photographing the Ospreys because they are perching in the nearby trees, hovering over the water, or launching into a dive.

Other fishing birds at the pond include Gray Herons, Common Mergansers, Lesser Black-backed Gulls, Hooded Crows, Eurasian Magpies, and Eurasian Jackdaws, plus occasionally other raptors such as Northern Goshawks and Common Buzzards.

The Osprey Foundation would like visiting photographers to keep in mind that volunteers produce the infrastructure and services in the center, and the center doesn't necessarily compare favorably with the standards in professionally operated commercial facilities. All of the revenue from renting the blinds is used for Osprey conservation at the center.

MARKUS VARESVUO

ICELAND

Iceland's position between two continents, Europe and North America, makes it an interesting location for bird photographers.

In Europe, Barrow's Goldeneyes, Harlequin Ducks, and Common Loons breed only in Iceland. Many other interesting species are relatively easy to see in Iceland, and many of them can be photographed, such as Red-necked Phalaropes, Red Phalaropes, Black-tailed Godwits, Pink-footed Geese, Greater Scaups, Great Skuas, Northern Fulmars, Northern Gannets, Gyrfalcons, and in winter, Iceland Gulls. At least for Gyrfalcons and Red Phalaropes, you must have a license to photograph at their breeding grounds.

It's not just the fascinating species; with its expansive, nearly treeless landscapes, snow-capped mountains, and glacier lakes, Iceland is a spectacular setting for your images. The northern edge of Iceland is in the Arctic Circle, meaning that at the end of June there is light almost throughout the whole night, and because it comes from a very low angle, the quality is beautiful. June is the best time to photograph birds in Iceland—because of the light, and because of the birds. For example, at the end of June the dashing Harlequin Ducks leave their breeding grounds in the Mývatn area and head for the sea, where they are difficult to photograph.

A good road, about 1,300 km (808 mi) long, circles Iceland, and accommodation can easily be found almost anywhere. The best strategy for traveling is to fly to Reykjavík, rent a car, and go explore.

In this chapter I will highlight three areas that I have found especially good for bird photography: Lake Mývatn with its many birds, Langanes in the northeast, and in the southeast the area between the glacier Vatnajökull and the sea, particularly the glacier lake Jökulsárlón.

Driving eastbound from Reykjavík, the distance to Lake Mývatn is about 500 km (311 mi). Count on taking 8 to 10 hours for the drive so you can travel at a relaxed pace and stop to photograph whatever comes your way. Common Snipes and Black-tailed Godwits perching on fence posts along the road can prove irresistible. During the last 100 km (62 mi) before reaching Mývatn, you should see Red-necked Phalaropes on little ponds by the road, and on some of the bigger lakes you'll probably spot the first Common Loons.

In Iceland, the Common Snipe is very common indeed *(Gallinago gallinago)*
Canon EOS-1Ds Mark II, 500mm f/4.0 plus 1.4x extender, 1/500 second, f/7.1, ISO 500, one-shot focus with a central focusing point, beanbag, car as a blind. Iceland, June 2006.

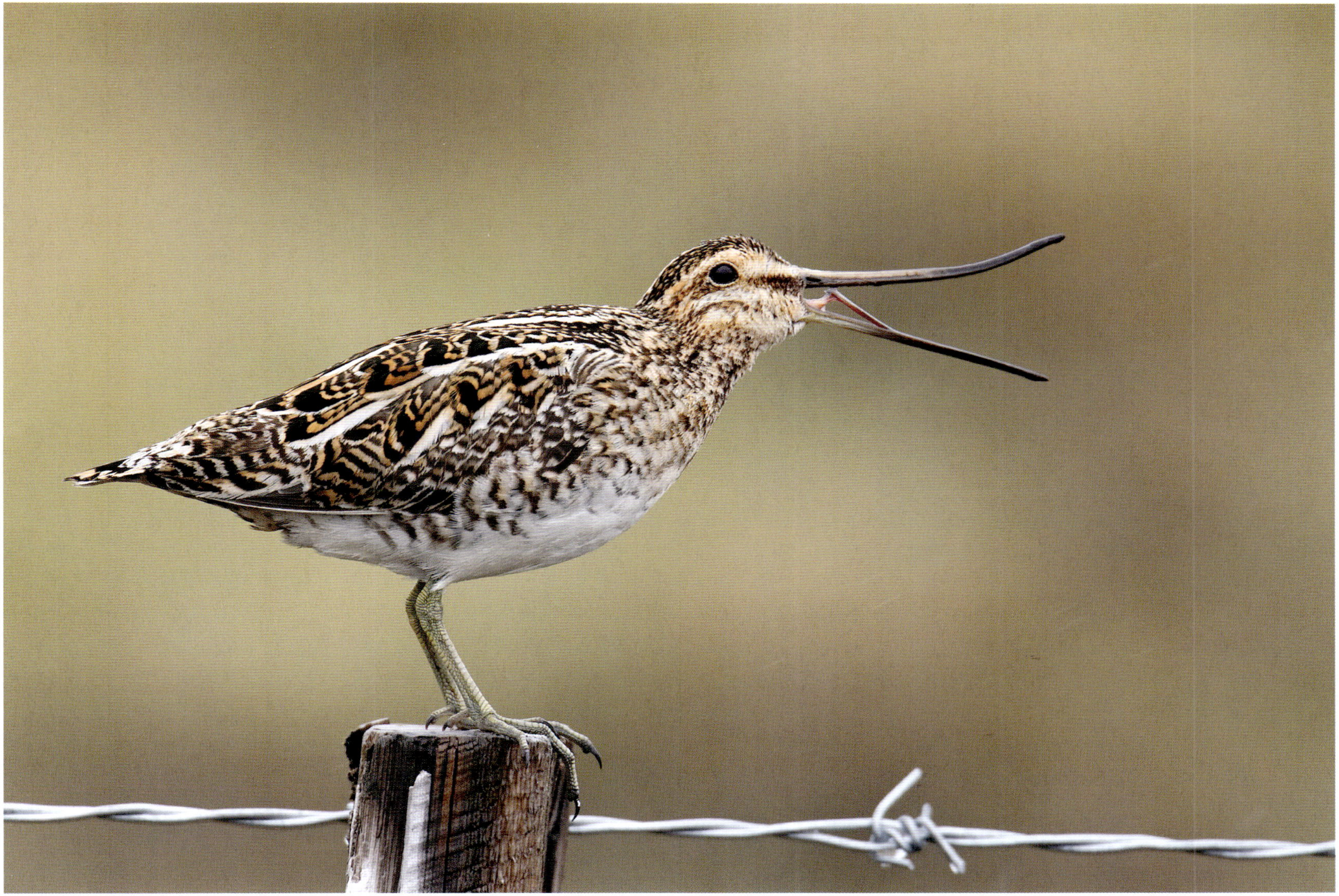

Markus Varesvuo

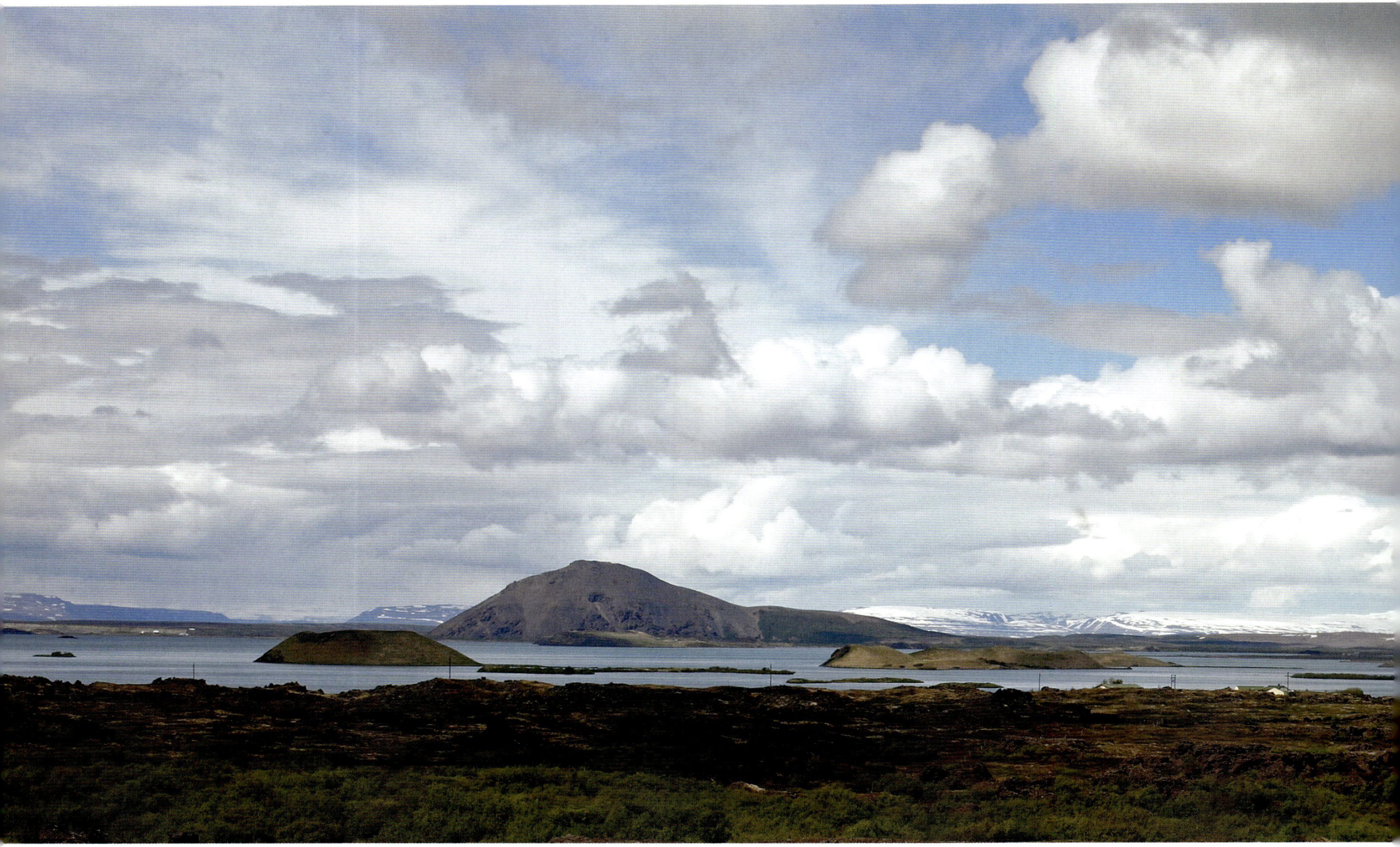

Markus Varesvuo

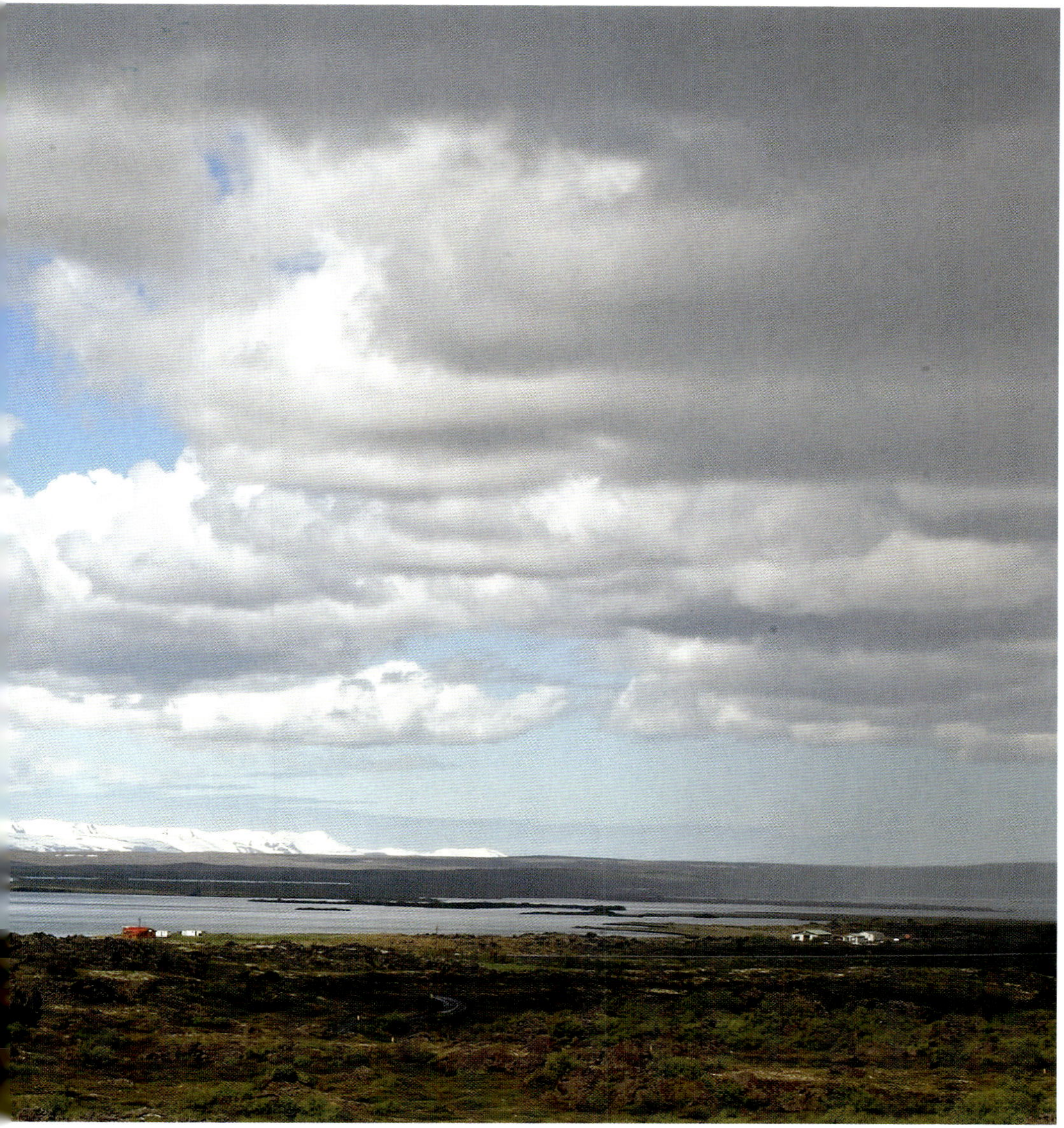

Mývatn

Lake Mývatn is famous for its waterbirds; it has 14 breeding species, and some in great numbers. Mývatn is a big lake (37 km^2/14.3 mi^2), but it's only 2 m (6.6 ft) deep in the middle. The lake is also famous for its midges, which are a great source of food for many birds and a royal pain for a photographer. I recommend investing in a midge-net hat.

Some 300 Barrow's Goldeneye and Harlequin Duck pairs, plus a couple of Common Loon pairs, breed in the area. The Harlequin Ducks prefer fast-flowing water and favor the River Laxá in particular. When you follow the river you are bound to bump into Harlequin Ducks. They are used to people fishing in the area and are actually quite trusting, so blinds aren't necessary even for closeups.

It's easy to see the great numbers of birds on the main lake, but it's not so

Markus Varesvuo

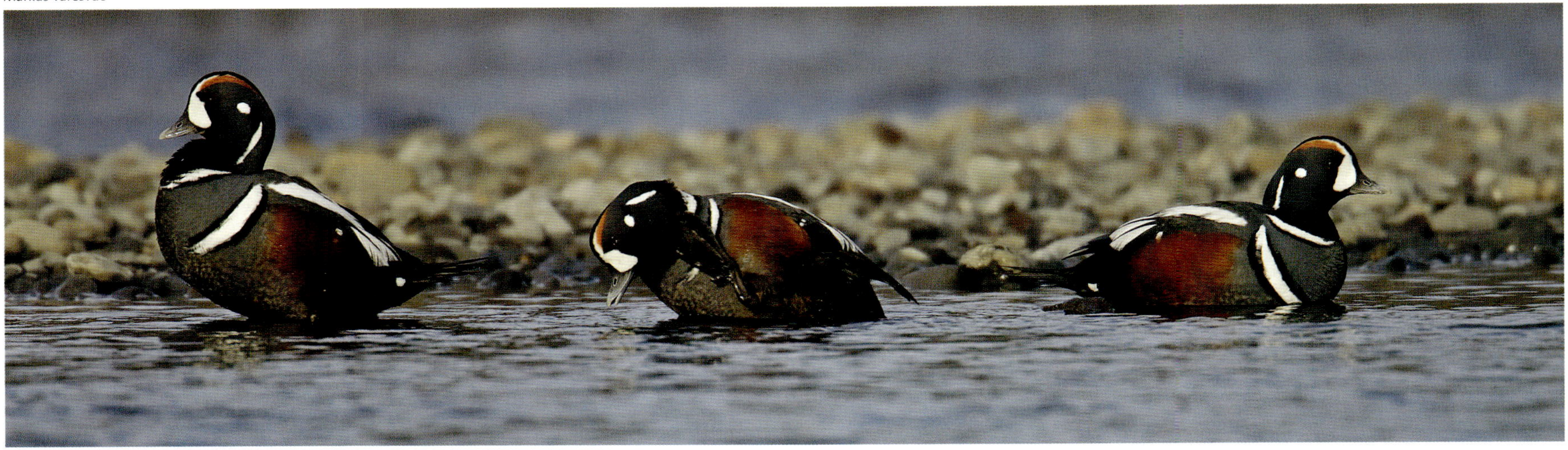

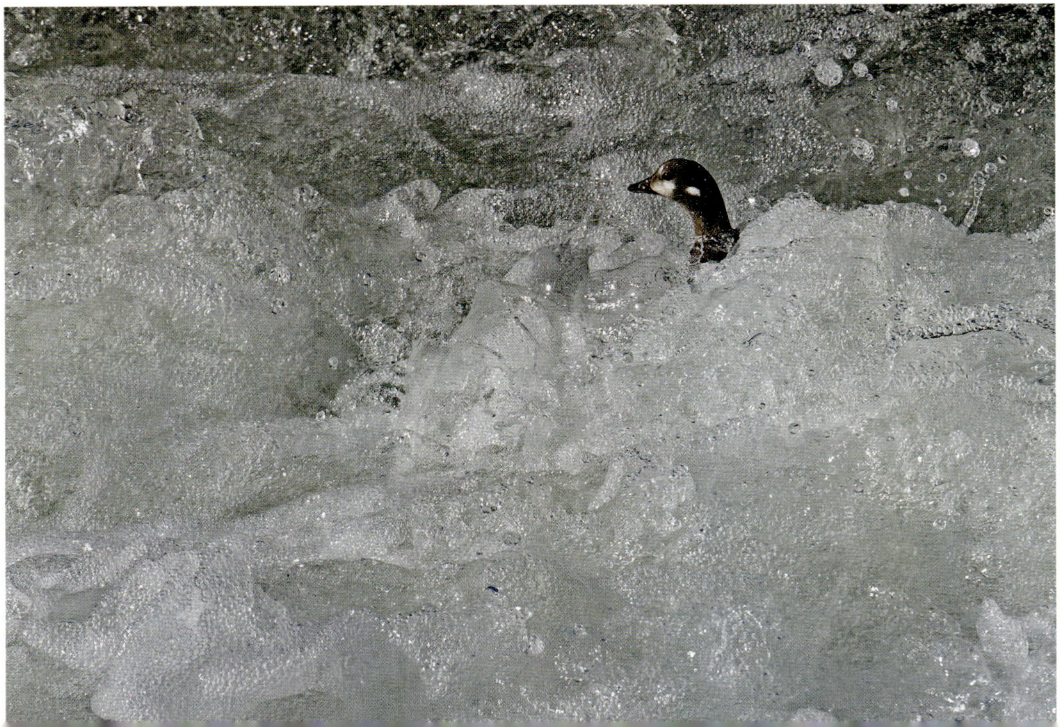

Markus Varesvuo

The colorful Harlequin Ducks gather together in small flocks at the end of June and move from the Mývatn area out to the ocean *(Histrionicus histrionicus)*
Canon EOS-1D Mark II, 500mm f/4.0 plus 1.4x extender, 1/1000 second, f/5.6, ISO 400, one-shot focus with a central focusing point, Citzo tripod, Manfrotto 501 video head. Iceland, June 2006.

Harlequin Ducks aren't afraid of the turbulent streams; they ride the surf with ease from one calm spot to another *(Histrionicus histrionicus)*
Canon EOS-1D Mark II, 500mm f/4.0, 1/1000 second, f/10.0, ISO 500, continuous focus with a central focusing point, handheld camera. Mývatn, Iceland, June 2006.

easy to photograph them. Luckily there are quite a few smaller ponds close to the main lake, and they draw a lot of birds too. Setting up a blind on the shore of a small pond is the best way to get good images, and by getting in the blind late in the afternoon and photographing through the evening and the night, until the quality of light turns hard again in the morning, you'll get the best light conditions. You should see at least Barrow's Goldeneyes, Common Scoters, Greater Scaups, Long-tailed Ducks, and Gadwalls. In mid-June many are still on display, so you can expect quite a few courtship rituals and battling males.

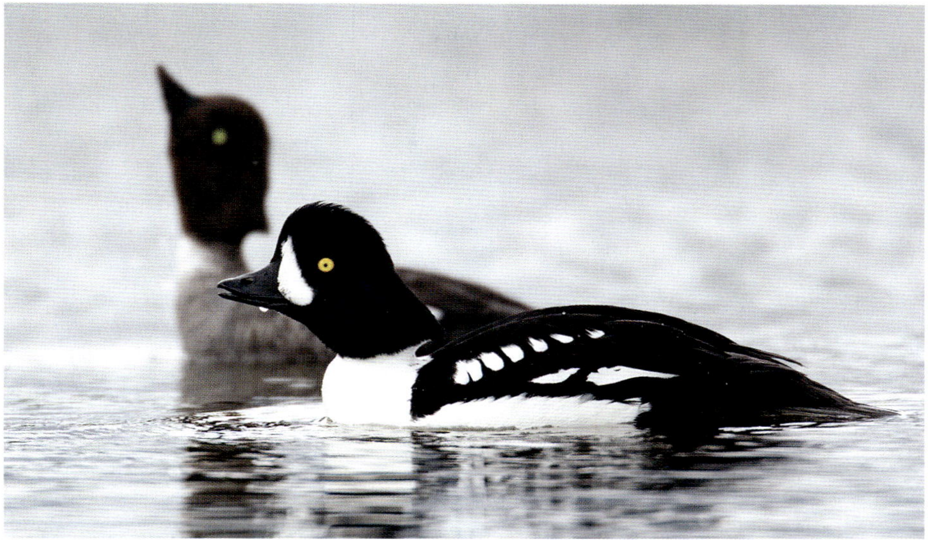

Markus Varesvuo

A Barrow's Goldeneye pair in display *(Bucephala islandica)*
Canon EOS-1Ds Mark II, 500mm f/4.0 plus 2.0x extender, 1/250 second, f/8.0, ISO 400, one-shot focus with a central focusing point, Gitzo tripod, Manfrotto 501 video head, blind. Mývatn, Iceland, June 2006.

A male Greater Scaup taking off *(Aythya marila)*
Canon EOS-1Ds Mark II, 500mm f/4.0 plus 1.4x extender, 1/1250 second, f/5.6, ISO 800, continuous focus with 45 focusing points, Gitzo tripod, Manfrotto 501 video head, blind.
Mývatn, Iceland, June 2006.

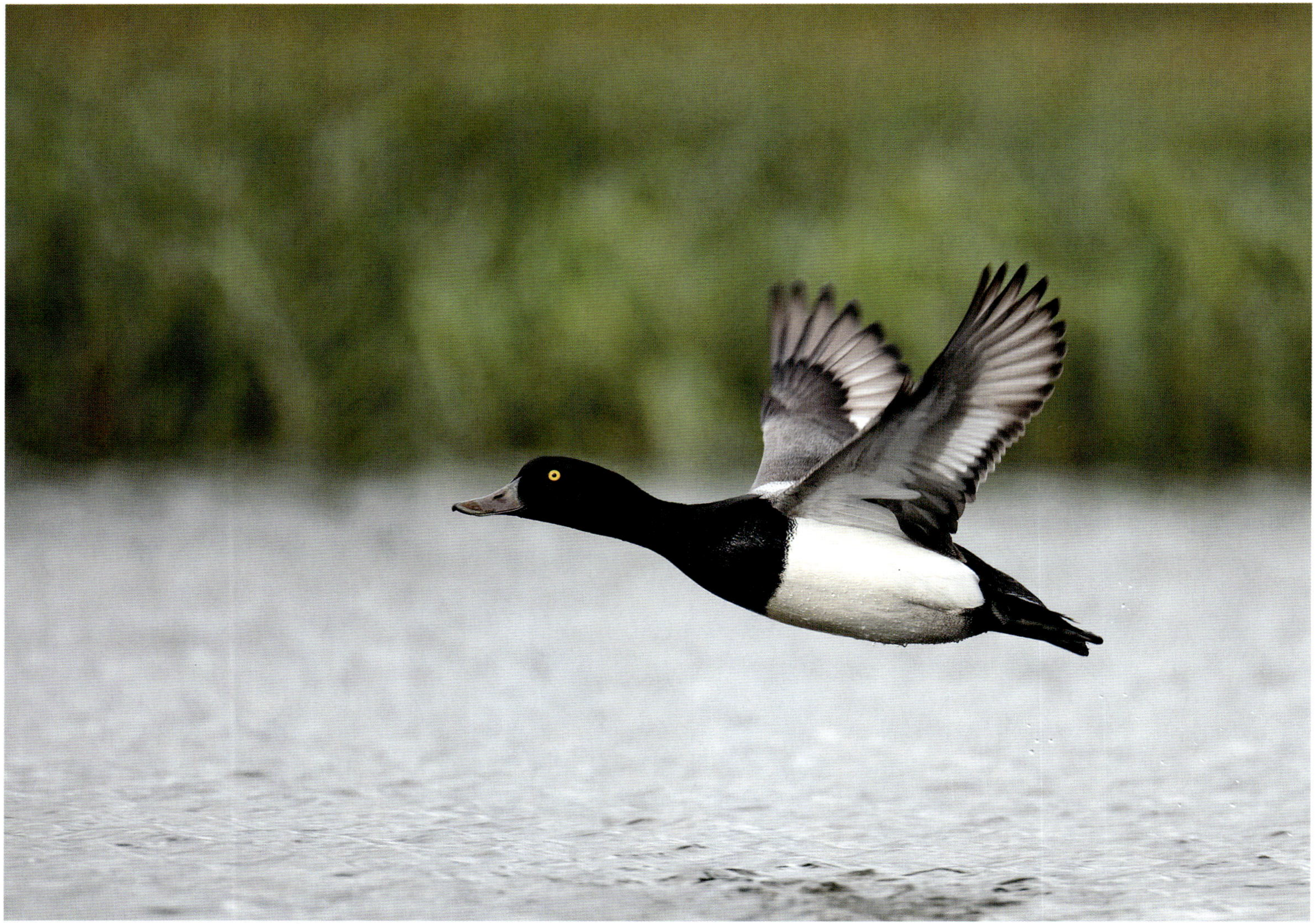

Markus Varesvuo

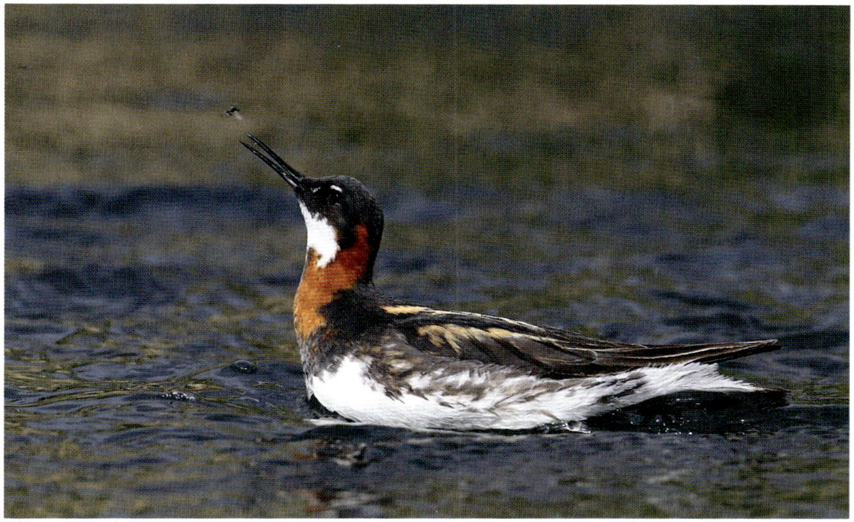

Markus Varesvuo

Red-necked Phalarope hunting midges *(Phalaropus lobatus)*
Canon EOS-1D Mark II, 500mm f/4.0, 1/2000 second, f/5.6, ISO 800, continuous focus with 45 focusing points, Gitzo tripod, Manfrotto 501 video head. Mývatn, Iceland, June 2006.

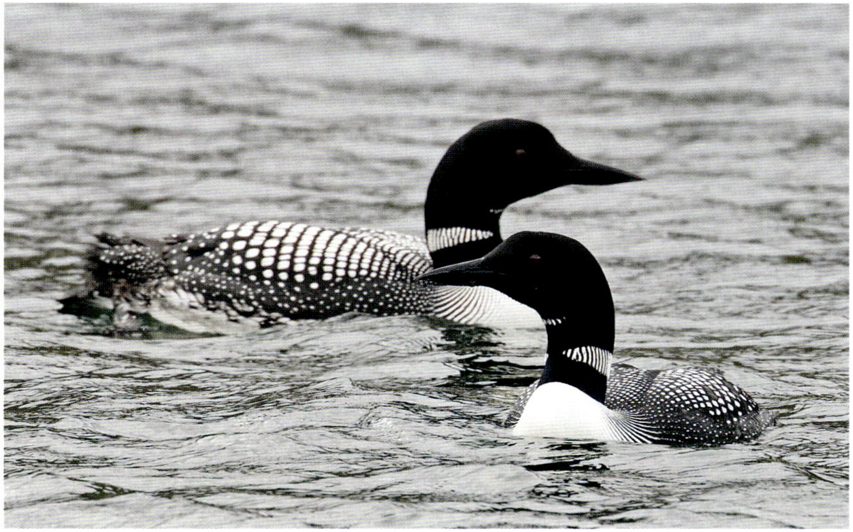

Markus Varesvuo

The Common Loon is quite confident with people *(Gavia immer)*
Canon EOS-1D Mark II, 500mm f/4.0 plus 1.4x extender, 1/640 second, f/7.1, ISO 800, continuous focus with a central focusing point, Gitzo tripod, Manfrotto 501 video head. Iceland, June 2006.

The Mývatn area has also some waders, Whimbrels and Red-necked Phalaropes being the most common, and the latter especially is very photographer friendly. Red-necked Phalaropes are specialized in picking up insects from the surface of the water, but they can hunt them in the air too.

On my latest trip to Iceland in June 2006, I saw one Common Loon pair in the Mývatn area, but I couldn't photograph them because they kept their distance and favored the middle of the lake. During my fortnight, I saw six pairs without searching for them, some on smaller lakes, where they could be photographed by either calmly and quietly

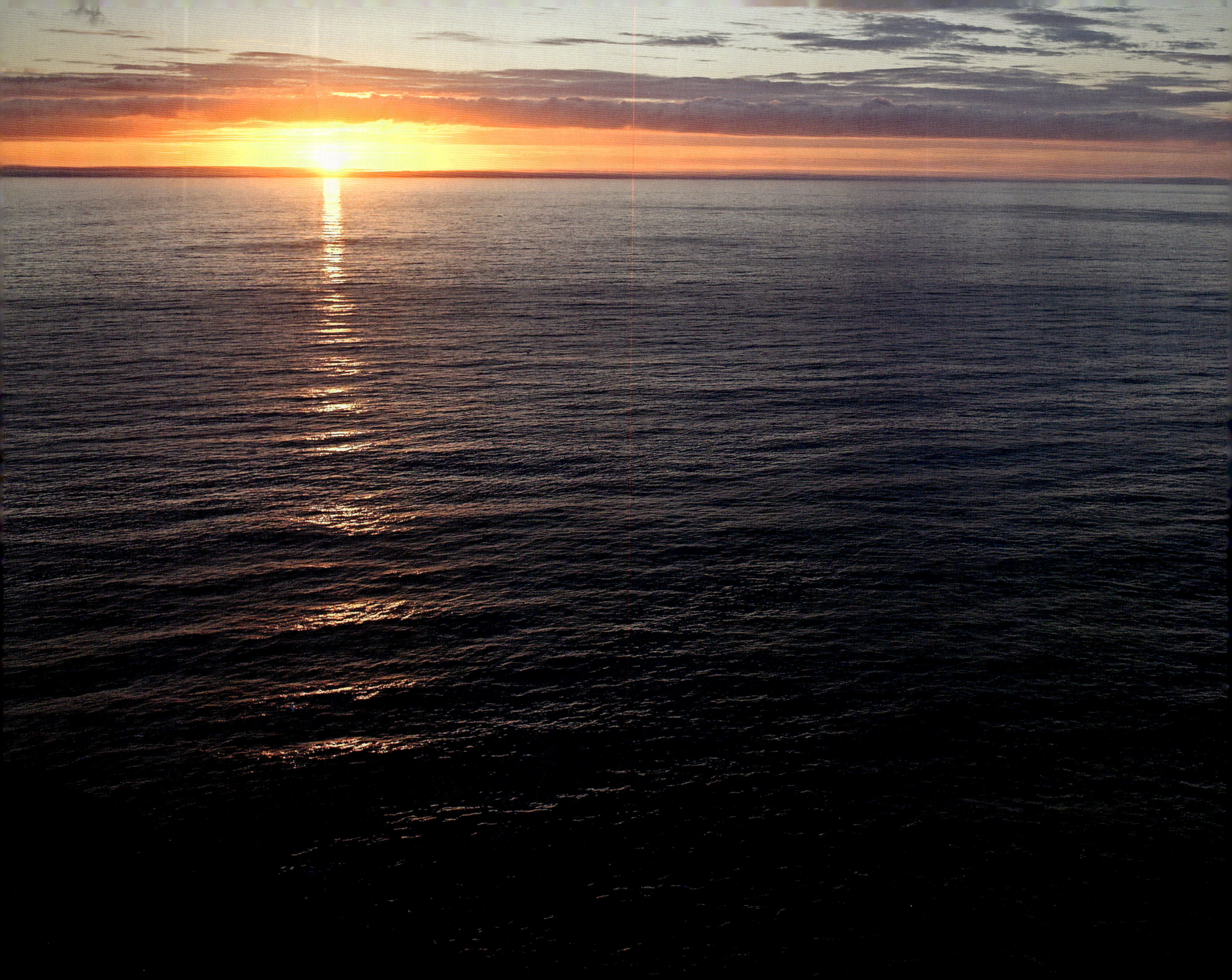

Markus Varesvuo

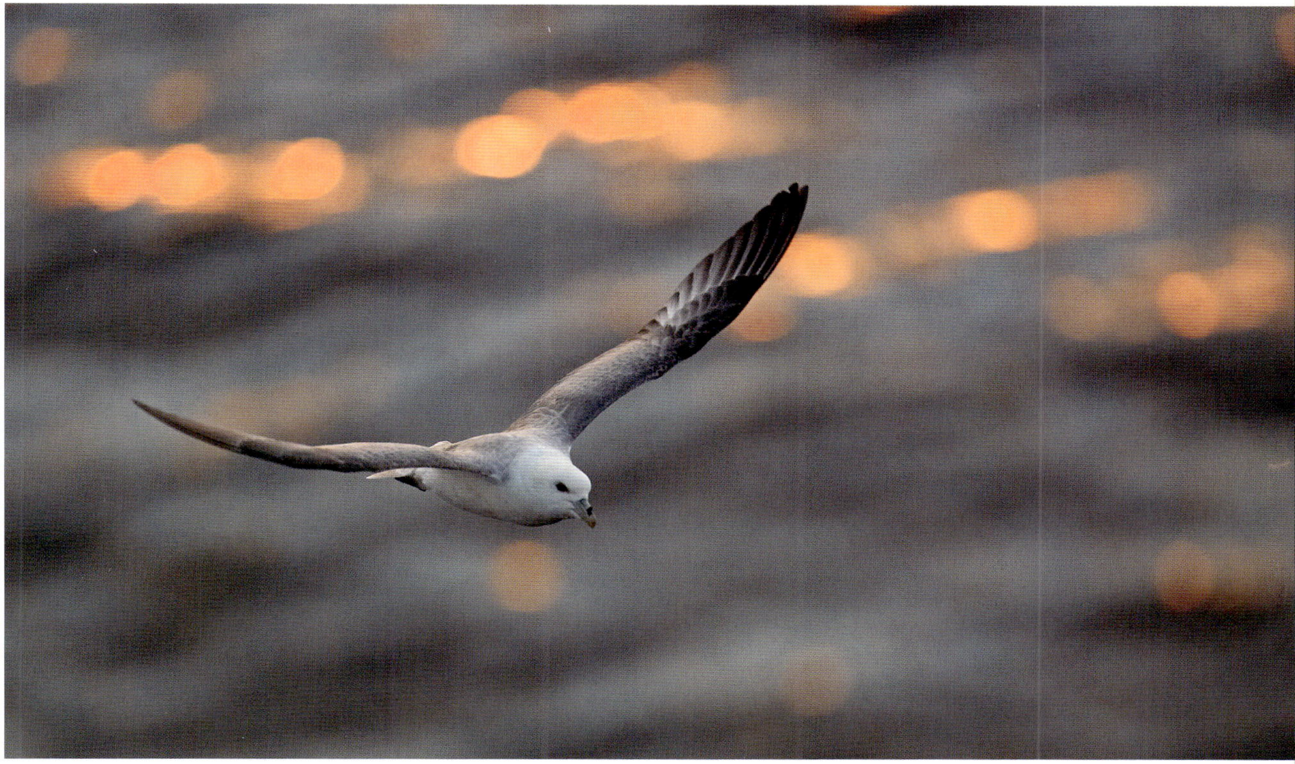

Markus Varesvuo

A Northern Fulmar above the waves kissed with the golden light of the sun
(Fulmarus glacialis)
Canon EOS-1Ds Mark II, 500mm f/4.0, 1/1000 second, f/4.0, ISO 800, continuous focus with 45 focusing points, handheld camera. Langanes, Iceland, June 2006.

Langanes

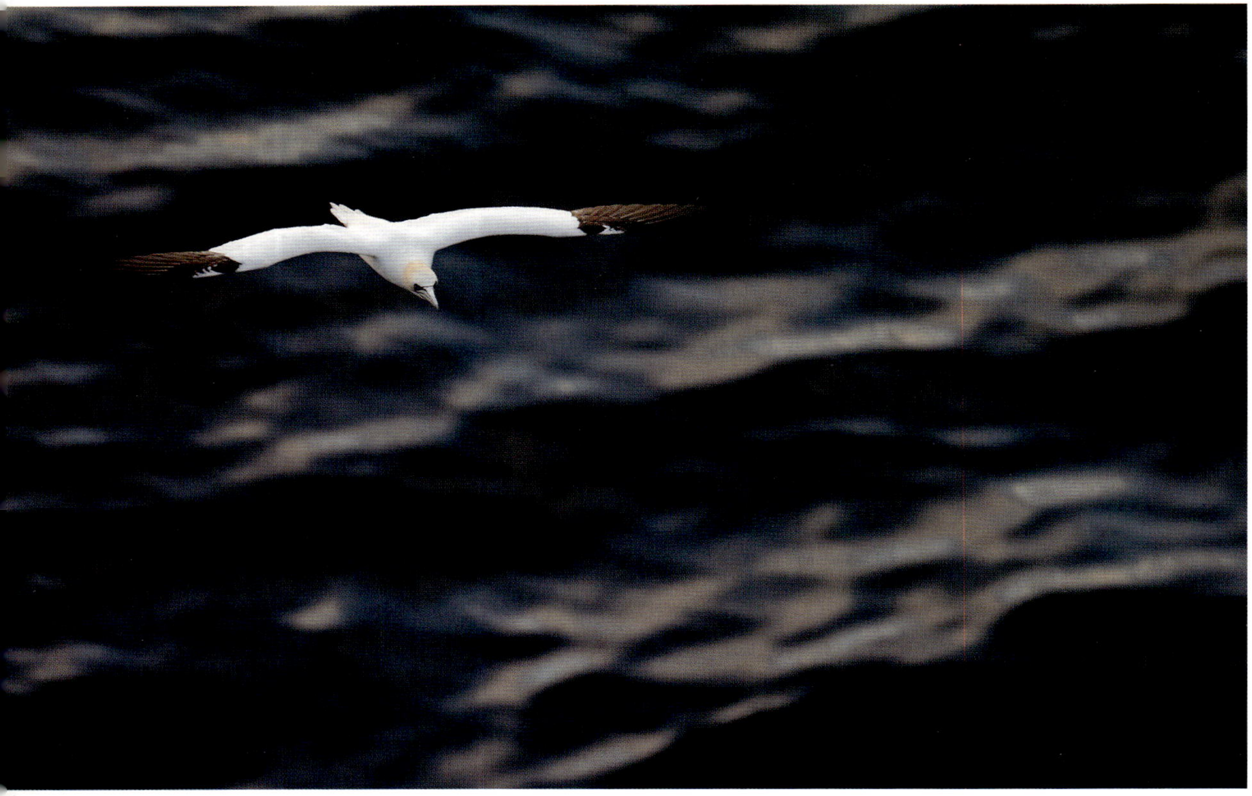

Markus Varesvuo

A Northern Gannet gliding in the air *(Morus bassanus)*
Canon EOS-1Ds Mark II, 500mm f/4.0, 1/400 second, f/4.0, ISO 640, continuous focus with 45 focusing points, handheld camera. Langanes, Iceland, June 2006.

Markus Varesvuo

waiting on the shore or from a blind. Common Loons are quite trusting, and some of the ones I saw swam closer, as if they were curious to see what I was up to. The population in Iceland is estimated at 300 pairs.

In the northeast, big seabird colonies live on the steep westerly cliffs of the Langanes Peninsula, which extends 40 km (24.9 mi) into the North Atlantic Ocean. An unpaved, rough dirt road with enough potholes to last you a lifetime leads to a lighthouse right at the tip of the peninsula. The road is best left to a four-wheel drive vehicle. About halfway to the tip is Skoruvík, with a big seabird colony on the steep cliffs reclining almost vertically into the ocean.

The site is known especially for its Northern Gannet colony, which is one of the biggest in the world. Most of the birds breed on a separate, isolated rocky column (Stórikarl), but some of them are on the mainland cliffs. This is the only Northern Gannet breeding colony on mainland Iceland, together with puffins, Common Murres, Black-legged Kittiwakes, Northern Fulmars, and the odd Thick-billed Murres and Glaucous Gulls.

With some of the birds nesting high above the sea close to the top of the cliff, it's possible to photograph them from the edge of the peninsula. But if you want to photograph the Thick-billed Murres and the Northern Gannets, you have to descend the cliff several tens of meters to be close enough. This requires extreme caution and nerves of steel because falling means death. I secured myself to the car with a long rope from the waist.

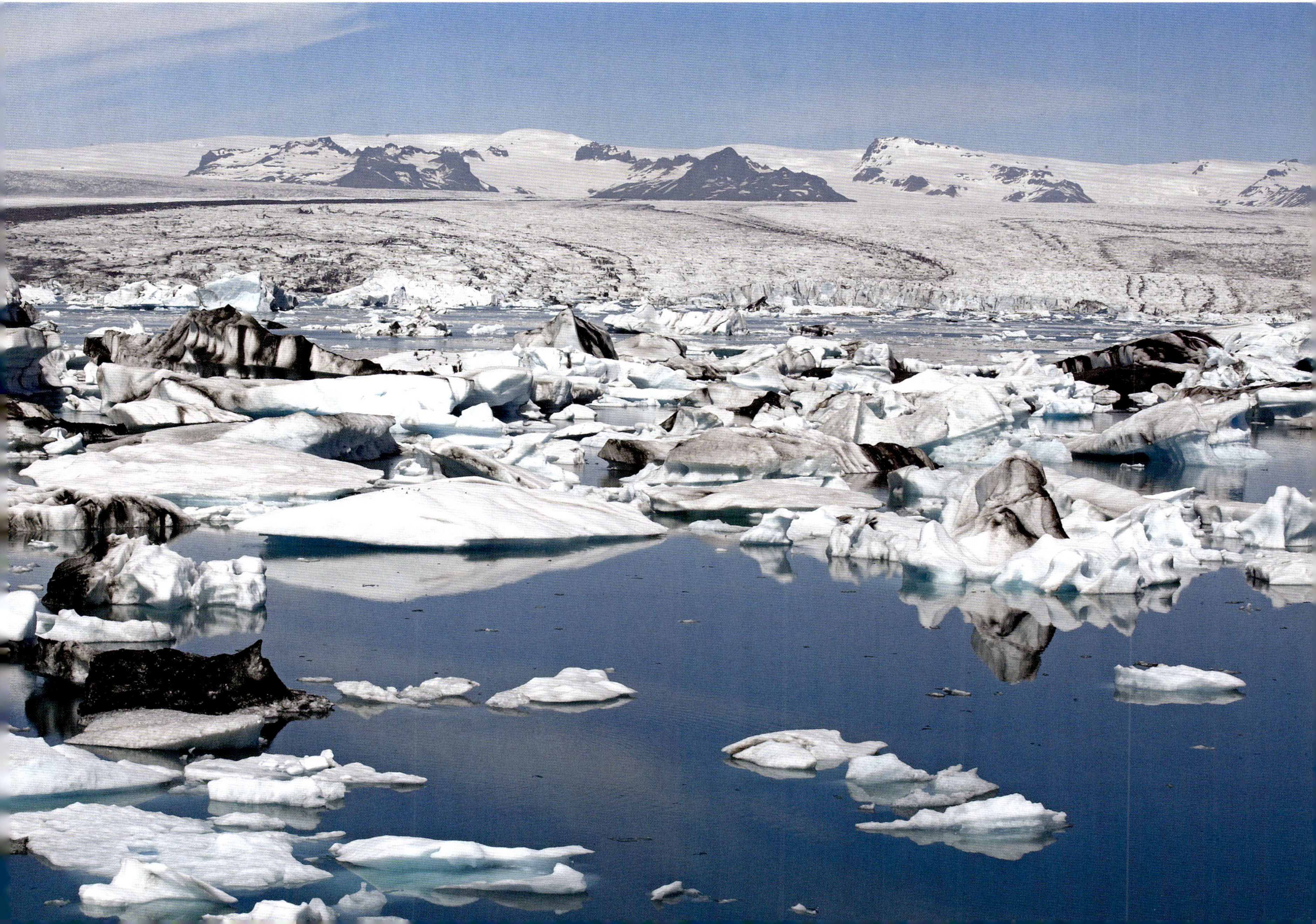

An Arctic Tern hovering over a glacier lake *(Sterna paradisaea)*
Canon EOS-1D Mark II, 500mm f/4.0, 1/1600 second, f/5.6, ISO 500, continuous focus with 45 focusing points, Gitzo tripod, Manfrotto 501 video head. Jökulsárlón, Iceland, June 2006.

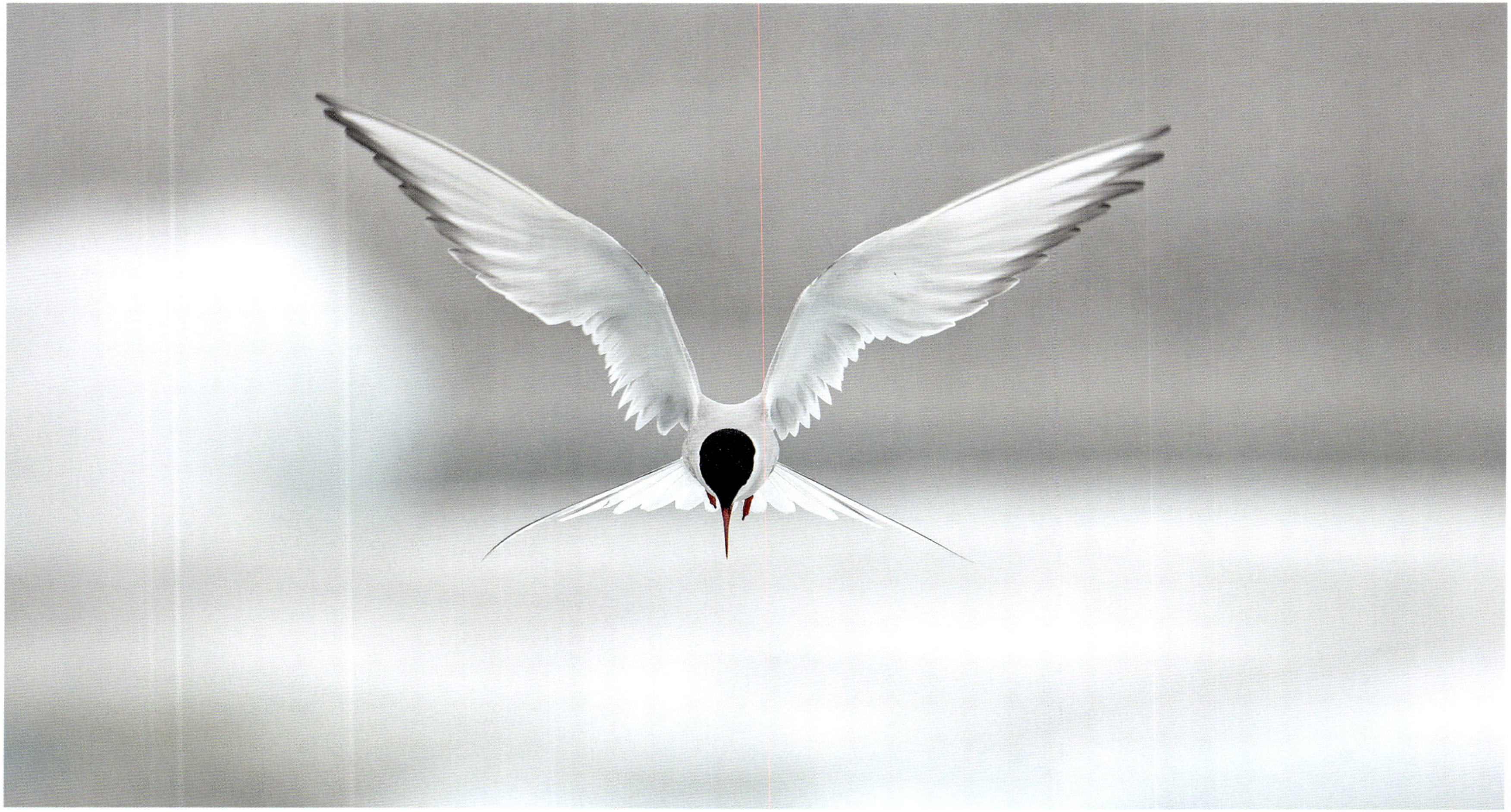

Markus Varesvuo

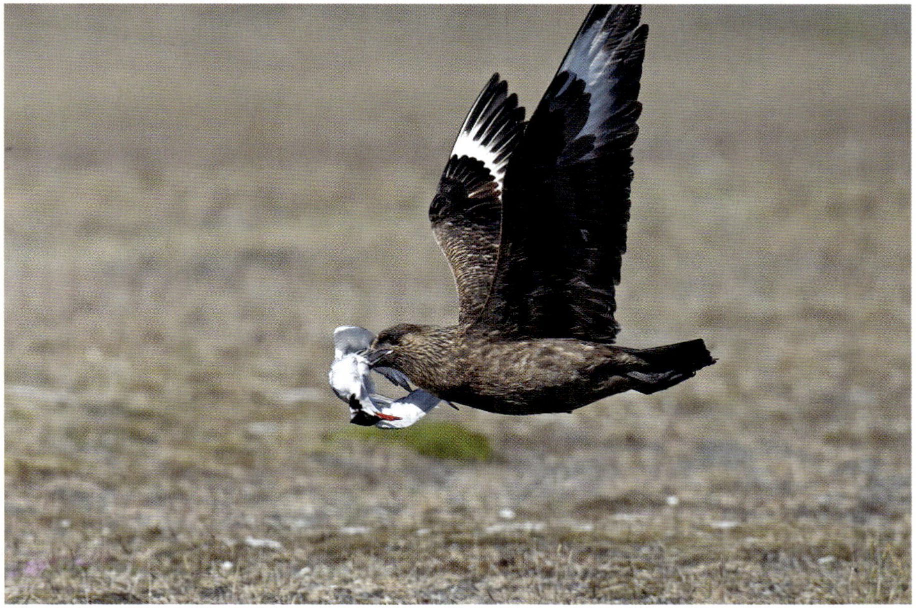

Markus Varesvuo

A Great Skua clutching an Arctic Tern in its beak *(Stercorarius skua, Sterna paradisaea)*
Canon EOS-1D Mark II, 500mm f/4.0, 1/2000 second, f/6.3, ISO 500, continuous focus with 45 focusing points, Gitzo tripod, Manfrotto 501 video head. Jökulsárlón, Iceland, June 2006.

I spent two cloudless nights at the Northern Gannet cliffs. The sun dipped below the horizon only briefly, and it was a feast of fabulous, low-angle light. From where I was photographing, I could take closeups of the nesting Northern Gannets and Thick-billed Murres and also capture Northern Gannets and other seabirds directly from above as they flew past me, with the sea below as the background.

My third favorite location is a large area, hundreds of square kilometers, that lies between the sea and the glacier Vatnajökull. Arctic Tern colonies breed there, as do Great Skuas and Red-throated Loons, plus a few dozen strictly protected Red Phalaropes.

A visit to the glacier lake of Jökulsárlón is a must. The river that runs from the lake into the sea has lots of fish, and the Arctic Terns fish actively on the lake in the hundreds, posing beautifully against the huge blocks of ice floating in the water. In the dark-free nights you can take images where the ice reflects light back onto the wings of the white terns in delicate hues of blue green.

Hundreds of Great Skua pairs breed in the area, and some of them have specialized in eating the Arctic Terns. The skuas can't catch a tern in flight, but I got to witness one skua's strategy. The Great Skua was circling above the terns as they were fishing, waiting for a tern to dive after a fish. As it reemerged from the water, the skua caught it by surprise. It killed the tern and flew away to a more quiet place where it could pluck its catch and feed in peace.

Great Skuas are relatively easy to photograph, but anyone coming too

Markus Varesvuo

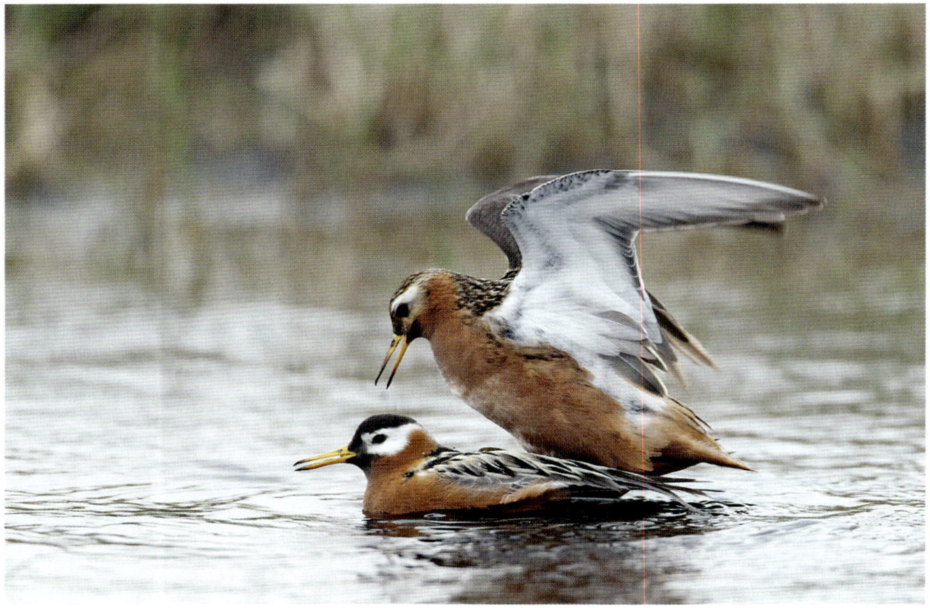

Red Phalaropes mating *(Phalaropus fulicarius)*
Canon EOS-1Ds Mark II, 500mm f/4.0 plus 1.4x extender, 1/400 second, f/6.3, ISO 400, continuous focus with a central focusing point, Gitzo tripod, Manfrotto 501 video head. Iceland, June 2006.

close to their nest is chased off with merciless dive bombing.

There are plenty of small ponds where dozens of Red-throated Loon pairs breed. The Red Phalaropes that breed in the area are under protection, and photographing them requires permission from the authorities. It's estimated that about 100–200 pairs breed in Iceland.

The range of fascinating bird species to photograph is not the only way Iceland can lure a photographer; the wonderful sights and the volcanic soil add to Iceland's magic.

MARKUS VARESVUO

EILAT, ISRAEL

There are many bird species along the migration pathways and avian highways of Israel.

For a bird photographer Eilat works best from March to May. Over the years I've been there close to 10 times. After a gap of several years, I was there again in 2009: two weeks in March and a week in May. Eilat has seen many changes in the past two decades, but it hasn't lost its lure as a great bird place. It's still one of the most exciting locations in the Western Palearctic for photographing birds.

Eilat is in the southern tip of Israel, on the northern edge of the Red Sea, along the main flyways of birds migrating between Europe and Africa. Eilat's annual spring migration of raptors is unique in the Western Palearctic. Raptors pass Eilat in numbers ranging from about a half million to more than 1 million, depending on the year. In addition, great numbers of passerine birds, waders, and some herons and egrets, waterbirds, and raptors stop to rest and feed in Eilat and the neighboring areas. The region also has its own avifauna, so there is no shortage of birds to see and photograph.

Eilat has many biotopes to offer the tired and hungry birds, starting from the parks in the city center, which attract wagtails, phylloscopus warblers, pipits, buntings, sylviidae warblers, and shrikes.

The salt ponds and reservoirs north of Eilat draw great numbers of waders as well as flamingoes, herons and egrets, gulls, and some terns.

Farther north, you will come to large irrigated areas of agricultural land with wheatears, pipits, larks, shrikes, doves, and bee-eaters. The agricultural lands are quite extensive nowadays from Eilat to Yotvata, with its kibbutz center about 40 km (25 mi) north on the southern edge of the Negev Desert. A further 30 km (19 mi) north brings you to kibbutz Neot Semadar (formerly known as Shizafon) in the Southern Negev Desert. As an oasis in the desert, Neot Semadar is a powerful attraction to birds, and thus bird photographers.

Many bushes and acacia trees growing in the arid land of Eilat offer food and shelter to small birds, especially warblers, such as the sylviidae, phylloscopus, and Icterine.

Eilat's northern shore is still relatively unbuilt, and you have a good chance of seeing birds that are fairly exotic in the Western Palearctic, such as Brown Boobies and Red-billed Tropicbirds, and to photograph many other interesting species, such as the White-eyed Gull, the Western Reef Heron, the Little Tern, and the White-winged Tern.

I recommend renting a car, not just for getting around, but also for photographing. Some of the salt ponds are circled by roads, offering good opportunities for photographing waders from the car. The irrigated lands, grain stores, cattle farms, and heaps of manure are frequented by a wide variety of species, and it's easy to photograph the birds from a car.

In Eilat I tend to get up early so I can either get to the salt ponds before sunrise and photograph waders in the beautiful morning light, or so I can go to the parks or other areas with shrubs and

Eilat is not good just for its rare and exotic species, it's also great for photographing the more common migratory birds, such as this Barn Swallow in flight *(Hirundo rustica)*
Canon EOS-1D Mark III, 500mm f/4.0, 1/2000 second, f/6.3, ISO 1600, continuous focus with an extended central focusing point, handheld camera. Eilat, Israel, March 2009.

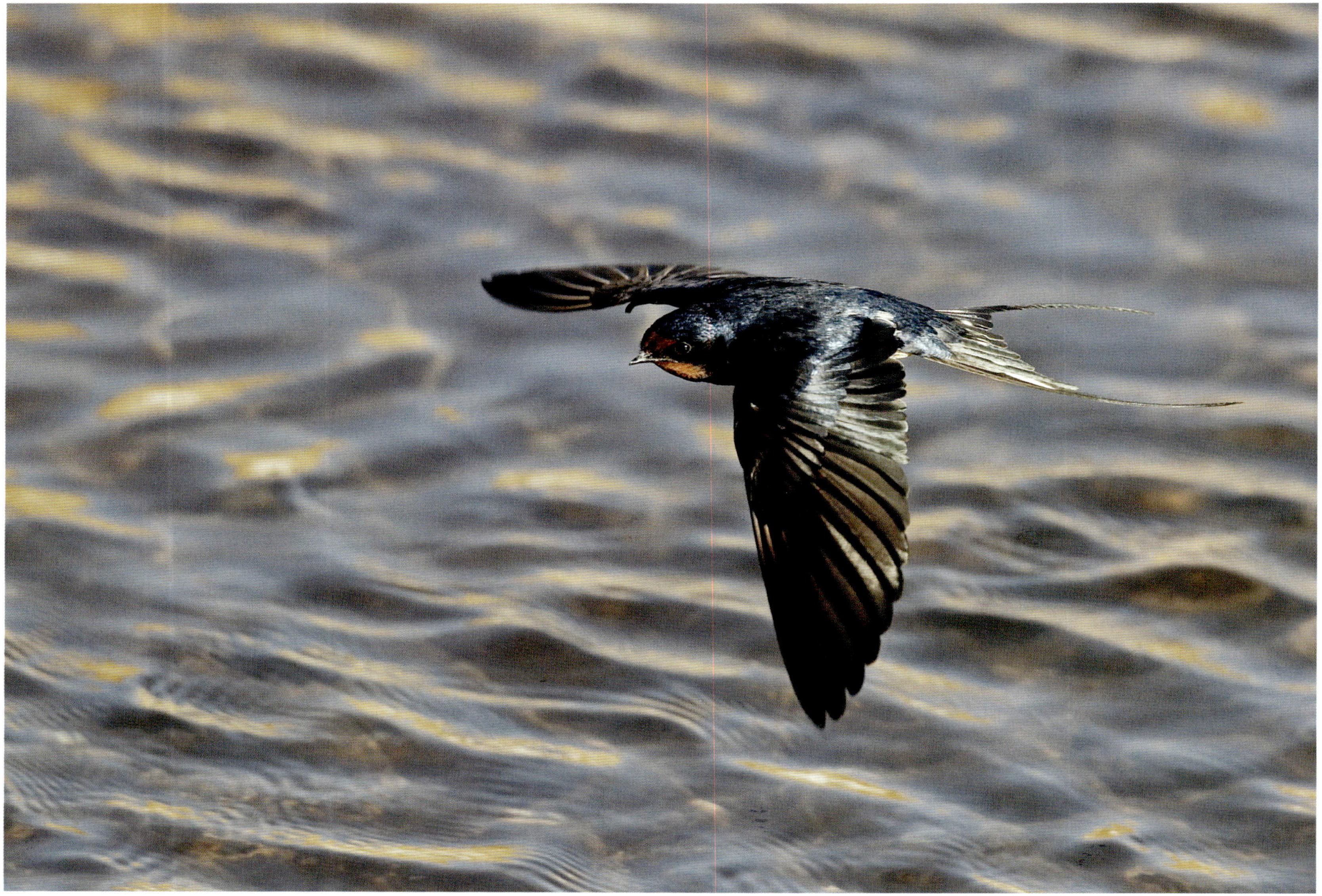

Markus Varesvuo

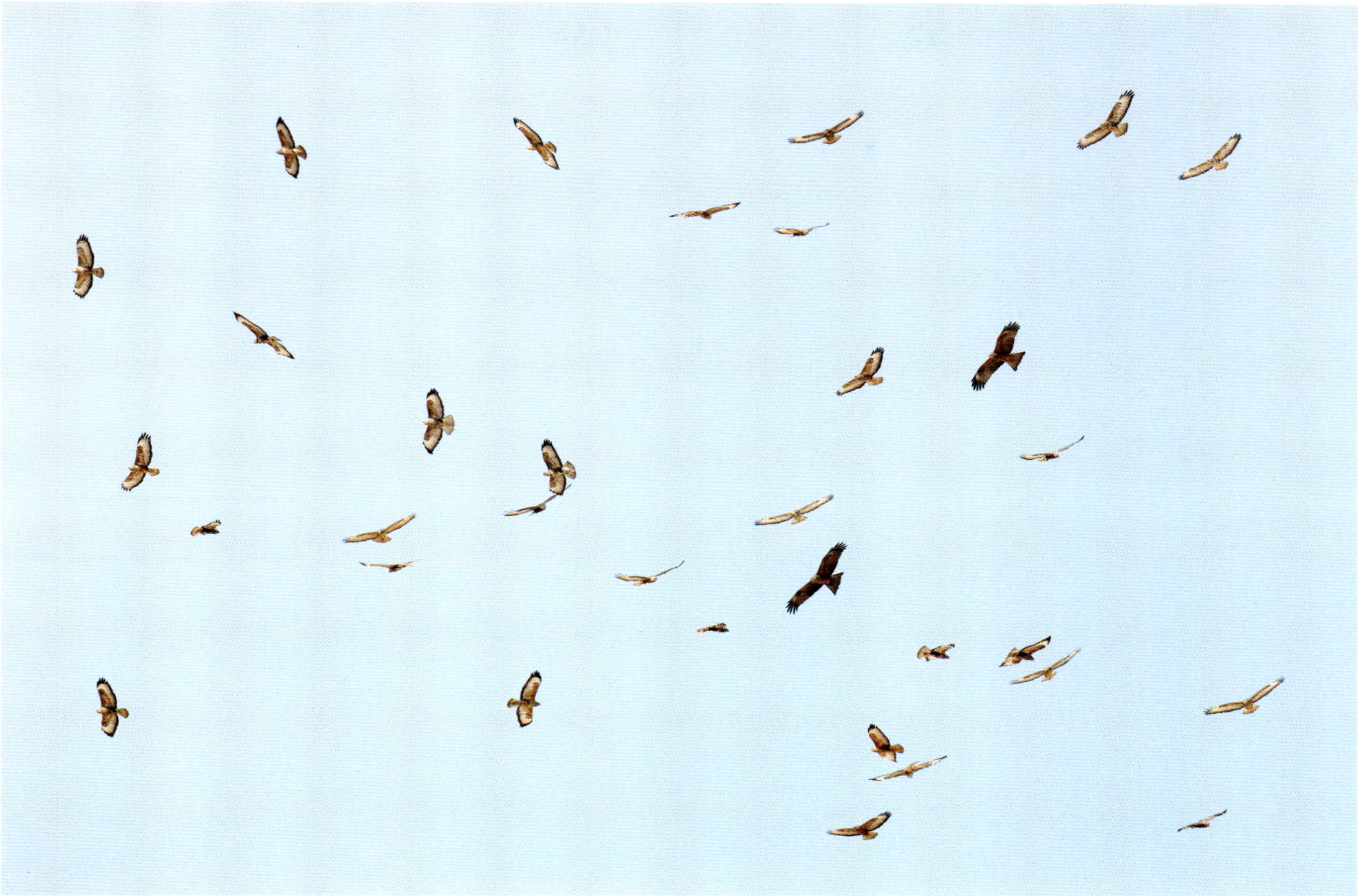

Markus Varesvuo

Eastern Common Buzzards and Black Kites on migration above Eilat *(Buteo buteo vulpinus, Milvus migrans)*
Canon EOS-1Ds Mark III, 500mm f/4.0, 1/1000 second, f/7.1, ISO 500, continuous focus with an extended central focusing point, Gitzo tripod, Manfrotto 501 video head. Eilat, Israel, March 2009.

You'll have fairly good opportunities to photograph migrating Steppe Eagles in Eilat *(Aquila nipalensis)*
Canon EOS-1D Mark III, 800mm f/5.6, 1/2000 second, f/7.1, ISO 1600, continuous focus with an extended central focusing point, Gitzo tripod, Manfrotto 501 video head. Eilat, Israel, March 2009.

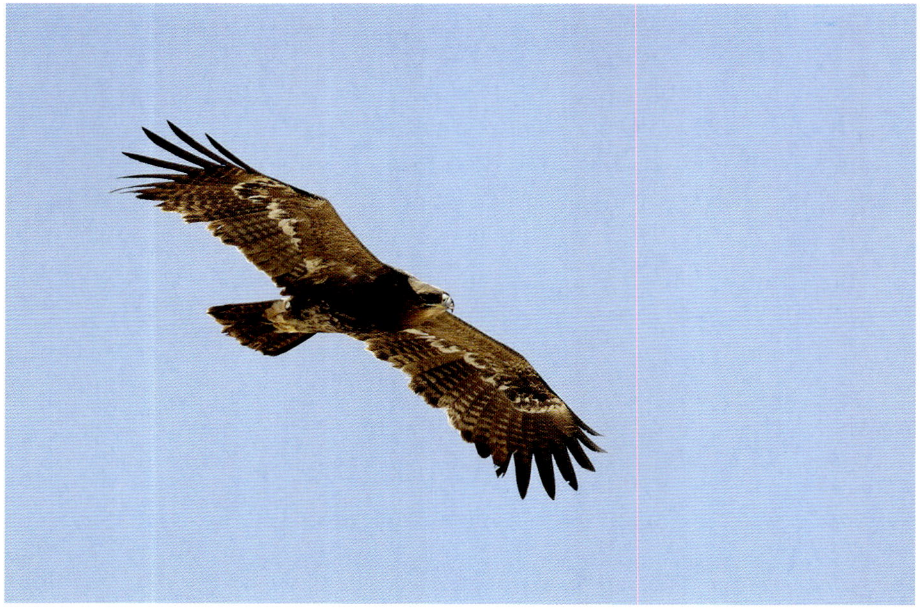

Markus Varesvuo

bushes where I can photograph small birds. After a good hour or so I head for the mountains, which is the main path for raptors on migration. The drive takes only about 10 minutes northwest from the city center, along the road to the Ovda Airport. The sand and ground are quite light in the mountains and reflect light into the air, lighting the birds' undersides nicely.

The migration often starts 60–90 minutes after sunrise. The ideal time for photography lasts only two hours or so, before the warming temperatures create thermals that the birds use to gain altitude, making them fly beyond the reach of your camera. Also, as it gets warmer, the heat haze gets stronger, and even if the raptors were still flying low on some days after midmorning, your images would end up blurry, especially with lenses longer than 500mm. Most times the raptor sessions are over by midmorning, which leaves you enough time to catch breakfast at your hotel. Then there's still time to reexplore the parks or the fields and plantations. The middle of the day, when the light is harshest, is best used for a siesta. After all, there's a lot to do from about 3:00 in the afternoon to sunset.

The dominant raptor species on migration in March and April is the Eastern Common Buzzard, with daily numbers reaching into the tens of thousands. Other plentiful species include the Black Kite and the Steppe Eagle, tens of thousands of which pass through and over Eilat during the course of the spring migration. Among these main species you can spot Long-legged Buzzards, Short-toed Eagles, and Egyptian Vultures and Harriers—the Western Marsh, Pallid, and Montagu's.

The main migration pathway is in the hands of the wind, so to speak, and can change as the day passes. You need to anticipate and stay ahead of the weather so that you find yourself in the right place at the right time. You won't get it right every day, but sometimes each piece falls into place, and you're exactly where the raptors are, and they are low enough, and all you can do is photograph to your heart's content.

If you stay for a fortnight you'll get a good overview of the spring migration. You'll witness the migration peaks for many small bird species, and the ensuing decrease of their numbers in the area, and the concurrent increase of other species as they are nearing their

Markus Varesvuo

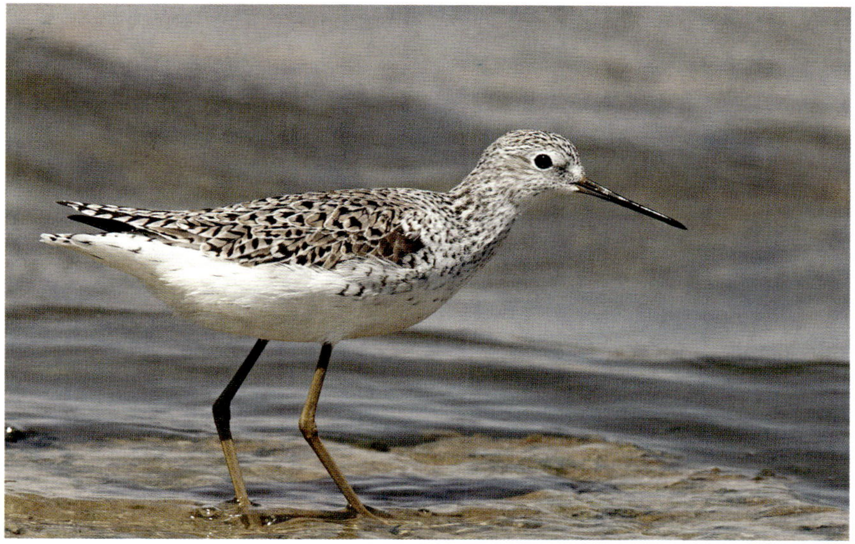

A Marsh Sandpiper in its breeding plumage by the side of a freshwater reservoir *(Tringa stagnatilis)*
Canon EOS-1Ds Mark III, 800mm f/5.6 plus 1.4x extender, 1/500 second, f/14.0, ISO 500, one-shot focus with a central focusing point, beanbag, car as a blind.
Eilat, Israel, March 2009.

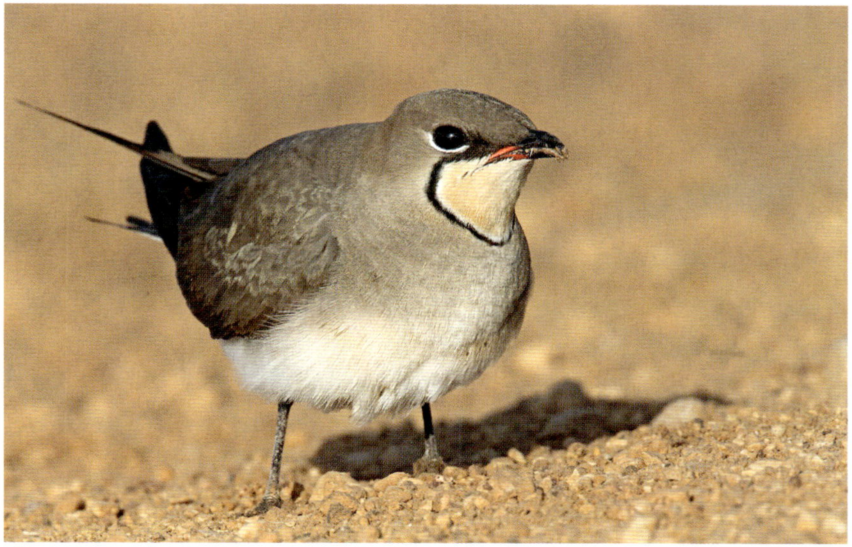

Markus Varesvuo

The Collared Pratincole is one of Eilat's many fascinating wader species *(Glareola pratincola)*
Canon EOS-1Ds Mark III, 800mm f/5.6 plus 1.4x extender, 1/160 second, f/22.0, ISO 400, one-shot focus with a central focusing point, beanbag, car as a blind.
Eilat, Israel, March 2009.

A male Rueppell's Warbler *(Sylvia rueppelli)*
Canon EOS-1Ds Mark III, 800mm f/5.6 plus 1.4x extender, 1/400 second, f/9.0, ISO 500, one-shot focus with a central focusing point, beanbag, car as a blind. Eilat, Israel, March 2009.

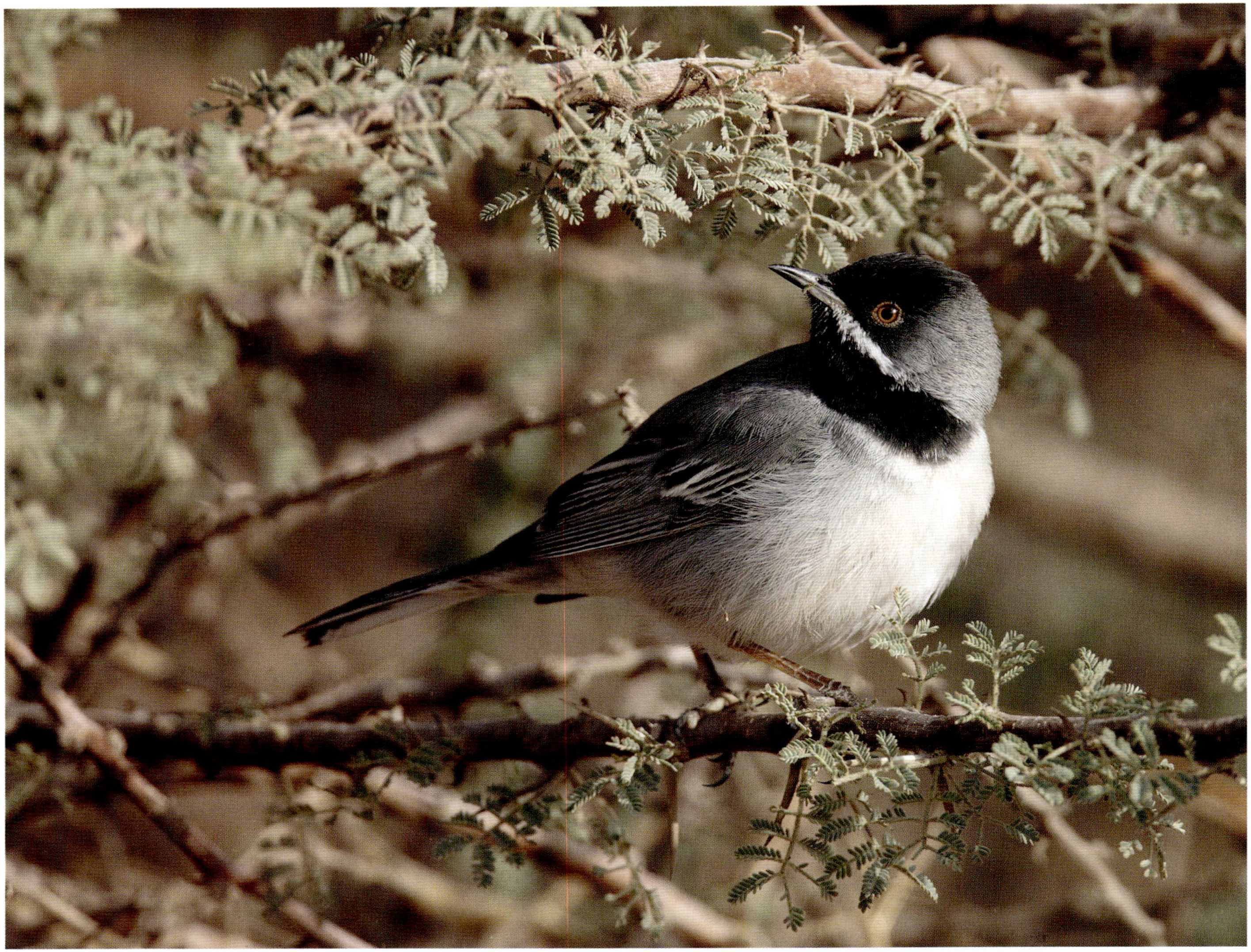

Markus Varesvuo

Markus Varesvuo

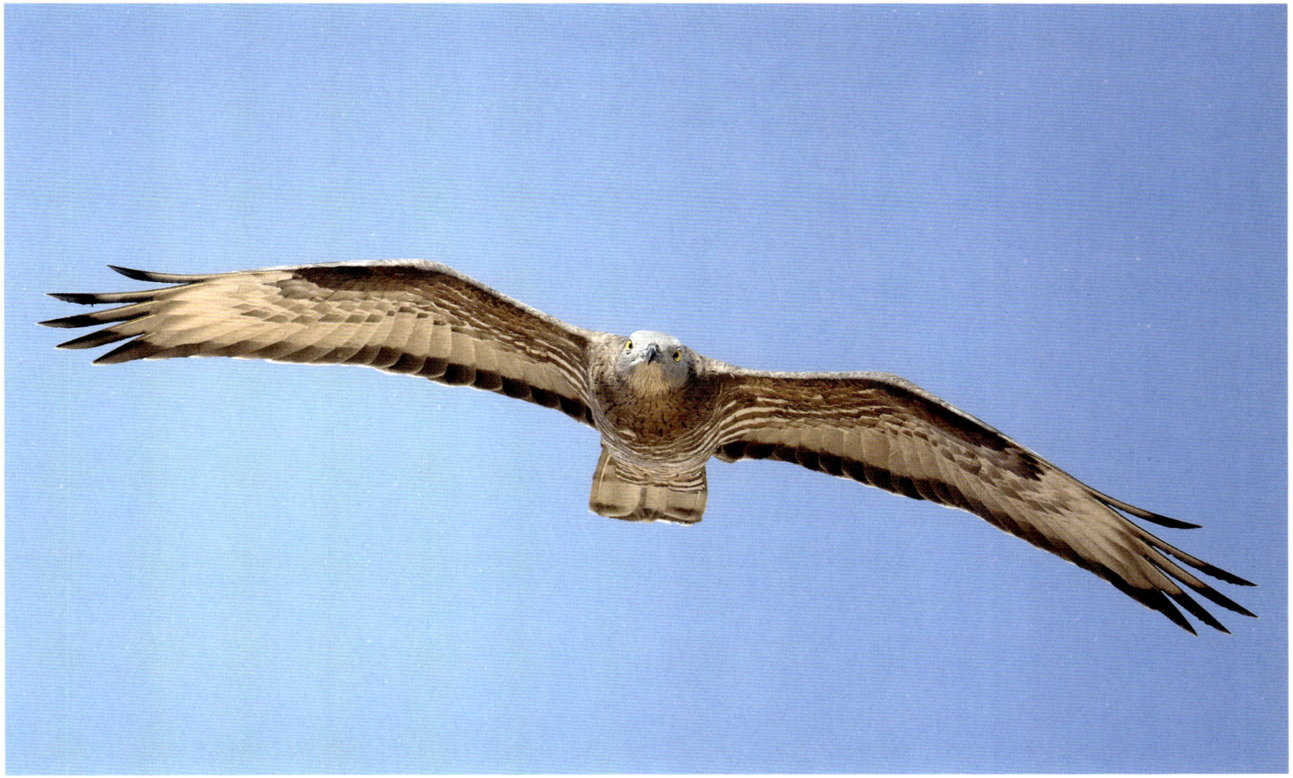

European Honey-buzzards can come eye to eye with a photographer in Eilat *(Pernis apivorus)*
Canon EOS-1D Mark III, 800mm f/5.6, 1/3200 second, f/5.6, ISO 1600, continuous focus with an extended central focusing point, Gitzo tripod, Manfrotto 501 video head. Eilat, Israel, March 2009.

migration peaks. The changing of the species works well for a bird photographer; there's something new to work with every day.

The same is evident with the waders as species come and go at the salt ponds. In March especially, look out for Marsh Sandpipers, Collared Pratincoles, Black-winged Stilts, and Plovers (the Kentish, the Caspian, and the Greater Sand), among others.

March is a good month for photographing many small birds on migration. Rueppell's Warblers can be seen in the bushes and parks toward the end of the month. Using bird sounds is a good way to attract some inquisitive individuals to a bush near you, as they come to check the source of the sound. They aren't on their breeding grounds, and employing the lure only briefly will not disturb them. The beautiful Subalpine Warbler comes in lower numbers, and it is not particularly easy to photograph. Eastern Bonelli's Warblers and Eastern Olivaceous Warblers are common toward the end of the month and are easier to photograph. The boldly colored Woodchat and Masked Shrikes, Black-eared and Desert Wheatears, plus Cretzschmar's and Ortolan Buntings are relatively easy to photograph from a car because they feed on the agricultural lands. The Red-rumped Swallows' migration peaks shortly after mid-March, and that's when they are common in the area.

The Levant Sparrowhawk's migration peak, which often coincides with the third week of April, is short, intensive, and difficult to photograph. The birds migrate in flocks, on a good day in numbers exceeding 10,000. In early April, Eastern Common Buzzards are still seen regularly on migration, and Black Kites migrate well into the second half of April. As April turns into May, European Honey-buzzards start to migrate in massive numbers, often peaking during the first week of May. With about 500,000 individual birds, the European Honey-buzzard is the most numerous of all the raptors that migrate through Eilat in spring. Photographing them is done with the same approach as with other raptors.

During April the numbers of European Bee-eaters and Blue-cheeked Bee-eaters grow steadily, peaking at the end of April and early May. The European Bee-eaters are far more common than the Blue-cheeked Bee-eaters, and photographing them is quite easy because they hunt above the fields or rest on the ground or in the trees.

Markus Varesvuo

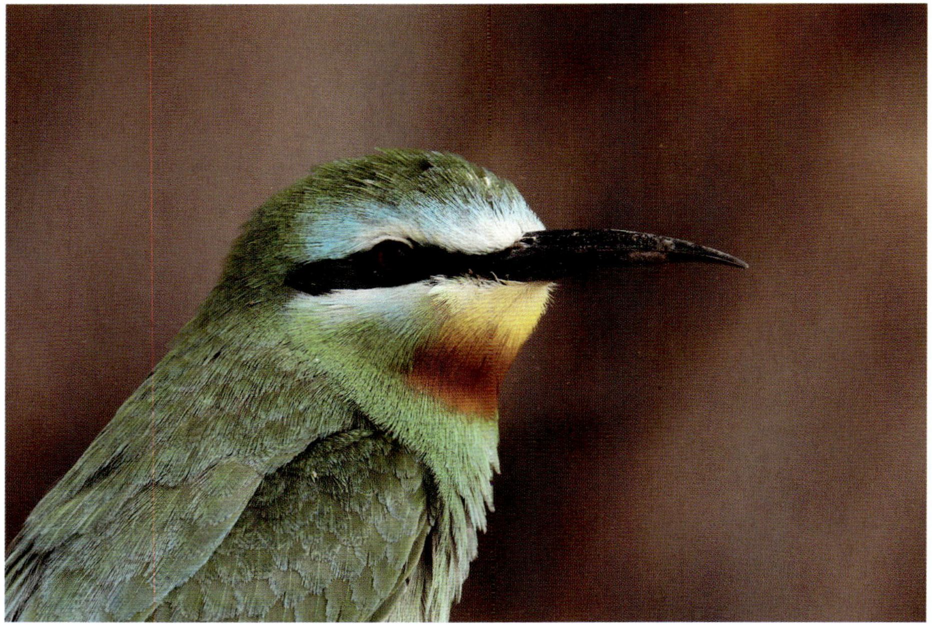

With a bit of luck, you can photograph Blue-cheeked Bee-eaters from a very short distance *(Merops persicus)*
Canon EOS-1Ds Mark III, 800mm f/5.6 plus 1.4x extender, 1/100 second, f/16.0, ISO 500, one-shot focus with a central focusing point, beanbag, car as a blind. Eilat, Israel, March 2009.

In May you can see White-winged Terns, Black Terns, and the occasional Gull-billed Tern at the fresh water pools. There are more and more typical waders in their breeding plumage as May advances, with especially good opportunities for Little Stints and Curlew Sandpipers.

Bluethroats, Redstarts, Common Nightingales, Rufous-tailed Scrub-robins, and Warblers, such as the Icterine, the Eastern Olivacous, and the Booted, stop in Eilat to rest and feed.

In addition to the migrating birds there are many intriguing breeding species in and around Eilat. Lichtenstein's

Markus Varesvuo

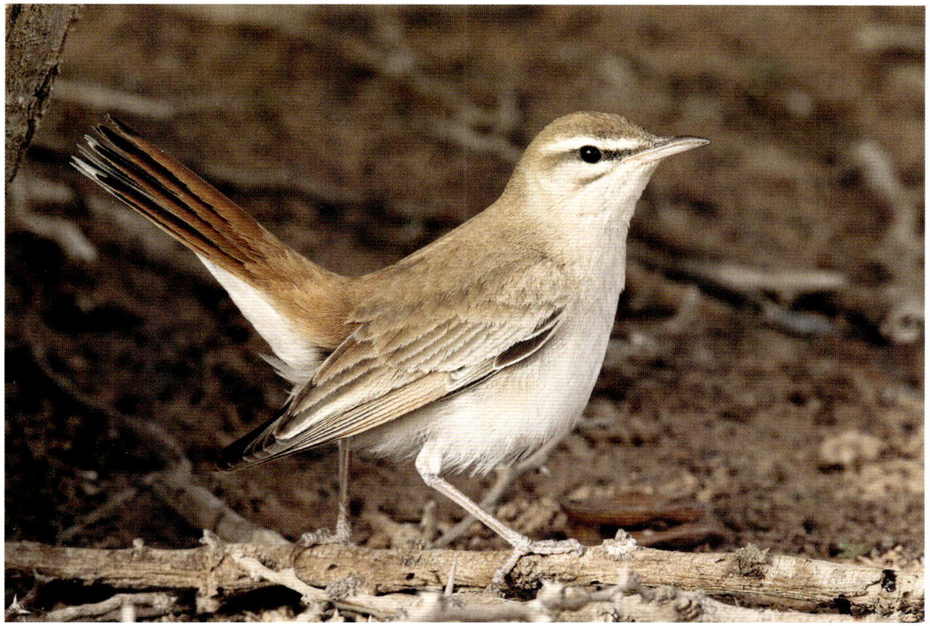

Rufous-tailed Scrub-robins prefer to stay in the cover of bushes *(Cercotrichas galactotes)*
Canon EOS-1Ds Mark III, 800mm f/5.6 plus 1.4x extender, 1/160 second, f/16.0, ISO 800, one-shot focus with a central focusing point, bean-bag, car as a blind. Eilat, Israel, March 2009.

Markus Varesvuo

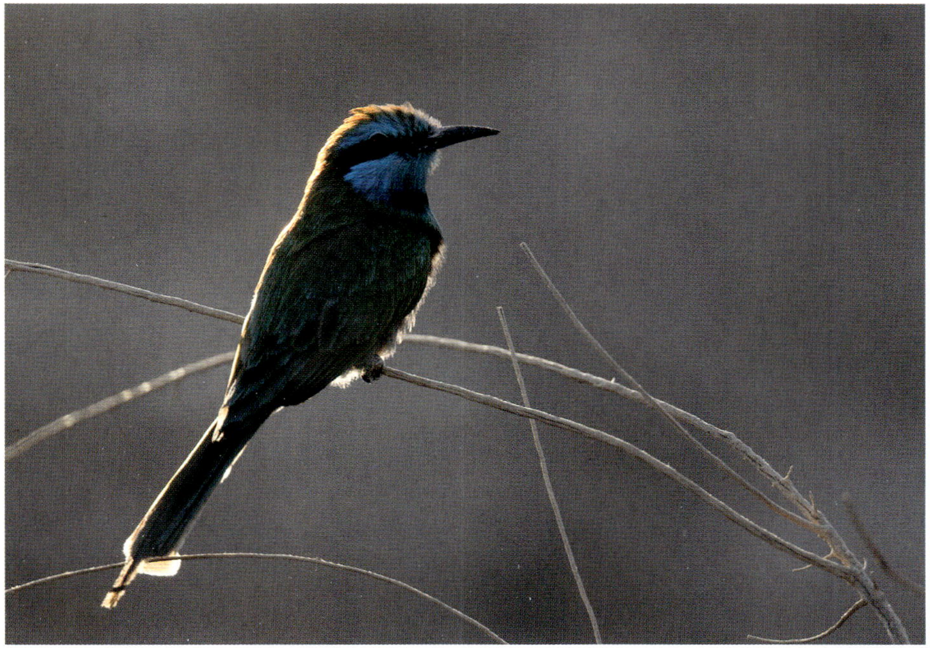

A Green Bee-eater bathing in the soft evening light just before sunset *(Merops orientalis)*
Canon EOS-1Ds Mark III, 800mm f/5.6 plus 1.4x extender, 1/100 second, f/8.0, ISO 200, one-shot focus with a central focusing point, bean-bag, car as a blind. Eilat, Israel, March 2009.

Sandgrouse, Sand Partridges, Green Bee-eaters, Sinai Rosefinches, Tristram's Starlings, Arabian Babblers, and Greater Hoopoe-Larks are good examples of birds to pursue on days when there is no migration.

For more information about Eilat and the neighboring regions, see *A Guide to the Birding Hot-Spots of Israel* by Hadoram Shirihai (Society for the Protection of Nature in Israel, 2000).

Lichtenstein's Sandgrouse are best seen in late evening at places where they can come to drink, but with some luck you can bump into them in broad daylight *(Pterocles lichtensteinii)*
Canon EOS-1Ds Mark III, 800mm f/5.6, 1/25 second, f/5.6, ISO 800, one-shot focus with a central focusing point, beanbag, car as a blind. Eilat, Israel, May 2009.

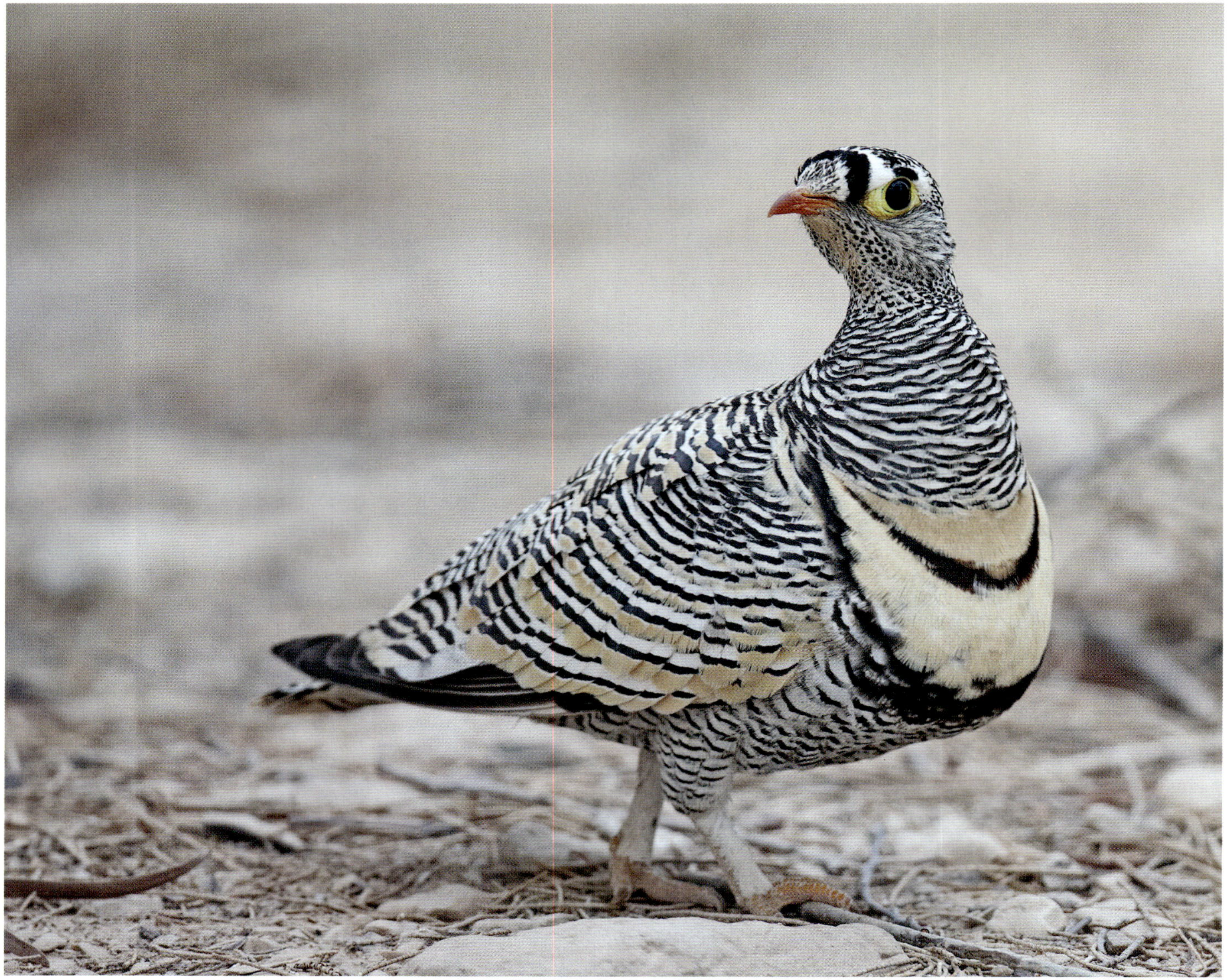

Markus Varesvuo

MARKUS VARESVUO

VARANGER PENINSULA, NORWAY

Dream species can be found in arctic settings.

The Varanger Peninsula on the southern edge of the Barents Sea is in the Finnmark province in northeast Norway. Even though it's 400 km (249 mi) north of the Polar Circle, the sea around it is open all year due to the warming effect of the Gulf Stream's Norwegian Current. A lot of arctic seabirds winter on Varanger, especially Steller's Eiders and King Eiders that come here in the thousands. Other waterbirds include Long-tailed Ducks and Common Eiders.

With enough light and before the wintering birds have left, the best time for photographing the Steller's and King Eiders stretches from the end of February throughout March. By the beginning of April, the birds start heading for their breeding grounds in northern Russia, and by mid-April they become much scarcer in the region.

In the 1990s it was easy to photograph these beautiful ducks in the harbors in Vadsø on the southern coast of the peninsula, and in Vardø on the eastern edge. The birds flocked in the harbors, feeding on the surplus fish and discards from the local fish factories. Vadsø harbor, for example, had at least 1,000 Common Eiders, 500 King Eiders, and hundreds of Long-tailed Ducks in February 1993.

Sides of the quays in Vardø harbor and the tip of the breakwater have long been traditional sites for photographing Long-tail Ducks and King Eiders.

The fish industry in Vardø and Vadsø is not as big as it used to be, and the same applies to the seabird flocks—Long-tailed Ducks occur in small numbers along with the odd King Eider. The population numbers themselves haven't been reduced, but the birds are scattered out at sea around the peninsula.

In the past few years, Båtsfjord on the northern coast has become a better place to photograph both Long-tailed Ducks and King Eiders.

Another option worthy of consideration is to rent a boat with a skipper and sail out into the sea where the birds are. This requires calm winds, because stronger winds raise the waves, which can get quite high in the Arctic Ocean, making photography difficult or impossible.

In March and April, the Hornøya bird island just outside Vardø offers fantastic photo opportunities. Tens of thousands of seabirds breed on the island, and by mid-March most of the species that breed on the island have returned from their wintering grounds wearing their dashing breeding plumages. Although the island is a bird refuge, the limitations restricting free movement don't come into force before the beginning of the breeding season in early May, so you can walk around the island freely and photograph in all the good spots. March usually still has lots of snow and snowfall, giving your images truly arctic settings. The snow reflects light back into the air, adding an extra glow to the birds' undersides.

The website www.varanger.com contains information about the area, including useful contacts, transportation to Hornøya, and accommodations on the island. There is no regular boat connection to the island before May, so a boat trip would have to be booked in

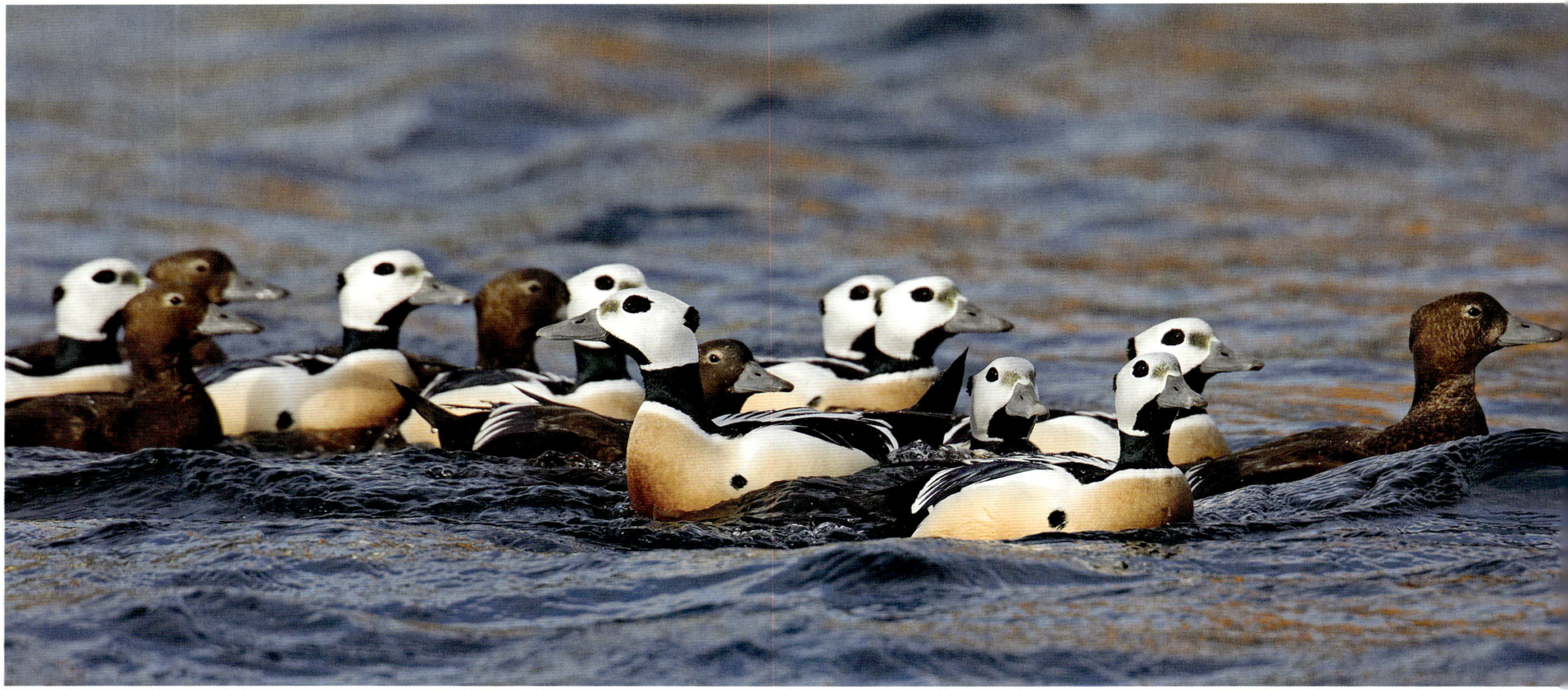

Markus Varesvuo

Steller's Eiders often move in flocks *(Polysticta stelleri)*
Canon EOS-1D Mark II, 500mm f/4.0 plus 1.4x extender, 1/2000 second, f/7.1, ISO 500, continuous focus with 45 focusing points, Gitzo tripod, Manfrotto 501 video head. Båtsfjord, Norway, March 2007.

A handsome Steller's Eider male captured in flight *(Polysticta stelleri)*
Canon EOS-1D Mark II, 500mm f/4.0, 1/2000 second, f/4.5, ISO 400, continuous focus with 45 focusing points, handheld camera. Vardø, Norway, April 2006.

Markus Varesvuo

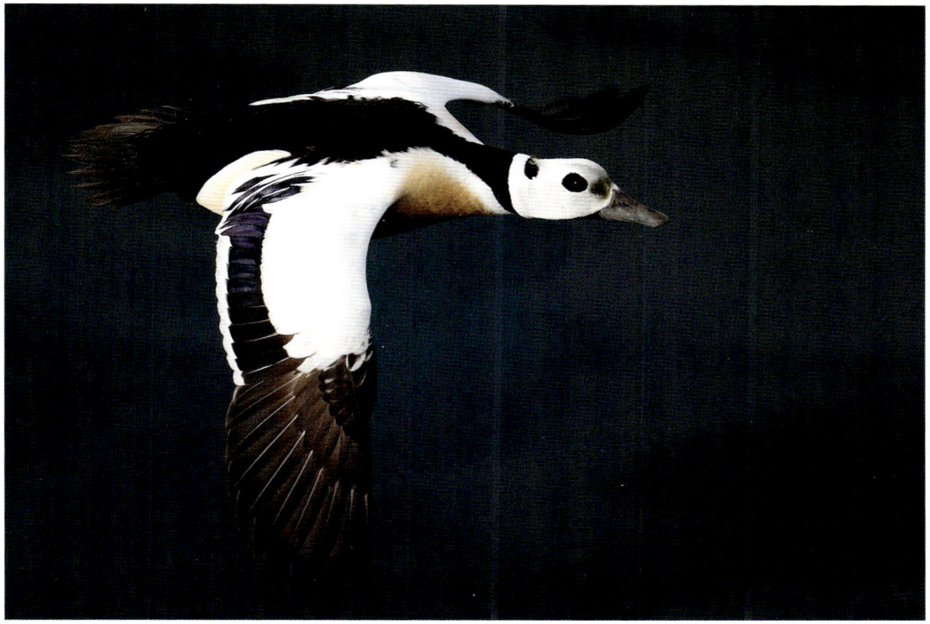

A King Eider in the Båtsfjord harbor, taken from a floating quay *(Somateria spectabilis)*
Canon EOS-1D Mark II N, 500mm f/4.0 plus 1.4x extender, 1/1000 second, f/10.0, ISO 400, continuous focus with an extended central focusing point, Gitzo tripod, Manfrotto 501 video head. Båtsfjord, Norway, April 2006.

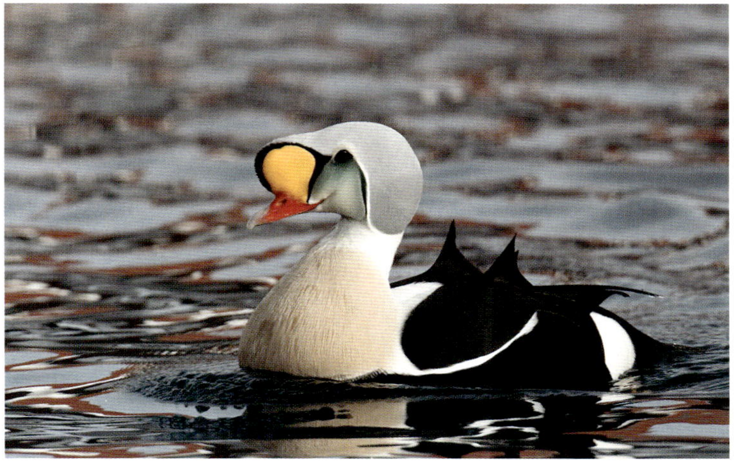

Jari Peltomäki

Overnighting is possible on the Hornøya bird island in the lighthouse keeper's house

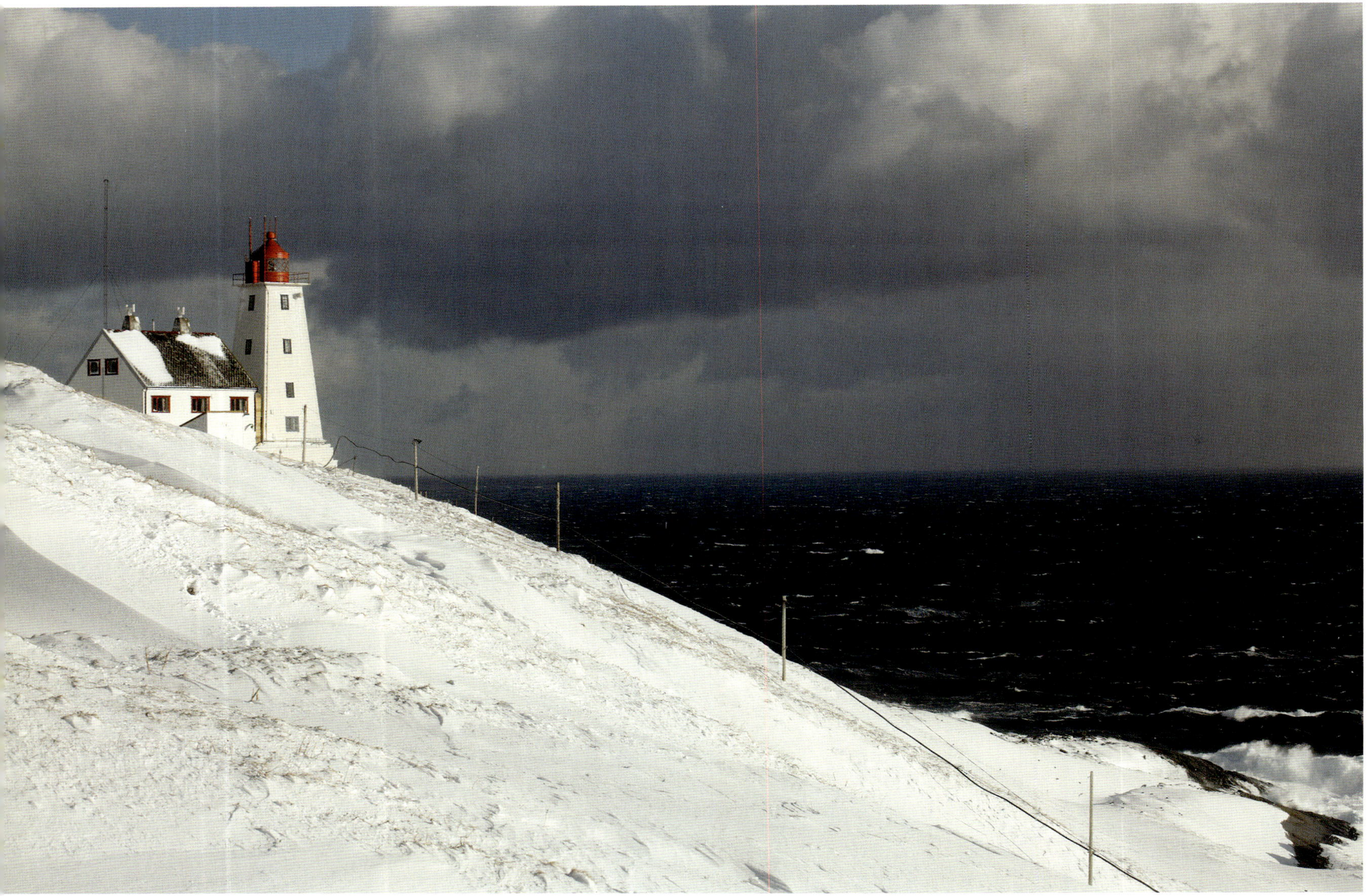

Markus Varesvuo

advance. Getting to the island in early spring can be difficult, especially in windy weather, because the main quay is not in use yet and the service quay on the other side of the island is particularly prone to the winds. The weather can turn bad fast, and stay bad for days, meaning that the boat cannot come to pick you up from the island. It's good to stock up on extra food and water.

Hornøya's breeding birds include great numbers of Puffins, Common Murres, Black-legged Kittiwakes, Razorbills, European Shags, Herring and Great Black-backed Gulls, plus lower numbers of Thick-billed Murres, Black Guillemots, Great Cormorants, and Ravens. The sheer volume of birds is portrayed in the image of the Common Murre flock in the chapter "Look for New Angles."

From the top of the island you can photograph the birds from above as they fly past their breeding cliffs, or when they land on a nesting rock, with the dark cliffs in the background or the sea shimmering in the distance. The settings are superb, and with the birds constantly flying around, getting good images is only a matter of how much you are willing to stay out there and shoot.

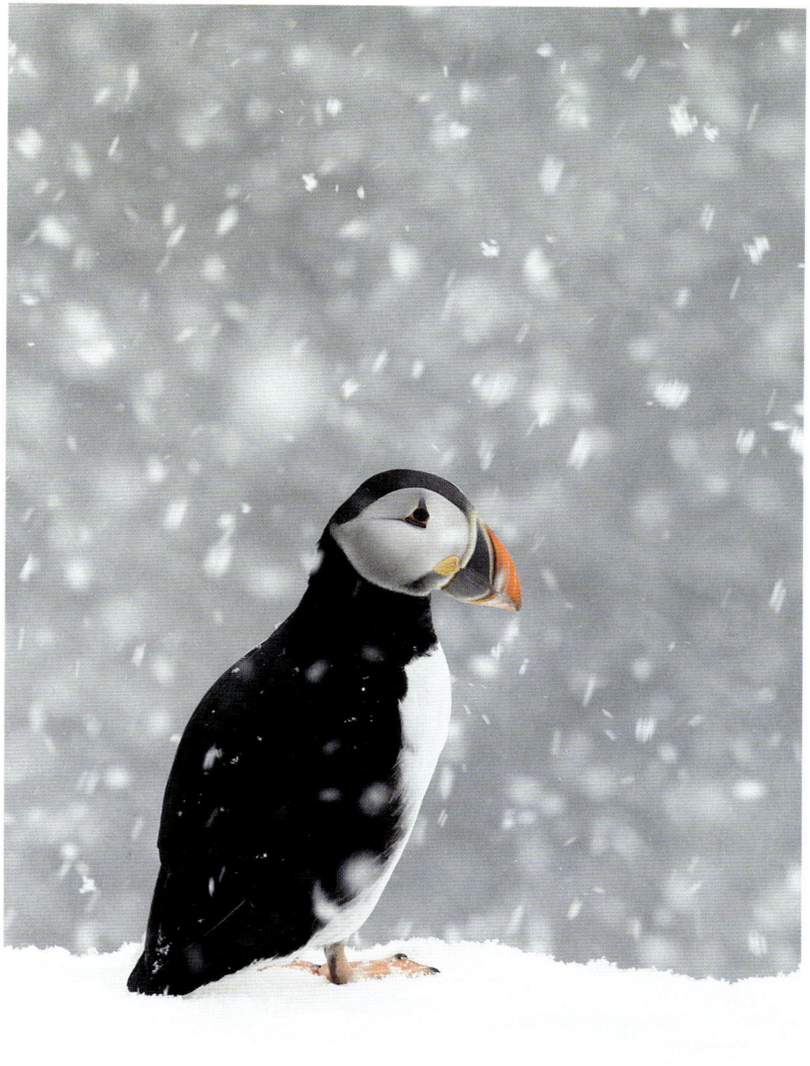

Markus Varesvuo

An Atlantic Puffin in a snowstorm *(Fratercula arctica)*
Canon EOS-1D Mark IV, 500mm f/4.0, 1/125 second, f/10.0, ISO 250, one-shot focus with a central focusing point, Gitzo tripod, Manfrotto 501 video head. Hornøya, Norway, March 2010.

Markus Varesvuo

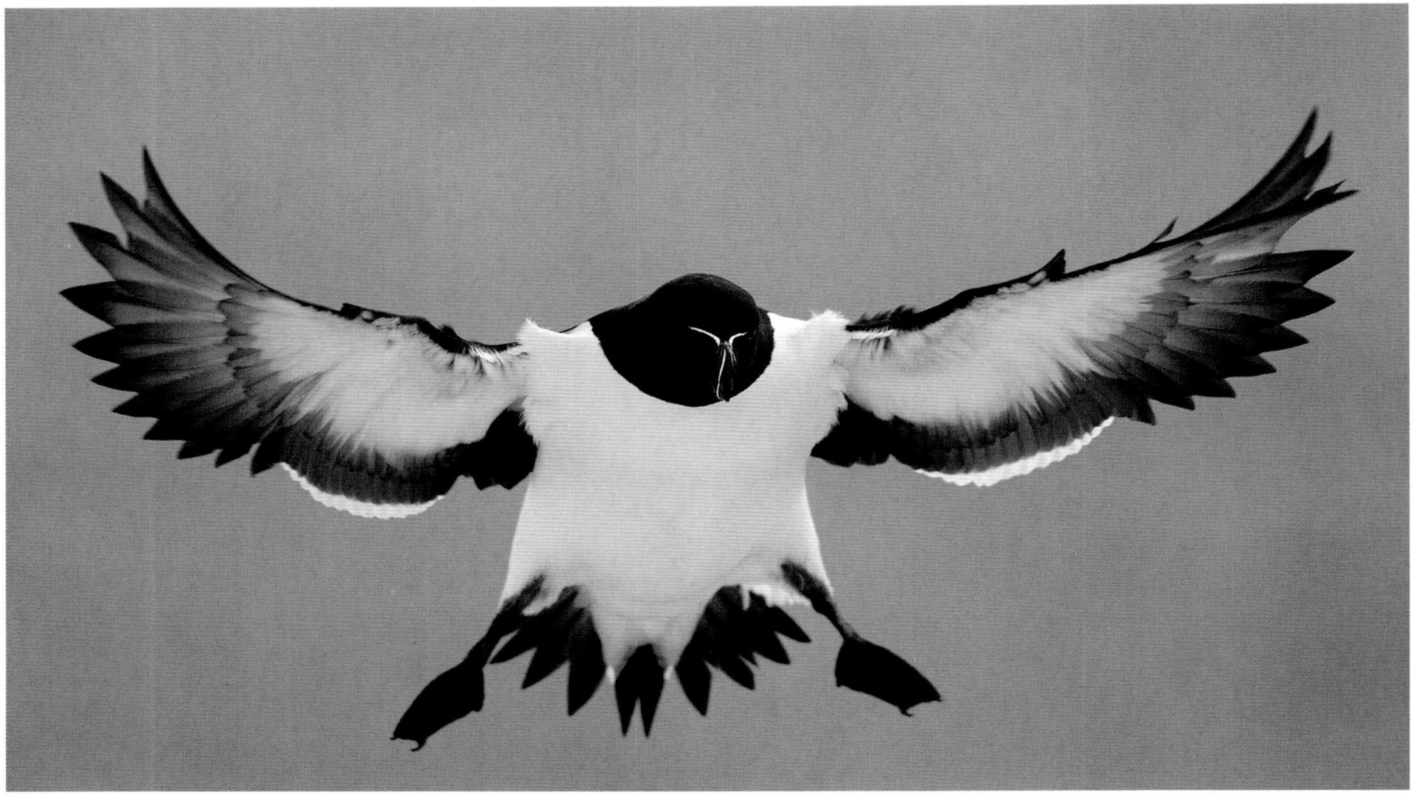

A Razorbill braking *(Alca torda)*
Canon EOS-1D Mark IV, 500mm f/4.0, 1/3200 second, f/5.0, ISO 1250, continuous focus with an extended central focusing point, handheld camera. Hornøya, Norway, March 2010.

The Common Ravens patrol the island, close to the steep cliffs, and they seem to be quite fearless. If you stand on the edge (within a safe distance, of course, because a fall would be lethal) and wait patiently, you will get good chances to photograph Common Ravens.

In addition to the breeding birds, there are daily sightings of White-tailed Eagles and Glaucous Gulls. One of the most sought-after birds on Hornøya is the Gyrfalcon. In early spring it hunts sporadically on the island, and in some years it isn't spotted at all. During a weeklong stay in 2009 I saw a Gyrfalcon almost daily, whereas on a two-week trip the following year I didn't see it once.

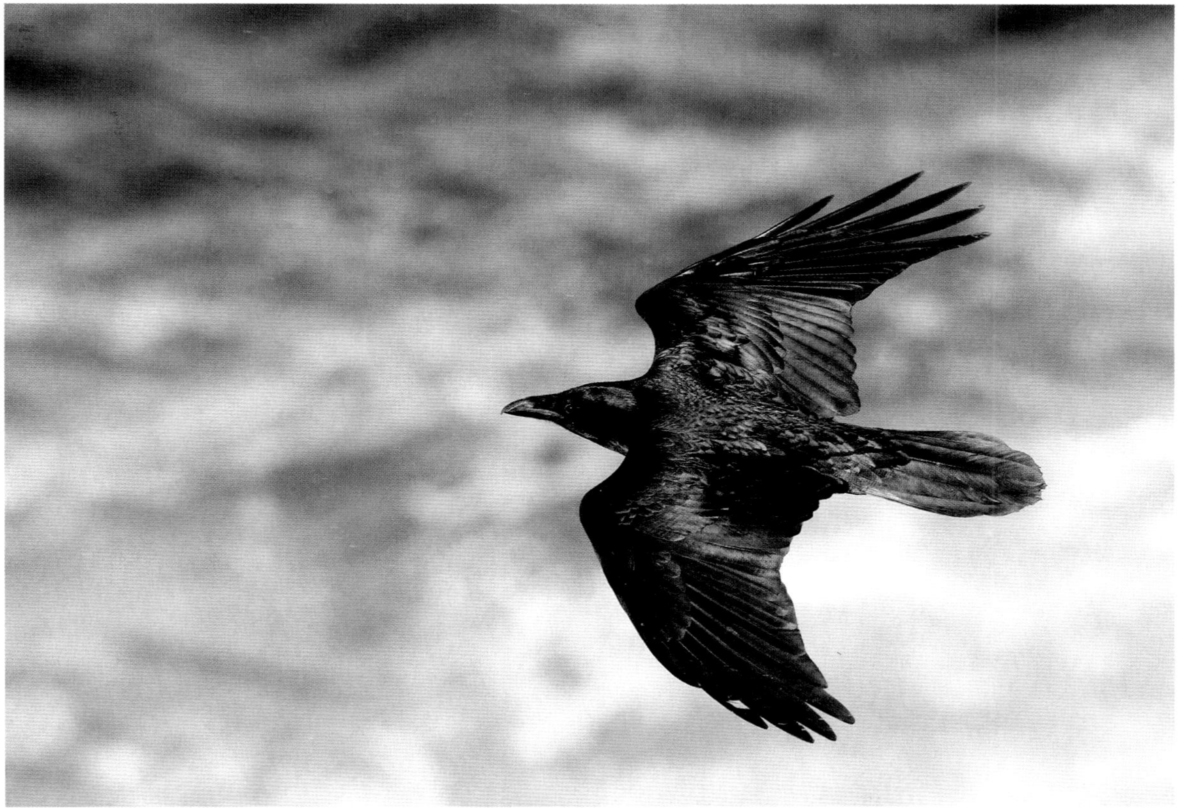

Markus Varesvuo

A Common Raven flying with the sea in the background *(Corvus corax)*
Canon EOS-1D Mark III, 500mm f/4.0, 1/2000 second, f/9.0, ISO 1250, continuous focus with a central focusing point, handheld camera. Hornøya, Norway, April 2009.

Snow reflects light on the undersides of a Gyrfalcon's wings *(Falco rusticolus)*
Canon EOS-1Ds Mark III, 500mm f/4.0 plus 1.4x extender, 1/2000 second, f/6.3, ISO 800, continuous focus with an extended central focusing point, handheld camera. Hornøya, Norway, April 2009.

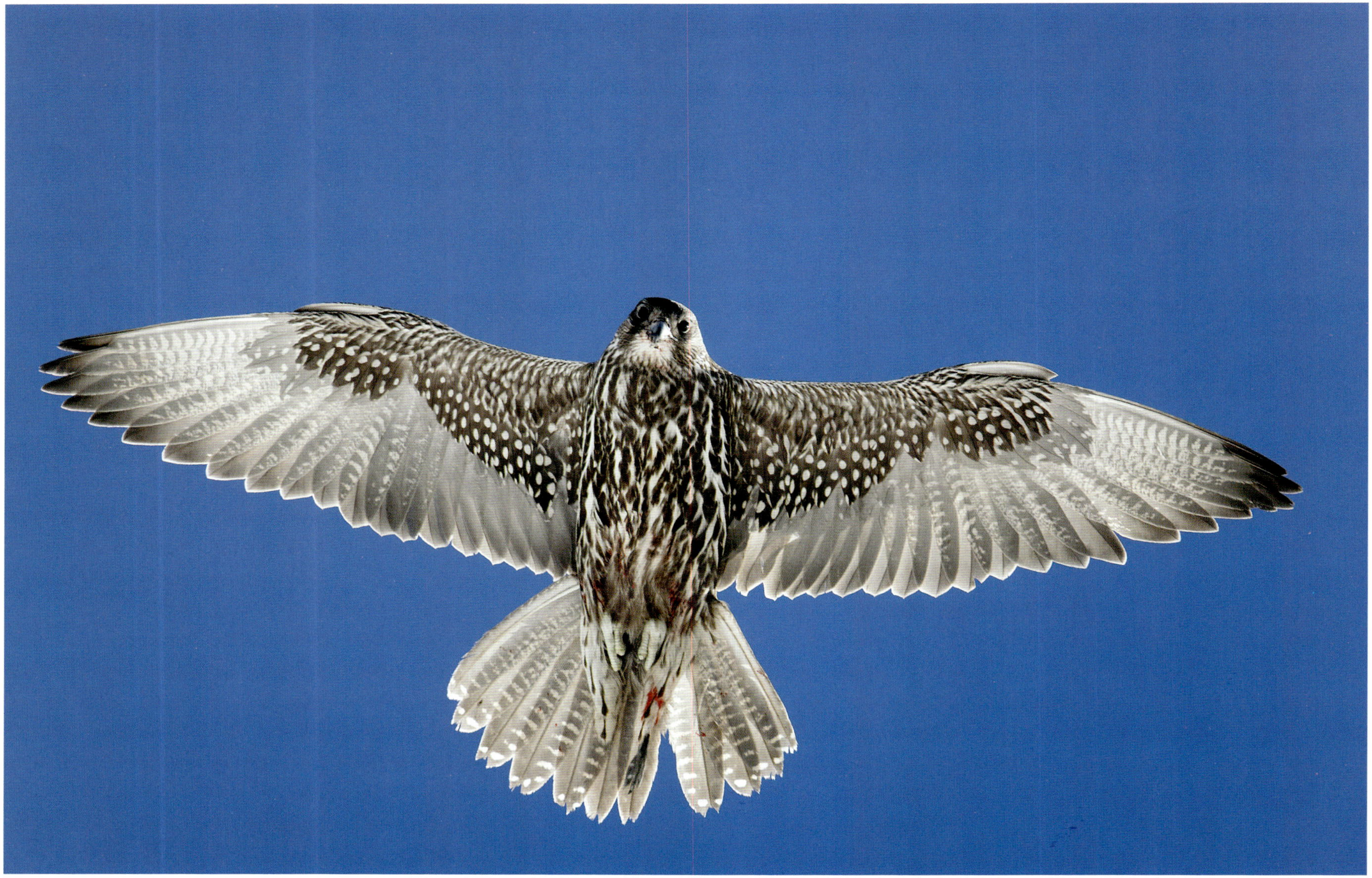

Markus Varesvuo

Most birding tourists and bird photographers visit the island in the summer because there are regular, daily boat trips to the island, and landing is much easier than in late winter. There are more birds, but moving around the island is restricted and due to the boat connection timetables, you miss the best light conditions of early morning and late evening. Plus there is no snow to soften the sunlight. Despite these handicaps, Hornøya is worth a visit in the summer. You can stay overnight if there is room in the lighthouse keeper's house, which is more or less staffed by researchers in the summer.

In the summer season, June and early July are the best times for bird photography. In the beginning of June the breeding birds have arrived, small birds are eagerly singing, and waders are displaying openly. From mid-June to mid-July the sun doesn't set at all.

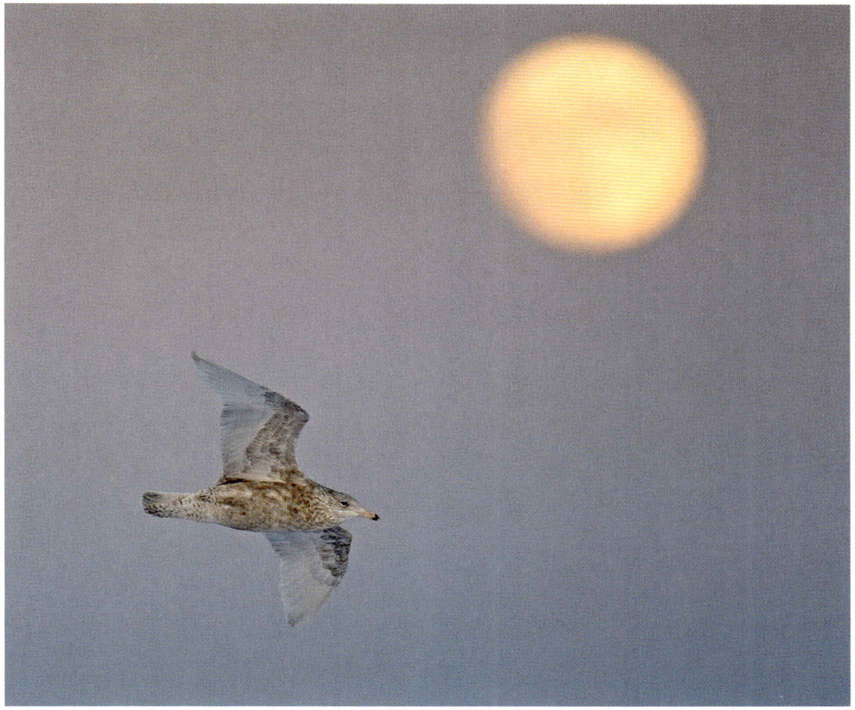

Markus Varesvuo

A Glaucous Gull and the moon *(Larus hyperboreus)*
Canon EOS-1D Mark III, 500mm f/4.0, 1/640 second, f/4.0, ISO 1600, continuous focus with a central focusing point, Gitzo tripod, Manfrotto 501 video head.
Hornøya, Norway, April 2009.

Markus Varesvuo

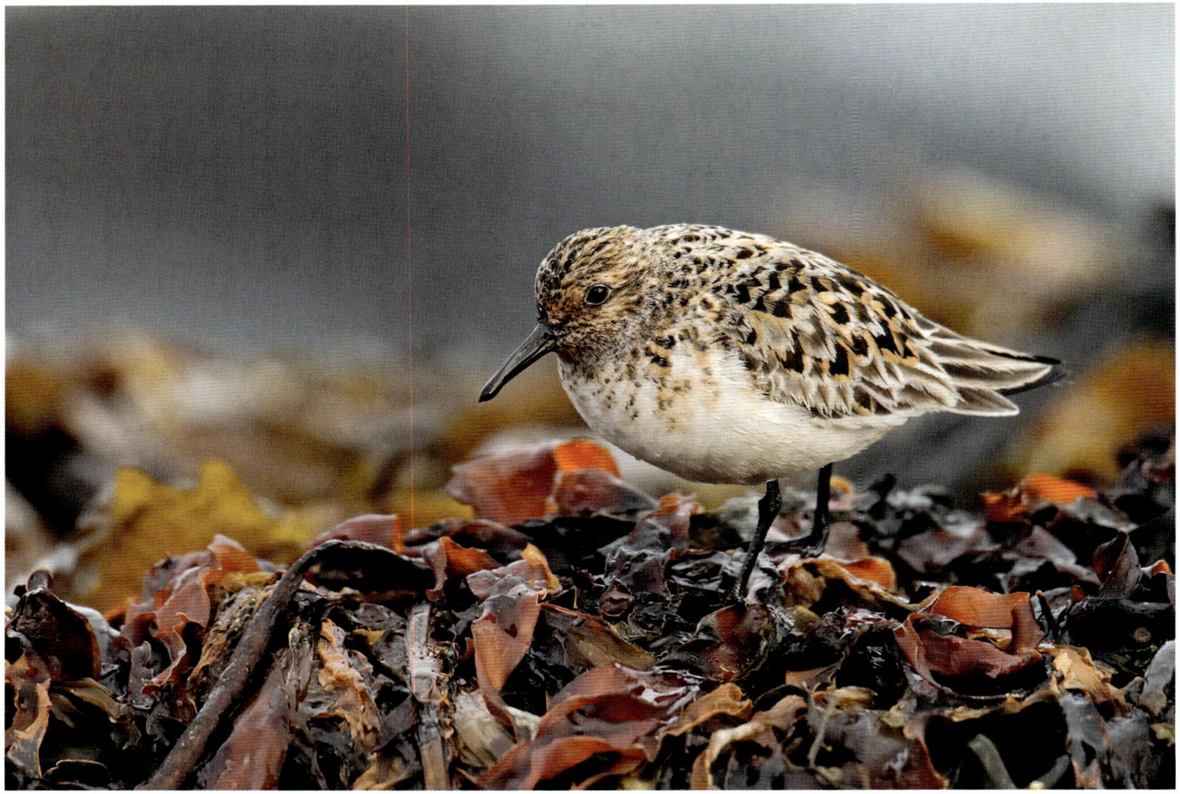

A Sanderling posing on the colorful seaweed on Hamningberg's wader shore *(Calidris alba)*
Canon EOS-1Ds Mark II, 500mm f/4.0 plus 1.4x extender, 1/200 second, f/6.3, ISO 500, one-shot focus with a central focusing point, Gitzo tripod, Manfrotto 501 video head. Hamningberg, Norway, June 2007.

About 40 km (25 mi) northwest from Vardø lies a little village called Hamningberg, and on its western edge is a shallow pebble shore covered in seaweed. It's very popular among waders; in early June Little Stints, Curlew Sandpipers, and Sanderlings can be spotted in their breeding plumage. Common Ringed Plovers, Eurasian Oystercatchers, and Ruddy Turnstones are common, and Snow Buntings visit the shore frequently to fetch insects for their young. When the wind is blowing from the north, Northern Gannets can be photographed in the eastern corner of the village as they fly close to the shore.

Hamningberg is the end of the road, so the way back is through Vardø toward Vadsø. En route, at Komagvaer, on the western side of the road is a large wetland area with bogs and small ponds where many species breed, such as Ruffs, Dunlins, Wood Sandpipers, Red-necked Phalaropes, Whimbrels, and Bar-tailed Godwits. A few Red-throated Loon pairs nest in the ponds, and it's relatively easy to bump into

A Red-necked Phalarope landing *(Phalaropus lobatus)*
Canon EOS-1D Mark II, 500mm f/4.0, 1/2500 second, f/4.0, ISO 400, continuous focus 45 with a central focusing point, handheld camera. Komagvaer, Norway, July 2009.

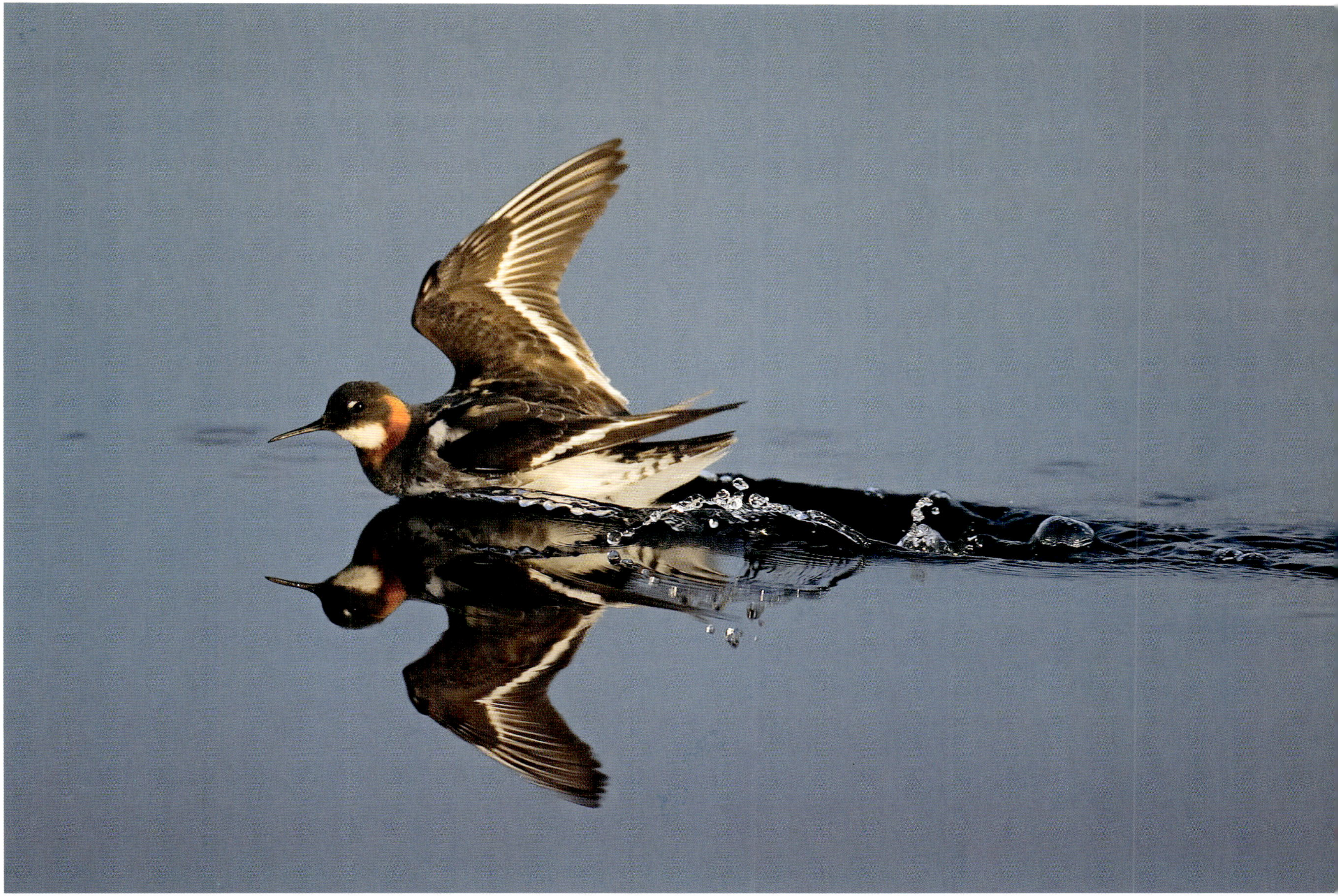

Markus Varesvuo

Markus Varesvuo

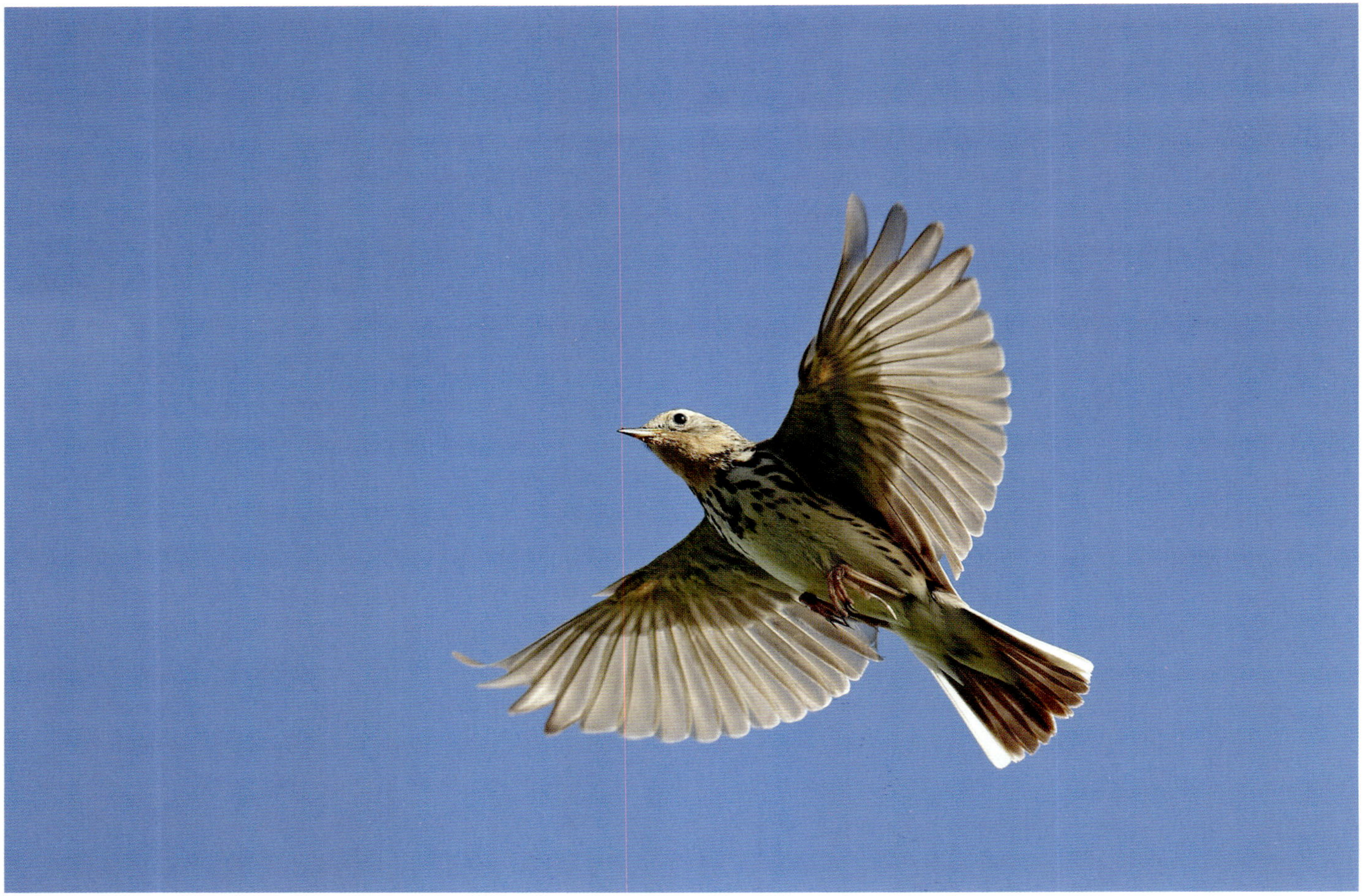

A Red-throated Pipit in flight ***(Anthus cervinus)***
Canon EOS-1D Mark III, 500mm f/4.0, 1/2500 second, f/6.3, ISO 800, continuous focus with 45 focusing points, handheld camera. Norway, July 2008.

Markus Varesvuo

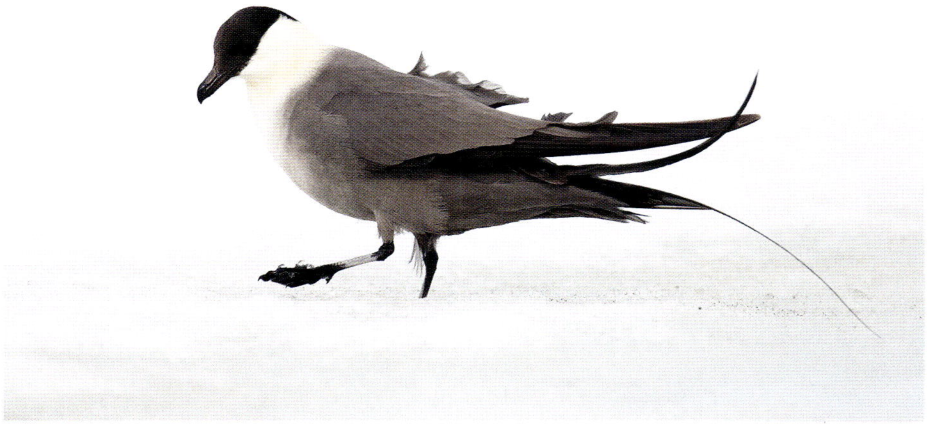

Long-tailed Jaegers arrive to the Varanger highlands when large areas are still covered in snow *(Stercorarius longicaudus)*
Canon EOS-1D Mark II, 500mm f/4.0, 1/1250 second, f/6.3, ISO 400, one-shot focus with a central focusing point, Gitzo tripod, Manfrotto 501 video head. Norway, June 2005.

Willow Ptarmigans. Lapland Longspurs, Bluethroats, and Red-throated Pipits are fairly common, too. This is a nature reserve, and you have to make sure that you're not disturbing the birds, especially in the nesting season. Off-road driving in a nature reserve is strictly forbidden, so you cannot deviate from the roads no matter how picturesque the bird is or how even or easy the terrain looks.

Another good stop along the road back toward Vadsø is the Ekkerøy Island, where thousands of Kittiwake pairs breed, as do a number of other seabirds. Ekkerøy is actually a high cape connected to the mainland by a narrow causeway. The seabirds nest on a steep cliff facing south. The top of the high point is a moor, where Lapland Longspurs nest, and some years a few Parasitic Jaegers nest there as well. The northern edge is a gentle slope with old meadows where several pairs of Red-throated Pipits nest every year.

The road to the Varanger Peninsula's highlands goes past Vadsø through Varangerbotn to Tana, and from there toward Båtsfjord and Berlevåg on the northern coast. Nesseby, between Vadsø and Varangerbotn, has nice wader shores near the Nesseby Church. Another good spot to check is a small freshwater pond in a point pushing out to the sea west of the church.

Høyholmen, about 40 km (25 mi) from Tana toward Båtsfjord, offers good opportunities for photographing Temminck's Stints and Parasitic Jaegers. The Lesser White-fronted Goose is a random visitor.

The distance from Tana to Båtsfjord is about 100 km (62 mi). At about the halfway point you enter the Varanger Peninsula National Park, which is an

Markus Varesvuo

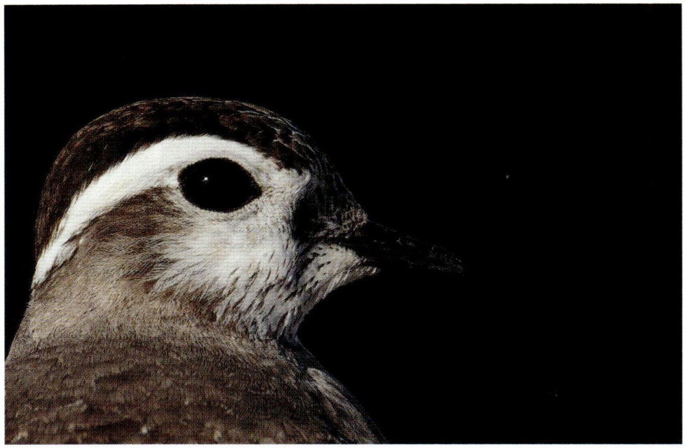

Eurasian Dotterels are best found on the peaks of the arctic hills *(Charadrius morinellus)*
Canon EOS-1Ds Mark III, 500mm f/4.0 plus 2x extender, 1/400 second, f/18.0, ISO 500, one-shot focus with a central focusing point, Gitzo tripod, Manfrotto 501 video head. Norway, July 2008.

extensive and open highland area with ponds and lakes surrounded by bogs and no trees; it is excellent for birding, with breeding Red-throated Loons, Long-tailed Jaegers, Eurasian Dotterels, Rock Ptarmigans, Willow Ptarmigans, Long-tailed Ducks, Red-necked Phalaropes, Temminck's Stints, Ruffs, Rough-legged Hawks, Lapland Longspurs, Bluethroats, and Horned Larks. Large areas are still under snow and ice in early June, but by the beginning of July most of it has melted with only some snow lingering in the highest altitudes or shade.

Rock Ptarmigans and Eurasian Dotterels are relatively easy to find by walking around the tops of the arctic hills. Both species are very confident and are usually agreeable to being photographed.

The Varanger Peninsula offers great opportunities for photographing many charismatic bird species in great settings. Add the spectacular light conditions in the dark-free nights, and in the late winter with early spring snowpack and snowbanks reflecting light abundantly and excessively, and you have a combination that isn't just mildly addictive!

JARI PELTOMÄKI

HOKKAIDŌ, JAPAN

Hokkaidō Island offers great winter birding opportunities, delightful cuisine, and relaxing Japanese baths.

Hokkaidō Island in northern Japan is one of my favorite locations for photography in the world. I have been to this rather arctic island twice in February to photograph birds. The weather on Hokkaidō in winter resembles spring on the Varanger Peninsula in Norway, and some of the snowstorms can definitely be heavy!

Blakiston's Fish-Owls, Red-crowned Cranes, and Steller's Sea-Eagles are the main targets on Hokkaidō, but the island also offers good chances for Black Kites, White-tailed Eagles, Pintails, and Whooper Swans. The fishing ports attract Scaups, Red-breasted Mergansers, Goosanders, and Harlequin Ducks. They are easily photographed, especially if you use a car as a blind. Many gulls favor the ports, too. For a bird photographer, Hokkaidō in winter is full of great opportunities!

Hokkaidō can be reached from Tokyo by plane or bullet train. A flight from Tokyo to the Kushiro Airport takes about an hour. The island has lots of lodging at various levels. Renting a car is easy, but the roads can be icy and covered with snow. You will find great cuisine at Hokkaidō, and a Japanese bath puts a crown on any day.

Red-crowned Crane

The main three feeding stations for Red-crowned Cranes on Hokkaidō are Akan, Tsurui Ito Tancho, and Tsuruimidai, all of which are close to the city of Kushiro. Thanks to the regular feeding, the cranes are relatively used to people and will come close to photographers. The biggest problem is to single out one or two individual birds, because whenever the cranes start their signature dance there are always other birds either in front of them or in the background. To make sure you'll end up with good images, it's necessary to spend a lot of time at the feeding stations. The Red-crowned Cranes are very photogenic in snowfall or flying against a blue sky.

In my opinion, Akan along road 240 is the best feeding station, and it's also the most popular place for photographing Red-crowned Cranes. On clear mornings the place is backlit for a brief moment when the sun rises from behind the hill and creates a beautiful setting. But if it's very cold, the cranes might not come to the feeding at all; instead they will spend the morning in a nearby open-water river. In the afternoon at 2:00 the station keeper feeds the cranes live trout, and then there may be hundreds of photographers! Many arrive several hours in advance to get the best places in the front row. A number of them come to photograph the White-tailed Eagles diving into the midst of the cranes in hopes of catching trout. The situations can be truly magnificent, especially when, in midair, the cranes kick the eagles as the eagles approach with their claws out, ready to grab a fish. Occasionally there are also some hopeful Steller's Sea-Eagles, but they aren't comfortable with diving in too close to the photographers, so they tend to settle on snatching fish from the White-tailed Eagles.

The Otowa Bridge near Tsurui is another classic spot for photographing Red-crowned Cranes as they roost in the river. But the birds are mostly quite far away, and the place is better for taking landscape images of the cranes in their environment. Some of the images I've seen from the Otowa Bridge are great, but to get good shots the circumstances must be just right—preferably clear skies and very cold temperatures, which makes the birds along the open-water river become sugar-coated with frost and turns the water to steam. Early mornings offer the best light conditions, with the rising sun lending color to the frosty trees and steam. Still, evening can yield great images, when the cranes return to roost for the night. There's a chance for landscape images of the cranes in the winding river from a high point on a hill north of the bridge.

Steller's Sea-Eagle

Despite its name, Lake Fuhren is actually a sea bay that freezes over in the winter. It's a good spot for photographing Steller's Sea-Eagles. In some winters, hundreds of Steller's Sea-Eagles and White-tailed Eagles gather on the ice in front of Lake Sunset Restaurant along road 44. The restaurant owner is a photographer and feeds the eagles fish on the ice every day. Some of the fishermen take photographers farther out on the ice in a sled, where it's possible to photograph eagles in a slightly different setting.

Still, the best place to shoot Steller's Sea-Eagles is Rausu. Usually by the middle of February the Sea of Okhotsk has pushed drift ice into the Nemuro Bay, where the ice stays for a couple of weeks. The eagles have grown accustomed to fish guts from the fishing boats, and during the drift ice season a dozen tourist boats leave the harbor every morning at 5:00 and 9:00, taking photographers out to the eagles on the

A pair of Red-crowned Cranes calling, taken at the Akan Crane Centre *(Grus japonensis)*. I angled my camera to conceal a restless background behind a wall of snow in the foreground.
Nikon D300S, 70–200mm f/2.8, 1/500 second, 110mm, f/8.0, ISO 200, one-shot focus with one focusing point, handheld camera. Akan, Hokkaidō, February 2010.

Jari Peltomäki

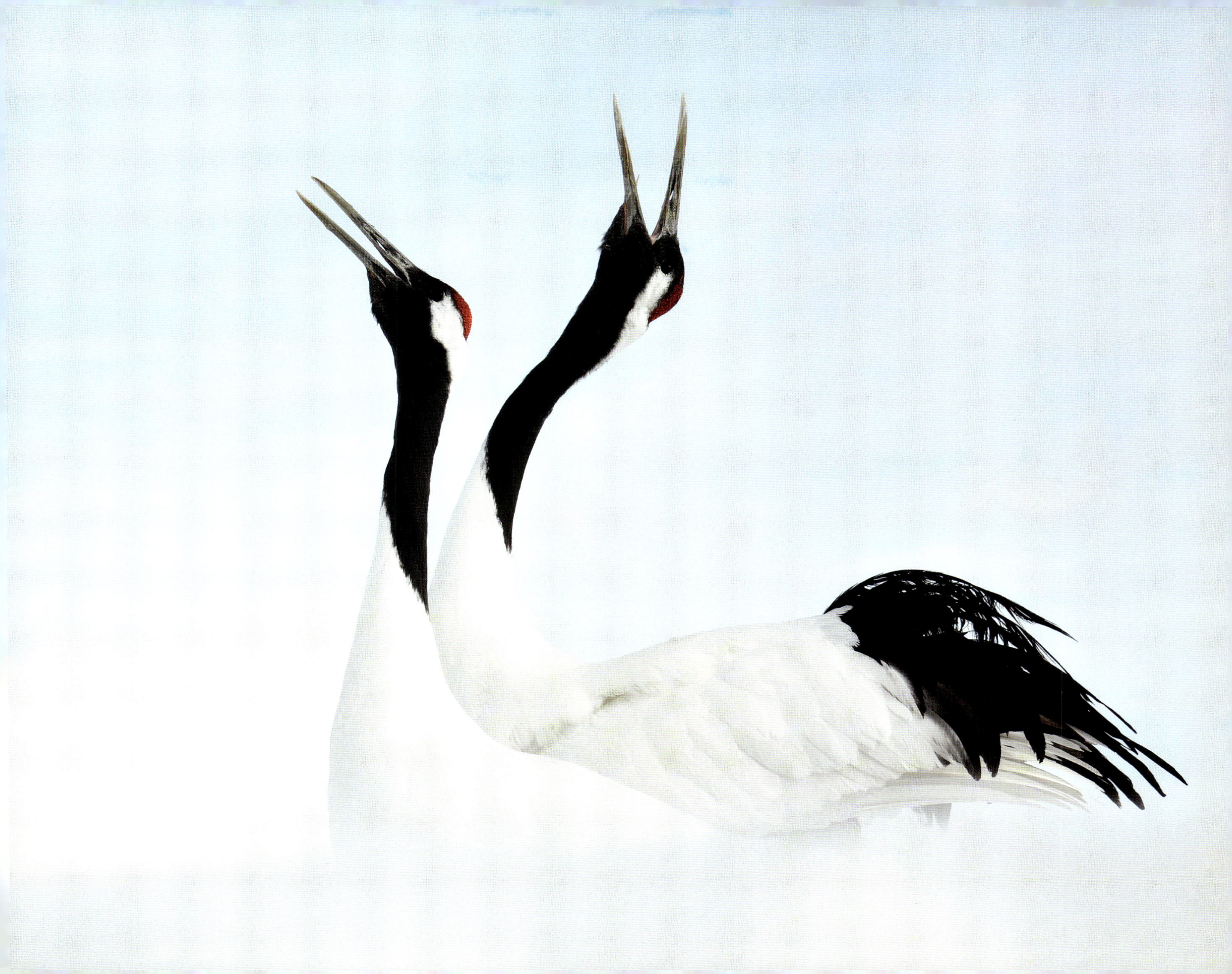

In the winter boat trips are arranged from the town of Rausu to the drift ice, where it's possible to get very close to the White-tailed Eagles and the majestic Steller's Sea-Eagles *(Haliaeetus albicilla, Haliaeetus pelagicus)*
Nikon D3S, 500mm f/4, 1/640 second, f/9.0, ISO 2500, continuous focusing with 51 points, Gitzo monopod with Wimberley Sidekick. Rausu, Hokkaidō, February 2010.

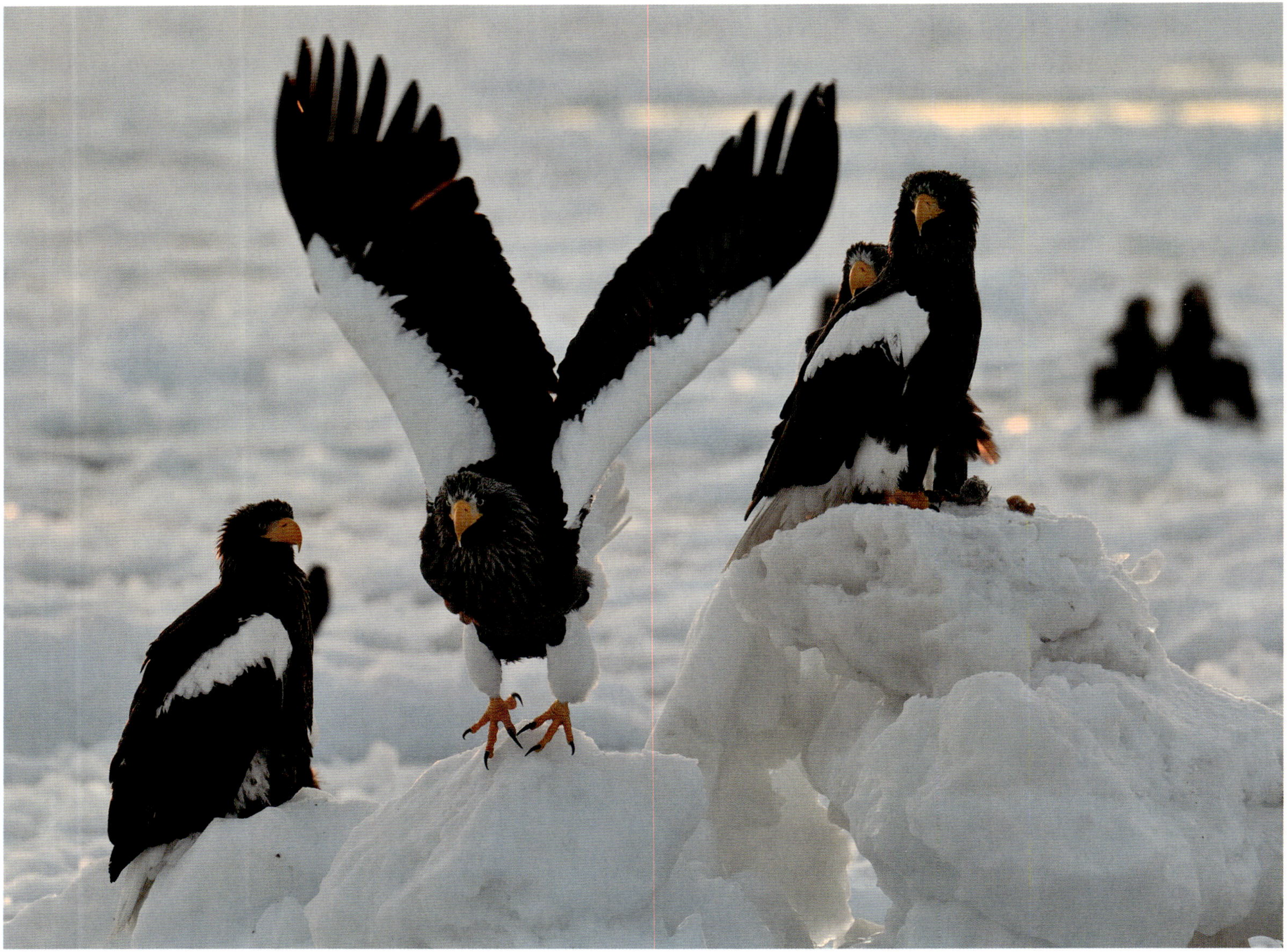

Jari Peltomäki

drift ice. The photo trips last about four hours, depending on how long it takes the boats to reach the drift ice. Sometimes it takes just 10 minutes, other times it can take well over an hour.

When the weather is clear I recommend taking the 5:00 boat. The eagles can be photographed with the sunrise in the background, and in general, the light is much nicer than later on. If it is cloudy, the 9:00 trip might be better. After you have reached the drift ice, the fishermen choose the highest peak and cover it with fish guts. Then they drive back a little and wait for the gulls, Large-billed Crows, and eagles to come and feed on the fish. By the time the eagles have come in by the dozens, the boats start to slowly move closer again. On the 5:00 trip, the sun rises about this time, so the eagles are backlit. By the time the sun has risen above the horizon, the boat is very close to the eagles and it's time to use a 500mm telephoto lens to take extreme closeups of Steller's Sea-Eagles and White-tailed Eagles. On my first trip I couldn't believe how the eagles were not the least bit worried about the 10 or so photographers bustling about on the boat deck.

On the boat I prefer using a monopod and a Wimberley Sidekick. The monopod takes the weight of the camera and makes following the flying eagles easier than when handholding the camera. The boat engines are switched off for long periods of time while the eagles are feeding, so the deck is not vibrating all the time. A monopod is easier in a crowd than a tripod.

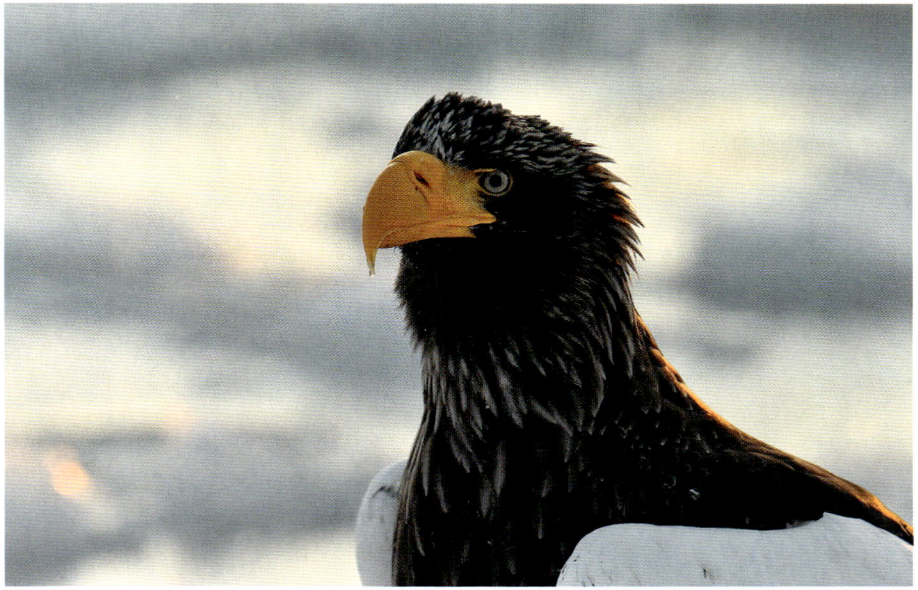

Jari Peltomäki

This backlit profile of a Steller's Sea-Eagle was photographed on an early morning boat trip from Rausu *(Haliaeetus pelagicus)*. The only way to get this close to the eagles on Hokkaidō is from a boat. Nikon D3S, 500mm f/4, 1/2000 second, f/8.0, ISO 6400, one-shot focus with one focusing point, Gitzo monopod with Wimberley Sidekick. Rausu, Hokkaidō, February 2010.

During the morning session the eagles get fed from several ice floes. Usually the fishermen throw fish from the boat into the open sea, and some of the eagles come fishing for them. Having photographed eagles at close range from a Japanese boat, I swore I would never again spend a single day in a White-tailed Eagle blind in Finland, but I have to admit my resolution did not last long. The material from a blind is just completely different.

Jari Peltomäki

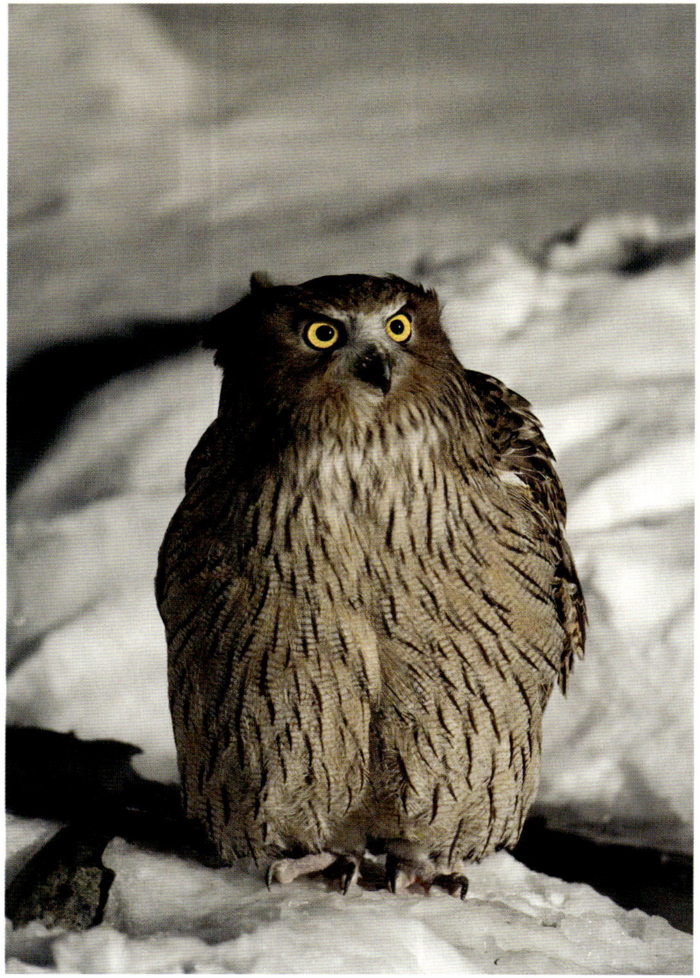

A Blakiston's Fish-Owl spotlighted by halogen lamps *(Ketupa blakistoni)*. Additional light hits the bird from fellow photographers' flashes.
Canon EOS-1D Mark III, 500mm f/4, 1/40 second, f/4.0, ISO 3200, one-shot focus with one focusing point, beanbag on car window. Washinado-yado, Hokkaidō, February 2008.

Blakiston's Fish-Owl

The rare Blakiston's Fish-Owl is a dream species to every bird photographer traveling to Hokkaidō.

On the shores of a river crossing the yard of the Japanese Washino-yado inn just outside the township of Rausu stands an old bus acting as a heated blind for photographers. Blakiston's Fish-Owls can also be photographed from a car, but good locations are few and far between, so you should negotiate with the innkeeper to get a specific parking spot, and get there with plenty of time before sunset. The Blakiston's Fish-Owls are fed with fish in pools made among the rocks in the river, and the owls' fishing activities look very natural. The fishing area is lit by spotlights and the use of flash is banned. Usually these large and magnificent owls announce their arrival with deep hollow hoots. During the night several owls may visit the location, but sometimes it's a long wait for just one bird.

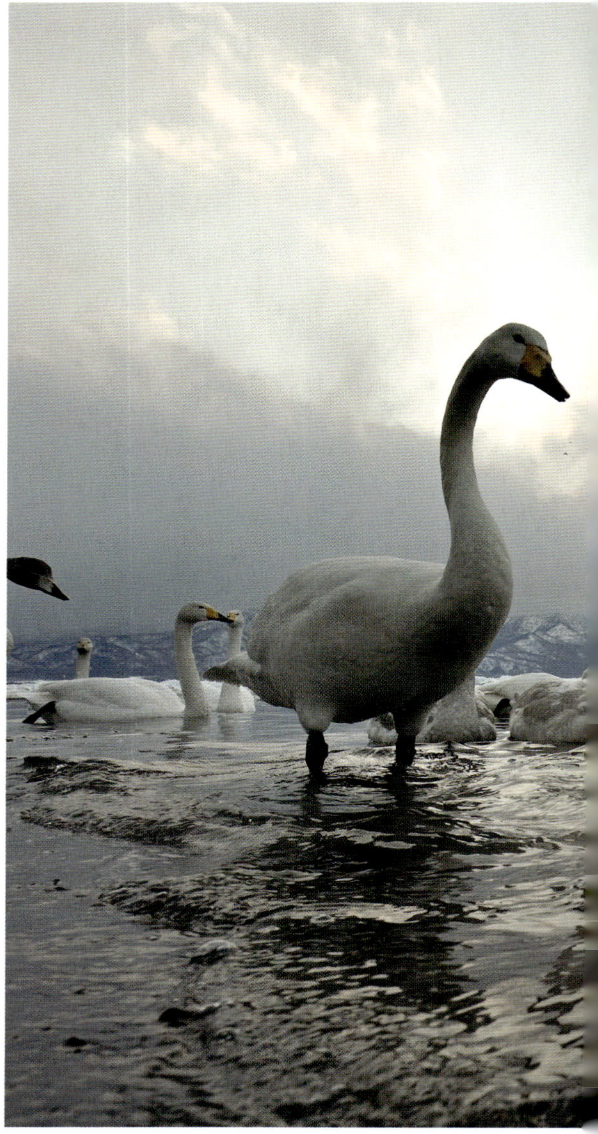

Whooper Swans are fed in winter on Lake Kussharo, where they can be photographed with wide lenses *(Cygnus cygnus)*
Nikon D3S, 14–24mm, 1/320 second, 19mm, f/13.0, ISO 1600, continuous focus with 51 focusing points, handheld camera. Lake Kussharo, Hokkaidō, February 2010.

Jari Peltomäki

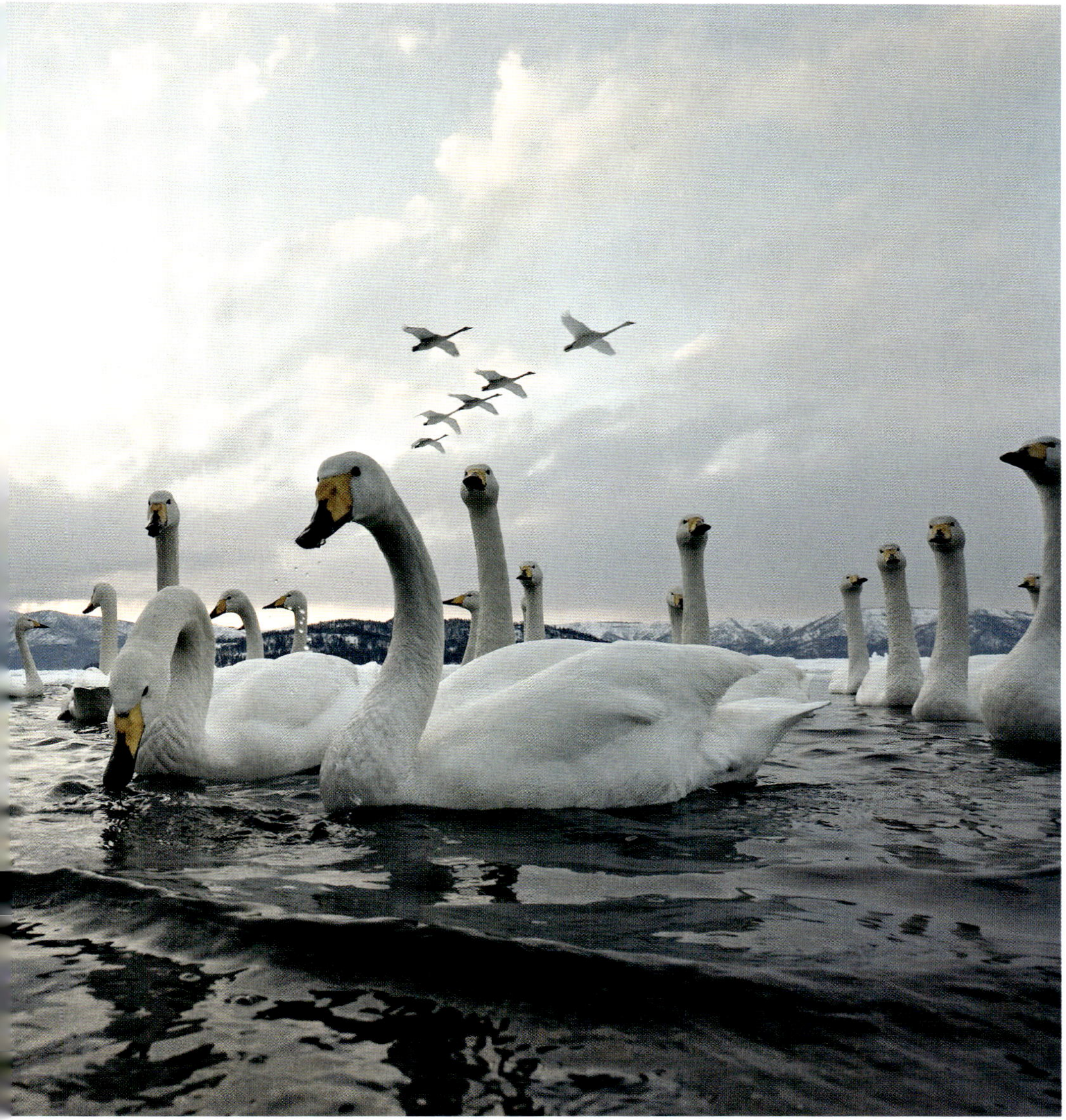

Lake Kussharo

Whooper Swans winter all over Hokkaidō, but Lake Kussharo is probably one of the most famous spots. The shores stay open with heat coming from hot springs, and the swans are also being fed. You can shop locally for grain and bread crumbs to feed them. It's the feeding that makes the swans so approachable on Hokkaidō. In February 2010, the fearless and photographer-friendly Lake Kussharo swans inspired and amused Hannu Hautala, the Grand Old Man of Finnish wildlife photography who has more swan photography under his belt than he cares to remember.

The Grand Old Man of Finnish nature photography, Hannu Hautala, is surrounded by the confident and cooperative Lake Kussharo swans.

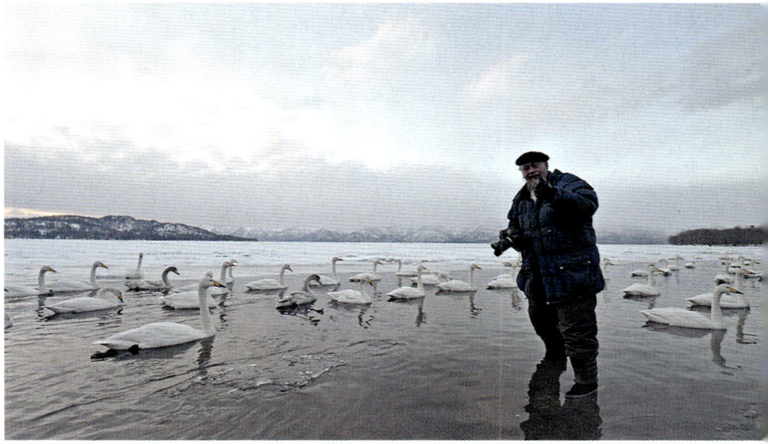

JARI PELTOMÄKI

LAKE KERKINI, GREECE

Lake Kerkini is the best place in the world to photograph Dalmatian Pelicans.

Lake Kerkini is in north Greece close to the Bulgarian border. It's a 110 km^2 (42.5 mi^2) reservoir that was formed in 1932 on a large flood plain of the River Strymon when the river was dammed. The river brings in silt that has created a large delta on the lake. The regulated water level varies about 5 m (16.4 ft) in a year; the highest level is in summer and the lowest level is at the end of autumn. When the water is low, the alluvial deposits are exposed and attract the migrating birds to land for rest, and some birds winter there. Fish-eating birds find a lot of food in the shallow waters.

Lake Kerkini is one of Greece's most valuable wetlands. Many endangered or rare European species breed there. More than 300 species have been observed on the lake and in the neighboring areas, with more than 140 of them breeding in the area. Nesting platforms have been built for Dalmatian Pelicans, and now this endangered species belongs to the area's breeding avifauna.

A big colony of Great and Pygmy Cormorants, Egrets (Great, Little, and Eurasian Spoonbill), Herons (Gray, Black-crowned Night, Squacco, and Purple), and Glossy Ibis breed on the River Strymon delta. Boat trips to the area are great in the winter because that's when it's easy to photograph Great Cormorants and Gray Herons in their breeding plumages, and you can sometimes see Spotted Eagles as they circle in the sky. The Dalmatian Pelicans' nesting platforms are near the river delta, and the birds start to claim their nests already in February. They must not be approached because disturbance can cause the pelicans to abandon their nests.

Up to 130 species can be seen on the lake and the neighboring areas in winter; the number of birds wintering on Lake Kerkini is huge. The lake is also one of the main wintering locations in Europe for the endangered Lesser White-fronted Geese.

In winter the lake's southern part gathers Dalmatian Pelicans, gulls, Great Cormorants, Pygmy Cormorants, and grebes as they follow the fishing boats in hopes of catching some food. The easiest place for observing them is in the village harbor in Lithotopos and near the fishing huts close to the village. The pelicans can be photographed at close range when the fishermen bring fish onto the shore; the pelicans follow the fishing boats on the lake like a pack of

A Dalmatian Pelican *(Pelecanus crispus)*
Canon EOS-1D Mark III, 500mm f/4.0, 1/500 second, f/9.0, ISO 800, manual focus, Gitzo tripod, Manfrotto 501 video head. Lake Kerkini, Greece, January 2009.

Jari Peltomäki/Wild Wonders of Europe

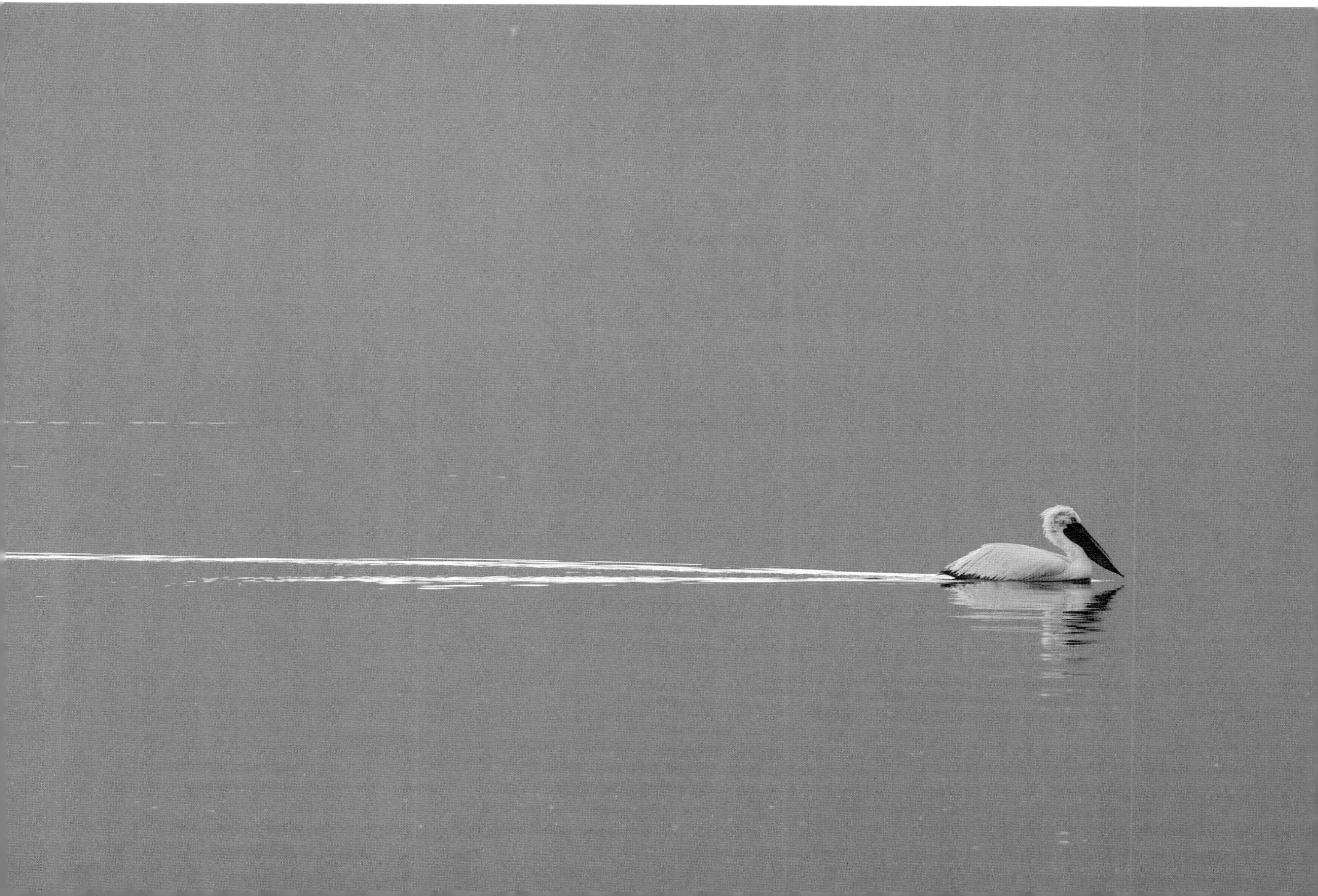

Dalmatian Pelicans, from young to old *(Pelecanus crispus)*
Canon EOS-1D Mark II, 500mm f/4.0 plus 1.4x extender, 1/1000 second, f/14.0, ISO 200, continuous focus with 45 focusing points, Gitzo tripod, Manfrotto 501 video head. Lake Kerkini, Greece, January 2005.

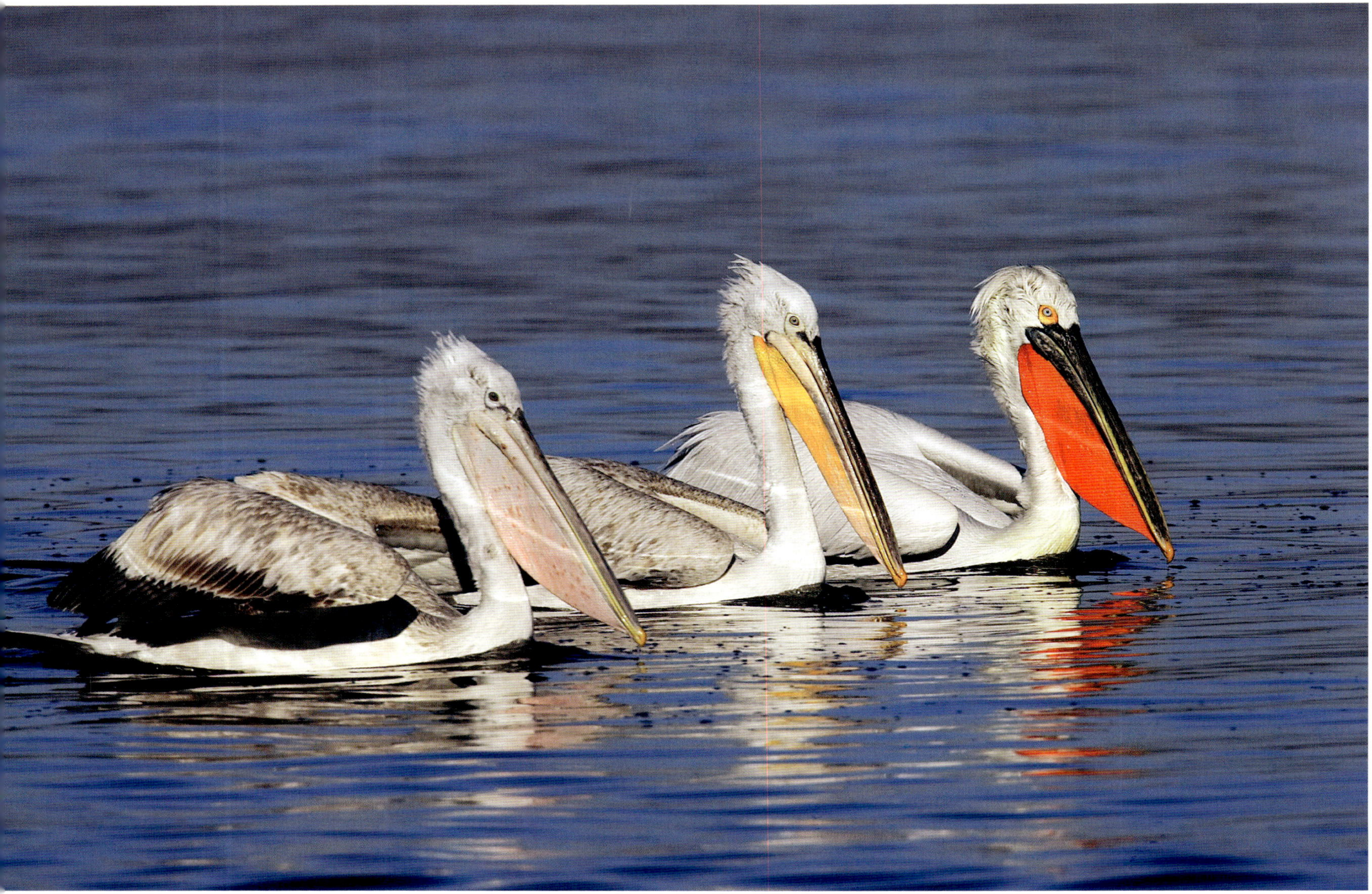

Jari Peltomäki

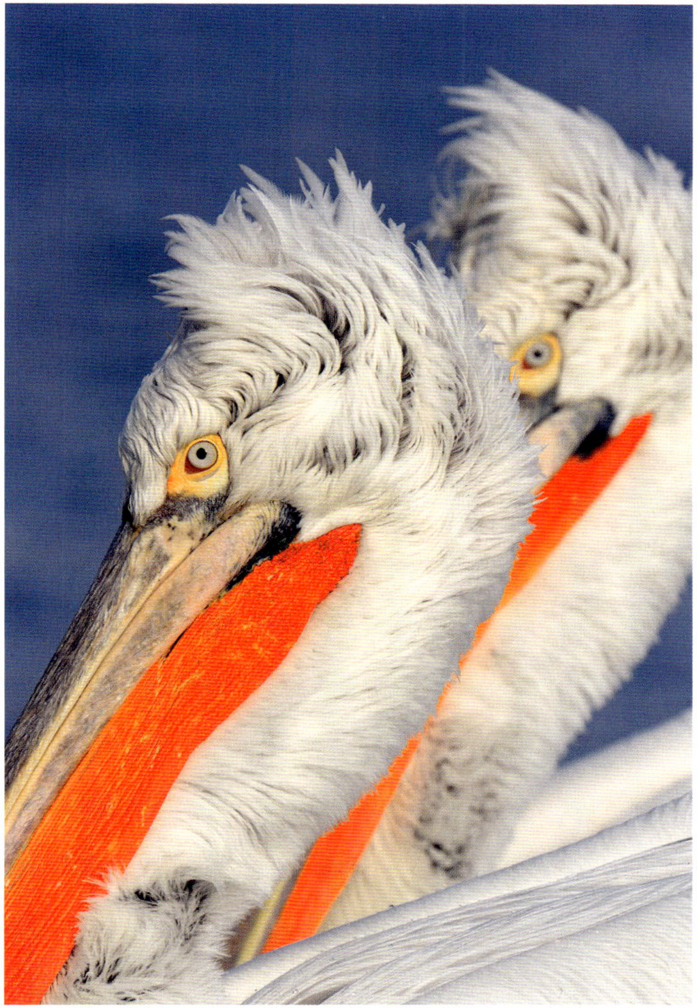

Dalmatian Pelicans posing *(Pelecanus crispus)*
Nikon D3S, 500mm f/4.0 plus 1.7x extender, 1/2000 second, f/14.0, ISO 1600, continuous focus with 51 focusing points, Gitzo tripod, Manfrotto 501 video head. Lake Kerkini, Greece, January 2010.

dogs. The fishermen don't mind giving a share of their catch to the pelicans, but you can also buy some of the fish and feed it to the pelicans—more food for the birds and better photo opportunities for the photographer. I've been on Lake Kerkini several times over the years, and January and February are good for photographing the Dalmatian Pelicans.

Lake Kerkini is quite easy to get to. The nearest airport is in Thessaloniki, where you can rent a car. It takes about two hours to drive to the lake. The Kerkini Wetland Information Centre, where you can see an exhibit about the lake and get brochures with more information, is in the Kerkini village on the western shore and is open in the morning.

There are accommodations and places to eat everywhere. I've stayed in the Oikoperiigitis hotel in Kerkini village (www.kerkinihotel.com) and the Erodios hotel in Lithotopos village (www.hotel-erodios.com). Erodios is closer to the best pelican areas, whereas the Oikoperiigitis is closer to the River Strymon delta. You can book boat trips on the river at the hotel, and a local guide named Dimitris Vavylis is a good contact when negotiating with the fishermen; he can also help organize a photo trip in the area. You can find out more about Dimitris on his website (www.wildmoments.gr).

Jari Peltomäki

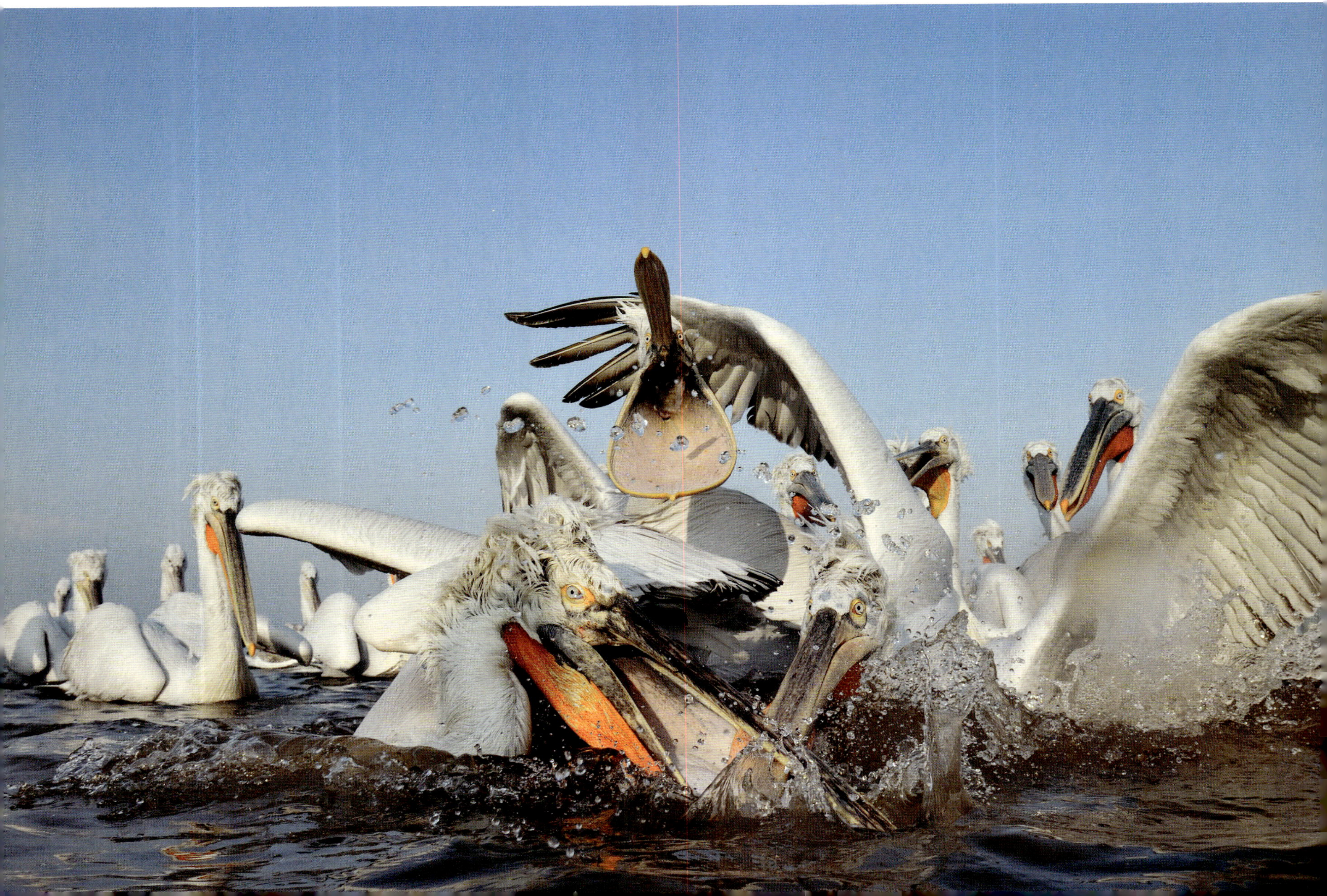

JARI PELTOMÄKI

BOSQUE DEL APACHE, NEW MEXICO

The Bosque is an excellent place to practice taking flock images.

The Bosque del Apache National Wildlife Refuge is in Socorro, in the Rio Grande Valley in New Mexico. Snow Geese and Ross's Geese winter there, numbering in the tens of thousands, and also about 10,000 Sandhill Cranes. The place offers great opportunities for taking flock images, as well as portraits and flight shots. The birds are fearless and feed confidently near photographers standing calmly by their tripods. When I was trying to find a really low angle to shoot from, I noticed that the birds were not used to people lying on the ground; they were very suspicious of me because I was behaving differently. The more openly the photographer was in sight, the closer the birds came! After the wariness of the birds in Europe, this was decidedly delightful.

Bosque del Apache has fairly large areas of fresh water, where the geese and cranes roost. The birds seem to favor certain areas over others, and this changes from one year to another. Make sure to get out early, a couple of hours before sunrise, because the beautiful sunrises can take your breath away, especially if there are clouds in the sky. Besides, if you're not out early enough, you'll probably miss the spectacle of the geese bursting up into the sky en masse. With a bit of luck, you may be in the right place at the right time—it's a fabulous moment to have thousands of Snow Geese flying just a few yards over your head!

The geese and cranes are fed at the refuge, and the corn is grown in large fields along its edge. Sometimes the birds feed right by the side of the road, where you can try your hand at flight shots. Throughout the day there may be huge flocks lifting off simultaneously; the coyotes and the Bald Eagles take their fair share from the throngs, and when they hunt, they scare the flocks up into the air.

Large numbers of waterbirds and raptors winter in Bosque del Apache. When you drive along the roads inside the refuge you come across many species, and you can use your car as a blind to photograph species such as Northern Shovelers, Northern Pintails, American Wigeons, American Kestrels, Red-tailed Hawks, and Northern Harriers. The Greater Roadrunner is also a common sight along the roads inside the refuge and is best photographed from the car.

Bosque del Apache is teeming with wintering birds from October to March, and most of the visiting photographers come in November and December. The annual week-long Festival of the Cranes is held in November, with up to 10,000 visiting photographers. The visitor center has feeding stations and you can photograph such species as Gambel's Quail, White-crowned Sparrow, and Red-winged Blackbird.

Dalmatian Pelicans reaching for fish and splashing water on my lens *(Pelecanus crispus)*
Nikon D3S, 24–70mm f/2.8, 1/2000 second, 24mm, f/11.0, ISO 1600, continuous focus with 51 focusing points, ground pod, Manfrotto 501 video head. Lake Kerkini, Greece, January 2010.

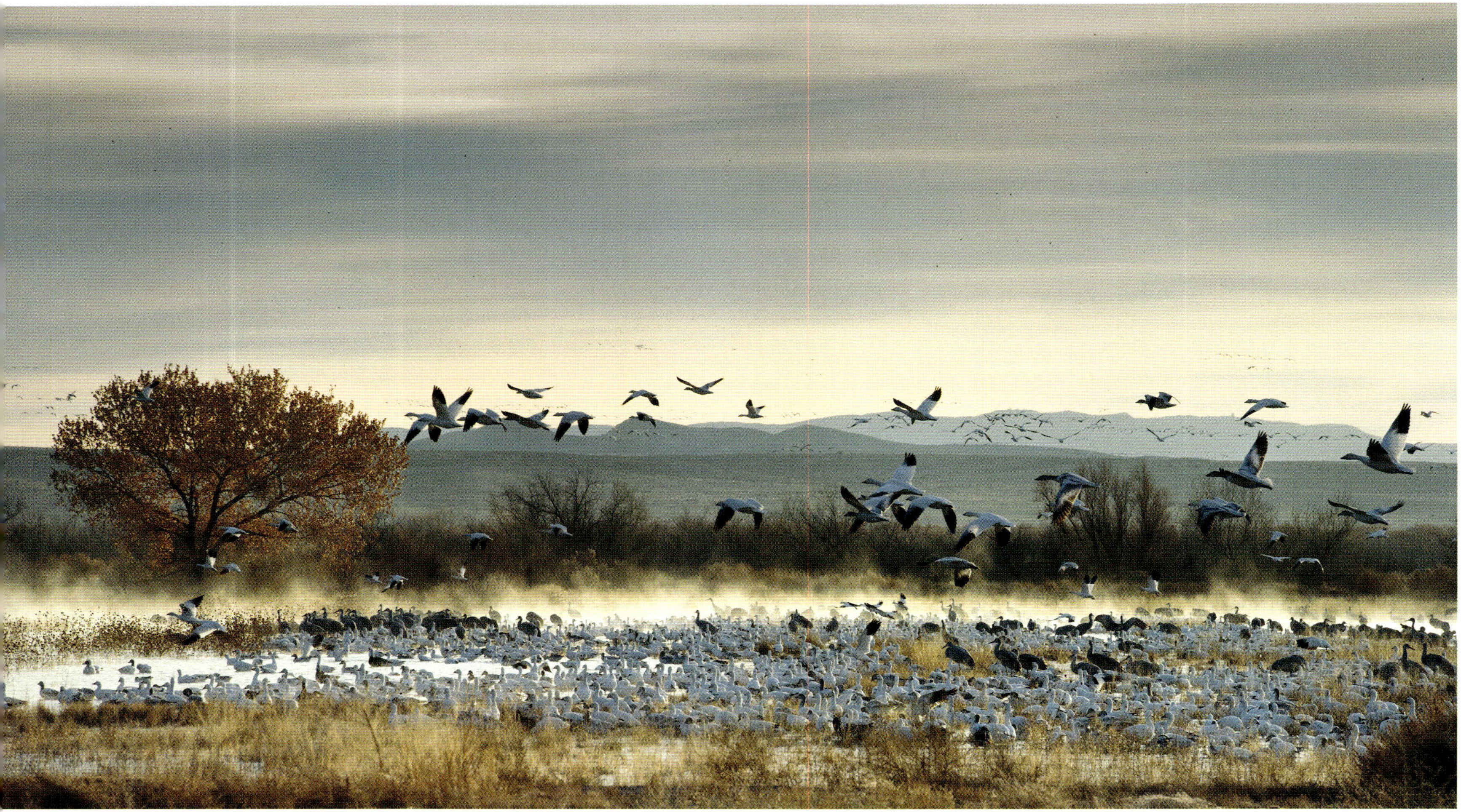

Jari Peltomäki

After the cold night, a mist rises from the warm water; the mist shows up especially well when backlit
Nikon D3S, 70–200mm f/2.8, 1/2000 second, 200mm, f/10.0, ISO 1600, handheld camera. New Mexico, December 2010.

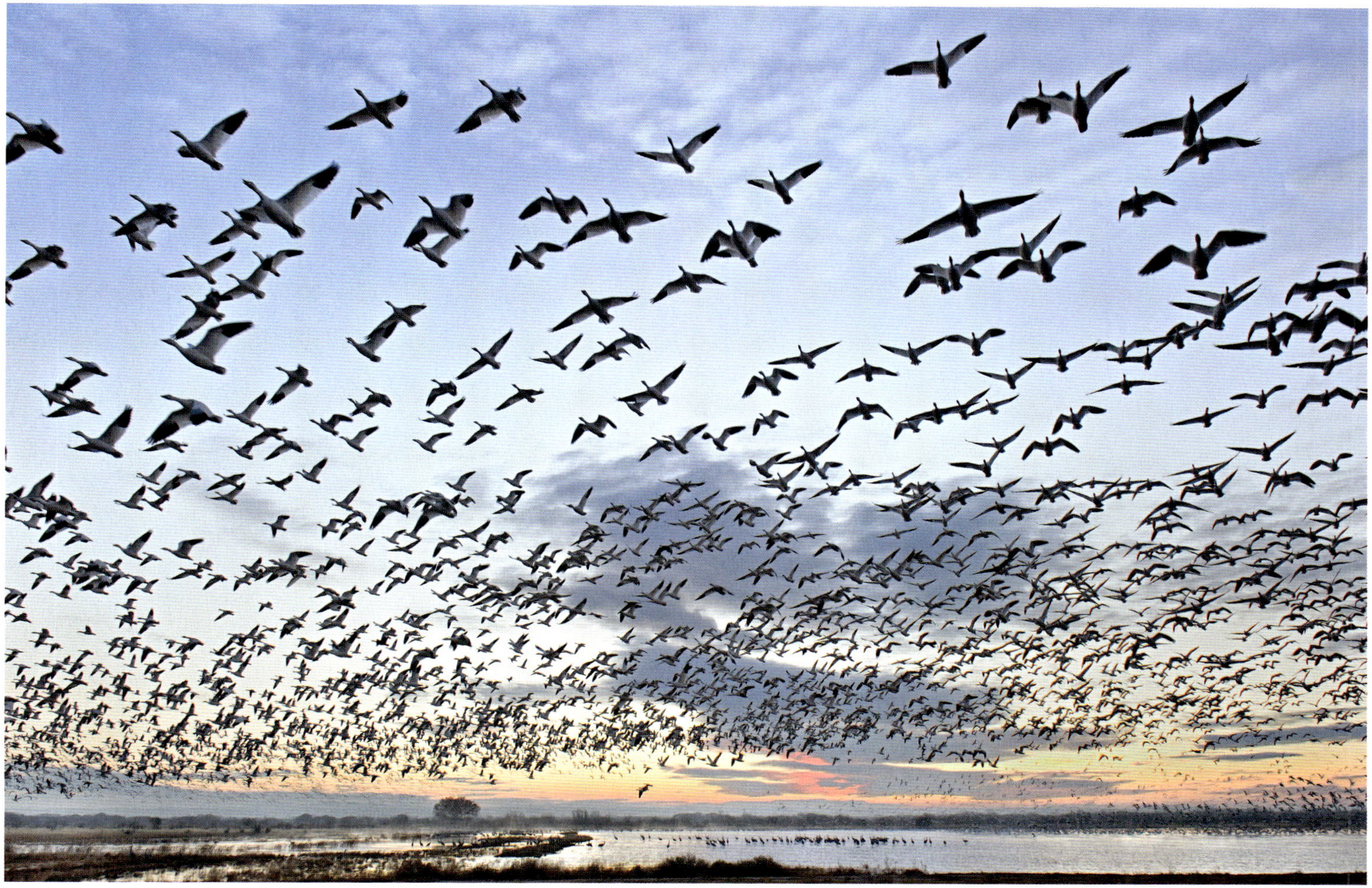

Jari Peltomäki

Early morning flight of Snow Geese in superb conditions *(Chen caerulescens)*
Nikon D3S, 24–70mm f/2.8, 1/400 second, 24mm, f/6.3, ISO 3200, handheld camera. New Mexico, December 2010.

Jari Peltomäki

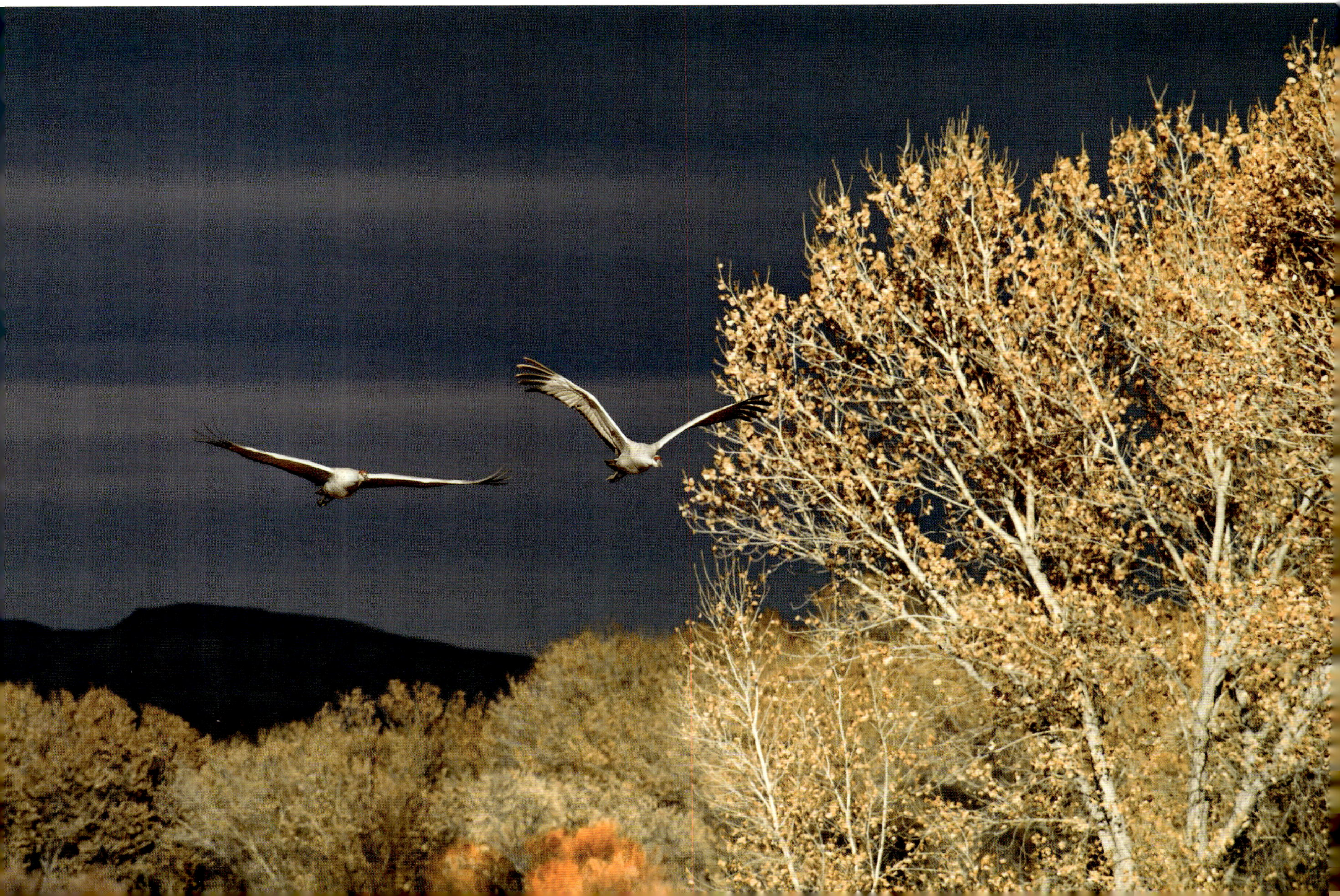

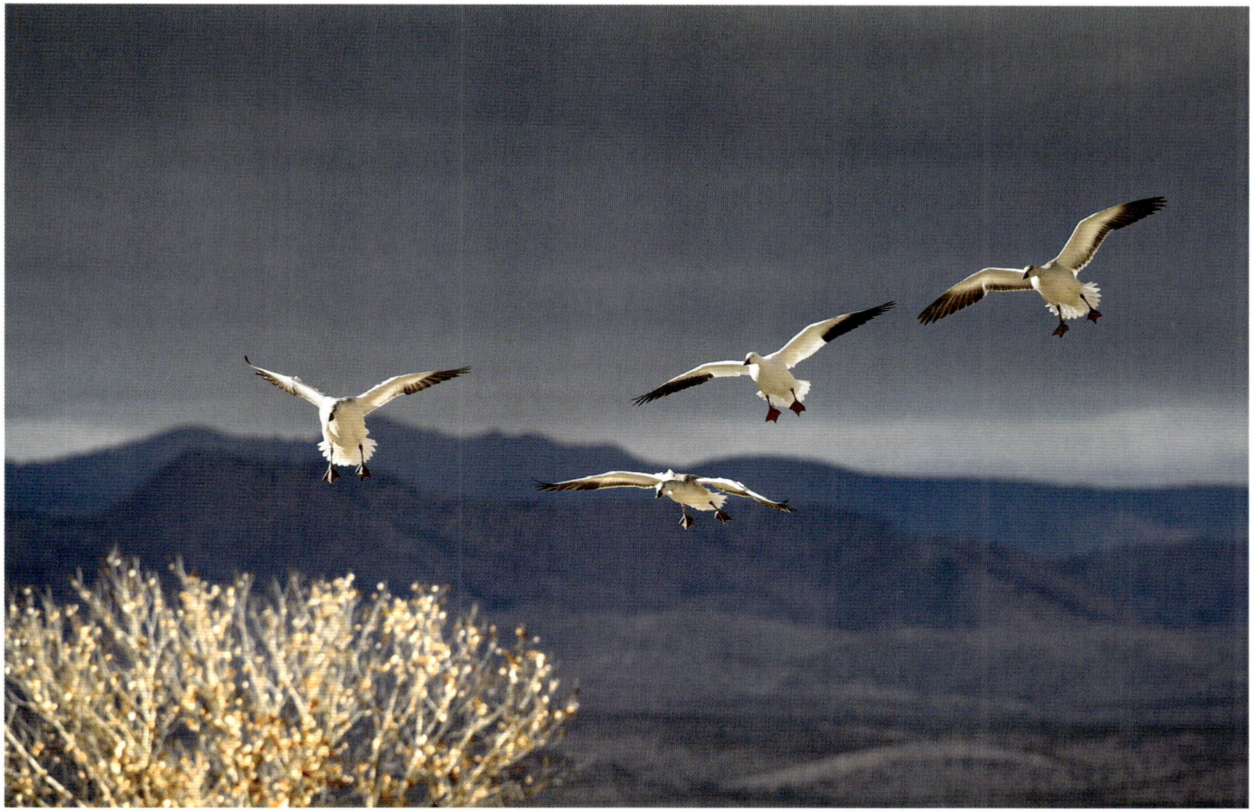

Jari Peltomäki

Snow Geese landing in a field to feed ***(Chen caerulescens)***
Nikon D3S, 200–400mm f/4.0, 1/1250 second, 400mm, f/6.3, ISO 400, Gitzo tripod, Manfrotto 701 video head. New Mexico, December 2010.

Sandhill Cranes heading toward their roosting grounds ***(Grus canadensis)***
Nikon D3S, 200–400mm f/4.0, 1/2000 second, 400mm, f/10.0, ISO 800, Gitzo tripod, Manfrotto 701 video head. New Mexico, December 2010.

Sandhill Cranes flying back to the feeding fields from their roosts in early morning light *(Grus canadensis)*

Nikon D3S, 200–400mm f/4.0, 1/1250 second, 200mm, f/8.0, ISO 800, Gitzo tripod, Manfrotto 701 video head. New Mexico, December 2010.

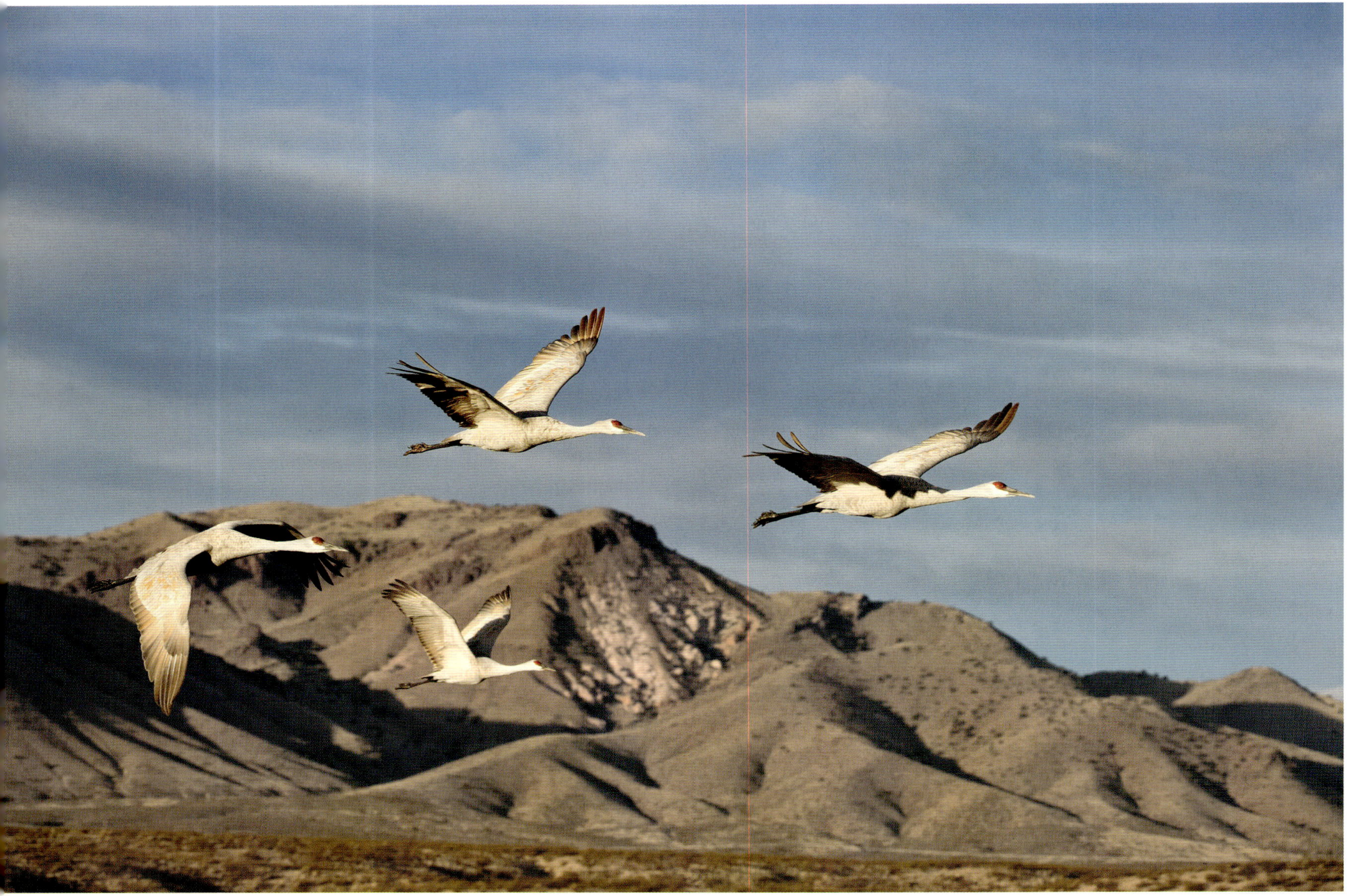

Jari Peltomäki

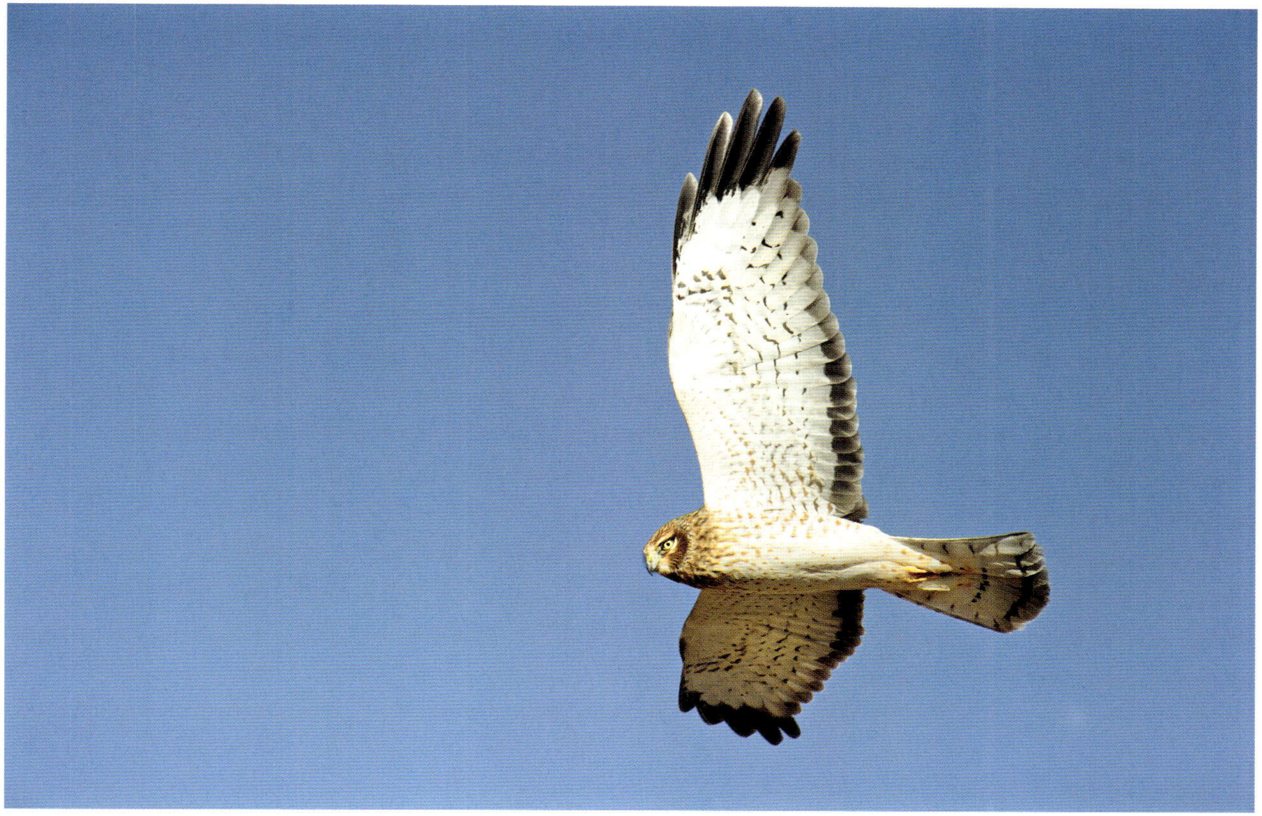

Jari Peltomäki

Northern Harriers along the roads of the refuge are quite easily photographed from the car *(Circus cyaneus)*

Nikon D3S, 200–400mm f/4.0 plus 1.4x extender, 1/3200 second, 560mm, f/8.0, ISO 800, car as a blind. New Mexico, December 2010.

Jari Peltomäki

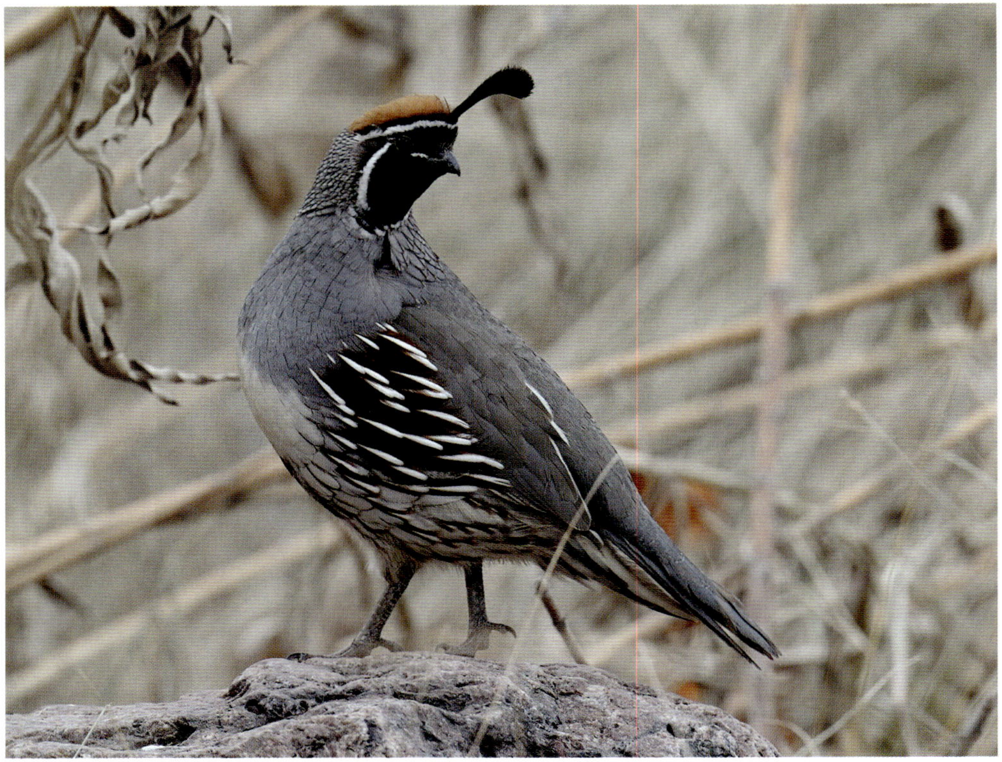

Gambel's Quail at the visitor center's feeding station *(Callipepla gambelii)*
Nikon D3S, 200–400mm f/4.0, 1/1250 second, 400mm, f/8.0, ISO 800, Gitzo tripod, Manfrotto 701 video head. New Mexico, December 2010.

There is also a feeding pond behind the New Mexico Institute of Mining and Technology in Socorro where you can photograph American Wigeons, American Coots, and Ring-necked Ducks at close range. The city parks with their berry trees and bushes draw berry-eating birds in winter, such as American Robins and Cedar Waxwings.

The closest decent-sized airport is in Albuquerque, which is a couple of hours' drive from Socorro, where you can find accommodations and restaurants. The drive from Socorro to the Bosque takes about 30 minutes (about 40 km/25 mi).

Arthur Morris, one of the world's leading bird photographers, organizes hugely popular photo tours to the Bosque every November. Those wanting to travel on their own can buy Arthur's very useful Bosque Site Guide from his online store (https://store.birdsasart.com/shop). The PDF guide includes annual updates to the best and always changing bird sites!

You can find more information about Bosque del Apache at www.friendsofthebosque.org.

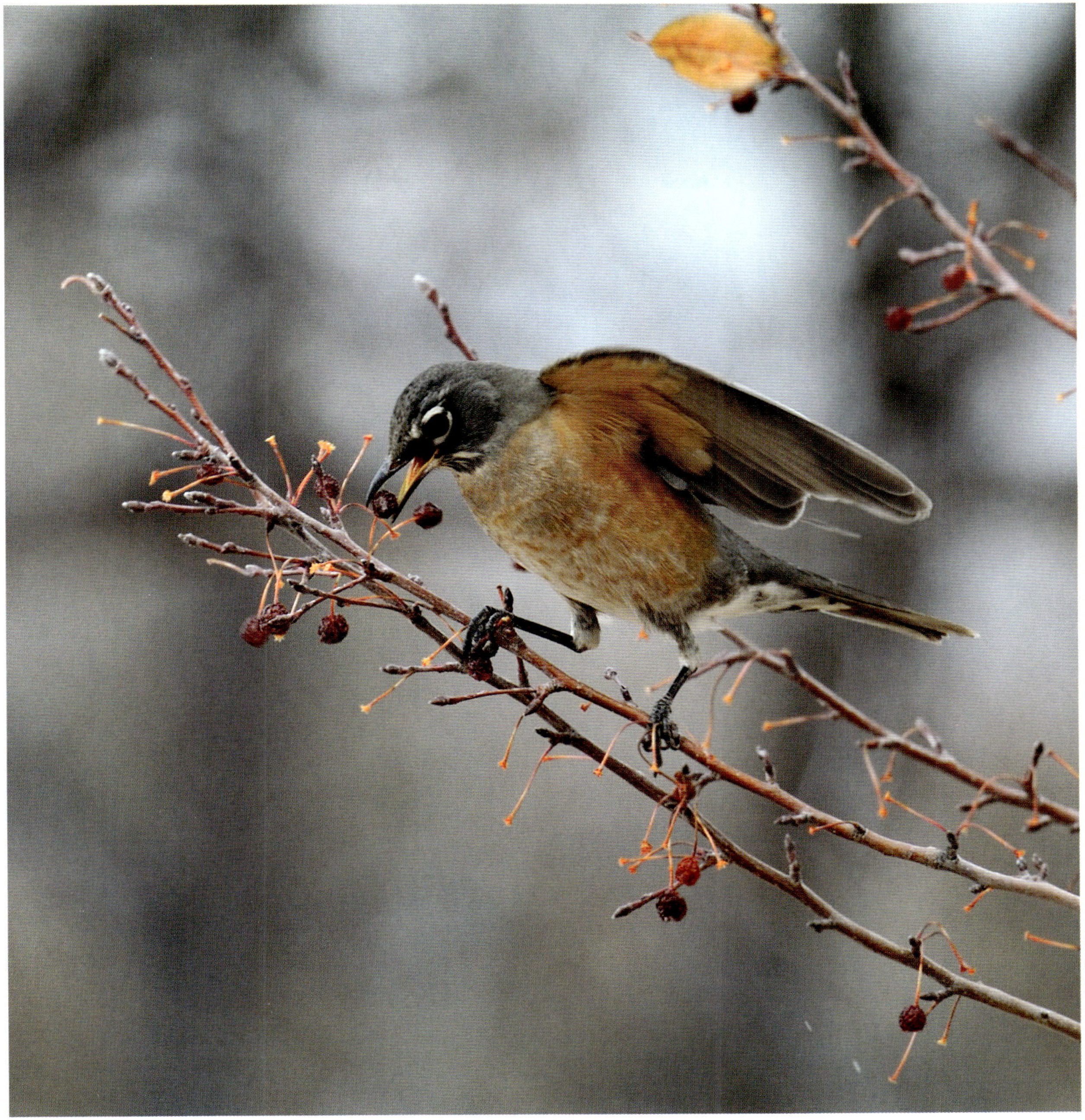

Jari Peltomäki

An American Robin feeding in one of the city parks in Socorro *(Turdus migratorius)*
Nikon D3S, 200–400mm f/4.0, 1/1250 second, 400mm, f/8.0, ISO 800, Gitzo tripod, Manfrotto 701 video head. New Mexico, December 2010.

BENCE MÁTÉ

HUNGARY

Hungary has many areas with abundant bird life; the Hortobágy and Kiskunság National Parks are in the top league in Europe.

Hortobágy

The Hortobágy National Park is not only a UNESCO World Heritage site, it's also a veritable treasure trove to bird photographers. On the whole, the park is still an age-old grassland biome, the puszta, and part of the Eurasian steppe that is a habitat for many bird species. Hortobágy is especially famous for its Red-footed Falcons and Great Bustards as well as huge crane flocks that gather in the autumn.

In winter there are good opportunities for blind photography targeting White-tailed Eagles, Imperial Eagles, and Common Buzzards. In the Hortobágy area you can also photograph Little Bitterns, Pygmy Cormorants, Ferruginous Ducks, Middle Spotted Woodpeckers, European Rollers, and European Bee-eaters.

Kiskunság

Even after 12 years as a bird photographer, and having photographed in more than 15 countries, I can still say that my favorite location is the region where I have lived since I was born. The Kiskunság National Park has one of the most varied avifaunas in Europe. Seasonal changes give each month some particular phenomenon that makes it easy to

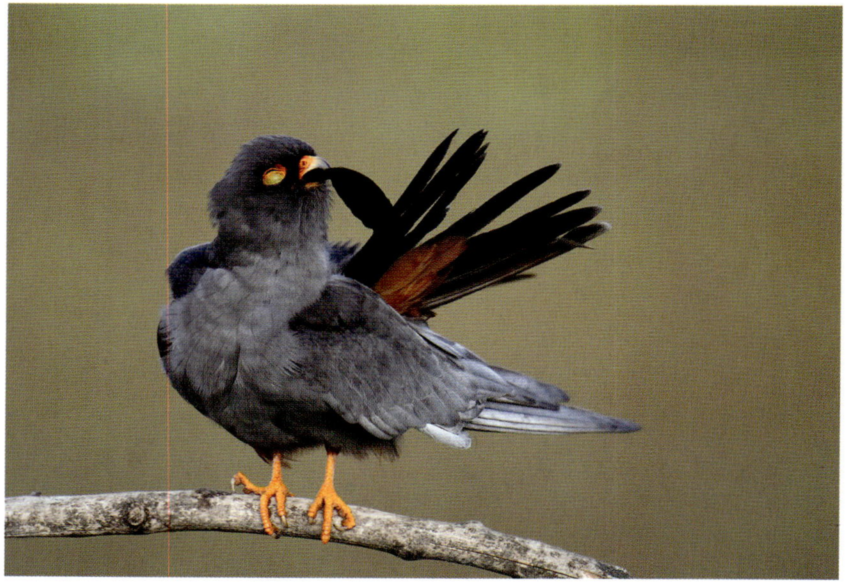

Markus Varesvuo/Wild Wonders of Europe

Hortobágy is well known for Red-footed Falcons *(Falco vespertinus)*
Canon EOS-1D Mark III, 500mm f/4.0, 1/500 second, f/4.0, ISO 1600, one-shot focus with a central focusing point, Gitzo tripod, Manfrotto 501 video head, blind. Hortobágy, Hungary, May 2008.

Great Reed-Warbler fishing *(Acrocephalus arundinaceus)*
Nikon D700, 300mm f/2.8, 1/60 second, f/8.0, ISO 640, manual focus, Gitzo video head, floating blind. Pusztaszer, Hungary, 2010.

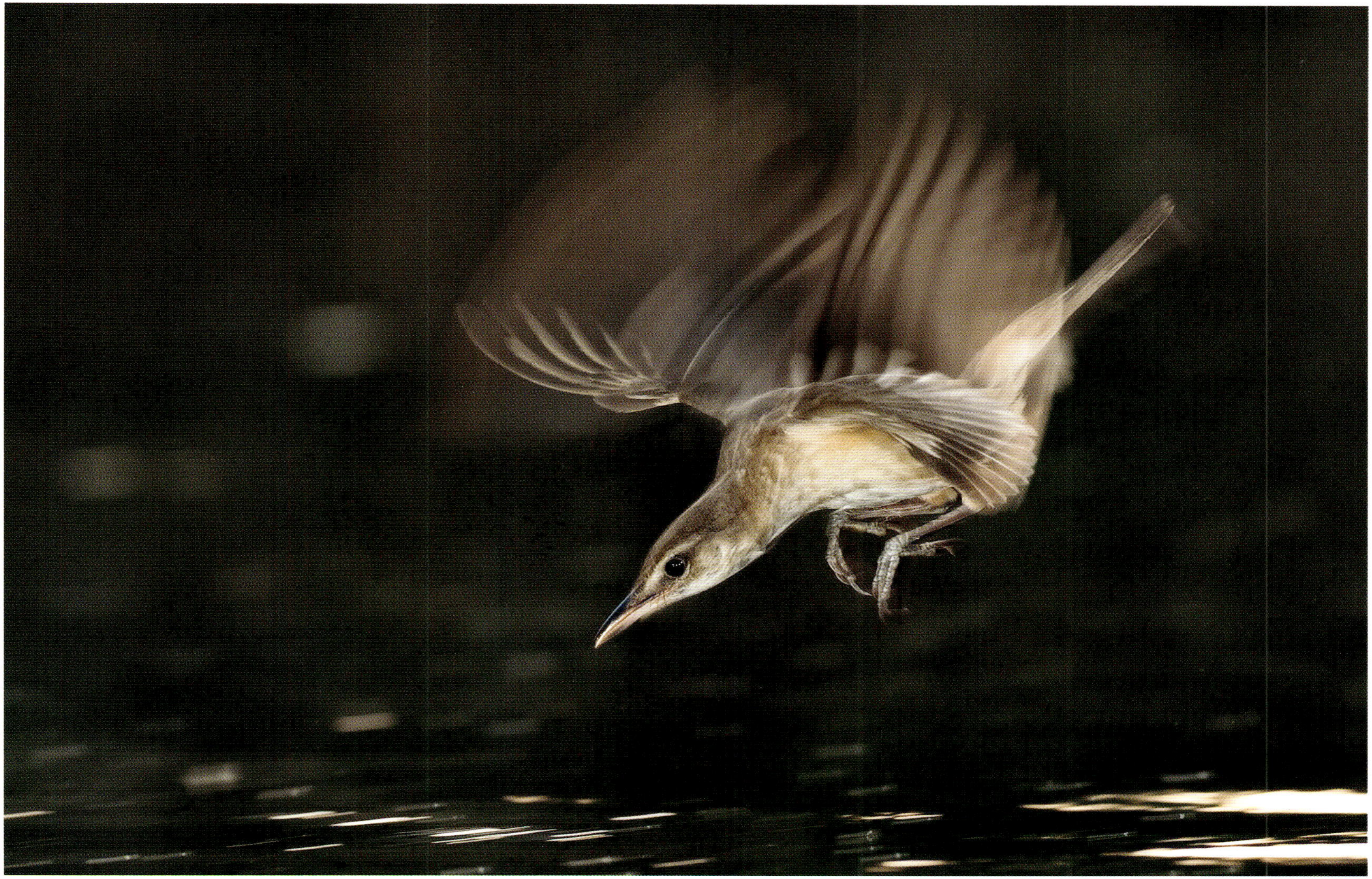

Bence Máté

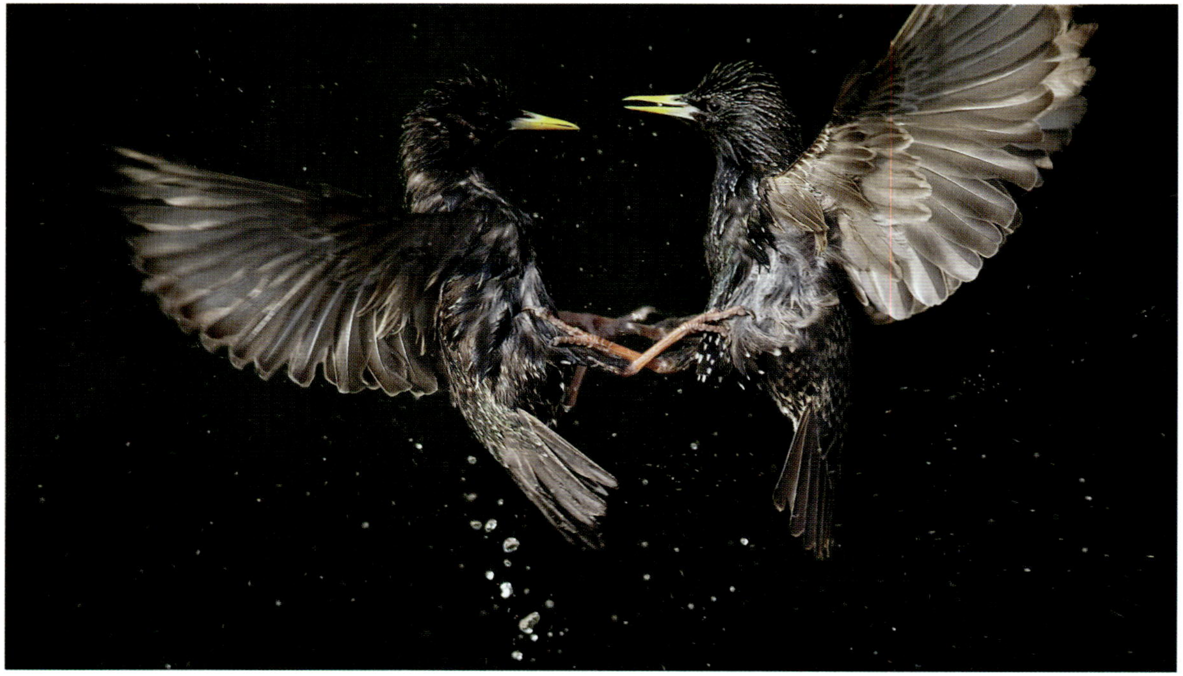

It's possible to see and photograph more than 40 species at the drinking station blinds. European Starlings *(Sturnus vulgaris)*.
Canon EOS-1D Mark III, 300mm f/2.8, 1/1600 second, f/2.8, ISO 1600, prefocus, Gitzo tripod, Manfrotto 501 video head, blind. Pusztaszer, Hungary, May 2008.

Markus Varesvuo/Wild Wonders of Europe

plan many different types of photography projects.

I organize photography trips in the Kiskunság area, where I have renovated an old farm into a nature photography center. We're about 140 km (87 mi) southeast of Budapest in an area with forests, wetlands, and steppes. The distances between the locations are short. High season starts around April 20 and slows down in the second week of June.

In the past couple of years I have built numerous photo blinds in the area; the best include the following:

- Six forest blinds with drinking ponds, each of which gets about 15–20 species and between 100 and 1,000 individuals on a daily basis. The most interesting species are Eurasian Sparrow Hawk, Northern Goshawk, Common Nightingale, Hawfinch, European Turtle Dove, European Green Woodpecker, and Black Woodpecker.
- A tower blind in the farmyard with good opportunities to photograph Common Kestrels and European Rollers that nest in boxes mounted near the blind. Other species that frequently visit the tree canopies next to the tower are Common Cuckoos and Eurasian Golden Orioles.

There are excellent opportunities in Kiskunság for almost all European egret and heron species. Little Bittern *(Ixobrychus minutus)*.
Nikon D300, 300mm f/2.8, 1/3200 second, f/4.0, ISO 640, manual focus, Gitzo video head, floating blind. Pusztaszer, Hungary, 2009.

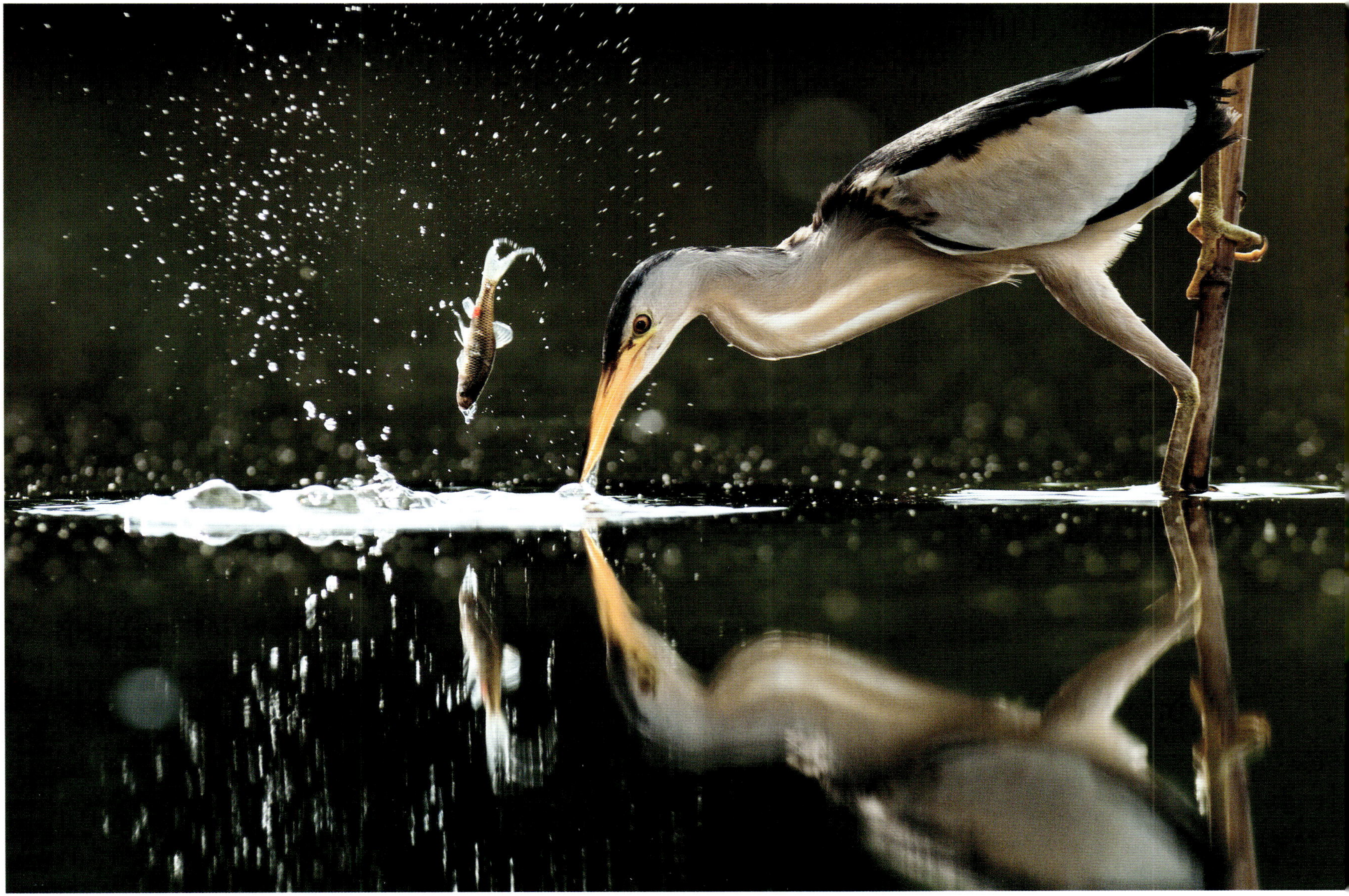

Bence Máté

Markus Varesvuo/Wild Wonders of Europe

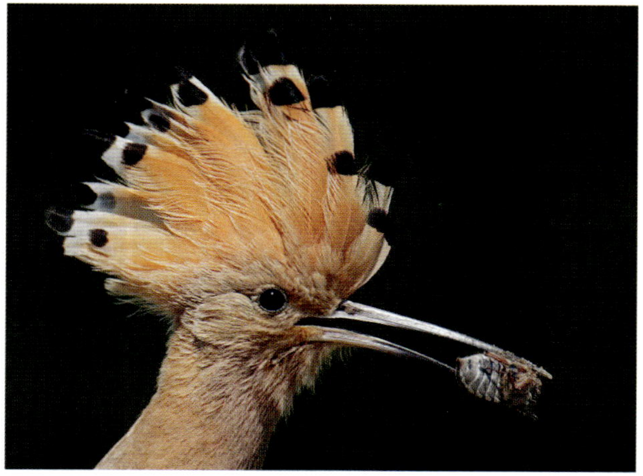

Eurasian Hoopoes can be discreetly observed and photographed at close range from the blinds *(Upupa epops)*
Canon EOS-1Ds Mark III, 500mm f/4.0 plus 2x extender, 1/640 second, f/10.0, ISO 500, one-shot focus with a central focusing point, Gitzo tripod, Manfrotto 501 video head, blind. Pusztaszer, Hungary, May 2008.

Bence Máté

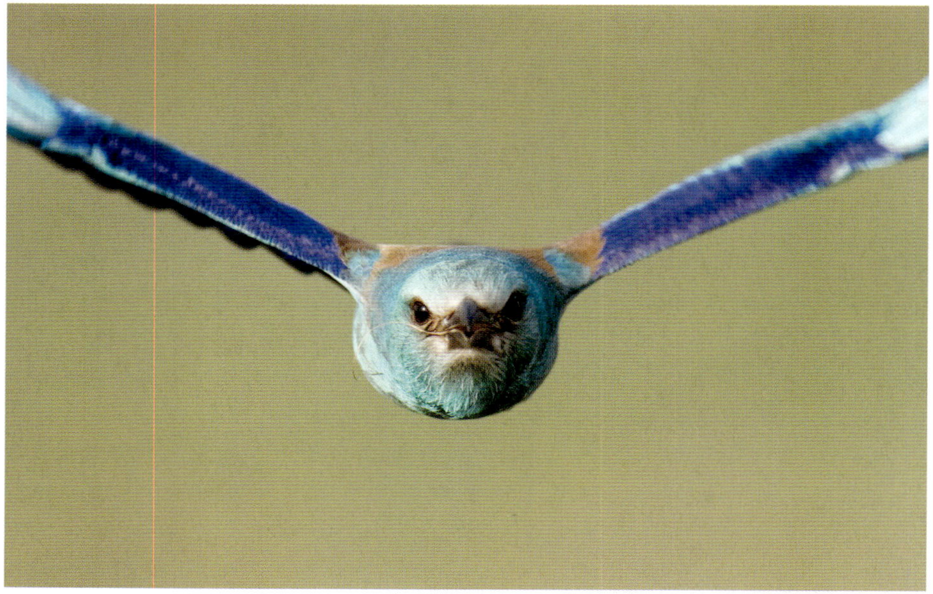

Hungary is ideal for photographing one of Europe's most colorful birds, the European Roller *(Coracias garrulus)*
Nikon D200, 300mm f/2.8, 1/750 second, f/4.0, ISO 400, manual focus, Gitzo tripod and video head, blind. Pusztaszer, Hungary, 2007.

- Two shore blinds by a lake with the largest egret and heron colony in Central Europe. About 500–1,000 pairs of Eurasian Spoonbills; Great and Little Egrets; and Squacco, Gray, Purple, and Night Heron pairs nest on the lake. The blinds have big windows with almost unrestricted views to the birds; the glass is semireflective, so the birds can't see the photographer.
- Two blinds near two nest boxes built for European Rollers. They are ideal for Roller photography.
- Two blinds near two separate Eurasian Hoopoe nest holes. The pairs raise one or two broods each year.

You can also pitch tent blinds in the farmyard, where I have a small nesting colony of about five to seven European Bee-eater pairs.

You can find more information at www.hidephotography.com.

Flight shots of egrets and herons are possible from a semiopen tower blind near the breeding colonies. Purple Heron *(Ardea purpurea)*.
Canon EOS-1D Mark IV, 800mm f/5.6, 1/2500 second, f/8.0, ISO 1250, continuous focus with an extended central focusing point, Gitzo tripod, Manfrotto 501 video head. Pusztaszer, Hungary, June 2010.

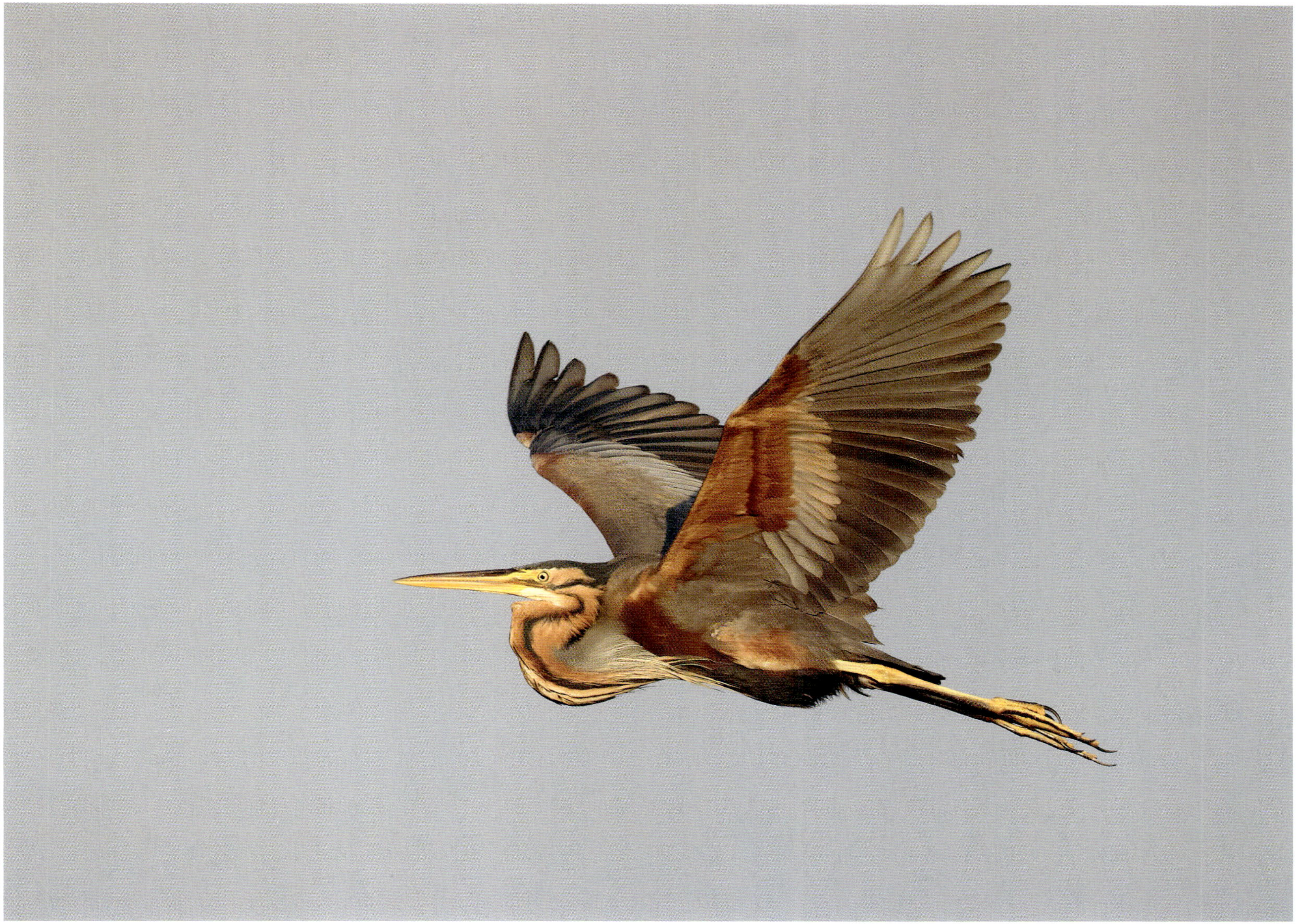

Markus Varesvuo

BENCE MÁTÉ

COSTA RICA

Costa Rica has more than 800 bird species and many different biotopes, including rainforests and the exotic birds that inhabit them.

After completing close to 30 photo blinds in Hungary, I wanted to see if the same concept could work in another location. I set out with a small group of people to Costa Rica, a whopping 10,000 km (6,214 mi) away from my home village, with a plan to build functional, high-quality bird photo blinds.

As a result of our six-month building project, we completed a combination of blinds in the Laguna Del Lagarto area that offer good settings for photographing typical rainforest species—toucans, aracaris, honeycreepers, colibris, and King Vultures—in ideal settings. To attract the world's most colorful vulture, the King Vulture, we built an underground blind and provided carcasses for feeding. And we built four more blinds to attract 15–20 species of birds daily, to within a good photography distance, with bananas and other fruits.

La Laguna Del Lagarto Lodge has 500 hectares of land, and 100 hectares of it is unmanaged rainforest. The lodge offers high-quality accommodations with phone connections (no Internet). You can find more information at www.hidephotography.com.

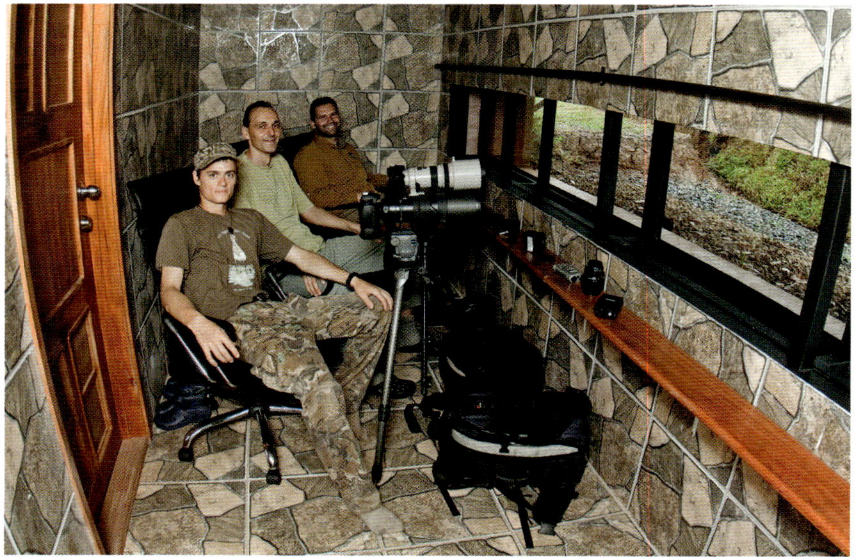

Bence Máté

A view from inside the King Vulture blind. The blinds were built to offer comfortable working conditions.

Bence Máté

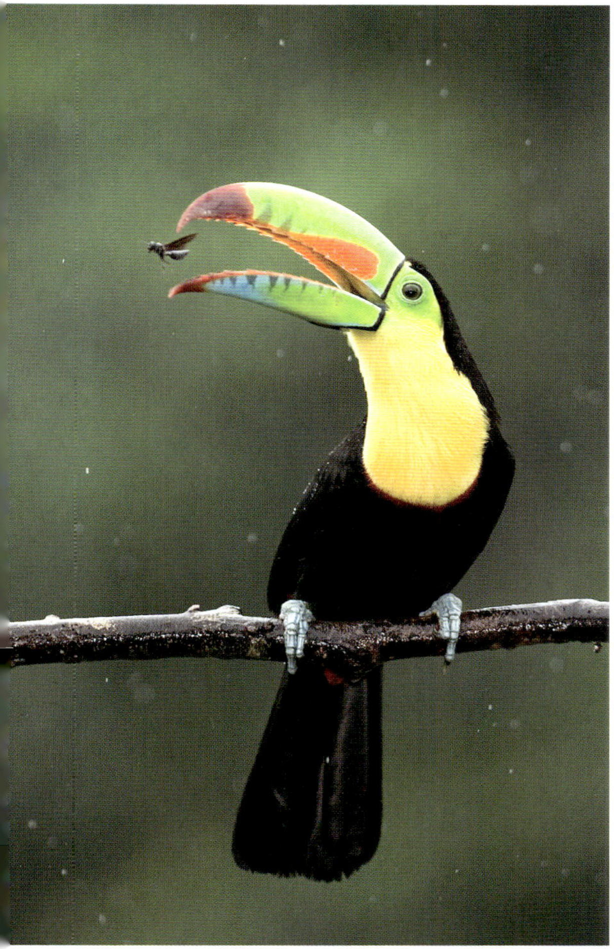

The Keel-billed Toucan is popular among photographers who come to Costa Rica *(Ramphastos sulfuratus)*
Nikon D700, 300mm f/2.8, 1/1600 second, f/4.0, ISO 800, manual focus, Gitzo tripod and video head, blind. Costa Rica, 2010.

Bence Máté

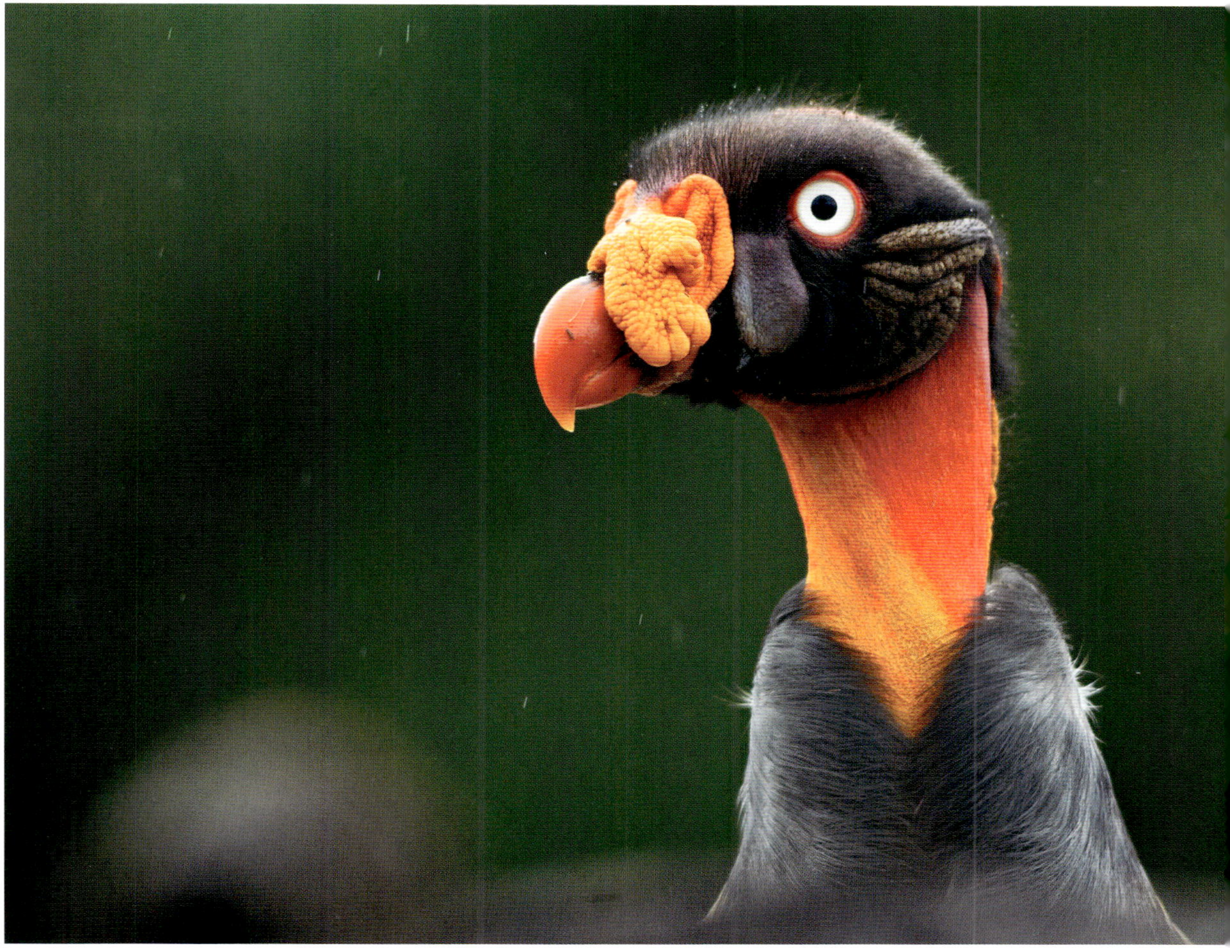

King Vulture *(Sarcoramphus papa)*
Nikon D300, Sigma 300–800mm f/5.6, 1/400 second, f/7.1, ISO 800, manual focus, Gitzo tripod and video head, blind. Costa Rica, 2009.

BENCE MÁTÉ

BRAZIL

A vast array of species gives photographers a nearly endless stream of opportunities.

In 2010 we built photo blinds in our third destination: Xaeres Lodges in Pantanal, southwest Brazil. Tropical Pantanal is the largest wetland in the world, with an estimated 1,000 bird species. The 4,000-hectare farm has eight photo blinds. The high season is August to October, which is the dry season.

Xaeres offers a unique opportunity to photograph Hyacinth Macaws from a specially built tower blind. These macaws forage in colonies and come to feed near the tower blind in flocks on a daily basis. About 1 m (3.3 ft) long from head to tail, Hyacinth Macaws are endangered, with only about 5,000 pairs left in the world.

There are two drinking pond blinds that attract several colorful bird species every day, and they are also occasionally visited by mammals. In addition, five one-person blinds are available for photographing caracaras. Feeding also attracts Black Vultures and Turkey Vultures, and there are often fights between the vultures and the caracaras.

Located deep in the rainforest, about 130 km (81 mi) from the closest village, Xaeres offers high-quality, air conditioned accommodations with phone connections and Internet access via satellite. You can find more information at www.hidephotography.com.

The Hyacinth Macaw is the largest parrot in the world *(Anodorhynchus hyacinthinus)*
Nikon D300, 300mm f/2.8, 1/160 second, f/2.8, ISO 400, manual focus, Gitzo tripod and video head, blind. Pantanal, Brazil, 2009.

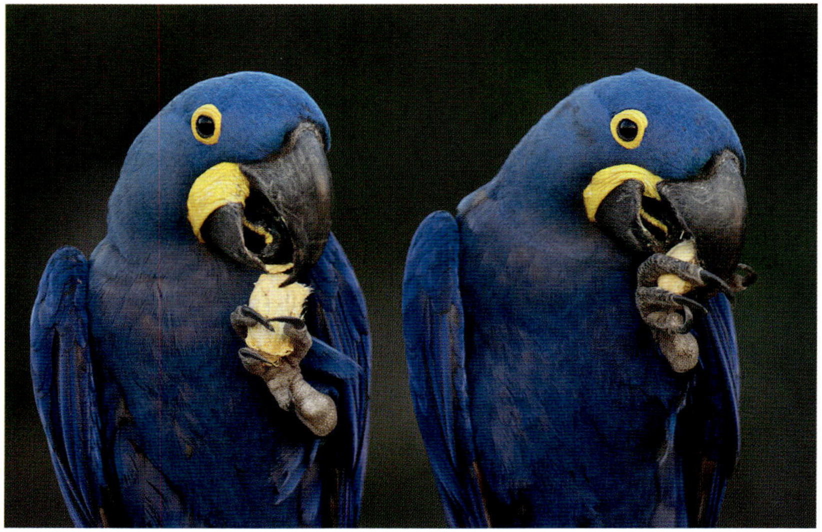

Bence Máté

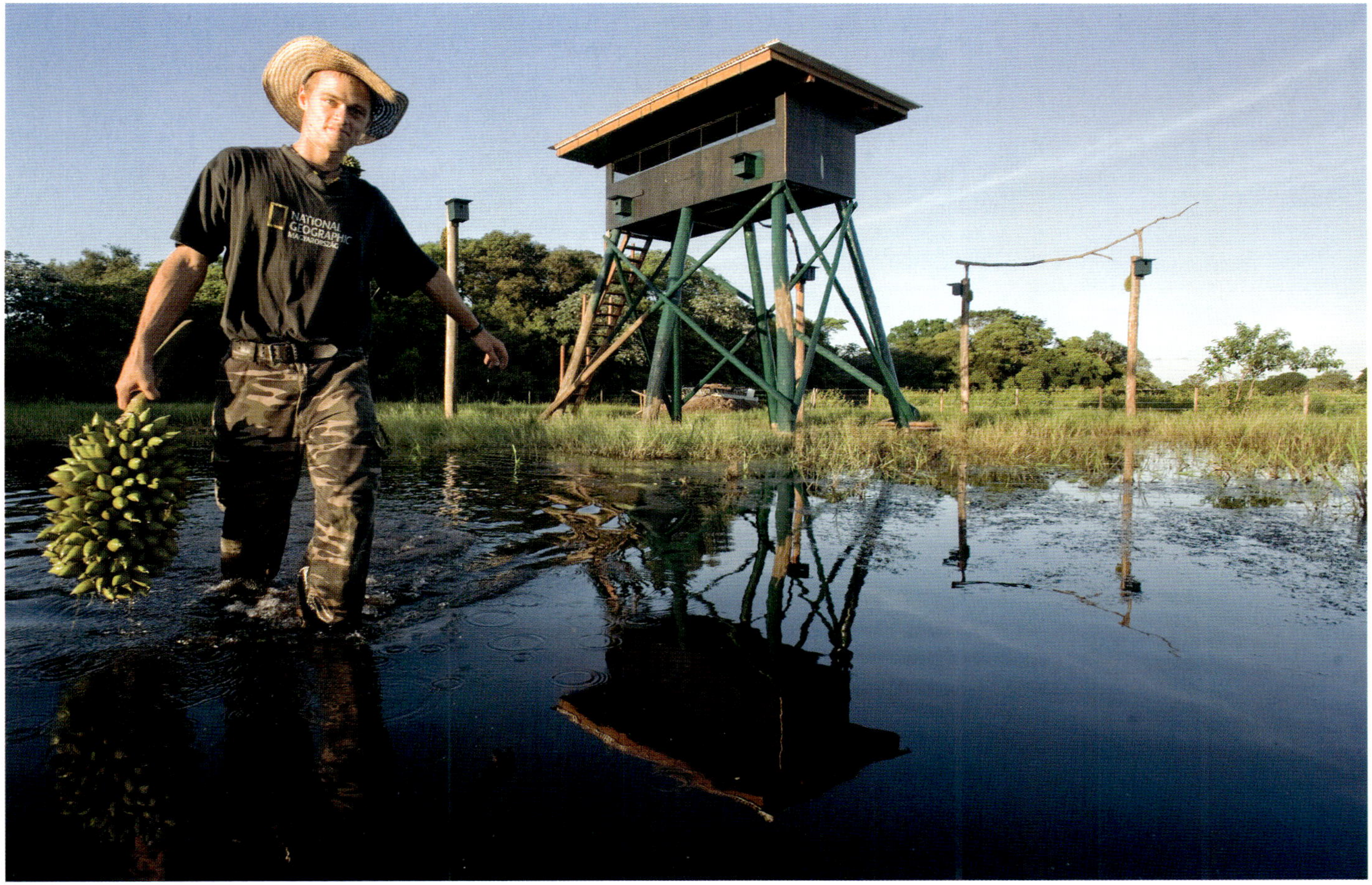

Pelican

A tower blind built on the Xaeres farm in the Pantanal offers good opportunities to photograph Hyacinth Macaws *(Anodorhynchus hyacinthinus)*

MARKUS VARESVUO

PROMOTING AND SELLING YOUR IMAGES

From the depths of hard drives to the big outside world.

Most bird photographers are amateurs who photograph for their own pleasure, but it's nice to show your best shots to at least friends and fellow photographers. Many photographers want to reach wider audiences, too.

Matching your material with a wider audience is easier than ever before. The lowest threshold is on the Internet, such as personal websites or community websites like Facebook. The photographer decides what gets published.

It's good to keep in mind, though, that the Internet is bursting with images, and drawing a larger crowd to your material can prove challenging. If you're going to set up your own website, it should be interesting and easy to use so your visitors want to come back. Consider each image carefully and be very critical of the images you publish. Update your material frequently.

There are many websites that conditionally host photographers' material. To get on such a website normally requires some kind of proof of your photographic skills. This is easier than setting up and running your own website, but the drawback is that your material fights for space with the work of other photographers, and you can't influence what level of images is published on the site in general. A big advantage, on the other hand, is that the website has a full-fledged audience that visits regularly.

If you want to get your work into printed publications, the threshold rises steeply. A good place to start is your local ornithological societies' papers and magazines. The editors select the images, so you have very limited say in what gets published. You narrow down the images you want to offer as candidates and choose where to submit your material. Some bigger, well-funded societies pay a fee, albeit often a small and symbolic one, but photographers should consider their contributions to be conservation work instead of a business deal.

Amateurs who invest heavily in their photography have an added interest in generating some extra revenue with image sales, often through their own websites or commercial image banks. Any larger-scale image sales tends to require patient groundwork, which consists of acquiring good photos in the first place, but also promoting yourself, your style, and your stock; for example, by being successful in photo competitions or giving talks to larger audiences or organizing exhibitions (see also the chapter "Spice Up Your Slideshow"). Getting into the best image banks is difficult; it often means submitting an extensive portfolio of your work, your personal approach to photography, and preferably some success in major competitions.

The singing Thrush Nightingale is one of my best-selling images *(Luscinia luscinia)*
Canon EOS-1D Mark II, 500mm f/4.0 plus 1.4x extender, 1/200 second, f/5.6, ISO 400, one-shot focus with a central focusing point, beanbag, car as a blind. Estonia, May 2005.

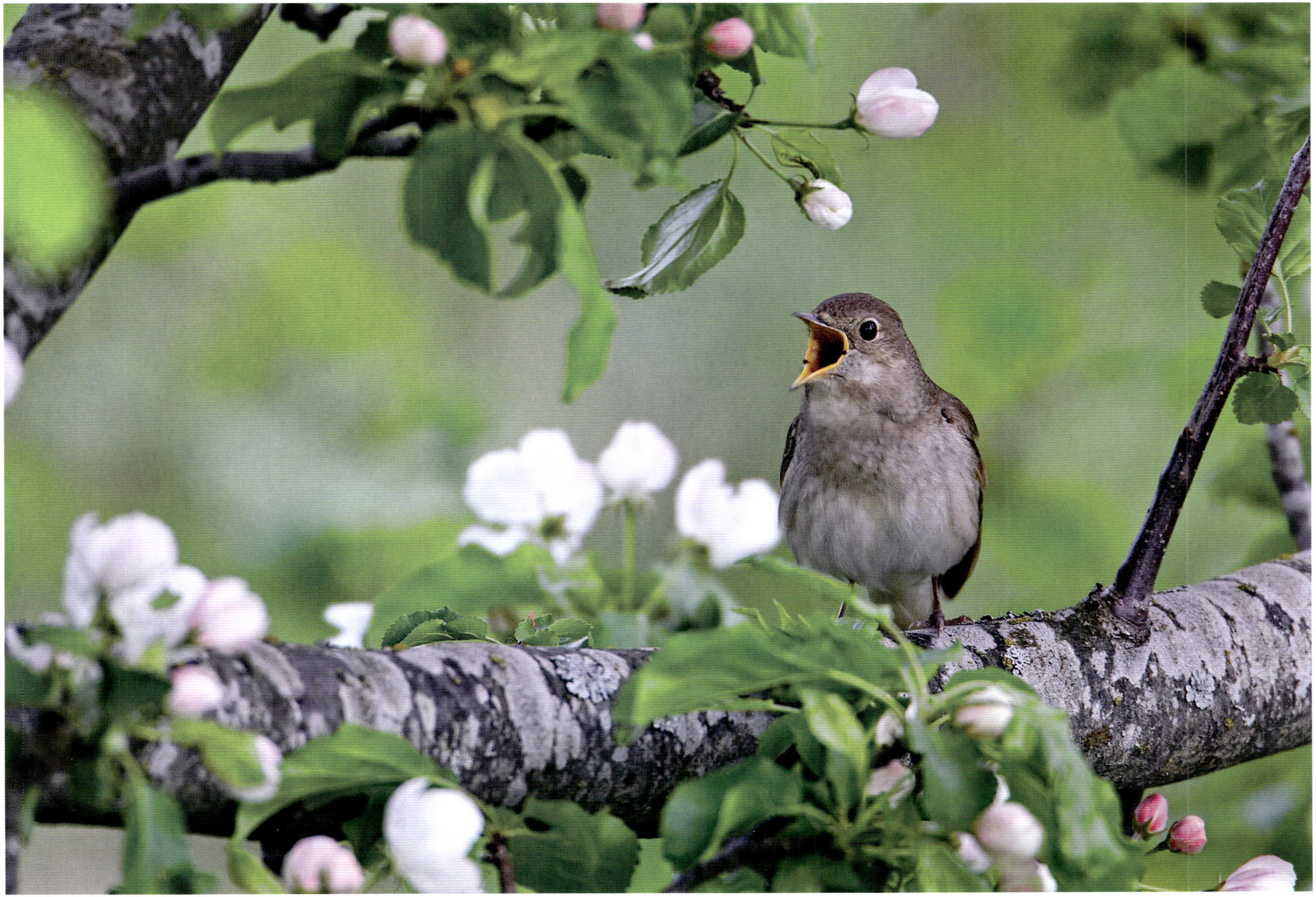

Ma-kus Varesvuo

As a rule, big local and national newspapers and nationwide photography and nature magazines pay a fair fee for image use. Books with a sizeable number of bird images aren't published that often, and photos are usually chosen by professional image researchers who make their selections from extensive archives in image banks and from professional photographers, so getting material in from outside the inner circle isn't so easy. Competition is really hard, and the usage fees are only slightly higher in books than in newspapers and magazines. However, bird images are used regularly and frequently in other types of publications, such as calendars, postcards, and educational and promotional material plus exhibitions in nature centers.

If you aspire to become a full-time bird photographer, you should realize that the challenges can be fairly daunting. More often than not, in addition to image sales you'll have to find several ways to make money; for example, making your own books, giving talks, renting out photo blinds, or arranging photo tours. Some of these methods work only if you have already been able to build a name for yourself.

The smaller your native country, the more important it is that you widen your horizons across national borders. In Europe, you should regard all of Europe as your home market, at least for image sales and maybe also for books. Otherwise it will probably be unrealistic to expect to make a living from your photography. On the whole, bird species are surprisingly the same in most European countries; for example, a Red-throated Diver image taken in Finland can be sold everywhere in Europe. And you will improve your chances by having material to offer from outside your own country.

Prospering on a European level, or even globally, requires an extensive stock of material and representation in the biggest countries in Europe through a good, reputable image agency. This can be done by giving your material to one good global agency that has an office or a partner agent in the most important markets. This is a good strategy because the photographer has to deliver material to only one dealer who then brokers the material further. The disadvantage is that the normal royalty share of 50–50 applies only to regions in which the agency has direct representation. If the agency uses a third partner—another agent, for example—the photographer gets only 25 percent of the net sales.

Another option is to negotiate an agreement with a good agent in each key market and thus get a 50–50 share of the image sales in all regions. This requires granting exclusivity in a region to each agency, which means more work in both agreement negotiating and submitting new material to each partner separately. And it's not guaranteed that you will get your first-choice agent.

Remember to negotiate the right to sell your images directly in all markets. This seems to be standard practice with most agencies.

To receive quarterly royalties that keep you at least somewhat happy, you must have thousands of images in stock. The agencies are very strict with their image selections, and it can take years to build up a solid amount of images at your agency.

You should also aim for good direct sales outside your home market. This can be facilitated with a website of international quality and an extensive stock of good-quality images. Note that a solo photographer can seldom offer the same range of choices as an agency, and image researchers prefer using services they've used in the past, as opposed to wading through more or less unknown websites and picking up an image here and there.

A viable option is to hook up with fellow photographers and make a website together. By joining forces you can offer a far wider range of images than you could on your own, giving more options to image buyers and thus lowering the threshold for them to start buying from you on a regular basis.

An example of this type of joint venture is www.birdphoto.fi, founded in 2003 by four photographers (Arto Juvonen, Tomi Muukkonen, Jari Peltomäki, and Markus Varesvuo). As we're writing this book, the site has more than 41,000 images, mostly of European species, and the main page is visited more than 800,000 times per year. Patience and hard work has made this website a good source of images to many picture editors and image researchers. The four photographers have been involved in many projects in the past 10 years, such as providing images for bird books in Germany, France, Sweden, the United Kingdom, Finland, South Africa, and the United States, to name a few. Bird sounds were added to the website early on, provided by renowned ornithologist and bird guide Hannu Jännes.

The website serves as a good example of how rival photographers can join forces in cooperation, and all gain from the endeavor.

BENCE MÁTÉ

NATURE PHOTO COMPETITIONS

A photo competition can be a springboard to success.

We photographers want to show our work. One of the best ways to gain wider publicity is to do well in photo competitions. The feedback from competitions and audiences helps us develop our artistic eye and technical skills. The publicity can also work in favor of nature conservation. In theory, getting your images out to the public can be quick and easy, but in reality it's more difficult. After you've shot the material, you need to go through it, select those worth saving (be brutal) and delete the rest, process the RAW files, then archive, edit, save, and publish them. This entails quite a bit of work. As described earlier, your channels for showcasing your work are community sites, forums, photo agencies, websites, talks, exhibitions, promotional material, magazines, books, and nature and wildlife photo competitions, which we will explore in this chapter.

When you compare the amount of work invested with the publicity gained, it can be said that success in a nature photo competition has the best input-to-output ratio, but the success will not come easy. Nature photo competitions have an important role in the evolution of nature and wildlife photography because wholesome competition encourages the competitors to push the boundaries in their search for the fresh and the novel—to evolve. Also, the competitions offer the photographers a forum in which they can compare and evaluate their skills and vision, while the audience has an opportunity to see the best of contemporary nature photography.

Before deciding whether to take part in a competition, I study the entry rules with these points in mind:

1. I find out why the competition has been organized and what rights the organizers want to the images that are entered. If they want more than the right to use the images in promotion and marketing of the competition, I do not enter. (Some rules state that by entering, the participant forfeits all rights to the submitted images. Needless to say, I do not enter such competitions.)
2. If the main theme, categories, or awards are not specifically itemized, the competition is probably not worth entering.
3. If I decide to enter, I read every detail of the rules and instructions. I was once disqualified after my image was chosen as a category winner because I read the rules carelessly and missed a clause that later caused my image to be disqualified. I learned my lesson and now read the rules very carefully, even when the competition is familiar, because there may be changes to the rules every year.

While I read through the rules, I pay special attention to the following questions:

What type of images are the organizers inviting to the competition, and what were the winners like in previous years? Some competitions seem to choose the same style of image every year, even if the jury changes. If the names of the

Markus Varesvuo 2003

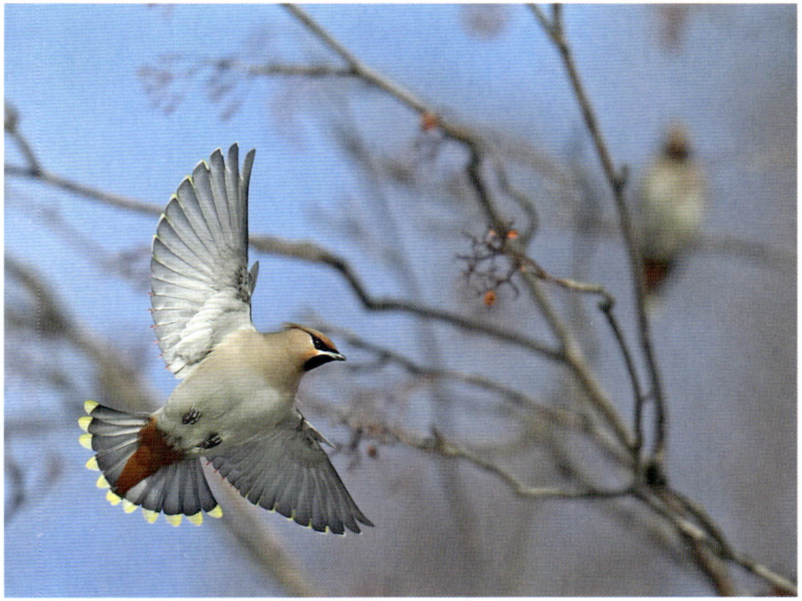

Bohemian Waxwing *(Bombycilla garrulus)*, 2003 winner

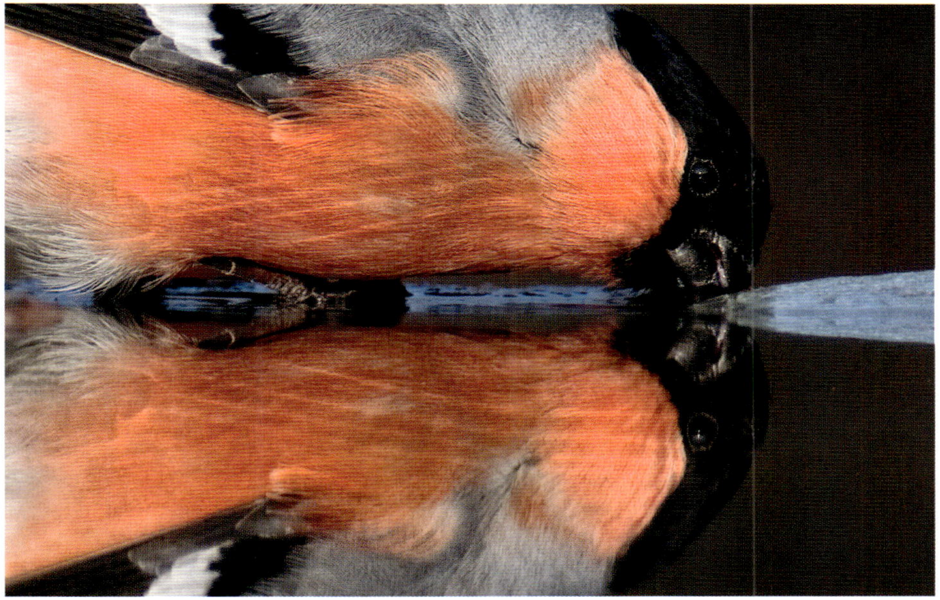

Eurasian Bullfinch *(Pyrrhula pyrrhula)*, 2005 winner

Bence Máté 2005

Jari Peltomäki 2004

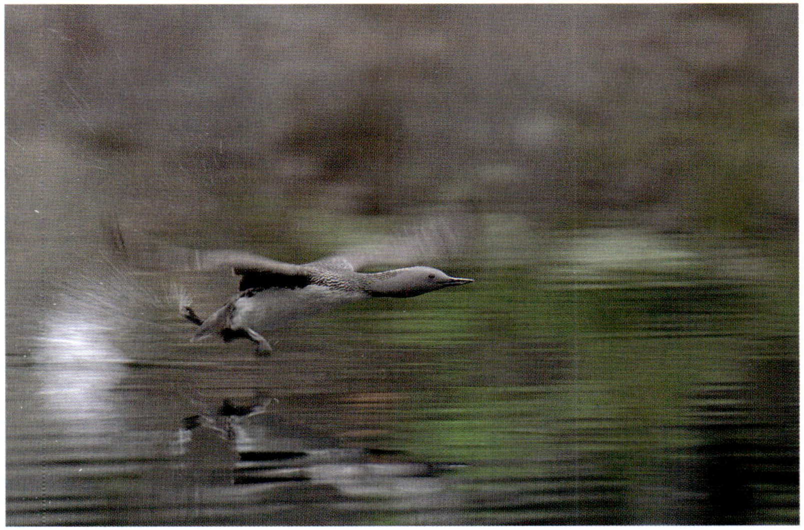

The International Wildbird Photographer was an international photo competition organized in Britain from 2003–2008. The authors of this book won the title in consecutive years with the following images. The awards brought the photographers publicity that opened new doors and opportunities.

Red-throated Loon *(Gavia stellata)*, 2004 winner

jury members are published before the entry deadline, it can be useful to have a look at who they are and what type of trends they favor in photography, or more importantly, what types of photos never seem to do well.

How many categories can I enter, and what is the maximum number of images I can submit?

What are the technical requirements? What is the required size of the high-resolution digital files? What is the maximum cropping ratio?
Regrettably, the technical requirements often seem to reflect an insufficient level of technical understanding among the organizers. Understandably, they want the entries to be as big as possible so they can be published in all kinds of media, exhibitions, books, and newsletters—both digitally and in print. This is, however, an area that requires specific expertise, and the organizers don't always seem to realize that they should make sure someone on the team has it. Yes, pixels can give some indication of the potential uses of the digital file, but maximum print size has more to do with the size and quality of the camera sensor; pixels are not equal in all cameras. Competition rules often state a requirement for minimum pixels, but cropping within the required pixels is unlimited. Also, you may see a minimum requirement of 6 megapixels, but the cropping is limited to 20 percent of the original, which does not seem very logical. As competitors we must comply with the rules, but we can also hope that one day somebody checks the size requirements and gets them right.

What are the ethical requirements?
Make sure that the images you enter meet the criteria defined by the organizers.

What kind of digital adjustments are allowed?
Apart from the artistic categories, the organizers of nature photo competitions want to see images that accurately match the events seen through the viewfinder. The rules do not always explain in detail what can be done to the digital file. It's the organizers' responsibility, and it is in their best interest, to select competent judges who can tell a fake image from an authentic one. The organizers will request to see the original RAW file of images that make it to the final round of judging, and if the competition entry greatly differs from the RAW file, the entry may be disqualified.

How are the entries sent to the competition?
Entering competitions is almost exclusively digital, which is the easiest and fastest method. I take part only in competitions where entries are sent digitally.

Can I enter an image that has been awarded in another competition?
Most organizers would like to have previously unseen images as their competition winners, because of the novelty value, but on the other hand, a lot of high-quality material might then be missing from their competition.

What is the competition closing date?
Based on empirical findings among my peers and myself, 9 out of 10 competitors seem to submit their entries during the last week before the deadline. You may want to be smarter, because uploading your images can take longer in the final days, or the servers may get overloaded and crash at a critical moment, meaning that you do not get your images submitted before the competition closes.

When are the results announced?
This is important, if you consider taking part in another competition where the rules state that a previously awarded

image is not eligible. Even if the results from your first competition are not yet public but you have been notified that your image won, you cannot enter that image in the next competition if the rules forbid it.

Photographers send their images to nature photo competitions wanting to win, but it's good to remember that you are vying for awards in art; hence, the approach is a matter of taste, which isn't easily measured and is widely varied. There is no such thing as the best image, only the opinion of a certain jury over a limited sampling; there is no one wildlife photographer who is the best. But each competition has a lot of great images, and to reap the awards photographers need a hefty dose of luck. And be patient; don't lose faith even if the awards seem to avoid you. After all, this is just wholesome, friendly rivalry.

Good luck!

BENCE MÁTÉ

SPICE UP YOUR SLIDE SHOW

A good narrative supports the images and adds interest to your presentation, as does well-chosen music that is skillfully synchronized.

Trends come and go, and photographers have their preferences, but normally when wildlife photographers give a talk, they show their images while sharing stories and facts about them, or they give audiovisual slide shows with images and music. A presentation can have both, because each component serves a different purpose. Used together, they can give the audience a more balanced experience.

I gave my first slide show in 2000 with 34 color slides that were loaded in the magazines of two projectors stacked on top of each other. With self-made blades that could be opened and closed like shutter curtains, I changed the slides manually to the rhythm of the music with the blades creating a simple cross-fade technique. The speed was limited to the speed of the projectors. Compared to this, the sky really is the limit nowadays when you put together a slide show; you can merge images and music almost any way you want, using different techniques and styles. Wings Platinum (for PC) and FotoMagico (for Mac) are good examples of applications that play a number of music and photo tracks simultaneously. Keep in mind, though, that the technical possibilities are tools, not the be-all and end-all of your slide show, and they should be used smartly.

Not all images need to be shown in full; sometimes a glimpse of an image can be used between two more powerful images, either to give extra information or to build a bridge between two separate images. Successive frames can be shown in rapid sequence, imitating a motion picture. Transitions between images can be made more animated by zooming in or scanning through the picture. You can break the basic rhythm of your slide show with both faster and slower-paced intervals; you can use transitions every 10 seconds with a batch of suitable images, and at other places you can create lingering, peaceful lulls, where a strong image keeps your audience captivated for much longer.

Rhythm is also important in presentations that are built on images and narration. Select powerful images that are rich in detail or emotion when you want to stop and tell a longer story; likewise, add a few batches of related images that can be shown in rapid succession without commentary.

How to Make a Slide Show

1. *Concept and audience*
   Your slide show has a purpose, be it entertainment, information, or showcasing your work. Focusing on that goal and your audience in the beginning helps you make a presentation that the audience can relate to. The nature of the event is also a factor; you would probably make a different type of presentation to your peers than to a more generic or heterogeneous audience.
2. *Image selection*
   In an ideal situation, you will have an idea for a slide show when you

Markus Varesvuo

Don't make a boring slideshow. Engage and entertain while you educate. Share a funny story or two; playing with stereotypes and sharing a kind of self-deprecating humor tends to go over well and has been known to travel across borders. Here is a typically Finnish crow *(Corvus corone cornix)*.
Canon EOS-1D Mark II, 500mm f/4.0 plus 1.4x extender, 1/400 second, f/7.1, one-shot focus with one focusing point, Gitzo tripod, Manfrotto 501 video head, blind. Liminka, Finland, May 2006.

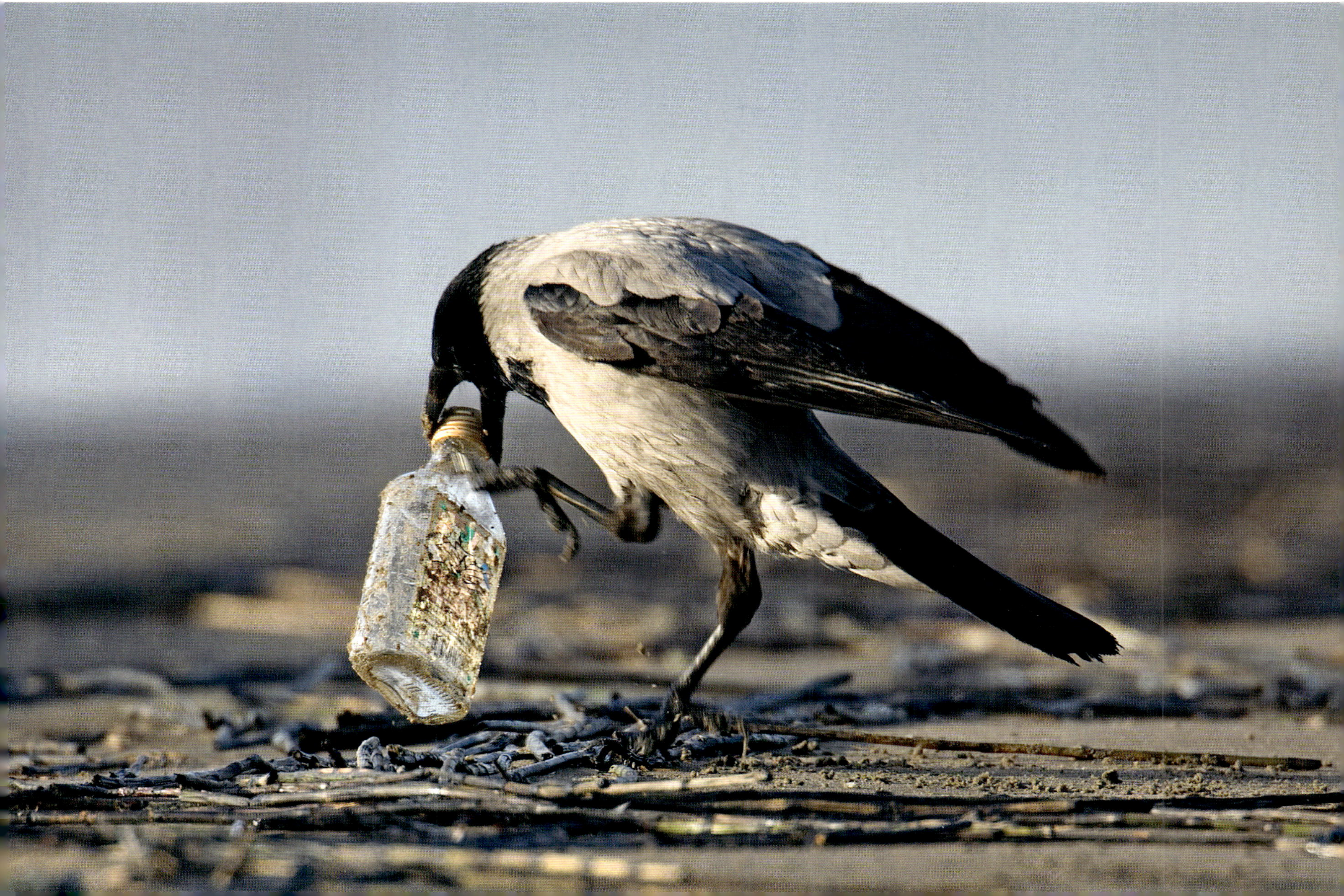

are selecting photos, but normally a slide show is created with existing images. Sometimes you can complete a presentation with some fresh material taken specifically for it. The main thing to keep clear in your mind, though, is that the images you use should cover a wide range of variations. A basic flaw, seen regrettably often, is that too many images are repetitive.

3. *Select the music, or have it composed*
   I favor slide shows that have music; to me music plays an almost equal role in a presentation. Movie soundtracks are tailor-made for slide shows; they are, after all, made to accompany images. They come in endless variations in style, and fast-changing moods and tempos are typical. Production music (also called archive music or catalog music) offers an even wider range of possibilities, and it is probably easiest to obtain permission to use this kind of music. You can also have music composed specifically for your slide show. Last but not least, there are other sounds to consider, such as those from the natural world.

> Music and other recordings, like bird songs, fall under copyright laws, and you must obtain permission and pay any applicable fees before you can use them in public. Unauthorized use of copyrighted material is a criminal act.

4. *Slow cross-fade*
   One of the most interesting features in digital slide show applications is creating a new image out of two existing images by using a slow cross-fade in the transition between two images; for a brief moment two images become one.
5. *Synchronize the images with the music*
   Carefully selected music that is skillfully synchronized with image transitions supports your slide show. The transition technique is successful when it boosts the overall dramatic effect and creates anticipation that carries your story from one image to the next. The applications mentioned earlier have relatively easy tools for creating a good slide show.
6. *Test to see if your slide show works*
   Allow time to show your final result to a test audience and use the feedback to improve your slide show before your premiere. You can become too attached to your images and possibly blind to the fact that some of them have no real meaning in the slide show. It's better to leave your audience wanting more than to numb them with an overly long presentation—less *is* more.

It's natural to want to show your best images, but don't overlook an average shot; it might serve a purpose in your presentation, maybe in creating a brief respite between the exciting peaks. Selecting the images can be a hard task, and building a slide show with narration or music can take up to several weeks. These are not necessarily areas that greatly interest a wildlife photographer. Even so, photographers who have extensive and powerful material should master this task. A well-constructed, impressive slide show is one of the best ways to showcase your work.

JARI PELTOMÄKI

BIRD PHOTOGRAPHY NOW AND IN THE NEAR FUTURE

Because of the rising popularity of bird photography, we are inundated with images. The challenge to produce unique and original images is increasingly more difficult.

To most amateur bird photographers the ultimate goal is a basic, decently exposed, sharp picture of a bird. Thanks to modern advanced technology, there are many easy and inexpensive ways to show your images, which has flooded the market with endless streams of more or less the same portraits of practically every species.

With this book we hope to provide some technical advice in addition to new ideas for taking better and more diverse pictures. The book is primarily for fledgling bird photographers, but even more advanced photographers will find good tips. Anyone can face a sudden and special situation out in the field, and it's good to be fast, confident, and deliberate when trying to capture something rare that you might see only once in your lifetime. A high level of readiness comes with technical confidence and the skill to see the opportunities in any given situation. The latter can be practiced by analyzing other people's work and by teaching yourself to do things differently.

The market for bird images is starting to be full of good stuff. The abundance is also raising viewers' expectations. Merely 10 years ago, a sharp, well-exposed basic portrait of a White-tailed Eagle was a rare treat. Now the species is making a comeback, and it's possible to photograph it in several places. You could say that White-tailed Eagle images have suffered from inflation because there are so many fantastic images. This means that you need to have a truly exceptional White-tailed Eagle image for it to stand out from the rest.

To stay ahead, you have to constantly reinvent—find new angles and surprise your audience. Copying old or new masters is not the way forward; instead, you should find your own style. By studying what's out there, by learning about photography, and by pushing the limits, you can build your own brand. Get off the beaten path and aim for something original that helps your image stand out.

We have said quite a few times that good technical quality is a prerequisite, but remember that some rules were made to be broken. There can be situations or styles that merit qualities other than technical ones, making even a critical viewer prone to forgive technical flaws when faced with something breathtaking.

Despite the present volume of bird images, it can't be said that every possible bird image has been taken. The same subjects can be approached from different angles, and each situation, with its variants of light conditions and action, is somewhat unique.

The most important thing is to spend as much time in the field with a camera as possible, and also to plan and visualize potential situations in advance. A specialist will focus on subjects that most people will pass, because rare footage will always be in demand, whereas a jack-of-all-trades will shoot anything! A professional can find success with both strategies.

Jari Peltomäki

Backlight enhances the details in this White-tailed Eagle's outspread wings and tail feathers as it lands *(Haliaeetus albicilla)*
Canon EOS-1D Mark III, 70–200mm f/2.8, 1/1600 second, 200mm, f/5.0, ISO 1600, continuous focus with an extended central focusing point, Manfrotto 501 video head attached to the blind's camera plank. Vehmaa, November 2008.

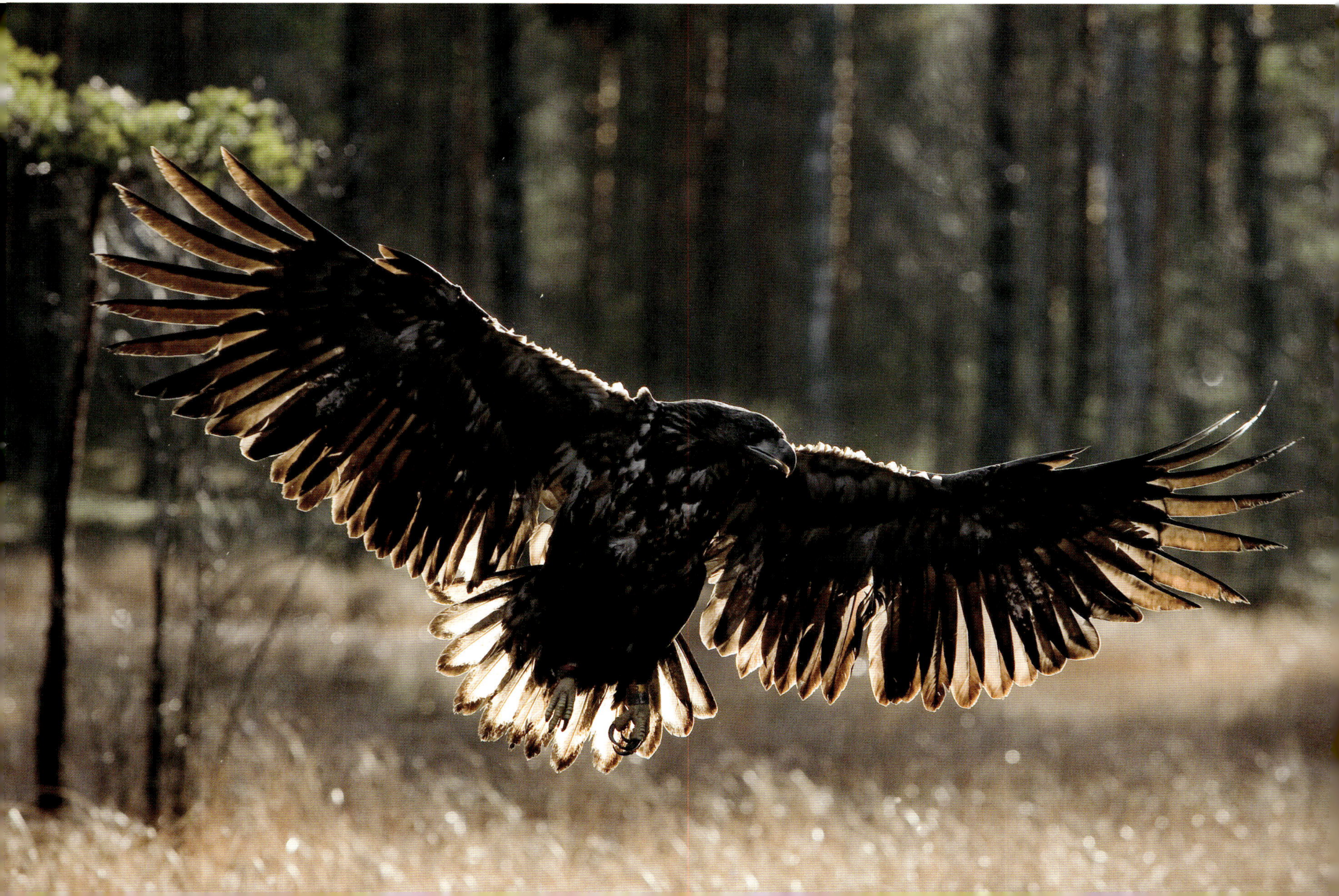

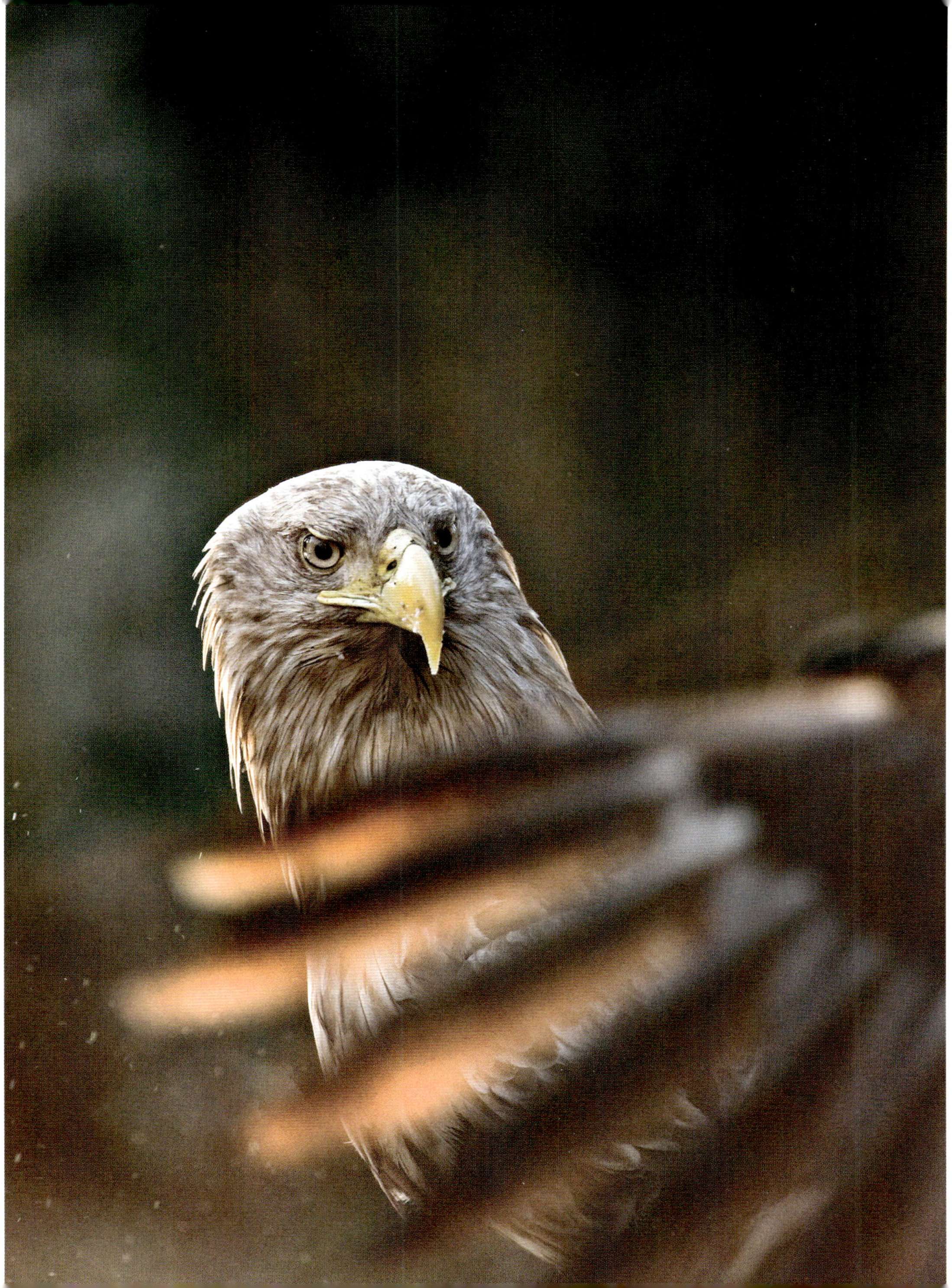

Jari Peltomäki

The tip of another eagle's wing makes this portrait of an old White-tailed Eagle more intriguing *(Haliaeetus albicilla)*
Canon EOS-1D Mark III, 500mm f/4.0 plus 1.4x extender, 1/500 second, f/5.6, ISO 800, continuous focus with an extended central focusing point, Manfrotto 501 video head attached to the blind's camera plank. Vehmaa, November 2008.

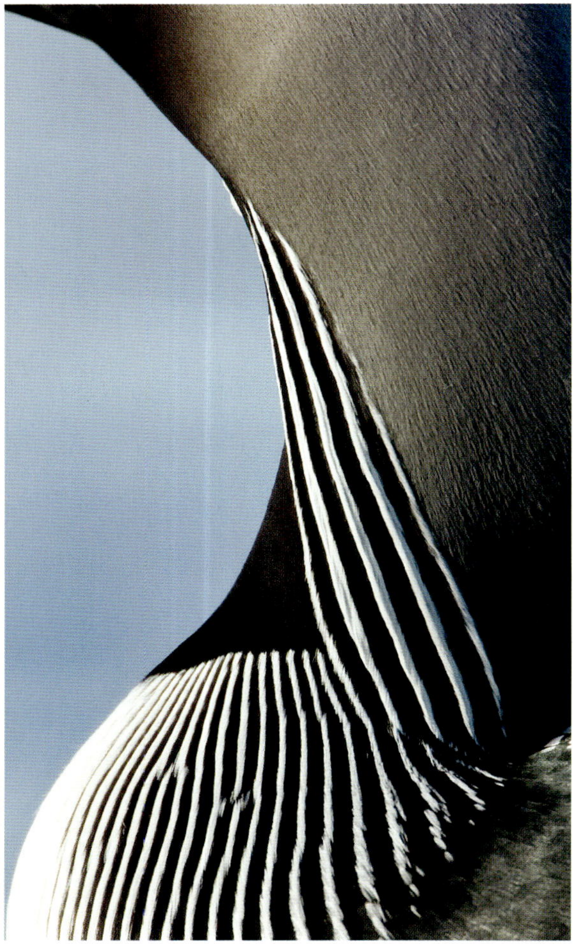

Jari Peltomäki

Birds have so many fantastic details, such as the plumage design on this Arctic Loon's neck *(Gavia arctica)*
Canon EOS-1D Mark II, 500mm f/4.0 plus 2x extender, 1/80 second, f/8.0, ISO 200, manual focus, Gitzo tripod, Manfrotto 501 video head. Vaala, Finland, June 2005.

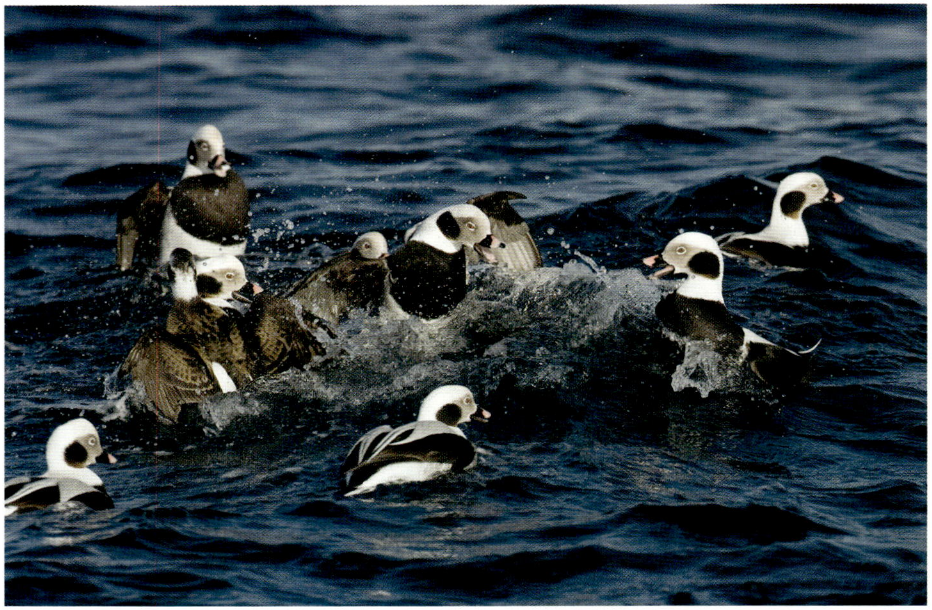

Jari Peltomäki

You might be able to catch something like this only once in a lifetime. Long-tailed Duck males fighting over a female *(Clangula hyemalis)*.
Canon EOS-1D Mark II N, 500mm f/4.0, 1/2000 second, f/8.0, ISO 400, continuous focus with 45 focusing points, handheld camera, boat. Varangerbotn, Norway, March 2006.

Great Gray Owl on the snow *(Strix nebulosa)*
Canon EOS-1D Mark II, 70–200mm f/2.8, 1/1000 second, 153mm, f/4.0, ISO 400, one-shot focus with a central focusing point, handheld camera. Kempele, March 2005.

The Future of Bird Photography

Increasingly, many people have the means to acquire high-quality camera equipment that helps them take technically good images. Commercial blinds can be rented and guide services can be bought. All this has helped to increase the image supply, which has led to lower pricing. Some offer their images for very low rates—even for free. Many seem to be happy with being credited as the photographer. This spells trouble for the overall progress in bird photography.

Novice photographers should reflect on their motives for a moment. If they photograph birds because it's a great way to spend one's free time, and the end goal is to bring joy to oneself, then they can focus on enjoying some great experiences, collecting lovely memories, and taking good pictures.

But if you want bird photography to help bring food to the table or even become a full-time profession, it's important to realize that the competition among photographers is not getting any easier, and the explosion of good material on the Internet is not going to make life easy for a bird photographer.

All the same, a technically faultless, visually interesting, consummately produced bird image still has commercial value, even if it's accurate to say that it's a buyer's market. Success rarely comes easily; instead, hard work and a strong vision can help you gain a foothold in the world of bird photography and be successful.

Bird photographers need patience and perseverance to spend the necessary amount of time with a photo

Jari Peltomäki

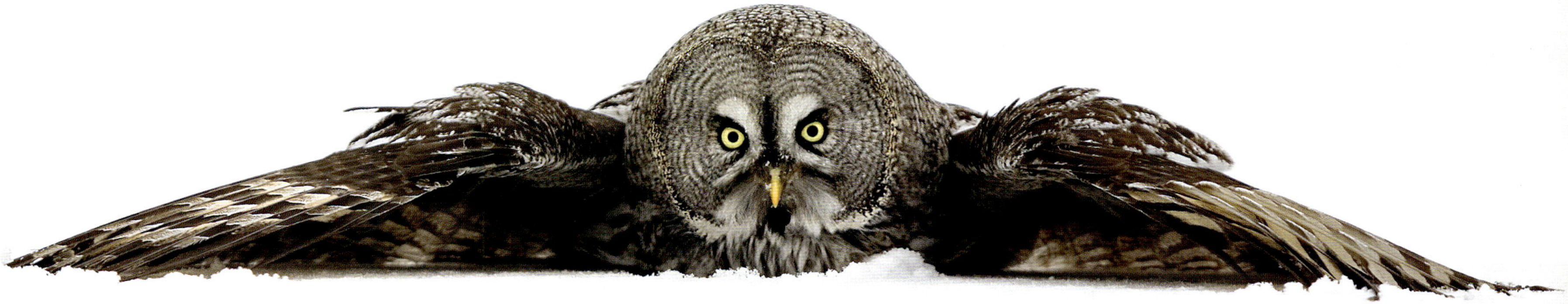

project, yet at the same time we need to be dynamic and quick to adapt our ways in a rapidly changing world. This applies to both work in the field and work done on the computer to process and archive the image files, and to publish and promote them.

There is no one road to success, nor is there one truth—the only sure thing is that bird photography is fun and interesting!

Show Your Images and Ask for Feedback

No one is born a master—it's a long road of learning and growing. It is fairly common among photographers, especially in the early stages of one's career, to feel that one's images are somehow better and more special than others. This stems from knowing that the images required great sacrifice and personal suffering and from being giddy with joy at the successful result. Unfortunately, this euphoria is seldom clear to the audience. The viewers, blissfully unaware of the hardships encountered, judge the image wholly and totally from their own varied premises and base it on the image's perceived exceptionality or beauty.

On the other hand, it's important not to underestimate your work. Trust your vision, even if some of the feedback is less encouraging. There's the old saying that envy burns hotter than lust, and sometimes your image can raise stinging criticism that stems more from envy than genuine examination of your work.

A good way to get constructive criticism and help in evaluating your work realistically is to share it widely with fellow photographers, for example on nature photo forums and websites. You will notice that feedback given with real names is often overly positive—it's not so easy to give genuinely constructive and helpful criticism. This seems to apply to Facebook especially well. One way to gauge the success of your image is the amount of attention it gets—the better your image is, the more comments it's likely to get.

We tend to share our images mostly among our photographer friends, but you should try to widen your audience; it gives you a broader understanding of which images appeal to larger audiences. I've entered a few images in competitions, based on how my audiences responded to them as I gave talks, and those images often did well.

Start by showing your images to a small crowd and gradually work your way to bigger audiences. This gives you experience and confidence, and when you eventually stand in front of a really big audience, you won't be incapacitated by nerves. Local camera clubs offer good opportunities for practice, and you can progress to national and international forums. The wider the audiences, the more varied the feedback, which can give you valuable insights to your perspectives and ideas. More experienced photographers can give useful tips and advice on how to improve your images and your presentation techniques. You don't have to agree with everybody, but exchanging opinions and listening to one another helps each and every one of us to grow.

For me, the Picture of the Week contest on our website (www.birdphoto.fi) has probably helped me to grow professionally more than any other single factor. People can rate and comment on our images without revealing their own identities, and sometimes the feedback is ruthless. But the viewers have taught

Capturing a Snowy Owl from a slightly unusual angle and in exceptional light conditions help to make a more interesting image *(Bubo scandiacus)*
Canon EOS-1D Mark III, 500mm f/4.0, 1/2500 second, f/7.1, ISO 400, continuous focus with an extended central focusing point, handheld camera. Canada, March 2009.

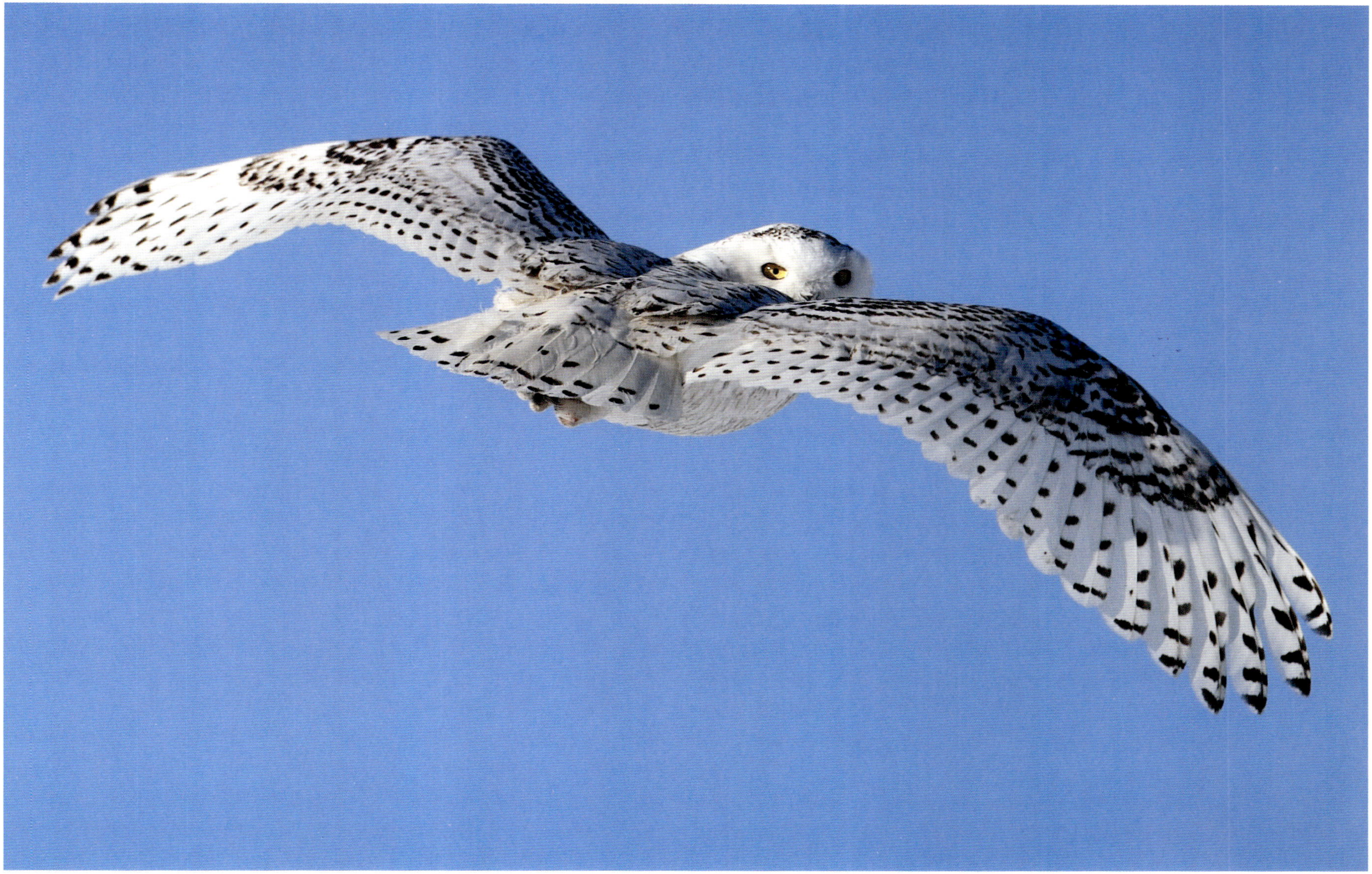

Jari Petlomäki

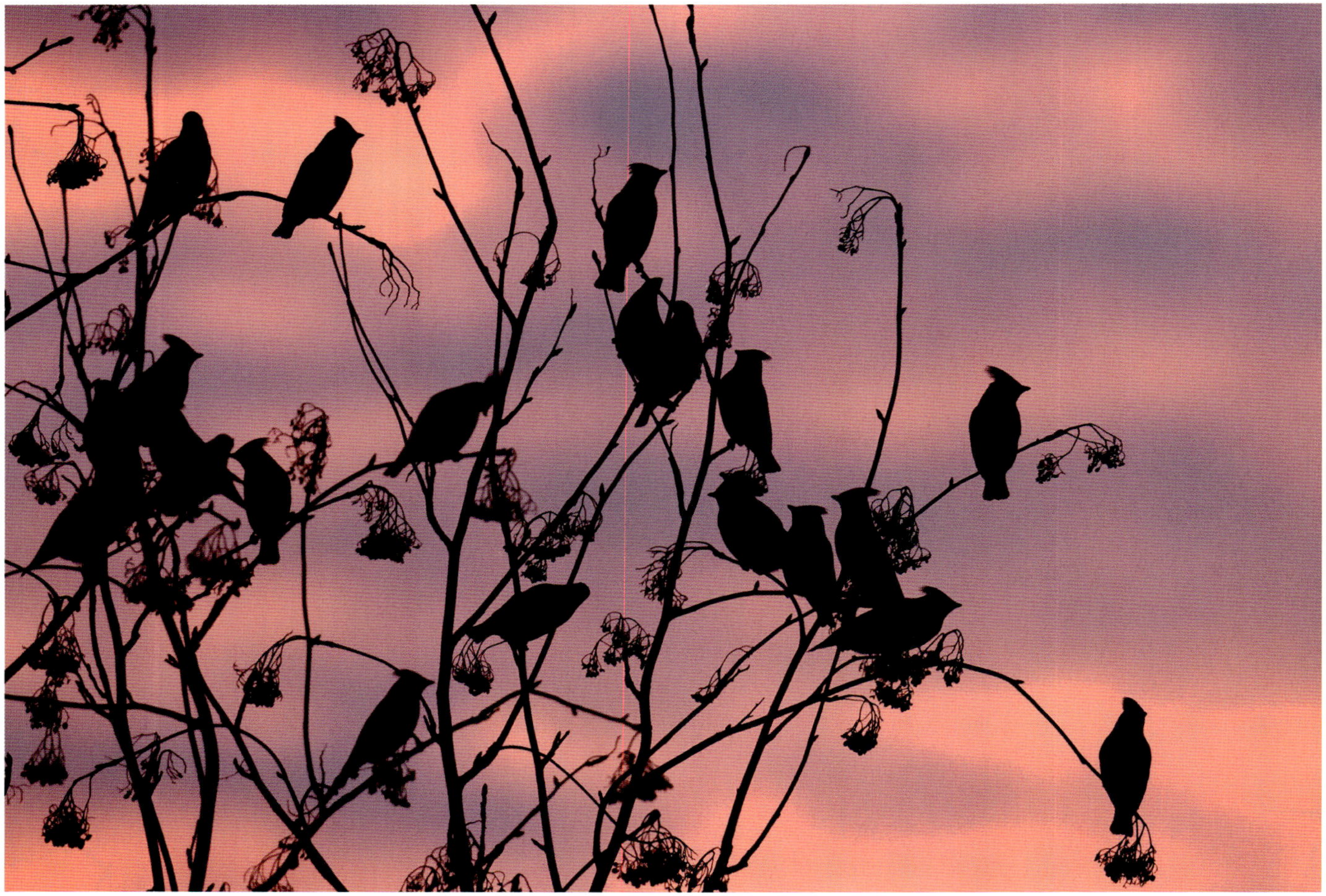

Jari Peltomäki

When I took this Bohemian Waxwing image one dark morning, I told myself it would be a useless image *(Bombycilla garrulus)*. Instead, it has been sold many times, so it's a very good image!
Canon EOS-1D Mark II N, 500mm f/4.0, 1/200 second, f/5.6, ISO 1000, one-shot focus with a central focusing point, handheld camera. Oulu, Finland, December 2006.

Jari Peltomäki

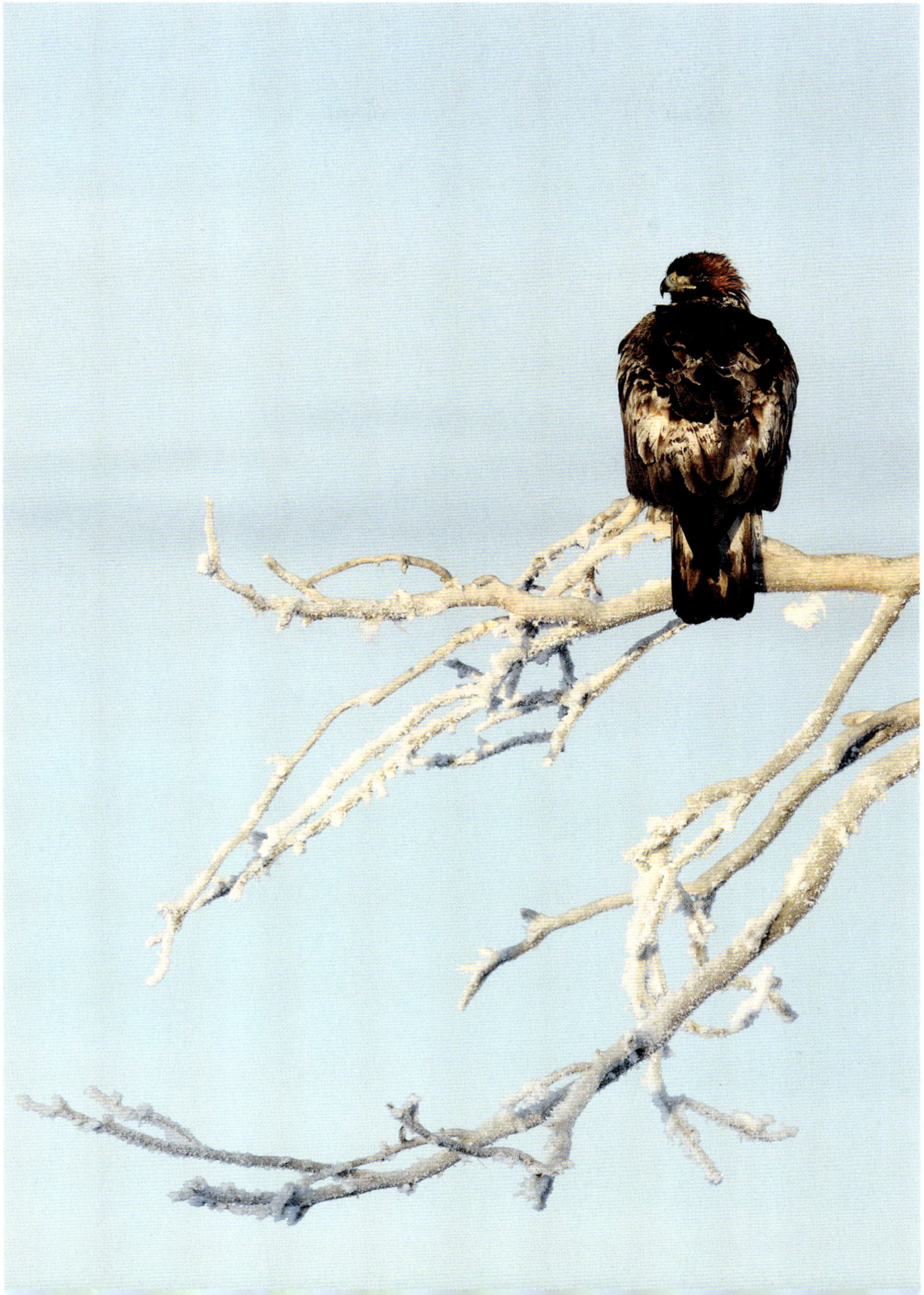

Composition is important. Golden Eagle *(Aquila chrysaetos)*.
Nikon D3S, 200–400mm f/2.8, 1/1000 second, 153mm, f/4.0, ISO 400, one-shot focus with a central focusing point, handheld camera. Utajärvi, Finland, January 2011.

me to look at my images more critically, and it has also been fun to see how the images that really are the best are in the top 10 at the end of the year. This open and direct competition between friends and colleagues has also proved to be a kick in the rear as we hotly pursue the best-ever image.

Value Your Work and Enjoy It

A healthy dose of self-criticism is a virtue because it's a driving force, and it motivates you to become even better. But like everything else, it's a balancing act, and too much of it is not a good thing. You need a touch of self-satisfaction, too. Who values your work if you don't? Don't compare your images too much with other people's work; instead, try sticking to your guns—this might even earn you your own hallmark. Latching onto ideas or being influenced by great images is only natural, but they should be impressions on one's own vision, not something to be copied. In the end, what matters is that your work pleases you. The commercial angle is well captured by Hannu Hautala, the Grand Old Man of Finnish nature photography: "A sold image is a good image." There is no one way to photograph birds nor to set a value on an image.

Positive experiences and feelings are the driving forces behind bird photography. Be proud of your achievements, be they skillful exposures, balanced compositions, good timing in action photos, or careful preparations that led to successful images. Take pleasure in your friends' achievements, and if you feel yourself turning green with envy at other photographers' fantastic images, tell them so. The next great image might be yours!

A nature photo can have elements of humor, drama, tragedy, suspense, mystery. A nature photo can be a document, a serenade to nature, a work of art, a piece of interior decoration. Nature photos can be used to promote conservation, to raise awareness, to catch attention, to educate, to fill with joy, to thrill.

A good bird image inspires and moves. A brilliant bird image fills you with awe. A camera is not just a technical device to capture something; photographers use their cameras to convey their visions of what they see to their audience. The more a photographer invests in the image, the more powerful its effect on the audience.

Every good image has a story that touches the viewer's imagination. The story is not created by pressing the shutter release, it stems from the photographer's own, individual, and unique vision.

Index